ADDISON-WESLEY

Environmental Science

ECOLOGY AND HUMAN IMPACT

Bernstein ◆ Winkler ◆ Zierdt-Warshaw

TEACHER'S EDITION

Addison-Wesley Publishing Company

Menlo Park, California • Reading, Massachusetts • New York
Don Mills, Ontario • Wokingham, England • Amsterdam • Bonn
Paris • Milan • Madrid • Sydney • Singapore • Tokyo
Seoul • Taipei • Mexico City • San Juan

Reviewers
Content/Multicultural

Dr. Harold J. McKenna
Professor of Environmental
    Science Education
City College School of
    Education
New York, NY

Dr. James Gavan
Department of Anthropology
University of Missouri
Columbia, MO

Anne Tweed
Science Department
    Coordinator
Eaglecrest High School
Aurora, CO

Pat Browne
Office of Multicultural
    Education
Crispus Attucks Multicultural
    Center
Indianapolis, IN

Dr. Paul Ecklund
Division of Biological Sciences
Cornell University
Ithaca, NY

Project Team Acknowledgments

Editorial
Dennis Colella, Joanne Raisner,
Robin O'Keefe, Eric Hill, Denise
Maraschin, Iris Martinez Kane

Design
Debbie Costello, Ellen Kwan

Production
Jenny Blackburn, Steve Rogers,
Ben Schroeter, Ellen Williams,
Bill Hollowell, Trevin Lowrey,
Beowulf Thorne, Dan Robbins

Production Editorial
Nina Pohl, Chris Hofer

Photo Edit
Karen Koppel, Margee Robinson,
Roberta Spieckerman

Manufacturing
Sheila Scott, Alison Fry

Marketing Services
Greg Gardner

Market Research
Shirley Black

Permissions
Marty Granahan

Contributing Writer
Sylvia Velasquez

 Text printed on recycled paper

Front Cover Photograph: Pat O'Hara/Allstock
Back Cover Photograph: S. Nielsen/DRK Photo

The sky blue eggs of the American robin are common in rural and urban areas throughout the United States. The eggs contain the next generation, and therefore the future of the species. The bird's nest and eggs symbolize the fragility of the environment and the dependence of all living things on a healthy, safe world in which to grow.

CONTENTS OF THE TEACHER'S EDITION

Addison-Wesley Environmental Science: Ecology and Human Impact has been developed as a complete, flexible, laboratory science program for all students. The program can be used as a full-year course for students with average, or below average, reading and comprehension abilities. The program can also be used as a half-year elective science course. The Student Edition can be supplemented with reproducible worksheets from the components books and ancillary materials.

Student Edition

The Student Edition is organized into 7 units and 25 chapters. The first 11 chapters focus on the basic principles of ecology. Chapters 12 through 25 explore the role and impact of human activities on natural systems.

Throughout the text, students are given frequent opportunities to evaluate viewpoints and to develop their own opinions. The intent of *Addison-Wesley Environmental Science* is not to persuade students to adopt a predetermined philosophy. Instead, the program is designed to inform and to encourage students to develop viewpoints through sound reasoning.

Annotated Teacher's Edition

The comprehensive Annotated Teacher's Edition contains all the information needed to teach an exciting, complete, hands-on science course. Teaching tips, answers to in-text questions, and suggestions for cooperative learning and multicultural perspectives are included directly on the pages where they are appropriate. Additional pages in the front of the Teacher's Edition include a chapter planning guide, a chapter overview, teaching strategies, demonstrations, advance planning for laboratory activities, resources, and answers to end-of-chapter review questions.

Laboratory Manual

The Laboratory Manual provides students with an opportunity to practice the skills involved in conducting a scientific investigation. The manual contains 34 investigations.

The Teacher's Edition of the Laboratory Manual provides instructions, safety notes, preparation guides, and teaching suggestions to ensure that the laboratory portion of the course is safe and meaningful. Answers to questions are overprinted on the pages of the Teacher's Edition.

Teacher's Resource Package

The teacher's resource package contains four supplementary booklets.

- **Review Book** contains a review worksheet for every section within the chapter, as well as chapter vocabulary activities.
- **Skills Book** contains two worksheets for every chapter, one featuring a study skill and one featuring a process skill.
- **Issues/Case Studies** explores real-life issues in environmental science. Students are presented with opposing viewpoints and encouraged to form their own opinions.
- **Test Book** includes two tests for every chapter in the student edition. Form A tests are multiple choice for quick grading and assessment. Form B tests use higher-order and critical-thinking skills in a short-answer format. The book also contains two multiple choice mid-term exams and one final exam.

SelecTest Computer Test Bank

The test bank software provides a test-generating tool for teachers. Test questions for each chapter can be selected on the basis of the type of question or chapter reference. The program allows teachers to edit or add new test questions. A booklet containing all the test bank questions and answers is included. Software is available for users of IBM-PC and Macintosh computers.

Ancillary Options

Addison-Wesley publishes several related products that can be used as supplements to enrich your Environmental Science class. The chapter planning guides in the Teacher's Edition include the following three products:

- *One Minute Readings: Issues in Science, Technology, and Society*, Richard F. Brinkerhoff, 1992.
- *Multiculturalism in Mathematics, Science, and Technology: Readings and Activities*, 1993.
- *CEPUP: Chemical Education for Public Understanding Program*, Lawrence Hall of Science, University of California at Berkeley, 1990.

Unit Openers

Each of the seven units begins with a two-page visual spread. The photographs in the spread represent major topics covered in the unit. Each unit is also represented by a pictographic symbol from one of seven human societies, ancient or modern. The symbol represents a concept that weaves together many of the ideas within the unit. The unit opener pages also contain an explanation of the symbol and its relevance to environmental science.

Chapter Openers

The first page of each chapter includes a photographic and written introduction to help students place the chapter into the larger environmental scope. The chapter introduction also includes a list of the sections inside the chapter that can be used as a study guide. The pictographic symbol introduced in the unit opener appears on the chapter opener as well, tying together the chapters within the unit.

Addison-Wesley Environmental Science is... STUDENT-FRIENDLY!

Writing Style is clear, comprehensible, and engaging, designed to excite students with a wide range of interests and abilities.

Word Power shows the derivations of some of the key terms in the text.

Section Reviews help students master the section content and apply thinking skills to the new concepts.

Think Critically enables students to test their understanding of issues and ideas by applying them to new situations.

Links to other subjects show how concepts in environmental science relate to other areas of study.

Field Activities show how you can take environmental science issues out of the classroom and into the environment and community.

Datelines bring the history of environmental science issues to life by connecting real events to the concepts of ecological interactions.

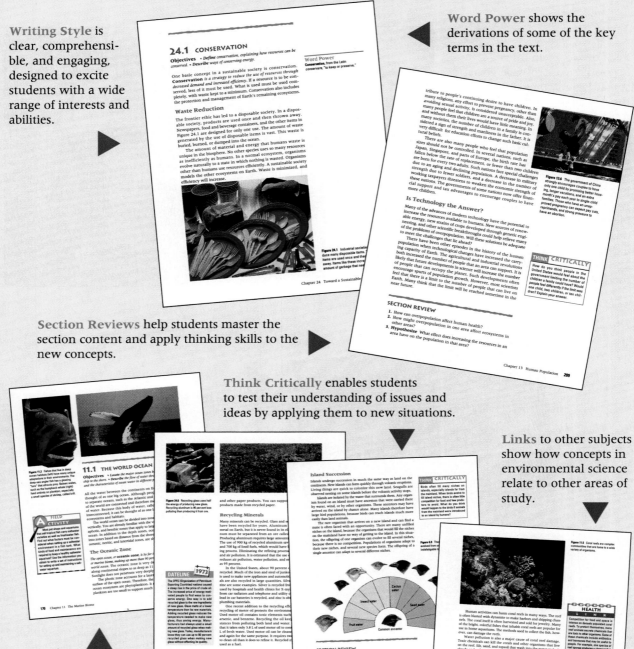

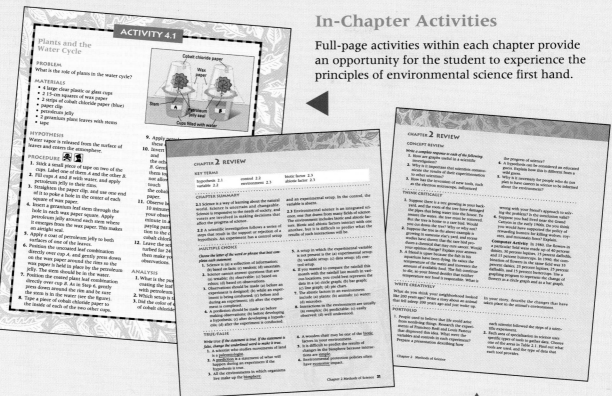

In-Chapter Activities

Full-page activities within each chapter provide an opportunity for the student to experience the principles of environmental science first hand.

Chapter Review

Each chapter ends with a comprehensive review that allows students to test their knowledge of the chapter content and concepts.

- **Chapter summary** reviews the contents at a glance.
- **Short-answer questions** check knowledge of the main ideas.
- **Think Critically** helps students focus on issues and sharpens their decision-making skills.
- **Writing Activities** allow students to develop and apply their writing skills to concepts and current events.
- **Portfolio** provides suggestions for long-term projects that students may choose to undertake to further develop concepts introduced in the text. An essay on how to integrate portfolios into your curriculum is also included in the Teacher's Edition.

- **End of Chapter Activities** provide an additional opportunity to experience the principles of environmental science.

Frontiers chronicle new developments in the field of environmental science that relate to issues in the chapter.

Feature Essays in every chapter take environmental science out of the classroom and into the headlines.

People and the Environment explores the relationship between humans and their role in the world's ecosystems.

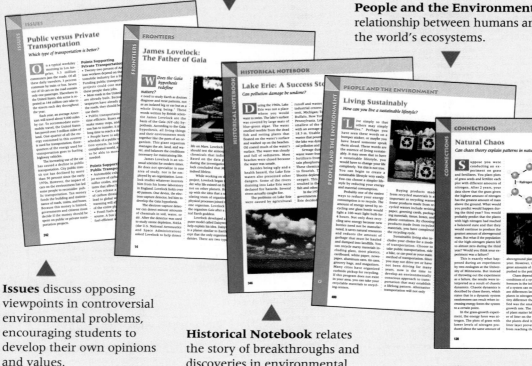

Issues discuss opposing viewpoints in controversial environmental problems, encouraging students to develop their own opinions and values.

Historical Notebook relates the story of breakthroughs and discoveries in environmental science, illustrating the ongoing nature of scientific research.

Connections show the integrated nature of issues in environmental science, connecting topics in the text to other disciplines.

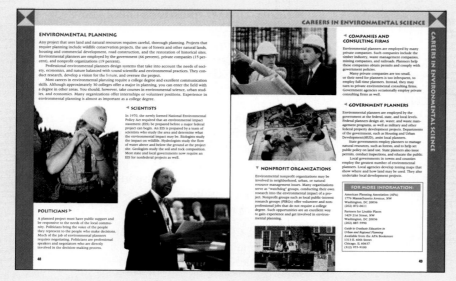

Career Pages at the end of each unit introduce students to the professional world of environmental science and management. Each spread also includes additional sources of information that students may choose to explore on their own.

Unit Pages in the front of the Teacher's Edition provide an overview of the unit contents, a list of audiovisual resources, and any advance preparation needed for activities and demonstrations in the upcoming unit.

Lesson Cycle Guides that follow the chapter planning grids in the Teacher's Edition help you structure your lessons with *Skill Objectives, Motivate, Teaching Strategies,* and *Evaluate* suggestions.

Chapter Planning Grids in the Teacher's Edition help you plan your lessons and direct you to related materials in other components of the program.

Chapter Resource pages provide answers to questions in the feature essays and the end of chapter review, as well as teaching tips and material preparation needed for the activities in the Student Edition.

Today's teachers are challenged with the task of meeting the needs of diverse student populations who bring to the educational forum unique sets of abilities, interests, and learning styles.

Positive Learning Environment

All students should be provided with a positive educational environment with optimum opportunities for success. The following strategies may help teachers structure learning for populations consisting of students with different ability levels, physical, visual, or hearing impairments, and limited English proficiency.

Ability Levels

Based on individual needs of students, classroom management, and teaching styles, the components and ancillaries of *Addison-Welsey Environmental Science* may be used at different levels, as deemed necessary by the teacher. Suggestions for use of chapter sections, features, worksheets, and ancillaries are provided in the chapter planning guides. Listed below are other strategies for teaching students of varying ability levels and for implementing the text features.

- Speak clearly and slowly using body language and gestures.
- Approach concepts in several different ways and provide relevant, common examples.
- Use hands-on activities and demonstrations to reinforce concepts.
- Encourage a variety of responses, including speaking, drawing, demonstrating, and writing.
- Check for understanding and comprehension frequently.
- Use cooperative learning groups for activities and investigations and actively encourage individuals to participate within their groups.
- Have core-level students complete the worksheets in the Review Book and the Skills Book as homework.

Physical, Visual, or Hearing Impairments

The specific nature and severity of the physical, visual, or hearing impairment of a student will determine the degree to which classroom management techniques and teaching methods will need to be adjusted. It is important for the classroom teacher to work in close cooperation with the student, his/her parent, and the school guidance counselor to determine what the student's needs are. Other provisions for students with physical, visual, or hearing impairments include the following.

- Make sure that aisles are unobstructed and wide enough to accommodate wheelchairs and that materials and equipment are within reach of the student.
- If deemed appropriate by the guidance counselor, enlist the aid of one or more students to physically assist the student as necessary.
- Do not exclude students with physical challenges from participation in activities. Instead, provide these students with roles such as timekeeper or activity manager.
- Seat students with limited vision or hearing problems close to the front of the classroom and always face the class when speaking.

Limited English Proficiency (LEP) Students

Science presents three levels of challenges to students with limited English proficiency—overcoming a language barrier, achieving mastery in science, and addressing social concerns. The following teaching strategies are designed to help teachers create a positive educational environment:

- Relate and incorporate cultural content into discussions. Stress relevant examples.
- Provide tools, such as picture dictionaries, and other visual learning resources.
- Use illustrations with labeling exercises to build and reinforce vocabulary.
- Have students keep a "dictionary" of key terms and words that includes the term in English, the term in their primary language, and the definition. Encourage students to illustrate their dictionaries.
- Encourage students to use English primary-language dictionaries.
- Use remedial or average vocabulary and skills worksheets.
- Provide opportunities for students to communicate nonverbally.

THE LESSON CYCLE

Like many events in nature, learning is an ongoing process that occurs in cycles. Similarly, lesson planning should reflect the stages of the learning cycle. The first phase of the lesson cycle is often called the Planning Phase. This phase includes task analysis, in which the teacher selects objectives at the appropriate level and identifies the content to be taught. Once these decisions are made, the teacher proceeds to the second phase, or the Teaching Phase during which he or she plans the daily lesson and incorporates the appropriate teaching steps into the instructional design. The Teaching Phase uses a lesson plan that includes the following elements.

Focus/Motivate is a procedure for generating student interest in the learning that is to follow. The focus is often referred to as the anticipatory set. The anticipatory set develops student readiness by involving the learner in a relevant way. The focus should also use a technique called transfer to connect prior knowledge to the current instruction. Other techniques of focus include asking divergent questions, role playing, telling stories or anecdotes, showing pictures and cartoons, and using open and closed inquiry methods.

Objective/Purpose is a teacher communication that informs students what they will need to know or be able to do at the end of the instruction. The objective also states why the learning is important, useful, and relevant for the student.

Explanation is the method selected by the teacher to present the objective (information) to the learner. Explanation techniques may include the use of definitions, rules, process steps, and examples.

Modeling is what the teacher does to cause the learner to recognize or imitate the learning. Modeling allows for a visual demonstration of the learning process. Techniques of modeling include both visual and verbal demonstrations, showing examples of an acceptable finished product.

Knowledge and Comprehension Check involves assessing students' understanding of the learning. Techniques for assessing mastery include posing key questions to the students and asking them to explain the definitions, concepts, and attributes in their own words. The ability to defend viewpoints is a particularly important indicator of comprehension in Environmental Science.

Monitoring and Adjusting is the process of observing learner behavior, as well as the learning environment, during instruction and making necessary changes in the instruction to achieve the desired results.

Guided Practice is individual student practice of the concepts. This practice is monitored by the teacher by guiding the student through the problem, skill, or work to be done and providing feedback to the student.

Reteaching occurs when learning has not taken place or when students have not mastered the objectives. Like the monitoring and adjusting step, reteaching involves changing the instructional mode to achieve the desired results.

Independent Practice involves student practice of the learned concepts without teacher assistance. Two psychological principles should be considered to evaluate the appropriate amount of practice: (1) Massing practice at the beginning of learning makes for fast learning, and (2) Distributing practice after material is learned makes for long remembering. In keeping with these psychological principles, new material should be practiced briefly, intensely, and frequently. As students internalize the material, practice should become less frequent and be spaced further and further apart.

Enrichment occurs after learning has taken place, and following guided and independent practice. The enrichment step extends knowledge by providing students with higher-level activities.

Closure is bringing the lesson to a logical conclusion. Involve students in the lesson closure by having them use their own words to summarize what they learned.

Planning and Pacing Guide

Addison-Wesley Environmental Science is designed and organized to be flexible and adaptable to a variety of curricula. The text can be used as a full-year course for core, standard, or advanced students. It can also be used as a half-year course for students seeking an elective science class. The following charts are provided to help you plan and pace your lessons according to the needs of your schedule and your students. More detailed planning guides are included in the teacher's pages for each chapter. Those guides provide additional suggestions for enriching your lessons with ancillary materials for your core, standard, and advanced students.

The suggested number of days for each chapter of the core and standard full-year curricula are based on a 180-day school year. The half-year course is based on a 90-day term for standard students. Although the half-year course begins with Chapter 12, the chart provides suggestions for review sections from the first part of the text. A review of these sections would be particularly valuable to students who have not had a recent course in life science or biology.

KEY: A = Activity
F = Field Activity
E = Enrichment Essay
* = Recommended for review
- = Not recommended

Unit	Chapter	CORE Days	CORE Sections	CORE Features	STANDARD Days	STANDARD Sections	STANDARD Features	1/2 YEAR Days	1/2 YEAR Sections*	1/2 YEAR Features
1	1	7	All	A1.1, F, E	7	All	All	-	1.2, 1.3	-
	2	8	All	A2.2, F, E	6	All	All	-	2.2	-
	3	5	3.2, 3.3	A3.2, E	5	All	A 3.1, F, E	-	3.3	-
2	4	10	All	All	9	All	All	-	4.1, 4.2	-
	5	9	All	A5.2, F, E	8	All	All	-	5.1	-
	6	8	6.1, 6.3, 6.4	A6.2, F, E	8	All	All	-	6.1	-
3	7	6	All	All	5	All	All	-	-	-
	8	6	All	A8.1, E	5	All	All	-	-	-
	9	6	All	A9.2, F, E	5	All	A9.1, F, E	-	-	-
	10	6	All	A10.2, F, E	5	All	All	-	-	-
	11	6	All	A11.1, E	5	All	All	-	-	-
4	12	8	All	A12.1, E	7	All	A12.1, F, E	5	All	All
	13	8	13.1, 13.2	A13.2, F, E	7	All	All	5	All	A13.1, F, E
	14	9	All	A14.2, F, E	8	All	All	7	All	A14.1, F, E
5	15	9	15.1, 15.3, 15.4	A15.2, E	9	All	All	8	All	A15.1, F, E
	16	8	All	A16.1, A16.2, E	8	All	All	6	All	All
	17	9	17.1, 17.2, 17.3	All	9	All	All	7	All	All
6	18	-	-	-	8	All	All	6	All	All
	19	9	19.1, 19.2, 19.4	A19.1, A19.2, F2, E	9	All	All	8	All	A19.1, F1, E
	20	-	—	-	8	All	All	6	All	All
	21	8	21.1, 21.2, 21.4	A19.2, F, E	8	All	All	7	All	A19.1, F, E
	22	10	All	A22.2, F, E	9	All	All	8	All	All
7	23	9	All	All	8	All	All	7	All	All
	24	8	All	A24.1, F, E	7	All	All	5	All	A24.2, F, E
	25	8	All	A25.1, F, E	7	All	All	5	All	A25.2, F, E

Skills Matrix By Chapter

Addison-Wesley Environmental Science provides students with frequent opportunities to learn and practice a variety of thinking skills and process skills that will be of value not only in the science classroom, but in their future lives and careers as well. The skills of analyzing, experimenting, explaining, and describing appear in every chapter and are therefore not included in this chart.

	THINKING SKILLS											PROCESS SKILLS									
	Apply	Compare/Contrast	Deduce	Define	Discuss	Evaluate	Hypothesize	Infer	Integrate	Predict	Relate	Calculate	Classify	Computer	Diagram/Illustrate	Examine/Observe	Graph	Identify	List	Locate	Measure
1	•	•					•	•	•						•	•	•	•	•	•	•
2	•						•	•				•		•	•						
3	•					•	•			•	•			•	•						
4				•		•	•	•		•				•				•	•		
5						•				•		•		•			•	•			
6		•		•						•	•			•	•	•					•
7			•					•		•					•						•
8		•			•		•	•			•			•				•	•	•	
9		•					•		•	•					•				•		
10	•						•	•		•									•		
11	•	•					•	•		•									•	•	
12	•							•		•											
13							•	•				•		•							•
14	•	•				•		•		•									•		•
15		•						•		•							•		•	•	
16				•				•		•					•	•					
17	•				•		•	•	•						•						•
18		•					•	•		•								•	•		
19	•				•		•	•		•					•	•		•	•		
20		•					•	•		•											
21			•				•			•					•	•		•			
22		•				•	•			•									•		
23		•	•		•		•	•	•	•											
24	•			•			•	•		•	•			•					•	•	
25	•							•		•							•		•		

COOPERATIVE LEARNING

Cooperation and collaboration are instrumental parts of the science process.

Cooperative learning is a teaching approach that requires students to work collaboratively to carry out structured activities. To accomplish a cooperative task, students work in small groups to solve a problem or create a product to which each group member contributes and for which each member is held equally accountable. Interdependence among group members is essential for the group as a whole to be successful in achieving its designated goal.

The cooperative-learning approach provides students with an opportunity to develop positive social skills that are beneficial in everyday life as well as in the classroom. Process- and critical-thinking skills are extended as students become aware of the methods their teammates use to solve problems. In addition, students often find that in sharing information with team members, they come to a better understanding of the concepts they are studying.

Cooperative-Learning Groups

Cooperative-learning groups should range in number from two to six, with each group having three to four members. Once a group is established, it must remain together until the activity is completed. Do not dissolve a group that is having difficulty working together socially or staying on task. Keeping the group intact helps students learn the social interaction skills needed to solve problems or complete tasks through cooperation and collaboration.

Suggested Roles in Cooperative Groups

Members of a cooperative-learning group must assume a variety of roles for the group to collaborate effectively. The roles students assume will largely be determined by the nature of the project. For example, the roles required to work cooperatively on a laboratory assignment may be very different from the roles needed for a debate or a research activity. Some suggested roles are described here.

- **Principal Investigator** The Principal Investigator manages the tasks within the activity and insures that all members understand the goals and content of the activity. The Principal Investigator serves as a liaison between the teacher and the group.
- **Primary Researcher or Activity Manager** The Primary Researcher/Activity Manager assumes the role of group manager for activities involving research. The Primary Researcher should explain the task to the group and identify the resources the group will use.
- **Materials Manager** The Materials Manager assembles and distributes the materials and equipment needed to carry out an assignment. The Materials Manager also reports damaged, poorly operating, or unsafe equipment to the teacher.
- **Data Collector/Organizer** The Data Collector/Organizer coordinates the group data and certifies each group member's contributions to the activity. This student may also be responsible for reporting the results of an activity either in writing or orally to the class or to the teacher. Occasionally, the tasks of the Data Collector/Organizer may be split among several students such as Data Collector, Data Organizer, and/or Presenter.
- **Presenter** The Presenter reports the results of an activity. The Presenter may field questions posed by classmates or the teacher about the group's activity or delegate specific types of questions to other members of the group as a panel discussion.
- **Timekeeper** The Timekeeper is responsible for keeping track of time, monitoring noise level, checking the results of an activity for accuracy, and making sure proper safety precautions are observed by all group members.

Self-Evaluation

Encourage students to become involved in the evaluation process by providing time for them to reflect on the activity. Remind students that for all projects, you may call on any member of a group to explain what the group has done. Also remind students that the nature of cooperative activities is such that individual members of a group succeed only when the group as a whole succeeds. Thus, the success of the group is reflected by the individual contributions of each group member.

CONCEPT MAPPING

Concept mapping is a technique that helps students learn in a more substantial way: students draw maps that link together main ideas in a particular format. Concept mapping relies on a basic learning principle. People learn best by adding new information to what they already know. Typically, students are trained to memorize facts and concepts. Often, students only remember new information for a short time. Unless memorizing new information is continually reinforced, students quickly forget what they have learned.

Concept mapping has several benefits that help students:

- make connections between things they already know and new ideas.
- learn how to organize information and establish relationships between ideas.
- find new meaning in the things they are learning.

Concept mapping helps teachers:

- introduce new concepts to students in an interesting way.
- determine student misconceptions.

Most importantly, concept mapping can give both teachers and students new insights.

Teaching Concept-Mapping Skills

The best way to teach students about concept mapping is by practice. You may wish to assign concept mapping as a closure activity at the completion of each chapter. Review the concept-mapping instructions on page x of the student text with your class. To help students get started with concept mapping, you can prepare several incomplete maps with fill-in blanks. Have students write the missing concept and link-ing words in the blanks. Also, you can prepare lists of scrambled concepts and linking words and ask students to put the words into the correct category.

To encourage students, show them examples of good maps. Good maps show concepts linked in a logical arrangement and do not contain misconceptions. A suggested concept map for Chapter 1 appears below. Remember that concept maps are intended to be flexible tools for learning. Stress to the students that there is more than one correct way to do a concept map. Reinforce the idea that concept maps are a tool to help students learn in their own way.

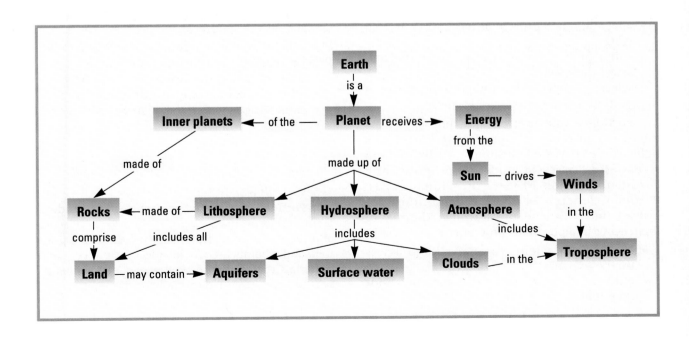

PORTFOLIOS IN SCIENCE

Traditional tests can't tell teachers and parents all they need to know about students' problem-solving, critical-thinking, attitudes, and interpersonal communications skills. Portfolios are a more accurate way to assess students' mastery of knowledge and skills.

Portfolios are collections of representative work done by students during the year. Portfolios are valuable in several ways. By encouraging students to create portfolios, teachers enable students to assess and revise their own work, to develop the ability to identify their own strengths and weaknesses, and to set goals for learning. Because students choose the items for their portfolios, portfolios are a powerful tool for teachers to gain an understanding of student achievement, knowledge, and attitudes.

The decision to use portfolios requires input from teachers, administrators, and members of the community. Portfolios require a significant amount of time for planning and managing. Keep in mind that using portfolios is a continuously developing process.

Initially, teachers should establish a portfolio protocol in the classroom to guide students through each of the following steps of the portfolio development process. The protocol might include:

- identifying the characteristics of good academic work.
- applying criteria for good work to their own work.
- using peer-revision groups to refine and assess their work.
- selecting work so that the portfolio creates a portrait of the student as a learner.

Portfolios can be used as a tool for assessment. For instance, periodic portfolio reviews help to identify each student's strengths and weaknesses, assess a student's progress, and adjust instruction to meet individual needs. Portfolio conferences offer an opportunity for insights into each student's learning. The role of the teacher in a portfolio conference is to:

- encourage students to analyze and assess their own work.
- guide students to draw conclusions about their work.

- provide reinforcement.
- participate in conversations with students.

Many kinds of student work can be included in portfolios. Some examples of items that are suitable for portfolios are:

- open-ended projects that show problem-solving, and critical-thinking skills
- lab reports that display the use of science process skills
- collected data entries and logs
- items that illustrate creative expressions such as audio and video tapes, art, and photo-albums
- journals that record a student's reactions, reflections, and feelings
- computer readouts and disks
- written critiques
- rough drafts and final copies of "acceptable," "unacceptable," and "important" pieces
- selected samples of specific content presented over time
- group assignments and ideas from "brain-storming" sessions
- work that shows progress and the ability to reflect on one's intellectual growth
- written work and other projects that offer evidence of progress and goal setting

Students can select what they want for their portfolios within the guidelines set by the teacher, student, or the nature of the content. For example, students could be asked to choose two examples for categories such as:

- something that was difficult
- what you did to start figuring it out
- something new that you learned
- a solution you reached
- topics for which you need to keep searching for ideas
- two things that you would like to forget
- two things you are proud of

Portfolios can be what each teacher/student team decides to make them. It is up to the teacher and the student to decide what will go into a portfolio and what its use will be. Ideas for projects, and materials that could become a part of a student's portfolio are suggested throughout this book.

LABORATORY SAFETY

Good planning and common sense can make the science laboratory a safe and enjoyable learning environment.

Safety in the Laboratory

Safety should always be of prime importance in the science classroom and laboratory. Although students must be made aware of safe and appropriate laboratory behavior, accountability for student safety rests with the school administrators, faculty, and staff. As the classroom teacher, it is important to be aware that accidents resulting in injury can occur in the classroom or laboratory at any time. However, by making yourself and your students aware of potentially dangerous situations, the risk of accidents can be minimized.

Where to Begin

Safety regulations vary from state-to-state, district-to-district, and school-to-school. Before beginning any demonstration or laboratory investigation, you must familiarize yourself with all federal, state, and local safety regulations as well as specific guidelines established by your district or school. Such guidelines will provide you with information about materials that are prohibited for use in the classroom and those that require special conditions for use. In addition, such guidelines provide instruction about ventilation, chemical storage, disposal procedures, and the appropriate procedures for handling accidents and emergencies.

General Safety Information

At the beginning of the school year and periodically throughout the year, review with students what to do in case of fire. Display a list of these instructions, along with a map showing the locations of fire exits, in a prominent location. Make sure students know the locations of and are instructed on the proper use of the following:

- fire alarm
- first-aid kit
- eyewash facilities
- fire blanket
- dry-chemical fire extinguisher

In addition, make available to *each* student the following protective clothing:

- safety goggles
- laboratory gloves
- laboratory apron

Caution students about wearing appropriate attire in the laboratory. Loose-fitting clothing should be properly confined, and when open flames are in use, long hair should be tied back. Encourage students to report all accidents immediately, no matter how minor.

Never permit students to work in a laboratory alone. In addition, make sure students understand that the laboratory is a place for serious study and no irresponsible behavior will be tolerated.

Safety Symbols and Guidelines

A variety of safety symbols are used throughout the text and Laboratory Program to alert students to potential hazards. At the beginning of the school year, review with students the Safety Notes included on page xi of the text. Before students begin to perform any in-text activity or laboratory investigation, review the meanings of the symbols and any caution statements that appear in the investigation.

Field Study/Trip Safety

Field studies and trips can be exciting and valuable teaching tools in science; however, as with a laboratory environment, field activities can pose dangers to students. Before students conduct field studies or go on field trips, it is suggested that teachers do the following:

- Find out if any students have any restrictions due to medical conditions that may be aggravated by outdoor activities.
- Inform parents of the intended trip and obtain consent forms that permit the students to participate.
- Visit the site to look for potential dangers before taking students out.
- Tell students ahead of time that they will be going on a field study or trip. Discuss proper attire for the trip as well as rules of conduct that must be followed.
- Warn students about coming into contact with poisonous plants, such as poison ivy, oak, or sumac. Also instruct students not to try to touch or catch animals they may encounter.
- Carry a first-aid kit.

MATERIALS FOR LABORATORY ACTIVITIES

The following supplies are needed for the laboratory activities in the Student Edition of *Addison-Wesley Environmental Science*. A list of suppliers can be found on p. T20 of this Teacher's Edition.

Item	Quantity per Group	Chapter	Item	Quantity per Group	Chapter
Acetate	4 sheets	8	Fireproof pad	1	14
Aluminum foil	1 100-cm piece	3	Flask, 1 L	1	20
	1 5-cm square	16	Food coloring	1 bottle	11
Aphids, live	5	12	Food samples	small amounts of 4 different foods	14
Apple peelings	from 1 apple	18			
Baby food jar, empty	1 per student	13	Geranium leaves (with stem)	2	4
Bag, medium-size paper	1	8	Glass slides with coverslip	5	5
Balance	1	18		1	6, 20
Beaker, 100-mL	1	5	(without coverslip)	5	22
Beakers, 250-mL	1	1, 11	Glass tubing	1 piece bent at a right angle	20
	5	17			
Beakers, 500-mL	1	6, 11, 20	Gloves, heat-resistant	1 pair	14
	3	15	Glue	1 stick	8, 9, 23
Beaker, 1 L	1	6, 10	Glycerine	5 g	20
Biuret's solution	25 mL	14	Graduated cylinder (10 mL)	1	5
Blotting paper	1 sheet	4	Graduated cylinder (100 mL)	1	5, 9, 10, 14, 17, 18, 21
	4 sheets	24			
Blue litmus paper	3 strips	15	Grapes	3	4
Bolt	1	17	Graph paper	1 sheet	1, 5, 6, 15, 22
Bread, white	1 slice	4		1 sheet per pair of students	23
	15 g	14	Grass seeds	1 pinch	6, 8
Brine-shrimp eggs	1 small container	11	Gravel, rocks, soil	combined to fill bottom of large jar	8
Bunsen burner	1	18			
Cardboard	1 piece (9" x 12")	20	Grease pencil	1	4, 17, 18, 19, 21
Cardboard box, large, black with lid	1	17		1 per student	13
			Hammer	1	15, 17
Cheese, Roquefort	1 chunk	4	Hand drill	1	17
Clams	2 live	11	Hand lens	1	4, 24
Clamp	1	1	Hand lens (or dissecting microscope)	1	11
Clock with second hand	1	10, 12			
Chlorella culture	20 mL	21	Hand lens (tripod type)	1	9
Cloth rag	1	15	Hot plate	1	20
Clover seeds	1 pinch	6, 8	Ice	1 (to fill 9" x12" pan)	11, 20
Cobalt chloride paper (blue)	2 strips	4	Index card	1 (per pair of students)	23
Coins		20	Jar, clear plastic or glass with tight-fitting lid	1	8
Colored pencils	2 different colors	1			
	6 different colors	23	Jars, 500-mL with lid	4	16
	1 set per student	25	Jar, 1-L without lid	1	18
Compass	1	9	Jar, 4-L with lid	1	19
Cork stopper	1 4-cm base diam.	14	Jars, without lid	2	9, 11
Cotton balls	1 handful	11	Laboratory apron	1	14
Cotton-tip swab	1	12	Land isopods	5	3, 8
Coverslip	1	10	Laundry starch, liquid	300 mL	24
Crayon	1	17	Leaf, fresh green	1	12
Crickets	5	8	Leaves, decayed (humus)	50 g	18
Crucible	1	18	Light bulb (100-watt)	1	22
Cryptobiotic tardigrade	2	10	Light source (window)	1 per class	21
Cups, large (clear plastic or glass)	4	4	Lima bean seeds	3	2
Cups, paper	3	6	Lima beans	2	5
Cups, plastic foam	2	9	Lima beans, mashed, cooked	15 g	14
	5	11	Magazines, old	1 large stack	24
Depression slide	1	10	Marking pen	1	3, 9, 11, 15
Detergent solution (5%)	10 mL	19	(red)	1 per pair of students	23
Dill pickle	1 slice	4		1 set	24
Dominoes	15	16	Masking tape	1 roll	3
Droppers	2	5		2 pieces	4
	1	6, 10, 11, 12, 20, 21		3 pieces	15, 21
				5 pieces	22
	1 per student	13	Matches	1 box	14
Dry yeast	1 small container	11	Mealworms	5	8
Earthworms	5	8	Metal pie tin	1	3
Egg white, cooked	15 mL	14	Meter stick	1	9, 13
Eggbeater	1	24	Methylene blue	1 dropperful	5
Electric fan	1 per class	17		30 mL	18

Item	Quantity per Group	Chapter	Item	Quantity per Group	Chapter
Methylene blue (diluted)	30 mL	21	Salt	8 mL	11
Metric measuring spoons	1 set	11, 20		35 g	11
Metric ruler	1	1, 6, 10, 14, 16		250 mL	17
	1 per pair of students	23	Salt solution (5%)	10 mL	19
Microscope	1	5, 6, 20	Sand	250 mL	17
Microscope, dissecting	1	10	Saucers	2	2
Microscope, binocular (or hand lens)	1	22	Scissors	1	3, 4, 12, 17, 22, 23
Mixing bowl, large	1	24		1 per pair of students	23
Modeling clay	1 small ball	16	Shoebox with lid	1	3
Mung bean seeds	12	8	Shoebox without lid	1	11
Nail	1 small	17	Shovel (or trowel)	1	18
Newspapers	3 full sheets	17	Sodium hydroxide	4 pellets	16
	1 sheet	24	Soft drink bottles, plastic	2 2-L	22
Newspapers	1 large stack	23	Soil, garden	3 cups	6
Nitrate solution (4%)	100 mL	21		1 cup	9
Notebooks	1 per student	19, 23, 24, 25		2 g	18
Nuts (hardware)	3	17	(3 different types)	250 mL each type	18
Oil solution	10 mL	19	Soil (containing dead conifer needles)	240 mL	9
Orange	1 wedge	4			
Pan (with screening inside)	1 large square	24	Soil, grass, leaves	combined to fill 1000-mL beaker	6
Paper, unruled	1 sheet	5, 23			
	3 sheets	6	Solid waste pieces (glass, paper, metal, fruit, plastic, or wood)	1 L in all	19
Paper, ruled	1	6, 8, 15, 16, 21, 25			
			Spatula	1	10
	1 per student	13	Sponges	2	2
Paper, white construction	4	6	Spoon, plastic	1	20
	1	9	Steel wool	small bunch	1
	1 piece 20-cm by 20-cm	23	Stock solution	1 L per class	13
Paper, dark construction	1 sheet	18	Stopwatch	1	16, 17
Paper clips	1	4, 14	Stream table	1	10
	152	12	Sugar	3 g	18
Paper towel	2	3	Sulfur coal	1 small rock sample	15
	6	9	Tape	8 pieces	19
	1	12		1 roll	22
	4 Petri-dish size pieces	19	Test tubes	1	1, 14
Pencils	1	1, 6, 15, 16, 21, 23		4	5
				5	14
	4	9		3	21
	1 per student	13, 23, 24, 25	(with stopper)	3	18
Petri dishes with lids	5	4, 22	(with screw cap)	3	20
	1	12	Test-tube clamp	1	14
	4	18	Test-tube rack	1	5, 14, 18, 21
Petri dish without lid	1	11	Thermometers	2	11, 22
Petroleum jelly	5 g	4, 22		1	14
pH paper	1 slip	6		5	17
Phenol red indicator	1 dropperful per student	13	Thread spool, empty	1	17
Phenolphthalein solution	1 dropperful	16	Tongs	1	18, 19, 20
Phosphate solution (4%)	100 mL	21	Toothpicks	100 to 200 per class	2
Pie tins, foil	3 or 4	17	Triple-beam balance	1	14
Plastic wrap	5 10-cm squares	11	Tuna fish (packed in water)	15 g	14
	1 5-cm square	16	Tweezers	1	16
	1 20-cm square	22	Twist-tie	1	16
Posterboard	1 large sheet	24	Washer	1	17
Potato, cooked	15 g	14	Watch (or small clock)	1 per class	2
Potting soil mix	200 g	19	Water, distilled	1 dropperful	10
	3 L	19		100 mL	21
	700 g	22		100 mL	20
Pyrite	1 small rock sample	15	Water, pond		21
Radish seeds	3	2	Water samples (such as dishwater, rainwater, or pond water	5 mL each	21
	40 approx.	19			
Reference sources		6, 8, 9, 11, 12, 23			
			Water, tap	500 mL	6
Rice grains, uncooked	150	23		1.5 L	15, 16
Ring stand	1	1, 14, 18, 22		10 mL	19
Rocks, sand, gravel	1 pie tin full	3		250 mL	18
Rolling pin	1	24		1 L	19
Rubber band	1	18, 22		600 mL	24
Rubber gloves	1 pair per student	13	(at room temperature)	250 mL	17
Rubber hose	1 4-m piece	10	(aged)	1 L	11
Rubber stopper, 1 hole	1	20	Wax paper	2 15-cm square pieces	4
Rubber tubing	1 m	20	Wire gauze	1	18
Safety goggles	1 per student	13	Wood	1 flat piece (20 cm by 40 cm)	3
	1	14, 16, 18		1 scrap piece about 3 cm by 30 cm	17

Equipment and Material Suppliers

Analytic Scientific
11049 Bandera Rd.
San Antonio, TX 78250

Arbor Scientific
P.O. Box 2750
Ann Arbor, MI 48106-2750

Carolina Scientific Co.
2700 York Rd.
Burlington, NC 27215

Central Scientific Co.
11222 Melrose Ave.
Franklin Park, IL 60131

Edmund Scientific Co.
101 Gloucester Pike
Barrington, NJ 08077

Fisher Scientific Co.
Educational Materials Division
4901 W. Le Moyne St.
Chicago, IL 60651

Hubbard Scientific
3101 Iris Ave. Ste. 215
Boulder, CO 80301

Lab Safety Supply Inc.
401 S. Wright Rd.
P.O. Box 1368
Janesville, WI 53547-1368

Nasco West Inc.
P.O. Box 3837
Modesto, CA 95352

Sargeant-Welch Scientific
7300 N. Linder Ave.
Skokie, IL 60077

Audiovisual Suppliers

Bullfrog Films
P.O. Box 149
Oley, PA 19606

Time-Life Video
1271 Avenue of the Americas
New York, NY 10020

Coronet/MTI Film and Video
108 Wilmot Rd.
Deerfield, IL 60015-9925

Encyclopedia Britannica Educational Corporation
Learning Materials
310 S. Michigan Ave.
Chicago, IL 60604-9839

Films for the Humanities and Sciences
P.O. Box 2054
Princeton, NJ 08543-2053

Centron Films
108 Wilmot Road
Deerfield, IL 60015-9990

National Geographic Society Educational Services
P.O. Box 98019
Washington, D.C. 20090-8019

Optical Data Corporation
30 Technology Dr.
Warren, NJ 07059

Phoenix/BFA Films
468 Park Avenue South
New York, NY 10016

National Film Board of Canada
1251 Avenue of the Americas
New York, NY 10020

Unit Overview

Unit 1 develops an awareness of the environment by presenting Earth as the only known viable habitat for people and other organisms. Chapter 1 focuses on the unique characteristics of Earth that make it capable of supporting life. In Chapter 2, students are introduced to the methods and skills used by scientists and others who study the environment. The importance of environmental study is stressed as it relates to everyday decision making. The unit concludes in Chapter 3 with a discussion of how Earth has changed through time and how these changes have affected the Earth's ability to support life. In the final section of Chapter 3, the discussion of the needs of individual organisms is expanded to the ecosystem level.

Introducing the Unit

Class Activity   Display a bag of soil, a beaker of water, a stoppered test tube filled with air, a potted plant, and a photograph of an animal. Ask students what these objects have in common. Explain that each object represents a distinct and interesting part of Earth. Have students list ways in which they think each object relates to Earth. Tell students to save their lists for later use. Encourage students to revise their lists as they read the unit.

Class Activity   Display a world map, a globe, and a photograph of Earth as seen from space. Have students study the three views of Earth and write a paragraph in their notebooks or journals explaining how the information conveyed by each view differs. Ask students to use the Earth models to speculate about what percentage of Earth is covered by land and what percent by water. Have students add this information to their notebooks or journals. Ask students to make a list of features of Earth that are not shown by the models. Tell students that this unit presents data about many of Earth's features.

Teacher Resources

Audiovisual
The Living Earth, film/video, 25 minutes, National Geographic Society, 1991.
An Ecosystem: A Struggle for Survival, film/video, 22 minutes, National Geographic Society, 1975.
Gaia, video, 45 minutes, Bullfrog Films, 1990.

Computer Software
Ecology, Apple II, Merlin Scientific Limited.
Community Dynamics, Apple II, Educational Media Equipment Company.
Sim Earth, Macintosh, Maxis.

Suggested Readings
Brewer, Richard and Margaret T. McCann. *Laboratory and Field Manual of Ecology*, Saunders, 1982.

Advance Preparation

Chapter 1
Field Activity   Gather rulers and wide-mouthed jars (plastic, if possible).
Activity 1.1   Provide graph paper to students.
Activity 1.2   Gather steel wool, test tubes, ring stands clamps, and metric rulers.

Chapter 2
Field Activity   No materials required.
Activity 2.1   Buy several boxes of toothpicks.
Activity 2.2   Purchase radish and lima bean seeds, sponges, and plastic saucers.

Chapter 3
Field Activity   Gather bottle caps for the activity. Bring several different types of food to class. (Suggestions: ground beef, sugar cubes, apples, uncooked pasta, potatoes, bread cubes, and pieces of fruit.)
Activity 3.1   Gather shoe boxes with lids, aluminum foil, masking tape, scissors, and paper towels. Purchase land isopods from a biological supply house.
Activity 3.2   Obtain flat pieces of wood (20 cm x 40 cm), rocks, sand, gravel, metal pie tins, and markers.

Chapter 1 Planning Guide

Section	Core	Standard	Enriched	Section	Core	Standard	Enriched
1.1 Parts of Earth	•	•	•	**1.3 The Air**	•	•	•
Section Features Dateline 1972, p.3	•	•	•	**Section Features** Biology Link, p. 9		•	•
Physics Link, p.4	•	•	•	Word Power, p. 11	•	•	•
Blackline Masters Review Worksheet 1.1	•	•		**Blackline Masters** Review Worksheet 1.3	•	•	
Skills Worksheet 1A	•	•		**Laboratory Program** Investigation 1	•	•	•
Ancillary Options One Minute Readings, p. 80		•	•	**1.4 The Biosphere**	•	•	•
1.2 Earth's Land and Water	•	•	•	**Section Features** Dateline 1991, p. 13	•	•	•
Section Features Field Activity, p. 6	•	•	•	Frontiers, p. 14		•	•
Think Critically, p. 7	•	•	•	Activity 1.2, p. 17		•	•
Activity 1.1, p. 8	•	•	•	**Blackline Masters** Review Worksheet 1.3	•	•	•
Blackline Masters Review Worksheet 1.2	•	•		Skills Worksheet 1B	•	•	
Issues and Case Studies 1		•	•	**Ancillary Options** CEPUP Risk Comparison, p. 13		•	•
Ancillary Options Multiculturalism, p. 19		•	•				
One Minute Readings, p. 104			•				

Every chapter has two corresponding tests in the Test Book and one Vocabulary Review Worksheet in the Review Book.

Chapter Overview

Chapter 1 introduces the main themes of environmental science and ecology by focusing on the planet Earth—the living space shared by all organisms. Section 1.1 presents the unique traits of Earth that permit the planet to support life. Sections 1.2 and 1.3 concentrate on the features of the lithosphere, hydrosphere, and atmosphere that are important to living things. The chapter concludes in Section 1.4 with a discussion of the biosphere—the part of Earth that sustains all life.

Advance Planner

- Bring in old magazines and scissors for the activity in the Introducing the Chapter section.

Section 1.1
- No materials required.

Section 1.2
- Provide pebbles, white glue, and plastic bowls for the activity in the Motivate section.
- A world map and map of the United States are needed for the Demonstration.
- Provide outline maps of the world for the closure activity in the Evaluate section.

Section 1.3
- No materials required.

Section 1.4
- Provide students with magazine photographs of organisms for the activity in the Motivate section.

Introducing the Chapter

Arrange students in groups of three. Provide each group with a stack of old magazines. Write the terms *Land*, *Water*, and *Air* on the chalkboard and have students cut out five examples of organisms that live in each kind of environment. Tell students to combine their examples with those of other students to create a classroom bulletin board display.

Alternatively, divide the class into eight approximately equal-sized groups. Assign each group a planet, other than Earth, on which to conduct library research. Have each group find the following information for their planet: distance from the sun, period of revolution, period of rotation, whether the planet has seasons, the type of atmosphere, and surface temperatures. Ask each group to predict whether the planet is capable of supporting life.

Section 1.1 Parts of Earth

pp. 3–4

Performance Objectives
- Locate Earth in a diagram of the solar system.
- Identify and describe the three spheres of the Earth.

Skills Objective
- Infer how the distance of a planet from the sun affects temperatures on the planet.

Section Vocabulary

atmosphere   hydrosphere   lithosphere
organisms

Motivate

Provide students with 1-L plastic beverage bottles with caps, balances, water, and table salt. Have students measure out 35 g of salt with the balance. Have them add the salt to the bottle, and fill it with water. They should cap the bottle tightly, and shake the bottle to mix the salt and water. Ask students how the water in the bottle differs from water that comes from the faucet. Explain that almost 70% of Earth's surface is covered by salt water, somewhat like that in the bottle.

Teaching Strategies

Discuss   Ask students to hypothesize about why people can survive longer without food than without water. (Water makes up a larger percentage by mass of the body than any other compound.) Tell students that most of the chemicals in an organism are dissolved in water and most of the chemical reactions require the presence of water.

Reteach   On the chalkboard, create a concept map that shows the components of the biosphere. Write the term *Biosphere* near the top of the chalkboard. Draw a circle around the term. Write the terms *Lithosphere*, *Hydrosphere*, and *Atmosphere* below, and circle each term. Connect the circles into a concept map. Write the words *Life-supporting zone*, *Land*, *Water*, and *Air* beside the appropriate circles. Have students copy the concept map into their notebooks.

Evaluate

Closure   Have students write out the topic sentence for each paragraph in the section and write a section summary.

Section 1.2 Earth's Land and Water

pp. 5–7

Performance Objectives
- Describe the three main types of rocks that make up the lithosphere.
- Explain why fresh water is a valuable resource for organisms.

Skills Objectives
- Analyze how salinity varies according to the size of a body of water.
- Measure rainfall using a rain gauge.

Section Vocabulary

aquifers   artesian wells   igneous rock
metamorphic rock   sedimentary rock

Motivate

Write the term *Rocks* on the chalkboard. Beneath this term, write the terms *Sedimentary rock, Igneous rock*, and *Metamorphic rock*. Draw circles around each term and connect the circles to form a concept map. Have students copy the concept map into their notebooks for later use. Tell students that all of the rocks on Earth are classified into one of these three groups.

Teaching Strategies

Enrich   Have interested students research the rock cycle. Ask students to create a diagram that shows the processes involved in the rock cycle and the types of rocks produced through these processes.

Activity   After students have read the text on the lithosphere on pages 5–6, have them add to the concept maps described in the Motivate section above. Tell students to add information to their concept maps that identifies how each rock type forms and also lists examples of each type.

Evaluate

Closure   Provide students with an outline map of the world. Ask students to create a color-coding system to identify the lithosphere, the salt water parts of the hydrosphere, and the freshwater parts of the hydrosphere. Encourage students to label the continents, the oceans, and any lakes or rivers.

Section 1.3 The Air

pp. 9–11

Performance Objectives
- Diagram the layers of the atmosphere.
- Describe the characteristics of each layer.

Skills Objective
- Apply changes in the characteristics of the atmosphere to their effects on organisms.

Section Vocabulary
ozone   stratosphere   troposphere

Motivate
Explain that many people think that the atmosphere is made up of a single substance, air. Review the composition of air by writing the following table on the chalkboard. Have students construct a bar graph based on the table.

Composition of Air
Nitrogen 78%   Oxygen 21%
Carbon dioxide 0.04%   Other matter 0.06%

Teaching Strategies
Misconception   Students sometimes think that plants require carbon dioxide, but not oxygen, for survival. Briefly discuss the processes of photosynthesis and respiration. Make sure students understand that plants require carbon dioxide for photosynthesis. Explain that plants, like other organisms, must also carry on respiration to meet their energy demands. Therefore, plants also require oxygen.

Reteach   Review the locations and characteristics of each layer of the atmosphere with students. To help students remember the names of the layers of the atmosphere from the layer closest to Earth's surface to the layer farthest from Earth's surface, have students draw a vertical arrow and write the following information next to it.

> Thermosphere (more than 85 km)
> Mesosphere (85 km)
> Stratosphere (50 km)
> Troposphere (8–18 km)

Evaluate
Closure   Have students create a table identifying the main characteristics of each atmospheric layer. Ask students to include the following information: layer name, distance from Earth's surface, temperatures, and importance to living things.

Section 1.4 The Biosphere

pp. 12–13

Performance Objectives
- Describe the location of the biosphere.
- Explain how organisms interact with the biosphere.

Skills Objectives
- Analyze the importance of the parts of the biosphere to food production.
- Observe ways in which people interact with the biosphere.

Section Vocabulary
biosphere

Motivate
Bring in magazine photographs of organisms in their natural habitats. Give one photograph to each student. Ask each student to write a caption that explains how the organism in the photograph interacts with the lithosphere, hydrosphere, and atmosphere.

Teaching Strategies
Reinforce   Write the terms *Lithosphere*, *Hydrosphere*, and *Atmosphere* on the chalkboard. Challenge students to provide examples of organisms that inhabit each part of Earth. List student responses beneath the appropriate heading. As a class, discuss the lists to determine whether each organism is in its correct environment. Reclassify organisms as needed. Discuss how each organism actually depends on all three parts of Earth to meet its needs.

Discuss   Have a volunteer read the last two paragraphs on page 13 aloud. As a class, discuss how each change in the biosphere mentioned in these two paragraphs affects other living things. For example, ask students to speculate about how a volcanic eruption might affect organisms. (Responses may indicate that lava flows might kill organisms directly, destroy plants that some animals use as food, raise temperatures, or give off toxic gases.)

Evaluate
Closure   Have students write a brief definition of the term *biosphere* and explain the importance of the biosphere to organisms. Ask students to describe how a specific organism depends on each part of the biosphere to meet its needs.

Chapter Resources

Teaching Tip for Feature
Frontiers: James Lovelock, The Father of Gaia
- Point out that the term *homeostasis* is applied to the ability organisms have to keep conditions within their bodies constant. Explain that according to Lovelock, the planet Earth has this same ability.

Teaching Tip for Field Activity
- Make sure students place jars in open areas.

Answers to Field Activity
Responses will vary.

Teaching Tips for Activities

ACTIVITY 1.1

Time 30–35 minutes
Group Size Students work individually.
Hypothesis The stream discharge increases or decreases according to the amount of rainfall.
Safety Tips No safety precautions are required.

Analysis
1. 3 hours. The increased rainfall had to run off the ground and flow to the measurement location.
2. The stream discharge curve is higher, due to the much larger amounts of water involved.
3. The rainfall curve begins to rise steeply, but reaches a plateau before falling off. The stream discharge curve begins to rise slowly, rises to a steep peak, then falls steeply down and levels off.
4. Answers will vary. The stream discharge level should be approximately 950 m³/s, because the 11 PM rainfall will not have reached the measurement point.

Conclusion
After sufficient time for runoff to build up, the stream discharge increases and decreases with the amount of rainfall.

ACTIVITY 1.2

Time Day 1: 10 min; Day 2: 5 min; Day 3: 5 min
Group Size 2 students
Hypothesis The percentage of oxygen in a sample of air can be estimated by measuring the volume of air remaining after the oxygen has reacted with iron.
Safety Tips Have students wear gloves.

Analysis
1. The steel wool began to look rusty.
2. Yes. The oxygen chemically combined with the steel wool to form iron oxide, or rust.
3. Possible sources of error include the presence of dissolved oxygen in the water.

Conclusion
Responses will vary, but should be close to 20% oxygen, the actual value.

Answers to End of Chapter Questions

Concept Review
1. The troposphere.
2. Mercury, Venus, Earth, and Mars. The inner planets are rock, while the distant planets are gaseous.
3. Many chemical reactions that occur within the cells of organisms require water.
4. Plants produce much of the oxygen in the atmosphere and also help to regulate the amount of carbon dioxide in the atmosphere.
5. Conditions at the uppermost and bottommost layers of the biosphere are not adequate to support most forms of life.

Think Critically
1. Thus far, no life has been discovered on Mars. Temperatures on Mars are too cold for liquid water.
2. The high temperatures that form igneous rock are likely to destroy matter that would form fossils.
3. The lithosphere provides an anchoring point for the trees as well as a source of nutrients. Nutrients taken in by the plants are passed on to the animals that eat the plants for food.
4. Air contains less oxygen at high altitudes.
5. About 1 percent is liquid fresh water.

Graphic Analysis
1. South or Southeast
2. The direction they flow from
3. Yes, the westerlies in that area could blow air pollution from England to Scandinavia.

Chapter 2 Planning Guide

Section	Core	Standard	Enriched	Section	Core	Standard	Enriched
2.1 The Nature of Science	•	•	•	**Blackline Masters** Review Worksheet 2.2 Skills Worksheet 2A Skills Worksheet 2B	• • •	• • •	•
Section Features Word Power, p. 19 Think Critically, p.4 People and the Environment, p. 21	• •	• • •	• • •	**Ancillary Options** Multiculturalism, p. 33 One Minute Readings, p. 114	•	•	•
Blackline Masters Review Worksheet 2.1 Issues and Case Studies 2	•	• •	•	**2.3 Environmental Science**	•	•	•
Ancillary Options Multiculturalism, p. 95 One Minute Readings, p. 78 One Minute Readings, p. 119	• •	• •	• • •	**Section Features** Chemistry Link, p. 26 Fine Arts Link, p. 27 Dateline 1970, p. 28 Activity 2.1, p. 29	• •	• • • •	• • •
2.2 Skills and Methods	•	•	•	**Blackline Masters** Review Worksheet 2.3	•	•	•
Section Features Field Activity, p. 22 Literature Link, p. 23 Activity 2.2, p. 33	• • •	• • •	• • •	**Laboratory Program** Investigation 2		•	•

Every chapter has two corresponding tests in the Test Book and one Vocabulary Review Worksheet in the Review Book.

Chapter Overview

Chapter 2 provides an overview of the methods and skills used by scientists who study the environment. Section 2.1 presents an overview of the nature of science, stressing that science by its very nature is uncertain. Section 2.2 discusses the tools, skills, and methods scientists use to study the environment, including the steps involved in carrying out a controlled experiment. The chapter concludes, in Section 2.3, with the concerns of environmental scientists, how these concerns integrate information from other branches of science, and why the environment is of concern to all people.

Advance Planner

- Obtain flashlights and batteries for the activity in the Introducing the Chapter section.

Section 2.1
- Have old newspapers and magazines on hand for the Cooperative Learning activity.
- Obtain tabloid papers, science magazines, and other newspapers for the activity in the Enrich section.

Section 2.2
- Obtain sugar cubes for the exercise described in the Motivate section.

Section 2.3
- No materials required.

Introducing the Chapter

Provide each group of five students with a flashlight that does not work for one of the following reasons: the batteries are inserted incorrectly; the batteries have been removed; some or all of the batteries are dead; the bulb has been loosened or removed entirely. Tell students to turn on the flashlights. Once students realize their flashlights do not work, tell them they have five minutes to find the cause of the problem. One member of each group should list the suggestions posed by the other members. After five minutes, find out how many groups found the cause of the problem. Ask students to describe the methods the group used to find the cause. Point out to students that scientists use similar methods to answer questions they have about nature.

Section 2.1 The Nature of Science

pp. 19–20

Performance Objectives
- Explain why there is always uncertainty in science.
- Distinguish between subjects that can and cannot be studied scientifically.

Skills Objectives
- Infer why events that are good for the economy might be harmful to the environment.
- Apply new developments in science and technology to old ways of thinking.

Section Vocabulary
hypothesis

Motivate
Ask students what words come to mind when they hear the word *scientist*. List responses on the chalkboard. Have students copy these phrases into their notebooks for use again at the end of this section. Spend a few minutes reviewing each phrase listed. Tell students that in this section, they will learn about the nature of science and the concerns of scientists.

Teaching Strategies
Reteach   Repeat the definition of hypothesis (a possible explanation for a set of observations). Emphasize how a hypothesis differs from a wild guess by stressing that a hypothesis is based on observation and known information, rather than intuition and feeling. Tell students to assume that they have made the following observations: the sky is cloudy and gray, the wind has begun to blow, and the air feels moist. Have students form a hypothesis about what the weather conditions for the day might be. (Likely hypotheses will state that it will rain.) Discuss student hypotheses and the information they used to develop their hypotheses. Use the responses to explain how a hypothesis differs from a wild guess.

Enrich   Students often believe that if information appears in print, it must be true. To help students develop an understanding of the importance of evaluating sources, obtain several copies of tabloids, such as those found at supermarket checkouts that have headlines reflecting topics of a scientific nature (UFOs, AIDS cures, etc.). Also obtain articles with similar headlines in reputable newspapers such as the *New York Times*, *Los Angeles Times*, *U.S.A. Today*, and the *Washington Post*, along with magazines devoted to scientific endeavors, such as *Discover* and *Scientific American*. Show students the headlines in the tabloids and those of the other sources. Help students develop an understanding of how to evaluate sources to determine the reliability of the information contained in articles.

Reinforce   Explain to students that technology is applied science. Point out that devices such as televisions, VCRs, camcorders, and automobiles, as well as advances in medicine and other industries all involve technology. Encourage students to begin a technology timeline for their portfolios. Tell students to add information to their timelines throughout the study of this course. Encourage students to include a page with their timelines that identifies the benefits and drawbacks of each piece of technology listed.

Evaluate
Closure   As a class, review the list of terms generated during the exercise in the Motivate section. Have students cross out any terms that they no longer think are descriptive of scientists and explain why not.

Section 2.2 Skills and Methods

pp. 22–25

Performance Objective
- Describe the steps involved in conducting a scientific experiment.

Skills Objectives
- Infer the importance of communication skills in science.
- Observe characteristics of objects and events in the local environment.

Section Vocabulary
variable   control

Motivate
Provide each student with a cube of sugar. Tell students to write down all of their observations about the substance to try to identify it. Make a list of student observations on the chalkboard. Using the list, discuss the difference between an observation and a conclusion. After a few minutes, ask students if they were able to identify the substance based on their observations. If any students indicate that they tasted the substance, discuss why tasting generally should not be used to identify unknown substances.

Teaching Strategies

Reinforce   Explain to students that the steps scientists use to carry out their work are often collectively referred to as *scientific method*. List the steps involved in scientific method on the chalkboard. Explain that while all scientists use these steps in their work, there is no single scientific method that is used by all scientists. Explain this point by telling students that in some cases a problem might be solved at the research stage. In other cases, the research may provide only clues to solving the problem, in which case an experiment may be required. The results of an experiment may solve the problem or may require that further research be carried out. Use different colors of chalk to draw arrows that trace the various pathways scientists may use as they try to solve a problem.

Reteach   Have students find the meaning of the term *integrate* (to make whole or complete by adding or bringing together parts). Challenge students to use the definition of integrate to explain why environmental science is an integrated science. (Environmental science requires the use of information from many different branches of science.) Discuss examples of information from other sciences that might be useful in studying the environment.

Misconception   Students often look at scientists as being people in white laboratory coats who carry out experiments in a laboratory environment. Point out to students that while many scientists do work in laboratories, many others do most of their research in libraries or in the field. Use this as an opportunity to introduce the concept of field studies and their importance to environmental science and ecology.

Evaluate

Closure   Have students refer to the page in their notebooks that contains terms used to describe science and scientists. Again ask students to cross off any terms from the list that they no longer feel apply to scientists. Challenge students to add terms to their lists based upon the information learned in the last two sections.

Section 2.3   Environmental Science

pp. 26–30

Performance Objectives
- Give examples of how parts of the environment interact.
- Explain why policies must balance the needs of the environment with the needs of society.

Skills Objective
- Infer how a change in one part of the environment can bring about a change in another part.

Section Vocabulary
environment   biotic factors   abiotic factors

Motivate
Have students write descriptive terms and phrases that describe their current environment. Tell students to include terms that describe both the living and nonliving parts of their environment. Specify that they include parts of the lithosphere, hydrosphere, and atmosphere. Have students retain their lists for use in the Closure Activity.

Teaching Strategies

Enrich   Have students copy Table 2.1 into their notebooks leaving four to five lines of space between one *area* and the next. Tell students to expand their tables as they read about the contributions of other scientists to the study of the environment.

Reteach   Write the terms *biotic* and *abiotic* on the chalkboard. Divide each term into its word parts with slashes. Have students use a dictionary to find the meaning of each word part. (a- means "not" or "without," *bio-* means "living," *-ic* means "related to.") Relate the meanings of these word parts to the meanings of the terms *biotic* and *abiotic*.

Discuss   As a class, discuss some of the ways people interact with their environments. Be sure to discuss ways in which people use air, land, and water, and how each of these parts of the environment are related to the foods eaten by people. Explain to students that they will learn more about such interactions throughout this course.

Evaluate

Closure   Have students divide a sheet of paper into two columns: one titled *Biotic factors* and one titled *Abiotic factors*. Ask students to review the list of terms they generated for the exercise in the Motivate section and rewrite each term in the correct column.

Chapter Resources

Teaching Tip for Feature

People and the Environment: Environmental Research

- Encourage students to ask themselves the following questions to evaluate information.

What is the topic of the information?
What is the source of this information?
Is the source of the information qualified to make judgments regarding the topic?
Is the information current?
Is the information scientifically valid? (i.e., Was the sample on which the information was based representative? Is this information based on only one study or the results of several studies?)

Teaching Tip for Field Activity

- Limit the size of the area in which students will work. Remind students that good observations make use of all their senses, not just their sense of sight.

Answers to Field Activity

Responses will vary. Encourage students to re-observe their surroundings after completing the activity to determine the types of information they missed.

Teaching Tips for Activities

ACTIVITY 2.1

Time   1 class period
Group Size   Entire class
Safety Tips   Remind students not to put toothpick fragments in their mouths.

Analysis

1. So they can be recaptured
2. Some marked fish could die. This problem could be minimized by careful handling.
3. No, it only works in the lake because the fish cannot migrate to another habitat.

Conclusion

Answers will vary. Check student calculations for logic and accuracy.

ACTIVITY 2.2

Time   Day 1: 15–20 min; Days 2–5: 5–10 min
Group Size   3 students
Safety Tips   Have students wash their hands with soapy water after handling the seeds.

Analysis

1. Stored vegetables such as onions or carrots may develop roots over time.
2. Number of seeds, amount of light, temperature
3. Moisture; by testing only one variable differences observed between the experimental group and control can be attributed to that variable. Likely responses will support the hypothesis.

Conclusion

The hypothesis must be evaluated to assess whether it is supported by observations.

Answers to End of Chapter Questions

Concept Review

1. Likely responses include that graphs can display a great deal of information in a small amount of space and provide easily observable comparisons.
2. A greater number of people can interpret the results or duplicate the experiment.
3. As new tools have become available, more information has been gathered. The new information can validate or disprove previous information.
4. An educated guess takes into account information that is known to be true and accurate. A wild guess does not make use of existing information.
5. The environment affects everyone.

Think Critically

1. Accept all logical responses.
2. Accept all logical responses.
3. More than one variable was changed.
4. Accept all logical responses.

Computer Activity

Check student graphs for accuracy.

Graphic Analysis

1. Bar graph
2. Africa
3. Eastern Europe, United States
4. Yes, but a bar graph is the best choice because quantities are being compared.

Chapter Planning Guide

Section	Core	Standard	Enriched	Section	Core	Standard	Enriched
3.1 The Changing Environment		•	•	Issue, p. 41	•	•	•
				Activity 3.1, p. 42		•	•
Section Features				**Blackline Masters**			
Social Studies Link, p. 35	•	•	•	Review Worksheet 3.2	•	•	•
Dateline 1982, p. 36	•	•	•				
Activity 3.2, p. 47	•			**Ancillary Options**			
				One Minute Readings, p. 69		•	•
Blackline Masters				Multiculturalism, p. 25	•	•	•
Review Worksheet 3.1	•	•	•	**3.3 The Ecosystem**	•	•	•
Skills Worksheet 3A	•	•					
				Section Features			
Ancillary Options				Word Power, p. 43	•	•	•
One Minute Readings, p. 104			•	Dateline 1973, p. 43	•	•	•
Laboratory Program				**Blackline Masters**			
Investigation 3	•	•	•	Review Worksheet 3.3	•	•	•
3.2 Needs of Organisms	•	•	•	Skills Worksheet 3B	•	•	
Section Features				**Ancillary Options**			
Health Link, p. 38	•	•	•	Multiculturalism, p. 119		•	•
Field Activity, p. 38		•	•				
Think Critically, p. 39	•	•	•				

Every chapter has two corresponding tests in the Test Book and one Vocabulary Review Worksheet in the Review Book. There is also a Unit 1 test in the test book covering Chapters 1–3.

Chapter Overview

Chapter 3 explores the needs of organisms on a dynamic, ever-changing planet. Section 3.1 gives examples to illustrate how the lithosphere, hydrosphere, and atmosphere have changed over time. Section 3.2 defines the needs of organisms and relates how these needs are met by environmental resources. Section 3.3 discusses the structure of an ecosystem, and shows how changes within any of Earth's major spheres might affect the biosphere and the organisms within it.

Advance Planner

- Obtain paper towels, scissors, and isopropyl alcohol for the activity in the Introducing the Chapter section.

Section 3.1
- Obtain a sheet of butcher paper or other white paper 5 meters in length, a meterstick, and marker for the Demonstration.
- Obtain a map showing the locations of the crustal plates for the exercise in the Reteach section.

Section 3.2
- Obtain a small mammal, goldfish, or reptile for the exercise in the Motivate section.

- Have a potted plant available for the Demonstration.
- Gather materials students may need to carry out the experiments they design for the Closure activity.

Section 3.3
- Obtain strings, stakes, and a meterstick to measure and mark off the 1m² area for the exercise in the Motivate section.
- Have a large cardboard box available for the Activity.

Introducing the Chapter

Cut paper towels into 10-cm² pieces. Dip each towel into alcohol and squeeze out the excess liquid. Distribute one towel to each group of two students. Direct students to observe the towel using all their senses, except taste. Have students predict how the towel will change as time passes. Ask students to share their observations and predictions. Relate any changes in moisture content, chemical composition, and temperature that students observed or predicted to similar changes in the environment. Ask students to speculate about the effect of alcohol, if any, to any organisms living on the towel. Relate student responses to the use of alcohol as an antiseptic.

Section 3.1 The Changing Environment

pp. 35–37

Performance Objective
- Describe ways in which the three layers of the biosphere have changed over time.

Skills Objective
- Integrate knowledge from several fields of science to explain how ice ages are related to changes in the three spheres of Earth.

Section Vocabulary
tectonic plates   weathering

Motivate
Ask students to recall the Introducing the Chapter activity and discuss how the paper towel changed. Compare the changes observed in moisture content, chemical composition, and temperature to those that might occur in natural environments. Establish that while some changes in the environment are due to natural events, other changes result from human activities.

Teaching Strategies
Demonstrate   Draw a timeline representing the age of Earth on a strip of paper about 5 m long. Use a scale of 1 m = 1 billion years and 1 mm = 1 million years. Compare the time frame of human history with the time frame of Earth's history. Point out that Earth has undergone many changes since its formation. Ask students what some of these changes are and when they occurred. Have interested students research specific changes and add the information to the timeline.

Discuss   Ask students to describe some natural disasters that have occurred during the past two years. Examples may include forest or brush fires, floods, earthquakes, volcanic eruptions, and storms, such as hurricanes and tornadoes. Ask students to describe changes to the environment in the areas in which these disasters occurred. Lead students to focus on how organisms other than humans are affected by such changes.

Reteach   Use a map showing crustal plates to discuss how the seven major plates and thirteen smaller plates are floating on the lower part of the mantle. Use sheets of multicolored paper to demonstrate what happens when these plates collide. With the paper, also demonstrate the mountain-building processes of folding and faulting and the process of sea-floor spreading.

Evaluate
Closure   Have the class construct a chart listing events such as forest fires, floods, ice ages, El Niño, hurricanes, and volcanoes. Direct students to list one way each of these events changes the atmosphere, lithosphere, hydrosphere, and biosphere. Discuss the chart as a review of the main ideas in Section 3.1.

Section 3.2 Needs of Organisms

pp. 38–40

Performance Objectives
- List factors that affect an area's ability to support life.
- Predict how changes in the environment might affect organisms.

Skills Objective
- Predict how changes in climate may affect organisms living in a region.

Section Vocabulary
dormant   hibernation   territory

Motivate
Display a live goldfish, plant, small mammal, or reptile beside a model or photograph of the same organism. Ask what characteristics are used to used to identify something as living. (Examples include respiration, nutrition, irritability, excretion, motion, circulation, and growth.) Remind students that nonliving things do not carry out all these activities. Explain that organisms get the energy and materials needed for these activities from the environment.

Teaching Strategies
Demonstrate   Allow a plant to grow on a window sill. Tell students that a plant gets energy from the process of photosynthesis. Explain that the sun supplies light energy for this process and that the leaves of a plant seek light by turning and bending toward the sun. Demonstrate this phenomena, called phototropism, by having students observe the plant for 48 hours and discuss how the direction of the leaves changes.

Reteach   On the chalkboard, construct a chart with the headings *Organism, Materials Needed for Life*, and *Sources of Life Materials*. List the following organisms in the first column: frog, fish, owl, and dandelion. Complete the chart as a class. Discuss the completed chart and instruct students to copy it into their notebooks for use as a study tool.

Misconception   Many people think that bears hibernate. However, bears are not true hibernators. During true hibernation, an organism remains in a dormant state during which its temperature drops below normal, and its metabolic, heart, and respiratory rates slow. A bear's bodily functions do slow slightly during its winter rest, but the bear does not enter a truly dormant state. In addition, bears do awaken from their rest in winter months to seek food.

Evaluate

Closure   Have students design three separate controlled experiments to show that a plant needs three of the following: nutrients, air, water, light, living space, or a proper temperature. Instruct students to include a control and predict the outcomes of each experiment. After receiving approval, have interested students carry out their experiments. Beans, grasses, and radishes are fast-growing plants easily grown from seed.

Section 3.3 The Ecosystem

pp. 43–44

Performance Objectives
- Describe the structure of an ecosystem.
- Relate the concept of habitat destruction to the loss of biodiversity.

Skills Objectives
- Classify the components of an ecosystem such as species, habitat, range, population, and community.
- Apply an understanding of how human decisions and activities can result in habitat destruction and a loss of biodiversity.

Section Vocabulary

biodiversity   community   ecosystem
habitat   population   range   species

Motivate

Take the class outside. Assign each group of four students an area 1 m². The area may include a lot with weeds, a puddle, a bush, a sidewalk with cracks, or a section of a tree. Have students observe and describe the biotic and abiotic factors of their assigned areas and report their findings to the class. Explain that each area may be considered an ecosystem because the biotic and abiotic components of an environment exist along with their interactions.

Teaching Strategies

Activity   Ask each student to remove one shoe and deposit it into a large box at the front of the class. Ask a pair of students to remove the shoes from the box and to arrange the shoes into smaller groups based upon similar characteristics. Have the remainder of the class try to explain the method used to group the shoes. Then allow several students to try different schemes of arrangements that result in smaller and smaller groupings of the shoes. Guide the class to see that the shoes are being arranged into groups based upon similarities of traits. Shoes in one group are more similar to each other than shoes in different groups. Point out that when scientists study organisms in their natural environments, they often focus on a single group of organisms called a species. Explain that organisms of the same species are much more similar than organisms of differing species. Explain that a species is a group of organisms having similar traits that can interbreed.

Reteach   Compile a list of familiar organisms on the chalkboard. Have the class identify the type of environment in which each organism listed is likely to be found. Write these suggestions to the right of each listed organism. Explain to students that these locations are known as the habitats of the organisms. Ask the class to explain the reasons why an organism lives in a particular type of habitat. (Reasons should include that the habitat provides the organism with food, protection from other organisms, a breeding ground, and an adequate temperature range.)

Discuss   Define population and community. Use photographs from magazines to show a variety of species living in an area. Identify which organisms in the photographs constitute a community and which constitute a population.

Evaluate

Closure   Have students write a brief summary or prepare a concept map that defines and shows the relationships among the terms *ecosystem*, *species*, *habitat*, *population*, and *community*.

Chapter Resources

Teaching Tip for Feature

Issues: The Mississippi Flood
* Have students research newspaper and magazine accounts of the 1993 Mississippi River flood.

Teaching Tip for Field Activity

* Have two groups test the same variety of food types to provide a basis for comparison.

Answers to Field Activity

Responses will vary, but they are likely to indicate that foods with strong odors or high sugar contents attracted the greatest numbers of insects.

Teaching Tips for Activities

ACTIVITY 3.1

Time   One class period
Group Size   4 students
Hypothesis   Land isopods prefer dark, moist conditions.
Safety Tip   Have students wash their hands after conducting the activity.

Analysis
1. Responses will vary depending upon hypotheses.
2. Answers will vary depending upon results.

Conclusion
Generally land isopods live in dark, moist habitats.

ACTIVITY 3.2

Time   Day 1: 10 min; Day 2: 15 min
Group Size   3 students
Hypothesis   Glaciers scrape Earth's surface and move rocks.
Safety Tip   Be sure students do not throw rocks or gravel fragments.

Analysis
1. They were pushed out of the way or run over.
2. Likely responses will include that the ice at the bottom part of the glacier melted slightly.
3. The wood was scratched by the sand and gravel frozen into the ice.

Conclusion
1. They scratch and wear away the surface and carry loosened particles to new locations.
2. An erratic is a boulder that was moved from one location to another through glacial activity.

Answers to End of Chapter Questions
Concept Review
1. Movement of tectonic plates and the actions of wind, water, gravity, and ice can all cause changes.
2. Photosynthesis and volcanic activity are not caused by humans. Changes caused by humans include an increase in carbon dioxide levels resulting from the burning of fuels and ozone depletion from CFC use.
3. Organisms obtain nutrients and energy.
4. Geographical range refers to the total area in which a species can live. Territory is the specific area in which an organism lives.
5. Areas that were once used as habitat by the mountain lion now serve as habitat for humans or have been converted to farmland.

Think Critically
1. As glaciers move across Earth's surface they remove particles of the lithosphere to new locations. Glaciers are part of the hydrosphere. As they melt, they change from solid water to liquid water. Temperatures in the atmosphere affect glacial movement.
2. Sunlight is converted to chemical energy and stored in the cells of the plant. This energy is transferred to animals that eat the plant and then to animals that eat the plant-eating animals.
3. If the food supply is limited to a small area, the range of the animal will also be small.
4. One species has slightly different habitats in different locations. The other species lives in a single habitat, and is at greater risk of extinction because a single event could destroy its entire habitat.
5. Organisms that once thrived have disappeared, areas that are now land were once seas.

Computer Activity
Bar graphs will show that the rain forests in each location will be greatly reduced in size by the year 2000.

Graphic Analysis
1. Northwest
2. Two
3. The North American and Pacific Plates meet there.
4. Closer together

Unit Overview

Unit 2 introduces the basic ecological concepts and ideas that frame the study of the environment. Chapter 4 provides an overview of how matter and energy are transferred through an ecosystem via food chains, food webs, and chemical cycles. Ecosystem dynamics are explored in Chapter 5 with an introduction to the interactions that help to define ecosystems. The discussion of ecosystem interactions continues in Chapter 6 through a presentation of the events that help to maintain balance in an ecosystem.

Introducing the Unit

Discussion   Obtain a copy of a chart that identifies and explains the four food groups, or a copy of the "eat right" pyramid, from a health teacher. Display the chart or pyramid and ask students the names of the organisms from which each food is derived. Use the exercise to lead students to recognize that all of the foods they eat come from other organisms. Continue this exercise until it is established that the ultimate energy source for all human food is the sun.

Class Activity   Provide students with world outline maps, while displaying a large world map at the front of the classroom. Point out that the shapes of South America and Africa and other evidence suggests that these continents were once joined as a single landmass called Pangaea. Tell students to cut out the continents on their map and reorganize them to form one landmass. Use this exercise to illustrate that Earth has changed over time.

Teacher Resources

Audiovisual

Population Ecology, film/video, 19 minutes, Encyclopaedia Britannica Educational Corporation, 1964.
Cave Ecology, video, 13 minutes, Centron Films, 1970.
Ecological Biology, video, 17 minutes, Coronet Film and Video, 1981.
An Ecosystem: A Struggle for Survival, film/video, 17 minutes, National Geographic Society, 1975.

Computer Software

Food Chains and Webs, Apple II, Prentice-Hall Media.
The Environment I: Habitats and Ecosystems, IBM.
The Environment II: Cycles and Interactions, IBM.
Cycles in the Environment, Apple II, Prentice-Hall Media.
Sim Life, Macintosh, Maxis.

Suggested Readings

Carson, Rachel. *Silent Spring: Twenty-fifth Anniversary Edition*, Houghton Mifflin Company, 1987.
Gore, Al. *Earth in the Balance: Ecology and the Human Spirit*, Penguin Books, 1992.

Advance Preparation

Chapter 4

Field Activity   Have field guides of insects, mammals, birds, and reptiles available for use.
Activity 4.1   Gather clear plastic and glass cups, wax paper, cobalt chloride paper, paper clips, petroleum jelly, geranium plants, and tape.
Activity 4.2   Gather petri dishes with lids, blotter paper, hand lenses, grease pencils, scissors, and small amounts of bread, Roquefort cheese, dill pickles, orange wedges, and grapes.

Chapter 5

Field Activity   No materials required.
Activity 5.1   Gather graduated cylinders (100-mL and 10-mL), 100-mL beakers, lima beans, glass slides, coverslips, methylene blue stain, droppers, microscopes, test tubes, test tube racks, aluminum foil, and graph paper .
Activity 5.2   Have graph paper available.

Chapter 6

Field Activity   Locate an abandoned farm field or vacant lot.
Activity 6.1   Obtain 500-mL and 1000-mL beakers, tap water, soil, grass, droppers, glue, slides, coverslips, microscopes, pH paper, and leaves.
Activity 6.2   Gather paper cups, soil, grass seeds, clover seeds, and metric rulers.

Chapter Planning Guide

Section	Core	Standard	Enriched	Section	Core	Standard	Enriched
4.1 Roles of Living Things	•	•	•	Think Critically, p. 61 Social Studies Connection, p. 63	•	• •	• •
Section Features Field Activity, p. 55	•	•	•	**Blackline Masters** Review Worksheet 4.3 Skills Worksheet 4B Issue and Case Studies 3	• • •	• • •	• •
Blackline Masters Review Worksheet 4.1	•	•	•	**4.4 Chemical Cycles**			
Laboratory Program Investigation 4		•	•	**Section Features** Biology Link, p. 65 Dateline 1750, p. 66 Activity 4.1	• • •	• • •	• • •
4.2 Ecosystem Structure							
Section Features Dateline 1972, p. 59 Activity 4.2, p. 71	• •	• •	• •	**Blackline Masters** Review Worksheet 4.4	•	•	•
Blackline Masters Review Worksheet 4.2 Skills Worksheet 4A Ancillary Options One Minute Readings, p. 28	• •	• •	•	**Ancillary Options** One Minute Readings, p. 46 CEPUP Chemical Survey, Act. 1		• •	• •
4.3 Energy in the Ecosystem							
Section Features Astronomy Link, p. 60	•	•	•	**Laboratory Program** Investigation 5	•	•	•

Every chapter has two corresponding tests in the Test Book and one Vocabulary Review Worksheet in the Review Book.

Chapter Overview

The relationship between matter, both biotic and abiotic, and energy in an ecosystem is the focal point of Chapter 4. Section 4.1 explains the roles of producers, consumers, and decomposers in an ecosystem. Section 4.2 expands on this idea by explaining how matter and energy are transferred through trophic levels via food chains and food webs. In Section 4.3, the relationship of energy and biomass in the ecosystem is investigated through the use of ecological pyramids. The chapter concludes in Section 4.4 with an explanation of how matter is recycled through the environment via the water, carbon-oxygen, and nitrogen cycles.

Advance Planner

Section 4.1
  • Obtain dominoes and a toy dinosaur for the exercise in the Motivate section.

Section 4.2
  • No preparation required.

Section 4.3
  • Peanuts in shells, a probe, and a Bunsen burner are needed for the Demonstration.

Section 4.4
  • A classroom aquarium containing plants and fishes is needed for the activity in the Reteach section.
  • Make overhead transparencies of Figures 4.11, 4.12, and 4.13 for the Closure exercise.

Introducing the Chapter

On the chalkboard, make a list of producers such as grass, trees, clover, and lettuce. Make a second list of consumers such as cows, deer, bison, and elephants. List lions, tigers, pythons, and wolves in a third column. Ask students to state the common characteristics of the organisms in each list. Point out that organisms are sometimes classified according to how they obtain energy.

Section 4.1 Roles of Living Things

pp. 53–55

Performance Objectives
- Identify the roles of producers, consumers, and decomposers.
- Describe the concept of trophic level.

Skills Objective
- Infer why the number of organisms at a given trophic level is smaller than in the preceding level.

Section Vocabulary

consumers   decomposers   producers   trophic level

Motivate

Set up a row of dominoes on a table. Place a toy dinosaur beside the dominoes. Ask students to speculate about why dinosaurs became extinct. Explain that one hypothesis about dinosaur extinction is that many plants died when large amounts of dust entered the atmosphere, blocking out the sunlight. Push over the first domino so that all the dominoes fall and explain that the lack of sunlight created a "domino effect". Explain that as sunlight became scarce, plants began to die. As plants became scarce, organisms that fed upon the plants starved to death. Animals that fed upon plant-eating animals also starved. In time, almost all the organisms died.

Teaching Strategies

Analogy   Explain that a plant is like a factory. Tell students a plant uses water and CO_2 as the raw materials to make its product (glucose). Point out that just as a factory needs electricity or other power source, plants also require energy to make products. This energy is provided by sunlight.

Enrich   Have interested students research adaptations for obtaining food, such as shapes of teeth, beaks, or claws, eye placement, body size, and color. Encourage students to prepare a visual display about the adaptations with explanatory labels.

Evaluate

Closure   On the chalkboard, prepare a chart with the following heads: *Producer*, *Primary consumer*, *Secondary consumer*, *Tertiary consumer*, and *Decomposer*. At the same time, have each student make their own list of the following: the names of one plant, five animals, and a type of fungus. Ask students to read the names of the organisms on their lists and have the class classify the organisms to complete the chart on the chalkboard.

Section 4.2 Ecosystem Structure

pp. 56–59

Performance Objectives
- Describe food chains and the food web.
- Examine the effects of ecosystem structure on population size and pollution.

Skills Objective
- Predict how introducing a new organism into an ecosystem may alter the food chain and affect existing populations.

Section Vocabulary

biological magnification   food chain   food web

Motivate

Write the word *acorn* on the chalkboard and have students copy it onto a clean sheet of paper. Beneath the word, have students list the name of an animal that feeds on acorns. Ask students to read the names they listed as you write the names on the chalkboard. Tell students to write the name of an animal that feeds on the animal they previously listed. Have students read their responses aloud as you write the names beneath the others. Connect some of the names with arrows to form a simple food chain. Explain that food chains show paths of food and energy transfer in an ecosystem.

Teaching Strategies

Reteach   Draw a food chain that consists of grass, grasshopper, mouse, and snake on the chalkboard. Develop the concept of a food web by introducing an owl into this ecosystem. Expand the food web by introducing a frog, a caterpillar, a rabbit, a robin, a hawk, and a house cat. Draw arrows in the appropriate locations. Explain that a food web is made up of several interconnected food chains and represents the feeding patterns in an ecosystem. Ask students to diagram three of the possible food chains shown.

Evaluate

Closure   Ask each student to devise a food chain. Ask how the removal of one type of organism affects their food chain. Have the students work together in cooperative groups to create a food web. Have each group predict how their food web will be impacted if an organism is removed. Review the food webs as a class. Explain that as food webs become more complex, the ecosystem becomes more stable.

Section 4.3 Energy in the Ecosystem

pp. 60–62

Performance Objectives
- Investigate the movement of energy through an ecosystem.
- Define *ecological pyramid*, and explain its relationship to energy in the ecosystem.

Skills Objectives
- Model the movement of energy in an ecosystem using an ecological pyramid.
- Infer that some energy at each trophic level is lost as heat.

Section Vocabulary
biomass   ecological pyramid

Motivate
Remove a peanut from its shell and place it on the tip of a probe. Place the peanut in the flame of a Bunsen burner until the peanut ignites. Explain to students that chemical energy stored in the peanut is being changed and given off as light and heat. Lead students to see that a consumer who eats the peanut gets the stored energy.

Teaching Strategies
Math Connection   Explain that in an ecological pyramid, about a 90 percent energy loss occurs at each trophic level. Tell students to assume that organisms at the producer level produce a total of 5,000 calories of energy. Have students calculate how many calories are available at the primary consumer, secondary consumer, and tertiary consumer levels of this pyramid (500 calories, 50 calories, 5 calories).

Reinforce   Have students work in cooperative groups to construct three-dimensional food pyramids. Suggest the use of boxes, colored paper, photographs from magazines, or original artwork. Tell students to label each trophic level in the pyramid.

Reteach   Using colored chalk, construct an ecological pyramid on the chalkboard. Label each trophic level and include the names of plants and animals that represent each level. Be sure students are able to distinguish between the producers and consumers. Using actual numbers, trace the amount of energy lost at each higher level of the pyramid. Show how the amount of energy affects the number of organisms each level can support.

Evaluate
Closure   Ask students to study a food web diagram. Have students use the food web to construct three food chains. Based on the food chains, ask students to create ecological pyramids and then summarize the relationship between biomass, energy, and number of organisms in an ecosystem.

Section 4.4 Chemical Cycles

pp. 64–67

Performance Objectives
- State the chemical composition of the human body.
- Describe and examine the water cycle, the carbon cycle, and the nitrogen cycle.

Skills Objectives
- Compare and contrast evaporation and transpiration.
- Infer the effects that carbon dioxide produced by the burning of fossil fuels will have on the carbon cycle.

Vocabulary
evaporation   legumes   transpiration

Motivate
Hold up a one dollar bill. Tell the class that the human body is said to be worth less than this dollar. Explain that the monetary value refers to the sum of the values of the raw materials (elements and compounds) that make up the body. Discuss examples of some of these raw materials, as listed in Table 4.1.

Teaching Strategies
Reteach   Direct students' attention to the classroom aquarium. Using the plants and fish in the tank as examples, challenge students to explain how carbon and oxygen are cycled throughout the aquarium.

Reinforce   Have students work in cooperative groups to create a visual display that shows the water, carbon-oxygen, and nitrogen cycles.

Evaluate
Closure   Prepare overhead transparencies of Figures 4.11, 4.12, and 4.13 with the labels deleted. Project each transparency onto a screen and challenge the class to supply the missing labels for each diagram.

Chapter Resources

Teaching Tip for Feature
Social Studies Connection: Food for the World
- Use an ecological pyramid to show how eating at a lower level on the food chain means a larger food supply.

Teaching Tip for Field Activity
- Provide students with field guides for various types of insects and animals.

Answers to Field Activity
Responses will vary depending upon observations.

Teaching Tips for Activities

ACTIVITY 4.1
Time   Day 1: one hr; Day 2: 15 min
Group Size   2 students
Safety Tip   Students should wash their hands after handling the cobalt chloride paper.

Analysis
1. To block the passage of water.
2. Setup B.
3. The paper in Setup A turned pink due to water.
4. Droplets of water should be seen in the top of Setup A due to condensation of transpired water.
5. Answers should reflect data.

Conclusion
1. Plants take in water through their roots and release water through their leaves.
2. Transpiration. The amount of transpired water entering the atmosphere can increase humidity and cloud formation, and lead to precipitation.

ACTIVITY 4.2
Time   Day 1: 30–35 min; Day 2: 10 min; Days 4, 6, 8, 10, 12, 14, and 16: 20–25 min
Group Size   5 students
Hypothesis   Different kinds of decomposers grow better on one or another kind of food.
Safety Tips   Remind students to use scissors carefully. Have students wash their hands with warm, soapy water after they handle the Petri dishes.

Analysis
1. Responses will vary. Students are likely to observe bacteria and some mold growth. Bacterial colonies lack the wispy fibers (mycelia) that molds have.
2. Yes. Actual results will vary.
3. Responses should indicate that the amount of food material decreased over time.

Conclusion
1. Mold growth is likely to be greatest on the bread and the cheese. Bacterial growth varies.
2. Decomposers break down organic matter.
3. The remains of dead organisms would accumulate, and nutrient cycling would not occur.

Answers to End of Chapter Questions
Concept Review
1. Producers manufacture food from raw materials. Consumers obtain food by eating other organisms.
2. The krill population increased. Then populations of organisms that fed on krill also increased.
3. About 90%; energy is lost largely as heat.
4. Accept all logical responses.
5. Nitrogen gas is not directly usable by plants.

Think Critically
1. Organic materials that rain down from upper levels serve as the nutrient sources of scavengers. Other consumers can use these scavengers as a food source.
2. Complex food webs are more stable because they provide many alternative food sources.
3. High temperatures increase the rate of evaporation.

Computer Activity
Graphs should show that only ten percent of the energy at one level is passed on.

Graphic Analysis
1. Breathing, fossil fuel burning, and agriculture affect the carbon cycle.
2. It is stored in rocks.
3. The largest amount of moving carbon occurs from CO_2 dissolved in the oceans. Other sources include volcanoes, fossil fuels, and living things.

Chapter Planning Guide

Section	Core	Standard	Enriched	Section	Core	Standard	Enriched
5.1 Habitats and Niches	•	•	•	**Ancillary Options** One Minute Readings, p. 28	•	•	•
Section Features Word Power, p. 73 Biology Link, p. 75	•	• •	• •	**Laboratory Program** Investigation 7	•	•	•
Blackline Masters Review Worksheet 5.1 Issues and Case Studies 5	• •	• •	• •	**5.3 Populations**	•	•	•
Ancillary Options Multiculturalism, p. 115		•	•	**Section Features** Think Critically, p. 80 Field Activity, p. 81 Dateline 1992, p. 82 Activity 5.1, p. 84 Activity 5.2 p. 87	• • • • •	• • • • •	• • •
Laboratory Program Investigation 6		•	•	**Blackline Masters** Review Worksheet 5.3 Skills Worksheet 5B	• •	• •	•
5.2 Evolution and Adaptation	•	•	•	**Ancillary Options** One Minute Readings, p. 112 Multiculturalism, p. 51	•	•	•
Section Features Historical Notebook, p. 79	•	•	•				
Blackline Masters Review Worksheet 5.2 Skills Worksheet 5A	• •	• •	•				

Every chapter has two corresponding tests in the Test Book and one Vocabulary Review Worksheet in the Review Book.

Chapter Overview

Chapter 5 provides an overview of ecosystem dynamics. Section 5.1 concentrates on distinguishing between habitat and niche, and discusses how changes in either of these factors could lead to the demise of an organism and possibly a species. This discussion is expanded upon in Section 5.2 through an introduction to the concepts of evolution and adaptation. The chapter concludes in Section 5.3 with a discussion of populations, their capacity for growth, and the limiting factors of the environment that prevent infinite population growth.

Advance Planner

Section 5.1
- An overhead projector and blank transparency is required for the activity in the Motivate section.

Section 5.2
- An overhead transparency of a world map is needed for the exercise in the Motivate section. Locate a biology text showing the route traveled by Darwin while on the *HMS Beagle*.

Section 5.3
- Have an overhead transparency of two graph grids made for the exercise in the Motivate section.
- Order *Paramecium caudatum* cultures from a biological supply house in time for the Activity. Obtain a microscope, glass slides, and coverslips.

Introducing the Chapter

Tell students that they are going to set up a classroom aquarium with a variety of freshwater plants and animals. Have students work in groups to compose a list of the materials they will need to set up and maintain their aquarium. Remind students that they need to consider both abiotic and biotic factors. As students develop their list of materials, tell them to include a description of why each material is needed. Encourage students to refer to Sections 3.2 and 3.3 as they compile their lists. Discuss the completed lists as a class. Have students in each group revise their lists as necessary. Tell students to retain their lists for use later in the chapter.

Section 5.1 Habitats and Niches

pp. 73–75

Performance Objectives
- Describe the concept of the niche.
- Examine how interactions between a species and its environment define the species' niche.

Skills Objective
- Infer how removal of an organism at one trophic level can affect other organisms in the ecosystem.

Section Vocabulary

niche   competitive exclusion
keystone predator

Motivate

Remind students that the habitat of an organism is the place in an ecosystem where the organism lives. Take students on a walk around the school grounds to make close observations of organisms in their habitats. Tell students to list five organisms they observe and to describe their specific habitats. Write the names of the organisms observed on an overhead transparency divided into columns titled *Organism, Habitat, Predicted niche,* and *Actual niche.* As a class, fill in the first two columns and have students copy the table into their notebooks. Explain what the term *niche* means and have students complete the *Predicted niche* column as a homework assignment. Explain that the last column will be completed at the end of this section.

Teaching Strategies

Reteach   Ask students to define the term *habitat.* (The place within an ecosystem where an organism lives.) Next ask students to define *niche.* (A niche is the role an organism plays in its environment.) Tell students that they can think of an organism's habitat as its home or address within an ecosystem. Its niche can be thought of as its job. Have students use this analogy to state their habitat and niche.

Enrich   Ask students what they think the phrase "survival of the fittest" means. Discuss responses as a class. Point out that this phrase is often used to describe one of the components of Darwin's theory of evolution. Explain that according to this idea, the most well-adapted organisms in a population survive to reproduce and pass their successful traits to their offspring. Have students explain how the idea of the "survival of the fittest" may relate to the principle of competitive exclusion.

Reinforce   Have students look up the word *keystone* in a dictionary and write the meaning in their journals. (Keystone: the one part of a number of things that supports or holds the other parts together.) Have students write a summary that explains how the meaning of the term *keystone* relates to the niche of a keystone predator.

Evaluate

Closure   Have students review the tables they created for the exercise in the Motivate section. Tell students to pay particular attention to their predictions of the niche of each organism and to revise their lists as necessary. Once all students have revised their lists, review the entries as a class.

Section 5.2 Evolution and Adaptation

pp. 76–78

Performance Objectives
- Explain how a species adapts to its niche.
- Describe convergent evolution and coevolution, and relate each to the concept of the niche.

Skills Objective
- Predict changes that may occur in an ecosystem if biodiversity is reduced.

Section Vocabulary

evolution   convergent evolution   coevolution

Motivate

Trace the route taken by Darwin aboard the *HMS Beagle* on an overhead transparency of a world map. As you trace the route, provide students with a brief description of Darwin's trip. Explain to students that the observations Darwin made on this journey led him to develop his theory of evolution.

Teaching Strategies

Biology Connection   Explain the impact of Darwin's theory of evolution on the science of taxonomy. Explain to students that prior to the acceptance of evolution, organisms were classified almost solely according to physical similarities. Evolutionary theory encouraged taxonomists to use relationships among organisms as the basis for classification.

Reteach   Repeat the definition of *evolution* for students. Emphasize that evolution relates to changes in an entire species over time; it does not refer to changes that an individual may undergo.

Reinforce To emphasize the differences between specialized species and generalized species, provide students with the following scenario.

An area with an active volcano is largely populated by two species of animals. Species A is a generalized species that lives in several different parts of the region and can eat several kinds of plants. Species B is a specialized species that lives only on the east side of the island and feeds on only one kind of plant. Tell students to imagine that the volcano erupts, sending molten lava across the eastern side of the island. Have students explain which species would be more likely to become extinct as a result of the eruption. Have students explain their responses.

Enrich Coevolution often occurs between parasites and their hosts. Have interested students conduct library research to find examples of parasites and hosts that have coevolved. Encourage students to report their findings to the class.

Evaluate
Closure Have students use the vocabulary terms in this section to create a concept map that explains the similarities and differences among the evolutionary processes discussed.

Section 5.3 Populations

pp. 80–83

Performance Objectives
- Explain how populations of organisms grow.
- Describe the factors that limit the growth of a population.
- Identify the shapes of growth curves that represent populations of different organisms.

Skills Objective
- Analyze and identify the limiting factors that can affect carrying capacity.

Section Vocabulary
exponential growth   carrying capacity
density-dependent limiting factor
density-independent limiting factor

Motivate
Make two graph grids on an overhead transparency. On one grid, plot data that shows arithmetic growth. On the other, plot data that shows exponential growth. Ask students how the growth patterns shown on the two grids differ. Explain that in nature, populations often tend to grow exponen-tially unless acted upon by outside factors. Have students speculate as to the kinds of factors that may limit population growth.

Teaching Strategies
Reteach Review the meaning of the term *population* with students. Be sure students understand that a population consists of organisms of the same species living in the same place at the same time.

Enrich Populations of certain organisms fluctuate over reasonably predictable intervals of time. Such fluctuations can be studied in populations of small arctic herbivores such as moles, mice, lemmings, and their predators; the Arctic fox and the snowy owl. Discuss the cyclic population explosions of lemmings on the tundra and the corresponding growth in the numbers of Arctic foxes and snowy owls. Guide students to the understanding that as the lemming population grows, food resources in the form of vegetation decrease. This food decrease results in starvation that leads to a decrease in the number of lemmings. Such population decreases occur about every three to four years. Organisms that display such patterns are referred to as "cyclic species."

Activity To further demonstrate the concept of the S-curve and carrying capacity, start a culture of *Paramecium caudatum*. Have students count the organisms using a microscope, glass slides, and coverslips. They can use the data collected to plot a growth curve for a period of about 14 days. Have them analyze the data and prepare a written report.

Biology Connection In his book *The Origin of Species*, Darwin stated that living things tend to produce many more offspring than will ultimately develop into adults. For example, huge numbers of eggs are produced by many marine species. Challenge students to discuss the "fate" of many of the eggs produced. Explain that the eggs, as well as the immature form of many marine organisms, are a vital part of complex marine food webs.

Evaluate
Closure Have students write a summary of this section beginning with a definition of exponential growth. The summary should include limiting factors and differentiate between density-dependent and density-independent limiting factors.

Chapter Resources

Teaching Tip for Feature
Historical Notebook: Accidental Tourists
- Invite a guest speaker from a local native plant society to discuss the impact of introduced species.

Teaching Tips for Field Activity
- Have students also investigate the factors that determine the carrying capacity of their homes.

Answers to Field Activity
The carrying capacity of the classroom is determined by the space and the number of desks and chairs.

Teaching Tips for Activities

ACTIVITY 5.1
Time   Day 1: 10 min; Day 4: 20–25 min
Group Size   2 students
Inference   The population density can be estimated by counting the individuals in a diluted sample and multiplying by the dilution factor.
Safety Tip   Tell students to wash their hands with warm, soapy water after handling the infusion.

Analysis
1. Check students' drawings for logic and accuracy.
2. Answers will vary, but should reflect a period during the growth phase.
3. Density first increased, then decreased.

Conclusion
Answers will vary.

ACTIVITY 5.2
Time   25 minutes
Group Size   Students work individually.
Inference   Human activities can cause a deer population to fluctuate greatly.
Safety Tips   No safety precautions required.

Analysis
In 1915, the deer population was below carrying capacity. In 1920, the deer population exceeded the estimated carrying capacity by 35,000. In 1924, the deer population exceeded the estimated carrying capacity by 70,000 members.

Conclusion
1. a. The deer population increased in number.
   b. The deer population increased dramatically in number as competition for grazing land decreased.
   c. The deer population had reached or exceeded carrying capacity.

2. Reducing a species' natural predators and competitors allows the population to grow out of control and exceed carrying capacity.

Answers to End of Chapter Questions
Concept Review
1. In Connell's experiments with barnacles, the downward spreading of species A was limited by the presence of species B.
2. The skulls are similar as a result of convergent evolution. Both animals were large carnivores.
3. A specialized species is one with a narrow niche, whereas a generalized species has a wide niche. A generalized species is more tolerant to change.
4. Food and predation are biotic factors that can limit or increase the size of a population. Water and temperature abiotic factors can limit or increase the size of a population.
5. S-shaped curves represent exponential growth and a leveling off, once the carrying capacity is reached.

Think Critically
1. Competitive exclusion would eventually lead to the extinction of one of the species.
2. As predators hunt and kill lame or diseased prey, the gene pool of the prey species is strengthened. Also, decreased numbers of prey animals result in less competition for limited resources.
3. A land environment is more subject to change than the environment on the ocean floor.
4. Accept all logical responses.

Graphic Analysis
1. Fruit fly population change over time.
2. In the middle of the time period shown on the graph. The population size is about one-half the carrying capacity.
3. Yes, at the carrying capacity
4. The resource limits have been reached.

Chapter Planning Guide

Section	Core	Standard	Enriched	Section	Core	Standard	Enriched
6.1 Relations in the Ecosystem	•	•	•	**Laboratory Program** Investigation 8	•	•	•
Blackline Masters Review Worksheet 6.1 Skills Worksheet 6A	• •	• •	•	**6.3 Balance in the Ecosystem**	•	•	•
Ancillary Options One Minute Readings, p. 35	•	•		**Section Features** Dateline 1972, p. 97 Word Power, p. 97 Astronomy Link, p. 98	• •	• • •	• • •
6.2 Ecological Succession		•	•	**Blackline Masters** Review Worksheet 6.3	•	•	•
Section Features Field Activity, p. 93 Biology Link, p. 94 Think Critically, p. 95 Frontiers, p. 96 Activity 6.1, p. 102	• • • •	• • • • •	• • • •	**Laboratory Program** Investigation 9		•	•
				6.4 Land Biomes	•	•	•
Blackline Masters Review Worksheet 6.2 Issues and Case Studies 4 Skills Worksheet 6B	• • •	• • •	• •	**Section Features** Activity 6.2	•	•	•
Ancillary Options Multiculturalism, p. 117		•	•	**Blackline Masters** Review Worksheet 6.4	•	•	•

Every chapter has two corresponding tests in the Test Book and one Vocabulary Review Worksheet in the Review Book. There is also a Unit 2 test in the Test Book covering Chapters 4–6.

Chapter Overview

Chapter 6 explains how an ecosystem, while dynamic in nature, can maintain relative balance and stability. Section 6.1 presents some of the many relationships that occur within an ecosystem. Section 6.2 addresses ecological succession and its role in producing a stable ecosystem. Section 6.3 focuses on interactions between biotic and abiotic factors that help maintain balance. The chapter concludes in Section 6.4 with an introduction to terrestrial biomes.

Advance Planner

- Order the film or video described in the Introducing the Chapter section.

Section 6.1
- Obtain photographs of spider webs for the activity in the Motivate section.

Section 6.2
- Obtain a piece of velcro for use in the STS Connection activity.

Section 6.3
- Obtain a double-pan balance and ten 1-gram masses for the activity in the Motivate section.

Section 6.4
- Make overhead transparencies of national weather maps for one week for the exercise in the Motivate section.
- Provide students with photocopies of outline maps of the United States, and markers or pencils of different colors for the Closure activity.

Introducing the Chapter

Show the class a film or video that includes time-lapse photography of biotic and abiotic factors undergoing change. Such films may include germinating plants, rapid seasonal changes, erupting volcanoes, or an area before and after an earthquake. Use the film as a springboard for a discussion on the dynamic nature of ecosystems and the ability of organisms to survive rapid and dramatic changes. Explain that although ecosystems undergo constant change, most ecosystems are able to maintain some form of stability.

Section 6.1 Relationships in the Ecosystem

pp. 89–91

Performance Objectives
- Explain the relationship between population sizes of predator and prey.
- Define *symbiosis* and state the effects of symbiotic relationships on populations.

Skills Objective
- Compare and contrast various types of symbiosis.

Section Vocabulary
parasitism   host   symbiosis

Motivate
Show students photographs of spider webs. Ask students why spiders build webs. Develop an understanding that spiders construct webs to capture prey, usually insects. Use this example to discuss the the roles of predator and prey.

Teaching Strategies
Misconception   Point out to students that predator–prey relationships involve not only animals. The consumption of plant material is by definition a predator-prey interaction.

Reteach   To illustrate how the size of a predator population affects the size of the prey population, relate the following scenario. Sea stars are a predator of oysters. At one time, oyster fishers commonly caught sea stars in their rakes. The fishers chopped the sea stars into pieces and returned the pieces to the ocean. Unknowingly, these fishers actually helped to increase the sea star population since sea stars can reproduce by regeneration. As a result, the oyster population dramatically decreased.

Enrich   Have students do library research to find the names of ten common parasites that affect people. Have students create a table in which they name the parasites and describe any related diseases.

Evaluate
Closure   Have students work in cooperative groups to create a concept map that shows the relationships among all the boldfaced and italicized terms in this section. Review some of the concept maps in class as a summary of the section.

Section 6.2 Ecological Succession

pp. 92–95

Performance Objectives
- Describe the process of primary and secondary succession.
- Illustrate the evolution of many species from a single ancestor during the process of island succession.

Skills Objectives
- Analyze changes in a community as evidence of secondary succession.
- Predict the effects of human activities designed to help a grassland community.

Section Vocabulary
primary succession   lichen
secondary succession

Motivate
Ask students to describe what happens to a lawn or garden that is left untended for a long time. Use their descriptions to introduce the idea that landscapes undergo change over time. Explain that such changes in the landscape over time are called succession.

Teaching Strategies
Discuss   Point out to students that the actions of wind, water, and animals are often responsible for the dispersal of seeds to a new area. Extend the discussion by having students conduct library research to find out what adaptations seeds have to aid in their dispersal.

STS Connection   Show students a piece of velcro. Explain to students that the inventor of velcro got the idea for the product from his observations of seeds that stick or cling to clothing and animal fur.

Enrich   Have interested students research succession in the Mount St. Helens area and prepare an oral report for the class.

Model   Have students working in cooperative groups use photographs, sketches, or other materials to create models that show the stages involved in one of the kinds of succession discussed in this section.

Evaluate
Closure   List the following terms on the chalkboard: *ecological succession, primary succession, secondary succession, pioneer community, climax community,* and *soil.* Have students describe an example related to each term.

Section 6.3 Balance in the Ecosystem

pp. 97–98

Performance Objectives
- Examine the concept of ecosystem balance and explain how humans affect that balance.
- Explain that disturbance is a natural part of all ecosystems, but that disturbances trigger changes in ecosystems.

Skills Objective
- Analyze the effects that present human activities will have on future ecosystems.

Motivate

Obtain a double-pan balance and ten 1-g masses. Place equal numbers of masses on each balance pan. Tell students that the masses on one pan represent predators, while those on the other side represent prey. Remove one of the prey from the balance and have students describe what happens. Ask students how the balance may be reestablished. Point out to students that other factors besides predator and prey may disrupt the balance of an ecosystem.

Teaching Strategies

Reteach   Relate the concept of homeostasis in organisms to balance in an ecosystem. Challenge students to identify the controls at work in each system. Relate this discussion to the Gaia hypothesis that was discussed in Chapter 1.

Misconception   At one time, many people thought that the ocean could rapidly recover from ocean dumping. However, this concept proved to be wrong. Evidence of damage created by toxins, oil, and other wastes dumped into oceans is now visible on shorelines around the world as well as in the tissues of fishes and other ocean organisms.

Evaluate

Closure   Write the following terms on the chalkboard: *temperature*, *predators*, *sunlight*, *water*, and *parasites*. Have students predict how an ecosystem would be affected by an increase or decrease in each of these factors.

Section 6.4 Land Biomes

pp. 99–101

Performance Objectives
- Define the concept of a biome and name the eight major land biomes.
- Illustrate where each of the eight major land biomes occurs.

Skills Objective
- Analyze how different land biomes affect human ways of living.

Motivate

Display national weather maps from your daily newspaper for one week. Have students summarize how weather conditions in different regions of the country changed throughout the week. Ask students what patterns are apparent in the weather conditions in different regions and challenge them to account for these differences. Explain that such changes over long periods of time determine climate and that climate, in turn, determines the types of organisms an area can support.

Teaching Strategies

Discuss   Have students use the data regarding climate and location of the various land biomes to predict the types of organisms that will live in each biome. Have students organize their predictions into a table or chart.

Enrich   Have students identify a city that they would like to visit in each biome shown on the map. Challenge students to use the data regarding climate to identify five articles of clothing that would be appropriate to the climate conditions.

Literature Connection   Have students use library sources to find a novel with the setting in a particular land biome. Have students read and write a report about the book they chose, pointing out how the characteristics of the biome affected the story.

Evaluate

Closure   Distribute outline maps of the United States. Have students use the world biome map in the text to identify the types of biomes located in the United States. Have students mark the location of each biome on their maps using a color-code system.

Chapter Resources

Teaching Tip for Feature
Frontiers: One of Each Organism
- Locate a book such as *Plant Hunters of the Andes* that describes a search for new species. Read a passage aloud to the class.

Teaching Tips for Field Activity
- Obtain necessary permissions.
- Provide meter sticks and hand lenses.

Answers to Field Activity
Responses will vary.

Teaching Tips for Activities

ACTIVITY 6.1
Time Day 1: 10 min; Day 3: 10 min; Days 4–14: 20 min
Group Size 3–4 students
Prediction The types of microorganisms found in aged tap water change over time.
Safety Tip Have students wash their hands with warm, soapy water after handling the aged tap water.

Analysis
1. Bacteria usually appear first in great numbers. The numbers of bacteria decrease over time as the populations of more complex organisms increase.
2. Certain populations may have become a food source for other populations.
3. As the number of organisms increased, waste materials accumulated. The pH became more basic due to ammonia and other nitrogen compounds.

Conclusion
Answers should be based on observations.

ACTIVITY 6.2
Time Day 1: 15 min; Days 2–21: 10 min
Group Size 2 students
Prediction Clover will dominate.
Safety Tips None

Analysis
1. Plants grown alone are likely to have longer roots and more numerous and darker leaves.
2. Same answer as question 1.

Conclusion
The grass and clover competed for light, space, water, and nutrients. When the plants in a grass and clover lawn are not cut and water is not limited, clover has an advantage because of its larger photosynthetic area and its root nodules.

Answers to End of Chapter Questions
Concept Review
1. Both predators and parasites use other organisms as their food source. Predators always kill the organisms they use as food, while parasites may cause illness but usually do not cause death.
2. In mutualism both organisms benefit. The yucca plant provides the moth with food and a habitat, while the moth aids in pollination of the plant.
3. Primary succession involves soil formation. Once soil is formed, small plants may grow. At each stage, the presence of new organisms encourages further growth and the introduction of new species.
4. Several different species of finches evolved, each of which fills a slightly different niche because it eats a different kind of food.
5. Lack of water in a desert makes plant life scarce.

Think Critically
1. The lynx population would be greatly reduced. In time, the hare population will increase, followed by an increase in lynx.
2. As one organism evolved, the other organism evolved adaptations to the changes in the first organism. In time, the organisms changed enough that neither could survive without the other.
3. If seed-eating mice are introduced to the island, competition for food will exist. A decrease in some species of finch populations will occur until mice and finch populations reach a state of equilibrium.
4. Because the type of plant life depends upon the temperature and rainfall. Other factors include sunlight, latitude, soil quality, and composition.

Computer Activity
See Figure 6.12, page 100.

Graphic Analysis
1. Rain forest
2. South America
3. North Africa, Central Asia
4. Northern regions of North America and Asia

Unit Overview

Unit 3 provides a detailed summary of the climate conditions, plants, and animals that characterize the world's terrestrial and aquatic biomes. Chapter 7 provides a glimpse into Earth's driest terrestrial biomes—deserts and tundra. Chapter 8 presents grassland regions such as steppes, prairies, and savannas. Chapter 9 focuses on the coniferous forest, deciduous forest, and tropical rain forest. In Chapters 10 and 11, the focus changes from terrestrial to aquatic biomes.

Introducing the Unit

Discussion   Display a world map and explain that certain areas of latitude are used to identify approximate locations of three large climate zones: tropical, temperate, and polar.

Teacher Resources

Audiovisual

Tundra, film/video, 12 minutes, Coronet Film and Video, 1989.
Grasslands, film/video, 12 minutes, Coronet Film and Video, 1989.
Rain Forest, film/video, 59 minutes, National Geographic Society, 1983.
Ancient Forests, film/video, 25 minutes, National Geographic Society, 1992.
A Desert Place, film/video, 30 minutes, Time-Life Video, 1976.
Animals of a Living Reef, video, 17 minutes, Centron Films, 1980.

Computer Software

Terrestrial Biomes, Apple II/IBM, Prentice-Hall Media.
Ecoadventures in the Rainforest, Macintosh, Chariot.

Suggested Readings

Gay, Kathlyn, *Rainforests of the World*, ABC-CLIO Inc., 1993.

Advance Preparation

Chapter 7
Field Activity   Gather thermometers, aluminum foil, and cardboard boxes.

Activity 7.1   Have graph paper available.
Activity 7.2   Have construction paper (white) and reference sources identifying desert organisms available.

Chapter 8
Field Activity   Select a location.
Activity 8.1   Have collecting bags, glue, and reference sources containing information about seed dispersal mechanisms available.
Activity 8.2   Obtain sheets of acetate, large clear containers with lids, gravel, rocks, soil, grass seeds, clover seeds, mung bean seeds, crickets, meal worms, land isopods, and earthworms.

Chapter 9
Field Activity   Make field guides of deciduous trees available to students.
Activity 9.1   Obtain styrofoam cups, marking pens, garden soil, soil from beneath a coniferous tree, jars, graduated cylinders, and paper towels.
Activity 9.2   Have reference material about lichens, glue or tape, metersticks, tripod type hand lenses, and compasses available.

Chapter 10
Field Activity   Gather jars, microscopes, and hand lenses for students to use.
Activity 10.1   Obtain the materials needed to make the stream table. Gather metric rulers, beakers, graduated cylinders, and a clock or watch with a second hand.
Activity 10.2   Obtain depression slides, spatulas, cryptobiotic tardigrades, droppers, coverslips, dissecting microscopes, and needles.

Chapter 11
Field Activity   Have reference books for maintaining saltwater aquariums available for use.
Activity 11.1   Obtain marking pens, styrofoam cups, 250-mL beakers, salt, metric measuring spoons, brine shrimp eggs, cotton balls, shoe boxes, plastic wrap, droppers, Petri dishes, hand lenses or dissecting microscopes, and dry yeast.
Activity 11.2   Prepare aged tap water. Gather salt, 500-mL beakers, jars, pans of ice, thermometers, food coloring, and live clams.

Chapter Planning Guide

Section	Core	Standard	Enriched	Section	Core	Standard	Enriched
7.1 Deserts	•	•	•	Skills Worksheet 7B		•	•
Section Features Social Studies Link, p. 111 Health Link, p. 112 Activity 7.2, p. 123	• • •	• • •	• • •	**Ancillary Options** One Minute Readings	•	•	
				7.3 Tundra	•	•	•
Blackline Masters Review Worksheet 7.1 Skill 7A Worksheet	• •	•		**Section Features** Dateline 1974, p. 116 Think Critically, p. 117 Word Power, p. 117 People and the Environment, p.119 Activity 7.1, p. 120	• • •	• • • • •	• • • • •
Laboratory Program Investigation 10	•	•	•				
7.2 Formation of Deserts	•	•	•	**Blackline Masters** Review Worksheet 7.3	•	•	•
Section Features Field Activity, p. 115	•	•	•	**Ancillary Options** Multiculturalism			•
Blackline Masters Review Worksheet 7.2	•	•	•				

Every chapter has two corresponding tests in the Test Book and one Vocabulary Review Worksheet in the Review Book.
Unit 2 test in the Test Book covering Chapters 4–6.

Chapter Overview

Chapter 7 discusses Earth's two most arid biomes—deserts and tundra. Section 7.1 presents the limiting, abiotic, and biotic factors that characterize a desert. Representative desert plants and animals are discussed with a focus on their specialized adaptations. Section 7.2 discusses the conditions that formed the deserts in the southwestern United States. Section 7.3 presents the characteristics of the tundra biome, including representative organisms and their adaptations.

Advance Planner

Section 7.1
- Obtain photographs of deserts in various parts of the world for the exercise in the Motivate section.
- Provide graph paper for the Activity.
- Have photocopies of world outline maps available for the activity in the Enrich section.
- Obtain a cactus as described in the Reteach section.
- Obtain an aquarium, wood chips, gerbils, and gerbil food for the activity in the Reinforce section.

Section 7.2
- Obtain a newspaper weather report for the exercise in the Motivate section.
- Obtain a sponge and a beaker of water to demonstrate the Analogy.
- Have a map of North America available and an Earth Science text for the discussion of air masses in the Earth Science Connection.

Section 7.3
- Provide students with graph paper for the activity in the Motivate section.
- Obtain moss or lichen samples from a biological supply house and sod samples from a local gardening center for the activity in the Reteach section.
- Obtain copies of bird migratory flyway maps for the activity in the Reinforce section.

Introducing the Chapter

Write the names of the following regions on the chalkboard: *Death Valley*, *Sahara*, and *Mojave*. Lead students to associate these regions with deserts. Write the names *Alaska* and *Siberia* on the chalkboard. Explain that each of these regions contains tundra biomes. Point out that although desert and tundra biomes seem very different, they actually share an important characteristic. Both are relatively dry because they receive less than 25 cm of precipitation each year.

Section 7.1 Deserts

pp. 111–113

Performance Objectives
- Describe the characteristics of a desert.
- Explain how desert organisms are adapted to live in their environment.

Skills Objective
- Infer why daytime summer temperatures in the desert are higher than those in other biomes.

Section Vocabulary
leaching   nocturnal   pavement   succulents

Motivate
Display pictures showing desert regions from various parts of the world. Have students list characteristics that seem common to all these regions. Have them generate a second list identifying differences among the regions. Discuss the lists as a class.

Teaching Strategies
Misconception   Many people associate the term *desert* with very hot areas. However, it is precipitation and not temperature that is the limiting factor of a desert. Explain that while daylight temperatures in some deserts are quite high, nighttime temperatures may drop to freezing.

Activity   Supply students with rainfall and temperature data from several desert regions. Have students construct graphs of the data. Use the activity to help students recognize that rainfall is the limiting factor in the desert biome.

Enrich   Distribute small world outline maps to students. Have students use colored pencils to show the locations of the world's deserts. Tell students to keep the maps in their portfolios for later use.

Reteach   Display a cactus and identify the features that serve as environmental adaptations (thick stem, spines, and root structure). Review how each of these structures permits survival in an arid environment.

Reinforce   A gerbil is a rodent that makes its home in desert regions. Set up a gerbil habitat by filling a 10-gallon aquarium half-full with wood chips. Have students observe how the gerbil burrows tunnels through the wood chips. Explain that gerbils, like many desert animals, are nocturnal. Leave lights shining on the tank at night and keep the tank in a darkened area during the day so students can observe the activities of this animal. When the cage is cleaned, have students note how little liquid waste the animal excretes.

Field Trip   Plan a trip to a botanical garden or nursery that has greenhouses set up for plants that grow in arid regions. Have students observe the types of plants grown and the conditions under which these plants are maintained.

Evaluate
Closure   Have students use their own sketches or pictures cut from magazines to create a desert scene that includes desert flora and fauna. Tell students to include labels that identify the annual temperature and precipitation data for their desert.

Section 7.2 Formation of Deserts

pp. 114–115.

Performance Objectives
- Illustrate the processes that cause deserts to form.

Skills Objectives
- Deduce the reasons farmers may try to raise more livestock on desert land than the land can support.
- Conduct a study of how the angle of the sun's rays affects temperature.

Section Vocabulary
desertification

Motivate
Read today's weather report. Have students name the factors that determine weather (temperature, precipitation, cloudiness, humidity, wind speed and direction, and air pressure). List these factors on the chalkboard. Ask students to define *climate*. Lead students to recognize that weather is a short-term description of atmospheric conditions, while climate describes long-term weather patterns.

Teaching Strategies
Analogy   Demonstrate how a sponge absorbs water from a beaker of water. Have students observe how the water level in the beaker changes as water is absorbed by the sponge. Tell students that air acts like a sponge in that it removes moisture from soil as it moves over land.

Earth Science Connection   Using a map of North America, describe how maritime polar air masses form over cold ocean regions, while tropical maritime air masses form over waters near the equator. Also identify continental polar air masses that form over cold land areas and continental tropical air masses that form over land areas near the equator. Explain that movement of these air masses is responsible for weather conditions.

Reteach   Have students recall that heat causes water to evaporate, while the cooler air temperatures influence condensation. Guide the class to realize that warmer air holds more moisture than cooler air. Remind students that temperatures decrease as you go higher in the troposphere. With the aid of a diagram, show how air moving over a mountain loses moisture to produce an arid region (called a rain shadow) on the far side of the mountain.

Evaluate
Closure   Have students prepare a chart with six columns. Head the columns as follows: *Biome, Average Yearly Rainfall, Average Yearly Temperature, Soil Conditions, Animal Characteristics, Plant Characteristics*. Tell students to fill in their chart for the desert biome. Have students keep their charts for use again throughout this unit.

Section 7.3 Tundra

pp. 116–118.

Performance Objectives
- Describe why the characteristics of the tundra make it a fragile ecosystem.
- Compare characteristics of tundra organisms and those of their relatives in warmer climates.

Skills Objectives
- Hypothesize how large bodies and small limbs are adaptations to tundra conditions.
- Analyze how the melting of permafrost could affect the tundra food web.

Section Vocabulary
   lichens   migration   permafrost

Motivate
Distribute graph paper and tell students they will be plotting data as follows: *Average monthly temperature* will be plotted as a line graph. On the same sheet of paper, average monthly rainfall will be plotted as a bar graph. Provide students with the following data for Point Barrow, Alaska.

Rainfall in cm: Jan,1.25; Feb, 2.0; Mar, 1.5; Apr, 2.0; May 1.75; Jun, 1.75; Jul, 2.5; Aug, 2.5; Sep, 2.0; Oct, 2.0; Nov, 1.25; Dec, 1.5. *Temperature in °C:* Jan, −29; Feb, −27; Mar, −23; Apr, −23; May −18; Jun, −7; Jul, 2; Aug, 6; Sep, 4; Oct −1; Nov, −12; Dec, −21.

Have students use their plotted data to describe the conditions of the tundra biome.

Teaching Strategies
Reteach   Display samples of moss or lichens and distribute small clumps of grasses to students working in groups of three. Have students examine the root or rhizoid systems that the plants use to absorb water. Note that a thick, shallow root system helps plants absorb moisture near the ground's surface. Tell students that deep roots would have difficulty penetrating the permafrost of the tundra.

Enrich   Tundra plants have difficulty reproducing from seeds because of the short growing season. Therefore, much of the growth of tundra plants results from vegetative propagation. Have students grow and display plants they develop using vegetative propagation methods. Sweet potatoes, carrots, tulips, and forsythia are excellent plants for such projects.

Reinforce   Have students examine a bird migratory flyway map and elicit explanations of why birds make these long trips. Contact a local birding club for a copy of local flyway maps or obtain copies of the maps from a birding book. Relate bird migration to migrations of other animals. Have students explain why migration is so important to tundra animals.

Enrich   Have interested students research various animals that live in the tundra and prepare reports about how these animals adapt to life in these regions. Ask students to include pictures of the animals that illustrate their adaptations.

Evaluate
Closure   Have students add information about the tundra to the table they began in the Closure activity for Section 7.2.

Chapter Resources

Teaching Tip for Feature
People and the Environment: Oil in the Tundra
- Use a map of Alaska to point out the pipeline route.

Teaching Tips for Field Activity
- Caution students to be careful when working with the thermometers to avoid breakage.
- Be sure students place both collectors in the same area and face them in the same direction.

Answers to Field Activity
Temperatures recorded will vary; however, boxes placed at greater than a 90° angle will warm up faster than those placed at a 90° angle.

Teaching Tips for Activities

ACTIVITY 7.1
Time One class period
Group Size 1–2 students
Prediction Climatograms will make it easier to see climate patterns.
Safety Tips None

Analysis
1. All four cities receive less than 25 cm of rainfall annually; however, only cities 2 and 3 are likely to be desert biomes.
2. The consistently low temperatures of cities 1 and 4 suggest they are tundra regions.
3. City 3 has higher temperatures than City 2.
4. City 1 is colder than City 4.

Conclusion
Responses are likely to indicate that climatograms show patterns more easily than data tables.

ACTIVITY 7.2
Time One class period
Group Size 1–2 students
Prediction Off-road vehicles could destroy the habitats of certain desert organisms and disrupt the desert food web.
Safety Tips None

Analysis
Responses will vary depending upon organisms used.

Conclusion
1. Likely responses will include that destruction of certain populations decreases the food supply.
2. Accept all logical responses.

Answers to End of Chapter Questions
Concept Review
1. Low precipitation prevents leaching of minerals. Dry soil is carried away by wind, reducing topsoil.
2. Desert rodents burrow during daylight hours to stay cool. They become active at night when less water will be lost as perspiration.
3. Both types of animals have body coverings that reduce water loss.
4. Shallow root systems obtain moisture near the surface; deep root systems reach down to the water table.
5. Desertification occurs as soils become prone to erosion and drying out.

Think Critically
1. Responses will vary, but are likely to suggest that habitat may be destroyed, vegetation may be destroyed and disrupt the food web, oil spills may damage the environment.
2. Such temperature differences result from the lack of moisture in the air.
3. Permafrost prevents the growth of plants with long, deep roots. Permafrost prevents the water that does fall in the tundra from being absorbed into deep soil layers, thus allowing for the formation of bogs. If the permafrost melted, the area might become submerged and in time trees could grow.
4. Temperature increases could cause permafrost in tundras to melt, forming wetlands and possibly forests. Temperature increases in desert regions may permit these areas to become larger as the air absorbs more moisture from soil.

Graphic Analysis
1. The far west and southwest
2. There is more rainfall.
3. Rainfall is higher there due to weather systems that move in from the Atlantic Ocean.

Chapter Planning Guide

Section	Core	Standard	Enriched	Section	Core	Standard	Enriched
8.1 Grasslands	•	•	•	**Blackline Masters** Review Worksheet 8.2 Skills Worksheet 8B	• •	• •	•
Section Features Field Activity, p. 127 Math Connection, p. 128		•	• •	**Ancillary Options** Multiculturalism, p. 123			•
Blackline Masters Review Worksheet 8.1 Skills Worksheet 8A	•	• •	• •	**8.3 Savannas**	•	•	•
Laboratory Program Investigation 11	•	•	•	**Section Features** Dateline 1954, p. 132 Archaeology Link, p. 133 Activity 8.1	•	• • •	• • •
8.2 Steppes and Prairies	•	•	•				
Section Features Word Power, p. 130 Think Critically, p. 131 Activity 8.2, p. 137	•	• • •	• • •	**Blackline Masters** Review Worksheet 8.3	•	•	•

Every chapter has two corresponding tests in the Test Book and one Vocabulary Review Worksheet in the Review Book.

Chapter Overview

Chapter 8 focuses on the biotic and abiotic factors that define grassland biomes. Section 8.1 discusses the locations of grasslands and limiting factors, such as rainfall, temperature, and fire, that help create and maintain these biomes. Sections 8.2 and 8.3 investigate the characteristics of three types of grasslands; steppes, prairies, and savannas. Information about soils, grass types, animal feeding patterns, and human impacts is presented.

Advance Planner

- Obtain samples of sod and weeds with roots intact for the activity in the Introducing the Chapter section.

Section 8.1
- Obtain packages of flour, oatmeal, rice, corn, and sugar for the activity described in the Motivate section.
- Provide students with world outline maps for the exercise in the Enrich section.
- Locate a reproduction of *M.C. Escher's Creation of Metamorphoses* or *The Fish and the Birds*.

Section 8.2
- A world map is needed for the Reteach section.

- 50-mL graduated cylinders, sand, and sod are needed for the Activity.

Section 8.3
- Order a filmstrip or video that shows different grasslands as described in the Motivate section.
- Obtain grass specimens for the Activity.
- Cut pictures of grassland animals from magazines for the activity in the Reteach section.

Introducing the Chapter

Ask several members of the class what they ate for breakfast. List the foods on the chalkboard. Tell students that most of the foods mentioned came from biomes called grasslands. Illustrate this by tracing each food back to its source. For example milk, butter, and cream come from cows which graze on grasses. Breads and cereals are derived from wheat, oat, rice, and corn—all of which are grasses.

Have students form cooperative groups. To each group distribute a small piece of sod and a large weed with roots intact. Have students examine the sod and the weed and write down their observations. Point out that although they may appear different, both the sod and the weed are types of grasses.

Section 8.1 Grasslands

pp. 125–127

Performance Objectives
- Describe the characteristics of a grassland.
- Identify where grasslands are located.

Skills Objective
- Suggest reasons why grass size and texture are related to climate.

Section Vocabulary
desert–grassland boundary

Motivate
Display a sack of flour, a box of oatmeal or rice, a can of corn, and a bag of sugar. Ask the class what all of these items have in common. Point out that all of the items are products of grasses.

Teaching Strategies
Discuss At one time, grasslands covered more than 40 percent of Earth's land surface. Explain that this percentage has been continually shrinking. Ask students to propose possible reasons for this shrinkage. Have students hypothesize about how this trend would affect future populations if it continued.

Enrich Distribute outline maps of the world. After studying each type of grassland, have students choose a color to represent each type of grassland and color in the appropriate area on the map.

Art Connection Display a reproduction of M.C. Escher's artwork such as *Creation of Metamorphoses* or *The Fish and the Birds*. Ask students to locate where one subject ends and the other begins. Tell them that a transitional area is sometimes called an interface. Using a beach as an example, lead students to recognize that an interface exists at the place where the land ends and the water begins. Point out that interfaces also exist between biomes. One such interface is located between a desert and a grassland, while another is located between a grassland and a forest. Inform students that the desert-grassland interface is called the desert-grassland boundary. Challenge students to explain what factors create this boundary.

Enrich Tell students that the amount of rainfall an area receives affects the size and texture of the grasses that grow there. Have students design an experiment to test the effects of rainfall on grass characteristics.

Evaluate
Closure Have students add information related to the grassland biome to the chart they started in the Closure activity for Section 7.2.

Section 8.2 Steppes and Prairies

pp. 129–131

Performance Objectives
- Compare and contrast the steppe and the prairie.
- Describe the importance of steppes and prairies to agriculture.

Skills Objective
- Identify changes in steppes and prairies that permit desertification to occur.

Section Vocabulary
bunchgrasses   humus   prairies   steppes sod-forming grasses

Motivate
Ask students what they think a prairie schooner might be. Explain that this name was given to the covered wagons used to move people and their household goods across the grasslands of central North America during the 1800s. Tell them that a schooner is a type of ship. Explain that the word *prairie* comes from a French word meaning '"grasslands." The people who traveled in covered wagons thought they were like ships that carried them over a sea of grass.

Teaching Strategies
Reteach Using a world map, have students locate the Great Plains of the United States, the Russian Steppes, the South African veldt, and the Argentinean pampas. Point out that all these areas are prairies. Show photographs of prairies and have students develop a list of prairie characteristics.

Activity Divide students into groups of three. Instruct them to use paper to make two funnels and to place the funnels into the tops of two 50-mL graduated cylinders. Have them place some sand into one funnel and the same amount of sod into the other. Then have them slowly pour 30 mL of water into each funnel and measure the amount of water that empties into each graduated cylinder. Have students determine the absorption capabilities of the sand and the soil. Ask students to relate their results to the impact of overgrazing and poor farming techniques.

Enrich Assign students reading from John Steinbeck's *The Grapes of Wrath*. Have students do library research on the Dust Bowl of the 1930s and identify the factors that created the Dust Bowl. Challenge students to identify measures being taken today to prevent the recurrence of such an event.

Reteach Have students identify animals that inhabit grasslands. Direct students to identify whether these animals are helpful or harmful in maintaining the grassland biome. Have students justify their responses.

Activity Have students construct a climatogram using the following data from a prairie region of Wyoming. Remind students that a climatogram shows temperature on a line graph and precipitation on a bar graph. Have students use their climatogram to describe the climatic conditions on a prairie.

	Jan	Feb	Mar	Apr	May	Jun
temp. (°C)	−3	−3	−2	0	6	18
precip. (cm)	0	0	2	4	6	5
	Jul	Aug	Sep	Oct	Nov	Dec
temp. (°C)	22	20	14	6	3	−2
precip. (cm)	5	4	3	2	1	1.5

Evaluate

Closure On the chalkboard, construct a chart comparing steppes and prairies. Include data about climate, height of grass, type of grass, and other conditions. Fill in the chart as a class and have students copy the chart for use as a study tool.

Section 8.3 Savannas

pp. 132–133

Performance Objectives
- Define savannas and state where they are located.
- Explain how savannas can support a wide range of organisms.

Skills Objective
- Hypothesize how enclosing a savanna with fencing could affect migrating animals in the area.

Section Vocabulary
> runners   savannas   tufts
> vertical feeding pattern

Motivate
Show a filmstrip or video of different grasslands. Direct students to observe the differences in plant growth between prairies and savannas. Have students list these differences in their notes. After the filmstrip, discuss students' observations.

Teaching Strategies
Language Connection The word *savanna* comes from the Spanish word *sabana*. In Cuba, grassy areas are called sabanas. The name of the capital of Cuba, Havana, is a corruption of the Spanish word for the grassland. The word *llanos*, the name for the savanna of Venezuela, means "grassy plains." The name for the savannas of Brazil, *campos*, comes from the Latin word *campus*, which means "field or plain." Students may know that many colleges have grassy open spaces. Such grounds have come to be called campuses.

Activity Have students construct a climatogram using the following data obtained from a savanna in India. Have students use the climatogram to describe the climatic conditions on a savanna.

	Jan	Feb	Mar	Apr	May	Jun
temp. (°C)	18	21	26	30	31	30
precip. (cm)	1	2.8	3.5	5	12.5	28
	Jul	Aug	Sep	Oct	Nov	Dec
temp. (°C)	28	27	28	26	22	18
precip. (cm)	30.3	38.8	22.5	10.8	1.3	.5

Activity Distribute grass specimens and have students observe and diagram the leaves, flowers, seeds, and roots of the grass. Ask students to describe the functions of each plant part. Discuss how runners help protect grasses from grazing animals and fires. Explain how overgrazing kills grasses.

Reteach Display photographs of grassland animals. Ask students to choose several animals and study the niche these animals occupy in the grasslands. Reports could show several of these animals in a food web, or demonstrate the concept of vertical feeding patterns. The reports could be presented as a diorama or poster including pictures of each animal.

Evaluate

Closure Have students create a table that summarizes the three different types of grasslands. Have them include climatic factors, soil conditions, and the flora and fauna of each.

Chapter Resources

Teaching Tip for Feature
Math Connection: Natural Chaos
- Explain that weather forecasting is often inaccurate due to chaos within the atmosphere.

Teaching Tips for Field Activity
- Caution students to obtain necessary permissions to observe an area as needed.
- Encourage students to watch for interactions involving insects, worms, or grazing animals.

Answers to Field Activity
Student responses will vary. Likely interactions include pollination by insects or burrowing by worms and small mammals. Harmful effects may include damage from trampling and evidence of overgrazing.

Teaching Tips for Activities

ACTIVITY 8.1

Time One class period
Group Size 4 students
Safety Tips Caution students to avoid contact with poison ivy, poison oak, or poison sumac. Have students wear long-sleeved shirts, long pants and closed shoes to avoid insect bites, and gloves to avoid handling plants that may induce allergic reactions.

Analysis
1. Responses will vary. Common dispersal methods involve wind, animals, or water.
2. Responses will vary. Seeds that become attached to clothing often have hooklike structures.
3. Likely responses will indicate yes.

Conclusion
1. Responses will vary. Dispersal methods are likely to include wind, water, or animals.
2. Walking through fields in which seeds become attached to clothing.

ACTIVITY 8.2

Time Day 1: 15 min; Day 7: 20 min; Day 8–30: 5 min
Group Size 4 students
Hypothesis Responses may vary, but should indicate possible food chains.
Safety Tips Caution students about the proper procedures for working with live plants and animals.

Analysis
1. Answers will vary. Causes of population changes include organisms being eaten, reproducing, or dying.
2. Answers will vary. In predator–prey relationships, the number of predators increases causing the number of prey to decrease. The trend then reverses.

Conclusion
Responses will vary depending upon hypotheses.

Answers to End of Chapter Questions
Concept Review
1. Climate—temperature and rainfall (abiotic); grasses dominant form of vegetation, burrowing animals and grazing animals (biotic).
2. Air spaces allow moisture to enter the soil.
3. Herded grazers are more likely to strip the land of vegetation through grazing and trampling in one area. Migrating grazers move from area to area, giving grasses a greater opportunity to regrow.
4. Overgrazing, poor farming practices, and droughts.
5. Steppes consist largely of short bunchgrasses. Prairies consist largely of sod-farming grasses. Savanna grasses are coarse grasses that grow by means of runners, and grow in tufts.

Think Critically
1. Runners help the grasses absorb moisture and prevent the grasses from being completely trampled.
2. Specialized species are more prone to extinction.
3. Once the soil structure collapses the soil is more prone to erosion by running water.
4. Grass fires clear away the old grass, increasing the amount of light for new germinating grasses.

Computer Activity
Graphs should generate a value in the range of 120–140 years.

Graphic Analysis
1. The wart hog, because it eats roots and grasses; and the dik-dik, because it needs less food compared to the rhinoceros.
2. The elephant and giraffe would probably do best, because trees would be undamaged and make too much shade for grasses.
3. The giraffes have long necks that can reach high trees. Dik-diks are small and can survive on small shrubs and grass.

CHAPTER 9 FOREST BIOMES

Chapter Planning Guide

Section	Core	Standard	Enriched
9.1 Coniferous Forests	•	•	•
Section Features Issues, p. 141	•	•	•
Activity 9.2, p. 153	•		
Blackline Masters Review Worksheet 9.1	•	•	
Skills Worksheet 9A	•	•	
9.2 Deciduous Forests	•	•	•
Section Features Word Power, p. 142	•	•	•
Biology Link, p. 142		•	•
Field Activity, p. 143	•	•	•
Historical Notebook, p. 145		•	•

Section	Core	Standard	Enriched
Blackline Masters Review Worksheet 9.2	•	•	
9.3 Rain Forests	•	•	•
Section Features Think Critically, p. 147	•	•	•
Biology Link, p. 149	•	•	•
Activity 9.1, p. 150		•	•
Blackline Masters Review Worksheet 9.3	•	•	•
Skills Worksheet 9B		•	•
Ancillary Options One Minute Readings, p. 33			•
Laboratory Program Investigation 12	•	•	•

Every chapter has two corresponding tests in the Test Book and one Vocabulary Review Worksheet in the Review Book.

Chapter Overview

Chapter 9 describes how climatic conditions affect soils and influence the biodiversity of the three major forest biomes. Section 9.1 discusses and shows the locations of coniferous forests and describes adaptations of plants and animals within this biome. Plants and animals of the deciduous forest are covered in Section 9.2, along with a description of the forest layers which serve as habitats. Section 9.3 focuses on the locations and climatic conditions of tropical rain forests. Deforestation and its effects on biodiversity within this biome are also examined.

Advance Planner

- Obtain wood samples for the activity in the Introducing the Chapter section. Keep the wood samples for reuse in Sections 9.1 and 9.2.

Section 9.1
- If you live in an area without conifers or deciduous trees, obtain leaf samples from a biological supply house. Save these samples for reuse in Section 9.2.
- A classroom map and outline maps will be needed for the activity in the Reteach section.
- Obtain samples of conifer cones for the activity in the Enrich section.

Section 9.2
- Make arrangements for the Field Trip.
- Have guide books identifying various kinds of trees available for the activity in the Enrich section.
- Have wood samples, a hammer, and nails available for the activity in the Reteach section.

Section 9.3
- Obtain coffee, chocolate, bananas, rubber bands, quinine tablets, and samples of rain-forest woods for the activity in the Motivate section.
- A large world map will be needed for the activity in the Reteach section.

Introducing the Chapter

Obtain samples of various kinds of wood. Cut the samples into small blocks and label each sample with a letter. Distribute a set of samples to pairs of students and ask them to describe the color, odor, and relative densities of each sample and record their observations in a table. Challenge students to identify the type of wood each sample represents. Conclude the activity by providing students with the correct identity of each wood sample.

Section 9.1 Coniferous Forests

pp. 139–141

Performance Objectives
- Describe the characteristics of the coniferous forest.
- Explain adaptations that enable organisms to survive in coniferous forests.

Skills Objective
- Deduce that conifer needles decompose slowly and suggest reasons for this slow rate of decomposition.

Section Vocabulary
conifers

Motivate
Have students construct a climatogram using the following data.

	Jan	Feb	Mar	Apr	May	Jun
temp. (°C)	–15	–12	–5	4	11	18
precip. (cm)	5.5	5	4.5	5.5	7	10.5
	Jul	Aug	Sep	Oct	Nov	Dec
temp. (°C)	20	18	15	6	–2	13
precip. (cm)	11	9	11	8	7	6.5

Tell students this climatogram represents a coniferous forest located near Quebec, Canada. Have students use their climatograms to describe the characteristics of this biome.

Teaching Strategies
Activity   Have students gather pine needles and compare them to the leaves of a deciduous tree. Point out that the needles have a waxy skin and a reduced surface area. Have students expose some pine needles and leaves to the air for several days and place other pine needles and leaves in a freezer for several hours. From the experimental results, develop the idea that the smaller surface area and waxy skin of the pine needles reduces the amount of water lost through evaporation. The waxy skin also helps protect the conifer from freezing.

Reteach   Use a classroom map to locate regions where coniferous forests exist. Have students color in these areas on smaller maps at their desks. Use this exercise to review the concept of ecotones.

Reinforce   Have students collect pictures of animals that live in a coniferous forest. Ask students to work in cooperative groups to construct food chains and food webs with the pictures.

Enrich   Assign students the task of surveying their neighborhoods for evergreen trees. Have them collect samples of different kinds of needles and cones and use a field guide to identify the type of coniferous tree each sample came from. Instruct students to mount some of their specimens for exhibition along with a short factual report.

Evaluate
Closure   Have students prepare a chart with two columns. In one column have them list the major environmental factors affecting the plants and animals in the coniferous forest. In the second column have them list the adaptations each plant or animal has for surviving in its biome.

Section 9.2 Deciduous Forests

pp. 142–144

Performance Objectives
- Identify the characteristics of the deciduous forest.
- Describe the organisms that inhabit the deciduous forests.

Skills Objective
- Integrate past human activities with changes in many of the world's deciduous forest biomes.

Section Vocabulary
deciduous

Motivate
Show the class some pine needles and point out that they come from a coniferous tree. Hold up some leaves and ask students what type of tree the leaves come from. Ask the class to describe the main differences between the two types of trees.

Teaching Strategies
Activity   Have students construct a climatogram using the following data from a deciduous forest near Nashville, Tennessee. Have students use the climatogram to describe the conditions of this biome.

	Jan	Feb	Mar	Apr	May	Jun
temp. (°C)	6	7	12	16	20	24
precip. (cm)	12	10	13	11	11.5	12.5
	Jul	Aug	Sep	Oct	Nov	Dec
temp. (°C)	27	26	22	17	12	6
precip. (cm)	12	10	9	8.5	10.5	12.5

Analogy Display a diagram of a deciduous forest. Tell students that just as people live on different floors in an apartment house, animals live at different levels in a forest. Point out that the upper level is the canopy, the middle level is the understory, and the bottom level is the forest floor. Have students suggest what animals are likely to live at each level.

Field Trip Arrange for the class to take a walk around a nearby area with many deciduous trees. Distribute guide books on tree identification. Have students collect leaf samples and make their own booklets to identify deciduous trees in the area. Assign some students the task of making tree maps.

Reteach Display samples of wood from maple, oak, walnut, and other deciduous trees. Point out that these trees are called hardwoods. Compare the hardwood samples with softwood samples from coniferous trees, using a hammer to drive nails into each type of wood. Have students discuss the types of products made from coniferous and deciduous woods.

Evaluate

Closure *Have students make a chart comparing coniferous and deciduous forests. Ask them to consider annual temperature and precipitation, amount of snowfall, length of growing season and intensity of light, diversity of organisms, migratory species, type of soil, and rate of decay of organic material.*

Section 9.3 Rain Forests

pp. 146–149

Performance Objectives
- Describe the characteristics of the tropical zone and of the rain forest.
- Illustrate the complexity and diversity of the rainforest ecosystem.

Skills Objective
- Hypothesize that plants on the rainforest floor often have very large leaves to capture the small amount of sunlight that filters through.

Section Vocabulary
  deforestation   rain forest

Motivate
Display a can of coffee, a chocolate bar, a banana, a rubber band, quinine tablets, and samples of rosewood, ebony, balsa, teak, or mahogany. Ask students what these items have in common. Point out that all are products of a tropical rain forest.

Teaching Strategies
Activity Have students construct a climatogram using the following data obtained from a tropical rain forest near Singapore. Have students use the climatogram to describe the conditions of this biome.

	Jan	Feb	Mar	Apr	May	Jun
temp. (°C)	27	27	27	28	28	28
precip. (cm)	22	17	18	19	20	18
	Jul	Aug	Sep	Oct	Nov	Dec
temp. (°C)	28	27	27	27	27	27
precip. (cm)	19	23	20	21	25	26

Reteach Display a large world map and point out the locations of the different climate zones. Have students use the climate zone information to describe the latitudes where tropical rain forests exist.

Reinforce Have students make a diagram that shows the vertical levels of a tropical rain forest and the animals that live and feed at each level. Point out that although many animals can move easily from one level to the next, most tend to remain within one level. Discuss the reasons for this behavior.

Discuss Have students define deforestation. Hold a pro and con discussion about rain forest destruction taking into account the various viewpoints of people and governments in the rainforest regions, as well as the viewpoints of people outside of rainforest regions.

Evaluate

Closure *Have students make a chart summarizing the characteristics of a rain forest. Have them include abiotic and biotic factors that describe this biome.*

Chapter Resources

Teaching Tip for Features

Issues: The Spotted Owl
- Locate newspaper articles describing ongoing efforts to log the remaining old-growth forests. Discuss steps that people are taking on both sides of the issue.

Historical Notebook: Year of the Fires
- You may wish to coordinate this feature with Laboratory Investigation 11, Chaparral and Fire Ecology, in the *Addison-Wesley Environmental Science Laboratory Manual*.

Teaching Tip for Field Activity
- The leaves can be labeled and mounted on colored paper and covered with plastic wrap.

Answers to Field Activity
Answers will vary.

Teaching Tips for Activities

ACTIVITY 9.1

Time   30 min
Group Size   2–4 students
Hypothesis   Conifer needles increase the water-holding capacity of forest soils.
Safety Tips   To avoid falls, have students clean up water and soil spills immediately.

Analysis
1. Coniferous forest
2. The jar under the plain soil
3. The stack of towels beneath the soil containing conifer needles

Conclusion
1. They increase it.
2. The needles increase the soil's water-holding capacity, encouraging plant growth.
3. Answers will vary.

ACTIVITY 9.2

Time   One class period
Group Size   2–3 students
Prediction   Lichens will grow better on the side where there is more moisture, usually the north side.
Safety Tips   If any students have allergies to plants or insects, take appropriate precautions. Remind students to avoid contact with poisonous plants such as poison ivy, oak, and sumac. In an area with tick infestations, tell students to carefully check their clothing and bodies for these organisms.

Analysis
1. Answers will vary.
2. To eliminate vertical variables

Conclusion
1. Answers will vary depending on data.
2. Accept all logical responses.

Answers to End of Chapter Questions

Concept Review
1. The triangular shape of conifers helps the trees shed snow. The needle-shaped leaves have a small surface area and are coated with a thick, waxy coating to prevent water loss. The organisms are adapted to low temperatures and snow.
2. The shedding of leaves enables the tree to conserve water. The decaying leaves enrich the soil and feed insects and other invertebrates.
3. Most of the nutrients exist in the living organisms. Thus, rainforest soils are thin and poor.
4. The diversity of rainforest plants and the variety of habitats that exist in the different forest levels
5. Deforestation is destroying forest biomes by upsetting food webs and eliminating ground cover which in turn results in erosion.

Think Critically
1. During summer, Earth's tilt causes the higher latitudes to receive more direct rays from the sun.
2. As populations grow, deciduous forests have been cleared to provide land for settlements and farming.
3. Refer to Figures 9.8 and 9.9.
4. The tropical rain forest has the greatest biodiversity, while the coniferous forest has the least.

Computer Activity
Check graphs for accuracy.

Graphic Analysis
1. Forest: 50%, Deforested Land: 0%
2. Forest: 25%, Deforested Land: 0%
3. Forest: 25%, Deforested Land: 75%
4. The soil dries out and is vulnerable to erosion.

Chapter Planning Guide

Section	Core	Standard	Enriched	Section	Core	Standard	Enriched
10.1 Aquatic Biomes	•	•	•	**Laboratory Program** Investigation 13		•	•
Section Features Field Activity, p. 155	•	•	•	**10.3 Flowing-Water Ecosystems**	•	•	•
Physical Science Link, p. 155		•	•	**Section Features** Chemistry Link, p. 161	•	•	•
Dateline 1977, p. 156	•	•	•	Think Critically, p. 162	•	•	•
Blackline Masters Review Worksheet 10.1	•	•	•	Historical Notebook, p. 163	•	•	•
Skills Worksheet 10A		•		Activity 10.1			•
10.2 Standing-Water Ecosystems	•	•	•	**Blackline Masters** Review Worksheet 10.3	•	•	•
Section Features Word Power, p. 159	•	•	•	Skills Worksheet 10B		•	•
Biology Link, p. 159		•	•	**Laboratory Program** Investigation 14	•	•	•
Activity 10.2	•	•					
Blackline Masters Review Worksheet 10.2	•	•	•				

Every chapter has two corresponding tests in the Test Book and one Vocabulary Review Worksheet in the Review Book.

Chapter Overview

Chapter 10 investigates the characteristics of freshwater biomes. Characteristics such as water salinity and depth are explored in Section 10.1. Section 10.2 identifies biomes classified as standing-water biomes. Section 10.3 investigates flowing-water biomes. Stream organisms, stream flow, and the amount of dissolved oxygen are studied, along with the effects humans have on such ecosystems.

Advance Planner

- Obtain 5–10 maps of your county or state for the activity in the Introducing the Chapter section.

Section 10.1

- Bring in a goldfish in a bowl for the discussion described in the Motivate section.
- Have a cylinder, water, a test tube, a Bunsen burner, and a ringstand and clamp assembly available for the Demonstration.
- Provide students with graph paper for the Activity.
- Obtain a photoelectric meter for the demonstration in the Reinforce section.

- Make a Secchi disk using a lid from a gallon paint can and black and white paint as described in the Enrich section.
- Have an evaporating dish and water available for the demonstration in the Reteach section.

Section 10.2

- Provide test tubes and stoppers to collect water samples for the Activity, or order prepared slides of phytoplankton from a biological supply house.

Section 10.3

- Obtain live goldfish and watches with second hands for the activity in the Motivate section.
- Have photographs of freshwater stream animals available for the exercise in the Reteach section.
- Have two beakers, water, sand, silt and pebbles available for the activity in the Model section.

Introducing the Chapter

Distribute maps of your county or state to groups of two to three students. Have each group identify bodies of water shown on the map and make a chart classifying them as standing freshwater, flowing freshwater, or salt water.

Section 10.1   Aquatic Biomes

pp. 155–156

Performance Objective

- Describe the factors that characterize the various types of aquatic biomes.

Skills Objectives

- Predict what will happen when saltwater fish are placed in freshwater.
- Observe microscopic organisms that live in freshwater ecosystems.

Section Vocabulary

benthic zone   photic zone   salinity

Motivate

Display a goldfish in a small bowl. Ask students what factors must be considered when keeping a goldfish as a pet. Make sure students mention fresh water. Discuss what makes fresh water different from salt water. Tell students that the amount of salt in the water is called the salinity.

Teaching Strategies

Demonstrate   Allow a tall cylinder of cold water to remain standing at the front of the classroom. Have students observe the bubbles that form in the water as the water warms. Gently heat a test tube of water while encouraging students to note the gas bubbles that appear on the inside of the test tube before the water begins to boil. Point out that the bubbles are air that was dissolved in the water. Explain that air dissolved in water provides the gases needed for aquatic organisms to carry on respiration.

Activity   The following chart lists the solubility of oxygen in fast-moving water at various temperatures. Have students construct a graph using these figures. Tell students to analyze the graph and explain what it shows. (They should conclude that as the temperature decreases the solubility of oxygen increases.)

Solubility of oxygen (g/100 g water)	Temperature (°C)
0.0069	0
0.0043	20
0.0031	40
0.0023	60
0.0014	80
0.0000	100

Reinforce   Use a photoelectric meter to demonstrate that light intensity decreases with depth. Shine a light through various amounts of water and allow students to record the meter readings. The light readings should decrease as the water depth increases. Relate light intensity to photosynthesis and populations of organisms at varying depths.

Enrich   Make a Secchi disk using the top of a gallon paint can. Fit a screw eye through the center of the lid and divide the lid into four sections. Paint opposite sections black and the others white. Explain to students that a Secchi disk is a device used to determine the depth to which light penetrates in an aquatic ecosystem. Explain that as the disk drops lower into the water, it becomes more difficult to see the white and black sections. Point out that in dirty or polluted water, visibility disappears nearer to the water surface than in cleaner, unpolluted water.

Reteach   Demonstrate that tap water contains dissolved salts by evaporating some tap water in an evaporating dish. Have students observe the resultant particles in the dish.

Evaluate

Closure   Have students summarize the factors used to characterize aquatic biomes. Ask how these factors differ from those used to describe land biomes.

Section 10.2   Standing-Water Ecosystems

pp. 157–160

Performance Objectives

- Identify the characteristics of different types of standing-water ecosystems.
- Explain the value of wetlands and the reasons for their decline.

Skills Objective

- Infer how public attitudes toward wetlands have contributed to the decline of migratory birds.

Section Vocabulary

phytoplankton   wetlands   zooplankton

Motivate

List the names of the kinds of aquatic ecosystems on the chalkboard in two columns. Place rivers, streams, and creeks in one column. Place lakes, ponds, marshes, and swamps in another column. Ask students what criteria were used for grouping these environments. Lead students to see that one column lists types of standing-water ecosystems while the other column lists types of flowing-water ecosystems.

Teaching Strategies

Reteach   Draw a cross section of a lake showing several levels of habitats. Ask the names of the organism that live in each level.

Reinforce   Ask the class to define *wetland* and then give examples and descriptions of different types of wetlands. List the examples and descriptions on the chalkboard. Have students copy this information in their notebooks. As a homework assignment, have students list representative types of plants and animals for each wetland ecosystem.

Activity   Have students examine water samples from standing-water ecosystems under the microscope. Supply students with samples of living plankton or prepared slides of various forms of plankton. Have students sketch the organisms they see and describe their differences and similarities.

Enrich   Allow students to choose one type of wetland and report on how the wetland is beneficial to the surrounding environment. Encourage interested students to report on Everglades National Park.

Enrich   The sundew, pitcher plant, and Venus flytrap are carnivorous plants that grow in bogs. Obtain specimens of these plants and demonstrate and discuss their unusual adaptations for survival.

Reteach   Have students construct aquatic food webs using original sketches or photographs cut from magazines. Have students work cooperatively to create a large classroom display.

Evaluate

Closure   Have students create an illustrated chart similar to Table 10.1 that includes examples of standing-water ecosystems located in their state.

Section 10.3   Flowing-Water Ecosystems

pp. 161–162

Performance Objective
- Describe how abiotic factors of gravity, erosion, and sedimentation affect stream ecosystems.

Skills Objective
- Apply information regarding oxygen content of moving water to explain why different parts of a stream will contain different amounts of oxygen in the waters.

Section Vocabulary
sediments

Motivate
The breathing rate of a fish can be determined by the number of times the gill covers move in and out per minute. Explain that fish breathe faster when there is insufficient oxygen present in their water. Prepare three beakers with water at about 10°, 20°, and 30°C. Add a goldfish to each beaker and assign groups of students to determine the breathing rates of the three fish. (After the measurements have been made, immediately return all three fish to their tank.) Have the groups compare their results and establish a hypothesis about how temperature affects the amount of oxygen dissolved in water.

Teaching Strategies

Reteach   Show specimens or pictures of animals that live in fast-flowing streams. Point out the adaptations such as streamlined bodies, suckers, and hooks. Specimens could include mayflies, stoneflies, blackflies, and dragonflies.

Model   Display one beaker containing water and pebbles and another beaker containing water, sand, and silt. Tell students that one beaker represents the bed of a fast-flowing stream while the other represents the bed of a slow-flowing stream. Challenge students to identify which stream is represented by each beaker and give the reasons for their choice. Have them describe some of the characteristics of each stream, such as the amount and source of oxygen, temperature of the water, and types of organisms living there.

Reinforce   Have students compare a moving-water biome with a still-water biome. Include such factors as source of oxygen, type of food chain (autotrophic or heterotrophic), and adaptations of organisms living in that biome.

Evaluate

Closure   Provide students with a list of all the aquatic biomes discussed as well as the terms *standing water ecosystem*, *flowing water ecosystem*, and *wetland*. Have students create a concept map that shows the relationships among these ecosystems.

Chapter Resources

Teaching Tip for Feature

Historical Notebook: Human Impact on the Nile River Delta
- Locate old magazines with photographs of archaeological sites before they were flooded by the waters behind the Aswan High Dam.

Teaching Tip for Field Activity
- Advise students to take samples from different levels in the water.

Answers to Field Activity

Slow-moving water rich in algae will have greater variety in the types and numbers of organisms.

Teaching Tips for Activities

ACTIVITY 10.1

Time 40–45 min
Group Size 2–4 students
Hypothesis The water flows at different rates on the inside and outside of a curve.
Safety Tip To avoid falls, have students wipe up any spills immediately.

Analysis
1. The rate of flow is fastest near the outside bank.
2. The outside slopes became more steep and the inside banks became less steep.
3. The meanders grew wider in a lateral direction.
4. The faster the water moved the greater the growth of the meanders in the lateral direction.

Conclusion

Water near the outside bank moves faster than water near the inside bank. The outside bank erodes, while sediments are deposited on the inside bank.

ACTIVITY 10.2

Time Day 1: 20 min; Day 2: 10 min
Group Size 2 students
Hypothesis Tardigrades are adapted to dry environments with occasional water.
Safety Tips None

Analysis
1. They are round, shriveled and inactive.
2. The body swelled, and a head, tail, and legs became visible. Movement also became observable.
3. They dried up, reentering the cryptobiotic state.

Conclusion
1. Tardigrades live in dry environments. Evidence for this is the cryptobiotic state.
2. If water is present intermittently

Answers to End of Chapter Questions

Concept Review
1. The Aswan High Dam flooded ecosystems at the head of the Nile River. Fertile soil was no longer deposited each year by the flooding of the Nile downstream.
2. The amount of light, the water depth, the amount of dissolved salts, and the flow rate.
3. A lake is the deepest type of standing water. A swamp is land soaked with water. A lake's producers are floating algae and benthic plants. A swamp has trees, shrubs, and plants adapted to oxygen-poor soil.
4. Depth affects the amount of sunlight that reaches producers which form the base of the food web.
5. Wetlands purify water, recharge aquifers, provide breeding areas for many organisms, and protect surrounding land from floods.

Think Critically
1. The size and depth of a lake tends to encourage greater biodiversity.
2. Salmon are born in the headwaters of a stream, spend years in the ocean, and return to the same headwaters to spawn. Any change in the habitats would destroy the cycle.
3. Accumulation of sediments in a stream could slow down the flow rate. This in turn could affect the evaporation rate, change the water temperature, affect the amount of dissolved oxygen, and change the salinity. Sediment accumulation also affects the stream bed. All of these factors affect animal life.
4. Warmer waters may not provide enough dissolved oxygen for fishes adapted to cold water.
5. It may result in less diversion of fresh water from freshwater ecosystems to meet the human needs, or provide a means for replacing water removed from freshwater ecosystems.

Graphic Analysis
1. The percentage of people with clean water increased.
2. Rural areas
3. The percentage of people without clean water decreased, so the supply of clean water increased.

Chapter Planning Guide

Section	Core	Standard	Enriched	Section	Core	Standard	Enriched
11.1 The World Ocean	•	•	•	Word Power, p. 173		•	•
Section Features				Think Critically, p. 174	•	•	•
Dateline 1985, p. 169	•	•	•	**Blackline Masters**			
Field Activity, p. 170		•	•	Review Worksheet 11.2	•	•	•
Activity 11.2. p. 181			•	**Ancillary Options**			
Blackline Masters				CEPUP Chemical Survey			
Review Worksheet 11.1	•	•	•	Solutions & Pollution Act. 2		•	•
Skills Worksheet 11A	•	•		**11.3 Intertidal Zones**	•	•	•
Ancillary Options				**Section Features**			
CEPUP Chemical Survey				Issues, p. 177	•	•	•
Solutions & Pollution Act. 1		•	•	Activity 11.1, p. 178	•	•	•
Laboratory Program				**Blackline Masters**			
Investigation 15	•	•	•	Review Worksheet 11.3	•	•	•
11.2 Neritic Zones	•	•	•	Skills Worksheet 11B		•	•
Section Features				Issues and Case Studies 5		•	•
Health Link, p. 173	•	•	•				

Every chapter has two corresponding tests in the Test Book and one Vocabulary Review Worksheet in the Review Book. There is also a Unit 3 test in the test book covering Chapters 7–11, and a mid-term test covering Chapters 1–11.

Chapter Overview

Chapter 11 discusses the life zones that make up the marine biome. Section 11.1 explores the features of the oceanic, neritic and intertidal zones and explains water temperature, salinity, density, and currents around the world. Section 11.2 examines photic, aphotic, and benthic regions of the neritic zone and describes coral reefs and estuaries. Section 11.3 investigates the intertidal zone, emphasizing the importance of salt marshes and mangrove swamps.

Advance Planner

Section 11.1

- Have photographs of marine animals available for the activity in the Motivate section.
- Obtain a 10-mL beaker, a tripod, water, a potassium permanganate crystal, tongs, a hot plate or Bunsen burner, and water for the Demonstration.
- Have a classroom map and outline maps available for the activity in the Reteach section.

Section 11.2

- Obtain coral samples for the activity in the Motivate section.

- Provide maps of coastal states for the Activity.
- Have cups, pebbles, sand, and silt for the activity in the Reteach section.

Section 11.3

- Have reference books about tidepool organisms available for the Cooperative Learning activity on page 175.
- Order films or videos that show salt marsh, mangrove swamps, and mud-flat ecosystems.
- Have modeling clay, aluminum roasting pans, strips of indoor-outdoor carpeting, and a small amount of mud available for the Activity.
- Obtain or make a stream table for use in the Demonstration.

Introducing the Chapter

Ask students to speculate about what life would be like in a totally aquatic environment. You may want to refer to examples from Jules Verne's novel *20,000 Leagues Under the Sea*. Have students design an underwater city in which they provide habitats for families, a means of transportation, schools, and farms. Have students create drawings of the designs and make a bulletin board or other visual display.

Section 11.1   The World Ocean

pp. 169–171

Performance Objectives
- Locate the major ocean zones based on their relationship to the shore.
- Describe the flow of water through the world ocean and the characteristics of ocean water in different parts of the world.

Skills Objectives
- Synthesize information to describe the type of winds that drive the Gulf Stream current by comparing different maps.
- Analyze the needs of organisms living in saltwater habitats.

Section Vocabulary
detritus   oceanic zone

Motivate
Display pictures of ocean animals such as whales, tuna, and sharks. Ask students what these animals have in common. (They are all free-swimming, wide-ranging marine animals.) Ask students what parts of the ocean these animals are likely to frequent. (Their characteristics suggest that they spend a great deal of time in the open ocean, far from land.) Explain that this part of the ocean is called the oceanic zone.

Teaching Strategies
Demonstrate   Place a 100-mL beaker on a tripod and fill it with cold water. Using tongs, place a small crystal of potassium permanganate into the water. Allow the crystal to settle on the bottom of the beaker and gently heat the beaker directly below the crystal. Have students observe the motion of the warm and cold water indicated by the movement of the color through the beaker. Relate the movement to the concept of density currents.

Reteach   Ask students to name as many of the major oceans and seas as they can. Make a list of the names on the chalkboard. Distribute outline maps of the world and have students label the locations of these oceans and seas. On the same map, have them draw and label the major ocean currents. Direct students to the map of world wind patterns on page 10, and ask them to explain the cause of surface ocean currents.

Reinforce   Draw a box on the chalkboard and tell students it represents the oceanic zone. Divide the zone into three sections: the photic zone, the aphotic zone, and the benthic zone. Ask students the names and characteristics of each zone and write this information in the appropriate box. Have students copy the diagram for use as a study tool.

Evaluate
Closure   Show pictures of various kinds of ocean life. Assign students the task of placing each in its proper zone. Then have students create food chains and food webs using these animals.

Section 11.2   Neritic Zones

pp. 172–174

Performance Objectives
- Describe the factors that define a neritic zone.
- Compare and contrast two types of neritic zone ecosystems.

Skills Objectives
- Infer the types of damage from which coral reefs can recover.
- Analyze the importance of the open ocean to the overall health of the biosphere.

Section Vocabulary
continental shelf   estuary   neritic zone
reef

Motivate
Display samples of coral. Have students study the coral with hand lenses and describe their observations. Explain that coral are living marine animals that live in colonies. Point out that as coral die, their skeletons remain in the water serving as a place where more coral can attach.

Teaching Strategies
Field Trip   Plan a trip to an aquarium that has several types of living coral on display. Have students investigate the animals they will see before they visit the aquarium. Make up a list of questions for the students to answer based upon their observations at the aquarium. Discuss the questions and their answers as a followup activity.

Activity   Provide students with maps of one or more coastal states, including the state in which you live, if appropriate. Ask students to define *estuary* and locate possible estuaries on the map. Have them identify the river supplying the fresh water to the estuary and predict what conditions, plant life, and animal life they would expect to find there. Have students do library research to see if their predictions were correct.

Reteach   Prepare several sets of three cups: one containing pebbles, one with sand, and one with silt. Distribute the sets to groups of students. Have students compare the sizes of the particles and speculate about the speed of flowing water that could move them. Challenge them to predict the size of particles found on the floor of an estuary. Have them explain their predictions.

Evaluate
Closure   Ask students to draw a diagram of the neritic zone. Have them label each level and list examples of plants and animals that live there.

Section 11.3   Intertidal Zones

pp. 175–176

Performance Objectives
- Explain the processes that contribute to the formation of salt marshes and mangrove swamps.
- List several human activities that damage intertidal habitats.

Skills Objectives
- Apply information to predict how the Mississippi River delta is affected by the construction of levees, dikes and other flood-control structures.

Section Vocabulary
intertidal zone   subsidence

Motivate
Show a videotape or film that includes images of salt marshes and/or mangrove swamps. Have students use information from the film or video to draw a diagram of a model food chain for each of these environments.

Teaching Strategies
Reteach   Show pictures or videotapes of salt marshes and mud flats. Have students write descriptions of these ecosystems. Ask them to include how these areas are being destroyed by humans. Allow them to suggest solutions for these problems.

Activity   Instruct students to build a model of a salt marsh by spreading some modeling clay up the sides of half a roasting pan. Shape the clay so that it creates gentle sloping land. A stream channel can be constructed in the clay. Place a small amount of water in the other side of the roasting pan to represent the ocean. Allow some muddy water to flow down the clay landform. Have students note how fast and how much muddy water enters the clean water. Direct students to empty the water and cut a strip of indoor-outdoor carpeting so that it will fit completely along the lower edge of the clay. Explain that the carpet represents a salt marsh. Have students again add the muddy water and note the speed and amount of particles that enter the clear water. Describe how a salt marsh affects flood control and water purification, and helps prevent soil erosion.

Enrich   Have students do library research on animals of the mangrove swamp and prepare illustrated reports. Mangrove swamp animals may include the green-backed heron, white ibis, brown pelican, mangrove snapper, American crocodile, blue crab, seahorse, mangrove tree crab, oyster, ungulate periwinkle, and the yellow rat snake.

Discuss   Present an example of an environmental issue such as a proposal to build an airport in a salt marsh. Have students organize a debate on the issue. Students can take the parts of various interest groups such as business organizations, the construction industry, politicians, environmentalists, fishers, and others. Have the class decide which arguments were most convincing and vote on the issue.

Reteach   Obtain sample plants and animals from an intertidal zone. Have students observe and identify adaptations that these organisms use for survival.

Demonstrate   Use a stream table to show how deltas form. Have students recall how swift-moving water erodes the land, while slow-moving water deposits sediments. Point out how these sediments enrich delta soils.

Evaluate
Closure   Develop a chart for a typical salt-marsh or mangrove swamp survey. The chart should include a list of plants, identification of dominant plants, a description of the soil and soil organisms, and a list of insects, birds, and animals.

Chapter Resources

Teaching Tip for Feature
Issues: Real Estate versus Salt Marshes
- Have students locate newspaper or magazine articles about recent salt-marsh development controversies.

Teaching Tip for Field Activity
- Have students evaluate which materials are vital for aquarium maintenance and which are optional.

Answers to Field Activity
Responses will vary.

Teaching Tips for Activities

ACTIVITY 11.1

Time Day 1: 30 min; Day 2–4: 15 min.
Group Size 3–4 students
Prediction Brine shrimp hatch and survive at high salt concentrations.
Safety Tips Have students wash their hands in warm soapy water after handling the setups.

Analysis
1. Answers should reflect student data.
2. Physical differences will likely be apparent.
3. Answers should reflect student data.

Conclusion
Answers should be consistent with data. Habitats of brine shrimp include tidepools and salt lakes.

ACTIVITY 11.2

Time One class period.
Group Size 2–3 students
Hypothesis The metabolic rate of clams will be slower in cooler water.
Safety Tips Caution students to work carefully with thermometers to avoid breakage. Have students wear laboratory aprons to protect their clothing.

Procedure
To prepare aged tap water, leave a container of water uncovered for 24 hours.

Analysis
1. Answers will vary.
2. Answers will vary.

Conclusion
1. Answers will depend on the hypothesis. Expulsion times should be slower for the clam in cooler water.
2. In general, shallower water will be warmer than deep water. The metabolic rates of clams are higher in warmer water.

Answers to End of Chapter Questions

Concept Review
1. Topsoil erosion makes the water surrounding a coral reef cloudy and reduces the amount of light available for photosynthesis.
2. High productivity is dependent upon an ample supply of sunlight for photosynthesis. A loss in the amount of sunlight would cause a decrease in the number of phytoplankton with a resulting loss in the numbers of zooplankton, small fish, and larger fish.
3. Draining marshes, rechanneling rivers, and filling in marshes have created farmland, pastures, and prime real estate for homes and shopping centers.
4. If the marshes are destroyed, migratory birds will lose their nesting and feeding grounds.

Think Critically
1. Coral grow in warm sunlit waters. If the depth of the water increases rapidly, the light will not reach them and they will not survive.
2. The pollution may have killed reef-building corals. The reef that once protected the coastline crumbled.
3. Accept all logical responses.

Graphic Analysis
1. Although each square meter of open ocean is less productive, the open ocean area is so vast that it has a higher total productivity.
2. There is more farmland than temperate deciduous forest. Although farmland has a lower productivity per square meter, its total productivity is greater.
3. Accept all logical responses.

Unit Overview

Unit 4 addresses environmental concerns as they relate to people. Chapter 12 discusses the survival needs of people and how they are met by the environment. Chapter 13 deals with human population growth and its impact on the global environment. The unit concludes, in Chapter 14, with the problem of how to feed a growing human population without devastating environmental resources.

Introducing the Unit

Discussion   Display a graph that shows the change in human population over the last 10,000 years. Ask students what type of growth curve is shown on the graph. Ask students to recall what happens over time to a bacterial population that shows a similar growth pattern. Use student responses to initiate a discussion about the carrying capacity of Earth as it relates to human populations.

Teacher Resources

Audiovisual

The House of Man II: Over Crowded Environment, film, 11 minutes, Britannica, 1985.
Diet for a Small Planet, film/video, 28 minutes, Bullfrog Films, 1973.
When the Bough Breaks: Our Children, Our Environment, video, 52 minutes, Bullfrog Films, 1991.

Computer Software

MECC Dataquest: The World Community, Apple II, MECC.
Sim City, Macintosh, Maxis.
World Geograph, Apple II, MECC.

Suggested Readings

Koren, Herman, *Handbook of Environmental Health and Safety*, Vols. 1 and 2., Pergamon Press, 1990.
Solkoff, Joel, *The Politics of Food*, Sierra Club Books, 1985.
Ehrlich, Paul R., and Anne H. Erlich, *The Population Explosion*, Simon & Schuster, 1990.
Doyle, Jack, *Altered Harvest: The Fate of the World's Food Supply*, Viking, 1985.

Advance Preparation

Chapter 12
Field Activity   No materials required.
Activity 12.1   Bring in reference sources regarding zinc supplies, paper clips, watches or a clock with second hand.
Activity 12.2   Obtain live aphids (available from a biological supply house), scissors, Petri dishes with lids, paper towels, droppers, fresh green leaves and cotton swabs.

Chapter 13
Field Activity   No materials required.
Activity 13.1   Bring in wax pencils and empty baby-food jars. Have safety goggles, rubber gloves, droppers, and phenol red indicator available. For stock solutions, use tap water and a dilute NaOH solution. All students receive tap water as a stock solution except for one student, who receives the NaOH solution. You may need to adjust the pH of your tap water prior to the activity to be sure that a drop of the base will be enough to make the indicator turn red.
Activity 13.2   Have meter sticks or metric tape measures available.

Chapter 14
Field Activity   No materials required.
Activity 14.1   For each group of 2–3 students, have available a ringstand, test tube clamp, test tube, paper clip, cork stopper (at least 4 cm diameter), fireproof pad, metric ruler, heat resistant gloves, triple beam balance, 100 mL graduated cylinder, matches, and food samples. Nuts, beans, cheese, and cereals work well. Have safety goggles and a lab apron available for each student.
Activity 14.2   Have five test tubes and a test-tube rack available for each group. Order Biuret's solution. Bring in samples of cooked egg white, potato, water-packed tuna, mashed lima beans, and white bread.

Chapter Planning Guide

Section	Core	Standard	Enriched	Section	Core	Standard	Enriched
12.1 A Portrait of Earth	•	•	•	Skills Worksheet 12A	•	•	•
Section Features Earth Science Link, p. 188 Activity 12.2, p. 199	•	• •	• •	**Ancillary Options** One Minute Readings, p. 3			•
				12.3 Sustainable Development	•	•	•
Blackline Masters Review Worksheet 12.1	•	•	•	**Section Features** Word Power, p. 194 Field Activity, p. 194 Activity 12.1, p. 197	• • •	• • •	• • •
• Ancillary Options One Minute Readings, p. 26		•	•				
12.2 Human Societies	•	•	•	**Blackline Masters** Review Worksheet 12.3 Issues and Case Studies 12 Skills Worksheet 12B	• •	• •	• • •
Section Features Dateline 1600 B.C., p. 191 Social Studies Connection, p. 193	• •	• •	• •				
Blackline Masters Review Worksheet 12.2	•	•	•	**Laboratory Program** Investigation 16	•	•	•

Every chapter has two corresponding tests in the Test Book and one Vocabulary Review Worksheet in the Review Book.

Chapter Overview

Chapter 12 introduces students to the idea that they are a part of nature. Section 12.1 presents a portrait of Earth as a living being consisting of a network of systems and interactions among biotic and abiotic factors. Section 12.2 describes the effects of hunter–gatherer, agricultural, and industrial societies on the environment. Section 12.3 develops the idea of how a sustainable development ethic differs from a frontier ethic in terms of its impact on the environment.

Advance Planner

Section 12.1
- No additional materials needed.

Section 12.2
- Have magazines with photographs of hunter–gatherer societies on hand for use in class discussion.
- Make arrangements for the Field Trip to an anthropological museum.
- Arrange for an anthropologist to speak to the class about hunter–gatherer, agricultural, and industrial societies.

Section 12.3
- Obtain items made from natural resources, such as a rubber ball, copper pipe, a potted plant, a piece of wood, and so on, for the activity in the Motivate section.
- Order live aphids from a biological supply house several weeks before doing Activity 12.2.

Introducing the Chapter

On the chalkboard, draw an outline of a human body. Around the outline, write the terms *respiration*, *perspiration*, *urination*, *ingestion*, and *excretion*. Ask students how each of these terms relates to keeping a human alive. Lead students to conclude that during these processes materials are taken from, and then returned, to the environment. Point out how these examples illustrate that humans are a part of nature.

Ask students to imagine they have become stranded on an island with only the clothes on their backs. The island contains a variety of shells, small rocks and stones, sticks, trees, and vines. Have students brainstorm how they can use these items to create tools they will need for survival. Relate this discussion to the characteristics of hunter–gatherer societies.

Section 12.1   A Portrait of Earth

pp. 187–189

Performance Objectives
- Describe Earth as a network of systems and connections.
- Explain how Earth is closed with respect to matter and open with respect to energy.

Skills Objective
- Analyze the Gaia hypothesis.

Section Vocabulary
Gaia hypothesis

Motivate
On the chalkboard, write the following sentence: "The portrait of Earth is one of systems and interactions." Have students look at Figure 12.1 on page 187 and explain how this statement relates to what is shown in the photograph. Challenge students to identify other systems and interactions that involve Earth.

Teaching Strategies
Discuss   Ask students why materials such as bottles, cans, and paper are recycled. Challenge students to relate the need for recycling with the idea that Earth is closed with respect to matter.

Analogy   Explain to students that the Earth can be viewed as a living organism. Explain that in this view, Earth's water is considered its blood, its land is considered its body, and its air is considered its breath. Have students speculate as to how the functions of the land, air, and water of Earth are similar to the body, breath, and blood of an organism.

Reinforce   Have students reread the feature on the Gaia hypothesis in Chapter 1. Have a class discussion of the feature, emphasizing how the ideas of the Gaia hypothesis fit in with the portrait of Earth as a network of systems and connections.

Evaluate
Closure   Have students write their own definitions of the term *systems*. Ask them to give examples of how Earth's systems are connected.

Section 12.2   Human Societies

pp. 190–192

Performance Objectives
- Identify hunter–gatherer, agricultural, and industrial societies.
- Describe how the impact of humans on the environment has increased over time.

Skills Objective
- Infer why hunter–gatherer societies cause less environmental damage than industrial societies.

Section Vocabulary
hunter–gatherer society   agricultural society
industrial society

Motivate
Obtain copies of magazines, such as *National Geographic*, that feature articles on hunter–gatherer societies. Display photographs of peoples from these societies. Ask students to describe how the lifestyles of these people appear to differ from their own. Ask students whether they think such societies are able to survive today and where they might be located. Explain that people still live in this way in many parts of the world.

Teaching Strategies
Field Trip   Arrange a field trip to an anthropological museum that has tools and other artifacts from hunter–gatherer cultures of the past. Have students make a list of ten different types of tools or artifacts and what they were used for. Encourage students to identify an object found in industrial societies that has replaced each tool or artifact on their list.

Enrich   Have students conduct library research on some of the past and present hunter–gatherer societies. As part of their research, have students speculate as to why many scientists and linguists are concerned about these societies disappearing from Earth. Have students speculate as to how industrialization affects such societies.

Guest Speaker   Invite an anthropologist to speak to the class about hunter–gatherer cultures of the past versus those of today. Before the speaker arrives, have students prepare questions they have about the lifestyles of hunter–gatherers. Give the questions to the speaker ahead of time to make sure all of the questions can be answered.

Reteach   Have students use a dictionary to find the meaning of the term *technology*. Explain to students that although the tools used by hunter–gatherer societies and agricultural societies differ from those used by many modern industrial societies, such tools are, in fact, examples of technology.

Ask students to explain why items such as ceramic bowls and weapons made from stones and twine can be considered technology.

Evaluate
Closure Have students create a concept map that compares and contrasts the three types of societies discussed in this section. Encourage students to refer to Table 12.1 as they develop their concept maps. Display several of the completed concept maps as a review of the section.

Section 12.3 Sustainable Development

pp. 194–195

Performance Objectives
- Define the frontier ethic and the sustainable development ethic.
- Describe the differences between a renewable resource and a nonrenewable resource.

Skills Objectives
- Observe and recognize activities that are evidence of the frontier ethic.
- Apply aspects of the sustainable development ethic in daily life.

Section Vocabulary
frontier ethic   sustainable development ethic

Motivate
Display the following items at the front of the classroom: can of motor oil, a piece of wood, a piece of copper pipe, a rubber ball, a potted plant, and a glass of water. Ask students what these items have in common. Explain that all of these items are classified as natural resources—materials produced by nature that are used by living organisms.

Teaching Strategies
Reteach Have students use a dictionary to find the meaning of the term *sustainable*. (Able to keep in existence, or to maintain). Have students relate this definition to the basic ideas in the sustainable development ethic.

Reinforce Have students construct a table that compares the basic ideas of the frontier ethic to those of the sustainable development ethic. Ask volunteers to summarize the differences between the three points of each ethic.

Enrich The idea of conservation of natural resources is closely linked to the principle of the sustainable development ethic which holds that resources are limited and are not all meant for human consumption. One method by which materials of today are being made to last longer is through recycling efforts. Show students an example of the recycling symbol. Have students find examples of products made from five different materials that contain this symbol. Have students combine their lists with those of their classmates to see how many different kinds of recycled materials they can identify.

Evaluate
Closure As a summary, have student volunteers come to the front of the class to present the main components of the frontier ethic and the sustainable development ethic in a point/counterpoint format. Have students summarize how the principles of each ethic differ.

Chapter Resources

Teaching Tip for Feature
Social Studies Connection: Conflict for a Tribal People

- Have students brainstorm factors that bind people together as a cultural group. (Examples include language, food, music, dance, and value systems.)

Teaching Tips for Field Activity

- Encourage students to photograph or videotape examples of the frontier ethic.
- Have interested students research the historical development of the frontier ethic.

Answers to Field Activity
Responses will vary.

Teaching Tips for Activities

ACTIVITY 12.1

Time   One class period
Group Size   4 students
Prediction   Yes, the world's zinc reserves will run out.
Safety Tips   No special safety precautions are required.

Analysis
1. Zinc is coated on iron to protect against corrosion. It is alloyed in copper to form brass and with other metals to form die-casting alloys. Zinc is used as the negative electrode in dry batteries.
2. The need is increasing exponentially. The need will be 8 million metric tons in 15 years. In 30 years, the need will be 84 million metric tons.

Conclusion
Students should state that the reserves could run out within 50 years. The effects described should be related to the uses of zinc from Question 1.

ACTIVITY 12.2

Time   Day 1: 15 min; Days 2–14: 10–15 min
Group Size   2 students
Inference   A population will decrease when the food supply gets smaller.
Safety Tips   Students allergic to plants or insects can be excused from the outdoor parts of the activity, and instead can be responsible for analyzing data collected by their partners. Used materials should be disposed of in a tightly sealed plastic bag, along with regular classroom solid wastes.

Analysis
1. The population may have increased at first, but then it decreased. Availability of food is the cause of both changes.
2. Students might relate the aphids to the human population and the leaf to our food supply. The lesson is to keep population size and resources in balance.

Conclusion
Answers will vary. Students might infer that population size decreases with a diminishing food supply. Their observations should be supportive.

Answers to End of Chapter Questions
Concept Review
1. The Gaia hypothesis states that Earth is a single living organism that regulates itself to maintain life.
2. The size of the population.
3. Coal-fired steam engines.
4. Overgrazing, poor farming methods, and excessive timber cutting.
5. Check essays for accurate definitions.

Think Critically
1. Accept all logical responses.
2. Advances in medicine and increased food supply.
3. Accept all logical responses.
4. Check paragraphs for logic and accuracy.

Graphic Analysis
1. In subtropical areas of the northern hemisphere.
2. The area was covered by glaciers.
3. Yes. They occurred near one another.
4. Near water. Fertile soils and ample water supplies exist in river deltas.
5. They may have walked across a land bridge between Asia and North America, or traveled by boat.

CHAPTER 13 HUMAN POPULATION

Chapter Planning Guide

Section	Core	Standard	Enriched	Section	Core	Standard	Enriched
13.1 History of the Human Population	•	•	•	Word Power, p. 205 Historical Notebook, p. 207	•	• •	• •
Section Features Biology Link, p. 201 Field Activity, p. 202 Activity 13.2, p. 213	• •	• • •	• •	**Blackline Masters** Review Worksheet 13.2 Skills Worksheet 13B	•	•	• •
Blackline Masters Review Worksheet 13.1 Skills Worksheet 13A	• •	• •	•	**Ancillary Options** One Minute Readings, p. 27		•	•
Ancillary Options One Minute Readings, p. 24	•	•	•	**13.3 Challenges of Overpopulation**	•	•	•
Laboratory Program Investigation 17	•	•	•	**Section Features** Dateline 1878, p. 208 Think Critically, p. 209 Activity 13.1, p. 213	•	• • •	• • •
13.2 Growth and Changing Needs	•	•	•	**Blackline Masters** Review Worksheet 13.3 Issues and Case Studies 7	• •	• •	• •
Section Features Social Studies Link, p. 204	•	•	•				

Every chapter has two corresponding tests in the Test Book and one Vocabulary Review Worksheet in the Review Book.

Chapter Overview

Chapter 13 presents an overview of how the human population has changed through time and the impact such changes have had on the environment. In Section 13.1, the history of the human population is discussed with a focus on societal evolution. Section 13.2 presents an overview of the science of demographics and explains why a knowledge of demographics is necessary to anticipate the needs of future populations. The chapter concludes, in Section 13.3, with a discussion of how natural resources, energy, and biodiversity are affected by overpopulation. As part of this discussion, reasons are presented as to why population growth is difficult to limit.

Advance Planner

Section 13.1
- Prepare an overhead transparency of two graph grids for the activity in the Reteach section. Have markers of different colors available.

Section 13.2
- Prepare the overhead transparency graph for the activity in the Motivate section.

Section 13.3
- Obtain yeast, water, sugar, test tubes, test tube racks, and stoppers for the activity described in the Motivate section.

Introducing the Chapter

Ask students to consider how they would be affected if the population size of their class doubled, while classroom resources, such as desks, chairs, and textbooks remained the same. Have students summarize their feelings in a brief essay. Ask volunteers to read their essays aloud as part of a class discussion on the effects of population growth.

Divide the class into three large cooperative learning groups. One group represents a hunter-gatherer society, the second represents an agricultural society, and the third an industrial society. Tell students that a new factory that uses large amounts of fossil fuels and energy is to be built in the area in which their society lives. Have groups discuss the effects the presence of the factory will have on their societal organization and population. Each group may want to assign societal roles and have students role-play during the discussion.

Section 13.1 History of the Human Population

pp. 201–203

Performance Objective

- Describe the major events that have affected the rate of human population growth throughout history.

Skills Objectives

- Analyze population trends in the local community for a 100-year period.
- Analyze whether arithmetic population growth would in time lead to overpopulation conditions.

Section Vocabulary
agricultural revolution   germ theory

Motivate
Tell students to imagine they have a magic penny. Ask them to quickly calculate how much money they would have in ten minutes if their penny, and the subsequent pennies that result from it doubled every minute. (They would have $10.24.) Show the calculations on the chalkboard as follows: 1 minute = 2 pennies; 2 minutes = 4 pennies; 3 minutes = 8 pennies; 4 minutes = 16 pennies; 5 minutes = 32 pennies; 6 minutes = 64 pennies; 7 minutes = 128 pennies; 8 minutes = 256 pennies; 9 minutes = 512 pennies; 10 minutes = 1024 pennies. Explain that if left unchecked, many populations would show a similar exponential growth pattern. Discuss the effects such population growth might have on resource availability.

Teaching Strategies
Literature Connection   Have students read Thomas More's *Utopia*. Have them present a summary of the book to the class in an oral report, or prepare a written summary.

Reteach   On an overhead transparency, draw two lines on a graph grid using different colored markers. Have one line represent arithmetic growth, while the other shows exponential growth. Challenge students to identify which line shows which type of growth. Make sure students understand that although differences in each type of growth are initially very small, the differences rapidly become large, as illustrated by the graphs.

Discuss Ask students what factors may have caused limited population growth in hunter–gatherer societies, while having a lesser impact on agricultural and industrial societies. (Possible factors include starvation, predation, and disease.) Discuss why the impact of these factors varies.

Reinforce   Have students create a timeline of all the events and changes in human population growth described in Section 13.1. Encourage students to use library resources, if necessary, to find out specific or approximate dates for important events, such as the development of the germ theory of disease.

Evaluate
Closure   Have students create a concept map that shows the relationships among all of the major concepts presented in this section. Students may want to use the section heads and subheads as a guide.

Section 13.2 Growth and Changing Needs

pp. 204–206

Performance Objectives

- Compare and contrast population growth trends in developing and industrialized nations.
- Infer reasons why emigration is higher in developing nations than in industrialized nations.

Skills Objective

- Calculate population growth for a region.

Section Vocabulary
demography

Motivate
On an overhead transparency, prepare a line graph with three curves: one showing growth trends of a hunter-gatherer society, one of an agricultural society, and one of an industrialized society. Do not label the curves. Tell students that each curve represents the population growth trend in a different type of society. Challenge students to identify the society represented by each curve.

Teaching Strategies
Reteach   Review the method for calculating population growth. Write the following data on the chalkboard: death rate = 4.5 people per thousand; birth rate = 12.5 people per thousand. Have students calculate the population growth using the formula given in the text.

Enrich   Ask students to research the societal organization of a specific country or culture and write a report on the society they chose. Have them identify the society as having a matriarchal or patriarchal organization, the type of society represented (hunter–gatherer, agricultural, industrial), and the family organization within the society. Tell students to relate their findings to the population growth trends of the society.

Reinforce Ask students to recall the Introducing the Chapter activity regarding the doubling of their classroom population. Tell students to imagine that the entire population of the school is now twice what it was last year, and is expected to double again in the coming year. Have students describe the effects of this exponential growth on resources, such as classroom space, locker availability, teachers, textbooks, administrators, health and cafeteria facilities, and bus transportation needs.

Enrich Explain the concept of zero population growth to students. After discussing the concept, have students conduct library research to determine in what areas of the world zero population growth is currently taking place.

Evaluate
Activity Students may be familiar with the census taken by the government every ten years. Briefly explain the role of the census in obtaining demographic information. Have students create a census form consisting of at least twenty questions. Remind students that their census must establish how population growth trends will affect resource availability.

Section 13.3 Challenges of Overpopulation

pp. 208–209

Performance Objectives
- Relate how overpopulation affects natural resources, energy demands, and biodiversity.
- Hypothesize how the availability of resources affects population growth.

Skills Objectives
- Hypothesize how population growth is affected by the availability of increased resources.
- Make decisions about government-controlled population growth.

Section Vocabulary
None

Motivate
Provide students with the materials necessary to establish a yeast culture. Directions for such an activity can be found in most high-school biology textbooks. Have students analyze the population growth of their cultures for a period of two weeks. Students should graph their data and explain why they think the population grew as it did.

Teaching Strategies
Reteach Remind students of the meanings of the terms *density-dependent limiting factor* and *density-independent limiting factor*. Have students reread the second paragraph of the section. Ask students whether the concept discussed in this paragraph is an example of a density-dependent or a density-independent limiting factor.

Enrich Have interested students read Paul Erlich's *The Population Bomb*, which deals with the effects overpopulation is placing on resource availability. Ask students to prepare a book report for inclusion in their portfolios.

Activity Have students work in groups to survey their local communities for evidence of problems caused by overpopulation. Encourage students to photograph or videotape their observations. Ask them to describe the reasons why each observation suggests a link to overpopulation.

Evaluate
Closure Initiate a classroom discussion about the benefits and drawbacks of increased population growth at the community level, the national level, and the global level. Lead students to recognize how population growth that is harmful for one region may be beneficial to another. You may wish to expand the discussion by pointing out trends in immigration and emigration that have occurred in the United States over the last twenty years. Examples of such trends include the immigration of peoples from other nations to the United States and emigration of the elderly from cities to more rural regions of the country.

Chapter Resources

Teaching Tip for Feature
Historical Notebook: The Great City of Copán.
- Have students write a report on an ancient society discussing the technology, the type of society that existed, and factors leading to its demise.

Teaching Tip for Field Activity
- Encourage students to use resources available through their local government to obtain the information needed.

Answers to Field Activity
Responses will vary, but are likely to show an increase in population.

Teaching Tips for Activities

ACTIVITY 13.1
Time   One class period
Group Size   Entire class
Hypothesis   A disease spreads through a population by the exchange of fluids between individuals.
Safety Tips   Students should wear safety goggles, laboratory aprons, and safety gloves while conducting this activity.

Procedure
All students receive tap water as a stock solution, except one student, who receives a dilute NaOH solution.

Analysis
1. Diagrams will vary.
2. Answers will vary.
3. Answers will vary.
4. The basic solution.

Conclusion
1. Accept all logical responses.
2. The chance of contamination would increase.

ACTIVITY 13.2
Time   20–25 minutes
Group Size   Entire class
Problem   What happens when too many people are crowded into a living space? What are the advantages of careful community planning?
Safety Tips   No special safety precautions required.

Analysis
1. Responses will vary.
2. Responses will vary, but students will probably focus on the fact that they are more crowded.

Conclusion
1. As population density increases and space decreases, the irritability factor increases. Most students will state that increased population density can adversely affect a community.
2. Responses will vary.

Answers to End of Chapter Questions

Concept Review
1. The discovery of the germ theory led to improvements in sanitation and an increased awareness of how disease was spread.
2. Responses may include factors such as increased infant mortality, famine, war, and disease.
3. Infant death rates have decreased largely as a result of improved prenatal and neonatal care.
4. Doubling time refers to the amount of time needed for the population of a region to double in size.
5. As the population increases, more people are competing for the same resources.

Think Critically
1. Accept all logical responses.
2. A growing human population deprives organisms of living space; people compete with organisms for limited resources; people may damage air or water quality. Accept all logical responses.
3. As industrialization occurs in an area, people who live as hunters and gatherers may be forced from their habitat. Without the habitat, the society would no longer exist.

Computer Activity
Check students' work for accuracy.

Graphic Analysis
1. Mexico. More money will be needed for children's services.
2. Sweden.
3. The life expectancy of men is shorter than that of women in the U.S. and Sweden.
4. Mexico. There will be a greater number of women of child-bearing age.

Chapter Planning Guide

Section	Core	Standard	Enriched	Section	Core	Standard	Enriched
14.1 Human Nutrition	•	•	•	Dateline 1982, p. 223	•	•	•
				Think Critically, p. 224			•
Section Features				**Blackline Masters**			
Field Activity, p. 217	•	•	•	Review Worksheet 14.3	•	•	•
Health Link, p. 218	•	•	•	Isues and Case Studies 10	•	•	•
Activity 14.1, p. 219		•	•	**Ancillary Options**			
Blackline Masters				One Minute Readings, p.11		•	•
Review Worksheet 14.1	•	•	•	**Laboratory Program**			
Skills Worksheet 14A	•	•	•	Investigation 19		•	•
Ancillary Options				**14.4 Sustainable Agriculture**	•	•	•
One Minute Readings, p. 17	•	•	•	**Section Features**			
14.2 World Food Supply	•	•	•	Social Studies Link, p. 225	•	•	•
Section Features				Activity 14.2, p. 229	•	•	
Issue, p. 22		•	•	**Blackline Masters**			
Blackline Masters				Review Worksheet 14.4	•	•	•
Review Worksheet 14.2	•	•	•	**Ancillary Options**			
Issues and Case Studies 8, 10		•	•	Multiculturalism, p. 35	•	•	•
Skills Worksheet 14B		•	•	CEPUP Chemicals in			
Ancillary Options				Food Act. 2			
One Minute Readings, p. 18	•	•	•				
14.3 Modern Farming Techniques	•	•	•				
Section Features							
Dateline 1972, p. 223	•	•	•				

Every chapter has two corresponding tests in the Test Book and one Vocabulary Review Worksheet in the Review Book. There is also a Unit 3 test in the Test Book covering Chapters 12–14.

Chapter Overview

Chapter 14 focuses on human nutritional needs and the challenge of meeting human food demands worldwide. Section 14.1 introduces the types of nutrients, along with nutrient-deficiency disorders. Section 14.2 discusses problems associated with meeting worldwide food demands. Section 14.3 introduces students to the benefits and drawbacks of various farming techniques of the past and present. The chapter concludes in Section 14.4 with a discussion of the principles of sustainable food production and the role of top-soil conservation.

Advance Planner

- Obtain a transparency of a food (nutritional) pyramid for the activity in the Introducing the Chapter section.

Section 14.1
- Make an overhead transparency of nutritional labels for the activity in the Motivate section.
- Arrange for a nutritionist or a dietician to speak with the class.

Section 14.2
- Bring in articles about food shortages in developing nations for the activity in the Motivate section.

Section 14.3
- Obtain photographs showing a variety of tools and farming methods as described in the Motivate section.
- Have students bring in pesticide containers with labels for the Activity.

Section 14.4
- Arrange for a financial planner to speak with the class about the commodities market as described in the Motivate section.

Introducing the Chapter

Show a transparency of a food pyramid. Discuss the concept shown by the pyramid with the class. Assign students the task of listing all of the foods they eat over a one-week period. Have students retain their lists for use in the Closure activity of Section 14.1.

Section 14.1   Human Nutrition

pp. 215–218

Performance Objective
- List the major groups of nutrients and the amount of energy provided by each type.

Skills Objective
- Analyze the importance of vitamins and minerals in the diet.

Section Vocabulary
carbohydrate   protein   essential amino acids   lipid   malnutrition

Motivate
Show nutritional labels from several food items on an overhead transparency. Discuss the information found on food labels such as number of servings per container, serving size, and the percent recommended daily allowance (RDA) of various vitamins and minerals. As a homework assignment, have students gather and analyze nutritional information from five food labels. Have students use the information to decide which of the foods analyzed is the most nutritious.

Teaching Strategies
Discuss   Information on food labels is determined and regulated by the Food and Drug Administration (FDA). In recent years, the FDA has been criticized for not requiring even more information on food labels. Ask students to identify the types of information they think need to be included on food labels.

Enrich   Have students use a reference book to find the causes of vitamin and mineral deficiency diseases such as rickets, beriberi, scurvy, night blindness, goiter, pellagra, and anemia. Ask students to construct a chart that identifies the disease, classifies it as a vitamin or mineral deficiency disease, identifies the missing nutrient in the diet, and lists foods that are rich in that nutrient.

Reteach   Have students identify the meanings of the word parts of the term *malnutrition*. Have students explain how the literal meaning of malnutrition relates to its scientific meaning.

Guest Speaker   Invite a nutritionist or the school dietician to speak to the class. Have the speaker emphasize the importance of a well-balanced diet and provide students with data regarding how many calories of food they should eat each day and what proportions of the total caloric intake each food type should make up.

Evaluate
Closure   Have students review the personal food list that they created as part of the activity described in the Introducing the Chapter section. Ask students to evaluate whether or not the foods they eat constitute a balanced diet.

Section 14.2   World Food Supply

pp. 220–221

Performance Objective
- Explain the effects of economics on the production of food.

Skills Objective
- Apply the principles of aquaculture to determine their effects on the environment.

Section Vocabulary
Green Revolution   cash crop   aquaculture

Motivate
Bring in newspaper or magazine articles that chronicle food shortages of developing nations, such as those in Ethiopia in the 1980s and Somalia in the 1990s. Include articles that discuss political factors involved in these food shortages as well as agricultural factors. Discuss the articles as a class.

Teaching Strategies
Enrich   Have students research the work George Washington Carver did with cash crops. Ask students to write reports about how Carver's research impacted the economy of the southern United States and how methods developed by Carver were used to improve soil quality.

Discuss   Take some time to discuss why farmers grow crops for sale to other nations, when people in their own countries often do not have enough food to eat. Point out that this situation is not unique to developing countries and happens in the United States as well.

Evaluate
Closure   Have students write a paragraph that summarizes the major ideas of Section 14.2.

Section 14.3 Modern Farming Techniques

pp. 223–224

Performance Objective
- Describe how farming techniques have changed during the past 50 years.

Skills Objective
- Infer how extinction of plants might impact future generations.

Section Vocabulary
None

Motivate
Show photographs of farmers employing various types of equipment and techniques. For example, juxtapose photographs of a plow being pulled by a mule or other animal and a modern tractor pulling some type of tilling device. Show other photographs that compare and contrast similar farming methods. Initiate a classroom discussion about the benefits and drawbacks of the methods shown in each photograph.

Teaching Strategies
STS Connection Discuss the impact of genetic engineering techniques on food crops. Such crops are genetically-altered to make them more disease-resistant or able to survive adverse climate conditions. Have students conduct library research to determine how biotechnology is used to transmit these desirable traits to plants.

Activity Have students bring in cans or boxes from pesticides used in the home. Set up the pesticide containers as stations throughout the classroom. Have students visit each station and list the active ingredient of each pesticide in a chart. Also have students record any warnings that appear on the pesticide labels. To extend the activity, have students find out which pesticides can no longer be used in the United States and write a report explaining why these pesticides were banned.

Evaluate
Closure Ask students to generate a list of terms related to farming and agricultural methods. List the terms on the chalkboard. Have students copy the terms into their notes and use the terms to create a timeline or concept map that describes how farming techniques have changed during the last 50 years.

Section 14.4 Sustainable Agriculture

pp. 225–226

Performance Objective
- Describe the basic components of sustainable agriculture and explain why they are desirable.

Skills Objective
- Apply the principles of sustainable farming to the term organic farming.

Section Vocabulary
sustainable agriculture

Motivate
Bring in the financial section of a newspaper that reports on the commodities market. Show the listings to students and have them identify the commodities (corn, wheat, beans, etc.). If possible, arrange for a financial planner to speak to the class about the commodities market.

Teaching Strategies
Reinforce Review the nitrogen cycle discussed in Chapter 3. Remind students of the importance of this cycle to plants and other organisms.

Demonstrate Fill two cafeteria trays with soil. Flatten and tamp the soil in one tray using a book or piece of wood. Run a fork across the surface of the soil in the other tray to simulate tilling. Expose both trays to air from a fan or blow dryer and have students observe the effects of the air on the soil. Repeat the activity to show the effects of water drainage on tilled and untilled soil. Use students' observations as a springboard to a discussion about the benefits and drawbacks of tilling on soil.

Enrich Ask students to visit a health food store to identify products that claim to be organically grown. Have students compare the prices of such products with similar products that do not make such claims. Discuss the advantages and disadvantages of using products grown organically versus those grown using modern agricultural methods.

Evaluate
Closure Write the phrases *crop rotation, reduced soil erosion, pest management*, and *reduced soil additives* on the chalkboard. Challenge students to explain how each term relates to the concept of sustainable agriculture. Ask students to identify other terms from the chapter relating to this concept.

Chapter Resources

Teaching Tip for Feature
People and the Environment: Rainforest Burgers
- More information on this subject is available in the book *Diet for a Small Planet*, by Frances Moore Lappe.

Teaching Tip for Field Activity
- Before the activity, discuss terms that appear on product labels that are intended to imply that the products are healthy. Such terms include Enriched, Fortified, Low-fat, Nonfat, Sugar-free, and so on.

Answers to Field Activity
Responses will vary.

Teaching Tips for Activities

ACTIVITY 14.1
Time One class period
Group Size 2–3 students
Hypothesis Fats will give off the most energy.
Safety Tips Make sure students wear laboratory aprons and safety goggles. Caution students to handle heated materials carefully, secure loose clothing, and tie back hair. Remind students to handle the thermometer carefully.

Conclusion
1. Responses will vary depending upon foods tested. Fats will release the most energy.
2. Responses will vary.

ACTIVITY 14.2
Time One class period
Group Size 2–3 students
Hypothesis Animal foods contain more protein that plant foods.
Safety Tips Students should wear laboratory aprons and safety goggles. Have students wash their hands immediately if they spill the Biuret's solution.

Procedure
In order of protein content (most to least) the foods are: tuna fish, egg white, lima beans, bread, and potato.

Analysis
1. Responses will vary depending upon predictions.
2. Like responses will indicate that animal products have more protein than plant products because the Biuret solution reacted to the animal products.
3. Accept all logical responses.

Conclusion
Likely responses will include either the tuna or the egg whites.

Answers to End of Chapter Questions
Concept Review
1. The machinery involved requires a large cash investment. Also, the water necessary to maintain crops is not always available, fuel is expensive, and pesticides cannot be purchased to maintain crops.
2. Saturated fats have the maximum number of hydrogen atoms. An unsaturated fat has fewer hydrogen atoms.
3. Benefits: aerates soil, returns nutrients to upper soil layers, destroys weeds, and improves drainage. Problems: uses energy, wastes water, causes erosion.
4. Cover crops are nonfood plants that are grown between growing seasons. Such plants reduce erosion and help to restore nitrogen to the soil.

Think Critically
1. The prices for products increase in the market. People who sell the higher-priced crops benefit. Consumers pay higher prices.
2. Accept all logical responses.
3. Crop rotation involves alternating the types of crops grown in a given field to allow the soil to replace lost nutrients.
4. Responses should indicate that if problems are not addressed they tend to worsen.

Graphic Analysis
1. Between 1957 and 1960.
2. Accept all logical responses.
3. It demonstrates increased resistance.

Unit Overview

Unit 5 explores the ways in which people use energy and the energy sources that are being investigated and developed as alternatives to fossil fuels. Chapter 15 surveys the fossil fuels that currently serve as energy sources for most of the world and alternative fuels that may meet the growing energy demands of an expanding world population. Chapter 16 discusses nuclear energy and evaluates this resource in terms of the potential danger of a nuclear accident. Chapter 17 presents other alternatives to nuclear and fossil fuels, including solar energy, wind energy, geothermal energy, and hydroelectric power.

Introducing the Unit

Discussion   Display an electric lamp, a dry cell, charcoal briquettes, a Bunsen burner, and an alcohol lamp. Ask what each of these objects has in common with the others. Lead students to recognize that all of these objects use energy to carry out their jobs. Briefly review the definition of energy and introduce the concept of energy transformations. Ask students to describe the energy transformations each object uses as it works.

Discussion   Display a potted plant. Ask students what the plant needs from its environment in order to survive. Relate the discussion of the importance of sunlight to plants, to the role of the sun as Earth's primary energy source. Explain to students that in addition to providing the energy for most living things, sunlight also provides the energy in wind, water, and organic fuels.

Teacher Resources

Audiovisual

Energy Supply, video, 36 minutes, Bullfrog Films, 1986.
Energy Efficiency, video, 23 minutes, Bullfrog Films, 1986.
Fossil Fuels, video, 20 minutes, Scott Resources, 1990.

Computer Software

MacNuke with the Radiation Detector, Macintosh, Vernier Software.

Suggested Readings

Worster, Donald, *Nature's Economy: A History of Ecological Ideas*, Cambridge University Press, 1977.

Advance Preparation

Chapter 15

Field Activity   Have graph paper available for students.
Activity 15.1   Have graph paper available for students.
Activity 15.2   Gather jars or beakers, masking tape or labels, marking pens, cloth rags, hammers, pyrite, sulfur coal, water, blue litmus paper, laboratory aprons, and safety goggles.

Chapter 16

Field Activity   Purchase home radon test kits.
Activity 16.1   Purchase sodium hydroxide pellets and gather jars with lids, phenolphthalein solution, water, plastic wrap, twist ties, aluminum foil, modeling clay, forceps, safety goggles, and laboratory aprons.
Activity 16.2   Gather dominoes, stopwatches, and rulers.

Chapter 17

Field Activity   Gather hand lenses and thin sheets of paper, such as lens paper, and small rocks.
Activity 17.1   Gather thermometers, 250-mL beakers, graduated cylinders, newspaper, large black cardboard boxes with lids, stopwatches or a wall clock with a second hand, salt, sand, and water at room temperature.
Activity 17.2   Gather hand drills, hammers, scrap wood, bolts, washers, nuts, foil pie tins, crayons, thread spools, scissors, small nails, and an electric fan.

Chapter Planning Guide

Section	Core	Standard	Enriched
15.1 The Need for Energy	•	•	•
Section Features Field Activity, p. 236		•	•
Blackline Masters Review Worksheet 15.1	•	•	•
Skills Worksheet 15A	•	•	
Ancillary Options One Minute Readings, p. 99	•	•	•
15.2 Coal		•	•
Section Features Geology Link, p. 239		•	•
Activity 15.2, p. 249	•	•	•
Blackline Masters Review Worksheet 15.2		•	•
15.3 Petroleum and Natural Gas	•	•	•
Section Features Dateline 1859, p. 240	•	•	•
Word Power, p. 240	•	•	•

Section	Core	Standard	Enriched
Issue, p. 242	•	•	•
Activity 15.1, p. 246		•	•
Blackline Masters Review Worksheet 15.3	•	•	•
Skills Worksheet 15B	•		
Issues and Case Studies 12	•	•	•
Ancillary Options One Minute Readings, p. 62			•
One Minute Readings, p. 65		•	
Laboratory Program Investigation 15	•	•	•
15.4 Other Organic Fuels	•	•	•
Section Features Dateline 1973, p. 243	•	•	•
Mathematics Link, p. 244		•	•
Blackline Masters Review Worksheet 15.4	•		•
Ancillary Options One Minute Readings, p. 64	•	•	•

Every chapter has two corresponding tests in the Test Book and one Vocabulary Review Worksheet in the Review Book.

Chapter Overview

Chapter 15 examines the use of fossil and biomass fuels as energy sources. Section 15.1 discusses how energy needs have changed over time. Section 15.2 describes coal formation. Section 15.3 explains the processes by which petroleum and natural gas were formed and ways in which these fuel sources are used. The chapter concludes, in Section 15.4, with a discussion of the problems associated with using fossil fuels and introduces alternate organic fuels.

Advance Planner

Section 15.1
- Bring in pictures of automobiles, televisions, gas stoves, and coal-burning locomotives as described in the Motivate section.
- Obtain a radiometer for the Demonstration.
- Obtain a Bunsen burner and a pinwheel for the demonstration in the Reteach section.

Section 15.2
- Order a film or video showing fossil formation and bring in fossil specimens for the activities in the Reteach sections.

- Obtain specimens of peat, lignite, bituminous coal and anthracite coal, along with several hand lenses for the Activity and the Reinforce sections.

Section 15.3
- Bring in a can of motor oil for the discussion in the Motivate section.
- Gather a 500-mL beaker, sand, water, clay, and salad oil for the demonstration in the Reteach section.
- Obtain a test tube, wooden splints, a stopper fitted with a glass tube, and matches for the Demonstration.

Section 15.4
- Bring in 200 mL of grape juice, a package of dry yeast, and a 500-mL flask with a stopper for the demonstration in the Reteach section.

Introducing the Chapter

Tell students to rub their hands together. Explain that several energy conversions are taking place. First, chemical energy from food is converted to mechanical energy as the hands move. The mechanical energy is then converted to heat energy.

Section 15.1 The Need for Energy

pp. 235–237

Performance Objectives

- Explain how changes in human societies have changed the demand for energy.
- Describe the structure of organic fuels.

Skills Objective

- Infer why a society based on hunting and gathering needs less energy than a society based on agriculture.

Section Vocabulary

fossil fuels   fuel   hydrocarbon

Motivate

On the chalkboard write the words *electricity, light, sound, nuclear, solar, chemical, mechanical,* and *heat.* Challenge students to identify what these words have in common. Show pictures of automobiles, televisions, gas stoves, and coal-burning locomotives. Tell students that energy stored in fuels is needed to operate these devices. Ask where the fuels acquire their energies.

Teaching Strategies

Demonstrate   Display a radiometer in low light and bright light. Have the class speculate about what causes the blades of the radiometer to turn. After students have expressed their views, explain that there is a small amount of air inside the bulb. When light strikes the dark sides of the blades, the light is absorbed and then converted into heat. The heat generated on the dark sides of the blades heats the air next to it, causing the air to expand and the blades to turn.

Reteach   Hold a pinwheel over a Bunsen burner and discuss how a Bunsen burner converts chemical energy in fuel to heat and light energy. The pinwheel turns when the heat energy is changed into mechanical energy. Have students develop a diagram that shows energy conversions involved in other activities.

Reinforce   Challenge students to identify a form of energy that is not a form of solar energy (nuclear and geothermal power are not). Lead students to recognize that the energy in coal, gas, and oil can be traced back to the sun.

Evaluate

Closure   Make a list of about ten activities, such as ringing a bell or striking a match. Have students describe the energy changes involved in each.

Section 15.2 Coal

pp. 238–239

Performance Objectives

- List the stages of coal formation and describe the characteristics of each stage.
- Locate the major coal deposits on a map of the United States.

Skills Objective

- Infer why peat is not considered to be a fossil fuel.

Vocabulary

anthracite coal   bituminous coal   lignite
peat

Motivate

Have students discuss popular motion pictures about dinosaurs and other prehistoric animals. Point out that scientific information about prehistoric animals comes from fossils. Ask what other uses fossil materials can have. Use this discussion as a springboard to identify coal, petroleum, and natural gas as fossil fuels.

Teaching Strategies

Reteach   Show a film or video on fossil formation. List the various kinds of fossils such as imprints, original remains, footprints, and petrified materials. Display any available samples of fossils.

Activity   Divide students into small groups and distribute specimens of peat, lignite, bituminous coal, and anthracite coal. Have students examine the peat with a hand lens, and describe peat components. Have students examine the coal specimens and describe properties such as luster, texture, and fracture.

Reteach   Review the differences between sedimentary and metamorphic rocks. Point out that bituminous coal and lignite are sedimentary rocks, while anthracite is metamorphic. Direct students to compare specimens of these rocks and identify their sedimentary and metamorphic properties.

Evaluate

Closure   Have students create a chart identifying the various forms of coal and peat. Ask students to list the properties of each substance and identify regions on Earth where each is located.

Section 15.3 Petroleum and Natural Gas

pp. 240–241

Performance Objectives
- Describe the characteristics of petroleum and natural gas.
- Explain how petroleum and natural gas are formed.

Skills Objective
- Compare and contrast the formation of petroleum versus the formation of coal.

Section Vocabulary
petroleum

Motivate
Display a can of motor oil and explain to students that this oil is obtained from crude petroleum. Have students identify other substances such as gasoline, fuel oil, kerosene, grease, wax, asphalt, lubricating oil, propane, butane, and ethane that all come from the distillation of crude petroleum.

Teaching Strategies
Reteach   Fill a 500-mL beaker one-quarter full of sand. Tell the class the sand represents a layer of sandstone that was once at the bottom of an ocean. Add water to the sand and show how the water moves between the sand grains just as ocean water would fill the pores of sandstone. Tell the class that plankton, other organisms, and their remains, also move into these pores. Discuss how decay, pressure, and heat create petroleum deposits. Pour some salad oil into the water. Ask students to notice that oil is lighter than water and forms a pool on top. Cover the sand with a layer of clay to represent an impervious layer of rock.

Demonstrate   Set a test tube containing several wooden splints on a stand. Ignite the splints and fit a stopper containing a glass tube onto the test tube. Point out the black residue that forms inside the test tube. Explain that this substance is carbon in the form of charcoal. Hold a burning splint to the end of the tube to ignite the gas coming from the tubing. Tell students that this gas is very much like natural gas which forms together with petroleum in oil pools.

Enrich   Have students do library research about the major oil-producing regions of the world. Ask them to find out the amount of oil in each deposit and the production rate. Have students estimate how long it will take for the supply at each location to run out.

Evaluate
Closure   Have students make a diagram of a cross-section of an oil well. Have them label the diagram and describe how the oil and natural gas formed.

Section 15.4   Other Organic Fuels

pp. 243–245

Performance Objectives
- Describe some of the problems associated with the use of fossil fuels.
- Compare biomass fuels to fossil fuels and give examples of bioconversion techniques.

Skills Objective
- Infer two ways that using garbage as fuel helps the environment.

Section Vocabulary
bioconversion   biomass fuel

Motivate
Ask students for examples of non-renewable resources. (These include metallic ores, nonmetallic mineral ores, and fossil fuels.) Tell students about the long gas lines created by the oil embargo of 1973. Show news photographs if available. Ask how such crises may be prevented in the future.

Teaching Strategies
Reteach   Place 200 mL of grape juice and some yeast into a flask. Stopper the flask and set it in a warm place. After several days, allow students to smell the contents of the flask. Tell students that starch and sugary compounds are converted to alcohol through the fermentation process. Point out that beers and wines are made in a similar manner. Explain that alcohol is being produced from plants to be used together with gasoline to run automobiles.

Enrich   Have students determine which octane rating of gasoline is best for cars. Have them investigate the mileage and performance of different gasoline formulations.

Evaluate
Closure   Have students make a list of biomass fuels describing their current and potential uses.

Chapter Resources

Teaching Tip for Feature
Issues: Public versus Private Transportation
- Have students hold a class debate on the issue.

Teaching Tip for Field Activity
- Have students prepare a survey questionnaire to record data. Have them arrange their observations in a table form so that construction of the graph will be easier.

Answers to Field Activity
Answers may vary, however, most homes in the same area will probably use similar energy sources.

Teaching Tips for Activities

ACTIVITY 15.1
Time   One class period
Group Size   Have students work individually.
Prediction   After the year 2000, the demand will begin to exceed the supply.
Safety Tips   No special safety precautions required.

Analysis
1. World oil production is much greater.
2. 1975. No, because the population continued to grow.
3. Mostly by imported oil.
4. Check calculations for accuracy.

Conclusion
1. Check response for logic and accuracy.
2. Accept all logical responses.

ACTIVITY 15.2
Time   Day 1: 25 min; Day 3: 15 min
Group Size   2–3 students
Prediction   Coal mining can produce acid wastes.
Safety Tips   Caution students to wear safety goggles while using the hammer and wipe up any spills immediately.

Analysis
1. The water in the jars represents water from springs, ground water, rivers, and streams.
2. The jar with only water in it was the control.
3. Pyrite is iron sulfide and the water in this jar was affected. Depending on the sample, the water in the jar with sulfur coal may also change.
4. A mild acid formed.

Conclusion
Answers will vary depending on predictions.

Answers to End of Chapter Questions
Concept Review
1. Coal, oil, and gas are fuels derived from the remains of organisms that lived long ago.
2. Biomass fuels are derived from living organisms and renewable resources.
3. The changing of sugar and starch in some plants into alcohol, which can be used as a fuel, is an example of bioconversion.
4. Coal, oil and natural gas are all hydrocarbons, which means they are composed of only carbon and hydrogen.
5. Hunter-gatherer societies require energy only for heat, light, and cooking, whereas an industrial society is more complex and has greater energy needs.

Think Critically
1. An increase in demand for biomass fuels would stimulate production of plants that are used for biomass fuels. It would raise plant prices and stimulate employment.
2. Fossil fuels would probably be found in recently uplifted areas of sedimentary rocks. Evidence of fossils would also be a good clue.
3. Offshore drilling and pumping of oil poses the problems of oil spills and habitat destruction.
4. Biomass fuels are considered renewable because they can be replaced in a very short amount of time, whereas fossil fuels take millions of years to replace.
5. Using more biomass fuels lessens the demand for fossil fuels and helps preserve these nonrenewable resources.

Graphic Analysis
1. 1884.
2. The 1973 oil embargo. Coal consumption increased.
3. Natural gas usage was not widespread before 1890.

CHAPTER 16 NUCLEAR ENERGY

Chapter Planning Guide

Section	Core	Standard	Enriched	Section	Core	Standard	Enriched
16.1 Atoms and Radioactivity	•	•	•	**Ancillary Options** One Minute Readings, p. 101	•	•	•
Section Features Word Power, p. 251	•	•	•	**16.3 Radioactive Waste**	•	•	•
Blackline Masters Review Worksheet 16.1	•	•	•	**Section Features** Field Activity, p. 257			•
Laboratory Program Investigation 20		•	•	Frontiers, p. 258	•	•	•
16.2 Reactions and Reactors	•	•	•	Dateline 1979, p. 260	•	•	•
Section Features Mathematics Link, p. 254		•	•	Mathematics Link, p. 260		•	•
Think Critically, p. 255			•	Activity 16.1, p. 259	•	•	•
Activity 16.2, p. 263	•	•		**Blackline Masters** Review Worksheet 16.3	•	•	•
Blackline Masters Review Worksheet 16.2	•	•	•	Skills Worksheet 16B		•	•
Skills Worksheet 16A	•	•	•	Issues and Case Studies 13	•	•	•
				Ancillary Options One Minute Readings, p. 97		•	•

Every chapter has two corresponding tests in the Test Book and one Vocabulary Review Worksheet in the Review Book.

Chapter Overview

Chapter 16 examines the atom and nuclear energy. Section 16.1 explores atomic structure and discusses isotopes, radioactive particles, and half-lives. Section 16.2 presents the fuels used in nuclear reactors and describes how nuclear reactions produce electricity. Section 16.3 deals with different types of radioactive wastes and methods presently used for their disposal. The dangers of a nuclear meltdown are examined.

Advance Planner

- Bring in the following items for the activities in the Introducing the Chapter section: mouse trap, ruler, gum drops, marshmallows, and toothpicks.

Section 16.1
- Obtain three jars, water, and sand for the activity in the Motivate section.
- Bring in a shoe box, a small ball, and some tape for the first Demonstration.
- Have a watch with a luminous dial and a Geiger counter available for the second demonstration.
- Arrange for a local dentist to provide you with an X-ray of a key as described in the Reteach section.

- Provide students with 50 pennies and one paper cup per group of four students for the Activity.

Section 16.2
- Obtain diagrams that show the control rods of a nuclear reactor.

Section 16.3
- Provide students with graph paper for the Activity.
- Arrange for a speaker from the electric utility company.

Introducing the Chapter

Demonstrate how a mouse trap is set and how it springs. Use a ruler to spring the trap to avoid injury. Have students assess the amount of energy required to set the trap compared to that used to spring the trap. Relate the small amount of energy needed to spring the trap to the way a small amount of mass in an atom can be used to generate large amounts of energy.

Have students construct models of atoms using marshmallows and gum drops. Direct students to use toothpicks to hold the marshmallows and gum drops together. Encourage students to work in groups to construct several different atomic models.

T86   Chapter 16 Preview

Section 16.1 Atoms and Radioactivity

pp. 251–252

Performance Objectives
- Describe the structure of the atom and the atomic nucleus.
- Explain how unstable nuclei become stable by releasing radiation.

Skills Objective
- Demonstrate an understanding of the term *half-life.*

Section Vocabulary
nucleus   isotopes   radiation   half-life

Motivate
Display three jars: one empty, one with water, and another with sand. Ask students what the contents of the jars have in common. (The air, water, and sand are all matter.) Ask the class to describe the properties of matter. Develop the idea that matter is composed of particles called atoms.

Teaching Strategies
Reteach   Construct atomic models of helium, lithium, beryllium, boron, carbon, nitrogen, oxygen, and fluorine. Use the models to discuss atomic mass, proton number, and atomic number. Have students draw diagrams of different atoms including the atomic mass and atomic numbers of each atom.

Demonstrate   Before the class arrives, place a ball inside a shoe box and seal the box. Display the box and ask volunteers to describe the contents of the box without opening it. On the chalkboard, list the descriptions. Use this exercise to guide students to recognize that it is possible to describe objects that cannot be directly observed.

Enrich   Have students write a report on the contributions made to the understanding of the atom by one of the following people: Democritus, John Dalton, William Crookes, J.J. Thomson, Ernest Rutherford, Niels Bohr, Robert Boyle, James Chadwick, Henry Mosley, Robert Millikan, Wilhelm von Roentgen, Marie Sklodowska Curie, Pierre Curie, Henri Becquerel, Lise Meitner, Enrico Fermi, Albert Einstein, and C.T.R. Wilson. As an alternative activity, have students research all these scientists and work together to develop a timeline of their contributions.

Demonstrate   Obtain an old watch that has a luminous dial. Use a Geiger counter to note the presence of radiation. Have students note the clicking sound and the reading on the meter. Move the probe close to and away from the source. Discuss also the concept of background radiation and have them suggest possible sources for this radiation.

Reteach   Bring in an X-ray of a key prepared by a local dentist. Relate the X-ray image to Becquerel's discovery of radiation emissions from pitchblende.

Activity   Direct groups of students to use 50 pennies to illustrate the concept of half-life. Have them shake 50 pennies in a cup and dump the pennies onto the desk. Tell students to separate the heads from the tails, count the number of tails and put them aside. Place all heads back into the cup and repeat the procedure until only one penny remains. Have all groups record how many pennies were tails in each trial and how many trials were needed before they ran out of pennies. Finally, have students tabulate the class results. Ask students to write a paragraph explaining how this activity illustrates the half-life of a radioactive element.

Evaluate
Closure   Have students draw a diagram of the isotopes of oxygen-16, oxygen-17, and oxygen-18. Tell them to include the atomic number and atomic mass for each isotope.

Section 16.2 Reactions and Reactors

pp. 253–255

Performance Objectives
- Illustrate the fission chain reactions that power nuclear reactors and breeder reactors.
- Diagram the structure and function of a nuclear reactor.

Skills Objective
- Predict what would happen to the nuclear fuel in a reactor if the water-cooling system and control rods stopped working.

Section Vocabulary
nuclear fission

Motivate
Ask students to explain the Law of Conservation of Mass–Energy. If no one responds, state the law and

explain its meaning. Tell students that they will see examples of this law as they read about how radioactive atoms are used to generate energy.

Teaching Strategies

Reteach Write $E = mc^2$ on the chalkboard. Ask students to explain what each letter in the equation represents and what the formula means. Point out that the speed of light is 3×10^{10} cm/sec and in the equation this very large number is squared. Guide students to recognize that even a very small mass loss produces a very large amount of energy.

Reinforce Emphasize that nuclear material is released as alpha particles, beta particles, and gamma rays. Describe alpha particles as helium nuclei because they are composed of two protons and two neutrons. On the atomic mass scale, normal helium nuclei are 4.0320 amu (mass of proton 1.0073, mass of neutron 1.0087). However, the mass of an alpha particle is 4.0015 amu. On the chalkboard, calculate the mass of a helium nucleus and show the difference in mass between helium nuclei and an alpha particle. Ask the class to speculate what happens to the lost mass during a nuclear reaction.

Reteach Emphasize that beta particles are high-speed electrons from the nucleus of an atom. Beta particles are thought to form when a neutron splits to form an electron and a proton. You can write a transmutation equation on the chalkboard to show how elements gain protons as they lose alpha particles.

Evaluate

Closure Have students write equations for the fission of U-238 and U-235. Have them explain how each fission reaction occurs and how it is controlled.

Section 16.3   Radioactive Waste

pp. 256–260

Performance Objectives
- Define radioactive wastes and explain the dangers that arise from such wastes.
- State the problems involved in the safe disposal of radioactive wastes.

Skills Objective
- Analyze what caused the Chernobyl nuclear accident and evaluate whether this factor can be eliminated from other nuclear plants.

Section Vocabulary
high-level wastes   low-level wastes
medium-level wastes

Motivate

Ask the class to list the advantages of nuclear energy as a substitute for fossil fuels. Have students create a second list that identifies disadvantages of nuclear energy. Have students save their lists and add to them as they read the section.

Teaching Strategies

Activity Write the following data on the chalkboard or on an overhead transparency.

Fishes	Temperature at which Fishes Die (°C)
goldfish	43
shad	37
largemouth bass	37
striped bass	35
Atlantic salmon	34
perch	33
trout	25

Direct students to graph the data. Ask how fishes could be affected by the placement of a nuclear power plant along a river. Have them describe which fishes would be affected most and which would be affected least.

Reteach As a class, create a chart on the chalkboard listing types of nuclear wastes, sources of the wastes, and any waste disposal methods. Have students copy the chart into their notebooks.

Guest Speaker Invite a representative from the local electric utility company to speak to the class about methods of generating power for your community. Ask them to discuss benefits and drawbacks of nuclear energy, as well as any future role nuclear energy is expected to play in local power generation.

Evaluate

Closure Have students debate the pros and cons for the use of nuclear energy as a means of generating electricity. Have them establish which interest groups would be for nuclear energy and which might be against its use. When nuclear accidents are discussed, be sure that the causes of these accidents are listed. Ask students what conditions might make the use of nuclear energy more acceptable.

Chapter Resources

Teaching Tip for Feature
Frontiers: Identifying a Waste Site
- Ask students to work in cooperative groups to design their own warning symbols.

Teaching Tip for Field Activity
- Have students create a map showing where radon gas was detected. Have students describe any patterns that emerge in their data.

Answers to Field Activity
Responses will vary.

Teaching Tips for Activities

ACTIVITY 16.1

Time Day 1: 20 min; Days 2 and 3: 10 min
Group Size 2 students
Inference The containers used to store nuclear waste can leak.
Safety Tips Sodium hydroxide is a caustic chemical. Instruct students to wear safety goggles and avoid contact with their skin. Instruct students on the use of the eyewash unit.

Analysis
1. The indicator changed color.
2. Responses will vary.
3. Responses will vary.

Conclusion
Responses will vary depending on inference.

ACTIVITY 16.2

Time 25–30 min
Group Size 2 students
Inference A nuclear chain reaction can be modeled as a domino effect.
Safety Tips None

Analysis
1. The dominoes fall faster when they are placed in a single line.
2. A chain reaction is illustrated when the dominoes are placed in the four rows.
3. The push on the first domino is like the slow-moving particle entering the nucleus of a radioactive element. The ruler represents a control rod.

Conclusion
The domino demonstration can be used to illustrate a chain reaction in a nuclear reactor, however the speed at which the dominoes fall and hit each other cannot be controlled as in a reactor.

Answers to End of Chapter Questions
Concept Review
1. The radon-222 nuclei are unstable, with a half-life of about 4 days, and they decay by giving off alpha particles. $Rn^{222} \rightarrow Po^{218} + He^4$
2. In a fission chain reaction, a nucleus is bombarded with subatomic particles. An unstable nucleus results. The nucleus splits into lighter weight nuclei and releases alpha particles. These particles, in turn, may strike nuclei of other elements. These newer elements become unstable and release particles that bombard additional nuclei.
3. Control rods absorb particles given off by splitting nuclei and slow the chain reaction.
4. Sources include uranium mine wastes, protective clothing worn by hospital and laboratory workers, or tracers used in industry.
5. The half-life of a radioactive material is the time it takes for half of it to decay into a more stable substance. As long as the substance gives off radiation it is still dangerous.

Think Critically
1. The atomic number of radon is 86. It emits an alpha particle and changes to polonium with atomic number of 84. There is no loss of additional particles.
2. The control rods at the Chernobyl plant kept the plant from exploding; the meltdown itself slowed down the reaction.

Computer Activity
Check student calculations for accuracy.

Graphic Analysis
1. Vermont.
2. No.
3. Mostly in the eastern U.S. Such a distribution pattern is not obvious from this information alone.
4. Yes, the same data is used.

Chapter Planning Guide

Section	Core	Standard	Enriched	Section	Core	Standard	Enriched
17.1 Solar Energy	•	•	•	**Blackline Masters** Review Worksheet 17.2 Skills Worksheet 17B	•	• •	• •
Section Features Field Activity, p. 265 Think Critically, p. 266 Dateline 1958, p. 269 Activity 17.1, p. 270	• • • •	• • • •	• •	**Ancillary Options** Multiculturalism, pp. 155–160		•	•
				17.3 Wind Energy	•	•	•
Blackline Masters Review Worksheet 17.1 Skills Worksheet 17A	• •	• •	• •	**Section Features** Literature Connection, p. 275 Activity 17.2, p. 281	• •	• •	• • •
Ancillary Options One Minute Readings, p. 100			•	**Blackline Masters** Review Worksheet 17.3	•	•	•
Laboratory Program Investigation 21	•	•	•	**17.4 Geothermal Energy and Nuclear Fusion**		•	•
17.2 Hydroelectric Energy	•	•	•	**Section Features** Social Studies Connection, p. 278	•	•	•
Section Features Frontiers, p. 273		•	•	**Blackline Masters** Review Worksheet 17.4	•	•	•

Every chapter has two corresponding tests in the Test Book and one Vocabulary Review Worksheet in the Review Book. There is also a Unit 5 test in the test book covering Chapters 15–17.

Chapter Overview

Chapter 17 presents energy sources being investigated as alternatives to fossil fuels. Section 17.1 explores methods by which sunlight can be harnessed to generate heat and electricity. Section 17.2 discusses methods of obtaining energy from moving water. Section 17.3 relates sunlight and wind and explores the use of wind as an energy source. Section 17.4 discusses geothermal energy and presents nuclear fusion as a possible future energy source.

Advance Planner

- Obtain a wristwatch and a calculator that use solar energy and a photo of a satellite showing solar panels.

Section 17.1
- Obtain a radiometer and black construction paper for the demonstration in the Motivate section.
- Have physics textbooks with light ray diagrams available for the activity in the Enrich section.

Section 17.2
- Obtain a photograph of a water wheel as described in the Motivate section.

- Have a pinwheel on hand for the demonstration in the Reteach section.

Section 17.3
- Have paper, pencils with erasers, and straight pins available for the activity in the Motivate section.
- Obtain a convection box for the demonstration in the Reteach section.

Section 17.4
- Order a video or film that explains how a volcanic eruption occurs as described in the Motivate section.
- Obtain a wall chart, illustration, or overhead transparency that shows the parts of a volcano.
- Provide students with outline maps of the world for the Closure activity.

Introducing the Chapter

Display a solar-powered watch, calculator, and a photo of solar panels from a satellite. Have students observe the solar-powered devices in use. Point out that like these devices, the satellite also uses sunlight as its energy source.

Section 17.1   Solar Energy

pp. 265–269

Performance Objectives
- Explain the importance of the sun in supplying energy to Earth.
- Describe how solar energy can be used to heat buildings and to generate electricity.

Skills Objectives
- Apply the ways in which solar energy can be used to reduce in air pollution.
- Observe a change caused by the energy in sunlight.

Section Vocabulary

solar energy   passive solar heating
active solar energy system   photovoltaic cell

Motivate

Display a radiometer in direct sunlight. Have students observe the movement of the device. Use a sheet of black construction paper to block the sunlight and have students observe what happens. Relate student observations to the idea that light is a form of energy because it can cause objects to move.

Teaching Strategies

Discuss   Explain to students that objects that are dark in color tend to absorb light energy, while those that are light in color tend to reflect light energy. In a similar way objects with rough textures tend to absorb more light energy than those with smooth surfaces. Relate these concepts to the use of dark, rough, construction materials in solar-powered homes.

Enrich   Have students research how light rays interact with different types of surfaces. Encourage students to refer to a physics text and create light ray diagrams that show how light acts when it strikes a highly polished surface such as a mirror.

Reteach   Review the characteristics of light and the electromagnetic spectrum. Challenge students to make a visual device that shows the correct sequence of colors that make up the visible spectrum.

Enrich   A Trombe wall is a structure used in the construction of solar-powered homes. Have students research the development of the Trombe wall and make a three-dimensional model that shows its features. Encourage students to include a summary with their model that explains how the model works.

Evaluate

Closure   Have students write a summary or make a concept map that compares and contrasts passive and active solar energy systems. Review the summaries or concept maps as a class.

Section 17.2   Hydroelectric Energy

pp. 271–272

Performance Objectives
- Describe two ways that moving water can be used to produce electricity.
- Discuss benefits and drawbacks to producing electricity through the use of hydroelectric power.

Skills Objective
- Justify viewpoints regarding benefits and drawbacks of hydroelectric power in a given area.

Section Vocabulary
hydroelectric power

Motivate

Display a photograph of a water wheel such as one used to grind grain. Explain to students that at one time such wheels were common along rivers. Ask students to describe how the wheel operates. Relate the water wheel to an electrical generator.

Teaching Strategies

Reteach   Place a pinwheel beneath a stream of water flowing from the faucet. Use the turning of the pinwheel as a demonstration of how the flowing water of a river can be used to rotate the turbines in a hydroelectric power plant.

Enrich   One of the largest tidal energy plants is located in the Rance Estuary in France. This plant, which was completed in 1967, generates 240,000 kilowatts of electricity using 24 units.

Evaluate

Closure   Have students create a diagram or flowchart that explains how energy is produced in a hydroelectric power plant. Have volunteers share their diagrams or flow charts with the class.

Section 17.3   Wind Energy

pp. 274–275

Performance Objectives
- Relate the energy of sunlight to the formation of air currents and winds.
- Explain how the energy in wind can be used to produce electricity.

Skills Objective
- Analyze whether wind energy is a viable source of energy in the region in which you live.

Vocabulary
aerogenerator

Motivate
Have students construct pinwheels using paper attached to a pencil eraser with a straight pin. Once students have constructed their pinwheels have them blow on them to try to get the pinwheels to turn. Ask students how the air they are blowing on the pinwheels is similar to wind. (Wind is also moving air.) Ask students whether or not wind can be used to do work. (Yes, as demonstrated by the pinwheel.) Explain that wind energy can be harnessed to produce electricity.

Teaching Strategies
Reteach   Set up a convection box to demonstrate convection currents. Use the box to explain the processes that result in wind formation.

Activity   Have students work in cooperative groups to design and make their own windmills. Have students explain their windmill designs and choice of materials.

Evaluate
Closure   Have students develop concept maps that show the similarities and differences between the processes involved in producing electricity from water and from wind. Review the maps as a class.

Section 17.4   Geothermal Energy and Nuclear Fusion

pp. 276–278

Performance Objectives
- Describe how geothermal energy is used.
- Explain how nuclear fusion could be a valuable source of energy in the future.

Skills Objective
- Analyze whether the conditions exist in their area to make geothermal energy a viable energy source.

Vocabulary
geothermal energy   nuclear fusion

Motivate
Show a video or film that explains the processes involved in a volcanic eruption. Review the concept that volcanoes are created by a buildup of pressure of heated materials within the earth. Ask students whether they think this energy might be harnessed to provide a useful energy source. Explain to students that such energy is called geothermal energy.

Teaching Strategies
Reinforce   Display an illustration or overhead transparency that shows the parts of a volcano. Discuss how magma and heat energy beneath the Earth's surface can travel to the surface.

Physics Connection   Explain that the watt is a unit of power equal to 1 joule (J) per second. The watt is named for Scottish engineer James Watt, the builder of the first useful steam engine.

Reteach   Students often get the processes of nuclear fission and nuclear fusion confused. To help students remember that fission is the splitting of atomic particles, point out that the word *fission* also describes the process by which organisms reproduce asexually by splitting in two—binary fission.

Activity   Have students create a table that compares nuclear fusion and nuclear fission.

Evaluate
Closure   Provide students with outline maps of the world. Have students identify locations in which geothermal energy is a viable energy source. Encourage students to also show regions where solar energy and wind energy are viable energy sources.

Chapter Resources

Teaching Tip for Feature
Frontiers: The Ocean Resource
* Have students prepare a flowchart of the steps involved in ocean thermal energy conversion.

Teaching Tips for Field Activity
* Caution students to be careful not to burn themselves as they carry out this activity.
* Have students extend the activity by repeating the experiment using different colors of paper.

Answers to Field Activity
Students should observe that as the sun's rays focus on the paper, the energy of the light changes to heat and ignites the paper.

Teaching Tips for Activities

ACTIVITY 17.1
Time   40–45 minutes
Group Size   5 students
Prediction   Water will store the most solar energy.
Safety Tips   Caution students to be careful with the thermometers and beakers to avoid breakage.

Analysis
1. The temperature rose the most in the beaker with air and least in the beaker with water.
2. The ranking should be air, paper, sand, salt, water.
3. The beaker with air will drop the fastest, while the beaker with water will drop the slowest.

Conclusion
1. Water stores heat better than any other material tested.
2. Answers will vary. Students may state that solar panels use water because it stores heat well.

ACTIVITY 17.2
Time   One class period
Group Size   3–4 students
Hypothesis   The design affects the ability of a windmill to use wind power to do work.
Safety Tips   Caution students to be careful with the sharp edges of cut pie tins.

Analysis
1. Length, angle, shape.
2. Two blades make a lighter design that can turn more rapidly.

Conclusion
Answers will vary depending upon designs tested.

Answers to End of Chapter Questions
Concept Review
1. Solar energy is nonpolluting and renewable.
2. By using any or all or these energy resources, less fossil fuels are needed. Therefore, the total amount of fossil fuels is conserved.
3. Air currents are up-and-down movements of air. Winds are horizontal movements of air.
4. The energy of the sun is expected to last for a very long time.
5. Nearness of a location to an accessible source of geothermal energy.

Think Critically
1. Accept all logical responses.
2. Solar energy comes directly from the sun. The sun causes the heating of the air that results in wind formation and provides the energy that drives the water cycle. Thus, the sun is involved in both wind energy and hydroelectric power.
3. Probably not, since the vents are located very far from the surface of Earth.
4. Hydroelectric power provides a relatively inexpensive energy source. The damming of a river, required for hydroelectric power, can disrupt habitats, causing some organisms to leave an area or die, while at the same time disrupting food chains.
5. As generators are turned, mechanical energy is changed in form to produce electrical energy.

Graphic Analysis
1. No, the liquid is recirculated.
2. North.
3. Check diagrams for logic and accuracy.

Unit Overview

Unit 6 explores Earth's land and water resources. Chapter 18 discusses the availability of minerals and soil. Chapter 19 explores problems associated with land pollution and land management. Chapter 20 discusses the importance of water as a resource. Chapter 21 discusses forms of water pollution and methods by which water pollution can be reduced. Chapter 22 explores the causes and effects of air pollution and noise pollution.

Introducing the Unit

Discussion   Display a globe or a world map. Point out the relative amounts of land and water on Earth. Discuss the amounts of water that are fresh, marine, frozen, and liquid. Emphasize that the amount of land and water available for use by humans and other organisms is limited.

Teacher Resources

Audiovisual
Downwind, Downstream, film/video, 60 minutes, Bullfrog Films, 1987.
Toxic Waste, videodisc, 60 minutes, National Film Board of Canada, 1991.

Computer Software
Water Pollution, Apple II/IBM, Educational Materials and Equipment Company.

Suggested Readings
Smith, W. Eugene, *Minamata*, Holt, Rhinehart, Winston, 1975.

Advance Preparation

Chapter 18
Field Activity   Have hand lenses and plastic bags available.
Activity 18.1   Gather glass markers, test tubes with stoppers, test-tube racks, balances, garden soil, safety goggles, wire gauze, crucibles, ring stands, Bunsen burners, tongs, sugar, methylene-blue solution, graduated cylinders, laboratory aprons, safety goggles and heat-resistant gloves.

Activity 18.2   Gather 3 types of soil, 1-L jars, water, partly decayed leaves (humus), apple seedlings, construction paper, rubber bands or tape, shovel or trowel.

Chapter 19
Field Activity   No materials required.
Activity 19.1   Gather wax marking pencils, plastic Petri dishes with lids, paper towels cut to fit the Petri dishes, radish seeds, 5% detergent solution, 5% salt solution, 5% oil solution, tape, tap water, potting soil mix, laboratory aprons and safety goggles.
Activity 19.2   Gather 4-L glass jars with lids, samples of glass, paper, metal, fruits, breads, plastic, and wood, potting soil, water, tongs, rubber gloves, laboratory aprons and safety goggles.

Chapter 20
Field Activity   Provide students with jars or vials in which to collect water samples.
Activity 20.1   Gather 500-mL beakers, metric measuring spoons, 1000-mL flasks, glycerine, pieces of glass tubing bent at right angle, 1-hole rubber stopper, rubber tubing, pans of ice, hot plates, plastic spoons, cardboard, coins, heat-resistant gloves, laboratory aprons, safety goggles.
Activity 20.2   Gather samples of pond water, 500-mL beaker, dropper, microscope slides with coverslips, microscopes, hot plates, tongs, heat-resistant gloves, laboratory aprons, safety goggles.

Chapter 21
Field Activity   No materials required.
Activity 21.1   Gather wax pencils, test tubes with screw caps, 100-mL graduated cylinders, 0.4% phosphate solution, 0.4% nitrate solution, *Chlorella* culture, dropper, light source, safety goggles, rubber gloves, laboratory aprons.
Activity 21.2   Gather water samples, test tubes, test tube racks, masking tape, and graduated cylinders.

Chapter 22
Field Activity   Have Petri dishes, vials, and pH paper available.
Activity 22.1   Gather 2-L soft drink bottles, scissors, tape, thermometers, potting soil, plastic wrap, rubber bands, 100-watt light bulbs, and graph paper.
Activity 22.2   Gather masking tape, microscope slides, petroleum jelly, Petri dishes with lids, and binocular microscopes or hand lenses.

Chapter Planning Guide*

Section	Core	Standard	Enriched	Section	Core	Standard	Enriched
18.1 Minerals and Their Uses	•	•	•	**Blackline Masters** Review Worksheet 18.3 Skills Worksheet 18B	• 	• 	• •
Section Features Earth Science Link, p. 288	•	•	•	**Ancillary Options** Multiculturalism, p. 39		•	•
Blackline Masters Review Worksheet 18.1	•	•	•	**Laboratory Program** Investigation 22		•	•
18.2 Obtaining Minerals	•	•	•	**18.4 Soil Mismanagement**	•	•	•
Section Features Think Critically, p. 292 Historical Notebook, p. 294	• •	• •	• •	**Section Features** Field Activity, p. 299 Dateline 1991, p. 300 Activity 18.2, p. 303	• • •	• • •	• • •
Blackline Masters Review Worksheet 18.2 Skills Worksheet 18A	•	•	•	**Blackline Masters** Review Worksheet 18.4 Issues and Case Studies 14	• 	• •	• •
Ancillary Options One Minute Readings, p. 66		•	•				
18.3 Soil and Its Formation	•	•	•				
Section Features Word Power, p. 295 Activity 18.1, p. 298	•	• •	• •				

Every chapter has two corresponding tests in the Test Book and one Vocabulary Review Worksheet in the Review Book.
*Chapter 18 is not recommended for core students in the Planning Guide on page T12. Recommendations for core students are shown here for teachers who choose to cover this chapter.

Chapter Overview

Chapter 18 introduces two important resources—minerals and soil. Section 18.1 emphasizes the importance of minerals. Section 18.2 presents common methods of obtaining minerals. Section 18.3 discusses soil and the processes involved in soil formation. Section 18.4 discusses human activities that have adverse effects on soil.

Advance Planner

- Bring in samples of soil, sulfur, copper, aluminum, graphite, and quartz for the activity in the Introducing the Chapter section.

Section 18.1
- Obtain an aluminum can, a glass jar, a pencil, a penny, a piece of jewelry, and a piece of wallboard for the activity in the Motivate section.

Section 18.2
- Display photographs of a dredging vessel and manganese nodules collected from the ocean floor for the activity in the Motivate section.

Section 18.3
- Obtain a small sedimentary rock and a hammer for the demonstration in the Motivate section.
- Provide students with clear plastic cups, different types of soil, and rock particles of varying sizes for the Activity.
- Provide students with samples of sand, silt, and clay, and hand lenses for the Closure activity.

Section 18.4
- Obtain soil, a shallow tray, a container, and water for the activity in the Motivate section.
- Obtain soil, a sifter, two funnels, filter paper, a container, and water for the Demonstration.

Introducing the Chapter

Display a container of soil and small samples of sulfur, copper, aluminum, graphite, and quartz. Challenge students to identify each substance on display. Ask what these samples have in common. Point out that minerals, such as those shown, compose a large part of soil. Ask students what other substances might be contained in soil.

Section 18.1 Minerals and Their Uses

pp. 287–289

Performance Objectives
- Identify some of the characteristics of minerals.
- List several ways that minerals are used.

Skills Objective
- Compare mineral use of the United States with that of other countries.

Section Vocabulary
mineral   ore

Motivate
Display an aluminum can, a glass jar, a pencil, a piece of jewelry, a penny, and a piece of wallboard. Ask students what all of the materials on display have in common. Lead students to recognize that all of these substances are made using one or more minerals. Explain that minerals are inorganic solids that have a definite chemical composition and a regularly occurring arrangement of atoms.

Teaching Strategies
Reinforce   Have students identify the properties of minerals. Write each property on the chalkboard as it is named. Ask: Why is it that diamond and graphite, both of which are pure carbon, do not fit the definition of a mineral? In what ways do these substances fit the definition?

Activity   Have students copy Table 18.1 into their notebooks. Challenge them to expand the table by adding five additional minerals and their uses. Have students form cooperative groups and combine their data. Hold a contest to see which group can come up with the largest table.

Evaluate
Closure   Have students create a concept map that explains the relationships among minerals, elements, compounds, ores, metals, and non-metals. Have students share their concept maps with each other to review the section concepts.

Section 18.2 Obtaining Minerals

pp. 290–293

Performance Objectives
- Describe methods for locating and extracting minerals.
- Identify and explain ways in which extraction methods may affect the environment.

Skills Objective
- Infer how recycling and reuse of materials can reduce pollution and conserve resources.

Section Vocabulary
None

Motivate
Display a photograph of a ship that is equipped to carry out dredging operations. Also display photographs of manganese nodules that have been mined from the ocean floor. Use the photographs to initiate a discussion about dredging and the types of minerals that are obtained in this way.

Teaching Strategies
Activity   Have students create a table that compares and contrasts methods of mineral extraction. Students should include a definition or description of each mining method, identify minerals that are obtained in the method, and identify how the type of mining adversely affects the environment. Ask students to identify ways to restore an area to its original condition after each type of mining operation has been completed.

Discuss   As a class, discuss ways to conserve minerals. Be sure to emphasize the value of reuse, recycling, and substitution as part of the discussion.

Evaluate
Closure   Have students revise the concept maps they started in the first section of the chapter. Their revised concept maps should include the three types of mining methods, the term *conservation*, and the principles of reuse, recycling, and substitution.

Section 18.3 Soil and Its Formation

pp. 295–297

Performance Objectives
- Describe the relationship between climate and soil formation.
- Identify different soil types and how they influence soil characteristics.

  • Think critically about the effect of vegetation removal on soil fertility.

Section Vocabulary
bedrock   parent rock   soil   soil profile

Motivate
Lightly strike a small sedimentary rock, such as shale or slate, with a hammer. Have students observe the small rock particles that break off the larger rock. Strike the rock again, and have students again observe the particles. Ask students what will happen to the size of the rock if you continue striking it with the hammer. Ask students to explain what will happen if you struck some of the smaller particles with a hammer. Explain to students that over time, the particles would continue to break apart into smaller and smaller particles. Explain that processes, which break rock into smaller and smaller particles occur in nature. Tell students that as rocks break apart, they combine with other particles to form soil.

Teaching Strategies
Reteach   Review the role of decomposers in the environment. Challenge students to explain the role of these organisms in the formation of soil. Extend the discussion by having students discuss the role of pioneer organisms, such as lichens, in soil formation.

Reinforce   Review the definitions of the terms *weathering* and *erosion* with students. Explain that while these processes are related they are not the same. Have students write a paragraph in which they describe the relationship between these two processes. Encourage students to incorporate a definition of each term in their paragraph.

Activity   Provide students with clear plastic cups, different types of soil, and rock particles of various sizes. Have students use the materials they are given to create a model soil profile for a mature soil. Have students label each layer (horizon) on their model.

Evaluate
Closure   Provide students with hand lenses and unlabeled samples of clay soil, sandy soil and silt. Have students identify each type of soil particle.

Section 18.4   Soil Mismanagement
pp. 299–300
Performance Objectives
  • Identify the causes of soil mismanagement.
  • Predict the possible effects of soil mismanagement.

Skills Objective
  • Analyze common farming and agricultural practices to determine their impact on soil and the environment.

Section Vocabulary
None

Motivate
Place some soil in a shallow tray and tilt the tray at an angle of about 30 to 35 degrees. Use a beaker to pour water onto the top of the tray. Have students observe the effect the water has on the soil. Explain that the process by which soil is carried away by such agents as running water or wind is called *erosion*.

Teaching Strategies
Reinforce   Review the nitrogen cycle, emphasizing its importance in helping soil remain nutrient-rich. Use this discussion to help students recognize how planting the same types of plants in an area year after year could deplete the soil of certain nutrients.

Demonstrate   To demonstrate the effect of compaction on soil, place equal amounts of soil in each of two funnels containing filter paper. Run the soil in one container through a sifter before placing it in the funnel. Point out that the sifter increases the number of air spaces in the soil. Compact the soil in the second funnel using a mortar. Pour equal amounts of water into each of the funnels. Have students observe the effect of soil compaction on water flow. Challenge students to explain why such compacted soil would be poor for the growth of plants.

Evaluate
Closure   Have students write a paragraph that addresses each of the objectives. Review the paragraphs as a class.

Chapter Resources

Teaching Tip for Feature
Historical Notebook: Out of the Soil and into the Ground
- Have students research the use of iron in different ancient cultures and prepare a display that shows various types of ancient iron tools. Challenge students to explain how each tool changed the lives of people.

Teaching Tips for Field Activity
- Caution students not to examine road cuts in areas that may be prone to falling rocks. Also encourage students to wear appropriate clothing.
- You may want students to collect and examine small soil samples. Have students view the samples with a hand lens to identify the sizes of the soil particles making up each layer.

Answers to Field Activity
Check students' sketches for logic and accuracy.

Teaching Tips for Activities

ACTIVITY 18.1
Time Day 1: 45 min; Day 2: 15 min
Group Size 2–3 students
Inference Living organisms give off carbon dioxide gas.
Safety Tips Remind students to tie back long hair, wear safety goggles, and use tongs to handle the hot crucible.

Analysis
1. To kill any living organisms.
2. Actual observations will vary, but the color changes in test tube A should indicate the presence of carbon dioxide.
3. Accept all logical responses.

Conclusion
Yes. The sample of unheated soil produced carbon dioxide, while the sample of heated soil did not.

ACTIVITY 18.2
Time Day 1: One class period; Days 2–5: 20 min
Group Size 2–3 students
Hypothesis: Earthworms will break down organic matter and make tunnels, mixing the soil.
Safety Tips Have students wash their hands with warm, soapy water after the activity.

Analysis
1. They were broken down further.
2. The layers of soil became somewhat mixed.
3. Answers will vary.
4. Accept all logical responses.
5. Accept all logical responses.

Conclusion
Accept all responses supported by evidence.

Answers to End of Chapter Questions
Concept Review
1. Reuse, recycling, and substitution.
2. Chemical weathering breaks apart rocks by altering their chemical composition. Mechanical weathering changes only the sizes of rocks.
3. Sand, silt, and clay. Sand is soil with the largest sized particles. Silt is composed of particles of medium size. Clay is made up of small, fine particles.
4. Climate affects the chemical makeup of soil in terms of nutrient content and also determines the ability of the soil to absorb or resist allowing water to pass through it.
5. Many agricultural methods deplete the soil of nutrients, aid in the process of erosion, or make soils unable to absorb water through compaction.

Think Critically
1. Soil in a grassland is more fertile because the minerals are not leached deep into the soil.
2. The political instability of a nation can make trade in minerals with that country impossible.
3. Accept all logical responses.
4. The agricultural process would suffer because nutrient-rich soil would no longer be washed into the delta region.
5. Soil is considered renewable because it is replaced over time. However, because soil takes so long to form and is being eroded or depleted of minerals at a faster rate than it is formed, some consider it a nonrenewable resource.

Graphic Analysis
1. North America and South America.
2. Silver, gold, magnesium, and platinum.
3. They must import all metals.
4. Iron, manganese, plantinum, lead, and nickel.
5. It may be more economical.
6. Most metals go to northern industrial nations.
7. By negotiations concerning the metals trade.

Chapter Planning Guide

Section	Core	Standard	Enriched	Section	Core	Standard	Enriched
19.1 Solid Wastes	•	•	•	**Ancillary Options** One Minute Readings, p. 54			•
Section Features Think Critically, p. 305 Social Studies Link, p. 306 Field Activity, p. 306	• •	• • •	• • •	**19.3 Topsoil Erosion**	•	•	•
				Section Features Activity 19.1, p. 318	•	•	•
Blackline Masters Review Worksheet 19.1 Skills Worksheet 19B	•	•	• •	**Blackline Masters** Review Worksheet 19.3	•	•	•
Ancillary Options One Minute Readings, p. 106 CEPUP Plastics Activity 6	•	• •	• •	**Ancillary Options** Multiculturalism, p. 161	•	•	•
				19.4 Controlling Land Pollution	•	•	•
Laboratory Program Investigation 23	•	•	•	**Section Features** Earth Science Link, p. 314 Economics Link, p. 316 Activity 19.2	• 	• • •	• • •
19.2 Hazardous Wastes	•	•	•				
Section Features Word Power, p. 309 Dateline 1990, p. 310 Field Activity, p. 310 People and the Env., p. 311	• • • •	• • • •	• • • •	**Blackline Masters** Review Worksheet 14.1 Issues and Case Studies 16	•	• •	• •
Blackline Masters Review Worksheet 19.2 Issues and Case Studies 15 Skills Worksheet 19A	• •	• • •	• •	**Ancillary Options** One Minute Readings, pp. 57–59 CEPUP Household Chemicals Activity 9		• •	• •

Every chapter has two corresponding tests in the Test Book and one Vocabulary Review Worksheet in the Review Book.

Chapter Overview

Chapter 19 focuses on land pollution and ways to control it. Section 19.1 discusses solid wastes and disposal methods. Section 19.2 describes hazardous wastes and problems associated with their disposal. Section 19.3 investigates causes of soil erosion. The chapter concludes in Section 19.4 with a discussion of hazardous waste disposal and environmental protection legislation.

Advance Planner

- Bring in household chemicals as described in the Introducing the Chapter section.

Section 19.1
- Arrange a field trip to a local landfill site.
- Have labels from household chemicals available for the discussion in the Reteach section.

Section 19.2
- Bring in articles describing the nuclear disaster at Chernobyl for the activity in the Motivate section.

Section 19.3
- Bring in two trays, dry soil, and dominoes for the demonstration in the Motivate section.
- Obtain or construct a stream table for the Demonstration.
- Make copies of outline maps of the world for the activity in the Closure section.

Section 19.4
- No materials needed.

Introducing the Chapter

Display containers of household chemicals such as paint thinner, turpentine, rubber cement, stain remover, pesticides, alcohol, paint, used motor oil, lye, acid, and cleaning fluid. Identify the substances as hazardous materials and explore the potential dangers of improper disposal. Challenge students to suggest proper disposal methods.

Section 19.1   Solid Wastes

pp. 305–307

Performance Objectives

- List examples of solid wastes and identify their sources.
- Identify past and present methods used to dispose of solid wastes.

Skills Objective

- Infer the effects a landfill located near an aquatic ecosystem may have on the organisms living there.

Section Vocabulary

solid wastes   landfill

Motivate

Explain that an investigation revealed that the Coast Guard discarded thousands of the lead/acid batteries used to power signal buoys by throwing the batteries into the ocean. Challenge students to identify potential hazards and dangers of such activities.

Teaching Strategies

Field Trip   Plan a trip to a local landfill site. Have students identify the types of wastes accepted at the site, the volume of wastes deposited daily, and the proposed closing dates.

Reteach   Review the physical and chemical properties of the household chemicals described in the Introducing the Chapter section. Examine the labels of some of the containers to find out the disposal methods recommended by the manufacturer.

Evaluate

Closure   On the chalkboard, write the terms *open dumping*, *sanitary landfill*, and *ocean dumping*. Ask students to write a brief description of each disposal method along with its advantages and disadvantages. Have students discuss which method(s) are least harmful to the environment.

Section 19.2   Hazardous Wastes

pp. 308–310

Performance Objectives

- Identify problems associated with hazardous wastes.
- Classify hazardous wastes according to their characteristics.

Skills Objective

- Apply knowledge of hazardous wastes to products used in the home.

Section Vocabulary

hazardous wastes

Motivate

Display and read aloud parts of newspaper and magazine articles about the nuclear disaster at Chernobyl. Discuss the number of people killed and injured, and the potential for future medical problems for people living nearby. Explain that consideration is being given to reopening the nuclear plant at Chernobyl. Ask students to present arguments as to why this should or should not happen.

Teaching Strategies

Reteach   Discuss the need to classify hazardous waste materials in order to design specific disposal methods. Divide students into cooperative learning groups and ask each group to develop a list of hazardous materials utilizing the EPA classification system. Have students identify the properties of each of the materials they list and suggest environmentally-sound disposal methods. You may want to have students prepare a chart to present their conclusions to the class.

Reinforce   Have students bring in copies of labels from household products containing hazardous materials. For each product, discuss the ingredients, their function, and an appropriate disposal method. Ask: What directions are given for use? What recommendations are given for storage, handling, emergency situations (including skin and eye contact), and accidental swallowing of these materials?

Evaluate

Closure   Have students list a variety of hazardous wastes and identify their use. Ask: What specific danger do each of these hazardous materials present? Have students classify the wastes according to the EPA system.

Section 19.3 Topsoil Erosion

pp. 312–313

Performance Objectives
- Identify ways in which soil is lost.
- Describe methods used in agriculture to prevent soil erosion.

Skills Objective
- Predict the effect a loss of water resources in a region may have on soil erosion.

Section Vocabulary
None

Motivate
Set up two small trays containing dry, loose soil. Insert a row of dominoes about 3 cm apart in one tray with the dominoes standing on their short ends. Tell students that the dominoes represent rows of trees. Turn a blow dryer on the high setting and aim the dryer first at one tray, then the other. Have students observe the effect the air coming from the dryer has on the soil in each tray. Discuss how plants can help reduce erosion caused by wind.

Teaching Strategies
Reteach   Write the word erosion on the chalkboard. Beneath this, write the terms *wind* and *running water*. Develop a definition for erosion emphasizing the differences between erosion and weathering. Provide examples of erosion carried out by wind and running water. Extend the discussion by pointing out that glaciers and waves are also agents of erosion.

Demonstrate   Use a stream table to compare erosion along a steep slope and a similar slope that has been terraced. You may also use the stream table to compare erosion in an area of bare soil and a section of sod. Have students observe and describe the differences in the rates of erosion. Ask them to make conclusions based on their observations.

Evaluate
Closure   Provide students with an outline map of the world. Have students reread the section and color in the areas of the world where topsoil erosion is occurring. Include those areas listed in Table 19.2. Challenge students to suggest what, if anything, these areas have in common.

Section 19.4 Controlling Land Pollution

pp. 314–317

Performance Objectives
- Identify and explain four methods for reducing the volume of wastes.
- Discuss benefits and drawbacks to various forms of waste disposal.

Skills Objective
- Infer how solid wastes of one country end up in other countries.

Section Vocabulary
biodegradable

Motivate
Explain that although many people think there is no safe disposal method for hazardous wastes, a number of new methods have been developed which are designed to protect the environment. Ask students to speculate on what these methods might be. Have students list their suggestions in their notebooks and save the list for use in the Closure activity.

Teaching Strategies
Reinforce   Explain that although new waste disposal technologies are constantly being developed, the best method for controlling land pollution is to reduce the amount of wastes being produced. Discuss such practices as recycling, reuse, and substitution.

Enrich   Have students conduct library research to identify federal legislation designed to protect and restore the land environment. Ask students to explain why these laws are important and what each law is designed to accomplish.

Evaluate
Closure   Have students refer to the lists they developed for the activity in the Motivate section and add terms based upon the information in the section.

Chapter Resources

Teaching Tip for Feature

People and the Environment: The Wismut Mines
- Have students research other mining-related diseases such as black lung and asbestosis. Encourage students to present their findings to the class.

Teaching Tip for Field Activity

- Alternatively, students can interview a gardener or nursery worker to find out about pesticides they use.

Answers to Field Activity
Responses will vary.

Teaching Tips for Activities

ACTIVITY 19.1

Time   Day 1: 25 min; Days 2–3: 10 min
Group Size   2 students
Hypothesis   Pollutants will reduce the percentage of radish seeds that germinate.
Safety Tips   None.

Analysis
1. Seedlings will likely grow best in the control dish, because of the lack of pollutants.
2. Responses will vary depending on results.

Conclusion
1. Responses should indicate that polluted water results in reduced plant growth.
2. Responses should indicate that plants grow better with clean water.

ACTIVITY 19.2

Time   Variable
Group Size   Have students work individually.
Prediction   Substances such as bread and plastic will decompose fastest.
Safety Tips   Have students use tongs to handle waste materials and wear laboratory aprons and safety goggles. Have students wash their hands thoroughly with warm, soapy water afterwards.

Analysis
1. The lid with uncovered soil
2. Water from uncovered soil was darker.
3. Lid with grass should take more time.

Conclusion
1. Yes; they slowed rainflow and erosion.
2. Covered soil is protected, lasts longer
3. Bare soil erodes fast. Need plant cover

Answers to End of Chapter Questions

Concept Review
1. Radioactive wastes are placed in water, sealed in stainless steel tanks that are encased in concrete and placed in concrete vaults deep underground.
2. In a sanitary landfill, wastes and soil are alternately layered and ultimately covered with a layer of soil. A secure chemical landfill is built in an area of nonporous bedrock to prevent leaching, and ultimately covered with a layer of clay.
3. The use of compost enriches soil as materials decompose to form humus.
4. Methods include: limits on packaging, recycling, reusing materials, and substitution.
5. Ocean dumping pollutes water, making it unsafe for wildlife. Increased levels of toxins in food fishes threaten food chains and endanger humans. The water becomes unsafe for recreation. Medical and other wastes may wash ashore and pollute beaches.

Think Critically
1. Radioactive particles can pass through a wide variety of materials. Also, radioactive materials emit particles for a long period of time.
2. In controlled incineration, complete burning takes place, destroying all hazardous wastes.
3. No. Wastes may leak and contaminate soil and groundwater. The area of the landfill may remain contaminated for many years possibly resulting in birth defects and cancer-related illnesses.
4. Gasoline and kerosene are easily washed downward in groundwater systems, contaminating drinking water. Also, these materials are highly flammable and can spread toxic fumes over an area.

Computer Activity
Check student graphs for accuracy.

Graphic Analysis
1. Deep well injection
2. The wastes could enter the groundwater supply.
3. Liquid hazardous wastes
4. Liquid wastes cannot pass through nonporous, impermeable rock.
5. To prevent wastes from entering the water supply
6. The characteristics of rock layers below the water table

CHAPTER 20 WATER

Chapter Planning Guide*

Section	Core	Standard	Enriched	Section	Core	Standard	Enriched
20.1 Uses for Water	•	•	•	**Ancillary Options** CEPUP Investigating Groundwater, Activities 1–5		•	•
Section Features Social Studies Connection, p. 324	•	•	•	**20.3 Water Treatment**	•	•	•
Blackline Masters Review Worksheet 20.1 Skills Worksheet 20B	•	• •	• •	**Section Features** Dateline 1993, p. 331 Think Critically, p. 332 Health Link, p. 333 Field Activity, p. 333 Activity 20.1, p. 334	• • •	• • • • •	• • • • •
20.2 Water Resources	•	•	•	**Blackline Masters** Review Worksheet 20.3	•	•	•
Section Features Word Power, p. 327 Social Studies Connection, p. 330 Activity 20.2, p. 337	• •	• • •	• • •	**Laboratory Program** Investigation 24		•	•
Blackline Masters Review Worksheet 20.2 Skills Worksheet 20A Issues and Case Studies 17	• •	• • •	• • •				

Every chapter has two corresponding tests in the Test Book and one Vocabulary Review Worksheet in the Review Book.
*Chapter 20 is not recommended for core students in the Planning Guide on page T12. Recommendatons for core students are shown here for teachers who choose to cover this chapter.

Chapter Overview

Chapter 20 investigates the availability of water for human consumption. Section 20.1 discusses residential, industrial, and agricultural water needs and the economic importance of water. Section 20.2 describes water resources and problems caused by overuse of water. Section 20.3 discusses water purification methods.

Advance Planner

- Obtain a used water meter from a local water company for the activity in the Introducing the Chapter section.
- Prepare an overhead transparency of a world map showing average annual precipitation for the discussion in the Introducing the Chapter section.

Section 20.1
- Arrange for a speaker from the water service company.

Section 20.2
- Have a 1000-mL beaker, water, and sand available for the Demonstration.
- Make a transparency of a map of the local drainage basin system for the activity in the Reteach section.

Section 20.3
- Have a jar and a classroom aquarium available for the discussion in the Motivate section.
- Contact a local water treatment plant to make arrangements for a class field trip.
- Have soil, gravel, clay, a large cylinder, water, a watch or clock with a second hand, filter paper, beakers, and aluminum trays on hand for the Activity.
- Obtain alum for the Demonstration.

Introducing the Chapter

Show how to read a water meter and calculate daily water use. Have students determine how much water their family uses in one day. Ask students why this daily consumption cannot be multiplied by 365 to get an accurate yearly consumption rate. (Responses should include that not all water use activities are carried out on a daily basis.)

Display a transparency of a map showing average annual precipitation for the world. Have students identify areas that receive the greatest and the least precipitation. Discuss how the amount of rainfall an area receives affects its population and economy.

Section 20.1   Uses for Water

pp. 323–326

Performance Objectives
- Describe the ways in which people use water.
- Explain why water conservation is important.

Skills Objective
- Infer ways in which water can be conserved.

Section Vocabulary
irrigation

Motivate
Have students brainstorm ways in which people use water. List their suggestions on the chalkboard. Have students copy the list of terms for use again later in the section.

Teaching Strategies
Activity   Direct students to calculate the average daily consumption rate for each activity listed in Table 20.1. Have students prepare a graph of the data. Ask students to identify uses for water not included in the table, and speculate about how much water each of these activities might use.

Guest Speaker   Contact a representative from your local water service company to speak to your class. Topics you may wish to have the speaker address include where the drainage basins for your water supply are located, the population size served by these water resources, and how much water is consumed locally for residential, industrial, and agricultural uses.

Reteach   Have students construct charts comparing four methods of irrigation. Charts should include information about suitable soil conditions and land topography as well as the pros and cons of each irrigation method. Encourage students to include a column listing the most appropriate types of crops for each type of irrigation.

Enrich   Have students do library research on hydroponics. They can set up a hydroponics experiment or create displays or models that demonstrate methods used in hydroponics.

Evaluate
Closure   Ask students to review the list of water uses they made during the Motivate activity. Have students work in cooperative groups to propose possible methods by which the amount of water used for each activity can be reduced.

Section 20.2   Water Resources

pp. 327–329

Performance Objectives
- Explain ways in which fresh water is naturally stored as a resource.
- Predict the effects of the depletion of an aquifer and the damming of rivers in ecosystems that rely on these water sources.

Skills Objective
- Predict what will happen to organisms in a bay when a nutrient-rich stream entering the bay is dammed.

Section Vocabulary
overdraft   water table

Motivate
Have students recall the water cycle studied in Chapter 3. Ask them to describe Earth's source of fresh water and the forms in which it exists. (Precipitation; runoff, lakes, ponds, groundwater.)

Teaching Strategies
Demonstrate   Half-fill a 1000-mL beaker with sand and pour about 300 mL of water into the sand. Have students observe the movement of the water through the sand and describe their observations. Explain to students that the bottom of the beaker represents an impervious layer of rock and the sand represents permeable rock layers. Compare the parts of this model to Figure 20.7. Identify on the model the zone of saturation, the zone of aeration, and the water table. To extend the demonstration, ask students to compare their observations to the movement of water through soil.

Reteach   Display a transparency that shows the locations of the drainage basins for your area. Trace the path of the water from the drainage basin to your community pointing out any reservoirs, dams, or human-made structures such as aqueducts and water purification plants that appear along the route. Discuss the purpose of each structure.

Discuss   Identify and discuss problems related to drought and overdraft. Have students conduct research on how different communities address these problems. They may prepare a written or oral report summarizing their findings.

Enrich   Have students construct three-dimensional models showing cross-sections of aquifers and artesian formations. Students may also produce diagrams showing how a water pump draws water from a well.

Evaluate

Closure Have students draw a diagram of an aquifer. Have them trace the movement of water from its source to a home.

Section 20.3 Water Treatment

pp. 331–333

Performance Objectives
- Explain why fresh water in many parts of the world is not potable.
- Trace the sequence of events involved in the purification of water.

Skills Objective
- Infer why ice served in regions with poor water quality may cause intestinal disorders in people.

Vocabulary
aeration   desalination

Motivate

Remove some water from a classroom aquarium. Ask students whether or not they would drink this water and ask them to justify their responses. Discuss reasons why untreated water should not be used for drinking purposes.

Teaching Strategies

Field Trip Visit a local water treatment plant. Have students note the processes occurring in the plant and the sequence in which they occur. Arrange for some students to photograph or videotape processes occurring in the plant for use in classroom discussions.

Activity Have students add three tablespoons of a prepared soil sample (consisting of equal parts of sand, gravel, and clay) to a large cylinder. Have them stopper the cylinder, shake it up, and then allow the water to stand undisturbed. As the water stands, ask students to observe the rate at which each type of material settles out. Next have students pour the water from the cylinder through a filter into a beaker. Have students use their observations to describe the processes of sedimentation and filtration.

Demonstrate Use the filtered water from the above Activity. Add a few drops of saturated alum ($Al_2(SO_4)_3 \bullet 18H_2O$) and ammonium hydroxide to the filtered water sample and allow the sample to stand for 20 minutes. Direct students to observe the water and note how the water becomes clearer. Challenge students to explain what occurs in the water after the chemicals have been added.

Reteach Ask students why chlorine is added to swimming pools. Discuss how chlorine kills disease-causing organisms.

Evaluate

Closure Have students construct a flow chart showing how water is purified in a water treatment plant. Have them identify the types of impurities removed during each stage of the water treatment process.

Chapter Resources

Teaching Tip for Feature
Social Studies Connection: The Great Dam of China
- Bring in a map of China and have students trace the path of the Yangtze River.

Teaching Tips for Field Activity
- Obtain samples of pond water from a biological supply company or use water from puddles.
- Have students centrifuge their water samples to increase the likelihood that protozoa will be visible.

Answers to Field Activity
Filtering removes many substances; however, depending upon the size of the filter paper pores, some microscopic organisms and most of the coloring will pass through.

Teaching Tips for Activities

ACTIVITY 20.1
Time   One class period
Group Size   4 students
Prediction   Evaporation and condensation should produce fresh water from seawater.
Safety Tips   Students should wear safety goggles. Assemble the stoppers and delivery tubes using only fire-polished glass tubing. Provide tongs, heat-resistant gloves, and pads for handling the heated flasks. Remind students to turn off the hot plates and allow time for glassware to cool before cleaning.

Analysis
1. To prevent water vapor from escaping into the air.
2. Step 1 should produce more precipitate than Step 6.
3. The water in the flask evaporated and condensed in the rubber tubing, then flowed into the beaker.

Conclusion
Responses will vary.

ACTIVITY 20.2
Time   One class period
Group Size   2 students
Hypothesis   Boiling kills microorganisms.
Safety Tips   Students should wear safety goggles. Remind students to wash their hands in warm, soapy water after handling the pond water samples. Have paper towels on hand to clean up

spills immediately. Provide heat-resistant pads and gloves and caution students to handle the heated beaker carefully.

Procedure
Order pond water from a biological supply company or make a hay–grass infusion.

Analysis
1. Moving organisms should be visible only in the unboiled water.
2. The unboiled water.

Conclusion
1. It kills microscopic organisms.
2. Responses will vary.

Answers to End of Chapter Questions
Concept Review
1. Water may be undrinkable due to pollution.
2. Water is delivered directly where it is needed, eliminating water loss due to evaporation.
3. The spaces between soil particles must allow water to flow through freely instead of pooling.
4. The zone or aeration is similar to the source of a river because water enters at both locations. The zone of discharge is similar to the mouth of a river in that water leaves both these places.
5. Reservoirs can flood a dry habitat, lower the water level downstream, or change the speed of stream flow thereby affecting the temperature and oxygen content of the water.

Think Critically
1. Freezing and boiling salt water causes the water to separate from the salt during physical changes.
2. Freezing removes most of the salts.
3. Winds must be taken into consideration when using overhead sprinkling systems because a strong wind could misdirect the water away from the plants.
4. The drip and trickle method is best for irrigating farms with steep slopes because it places the water at the roots of the plant and does not allow for too much loss from runoff.
5. Much of the Ogallala Aquifer is in arid regions and it is not receiving enough water to replenish itself.

Graphic Analysis
1. The sedimentation tank.
2. It passes through screens.
3. After filtering, and before the water is sent to the reservoir.
4. Aeration and sterilization.

Chapter Planning Guide

Section	Core	Standard	Enriched	Section	Core	Standard	Enriched
21.1 The Water Pollution Problem	•	•	•	**Blackline Masters** Review Worksheet 21.2 Skills Worksheet 21A	 • •	 • •	 • •
Section Features Biology Link, p. 339	•	•	•	**21.3 Radioactivity and Thermal Pollution**		•	•
Blackline Masters Review Worksheet 21.1 Issues and Case Studies 18	 • 	 • •	 • •	**Blackline Masters** Review Worksheet 21.4		•	•
Ancillary Options CEPUP Chemical Survey Act. 7		•	•	**Laboratory Program** Investigation 25	•	•	•
21.2 Chemical Pollutants	•	•	•	**21.4 Controlling Water Pollution**	•	•	•
Section Features Word Power, p. 343 Literature Connection, p.343 Think Critically, p. 344 Historical Notebook, p. 346 Dateline 1955, p. 347 Activity 21.1, p. 348	 • • • • • 	 • • • • • •	 • • • • • •	**Section Features** Dateline 1969, p. 351 Field Activity, p. 352 Activity 21.2	 • • •	 • • •	 • • •
				Blackline Masters Review Worksheet 21.4 Skills Worksheet 21B	 • •	 • •	 • •

Every chapter has two corresponding tests in the Test Book and one Vocabulary Review Worksheet in the Review Book.

Chapter Overview

Chapter 21 investigates problems associated with water pollution. Section 21.1 defines water pollution and describes the historical nature of the water pollution problem. Section 21.2 discusses chemical pollutants and the effects they have on ecosystems and humans. Section 21.3 presents problems associated with radioactive materials entering water systems and thermal pollution. The chapter concludes in Section 21.4 with a discussion of legislation designed to combat water pollution and issues that sometimes make such legislation difficult to enforce.

Advance Planner

- Bring in newspaper or magazine articles about outbreaks of water-borne diseases as described in the Introducing the Chapter section.

Section 21.1
- Arrange a field trip to a water treatment facility.

Section 21.2
- Obtain a color photo of the Chesapeake Bay taken by the Earth Resources Satellite. These images are available from the Chesapeake Bay Foundation.

Section 21.3
- Prepare an overhead transparency of a graph showing the solubility of oxygen in water at various temperatures, ranging from freezing through boiling, for the activity in the Motivate section.
- Obtain an indicator to test for the presence of dissolved oxygen, three test tubes, water, an ice bucket, and a Bunsen burner or other heat source for the Demonstration.

Section 21.4
- Bring in newspaper and magazine articles regarding water quality legislation at local, state, national and international levels.

Introducing the Chapter

Display newspaper and magazine articles about outbreaks of diseases such as typhoid, cholera, dysentery, and malaria. Point out that while such diseases are no longer common threats in the United States, they are a serious health threat in Africa, India, Asia, Latin America, and the Middle East. Indicate that millions of people suffer and/or die as a result of these diseases each year.

Section 21.1 The Water Pollution Problem

pp. 339–342

Performance Objectives
- Explain the link between water pollution and human disease.
- Identify the major causes of water pollution and their sources.

Skills Objective
- Diagram the relationships between sewage, contaminated water, pathogens, and humans.

Section Vocabulary
sewage   sewage treatment plant   pathogens

Motivate
Explain that in developing countries, waters from a single river may be used for transportation, irrigation, washing clothing, cooking, bathing, sewage discharge, garbage disposal, and burying the dead. Have students discuss how these uses may pose a serious health threat to all who come in contact with the river's waters. Point out that worldwide, water pollution is responsible for more illness than any other environmental influence.

Teaching Strategies
Enrich   Have students do library research on pathogens that contaminate water. Students should describe the diseases caused by these pathogens, the means by which the pathogens enter the water, and how they infect people. Ask students to find out in which countries these diseases are most common and propose measures to reduce their prevalence.

Reteach   Use Table 21.1 to review water pollutants and their sources. Discuss which pollutants are most closely associated with agriculture and urban runoff. Have students identify the sources of toxic chemicals.

Field Trip   Arrange a tour of a local water treatment facility. Before the tour, ask students to research five common types of pollutants. Have students find out how these pollutants enter water, and the steps required to remove them. After the tour, have students draw a diagram of the water treatment facility and label the various treatment components.

Evaluate
Closure   Prepare an overhead transparency of Table 21.1 that shows the sources but not the pollutant groups. Challenge the class to supply the missing data for the table.

Section 21.2 Chemical Pollutants

pp. 343–347

Performance Objectives
- Examine the sources and effects of inorganic and organic toxic chemicals.
- Describe the process of eutrophication and its effects on lake ecosystems.

Skills Objective
- Analyze the role of human error in toxic spills.

Section Vocabulary
toxic chemicals   heavy metals
eutrophication

Motivate
Ask students what words come to mind when they hear the word *toxic*. List responses on the chalkboard. Spend a few minutes discussing each response. Have students copy the responses into their notebooks for use in the Closure activity.

Teaching Strategies
Reteach   To develop the concept of eutrophication and its effects, display a color satellite photo of Chesapeake Bay. Discuss the significance of the various colors seen. Point out rivers that feed into the bay and color changes at various points along the rivers. Ask students to explain these differences.

Enrich   Discuss how companies are required to obtain a permit to transport organic chemicals over bridges, through tunnels, and along city streets. The decision whether to issue such a permit is often made in hearings before local government agencies. Have students discuss the pros and cons of such requests. Interested students may want to research how the hearing process works in their own city or town.

Evaluate
Closure   Have students write a summary that gives examples and lists differences between toxic organic and inorganic chemicals. Have them relate this information to the list prepared during the activity in the Motivate section.

Section 21.3 Radioactivity and Thermal Pollution

pp. 349–350

Performance Objective
- Explain the problems of radioactive and thermal pollution.

Skills Objective
- Predict causes of thermal pollution.

Section Vocabulary
thermal pollution

Motivate
Project an overhead transparency of a graph showing the solubility of oxygen in water at various temperatures, ranging from freezing through boiling. Point out that while the solubility of most solids increases with increasing temperature, the same is not the case with gases. Guide students to the understanding that gases, such as oxygen, become less soluble as water temperature increases. Ask: How does the changing solubility of gases relate to thermal pollution and its effect on fishes and other water animals?

Teaching Strategies
Demonstrate   Obtain an indicator to test for the presence of dissolved oxygen. Prepare three test tubes, one with water cooled to near freezing, a second containing water at room temperature, and a third with water heated to near boiling. Test each water sample for the presence of dissolved oxygen. Have students note the results of each test. Ask students to write a paragraph relating the test results to the graph they observed as part of the activity in the Motivate section.

Reteach   In a class discussion, have students generate a list of terms describing the uses of radioactive materials and ways in which radiation may enter and pollute the environment. List the terms on the chalkboard. Be sure to include the term background radiation to refer to radiation that comes from natural sources.

Evaluate
Closure   Have students write a brief summary that explains the sources of radioactive pollutants and illustrates the relationship between radioactivity and thermal pollution. Ask students whether it is possible to eliminate thermal pollution in the presence of nuclear power plants and radioactive wastes.

Section 21.4 Controlling Water Pollution

pp. 351–352

Performance Objectives
- Identify government attempts to control water pollution.
- Describe problems in enforcing laws regarding water pollution.

Skills Objective
- Justify a vote on a water pollution issue that has serious economic impact on a community.

Section Vocabulary
None

Motivate
Display newspaper and magazine articles that deal with legislation concerning water quality at the local, state, national, and international levels. Ask students why such legislation is needed and what effect, if any, such actions have on individuals and businesses.

Teaching Strategies
Discuss   Initiate a classroom discussion about the Clean Air Act. Have students explain why this act is not a set of laws for enforcement. Have students speculate about the effect such legislation is likely to have without enforcement policies to back it up.

Reinforce   Have students prepare a timeline of water pollution legislation. Encourage students to research each piece of legislation and add a brief summary of each to their timelines.

Evaluate
Closure   Present the following scenario to students. A rancher living along a river discovers that his cattle are becoming sick from drinking the river water. Upon further investigation, the rancher discovers that the problem stems from an upstream neighbor's use of pesticides, which are entering the river in the form of runoff. Ask: What recourse might the rancher have in this situation?

Chapter Resources

Teaching Tip for Feature
Historical Notebook: Lake Erie, A Success Story
- Obtain newspaper and magazine accounts of the pollution problem faced by Lake Erie during the 1960s. If possible obtain photographs to share with students that show the polluted status of the lake.

Teaching Tips for Field Activity
- As an alternative to making a table, you may wish to have students prepare a photo essay or home video that identifies pollutants and their sources.

Answers to Field Activity
Likely responses include solid wastes discarded into the water, oil floating along the water surface, detergents or fertilizers as indicated by large populations of algae. Accept all logical responses.

Teaching Tips for Activities

ACTIVITY 21.1
Time   Day 1: 1 class period; Days 2–6: 5–10 min
Group Size   2–3 students
Prediction   Phosphate and nitrate will both increase the growth of *Chlorella*.
Safety Tips   Have students wash their hands in warm, soapy water after handling materials. Have students wear safety goggles and lab aprons during the procedure on Day 1.

Analysis
1. There was little change. Descriptions will vary.
2. The algae grew densely, with a dark green color.
3. The algae grew densely, with a dark green color.
4. The tubes with nitrate and phosphate.

Conclusion
1. The tubes containing phosphate and nitrate contained the most algal growth.
2. Phosphate and nitrate are essential nutrients.
3. Check paragraphs for logic and accuracy.

ACTIVITY 21.2
Time   One class period
Group Size   2–3 students
Hypothesis   Bacteria break down organic matter and use up dissolved oxygen.
Safety Tips   Have students wear rubber gloves, safety goggles, and lab aprons.

Analysis
1. Responses will vary depending on water sources used, but a likely response will be pond water.
2. Greatest: pond water; least: distilled water. Answers may vary.
3. Oxygen.

Conclusion
1. Pond water: microorganisms; dish water: food or microorganisms.
2. Distilled water has been sterilized. Tap and well water are probably free of organisms.

Answers to End of Chapter Questions
Concept Review
1. Nuclear power plants, mine tailings, nuclear test sites, discarded weaponry, weapons research facilities, and medical wastes.
2. Heat can directly or indirectly harm organisms.
3. They can lead to eutrophication.
4. Heavy metals, acids, salts, and radioactive wastes.
5. Primarily sewage.

Think Critically
1. Sewage treatment occurs in several steps: screening, sedimentation and coagulation, filtration, and purification. Not all pollutants are removed.
2. Many forms of pollution may cause these conditions, including eutrophication, thermal pollution, or the presence of toxic chemicals. Physical and chemical studies should be performed to determine the types of pollutants.
3. Yes.
4. Reinforce oil tanks and increase monitoring mechanisms for tanker ships and personnel. No.
5. When threatened with stringent standards, corporations often threaten to move to other areas. These moves affect the local economy.

Graphic Analysis
1. Sewage treatment.
2. At the bar screen.
3. At the chlorination stage.
4. Sludge.
5. It is returned to surface waters.

Chapter Planning Guide

Section	Core	Standard	Enriched	Section	Core	Standard	Enriched
22.1 The Air Pollution Problem	•	•	•	Astronomy Link, p. 366	•	•	•
				Activity 22.1, p. 369		•	•
Section Features Dateline 1976, p. 359	•	•	•	**Blackline Masters** Review Worksheet 22.3	•	•	•
Blackline Masters Review Worksheet 22.1	•	•	•	Skills Worksheet 22A	•	•	•
Skills Worksheet 22B	•	•	•	Issues and Case Studies 19		•	•
Issues and Case Studies 21	•	•	•	**Ancillary Options** One Minute Readings, pp. 19, 52, 60		•	•
Ancillary Options One Minute Readings, p. 8	•	•	•	**22.4 Controlling Air Pollution**	•	•	•
22.2 Air Pollution and Living Things	•	•	•	**Section Features** Activity 22.2, p. 375	•	•	•
Section Features Health Link, p. 360	•	•	•	**Blackline Masters** Review Worksheet 22.4	•	•	•
Blackline Masters Review Worksheet 22.2	•	•	•	Issues and Case Studies 20		•	•
22.3 Global Effects of Air Pollution	•	•	•	**Laboratory Program** Investigation 26		•	•
Section Features Field Activity, p. 362	•	•	•	**22.5 Noise Pollution**	•	•	•
People and the Environment, p. 363		•	•	**Blackline Masters** Review Worksheet 22.5	•	•	•
Word Power, p. 365	•	•	•	**Ancillary Options** One Minute Readings, p. 87	•	•	•
Chemistry Link, p. 365	•	•	•				
Dateline 1978, p. 365	•	•	•				

Every chapter has two corresponding tests in the Test Book and one Vocabulary Review Worksheet in the Review Book. There is also a Unit 6 test in the test book covering Chapters 19–22.

Chapter Overview

Chapter 22 surveys the causes and effects of air and noise pollution. Section 22.1 defines air pollution and identifies various outdoor and indoor air pollutants. Section 22.2 discusses the effects of air pollution on living things. Section 22.3 deals with the topics of acid precipitation, ozone depletion, and global warming. Section 22.4 presents natural and human methods for controlling and minimizing air pollution. Section 22.5 discusses the problem of noise pollution.

Advance Planner
Section 22.1
- Borrow a hot air popcorn machine for the activity in the Motivate section.
- Obtain a filmstrip projector to use for the Demonstration.

Section 22.2
- Contact the American Lung Association for information and a guest speaker.

Section 22.3
- Have containers, vinegar, droppers, and small pieces of magnesium, marble, limestone, and calcite available for the Activity.

Section 22.4
- Arrange for a member of the Society of Automotive Engineers to speak to the class about pollution controls in automobiles.

Section 22.5
- Obtain tuning forks and a resonating box for the activity in the Motivate section.

Introducing the Chapter

Tell students the following investigation was done at a major highway. Samples of grass and soil were tested for the presence of metallic pollutants at various distances from the highway. The soil was also tested at different depths. Have students predict the results of this study, and infer the primary sources of the pollutants.

Section 22.1 The Air Pollution Problem

pp. 357–359

Performance Objectives
- Describe air pollution.
- Explain the historical background of air pollution.
- Identify common air pollutants.

Skills Objective
- Analyze and suggest ways to reduce the amount of air pollutants in the home.

Section Vocabulary

chlorofluorocarbons (CFCs)   oxides
particulates   photochemical smog
pollutants   radon

Motivate

Make some popcorn in a hot air popper before the class arrives, and hide the popper from view. Ask students if they can identify the source of the odor. Show them the source. Have students debate whether popping corn polluted the room. Challenge them to define pollution.

Teaching Strategies

Demonstrate   Darken the room. Use chalk dust and light from a filmstrip projector to show particulate matter. Explain that the very small mass of the particles and the movement of air keep the particulates afloat.

Reteach   On the chalkboard, use chemical equations to show the formation of oxides of carbon, nitrogen, and sulfur.

Evaluate

Closure   Have students identify and describe five sources of air pollution.

Section 22.2 Air Pollution and Living Things

pp. 360–361

Performance Objectives
- Identify the effects of air pollutants on human health.
- Describe the effects of air pollution on plants and animals.

Skills Objective
- Predict how industrial pollution would affect a person who smokes.

Section Vocabulary

emphysema   cancer

Motivate

Discuss how heart disease and cancer are the first and second leading causes of death in the United States. Have students speculate as to why air pollution is a factor in these two diseases.

Teaching Strategies

Reteach   Show transparencies of charts of statistical data on lung disease deaths. Relate the data to air pollution and discuss trends.

Guest Speaker   Arrange for a speaker from the American Lung Association or the American Cancer Society to speak with the class about the role of air pollutants in diseases of the lungs and cancer.

Evaluate

Closure   Have students make a chart listing the major air pollutants and their effects on human health.

Section 22.3 Global Effects of Air Pollution

pp. 362–368

Performance Objectives
- Identify the effects of acid precipitation and ozone depletion.
- Explain the greenhouse effect and global warming.

Skills Objective
- Think critically to evaluate evidence from ice cores and computer models about global warming.

Section Vocabulary

acid precipitation   greenhouse effect
global warming

Motivate

Have the class make a pH chart of common substances. Instruct them to divide the chart into equal sections and place the following substances in their correct pH location. Substances: lye 13.0; garden lime 12.4; ammonia 12.0; Milk of Magnesia 10.5; seawater and baking soda 8.5; blood 7.5; distilled water 7.0; milk 6.7; clean rain 5.6; tomato juice 4.2; apple juice 3.0; vinegar 2.7; lemon juice 2.2; and battery acid 1.0. Explain that acids can form in the atmosphere and fall to Earth in acid rain, with a pH between 5.4 and 2.2.

Teaching Strategies

Activity Allow students to observe the reaction of acids with various substances. Students can add a small piece of magnesium to vinegar in a jar. They can also add a few drops of vinegar to a piece of marble, limestone, or calcite.

Reinforce Draw a diagram of the layers of the atmosphere on the chalkboard. Locate the ozone layer and review its importance. Discuss where the ozone layer is wearing away and the possible effects of ozone depletion.

Evaluate

Closure Ask students to write a short paragraph that defines and lists the causes and effects of acid precipitation, ozone depletion, and global warming.

Section 22.4 Controlling Air Pollution

pp. 370–371

Performance Objectives
- Describe natural processes that help control air pollution.
- Explain human efforts to control air pollution.
- Identify federal legislation for curbing air pollution.

Skills Objective
- Analyze information to suggest things that one person can do to help reduce air pollution.

Motivate

List several air pollution sources on the chalkboard. Have students work in small groups for five minutes to suggest ways to reduce pollution from each source. Discuss the suggestions as a class. Have students copy the list of sources and record the suggestions discussed for use in the Closure activity.

Teaching Strategies

Discuss Tell students that deforestation is creating an air pollution problem. Have students discuss how deforestation may increase air pollution and how the problem can be reduced. If needed, review the processes of photosynthesis and respiration.

Guest Speaker The Society of Automotive Engineers has been working to decrease air pollution caused by automobiles. Invite a member of the society, or a local mechanic, to speak to your class.

Enrich Have students investigate various types of federal air pollution legislation and report on what a specific piece of legislation does.

Evaluate

Closure Have students update the list of sources and solutions for air pollution that they created for the activity in the Motivate section.

Section 22.5 Noise Pollution

p. 372

Performance Objectives
- Describe the problem of noise pollution.
- Explain measures and legislation for controlling noise pollution.

Skills Objective
- Analyze why signs prohibiting the honking of car horns might be posted on roads surrounding hospitals.

Motivate

Use a tuning fork to demonstrate how vibrating objects produce sounds. Demonstrate how volume and pitch can be changed. With another tuning fork and a resonating box, show how sound can be produced with sympathetic vibrations. After the demonstration, ask students to explain how sound can break glass. Relate this example to how loud sounds can cause injury.

Teaching Strategies

Activity Have students shut their eyes and note all the sounds they hear. Have them list these sounds and how often they occur. Have them classify each sound as pleasing or disturbing.

Reteach Introduce the decibel as a measure of loudness. Develop with the class a scale that lists the decibel (db) rating for various common sounds, such as thunder (110 db), and conversation (65 db).

Enrich Have students construct models of the ear. Have students identify each part of the ear and its function in detecting sounds. Have them explain how noise pollution can cause hearing loss.

Evaluate

Closure Ask students to write a paragraph summarizing causes and effects of noise pollution.

Chapter Resources

Teaching Tip for Feature
People and the Environment: Assault on the Past
- Students may directly observe weathering of inscriptions on headstones at a local cemetery.

Teaching Tips for Field Activity
- Have students work in cooperative groups. Encourage two groups to place their dishes in the same areas so students can compare the results.
- Remind students to place their dishes in places where they will be undisturbed. Caution students to obtain permission to place dishes on private property.

Answers to Field Activity
Responses will vary.

Teaching Tips for Activities

ACTIVITY 22.1

Time One or two class periods
Group Size 2–3 students
Hypothesis The greenhouse effect occurs when sunlight-heated air cannot escape.
Safety Tips Caution students to handle scissors and thermometer carefully.

Analysis
1. Check graphs for accuracy.
2. The sealed bottle became hotter.
3. Control: open bottle. Variable: being sealed off.
4. Accept all logical responses.

Conclusion
1. Responses will vary depending on hypotheses.
2. The extra plastic wrap will probably not affect the model. The first sheet is efficient in trapping most of the heat.
3. Accept all logical responses.

ACTIVITY 22.2

Time Day 1: 30 min; Day 2: 50 min
Group Size 2–3 students
Hypothesis The number and types of particulates vary in different locations.
Safety Tips Caution students to obtain permission to be on private property.

Analysis
1. The control slide provided a reference for comparison.
2. Responses will vary.
3. Responses will vary. Check students' descriptions for logic and accuracy.

Conclusion
1. Responses will vary depending upon hypothesis stated.
2. Responses will vary.

Answers to End of Chapter Questions
Concept Review
1. The atmosphere circulates, moving pollutants from one place to another. Also, air pollution produces the greenhouse effect and ozone depletion.
2. Bubbles in the ice are filled with air from various times in Earth's past.
3. Auto emissions can produce acid rain.
4. Smoking and air pollution. Smoking is avoidable.
5. Chlorine and fluorine from CFCs act as catalysts repeatedly.

Think Critically
1. Exposure to UV radiation can lead to skin cancer.
2. Economic considerations.
3. Ozone in the upper atmosphere acts as a shield against UV radiation. In the lower atmosphere it is an air pollutant.
4. Prevailing winds carry air pollution there.

Computer Activity
Check students' work for logic and accuracy.

Graphic Analysis
1. 1850: 288 ppm; 1950: 310 ppm
2. plus 7.6%
3. Accept all logical responses.

Unit Overview

Unit 7 presents the major environmental problems faced by the global commons, and suggests ways that people can reduce the adverse affects of their actions on the global ecosystem. Chapter 23 addresses the problem of loss of habitat and explores the need for maintaining biodiversity. Chapter 24 explores ways to attain a sustainable ethic that will help maintain the availability of resources for future generations. The book draws to a close in Chapter 25 with a discussion of activities in progress to correct past environmental damage and protect the environment for future generations.

Introducing the Unit

Discussion Display photographs showing various types of environmental damage, such as clear-cut forests, a smog-filled skyline, and evidence of land and water pollution. Ask students whether or not they would want to live in any of these areas and have them explain their responses. Use this discussion to introduce the need to improve environmental quality for future generations.

Teacher Resources

Audiovisual
The Diversity of Life, video, 25 minutes, National Geographic Society, 1993.
The House of Man I: Our Changing Environment, 17-minute film, Britannica, 1985.
The House of Man I: Our Crowded Environment, 11-minute film, Britannica, 1985.

Computer Software
Pollute, Apple II/IBM, Diversified Educational Enterprises.
Ecological Modeling, Apple II, Conduit.
Balance of the Planet, Macintosh, Chris Crawford Games.

Suggested Readings
Daly, Herman E., and John B. Cobb, Jr., *For the Common Good: Redirecting the Economy Toward Community, the Environment, and a Sustainable Future*, Beacon Press, 1989.

Naar, John, *Design for a Livable Planet: How You Can Clean up the Environment*, Harper & Row, 1990.
Koren, David C., *Getting to the 21st Century: Voluntary Action and the Global Agenda*, Kumarian Press, 1990.
Anderson, Bruce N., ed., *Ecologue: The Environmental Catalogue and Consumer's Guide for a Safe Earth*, Prentice Hall Press, 1990.

Advance Preparation

Chapter 23
Field Activity No materials required.
Activity 23.1 Gather index cards, red marking pens, #2 pencils, uncooked rice, paper 20 cm x 20 cm, metric rulers, scissors, graph paper, and colored pencils in six colors.
Activity 23.2 Gather newspapers, scissors, glue, or tape.

Chapter 24
Field Activity No materials required.
Activity 24.1 Gather newspapers, large mixing bowls, eggbeaters, water, liquid laundry starch, hand lenses, large square pans, screens, blotting paper, and rolling pins.
Activity 24.2 Gather marking pens of assorted colors, large sheets of posterboard, and magazines suitable for cutting.

Chapter 25
Field Activity No materials required.
Activity 25.1 No materials supplied by teacher.
Activity 25.2 Have colored pencils available.

Chapter Planning Guide

Section	Core	Standard	Enriched	Section	Core	Standard	Enriched
23.1 The Loss of Biodiversity	•	•	•	Word Power, p. 387	•	•	•
Section Features Biology Link, p. 381	•	•	•	People and the Environment, p. 389	•	•	•
Blackline Masters Review Worksheet 23.1	•	•	•	**Blackline Masters** Review Worksheet 23.3 Skills Worksheet 23B	• •	• •	• •
Ancillary Options One Minute Readings, p. 31	•	•	•	**Ancillary Options** Multiculturalism, p. 131	•	•	•
23.2 Humans and Habitats	•	•	•	**23.4 Controlling Habitat Destruction**	•	•	•
Section Features Dateline 1971, p. 385 Activity 23.2, p. 395	• •	• •	• •	**Section Features** Field Activity, p. 390 Biology Link, p. 391 Activity 23.1, p.392	• • •	• • •	• • •
Blackline Masters Review Worksheet 23.2 Issues and Case Studies 22 Skills Worksheet 23A	• •	• • •	• • •	**Blackline Masters** Review Worksheet 23.4	•	•	•
23.3 The Importance of Biodiversity	•	•	•	**Ancillary Options** One Minute Readings, p. 2	•	•	•
Section Features Think Critically, p. 387		•	•	**Laboratory Program** Investigation 28	•	•	•

Every chapter has two corresponding tests in the Test Book and one Vocabulary Review Worksheet in the Review Book.Unit 1 test in the test book covering Chapters 19–22.

Chapter Overview

The focus of Chapter 23 is habitat destruction and its effect on biodiversity. Section 23.1 introduces the loss of biodiversity in terms of extinction. Section 23.2 focuses on the role of humans in habitat destruction. Section 23.3 discusses how biodiversity benefits humans and the global ecosystem. The chapter concludes in Section 23.4 with suggestions for maintaining biodiversity.

Advance Planner

- Bring in aspirin, a pencil, orange juice, a sheet of paper, a bicycle tire, a chocolate bar, or other items for the discussion in the Introducing the Chapter section.

Section 23.1
- Provide students with outline maps of the United States for the Activity.

Section 23.2
- Have photographs of deforested regions available for the Motivate section.

Section 23.3
- Prepare an overhead transparency of a map that shows the locations of the world's rainforests, and make about a dozen construction paper cut-outs representing the state of Oregon (same scale as the map) for the activity in the Motivate section.

Section 23.4
- Obtain photographs of objects made from teak, mahogany, or ebony as described in the Enrich section.
- Arrange a class field trip to a zoo or wildlife preserve.

Introducing the Chapter

Display a variety of objects that are made possible through biodiversity. Ask students to identify the living things from which each object is produced. Ask students how their lives would be different if they no longer had these items.

Section 23.1   The Loss of Biodiversity

pp. 381–385

Performance Objectives

- Discuss extinction and how it occurs.
- Explain habitat destruction, the loss of biodiversity, and how they are related.

Skills Objective

- Relate the concepts of extinction, biodiversity, and habitat destruction.

Section Vocabulary

extinction   biodiversity   habitat destruction   alien species

Motivate

Ask each student to come up with the names of three or four different kinds of organisms. The goal is to develop a class list containing a total of 100 different species. Go down each row of students seeking names and ask a volunteer to write each name on the chalkboard. Continue until the list is complete. Explain that the list represents the number of organisms that are driven to extinction each day.

Teaching Strategies

Reteach   Use a geologic time scale to review natural extinction processes. Point out that geologic periods on the scale often coincide with the appearance of new varieties of organisms and the extinction of large numbers of other species.

Activity   Divide the class into four cooperative groups. Assign each group one quadrant of the United States. Have each group research two recently extinct species (one plant and one animal) for each state in their quadrant. Have students list the names of the organisms in the appropriate state on an outline map of the United States. Have groups pool their data to complete the map for all 50 states.

Evaluate

Closure   Have students write a summary explaining habitat destruction, the loss of biodiversity and how they are related.

Section 23.2   Humans and Habitats

pp. 383–385

Performance Objectives

- Explain the causes of deforestation and the impact of deforestation on biodiversity.
- Investigate the death of the Aral Sea and other aquatic habitat destruction.

Skills Objective

- Deduce the effects of deforestation on global warming.

Section Vocabulary

None

Motivate

Show students photographs of forest regions that have been stripped of their vegetation. Ask students what organisms may have once lived in these regions and write their responses on the chalkboard. Allow students time to generate a lengthy list that includes plants, animals, and fungi. Ask students to identify ways in which the organisms listed are important to each other (as part of food chains and food webs) and important to people (for food, clothing, medicines, and so on). Emphasize how loss of biodiversity in one biome affects people and the environmental balance.

Teaching Strategies

Discuss   Ask students to suggest reasons why deforestation occurs. Extend the discussion to show how each situation often leads to other problems. For example, the soils in forest lands cleared for farming often are unable to sustain crops. Ask students to suggest ways in which human demands can be met without deforestation.

Evaluate

Closure   Write the terms *deforestation, biodiversity, natural resources, habitat destruction,* and *population growth* on the chalkboard. Have students make a concept map relating these terms.

Section 23.3 The Importance of Biodiversity

pp. 386–388

Performance Objective
- State ways in which biodiversity benefits humans.

Skills Objective
- Contrast mass extinctions of the past with the one occurring today.

Section Vocabulary
wilderness

Motivate
Display an overhead transparency of an outline map of the world's rainforest areas. Remind students that Earth's rain forests are the areas of greatest biodiversity. Hold up a paper cutout representing an area the size of the state of Oregon. Explain that the cut-out represents the amount of rain forest being destroyed each year. Use the cutouts to cover up the rainforest areas. Ask students to estimate how long it will take for all of Earth's rain forests to be destroyed.

Teaching Strategies
Discuss   Discuss the variety of foods available worldwide. Point out that all foods are products of organisms. Ask students what happens to the variety of available foods as biodiversity is decreased. Have students imagine how their diet might change if two food sources were eliminated each day.

Biology Connection   Ethnobiologists are developing relationships with native rain forest populations to find out about their traditional medicines. It is hoped that the research will yield information about promising new drugs before their sources become extinct through deforestation. For more information about this topic, students can consult the December, 1993, issue of *Discover* magazine.

Enrich   Have students conduct library research to find the names of at least 15 different organisms from which medicines are obtained. Have students create a poster or display in which they identify the organism, the medicine made from the organism, and the illness the medicine is used to treat.

Evaluate
Closure   Ask students to create a list of five important human needs. Have them relate each need in some way to plant and animal life.

Section 24.4 Controlling Habitat Destruction

pp. 390–391

Performance Objectives
- Describe the social and economic factors behind habitat destruction.
- Explain the Endangered Species Act and how it is applied.

Skills Objective
- Analyze the possibility of building a replacement ecosystem.

Section Vocabulary
gene bank

Motivate
Discuss some of the problems involved in controlling habitat destruction. As an example, ask students what the needs of a small family living in a rainforest region might be. Ask students what resources the family may take from the environment to meet these needs. Next, ask students to imagine that an outside group offers this family large sums of money for resources that are found only on their property. Explain that similar occurrences take place in developing nations. As a result, such nations are at risk of completely depleting their resources.

Teaching Strategies
Enrich   Show photographs of objects made from rare and expensive woods. Such objects may include clocks, musical instruments, and furniture. Use the photographs to help students develop an appreciation for why certain woods are in high demand.

Field Trip   Arrange a field trip to a zoo or wildlife preserve that has rare or endangered species on display. Have students ask questions about the role of such facilities in preserving biodiversity.

Evaluate
Closure   Have students write a summary relating biodiversity, habitat destruction, and the Endangered Species Act.

Chapter Resources

Teaching Tip for Feature

People and the Environment: Plant Comebacks
- Discuss the benefits and drawbacks of reintroducing a native species to an area.

Teaching Tips for Field Activity

- Have students share their observations with their classmates by preparing a photo essay or home video.
- Caution students to avoid poisonous plants, wear proper clothing, and obtain permission before entering private property.

Answers to Field Activity

Responses will vary. Likely forms of destruction may include habitat destruction created by the clearing of land for construction or the trampling of grass by walking or vehicles.

Teaching Tips for Activities

ACTIVITY 23.1

Time One class period
Group Size 2 students
Hypothesis Availability of food can affect the size of a bald eagle population.
Safety Tips Caution students to work carefully with the scissors.

Analysis

1. Fish population decreases.
2. The eagle population may decrease in size or remain the same size. Answers will vary.
3. Eagle population will increase.

Conclusion

Responses should reflect data.

ACTIVITY 23.2

Time Variable
Group Size 3 students
Safety Tips No special safety precautions are necessary.

Analysis

1. Responses will vary.
2. Responses will vary.
3. Accept all logical responses.
4. Accept all logical responses.

Conclusion

1. Check reports for logic and accuracy.
2. Accept all logical responses.

Answers to End of Chapter Questions

Concept Review

1. The extinctions of many species of organisms in a short period of time. Refer to Figure 23.1.
2. Peoples living in these countries often clear forests for living space and food, as well as for a source of energy.
3. Developed countries encourage deforestation by paying high prices for forest products.
4. Rivers that once fed into the lake have been diverted.
5. A gene bank is a secure place where plants, seeds, and genetic materials are stored.

Think Critically

1. Introduced species may compete with existing species for resources and drive existing species out of the ecosystem.
2. Because many medicines are derived from rainforest organisms and many rain forest species have not yet been discovered.
3. As habitats are altered or destroyed, organisms that are unable to adapt may become extinct.
4. Wild strains often have desirable traits that can be genetically transferred to existing crops. Yes.
5. Protecting the habitat ensures that the species has everything it needs for survival.

Graphic Analysis

1. With an x shape. Four.
2. The Cambrian.
3. Yes. After the extinction rate peaks, the evolution rate increases, peaking shortly thereafter.
4. A mass extinction opens up niches, which organisms then evolve to fill.
5. A large mass extinction had just occurred, opening up many niches.

CHAPTER 24 TOWARD A SUSTAINABLE FUTURE

Chapter Planning Guide

Section	Core	Standard	Enriched	Section	Core	Standard	Enriched
24.1 Conservation	•	•	•	**Blackline Masters** Review Worksheet 24.2 Issues and Case Studies 23 Skills Worksheet 24B	• •	• • •	• • •
Section Features Word Power, p. 397 Field Activity, p. 398 Technology Link, p. 3994 People and the Environment, p. 400	• • •	• • • •	• • • •	**Ancillary Options** CEPUP Toxic Waste Activity 5		•	•
				24.3 Conserving Biodiversity	•	•	•
Blackline Masters Review Worksheet 24.1	•	•	•	**Section Features** Think Critically, p. 406 Activity 24.2, p. 409	•	• •	• •
Laboratory Program Investigation 29	•	•	•	**Blackline Masters** Review Worksheet 24.3 Skills Worksheet 24A	• •	• •	• •
24.2 Recycling	•	•	•	**Ancillary Options** Videotape "Spaceship Earth"	•	•	•
Section Features Dateline 1973, p. 402 Health Link, p. 403 Activity 24.1, p. 404	• • •	• • •	• • •				

Every chapter has two corresponding tests in the Test Book and one Vocabulary Review Worksheet in the Review Book.

Chapter Overview

Chapter 24 provides an overview of how people can change their behavior to ensure that resources enjoyed now will also be available to future generations. Section 24.1 develops the concept of conservation and relates it to the sustainable development ethic. The topic of conservation continues in Section 24.2 with a presentation of recycling, along with its benefits and drawbacks. The chapter concludes in Section 24.3 with a discussion of the need to preserve biodiversity and suggestions for how this goal can be attained.

Advance Planner

- Bring in an empty aluminum can, plastic bottle, a small stack of newspapers, and glass bottle for the discussion in the Introducing the Chapter section.

Section 24.1
- Arrange for a guest speaker from the local electric company to discuss home energy audits.

Section 24.2
- Bring in a can of motor oil for the discussion described in the Motivate section.

- Have sheets of recycled paper, new bond paper, and hand lenses available for the Activity.
- Have outline maps of the United States available for the research activity in the Enrich section.
- Have art materials available for the Closure activity.

Section 24.3
- Obtain a video of a nature preserve for the activity in the Motivate section. Alternatively, arrange for a field trip to a local nature preserve.
- Have outline maps of your state available for the Activity.

Introducing the Chapter

Display an empty aluminum can, an empty plastic bottle, a small stack of newspapers, and a glass bottle. On the chalkboard, write the terms *energy*, *natural resources*, and *sustainable development*. Ask students what the terms on the chalkboard have to do with the materials on display. Use their responses as a springboard to discussion about the major ideas that will be explored in this chapter.

Section 24.1   Conservation

pp. 397–399

Performance Objectives
- Define conservation and explain how resources can be conserved.
- Describe ways of conserving energy.

Skills Objective
- Apply principles of conservation to garbage disposal and energy use.

Section Vocabulary

conservation   source reduction

Motivate

Ask students what ideas come to mind when they hear the term *conservation*. As a class, discuss things that individuals do to employ the principles of conservation. List these suggestions on the chalkboard and have students copy the list into their notebooks. Encourage students to revise and add to their lists as they complete Section 24.1.

Teaching Strategies

Reinforce   Review the frontier ethic and the sustainable development ethic. Explain to students that the concept of conservation is one of the key components of sustainable development.

Activity   Have students generate a list of suggestions for how to conserve energy. Write the list on the chalkboard. Have students copy the list into their notebooks and place a plus sign beside each suggestion that they carry out in their daily lives. Have them place a minus sign beside those suggestions they do not carry out. Encourage students to continue this exercise each day for one month. At the end of the month, ask students how many of their minuses they were able to change to pluses.

Guest Speaker   Arrange for a representative from your local electric company to speak with the class about home energy audits. Ask the speaker to bring handouts or checklists that students can use to carry out their own energy audits at home. Have students identify places in their homes where energy is being wasted and suggest ways in which the situation can be corrected.

Activity   Explain to students how to read an electric meter. Have students read the meters at their homes once each week for a period of four weeks. Then ask students to implement some of the energy-saving suggestions from this section for a one-month period. Encourage students to again read the meter once each week to see if any changes in energy usage are observable. Have students summarize their findings in a report.

Evaluate

Closure   Have students create a topic sentence outline by writing a sentence that summarizes each paragraph in this section. Encourage students to share their outlines with their classmates.

Section 24.2   Recycling

pp. 401–403

Performance Objectives
- List materials that are currently recycled.
- Identify the benefits of recycling.

Skills Objective
- Predict the raw materials from which most plastics are made.

Section Vocabulary

recycling

Motivate

Display a can of motor oil. Ask students how motor oil is harmful to the environment. Then ask students to suggest ways in which motor oil might be made less harmful. If students do not suggest recycling, explain that today, many service stations now collect motor oil to send it for recycling. Ask students to suggest several ways in which recycling motor oil may benefit the environment.

Teaching Strategies

Activity   Display a sheet of recycled paper and another sheet of similar paper made from all new materials. Provide students with hand lenses and have them observe the quality of the two sheets of paper. Based on their observations, ask students what some of the drawbacks of recycled paper may be. Have students suggest suitable uses for recycled paper and uses for which new paper is necessary.

Reteach   Have students make a list of materials that are currently recycled. Beside each listed item, have students write one benefit of recycling the material. Review the lists as a class, encouraging students to add to their lists based on information included in the lists of others.

Enrich Have students conduct research to find out what states currently have some type of recycling laws and what types of materials are required to be recycled. Have students plot the information they gather on an outline map of the United States. Have students create a key that identifies the types of materials that are recycled in each state.

Activity Have students begin a recycling campaign at the school. Allow students to work in cooperative groups to design methods to encourage recycling among their classmates. Ask students to explain how they would change their campaigns for use in the community at large.

Evaluate

Closure Have students work in cooperative groups to make posters or other visual displays that summarize the amounts of different types of materials that are conserved through recycling. They should base their display on the statistics given in this section.

Section 24.3 Conserving Biodiversity

pp. 405–406

Performance Objectives
- Identify methods used to preserve biodiversity and assess their effectiveness.
- Relate the loss of biodiversity to the growth of the human population.

Skills Objective
- Hypothesize about the types of problems that could result if an endangered species was introduced into a new environment.

Section Vocabulary

preserve

Motivate

Show a video of a nature preserve, or take the class on a field trip to a local nature preserve. Explain to students what organisms the preserve is set up to protect and how the preserve was created. Discuss the funding required to set up the preserve and keep it in operation. Have students discuss whether they think tax dollars should be spent on such efforts and ask them to justify their responses.

Teaching Strategies

Discuss Initiate a class discussion about the reasons people should help to preserve biodiversity. Ask a volunteer to list the reasons on the chalkboard and have students copy the ideas into their notes. At the end of the section have students add to the list any new information that was learned in this section.

Enrich Encourage students to read Rachel Carson's book *Silent Spring*. Have students who read the book write a brief summary that explains what the book is about and how the ideas in the book relate to the topics covered in this chapter. Encourage students to share their summaries with the class.

Activity Provide each student in the class with an outline map of your state. Have students conduct research to find out the locations of any preserves in your state and the function of each preserve. If you live in a coastal state, be sure students include protected estuaries and salt marshes on their maps.

Evaluate

Closure Hold a class discussion about the need to protect biodiversity. Ask students what they as individuals can do to meet this need. Close the section by discussing organisms from your state that have become extinct.

Chapter Resources

Teaching Tip for Feature

People and the Environment: Living Sustainably

- Discuss how implementing many of the suggestions for living sustainably can also help save money.

Teaching Tips for Field Activity

- Have students form cooperative groups and combine their results. Ask students how the energy wasted per home becomes multiplied because of the number of people using and wasting energy.
- Provide students with examples of energy efficiency tags from large appliances. Review with students how the tag is read and the types of information that can be obtained from such tags.

Answers to Field Activity

Responses will vary. Likely responses will suggest using fluorescent lighting instead of incandescent bulbs, increasing insulation, installing weather stripping around doors, and caulking windows.

Teaching Tips for Activities

ACTIVITY 24.1

Time   One class period
Group Size   2 students
Inference   Recycling paper would save trees.
Safety Tips   Tell students to wash their hands after handling the slurry.

Analysis

1. The need for an even distribution of fibers.
2. To hold the fibers together
3. Results will vary.
4. Additional slurry, more applied pressure

Conclusion

1. Accept all logical responses.
2. Accept all logical responses.

ACTIVITY 24.2

Time   Variable
Group Size   3 students
Safety Tips   Caution students to handle scissors carefully.

Analysis

1. Responses will vary.
2. Responses will vary.

Conclusion

Accept all logical responses.

Answers to End of Chapter Questions

Concept Review

1. Source reduction is a lowering of the demand for a resource, reducing the amount used and wasted.
2. Responses will vary but may include keeping the thermostat turned down, taking shorter showers, and turning off lights and appliances when not in use.
3. There are many different types of plastics and most cannot be recycled together.
4. Aluminum, iron, steel, silver, copper, lead, and zinc.
5. Accept all logical responses.

Think Critically

1. Industrial societies generally waste large amounts of energy and materials; natural ecosystems do not.
2. Through efforts to minimize waste and conserve energy.
3. The recycling process does not produce pollution. Less energy is used because the recycled material need not be mined or manufactured.
4. Protecting an entire ecosystem ensures that the natural habitats and interactions of many species will be preserved.

Computer Activity

Check students' work for accuracy.

Graphic Analysis

1. Core preserves. Eight.
2. To allow organisms to move from one preserve to another
3. About 20–25 percent. Accept all logical responses.

Chapter Planning Guide

Section	Core	Standard	Enriched	Section	Core	Standard	Enriched
25.1 The Global Ecosystem	•	•	•	**Ancillary Options** CEPUP Investigating Groundwater Activities 6 and 7		•	•
Section Features Dateline 1977, p. 411	•	•	•	**25.3 Federal Policies**	•	•	•
Social Studies Link, p. 413	•	•	•	**Section Features** Field Activity, p. 418	•	•	•
Think Critically, p. 414	•	•	•				
People and the Environment, p. 415	•	•	•	**Blackline Masters** Review Worksheet 22.3	•	•	•
Blackline Masters Review Worksheet 25.1	•	•	•	**Ancillary Options** One Minute Readings, p. 117	•	•	•
Skills Worksheet 25A	•	•	•	Issues and Case Studies 24	•	•	•
Ancillary Options One Minute Readings, p. 110	•	•	•	**Laboratory Program** Investigation 30		•	•
25.2 Local Policies	•	•	•	**25.4 International Policies**	•	•	•
Section Features Word Power, p. 417	•	•	•	**Section Features** Activity 25.1, p. 422	•	•	•
Activity 25.2, p. 425		•	•	Skills Worksheet 25B		•	•
Blackline Masters Review Worksheet 22.2	•	•	•	**Blackline Masters** Review Worksheet 22.4	•	•	•
Issues and Case Studies 25	•	•	•				

Every chapter has two corresponding tests in the Test Book and one Vocabulary Review Worksheet in the Review Book. There is also a Unit 7 test in the test book covering Chapters 23–25, a midterm exam covering Chapters 12–25, and a final exam in the Test Book.

Chapter Overview

Chapter 25 focuses on legislative measures and policies designed to protect the global ecosystem. Section 25.1 discusses Earth as a global ecosystem with many forms of interactions, each of which draws upon the planet's limited resources. Section 25.2 discusses environmental protection measures that can be carried out at local and state levels and explores the role of citizens' groups. Section 25.3 examines the role of the federal government as it attempts to resolve environmental issues of national concern. The chapter concludes in Section 25.4 with a study of international environmental policies and related conflicts between industrialized and developing nations.

Advance Planner

Section 21.1
- No materials needed.

Section 21.2
- No materials needed.

Section 21.3
- Find and make copies of a newspaper or magazine article about pollution that has crossed state boundaries for the discussion in the Motivate section.

Section 21.4
- Bring in newspaper and magazine articles about the 1992 Earth Summit meeting, held in Rio de Janeiro, Brazil.

Introducing the Chapter

Ask students about any changes in their community that relate to health and the environment. For example, many communities have voted to construct sound barriers along local highways. Some communities regulate advertising posted on trees, electric utility poles, and fences. Challenge students to outline what steps might be involved in legislating a particular issue from the time the issue arises until a law is passed. Suggest that students revise their outlines after completing the chapter.

Section 25.1 The Global Ecosystem

pp. 411–414

Performance Objectives

- Describe the relationship between the environment, human behavior, and human values.
- Describe the steps involved in decision-making and policy-making.

Skills Objective

- Predict changes in competition for resources.

Section Vocabulary

risk assessment   cost/benefit analysis
supply-demand curve   supply   demand

Motivate

Write the term *global ecosystem* on the chalkboard. Ask students to brainstorm phrases describing human activities that affect the global ecosystem. Have students copy these phrases into their notebooks for use in the Closure activity.

Teaching Strategies

Reteach   Review the concept of supply and demand. Explain that the concept of supply and demand is a reasonably sound principle when applied to economics. However, in terms of ecological principles, supply and demand does not take into account the concept of limited or declining resources.

Enrich   Divide the class into cooperative groups and present the following scenario: A business group wants to open a factory in your town. The factory will mean jobs and an increased cash flow into the local economy. It will also drain local resources and add to an already serious pollution problem. Have each group debate the risks, costs, and benefits of such a request and present their collective arguments to the class.

Evaluate

Closure   Have students write a brief summary illustrating the relationships between supply, demand, decisions, policies and the environment. Ask them to relate the ideas in their summaries to the human activities they listed in the activity in the Motivate section.

Section 25.2 Local Policies

pp. 416–417

Performance Objectives

- Identify how environmental protection may be carried out at the local level.
- Describe reasons why policies may be more effective at a local level.

Skills Objectives

None

Section Vocabulary

None

Motivate

Ask students to describe the student council and its role. Point out that the student council participates in school policy-making, especially decisions that affect students. Compare the role of the student council to the role of citizen groups in the community.

Teaching Strategies

Discuss   Ask students if they have ever been involved in a letter-writing campaign, or witnessed a boycott, demonstration, or other form of protest. Have students discuss the issues that may have prompted them or others to take such actions. Develop the idea that groups of people are more likely to effect changes than an individual acting alone.

Reteach   Discuss the role of the federal government in managing health and environmental issues through such agencies as the EPA. Remind students that federal legislation can only be effective when states work within the recommended guidelines. Ask students what the federal government can do to pressure states to comply with federal legislation. Point out that federal funds may be withheld from states that do not comply with federal environmental mandates. Encourage students to research cases in which states have failed to comply with federal mandates and report on the economic consequences.

Evaluate

Closure   Have students work in cooperative groups to prepare a short presentation on how a health or environmental issue may be dealt with locally.

Section 25.3   Federal Policies

pp. 418–419

Performance Objectives
- Explain the necessity for federal intervention in local environmental issues.
- Identify opposing values and how they complicate policy enforcement.

Skills Objective
- Think critically about value issues involved in a fishing rights dispute.

Section Vocabulary
None

Motivate
Distribute copies of a newspaper or magazine article about an issue in which a type of pollution produced in one state affected the quality of life in a neighboring state. Ask: How might the state being polluted obtain relief from the problem? Have students discuss factors involved in the issue.

Teaching Strategies
Reteach   Remind students that erosion caused by wind and running water carries and transports materials over great distances. Point out that many materials carried by erosion may be the result of human activity. Challenge students to identify some of these materials and to list their sources. Have them relate the movement of materials in erosion to environmental issues and government intervention.

Enrich   Ask: What is meant by the expression *quality of life*? Have students define the expression in terms of their personal experiences, goals, and aspirations. Ask: How can health and/or environmental issues threaten quality of life? How can quality of life be protected? Discuss the role of local, state, and federal agencies in protecting quality of life.

Evaluate
Closure   Discuss the need for federal intervention in local environmental issues. Have students discuss how factors such as culture, tradition, and economics, may limit the ability of government, at any level, to mediate or intervene with certain issues.

Section 25.4   International Policies

pp. 420–421

Performance Objectives
- Recognize the conflict between developed and developing nations over environmental policy issues.
- Recognize the importance of individuals in policy development at all levels.

Skills Objective
- Infer the relationship between environmental protection and economic development.

Section Vocabulary
None

Motivate
Display newspaper and magazine articles about the 1992 United Nations meeting, called the Earth Summit, held in Rio de Janeiro. Have students identify the countries that attended, as well as the purpose of the meeting. Use the meeting's agenda and resolutions to help students develop an awareness of the importance of global dialogue and to point out issues of worldwide concern. Ask students to identify issues on which there may be little or no progress and ask them to suggest possible reasons for this.

Teaching Strategies
Reteach   Review some of the issues that lead to the divergent viewpoints of industrialized and developing nations. These issues include energy needs and consumption, pollution-related issues, use and management of resources, decision and policy making, economics, individual versus societal needs, and the question of whose best interests are being served. Examine how such issues make it difficult to reach an accord on certain global environmental concerns.

Enrich   Have students research some of the agreements that industrialized and developing countries have entered into. Ask: What is the purpose of these agreements? How will these agreements set the stage for a sustainable future? Explore how the issues described in the Reteach section may affect the situation.

Evaluate
Closure   Have students write a short summary or prepare a concept map of this section.

Chapter Resources

Teaching Tip for Feature
People and the Environment: Taking a Stand
- Have students conduct library research to learn more about environmental organizations and their many functions. How does a given organization use its resources to protect the environment?
- Encourage students to become environmentally educated citizens. Have them identify and understand critical environmental issues and the role they can play in helping to improve health, the environment, and quality of life.

Teaching Tip for Field Activity
- Have students prepare a questionnaire to quantify their data.

Answers for Field Activity
Responses will vary.

Teaching Tips for Activities

ACTIVITY 25.1
Time Variable
Group Size 2–3 students
Prediction Predictions will vary.
Safety Tips No special safety precautions required.

Analysis
1. Responses will vary depending on student predictions.
2. Accept all logical responses.

Conclusion
1. Responses will vary.
2. Responses will vary.

ACTIVITY 25.2
Time Variable
Group Size 2 students
Inference Inferences will vary depending on the community.
Safety Tips Remind students to stay together while surveying the area and obtain any necessary permissions before entering private property.

Analysis
1. Responses will vary.
2. Responses will vary.

Conclusion
1. Responses will vary.
2. Responses will vary.

Answers to End of Chapter Questions
Concept Review
1. Supply is the availability of a resource to be purchased. Demand is the amount of a resource that people desire and are willing to purchase.
2. Price increases as demand increases.
3. Money for research may be insufficient and real-life cause and effect models for new products and new technology are limited.
4. Not all things can be given an economic value. If an object is not given an economic value, its importance at the policy-making table will be reduced. Costs may be difficult to calculate if shared by many people.
5. Earth is a complex collection of ecosystems, all of which have been united through human interactions.

Think Critically
1. One of the competing species must adapt or face competitive exclusion.
2. Toxic waste contamination, soil erosion. Consider all logical responses.
3. Strengthen existing laws through compliance, monitoring, and enforcement. Accept all logical responses.
4. Conserve resources and protect the environment within your own community. Accept all logical responses.
5. Differences in values, attitudes, culture, religion, and education.

Graphic Analysis
1. These are the areas with the highest demand for water.
2. Accept all logical responses.
3. It may divert water from ecosystems that need it.
4. They may be reduced as groundwater supplies increase.

ADDISON-WESLEY

Environmental Science

ECOLOGY AND HUMAN IMPACT

Bernstein ◆ Winkler ◆ Zierdt-Warshaw

Addison-Wesley Publishing Company

Menlo Park, California • Reading, Massachusetts • New York
Don Mills, Ontario • Wokingham, England • Amsterdam • Bonn
Paris • Milan • Madrid • Sydney • Singapore • Tokyo
Seoul • Taipei • Mexico City • San Juan

Authors

Leonard Bernstein
Coordinator of Science
Community School District 12
Bronx, NY

Alan Winkler
Science Teacher and Resource
    Specialist
Brooklyn, NY

Linda Zierdt-Warshaw
Science Writer and Private
    Tutor
Boothwyn, PA

Content Reviewers
Content/Multicultural

Dr. Harold J. McKenna
Professor of Environmental
    Science Education
City College School of
    Education
New York, NY

Dr. James A. Gavan
Department of Anthropology
University of Missouri
Columbia, MO

Anne Tweed
Science Department
    Coordinator
Eaglecrest High School
Aurora, CO

Pat Browne
Office of Multicultural
    Education
Crispus Attucks Multicultural
    Center
Indianapolis, IN

Dr. Paul Ecklund
Division of Biological Sciences
Cornell University
Ithaca, NY

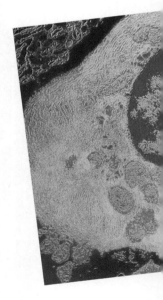

 Text printed on recycled paper

Front Cover Photograph: Pat O'Hara/AllStock
Back Cover Photograph: S. Nielsen/DRK Photo

The sky blue eggs of the American robin are common in rural and urban areas throughout the United States. The eggs contain the next generation, and therefore the future of the species. The bird's nest and eggs symbolize the fragility of the environment and the dependence of all living things on a healthy, safe world in which to grow.

ISBN 0-201-46888-3

1 2 3 4 5 6 7 8 9 10 - VH - 99 98 97 96 95

CONTENTS

PART II PEOPLE AND THE ENVIRONMENT

ACTIVITIES

CAREERS

ENRICHMENT ESSAYS

FRONTIERS

PEOPLE AND THE ENVIRONMENT

CONNECTIONS

ISSUES

HISTORICAL NOTEBOOK

CONCEPT MAPPING

Throughout your study of environmental science, you will be presented with many new concepts and information. One way to organize the information, so you can understand and remember what you have learned, is to make a concept map. A concept map is a graphic, visual representation of the information in a chapter or section. The process of making the concept map will help you to identify ideas that you do not understand, and to reinforce the ideas that you do understand. What makes a concept map most useful is the fact that you make it yourself.

Making a Concept Map

In a concept map, ideas are expressed as words or phrases enclosed in boxes. Boxes are connected by cross-links that state what the connection is between the ideas. The main idea is shown at the top of the map, and is linked to several general concepts. Each general concept, in turn, is linked to more specific ideas and finally, to examples. No ideas should appear more than once, and all ideas must be linked to others. Use the following steps to make a concept map.

- Identify the main idea and general concepts to be mapped. The name of the sections and subsections may help you identify the important ideas.
- Start making your map by placing the main idea at the top of your map and drawing a box around it. Draw lines to connect the main idea to the general concepts. Each concept should also be boxed.
- Choose linking words or phrases that explain the relationship between the boxed concepts.
- Continue to add more specific concepts and examples, boxing each one and linking it to other boxed words. Be sure to identify the relationships with linking words. Include as many links as you can.

Study hint: Do not be discouraged if you find concept mapping difficult at first. You may find it helpful to start by writing the important words on slips of paper. The slips can be moved around on your desk easily until you decide which arrangement works best. Sharing your concept map with other students may help you to understand the concepts better.

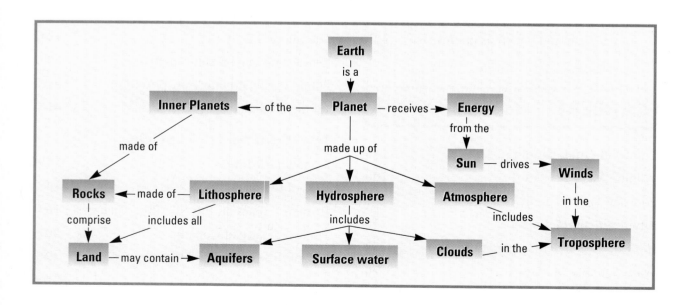

A science laboratory is a place where many exciting things can happen. It is also a place with many potential hazards and dangerous materials. Following sensible safety precautions will help to ensure that your experience in the lab is a positive one. Read the following guidelines before you begin working in the laboratory, and review them from time to time throughout your study of science.

Safety Guidelines

1. Read through the procedures of each laboratory activity before you come to class so you are familiar with the activities.
2. Know how to use and be able to locate all safety equipment in the laboratory including the fume hood, fire blanket, fire extinguisher, and eye washes. Also be sure to locate the nearest exit in case of an emergency.
3. Horseplay, running, or other unsuitable behavior can be dangerous in the laboratory.
4. Wear safety goggles when handling all hazardous chemicals, an open flame, or when otherwise instructed.
5. Wear an apron or a smock to protect your clothing in the laboratory.
6. Tie back long hair and secure any loose fitting clothing.
7. Never eat or drink in the laboratory.
8. Wash your hands before and after each activity in the lab.
9. Keep the work area free of any unnecessary items.
10. Wash all utensils thoroughly before and after each use.
11. Never smell or taste any chemicals unless instructed to do so by your teacher and the experiment instructions.
12. Do not experiment or mix chemicals on your own. Many chemicals in the lab can be explosive or dangerous.
13. When using scissors or a scalpel, cut *away* from yourself and others.
14. When heating substances in a test tube, always point it *away* from yourself and others.
15. Clearly label all containers with the names of the materials you are using during the activity.
16. Report all accidents to the teacher immediately, including breakage of materials, chemical spills, and physical injury.
17. Don't pick up broken glass with your hands. Sweep it up with a broom, and dispose of it in a container labeled for glass disposal.
18. Never return unused chemicals to their original containers. Follow your teacher's instructions for the proper disposal and cleanup of all materials, prior to the end of the lab period.
19. Make sure all your materials are washed and put away, and your work area is clean before leaving the lab.
20. Be certain that all Bunsen burners, gas outlets, and water faucets are turned off before leaving the lab.

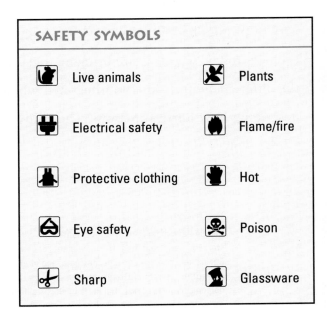

SAFETY SYMBOLS

- Live animals
- Plants
- Electrical safety
- Flame/fire
- Protective clothing
- Hot
- Eye safety
- Poison
- Sharp
- Glassware

UNIT 1

STUDYING EARTH

CHAPTERS

1 Planet Earth
2 Methods of Science
3 Change in the Biosphere

This symbol means *Earth*. It comes from medieval European astrology. In the past, scientists often studied the different parts of Earth in isolation. Subjects such as chemistry or physics had little to do with biology or ecology. Today, scientists are bringing together the different subjects into an integrated whole describing how Earth functions. The study of Earth involves many scientific disciplines.

People have measured the movement of the sun and stars for many centuries. The movements of celestial bodies help people keep time, navigate, and chart the changing seasons. Observations such as these helped scientists realize that Earth itself is a celestial body, one of a group of nine planets orbiting the sun.

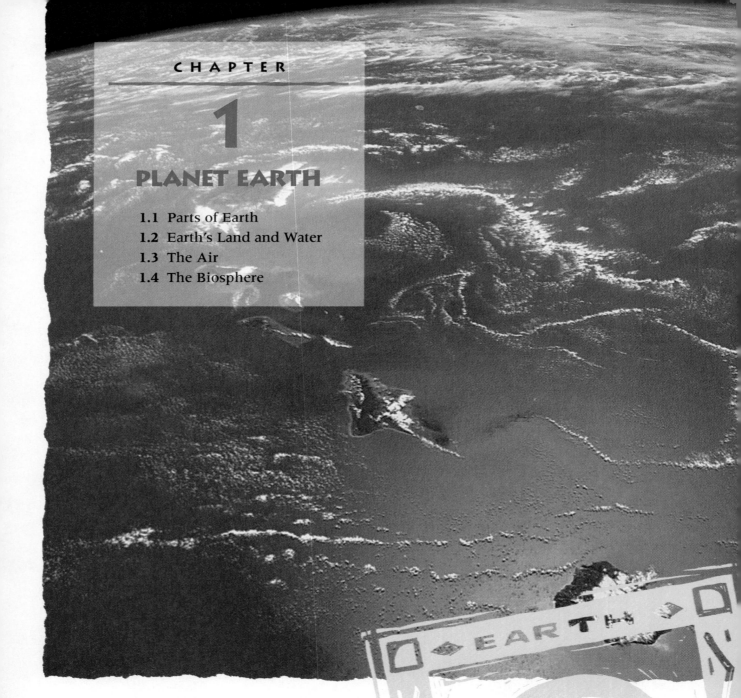

Earth is like a small island of life in the vastness of space. So far, no life of any kind has been found anywhere else in the universe. What conditions give Earth the unique ability to support life? Which parts of Earth are important to the living things that make this planet their home? Understanding how the planet supports its living population is very important. Without this understanding, Earth's inhabitants could damage, or even destroy, their only home.

1.1 PARTS OF EARTH

Objectives • *Locate* Earth in a diagram of the solar system.
• *Identify* and *describe* the three layers of Earth.

Earth is one of the nine planets in the solar system. As you can see in Figure 1.1, Earth is the third planet from the sun. Venus and Mars are Earth's closest neighbors.

Each of the nine planets has unique characteristics. These characteristics are determined mostly by the planet's density, composition, and distance from the sun. Mercury, Venus, Earth, and Mars are known as the inner planets. These planets are made mostly of rock. The other five planets are known as the outer planets. The outer planets are made mostly of gases, with the exception of Pluto, which is rocky like the inner planets.

Earth is the only planet known to support life. It is home to millions of different kinds of living things. *All living things can also be called* **organisms**. What characteristics enable this planet to support life? One of the most important reasons Earth can support life is the presence of liquid water. Although water exists elsewhere in the solar system, it is in the form of ice or vapor everywhere else. All organisms on Earth require some liquid water. Water is the main component of the bodies of organisms. For example, your body is at least 50 percent water. Water is also necessary for chemical reactions to take place within organisms.

Water can absorb, store, and release heat more slowly than rock does. Water absorbs heat during warm periods and releases it during cold periods. The abundance of water on the surface of Earth, therefore, helps to maintain a steadier surface temperature than other planets.

Encourage students to create a mnemonic sentence in which each word begins with the initial of each planet's name. If students develop their own sentences, they will remember them more easily.

DATELINE 1972

The United States launched Pioneer 10, the first human-made object to leave the solar system. The probe, launched to study Jupiter, contained a recorded greeting from the many cultures on Earth. The probe continues to travel through space, carrying its message to any intelligent life it may encounter in the universe.

Figure 1.1 The solar system consists of the sun and all the bodies that orbit the sun, including the nine planets and a belt of asteroids.

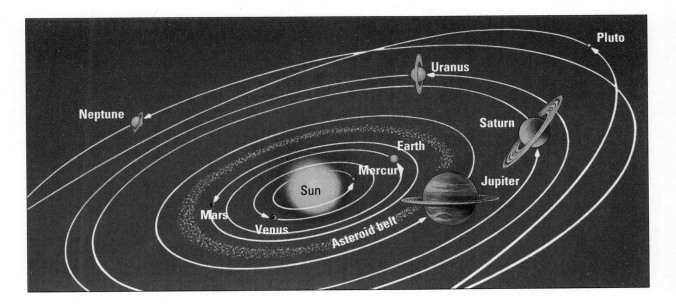

Figure 1.2 Visible light makes up only a small portion of the energy given off by the sun. Each type of wave has a specific wavelength.

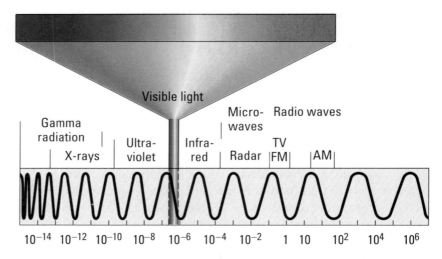

Wavelength (m)

10^{-14} 10^{-12} 10^{-10} 10^{-8} 10^{-6} 10^{-4} 10^{-2} 1 10 10^2 10^4 10^6

PHYSICS
L I N K

The microwaves in a microwave oven are radio waves with a wavelength of about 12.2 cm. The energy in the waves penetrates food and causes water, fats, and sugars in the food to absorb the energy as heat.

Another reason Earth is able to support life is the layer of air surrounding the planet. Air contains oxygen, which is needed by most living things. The layer of air also helps keep Earth's temperature in a range suitable for supporting life.

In addition to water and air, organisms also need energy. Energy from the sun travels to the planets in the solar system in the form of waves. Each type of wave has a different wavelength. Most waves are invisible. Waves in a narrow range of wavelengths, called the visible spectrum, can be seen by the human eye. Almost all the energy used by organisms originally comes from the sun.

Earth can be viewed as having three layers: the lithosphere, the hydrosphere, and the atmosphere. *The* **lithosphere** (LITH oh SFEER) *is the layer of land that forms Earth's surface.* The lithosphere includes all the rocks, soil, and sand that make up land. *The* **hydrosphere** HY droh SFEER) *includes all the parts of Earth that are made up of water.* The hydrosphere includes oceans, lakes, and rivers, as well as underground water and clouds in the air. *The* **atmosphere** (AT muh SFEER) *is the layer of air that surrounds Earth.*

All three layers of Earth are in constant motion. The hydrosphere flows through the ocean currents and waterways of the world. The lithosphere moves much more slowly, resulting in occasional earthquakes and volcanic eruptions. The movement of the atmosphere can be seen on television weather reports, as radar and computers track the movement of weather systems across the nation.

1. The hydrosphere includes oceans, lakes, rivers, clouds, and underground water.
2. The presence of an atmosphere and liquid water enable Earth to sustain life.
3. Mercury and Venus should be warmer; all the rest should be colder.

SECTION REVIEW

1. What parts of Earth make up the hydrosphere?
2. What characteristics of Earth enable it to support life?
3. **Infer** The temperature of a planet is determined, in part, by its distance from the sun. Which planets would you expect to be warmer than Earth? Which ones would be colder?

1.2 EARTH'S LAND AND WATER

Objectives • **Describe** *the three main types of rocks that make up the lithosphere.* • **Explain** *why fresh water is a valuable resource for organisms.*

If Earth were an organism, the lithosphere would be the organism's body, and the hydrosphere would be its blood. The hydrosphere flows to almost every part of the planet. The shores and riverbanks where the lithosphere and the hydrosphere meet are some of Earth's most heavily populated parts.

The Lithosphere

The lithosphere varies in thickness from about 10 to 200 kilometers (km). The rocks that make up the lithosphere can be divided into three main types: igneous rock, sedimentary rock, and metamorphic rock. The rocks are classified on the basis of how they formed.

Igneous Rock   Below the hard, solid lithosphere, Earth contains hot, melted rocks in liquid form. *When liquid rock cools, it solidifies to become* **igneous** (IG nee us) **rock**. The lava that flows from a volcano cools and turns into igneous rock. Granite and basalt are two common types of igneous rock.

Sedimentary Rock   Rocks break down slowly over time. The tiny pieces of rock that wear off become sediments that are carried away by wind and water. The sediments eventually settle down into layers. *As layers of sediments accumulate, they become compressed and cemented into* **sedimentary** (SED ih MENT uh ree) **rock**. Fossils are often found in sedimentary rock. Limestone and sandstone are examples of sedimentary rock.

Metamorphic Rock   Pressure and heat over long periods of time can cause igneous rocks and sedimentary rocks to undergo a change in structure. *Rock that has been transformed by heat and pressure*

Figure 1.3 When a volcano erupts, liquid rock called lava flows from the surface. The lava will cool to form igneous rock.

Figure 1.4 Granite is a common type of igneous rock (left). Conglomerate (center), which can contain fossils, is a sedimentary rock. Marble (right) is an example of metamorphic rock.

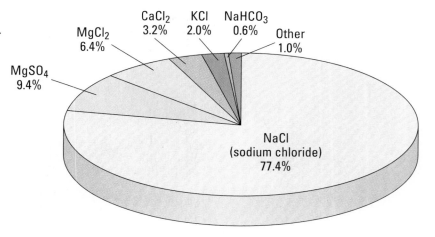

FIELD ACTIVITY

How much rain falls during a single rainstorm? You can measure rainfall by making a simple rain gauge. Attach a ruler to the side of a wide-mouthed glass jar, with the bottom of the ruler at the bottom of the jar. The jar should be the same width at the top and the bottom. Measure the depth of the water in the jar after it has been left outside during a storm.

Be sure students understand that the width of the jar does not matter. The wider the opening, the more rain will collect, but it will be distributed over a wider bottom.

is called **metamorphic** (MET uh MORF ik) **rock**. Marble and slate are familiar examples of metamorphic rock.

The Hydrosphere

When viewed from space, Earth appears mostly blue. This blue appearance is due to the fact that more than 70 percent of Earth's surface is covered by water. Because of its large proportion of water, Earth is sometimes called the water planet.

More than 97 percent of the hydrosphere is made up of salt water. As the name suggests, salt water is water that contains dissolved salts. About 35 grams (g) of salt are dissolved in each liter (L) of ocean water. The amounts of various types of salt in ocean water are shown in Figure 1.5. Sodium chloride (NaCl) is the salt you are familiar with as table salt. Most salt water is located in the oceans. Some lakes, however, such as the Great Salt Lake in Utah, also contain salt water.

Fresh water contains fewer dissolved salts than salt water does. Most lakes, ponds, streams, and underground water is fresh water. Fresh water makes up less than 3 percent of the hydrosphere. More than two-thirds of the fresh water on Earth is contained in frozen glaciers and ice caps. Although fresh water makes up a very small portion of the hydrosphere, it is the fresh water on Earth that supports most life forms. Because there is so little fresh water, it is a very valuable substance for most living things. The availability of fresh water is an important factor in the ability of an area to support life.

Fresh water can be divided into two types: surface water and groundwater. Surface water includes the water in lakes, streams, and rain runoff. Groundwater flows beneath the surface of Earth through small spaces in and between rocks. *An underground layer of porous rock that contains water is called an* **aquifer** (AHK weh fer). An aquifer may reach the surface of the ground, resulting in a natural spring.

Sometimes aquifers flow between two layers of rock that water cannot seep through. Pressure in the aquifer builds up from water

Figure 1.5 More than 75 percent of the salt in ocean water is NaCl, or table salt.

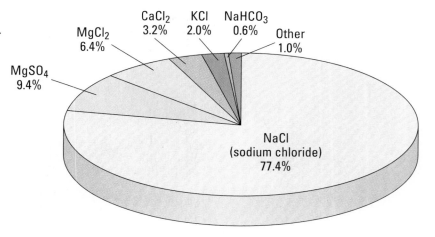

MgSO$_4$ 9.4%

MgCl$_2$ 6.4%

CaCl$_2$ 3.2%

KCl 2.0%

NaHCO$_3$ 0.6%

Other 1.0%

NaCl (sodium chloride) 77.4%

THINK CRITICALLY

Water, like all liquids, expands when it is heated. If the temperature of Earth's oceans were to rise, what would happen to the size of the oceans? What might happen to the land along the coasts of the continents?

Oceans would expand, and would cover a greater portion of land, flooding coastlines.

Figure 1.6 Natural springs occur where groundwater flows to the surface.

pressure and the weight of the heavy layer of rock above. If a well is drilled into such an aquifer, water will flow freely to the surface. *Wells in which water flows to the surface due to high pressure underground are called* **artesian** (ar TEE shun) **wells**. The name comes from an area in France where such wells are common.

Much of the fresh water used by people is pumped to the surface from wells drilled in aquifers. The water contained in aquifers is refilled very slowly, however. It takes many years for rainwater to seep through the soil and rocks of the surface to reach the aquifer. Because the water is pumped out faster than it is replaced, many aquifers in the United States are beginning to dry up. Many communities that currently depend on the water in aquifers will have to look elsewhere for a supply of fresh water in the future.

SECTION REVIEW

1. In which type of rock are fossils usually found?
2. Why is the presence of fresh water important to living things?
3. **Analyze** The amount of salt dissolved in the water of saltwater lakes is often greater than the amount of salt in ocean water. Why do you think this is true?

1. Fossils are usually found in sedimentary rock.
2. Fresh water is needed for many biological processes, but the supply is very limited.
3. As water evaporates from inland bodies of water, the salt becomes more concentrated in the water left behind.

ACTIVITY 1.1

Stream Discharge

PROBLEM

A stream-gauging station measures the volume of water flowing past a certain location each second. A rain gauge provides data on the number of centimeters of rain falling per hour. Data for a sample 12-hour period is shown in the table. What is the relationship between amount of rainfall and stream discharge?

MATERIALS

- graph paper
- 2 pencils of different colors

HYPOTHESIS

Write a hypothesis that pertains to the problem.

PROCEDURE

1. On a sheet of graph paper, construct a line graph that compares the rainfall and stream-discharge data. The graph you construct should have two vertical axes and one horizontal axis, as shown in the figure. Show rainfall in cm/h on the left vertical axis and stream discharge in m3/s on the right vertical axis. The horizontal axis shows the time.
2. Plot the data points for rainfall. Connect the points to produce a curve showing the amount of rainfall over time.
3. Use the other pencil to plot the data points for stream discharge. Connect the points to

produce a second curve showing stream discharge over time.

ANALYSIS

1. How much time passed between the heaviest rainfall and the greatest stream discharge? How do you explain this time difference?
2. How do the two curves compare in height? Give reasons for the difference.
3. How do the curves compare in shape and steepness? Give reasons for the differences.
4. Predict what the volume of stream discharge will be at 1:00 A.M. the following morning. Explain your prediction.

CONCLUSION

What is the relationship between rainfall and stream discharge?

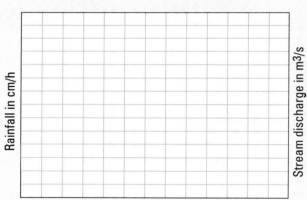

Time	Rainfall (cm/h)	Stream Discharge (m³/s)	Time	Rainfall (cm/h)	Stream Discharge (m³/s)
12:00 noon	0	220	6:00 P.M.	0.3	3400
1:00 P.M.	2.0	290	7:00 P.M.	0	2285
2:00 P.M.	5.9	440	8:00 P.M.	0	1420
3:00 P.M.	6.2	830	9:00 P.M.	0	1000
4:00 P.M.	3.2	1400	10:00 P.M.	0	950
5:00 P.M.	1.0	2000	11:00 P.M.	4.0	950

1.3 THE AIR

Objectives • *Diagram* the layers of the atmosphere.
• *Describe* the characteristics of each layer.

The atmosphere is an envelope of gases that surrounds Earth. The air you breathe is part of the atmosphere. Scientists have divided the atmosphere into four main parts, each with its own characteristics. These parts are arranged in layers around Earth. As you can see in Figure 1.7, the four main layers of Earth's atmosphere are the troposphere, the stratosphere, the mesosphere, and the thermosphere. Gases become thinner, or less dense, the farther they are from Earth's surface.

The atmosphere is made up of about 78 percent nitrogen and 21 percent oxygen. Water vapor, dust particles, and small amounts of other gases make up the remaining 1 percent of the air. Only about 0.04 percent of the air is made up of carbon dioxide. Carbon dioxide is a gas that is very important to life on Earth. Carbon dioxide is one of the ingredients used by plants to make food. Carbon dioxide also helps maintain the temperature of Earth.

BIOLOGY LINK

In the process of photosynthesis, plants, algae, and certain bacteria make sugars by combining carbon dioxide (CO_2), water, and energy from the sun. Animals and other organisms break down these sugars, releasing CO_2, water, and energy. In humans, much of the energy is used to maintain body heat.

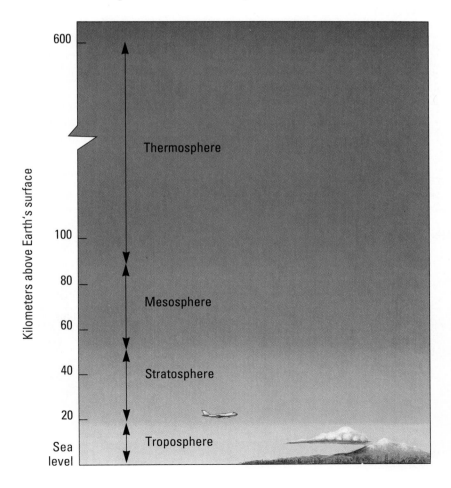

Figure 1.7 No one can say exactly where Earth's atmosphere ends. The gases simply get less dense as they get farther from the surface.

Animals and other organisms release carbon dioxide when they breathe. When you exhale, your breath contains carbon dioxide. Carbon dioxide is also released when materials such as wood, coal, and gasoline are burned. Many scientists are concerned that rising levels of atmospheric carbon dioxide due to human activities could affect Earth's climate.

Troposphere

The layer of the atmosphere that touches the surface of Earth is called the **troposphere** (TROHP uh SFEER). The troposphere extends to a height of about 8 to 18 km above Earth's surface. Most of the gas molecules in the atmosphere are in the troposphere.

Most land organisms live in the troposphere. The air you breathe is, therefore, part of the troposphere. The troposphere contains most of the water vapor in the atmosphere. This is the layer in which most weather occurs. The winds that carry weather across Earth are an important factor in the climate of an area. Figure 1.8 shows the major patterns of air currents that flow across Earth's surface.

Stratosphere

Beyond the troposphere, reaching a height of 50 km above Earth, is the **stratosphere** (STRAT uh SFEER). Most jet airplanes travel in the lower stratosphere. Weather disturbances that are common in the troposphere do not occur in the stratosphere.

The upper stratosphere contains a layer of gas called ozone. **Ozone** (OH ZOHN) *is an oxygen gas containing three oxygen atoms per molecule.* The oxygen you breathe in the troposphere contains only

Figure 1.8 Prevailing winds are caused by the rotation of Earth and by temperature differences. In which direction do winds usually blow where you live?

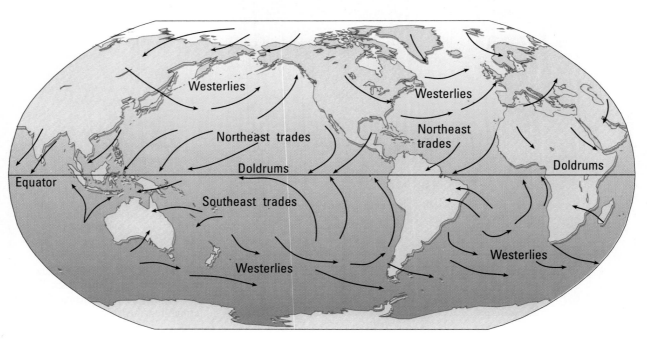

Figure 1.9 An aurora borealis (left) occurs in the thermosphere of the Northern Hemisphere. An aurora australis occurs in the Southern Hemisphere.

two oxygen atoms in each molecule. The ozone layer is very important to living things because it filters out most of the ultraviolet, or UV, radiation given off by the sun. Ultraviolet radiation is one of many types of electromagnetic waves produced by the sun. Without the filtering action of the ozone layer, the sun's UV radiation would destroy much of life on Earth.

Mesosphere and Thermosphere

Beyond the stratosphere is the *mesosphere* (MEZ oh SFEER), which extends about 85 km above Earth's surface. The mesosphere is the coldest layer of the atmosphere. Temperatures in the mesosphere can be as low as −100°C.

The *thermosphere* (THERM oh SFEER) is the outer layer of the atmosphere. Unlike the mesosphere, the thermosphere is a high-temperature layer of the atmosphere. In fact, temperatures as high as 2000°C have been recorded in this layer.

Gas molecules in one layer of the thermosphere are bombarded with rays from the sun. These rays cause the gas molecules to lose electrons, and they become ions. Because of these ions, this layer of the thermosphere is called the *ionosphere* (y ON oh SFEER). When gas molecules reunite with free electrons, light is given off. This process occurs most often near Earth's poles, resulting in a display of lights called an aurora (uh ROR uh).

Word Power

Troposphere, from the Greek *tropos*, "to turn," and the Latin *sphaera*, "ball."
Stratosphere, from the Latin *stratum*, "covering," and *sphaera*, "ball."
Mesosphere, from the Greek *mesos*, "middle," and the Latin *sphaera*, "ball."
Thermosphere, from the Greek *therme*, "heat", and the Latin *sphaera*, "ball."

SECTION REVIEW

1. Which layer of the atmosphere contains the ionosphere? Why does this layer have this name?
2. Approximately how high do airplanes fly? Explain why.
3. **Apply** People who live at sea level often have trouble breathing at the tops of high mountains. Why do you think this is true?

1. The thermosphere contains the ionosphere so called because of the presence of ions.
2. Airplanes fly in the lower stratosphere, about 20 km above Earth's surface, to avoid weather disturbances in the troposphere.
3. Because the gases in the atmosphere become less dense the farther they are from Earth's surface, the oxygen is less concentrated at high altitudes.

1.4 THE BIOSPHERE

Objectives • **Describe** *the location of the biosphere.*
• **Explain** *how organisms interact with the biosphere.*

Earth is home to trillions of organisms. Together, the parts of the lithosphere, hydrosphere, and atmosphere where life exists make up the biosphere. *The* **biosphere** (BY oh SFEER) *is all the parts of Earth that support life.* The biosphere reaches from the floor of the ocean to the tops of the highest mountains. All together, the biosphere is about 20 km (12.4 mi) thick. You may think that this sounds like quite a distance, but the biosphere really makes up only a thin layer surrounding the planet. If Earth were the size of an apple, the layer that supports life would be only about as thick as the apple's skin.

Although the biosphere is 20 km thick, most organisms live in an even narrower range. Deep below the surface of the ocean life is rare because the pressure is too high for most organisms. And few organisms live high upon the tallest mountains, because the oxygen is too thin and the temperatures are too cold. Most life on Earth exists between 500 m below the surface of the ocean and about 6 km above sea level.

The biosphere provides all organisms with the materials they need to live. While each individual organism may live mostly on land, water, or in the air, all organisms depend on materials from each of these three areas of Earth. For example, you live on the lithosphere, but breathe the air of the atmosphere, and drink the water of the hydrosphere. Although a bird may live in the air, it eats food that grew on the ground, which is part of the lithosphere. A fish depends on oxygen from the atmosphere dissolved in the water.

Figure 1.10 Spider monkeys (left), white crabs (center), and tundra brush are adapted to live in very different environments.

The leaves of the tree absorb CO_2 from the atmosphere and release oxygen and water vapor.

The tree absorbs groundwater with its roots and transports the water to the leaves.

Rocks and soil anchor the tree and contain important minerals and nutrients.

Within the biosphere, organisms live in a wide variety of environments. Some of the more unusual places where organisms live are shown in Figure 1.10. The Mexican spider monkey lives in the tops of trees in the rain forest. A community of worms, crabs, and fish lives near hot vents in the ocean floor. A variety of plants grow during the short cool summers in Denali National Park, Alaska.

Because all organisms depend on the biosphere to meet their needs, they are affected by changes in the biosphere. For example, a change in the composition of seawater can affect the organisms in the ocean. The eruption of a volcano can affect organisms that live on the surrounding land.

While changes in the environment can affect organisms, organisms can also cause changes to occur in their environments. The damming of a river by beavers would affect the flow of water. The release of harmful smoke by a factory could affect the atmosphere. Because organisms affect their environments and changes in the environment affect organisms, the biosphere is a very complex network of interactions.

Figure 1.11 Organisms interact with each part of the biosphere.

DATELINE 1991

A group of eight people moved into a seven-domed structure they called Biosphere II. The structure was designed to be a completely closed, self-sufficient environment in which all materials were recycled. Much of the scientific community questioned the value of the "experiment" because no new information was being sought.

Cooperative Learning
Have students work in groups to develop lists of ways they interact daily with each of the three parts of the biosphere. Groups can exchange lists and determine which items are essential.

SECTION REVIEW

1. What parts of Earth make up the biosphere?
2. List two ways in which you interact with each of the three parts of the biosphere every day.
3. **Analyze** In what ways does each part of the biosphere contribute to the production of the food you eat?

1. The biosphere is made up of parts of the lithosphere, the hydrosphere, and the atmosphere.
2. Answers will vary.
3. Answers will vary.

James Lovelock: The Father of Gaia

Does the Gaia hypothesis redefine nature?

1. All Living things and their environments work together like the parts of a giant organism.
2. Industry supports the idea that the planet is self-healing and can correct damage on its own, Environmentalists support the idea that the health of the planet requires care, or it will die.

"We need to study Earth as doctors diagnose and treat patients, not as an isolated leg or ear but as a whole living being." These words written by British scientist James Lovelock are the basis of the Gaia (GY-uh) hypothesis. According to the Gaia hypothesis, all living things and their environments work together like the parts of an organism. This giant organism manages the air, land, and water, and balances the conditions necessary for maintaining life.

James Lovelock is an unusual scientist for modern times. He does not specialize in one area of study, nor is he employed by an organization. Lovelock studies whatever interests him from his home laboratory in England. Lovelock holds over 40 patents. One device, the electron-capture detector, led him to develop the Gaia hypothesis.

The electron-capture detector can detect minute amounts of chemicals in soil, water, or air. After the detector was used to study ozone depletion, NASA (the U.S. National Aeronautics and Space Administration) asked Lovelock to help detect life on Mars. Lovelock said they should test the atmosphere for chemicals that indicate life. Based on the data gathered

Please Shut the Gate

Coombe Mill
Experimental
Station

during the investigation, Lovelock concluded that Mars was indeed lifeless.

While working on the Mars project, Lovelock began to wonder why life existed on Earth but not on other planets. He came up with the idea that a self-regulating team of organisms and physical processes joined to form one organism. Lovelock called the organism *Gaia* after a mythical Earth goddess.

Lovelock developed a computer model called Daisyworld to help explain his idea. Daisyworld is a planet similar to Earth, except that the only organisms are daisies. There are two types of daisies: dark-colored ones that absorb sunlight, and light-colored ones that reflect sunlight. Each type of daisy affects the

environment in its own way, and each is affected by changes in the environment as well. The quantity of each type of daisy determines the environmental changes. Together, the different types of daisies keep the environment in balance.

The implication of the Gaia concept is that the Earth and its biosphere can correct for small or gradual changes in the environment, maintaining a balance that supports life. If the balance is seriously upset, however, the organism could die. In this case, the organism would be the entire planet Earth.

What do other scientists think about Lovelock's ideas? Most researchers do not agree with the idea that the Earth itself is an actual organism. However, they do agree that there is a similarity between the checks and balances that occur among organisms and their environments, and the systems that maintain balance within an organism.

DECISIONS

1. Explain the Gaia hypothesis.
2. Two very different groups support the Gaia hypothesis, industry members and environmentalists. Why might each of these groups support Lovelock's theory?

CHAPTER 1 REVIEW

KEY TERMS

organism 1.1	igneous rock 1.2	artesian well 1.2	biosphere 1.4
lithosphere 1.1	sedimentary rock 1.2	troposphere 1.3	
hydrosphere 1.1	metamorphic rock 1.2	stratosphere 1.3	
atmosphere 1.1	aquifer 1.2	ozone 1.3	

CHAPTER SUMMARY

1.1 Earth is the third planet from the sun in the solar system. The presence of liquid water and an oxygen-containing atmosphere enable Earth to support life. Earth consists of the lithosphere, the hydrosphere, and the atmosphere.

1.2 The lithosphere is made up of three types of rocks: igneous, sedimentary, and metamorphic. The hydrosphere is made up mostly of salt water. Less than 3 percent of the water on Earth is fresh water. Much of the fresh water is contained in underground aquifers.

1.3 The atmosphere is made up of several layers of decreasing density. The troposphere contains water vapor, and most weather occurs there. The stratosphere contains the ozone layer, which absorbs harmful ultraviolet (UV) radiation.

1.4 The biosphere is the part of Earth occupied by organisms. The biosphere and the organisms interact with one another. The biosphere provides all the materials necessary to support life.

MULTIPLE CHOICE

Choose the letter of the word or phrase that completes each statement.

1. The five distant planets are made mostly of (a) gas; (b) water; (c) rock; (d) radiation. a
2. Earth can support life because of the presence of (a) heat; (b) oxygen; (c) liquid water; (d) rocks. c
3. Compared to visible light, the wavelength of ultraviolet light is (a) longer; (b) shorter; (c) the same; (d) brighter. b
4. Water makes up approximately what percentage of the human body? (a) 10; (b) 50; (c) 80; (d) 100. b
5. Fossils are usually found in (a) igneous rock; (b) sedimentary rock; (c) metamorphic rock; (d) lava. b
6. More than 97 percent of the hydrosphere is (a) salt water; (b) fresh water; (c) underground water; (d) ice caps and glaciers. a
7. Aquifers transport (a) water from reservoirs; (b) surface runoff; (c) ocean water; (d) groundwater. d
8. The most abundant gas in the Earth's atmosphere is (a) nitrogen; (b) oxygen; (c) carbon dioxide; (d) water vapor. a
9. The ozone layer is part of the (a) troposphere; (b) stratosphere; (c) mesosphere; (d) thermosphere. b
10. A fish interacts only with the (a) hydrosphere (b) atmosphere (c) lithosphere (d) biosphere. d
11. The layer of the atmosphere in which rainstorms occur is the (a) hydrosphere; (b) stratosphere; (c) troposphere; (d) thermosphere. c
12. Rocks formed from the cooling lava of volcanic eruptions are (a) igneous rocks; (b) lithospheric rocks; (c) sedimentary rocks; (d) metamorphic rocks. a
13. Temperatures in the themosphere can reach (a) −100°C; (b) 200°C; (c) 1000°C; (d) 2000°C. d

CHAPTER 1 REVIEW

WORD COMPARISONS

Write the letter of the second word pair that best matches the first pair.

1. Atmosphere: air as (a) land: water; (b) lithosphere: hydrosphere; (c) hydrosphere: water; (d) land: lithosphere. c
2. Aquifer: groundwater as (a) artesian well: spring; (b) ocean: current; (c) rain: ocean; (d) river: surface water. d
3. granite: igneous as (a) fossil: metamorphic; (b) sandstone: sedimentary; (c) metamorphic: granite; (d) sandstone: marble. b
4. Carbon dioxide: plants as (a) oxygen: animals; (b) nitrogen: atmosphere; (c) oxygen: carbon; (d) ozone: animals. a
5. Weather: troposphere as (a) ozone: ionosphere; (b) water vapor: troposphere; (c) aurora: ionosphere; (d) heat: mesosphere. c

CONCEPT REVIEW Answers on page T25.

Write a complete response to each of the following.

1. Which layer of the atmosphere is included in the biosphere?
2. Which of the nine planets are called the inner planets? In what way do the inner planets differ from the outer planets?
3. Why is liquid water important to living things?
4. How does the presence of plants on Earth affect the content of the atmosphere?
5. Why are organisms not equally distributed throughout the biosphere?

THINK CRITICALLY Answers on page T25.

1. Planet Mars has polar ice caps consisting mostly of frozen water. Mars also has an atmosphere containing carbon dioxide. Do you think any form of life could live on Mars? Why or why not?
2. Why are fossils not found in igneous rock?
3. Some animals live high in the tops of trees in rain forests and never touch the ground. In what ways do such animals depend on the lithosphere?
4. All commercial airplanes are equipped with oxygen masks for every passenger. Why do you suppose this is a necessary precaution?
5. Approximately what percentage of the water on Earth is liquid fresh water?

WRITE FOR UNDERSTANDING

Identify the topic of each paragraph in Section 1.2. Write a complete sentence that reflects the topic. Organize the topics into a summary of the section's contents.

PORTFOLIO

1. Research the environmental conditions on each of the planets in the solar system other than Earth. Evaluate each planet as a potential place for human colonization. Identify what challenges would be faced, and how they could be met.
2. Has the climate where you live changed during the past 100 years? Research weather history as far back as records are available. Make a graph or other visual representation of the information, and determine whether there has been a significant change.

GRAPHIC ANALYSIS   Answers on page T25.

Use Figure 1.8 on page 10 to answer the following.

1. If you lived on the west coast of South America, from which direction would the wind usually blow?
2. Are winds named for the direction they flow to, or the direction they flow from? Support your answer with an example.
3. Do you think the governments of the Scandinavian countries should be concerned about air pollution in England? Explain your answer.
4. The northeastern United States tends to have colder winters than the northwestern United States. Which winds contribute to this difference?
5. From which direction does the wind usually blow at the equator? Is this the same direction or the opposite direction from the rotation of Earth?

ACTIVITY 1.2

Answers and teaching strategies on page T25.

PROBLEM
What is the percentage of oxygen in the air?

MATERIALS
- pencil
- steel wool, small amount
- test tube
- ring stand
- clamp
- metric ruler
- beaker

HYPOTHESIS
After reading the entire activity, write a hypothesis that pertains to the problem.

PROCEDURE
1. Use the eraser end of a pencil to wedge a small amount of fine, moist steel wool into the bottom of a test tube.
2. Pour water into a beaker so it is approximately half-full.
3. Invert the test tube. Use the clamp and ring stand to hold the test tube upside-down and lower it to a position just above the surface of the water. Lower the test tube straight down into the water. *Note: Because the test tube is full of air, no water will enter it.* Label your setup with your name and store it where it will be undisturbed.
4. Observe the setup closely for several consecutive days. Record your observations. During this time, oxygen will be removed from the air in the test tube as it reacts with iron in the steel wool. Water will be drawn up into the test tube to replace the oxygen.
5. After two days, use a metric ruler to measure how far the water has been drawn up into the test tube.
6. To determine the percentage of oxygen in the original air inside the test tube, divide the length measured in Step 5 by the total length of the test tube. Multiply the quotient by 100.

ANALYSIS
1. Did you notice any changes in the steel wool after two days? Explain.
2. Was oxygen removed from the test tube? Explain.
3. What are the possible sources of error in this method of determining the percentage of oxygen in air?

CONCLUSION
What is the percentage of oxygen in air? Show the calculations you performed to obtain your answer.

CHAPTER

2

METHODS OF SCIENCE

2.1 The Nature of Science
2.2 Skills and Methods
2.3 Environmental Science

You may have heard news stories about new discoveries in science that contradict what scientists used to say. People often ignore what scientists say either because they cannot seem to make up their minds, or because they think scientists don't know what they are talking about. But what many people do not realize is that uncertainty and change are the very basis of science. The never-ending search for new information inspires scientists to explore every corner of Earth. From observing the violent birth of new land formed by a volcano to the delicate workings of a living cell, gaining new information contributes to the understanding of the biosphere.

2.1 THE NATURE OF SCIENCE

Objectives • *Explain* why there is always uncertainty in science.
• *Distinguish* between subjects that can and cannot be studied scientifically.

What is science? What do scientists do? You can probably name certain kinds of scientists, such as biologists, chemists, or physicists. What do these professionals have in common? Different kinds of scientists use different tools and techniques in their work. But the real work of a scientist takes place in the mind.

Science is a way of learning about the natural world. Often, books and classes about science offer little more than a collection of information. The information was learned by scientists throughout the years. The information itself, however, is not science. Science is the *process* by which the information was learned.

Uncertainty in Science

In some ways, the work of a scientist is similar to the work of a detective. The detective cannot go back in time to watch a crime being committed. Instead, the detective must solve a mystery by putting together pieces of evidence. The detective first gathers as much evidence as possible about the crime. Then, based on the evidence, the detective forms a likely explanation. If new evidence is brought to light that disproves the explanation, the detective will have to come up with a new explanation.

In a similar way, a scientist tries to find answers to the mysteries of nature. Just as the detective cannot watch the crime, the scientist often cannot see natural process at work. Instead, the scientist must make as many observations as possible about the subject. The scientist then forms an explanation for what was observed. *A* **hypothesis** (hy-POTH-eh-sis) (plural, hypotheses) *is a possible explanation for a set of observations.* A hypothesis is not just a wild guess. A scientist forms a hypothesis based on observations. Forming a hypothesis requires imagination and strong thinking skills.

If any bit of information fails to fit the hypothesis, the hypothesis must change. For example, you may observe that after a hard rain, the gutters on your street fill up with water. You form a hypothesis that all the water in the gutter comes from rain. The next sunny day, a neighbor up the block washes her car, and the gutter fills with water even though there has been no rain. You must reject your hypothesis and develop a new one. How could you restate your hypothesis about where the water in the gutter comes from?

Scientists can never be certain that they have observed all the information that exists. A new tool may be invented some day that allows further observations to be made. A scientist must always be

Word Power
Hypothesis, from the Greek *hypotithenai*, "to place under."

Figure 2.1 The transmission electron microscope (TEM) is a tool that enables scientists to see structures within a cell. Scientists had to change their ideas about some cellular structures when they saw images like this one produced by the TEM.

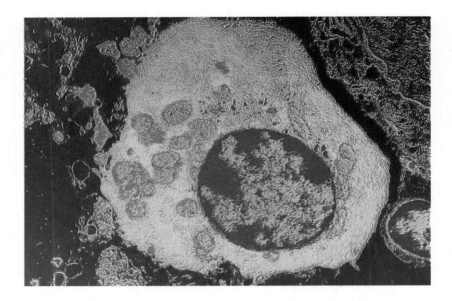

THINK CRITICALLY

Housing starts, or the construction of new homes, are an important indicator of economic health. But building new homes may also be harmful. Why do you think housing starts are good for the economy but sometimes bad for the environment?

Building homes employs many people, and is a strong sign that people are financially sound. But every plot of land that is converted to housing used to be home to other organisms.

ready to give up an old hypothesis in favor of a better one. Because new information can cause a scientist to change a hypothesis, science is always uncertain and changeable.

Science and Society

The progress of science is often driven by the needs and challenges of society. Feeding a hungry world, curing and preventing the spread of AIDS, and developing new energy sources are just some of the challenges of today's scientists.

To be studied scientifically, a subject must be observable and testable. Questions of ethics and personal values cannot be studied scientifically. For example, science cannot tell you whether or not you should keep a sack of money you found on a bus.

The products of science can be of great benefit to the world. Unfortunately, the products of science also have the potential to do great harm. People, including scientists, must be very careful about how new information is used. As a voter and a consumer of the products of science, you will be involved in making some decisions that have an effect on science. The more you know about the issues, the more informed your opinion will be.

SECTION REVIEW

1. Explain why a hypothesis is not just a wild guess.
2. Why are scientific ideas uncertain by nature?
3. **Apply** The United States government has established recommended daily allowances for many nutrients. The amounts recommended for some nutrients have changed over the years. Why do you think this has happened?

1. Unlike a wild guess, a hypothesis is based on observations.
2. New information can always appear, forcing scientists to change their ideas.
3. New information became available that made the old information inaccurate.

Environmental Research

Who's to say who's right?

1. Government, industry, and citizens, groups.
2. Data, perspective, and approach to the problem can affect the results of research.

In March 1989, an oil tanker spilled 265,000 barrels of oil into the icy waters of Prince William Sound off of the Alaskan coast. Intensive efforts were made to contain, collect, and clean up the spill. In May 1993, two groups of environmental scientists gathered to discuss the impact of the oil spill on the plants and animals in the area of the disaster.

One group of researchers was funded by the corporation that owned the oil tanker. This group said the area had made an amazing ecological comeback and that there were no longer traces of oil in the organisms. The other group of researchers was funded by the government. This group said the area was still suffering from the spill and that it may take years before some of the animal populations recover. How could the conclusions from the two groups vary so greatly?

The groups used different techniques to determine the amount of oil damage to the organisms. Who was correct? The job of answering the question of who was right fell upon a group of six federal and state officials in charge of administering the cleanup of the area.

Differences such as those in this example are common in environmental research. There is often disagreement among environmental researchers on both the data and the interpretation of the data. Another example of such disagreement involves predictions about global warming. Many scientists have predicted that the atmosphere will warm if global concentrations of carbon dioxide continue to rise in the atmosphere. The exact amount of warming predicted varies from 0.5°C to 4°C. Other researchers think that global warming will not occur at all. These scientists believe that the warming trend observed over the last several decades is due to natural cycles in Earth's atmosphere.

One reason it is difficult to reach conclusions in environmental research is that Earth is a complex system. Many different variables affect the dynamic interactions that take place on the planet. How environmental researchers approach these variables can affect the outcome of the results. Who decides when data are correct? Most often, it is government policymakers who decide which data to act upon.

Alerting policymakers to potential environmental problems is often the role of various "watchdog" groups. These groups use scientific data to inform citizens about environmental problems. They also pressure government officials to take action. Watchdog groups make sure that environmental issues are not ignored in the process of policymaking. Joining a watchdog group is one way a concerned citizen can get involved in environmental issues.

DECISIONS

1. Which people are involved in deciding what to do with environmental research data?
2. Why might the results of research on the same environmental problem differ?

21

2.2 SKILLS AND METHODS

Objective • *Describe the steps involved in conducting a scientific experiment.*

There is no single process or set of steps that all scientists use. The scientist must always be prepared to go backward, change direction, and be flexible. The scientist must be prepared for surprising results or unexpected information. One investigation may lead to another, and yet another. The result for the scientist may be a lifetime of investigation and learning. Although the exact steps may vary, a good scientific investigation must have certain features. Every investigation begins with an observation.

Observing and Questioning

Observations can be made directly with the senses, such as sight or touch. But many observations are made with the help of tools. Tools help extend the senses, allowing further observations and measurements to be made. A scale, for example, enables a scientist to measure the mass of a rock more accurately than by simply hefting it. A microscope enables a scientist to view things too small for the unaided eye to see. Some tools enable scientists to measure things that could not otherwise be observed at all. For example, a Geiger counter lets scientists measure radiation that the senses cannot detect.

Observations are followed by a question. The question is based on something that was observed. For example, a scientist may observe that grass does not grow in a certain area, and ask why. A scientist may observe that people who work in a particular building become sick often, and ask why. But remember that science cannot answer questions about ethics or values.

Researching

How would you feel if you spent years trying to solve a mystery, only to find that someone else had already solved it? An important step in solving a scientific mystery, or conducting an investigation, is to find out what others have already discovered about the topic. Perhaps the earlier work can save you some steps. Perhaps your hypothesis has already been supported or disproven. A trip to the library will help a scientist learn what work has been done on the subject.

Sometimes scientists deliberately repeat work that was done by others. Repeating an experiment is an important part of science. If someone repeats your experiment and does not get the same results, there may be a problem with your hypothesis. Experimental results that cannot be repeated are not considered valid.

FIELD ACTIVITY

An important skill in detective work is observing and noting details about your surroundings. Using a specific site on the school grounds, make as many observations as you can in 10 minutes, and write them down. Based on your observations, make a list of five questions; for example: What was the color of the car parked on the corner? Exchange your list with that of your classmates and see how well you each observed your surroundings.

Make sure all students are observing the same area. They can work in groups, as long as they exchange questions with someone who has observed the same area.

Figure 2.2 Much of the data used in environmental science comes from field studies. Field studies take place in any kind of environment, not just fields.

Hypothesizing

Once the scientist has found out about the work others have done, it is time to determine what direction the investigation will take. The next step is to develop a hypothesis. Recall that a hypothesis is a possible explanation for an observation. The scientist should try to think of several hypotheses. From all the possible hypotheses, the scientist then chooses the most likely one. The ability to develop hypotheses and then choose among them is one of the most creative, important parts of a scientist's work.

Suppose a scientist observes that grass does not grow in a certain part of a lawn. The observation may raise a question: Why does grass not grow in this area? The scientist can offer several hypotheses, one of which will be investigated. For example, one hypothesis may be that the area does not receive enough water. Another hypothesis may be that the area is too shady. The presence of a grass disease could be yet another hypothesis to explain the observation. Only one hypothesis can be investigated in one experiment.

Once a hypothesis has been chosen, the scientist makes a prediction. The prediction states what the results of the experiment will be if the hypothesis is true. In the previous example, the scientist may predict that if the area is given more water, grass will grow. Which hypothesis would this prediction support? Suppose the scientist's hypothesis is that a fungus is killing the grass. What prediction could be made to support this hypothesis?

Sometimes a scientist may conduct an experiment without a clear hypothesis. Such an experiment could answer a question that begins with "what would happen if...?" This type of experiment is used to produce further observations that could be used as the basis for a hypothesis later. For such an experiment to be valid, it must be considered part of a larger experiment. For example, you might conduct an experiment to see what would happen if you added bleach to your laundry. You might observe that some clothes are

LITERATURE LINK

The mythology of many ancient cultures, such as the Greeks and Romans, was an attempt to explain observations of nature. Unlike modern science, the ideas put forth in mythology were not tested or testable.

cleaner, some are faded, and others are not affected at all. From these observations you could develop a hypothesis such as "bleach causes colors to fade on cotton fabric." You could then predict that if you wash a bright-colored cotton tee shirt with bleach, it will fade. At this point, you are ready to design an experiment.

Designing an Experiment

Scientists use experiments to either support or reject their hypotheses. If the results of an experiment disprove a hypothesis, the scientist may develop a new hypothesis and design a new experiment. If the results support the hypothesis, has the hypothesis been proven? Although it is tempting to say yes, scientists must be careful not to jump to conclusions. There could be an even better explanation that no one has thought of yet. Only after many experiments have supported the hypothesis is the explanation considered proven. Even then, it may be disproven by a better explanation in the future. Designing a good experiment to test a hypothesis is a very important part of scientific studies.

Variables   A **variable** *is any factor that affects the outcome of an experiment*. An experiment must test one, and only one, variable at a time. The variable being tested in an experiment is the *experimental variable*. Consider once again the problem of grass growth. If the hypothesis was that the grass died because there was no water, the variable to be tested would be the presence of water. The scientist would have predicted that by changing the experimental variable—the presence of water—the grass would grow. To be a valid experiment, all other variables should remain unchanged.

Figure 2.3 If the data do not support the hypothesis, the scientist may choose a new hypothesis and start the process again.

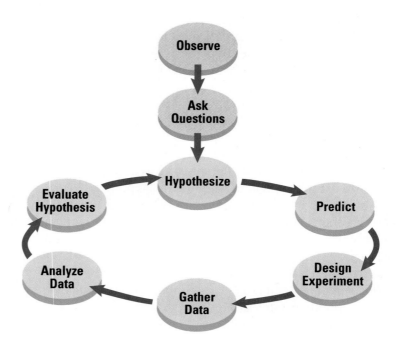

Experimental and Control Setups After the scientist has decided which variable to test, the next step is to set up the experiment. Suppose the scientist exposed the grassless area to more sunlight and gave the area more water. A few days later, new grass grew. The scientist cannot know whether it was the water, the sun, or both that caused the observed result. The skill in designing a good experiment is to isolate the one variable to be tested.

To test one variable at a time, an experiment must have two setups: an experimental setup and a control setup. In an experimental setup, the variable being tested is present. *In a* **control** *setup, the variable being tested is missing.* Recall that in the experiment about grass growth, the variable was water. The control setup would have all the other factors that were present when the original observations were made, including no water. The experimental setup would be identical to the control, except for the presence of water. Finally, the scientist makes a prediction: "If lack of water caused the grass to die, then the grass in the setup with water will live, and the control grass without water will die."

Collecting, Organizing, and Analyzing Data

Scientists must keep very careful records of their experiments. They must be careful to record not only the results of the experiment but also the steps they took to conduct the experiment. Once the data are collected, the scientist must decide what the results mean.

To analyze and interpret data, the scientist chooses a way to represent the data. Sometimes the data are organized into a table. A graph is often used to show patterns or trends in the data more easily. Some of the more common types of graphs are shown in Figure 2.4. Which type of graph would you use to show the results of the grass-growing experiment?

Once the experiment has been conducted and data have been collected and analyzed, the scientist communicates the work to others. Sometimes scientists share their work informally through conversations. To share work formally, scientists submit write-ups of their experiments to scientific journals. There are approximately 20,000 scientific journals. Each write-up must clearly show how the experiment was conducted, what the results were, and how the results can be interpreted.

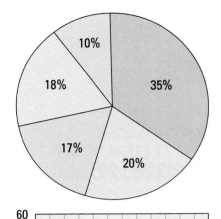

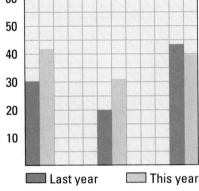

Last year   This year

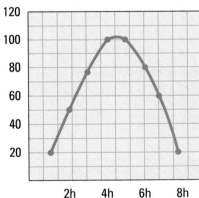

2h   4h   6h   8h

Figure 2.4 Circle graphs, or pie charts (top), show portions of a whole value. Bar graphs (center) are used to compare quantities. Line graphs (bottom) are used to show patterns of change, often over time.

SECTION REVIEW

1. How does an experimental setup differ from a control setup?
2. Why should a scientist conduct research before beginning an experiment?
3. **Infer** One of the most important skills a scientist can have is the ability to write well. Why do you think this is so?

1. In the control, the experimental variable is absent.
2. Research is conducted to determine what work has already been done on the subject.
3. Publishing write-ups of experiments is an important part of scientific communication.

2.3 ENVIRONMENTAL SCIENCE

Objectives • *Give examples of how parts of the environment interact.* • *Explain why policies must balance the needs of the environment with the needs of society.*

How would you describe your surroundings? If you are in a classroom, you might describe the tables and chairs, the posters on the wall, and the other students. You might also describe the lighting, the temperature, and a breeze from the window. If you were at home, at the mall, or camping in the woods, the surroundings you describe would be different. *Everything that surrounds an organism is its* **environment**. Environmental science is the study of the environments in which organisms live. As you learned in Chapter 1, all the environments in which organisms live make up the biosphere.

Why should people be interested in studying the environment? An organism's environment provides everything the organism needs in order to live. The environment provides food, water, shelter, air, and other resources. If conditions in the environment change, the organism may not be able to survive. Keeping the environment healthy is the first step in making sure that the biosphere can continue to support life in the future.

Environmental science is an integrated science. An integrated science is one that draws from many different fields of science. Because the environment includes organisms, environmental science includes some biology. Because energy and motion are part of the environment, environmental studies involve physics. Chemistry is part of environmental studies as well because all parts of the biosphere are made up of matter. Politicians, economists, sociologists, and other members of society are involved in environmental science as well.

Figure 2.5 Every environment has its own set of characteristics. What are the living and nonliving parts of each of the environments shown here?

Table 2.1 Areas of Study in Environmental Science

Area	Scientist	Subject
Water	Hydrologist	Flow of Earth's waters
	Oceanographer	Ocean environments
Air	Meteorologist	Weather and the atmosphere
	Climatologist	Global weather patterns
Land	Geologist	Structure and history of Earth
	Seismologist	Movements of Earth's surface
Organisms	Biologist	Structure and behavior of organisms
	Ecologist	Interactions of organisms and their environments
	Paleontologist	Prehistoric life and fossils
	Anthropologist	Structure of human societies

Table 2.1 shows some of the types of scientists that are involved in studying the environment. As you can see from the table, ecologists are scientists that study the interactions between organisms and their environments. What then is the difference between ecology and environmental science? Often the two terms are used to refer to the same thing. Indeed, you cannot study the environment without understanding the principles of ecology. The difference between the two fields of study is the role of humans.

The principles of ecology do not change simply by including humans in the picture. After all, humans are organisms and are part of the scheme of nature. Unlike other organisms, however, humans have the ability to create and enforce policy, and to affect the environment on a global scale. Environmental science incorporates the impact of human activities, both planned and unplanned, on the environment.

Parts of the Environment

All the factors that make up the environment can be divided into two categories: living and nonliving. *All the living parts of the environment are called* **biotic** (by-OT-ik) **factors**. Biotic factors in the classroom may include only humans and microbes too small to see. If you were camping, the list of biotic factors in your environment would be longer. The list might include plants, birds, mushrooms, insects, and so on.

All the nonliving parts of the environment are called **abiotic** (AY-by-OT-ik) **factors**. Abiotic factors include water, soil, and air, as well as temperature, wind, and sunlight. Some of the abiotic factors in an environment may once have been alive, such as your classroom's wooden chairs, which came from trees. Because the wood is no longer alive, it is therefore not a biotic factor.

FINE ARTS

L I N K

One way to record observations about your environment is through art. French painter Paul Gauguin (1848–1903) was fascinated with the plants, animals, and people of Tahiti. He made several trips to the islands and painted his impressions of the environment.

✳ **Multicultural Perspective**
Humans have survived in a wider range of habitats than most species. The Inuits of arctic North America have developed techniques that enable them to survive in one of the Earth's harshest regions. Have students research and share information on the lifestyle of the Inuits.

Environmental Interactions

Much of the research that is done in the area of environmental science involves interactions. Organisms interact with the biotic and abiotic factors in the environment. An organism may be affected by changes in the environment, and the environment can be affected by the organism. The change that occurred in the environment may, in turn, have an effect on another organism.

Sometimes it seems easy to predict how a change in the environment will affect other factors. For example, a particular species of butterfly can lay eggs on only one type of lupine flower. It is not difficult to predict what will happen to the butterflies if all the lupine flowers are destroyed. However, it is usually more difficult to predict how a change in one part of the environment will affect other parts. For example, there was once a thriving population of coyotes, deer, wolves, and mountain lions on the north rim of the Grand Canyon. In the early 1900s, the state of Arizona began rewarding hunters for killing the coyotes, mountain lions, and wolves because they were a danger to settlers and livestock. After 15 years, the hunted animals were almost completely wiped out. But these animals were the natural enemy of the deer, which were not being hunted.

Without wolves, coyotes, and mountain lions, the deer population soon grew to 25 times the size it had been before the hunting began. The deer ate all the available plants in the area. Eventually, the environment could no longer support so many deer, and approximately 60,000 deer died of starvation the following winters. Seventy years later, the plant growth in the area has not yet fully recovered. No one had predicted that the hunting would have such a destructive effect on the environment.

Figure 2.6 The tree responded to a change in its environment by adjusting the direction of its growth. The environment can also be changed by organisms, such as the change in the river caused by the beaver's dam.

Answers and teaching strategies on page T29.

The Capture-Recapture Method

PROBLEM

Every year, a team of biologists estimates the population size of a rare species of trout that live in Grass Lake. Grass Lake is polluted, but efforts are being made to clean it up. The biologists make their estimation using the capture-recapture method. The biologists float on rafts and capture fish on baited hooks. The fish are marked, tallied, and thrown back into the water. The biologists repeat the procedure a week later. Imagine you are a biologist on the team trying to answer this question: What is the size of the trout population in Grass Lake?

MATERIALS (per class)

- 100 to 200 toothpicks
- Watch or small clock

PREDICTION

The capture-recapture method will produce an accurate estimate of a population size.

PROCEDURE

1. For the first sampling, go with your class to the designated grass area. The borders of this area represent the shores of Grass Lake.
2. Previously, toothpicks were spread out over Grass Lake. Toothpicks have been cut in half. Each half toothpick represents a trout. Spend 2 minutes capturing toothpicks. Keep the toothpicks you capture in your hand, and return to class with them.
3. Mark the toothpicks in an agreed-upon manner without damaging them. Tally and record the number caught by the entire class. These are the marked trout in the total population.
4. Give your half toothpicks to a designated member of your class. The designated person will throw the marked toothpicks back in Grass Lake. They should be

randomly scattered across Grass Lake.
5. Return to Grass Lake with the rest of the class. Again, spend 2 minutes capturing toothpicks, and return to class with them.
6. Some of the toothpicks you've captured will probably be marked, indicating they had been previously captured. Separate these from the unmarked toothpicks.
7. Tally and record the number of toothpicks recaptured by the entire class. These are the marked trout recaptured.
8. Tally and record the total number of toothpicks, marked and unmarked, captured by the class during the second sampling. These are the total trout captured.
9. Return all toothpicks to your teacher.
10. Multiply the number of Total trout captured (Step 8) by Marked trout in total population (Step 3). Divide this product by the Marked trout recaptured (Step 7). the result is an estimate of the trout population in Grass Lake.

$$\frac{\text{Marked trout recaptured}}{\text{Total trout captured}} = \frac{\text{Marked trout in total population}}{X}$$

X = The size of the trout population in Grass Lake

ANALYSIS

1. To get an accurate estimate, why is it important that trout caught during the first sampling are returned to the lake unharmed?
2. What are possible sources of error with the capture-recapture method? How can these errors be minimized?
3. Could the capture-recapture method be used to accurately estimate the size of any population? Explain.

CONCLUSION

What is your estimate of the trout population in Grass Lake? Show the calculations you performed to obtain your estimate.

Figure 2.7 Citizens can voice their opinions by voting. Sometimes, however, people express themselves with protests and demonstrations to get their voices heard.

Making Decisions

Many changes that are taking place in the biosphere are the result of human activities. Many of these changes are harmful, and some could cause environmental disaster if they are allowed to continue. It may seem obvious that people should stop doing things that damage the environment. Unfortunately, deciding what needs to be done, and how to do it, are not such easy tasks.

The interactions that take place in the biosphere are very complex. As you have learned, it is not always possible to predict how one change will affect other parts of the environment. An organism may interact with its environment in ways scientists are not aware of. Whenever a public policy regarding the environment is put into effect, the government must try to predict what the impact of the policy will be. To do this, the government usually employs a team of researchers to study the interactions that will be affected.

Besides the impact a policy may have on the environment, the government must also consider the economic effect the policy may have on society. Public policies that regulate activities in an effort to protect the environment often end up costing people their jobs. A well-known example of the battle between preserving the environment and keeping jobs has been going on for years in the northwestern United States. In this region, efforts to protect old-growth forests and the organisms that live there have conflicted with the local economic concerns. The economy in the area depends heavily on the lumber industry, which would suffer from protection of the forest. In developing nations where food and fuel are scarce, the conflict between environmental issues and the needs of people are even more difficult to resolve.

Who should decide how, where, and when the environment is to be protected? Who will determine the steps that are to be taken in the future? There is no magic formula for solving these problems. One thing is clear, however. The more informed people are about how their activities affect the environment, the better prepared they are to protect the biosphere.

SECTION REVIEW

1. What is meant by the word *environment*?
2. Which parts of the environment respond to the activities of organisms, the biotic factors or the abiotic factors?
3. **Infer** Mosquito fish feed on young mosquitoes that can carry malaria. The young mosquitoes feed on tiny floating plants in ponds. Turtles feed on plants at the bottom of the ponds. These plants need sunlight from the surface. What might happen to the turtles if mosquito fish are brought into a pond?

1. An environment is everything that surrounds an organism.
2. Both biotic and abiotic factors can respond to the activities of organisms.
3. They could die, because a lack of mosquitoes increases the amount of floating plants, which reduces sunlight, which in turn reduces the number of plants available for turtles.

CHAPTER 2 REVIEW

KEY TERMS

hypothesis 2.1
variable 2.2

control 2.2
environment 2.3

biotic factor 2.3
abiotic factor 2.3

CHAPTER SUMMARY

2.1 Science is a way of learning about the natural world. Science is uncertain and changeable. Science is responsive to the needs of society, and voters are involved in making decisions that affect the progress of science.

2.2 A scientific investigation follows a series of steps that result in the support or rejection of a hypothesis. An experiment has a control setup and an experimental setup. In the control, the variable is absent.

2.3 Environmental science is an integrated science, one that draws from many fields of science. The environment includes biotic and abiotic factors. Biotic and abiotic factors interact with one another, but it is difficult to predict what the results of such interactions will be.

MULTIPLE CHOICE

Choose the letter of the word or phrase that best completes each statement.

1. Science is (a) a collection of information; (b) based on facts; (c) random; (d) uncertain. d
2. Science cannot answer questions that are (a) testable; (b) observable; (c) based on ethics; (d) based on observations. c
3. Observations should be made (a) before an experiment is designed; (b) while an experiment is being conducted; (c) before and during an experiment; (d) after the experiment is completed. c
4. A prediction should be made (a) before making observations; (b) before developing a hypothesis; (c) after developing a hypothesis; (d) after the experiment is conducted. c
5. A setup in which the experimental variable is not present is the (a) experimental setup; (b) variable setup; (c) data setup; (d) control setup. d
6. If you wanted to compare the rainfall this month with the rainfall last month in various locations, you could best represent the data in a (a) circle graph; (b) bar graph; (c) line graph; (d) pie chart. b
7. The abiotic factors in an environment include (a) plants; (b) animals; (c) water; (d) microbes. c
8. Interactions in the environment are usually (a) complex; (b) predictable; (c) easily observed; (d) well understood. a

TRUE/FALSE

Write true *if the statement is true. If the statement is false, change the underlined word to make it true.*

1. A scientist who studies movements of land is a <u>paleontologist</u>. f, seismologist
2. A <u>prediction</u> is a statement of what will happen during an experiment if the hypothesis is true. t
3. All the environments in which organisms live make up the <u>biosphere</u>. t
4. A wooden chair may be one of the <u>biotic</u> factors in your environment. f, abiotic
5. It is difficult to predict the results of changes in the biosphere because interactions are <u>simple</u>. f, complex
6. Environmental protection policies often have <u>economic</u> impact. t

CONCEPT REVIEW Answers on page T29.

Write a complete response to each of the following.

1. How are graphs useful in a scientific investigation?
2. Why is it important that scientists communicate the results of their experimentation to other scientists?
3. How has the invention of new tools, such as the electron microscope, influenced the progress of science?
4. A hypothesis can be considered an educated guess. Explain how this is different from a wild guess.
5. Why is it necessary for people who do not plan to have careers in science to be informed about the environment?

THINK CRITICALLY Answers on page T29.

1. Suppose there is a tree growing in your backyard, and the roots of the tree have damaged the pipes that bring water into the house. To restore the water, the tree must be removed. But the tree is home to a rare bird. Would you cut down the tree? Why or why not?
2. Suppose the tree in the above example is growing in someone else's yard, and recent studies have shown that the rare bird produces a chemical that may cure cancer. Would your opinion change? Explain your answer.
3. A friend is upset because the fish in his aquarium have been dying. He raises the temperature of the water and increases the amount of available food. The fish continue to die, so your friend decides that neither temperature nor food is responsible. What is wrong with your friend's approach to solving the problem? Is the conclusion valid?
4. Suppose you had lived near the Grand Canyon in the early 1900s. Do you think you would have supported the policy of rewarding hunters for killing wolves, coyotes, and mountain lions? Explain.

Computer Activity In 1980, the flowers in a particular field were made up of 40 percent daisies, 30 percent lupines, 15 percent daffodils, and 15 percent buttercups. In 1990, the combination of flowers in the same field was 35 percent daisies, 25 percent lupines, 25 percent daffodils, and 15 percent buttercups. Use a graphing program to represent the change of flowers as a circle graph and as a bar graph.

WRITE CREATIVELY

What do you think your neighborhood looked like 200 years ago? Write a story about an animal that fell asleep 200 years ago and just woke up. In your story, describe the changes that have taken place in the animal's environment.

PORTFOLIO

1. People used to believe that life could arise from nonliving things. Research the experiments of Francisco Redi and Louis Pasteur that disproved this idea. What were the variables and controls in each experiment? Prepare a presentation describing how each scientist followed the steps of a scientific experiment.
2. Each area of specialization in science uses specific types of tools to gather data. Choose one of the areas in Table 2.1. Find out what tools are used, and the type of data that each tool provides.

GRAPHIC ANALYSIS Answers on page T29.

Use the figure to answer the following.

1. The graph represents the amount of grain consumed per person per year in various parts of the world. The graph shows consumption in 1975 and expected consumption in the year 2000. Which type of graph is shown?
2. In what part of the world is consumption not expected to rise?
3. In what part of the world was grain consumption greatest in 1975? What part of the world is expected to be the greatest grain consumer in 2000?
4. Could this information be presented in a different form? Explain your answer.

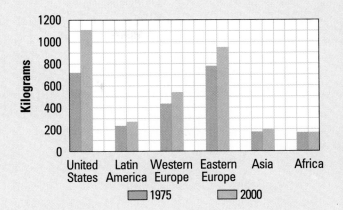

ACTIVITY 2.2

Answers and teaching strategies on page T29.

PROBLEM
How is a hypothesis tested and evaluated?

MATERIALS
- 3 radish seeds
- 3 lima bean seeds
- 2 sponges
- 2 Petri dishes
- wax marking pencil

HYPOTHESIS
Water is needed for seeds to germinate.

PROCEDURE

1. To test the hypothesis, place a wet sponge in one Petri dish. Pour a small amount of water in the dish. The top of the sponge should be moist but not submerged. Label this dish *experiment*.
2. Place a dry sponge in the other dish. Do not allow this sponge to get wet. Label this dish *control*.
3. Place 3 radish seeds and 3 lima bean seeds on top of each sponge. **Caution**: Wash your hands after handling the seeds because they are often coated with chemicals.
4. Keep the two dishes close together at all times. Keep all conditions, except moisture, the same for each setup. Be sure to keep the wet sponge moist.
5. Examine the seeds over the next few days.
6. Record the number of seeds that germinated from each setup in a data table.

ANALYSIS

1. Describe an observation of nature that might lead someone to develop the original hypothesis.
2. What factors did you control in this experiment?
3. What was the tested variable? Why is it important to test only one variable in an experiment? Do your observations support or reject the previously stated hypothesis? If necessary, restate your hypothesis.

CONCLUSION
Why is evaluating your hypothesis an important part of a good scientific experiment?

CHAPTER

3

CHANGE IN THE BIOSPHERE

3.1 The Changing Environment
3.2 Needs of Organisms
3.3 The Ecosystem

You might think as you look around that the world has always been the way it is now. Mountains have always been where they now stand. Ocean waves have been crashing on the shore for so long that giant rocks have been worn to sand. Rivers have flowed through the country-side for so long they have carved deep canyons along their paths. Rain forests have been growing long enough to develop life forms that exist nowhere else. Although it may seem that the world is a very stable, unchangeable place, the truth is just the opposite. All the parts of the biosphere are constantly moving, changing, and interacting—and they have been for billions of years.

3.1 THE CHANGING ENVIRONMENT

Objective • **Describe** *ways in which the three layers of the bio-sphere have changed over time.*

Humans have only lived on Earth for fewer than 0.5 million years. But Earth itself is approximately 4.5 billion years old. Change has been a part of Earth's nature since it first formed. Many rapid changes have taken place as a result of human activity.

Changes in the Lithosphere

The lithosphere is made up of several large movable plates called **tectonic** (tek-TON-ik)**plates.** Figure 3.1 shows the major tectonic plates of Earth's surface. Liquid rock below the surface rises through cracks between the plates deep in the ocean floor. As the hot, liquid rock meets the cool ocean water, the rock cools and hardens. New rock pushes the tectonic plates apart, causing them to shift position. When the plates shift, earthquakes can occur along the edges of the plates. Mountain chains rise when the movements of the plates cause parts of Earth's surface to buckle.

Besides the movement of tectonic plates, weather and flowing water also affect the shape of the land. *The breaking down of rocks by weather and water is called* **weathering.** *The broken down material is then carried off in the process of* **erosion** (eh-ROH-zhun). Together, the effects of tectonic plate movements, followed by weathering and erosion, have resulted in Earth's present land formations.

Figure 3.1 The surface of Earth is made up of several tectonic plates. Arrows show the direction in which the plates move.

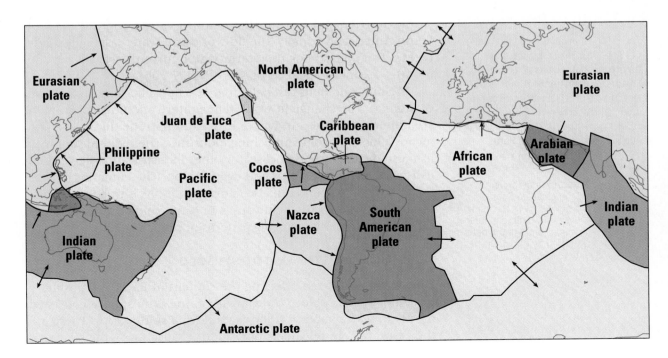

Changes in the Hydrosphere

Just as the shape and location of the land have changed over time, so have the shapes and locations of Earth's oceans. Some of the changes that have taken place in the hydrosphere have progressed slowly and steadily throughout time. Other changes occur in a series of cycles. Ice ages are cycles that take place over millions of years. El Niño is a change that occurs on a cycle of 4 to 7 years.

Ice Ages   An *ice age* is a long period of cooling during which huge ice masses, called glaciers, move from the poles and cover much of Earth's surface. After the ice age, the glaciers retreat back toward the poles. Scientists have found evidence of at least five major ice ages in Earth's history. The most recent ice age ended between 12,000 and 10,000 years ago, although some researchers think that the glaciers are still retreating.

The movement of glaciers causes significant changes in the shape of the land. The scraping of the ice across the land and the displacement of rocks result in large-scale weathering and erosion in some areas and the deposit of materials in other areas. Many of the geological features of the northern United States are the result of the last ice age, including the Great Lakes and the peninsula of Cape Cod.

No one knows what causes glaciers to advance and then retreat, although there are many hypotheses. Some scientists think that a wobbling of Earth on its axis is responsible for ice ages. What scientists do know, however, is that ice ages are associated with periods of global cooling.

El Niño   Every year near the end of December, a current of warm, nutrient-poor water flows southward along the coast of South America. Normally, the flow of warm water lasts only a few weeks. But sometimes the warm water current lasts for several months, a condition called El Niño (NEEN-yoh).

El Niño conditions can have a far-reaching effect on climate and economics. The change in water temperature and nutrient content are important to the survival of fish. A drop in the number of fish means a loss of income for fishing industries. The reduced supply of fish also means increased costs for other industries that depend on fish meal, such as poultry and egg farming. The climatic changes associated with El Niño can also damage crops. As is true for ice ages, no one knows exactly what causes El Niño conditions to occur. El Niño is one of many recurring patterns of change in ocean currents.

Changes in the Atmosphere

Organisms have been affecting the content of Earth's atmosphere since life began. Before there was life, the atmosphere consisted mostly of water vapor, carbon dioxide, and sulfur gases. These are the gases that are released from erupting volcanoes—the source of

Figure 3.2 Glaciers contain bubbles of air that were trapped when the glacier formed thousands of years ago. By analyzing the gas contained in the bubbles, scientists can compare the modern atmosphere to the atmosphere at the time the glacier formed.

The use of ice cores to analyze the atmosphere is explained more fully in Chapter 18.

Earth's early atmosphere. The very first simple organisms obtained energy from the chemicals in the ancient seas. Eventually, bacteria evolved that could combine water, carbon dioxide, and the energy in sunlight to produce food. This process, called photosynthesis, released the first oxygen into the atmosphere.

For approximately 3.5 billion years, oxygen, carbon dioxide, water vapor, and nitrogen have been cycling from the atmosphere, through the bodies of organisms, and back into the atmosphere. You will learn more about these cycles in Chapter 4. Although some of Earth's carbon is continually being cycled, much is stored in the bodies of organisms, both alive and dead. Coal and other fossil fuels, for example, contain stored carbon from long-dead organisms. The release of stored carbon into the atmosphere by burning organic matter may influence the temperature of Earth through a process called the *greenhouse effect.*

The greenhouse effect is just one way in which humans are having an impact on Earth's atmosphere. Ozone depletion in the stratosphere and increased pollution in the troposphere are also being caused by humans. But humans and other organisms are not the only factors that affect the atmosphere. Volcanoes continue to erupt just as they did when Earth was young. Major volcanic eruptions, such as the eruption of Mount Pinatubo in the Philippines in 1991, send gases into the atmosphere that are transported by winds around the world.

Figure 3.3 When Mount Pinatubo erupted, it sent gases and particles high into the atmosphere. Scientists estimate that the eruption caused temperatures around the world to be 0.5°C cooler than normal the following year.

SECTION REVIEW

1. Through what process does weather affect the shape of land?
2. In what ways does El Niño affect the economy?
3. **Integrate** Describe how ice ages are related to changes in the lithosphere, hydrosphere, and atmosphere.

1. Weather affects the shape of the land through erosion.
2. By affecting climate and water quality, farming and fishing industries are affected.
3. In ice ages, the state of water changes in the hydrosphere, air bubbles are trapped, and land is eroded in the lithosphere.

3.2 NEEDS OF ORGANISMS

Objectives • *List factors that affect an area's ability to support life.*
• *Predict how changes in the environment might affect organisms.*

As you have learned, the environment provides an organism with everything it needs in order to live. Every type of organism has a different set of specific needs. For example, you can easily see how your needs are different from those of a goldfish or a tree. Despite these differences, however, all organisms have certain needs in common. Water, a source of energy, living space, and a suitable climate are requirements of all living things.

Water

The presence of fresh water is one of the most important factors in the ability of land to support life. Water is needed for plants to grow, and plants and water are both necessary for an animal population to survive. The amount of rainfall on an area of land directly affects the abundance of life in that area.

Organisms that live in the oceans are not usually affected by local rainfall. But because they are completely surrounded by water, fish and other organisms in the oceans are affected by water quality. Temperature, nutrients, dissolved oxygen, and pollution are factors that affect water quality. Warm water contains less dissolved oxygen than does cooler water. Water that becomes warmer than normal often does not contain enough oxygen to keep most types of organisms alive.

Food and Energy

Almost all the energy used by living things comes from the sun and is stored in the form of food. Through photosynthesis, plants and algae can make food by capturing energy from the sun. Animals and other organisms get their energy by eating plants, or by eating animals that eat plants.

Food contains not only energy, but also minerals, vitamins, and other chemicals. These materials are used by organisms to build tissues and carry out biochemical reactions. *Together, all the substances that an organism requires from food are called* **nutrients.** Like most animals, you obtain nutrients by eating, or ingesting food through your mouth. Fungi, protists, plants, and some animals, such as small worms, can absorb nutrients directly into the cells of their bodies.

Some substances are stored and can build up in the cells of the body's tissues. If the substance is harmful, the tissues can become poisonous to other organisms. The buildup of poisonous materials in an organism's tissues allows poisons in the environment to pass from one organism to another.

HEALTH LINK

The average human body needs to take in about 2 L of water every day to remain healthy. In the United States, the average person uses an additional 240 L each day for bathing, washing clothes and dishes, and flushing the toilet.

Teaching tips for Field Activity appear on page T33.

FIELD ACTIVITY

Different organisms consume different foods. What foods do you think ants prefer? Choose an area around your school where ants are likely to live. Place several different types of foods in small bottle caps, and return the following day. Record your observations about the presence of ants. Which foods attracted the most ants?

Cooperative Learning
Have students pool their observations. In groups, students can analyze the results and develop a hypothesis about what quality of the foods attracted the ants. The group can then design an experiment to test their hypothesis.

Living Space

All organisms need space to live. Living space enables organisms to obtain the materials they need from the environment. For example, plants need space so they can get enough sunlight. They also need space for their roots to grow so they can obtain water and minerals from the soil. If trees grow too closely together, some will die.

Animals need space in which to seek food, water, shelter, and mates. Many animals claim specific areas as their own. *An area that is claimed as a living space by an individual animal is called a* **territory.** Animals that maintain territories are called *territorial animals.*

Many territorial animals mark their territory with scents to let intruders know that the area is off limits. Domestic house cats are a familiar example of a territorial animal. Cats have glands on their faces that produce scents with which they mark their territory. People often mistake the rubbing of a cat's face against their hand or leg as a sign of affection. Actually, the cat is just marking the person as part of its territory. Some animals defend their territories with sounds or gestures.

The size of a territory is determined by the type of animal. If there is not enough space for all the members of a population, they will compete for a territory, often to the death. Competition for space and the resources within the space is an important factor in the process of evolution. You will read more about evolution in Chapter 5.

THINK CRITICALLY

In many species of animals, territorial fighting involves sounds and gestures, but no physical contact. Why do you think such encounters may be more beneficial to the animals than violent fighting?

Because the winner is often injured in violent fights, the winner may be poorly fit to fight off the next challenger. By defending territory nonviolently, the winner remains strong, and the loser can try again elsewhere.

Figure 3.4 To keep animals as healthy as possible, many zoos try to reproduce the natural environments in which the animals live.

Figure 3.5 Different types of animals require different climates. The polar bear and the camel could not survive in each other's environment.

Warm-blooded animals are called endotherms. All others are ectotherms. It is a common misconception that ectotherms are cold-blooded. Instead, their temperature is controlled by the environment whether warm or cold.

Climate

Most organisms can survive only within a certain range of temperatures. The range of temperatures at which an organism can survive is its *range of tolerance*. The range of tolerance for a particular type of organism is a factor in the distribution of the organism around the world.

The temperature inside the body of most organisms is determined by the temperature of the environment. When the environment becomes cooler, so does the organism's body. Many organisms, especially plants that live in colder areas, survive the cold by becoming dormant. *When an organism becomes* **dormant** (DOR-munt), *the life processes within the body slow down.* Most dormant plants lose their leaves and stop growing. The growth of bacteria and other microorganisms can also be slowed by reducing the temperature of the surrounding environment. Why do you think refrigerators are used to keep foods fresh? Refrigerators slow the growth of food-spoiling organisms.

Birds and mammals, including humans, maintain a high body temperature regardless of the temperature of the environment. Because birds and mammals maintain a steady, warm body temperature, they are commonly called warm-blooded animals. Warm-blooded animals have a wider range of tolerance, and can remain active in more diverse climates, than other animals. But maintaining a high body temperature requires a great deal of food because producing and maintaining heat uses a lot of energy. Warm-blooded animals tend to need about ten times more food than other animals of the same size.

Like plants, many types of animals become dormant during periods of cold temperatures and low food supplies. *Dormancy in some animals is called* **hibernation** (HY-ber-NAY-shun). During hibernation, heart rate and breathing slow, the body temperature drops, and the animal enters a sleeplike state. Energy requirements during hibernation are very low, enabling the animal to survive a period when there is not enough food to maintain normal activities. This is especially important for warm-blooded animals.

SECTION REVIEW

1. In what ways does behavior among territorial animals differ?
2. How does hibernation help animals to survive?
3. Do you think that the amount of water used by each person in the United States has changed over time? If so, in what way? Explain your answer.
4. **Predict** Suppose a particular area was to experience a sudden change in rainfall and temperature that lasts a long time. Do you think the area would lose its ability to support life? Explain your answer.

1. Some use violence; others use sounds or gestures.
2. Hibernation reduces energy needs during a period of low food supply.
3. You could expect that the use of modern plumbing and machines have increased the amount of water used.
4. It would not lose its ability to support life, but it would support a different collection of organisms.

The Mississippi Flood

Who should pay for property damage on a floodplain?

1. Accept all well-defended answers. Students should realize that flood prevention has risks.
2. Responses will vary.

During the summer of 1993, the Mississippi River and many of its tributaries overflowed their banks. Thousands of people in eight states were evacuated. Seventeen people died. Billions of dollars worth of property and crops were destroyed by the rising waters.

The flooding of the Mississippi River basin is part of the river's natural cycle. Old rivers like the Mississippi regularly flood their banks. When they flood, rivers deposit rich sediment along the edges of the banks, areas known as floodplains. Rich soil is one reason that many farmlands exist along riverbanks.

A variety of factors contribute to flooding, including the amount of rain or snow, the type of vegetation on the floodplain, the type of floodplain soil, and the steepness of the terrain. Human activities affect some of these natural flooding factors. Farming, mining, and clear-cutting of trees reduce the amount of water that can seep into the soil. Construction along a floodplain decreases the amount of surface area that can absorb water. Levees built along one part of a river may lead to increased flooding farther down the river.

The federal government has spent much money on building flood-control projects along the Mississippi River. Some people believe more money should be spent on flood control and flood relief. Others disagree.

Supporting Points

• Land along a floodplain is flat and the soil is rich. Farmers should be allowed to plant crops in this rich soil because the food benefits many people.
• The river is convenient for transporting goods. Cities develop at river ports. Flood-control projects stimulate the economy.
• People have lived along the Mississippi River for a long time. A flood of this size will not occur again for many years.
• People live in areas that are prone to hurricanes, tornadoes, and earthquakes. Government money is used to help these areas.

Opposing Points

• People should be responsible for obtaining their own insurance if they live in an area that might flood.
• Billions of dollars were spent on flood-control projects that failed during the flood of 1993. The money spent on flood-control projects could be used for other projects that would benefit more people.
• The building of levees on the Mississippi River prevents the river from delivering sediment to the floodplain. Each year this results in major losses of marshlands, which would help control flooding.
• More than $8 billion has already been spent on flood-control projects.

DECISIONS

1. Do you think it is possible to live along a floodplain without being affected by the natural flooding of the river? How?
2. Do you think government money should be spent to help areas built along a floodplain? Explain your answer.

Answers and teaching
strategies on page T33.

Environmental Needs of Land Isopods

PROBLEM

What environmental conditions do land isopods need?

MATERIALS (per group)

- shoebox with lid
- 2 paper towels
- aluminum foil
- water (Part A)
- masking tape
- 5 land isopods
- scissors (Part B)

HYPOTHESIS

After reading the entire activity, write a hypothesis that relates to the problem.

PROCEDURE

To study the preference of land isopods for moisture or dryness, do Part A. To study their preference for lightness or darkness, do Part B.

Part A

1. Line a shoebox with aluminum foil.
2. Tape two paper towels side by side to the inside bottom of the shoebox. Place a strip of masking tape between the two paper towels.
3. Moisten one of the paper towels with water.
4. Place five isopods on the masking tape between the two paper towels. Place the lid on the shoebox. **Caution:** *Handle live animals with care and respect.*
5. Leave the shoebox undisturbed for 5 minutes. Make a data table like the one shown. Substitute *Moist Paper* and *Dry Paper* for *Condition 1* and *Condition 2*.
6. After 5 minutes, remove the lid. Quickly count the number of isopods on moist paper, on tape, and on dry paper. Record your results beside Trial 1 in the table.
7. Gently slide the isopods back onto the masking tape, and repeat steps 4–6 two more times.
8. Average the results of each column, and write the averages in the last row of the data table.

Part B

1. Follow steps 1 and 2 in Part A.
2. Cut the lid in half across the width, and cover half the shoebox with one of the pieces. **Caution:** *Handle sharp scissors with care.*
3. Place five isopods on the masking tape beween the two paper towels.
4. Leave the shoebox undisturbed for 5 minutes. Make a data table like the one shown. Write *Dark* and *Light* for *Conditions 1* and *2*.
5. After 5 minutes, remove the half lid. Quickly count the number of isopods on the dark half, on the masking tape, and on the light half. Record your results beside Trial 1 in the data table.
6. Gently slide the isopods back onto the masking tape, and repeat steps 4–6 two more times.
7. Average the results of each column, and write the averages in the last row of the data table.

ANALYSIS

1. Were you able to confirm your hypothesis? Explain why or why not.
2. Write a statement about the preference of land isopods for the factor studied.

CONCLUSION

Based on the class results, what can you infer about the environmental needs of land isopods? Describe their habitats.

Number of Isopods

Trial	(Condition 1)	Masking Tape	(Condition 2)
1			
2			
3			
Avg			

3.3 THE ECOSYSTEM

Objectives • *Describe* the structure of an ecosystem. • *Relate* the concept of habitat destruction to the loss of biodiversity.

An ecosystem is not simply a random collection of organisms and environmental factors. An ecosystem is a highly organized, structured environment in which all parts exist in a delicate balance. Ecosystems can be studied at a variety of levels, from individual species to the entire ecosystem.

Species

All organisms of the same type are members of the same species. *A* **species** *is a group of organisms so similar to one another that they can breed and produce fertile offspring.* All the members of a species have similar needs, such as the range of tolerance, size of territory, and types of food. Because they have the same needs, members of a species often compete with one another for resources.

The type of environment in which a particular species lives is its **habitat.** For example, the tops of the trees in a pine forest may be the habitat of a species of bird. A shallow, fast-moving, cold water stream may be the habitat of a species of trout. A rotting log is an ideal habitat for various species of insects, fungi, and microorganisms. The habitat provides the appropriate type of food, shelter, temperature, and so on that members of the species need to live. The destruction of habitat is a serious threat to the survival of many species.

The total area in which a species can live is called its **geographical range.** The size of the geographical range depends largely on the size of the area that has a suitable habitat. For example, the mountain lion requires a habitat with diverse plant life, a large hunting territory, and a variety of prey animals. Because its habitat was

DATELINE 1973

The U.S. Congress passed the Endangered Species Act of 1973 to protect disappearing wildlife. Twenty years later, there were 278 species of animals and 298 species of plants listed as endangered in the United States. There are more than 1 million species worldwide known to be endangered. Some scientists estimate that there are as many as 10 million more endangered species that have not been and may never be identified.

Have students compare the ecological meaning of the word *community* to the more common, social use of the word.

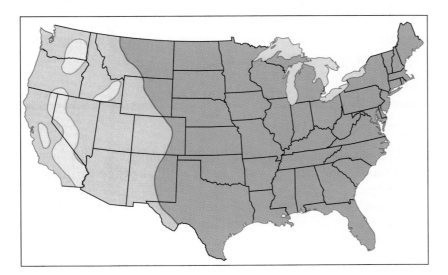

Figure 3.6 The geographical range of the mountain lion has been greatly reduced in the United States because of the destruction of its habitat. The mountain lion's range once included all green and orange areas. They now live only in the orange areas.

Figure 3.7 All the members of a species that live in an area are a population. All the populations in the area make up a community. The ecosystem consists of the community and the abiotic factors in the area.

once common, mountain lions ranged throughout the continental United States. Much of the mountain lion's habitat has since been developed for use by humans. As you can see in Figure 3.6, mountain lions are now restricted to a limited range in the Rockies and other western mountains.

Populations and Communities

All the members of a species that live in the same area make up a **population.** For example, all the dandelions in a field are a population. Ecologists sometimes think of a population as a single living unit. The ants in an anthill, for example, can be thought of as a single unit. Although individual ants hatch and die, the anthill population remains relatively unchanged. To study the effect of a factor on ants, a researcher would probably study a population rather than an individual ant.

Populations do not live alone in their environments. In any region, many different populations share the same living space. These populations interact with one another in a variety of ways. *All the populations that live and interact in the same environment make up a* **community.**

Ecosystems

An **ecosystem** *includes all the communities that live in an area, as well as the abiotic factors in the environment.* Ecosystems therefore include the water, soil, and climate in the area. A healthy ecosystem includes a wide variety of species in its community. *The variety of species in an ecosystem is known as* **biodiversity.**

If enough of a particular type of habitat is destroyed, the species that live in the habitat can die out completely, or become extinct. When species become extinct, biodiversity in the ecosystem is reduced. Much attention has recently focused on the loss of tropical rainforest ecosystems. These ecosystems contain many species that exist nowhere else. Destruction of the forests can mean the extinction of many species, and therefore a loss in both biodiversity and stability of the ecosystem.

SECTION REVIEW

1. What factors are included in an ecosystem?
2. What do you think is the geographical range for human beings?
3. **Apply** Some ancient cultures, such as the societies that live in rain forests, are shrinking as a result of the destruction of their habitats. Do you think human societies should be protected, as are endangered species of plants and animals? Explain your answer.

KEY TERMS

tectonic plate 3.1	territory 3.2	habitat 3.3	community 3.3
weathering 3.1	dormant 3.2	geographical range 3.3	biodiversity 3.3
erosion 3.1	hibernation 3.2	population 3.3	
nutrients 3.2	species 3.3	ecosystem 3.3	

CHAPTER SUMMARY

3.1 All three layers of the biosphere have been changing since Earth formed. Erosion and the movement of tectonic plates cause changes in the lithosphere. Ice ages and El Niños are examples of cyclical changes in the hydrosphere. Changes in the atmosphere have resulted from organic and volcanic activities.

3.2 Organisms obtain what they need to live from their environments. These needs include water, energy, living space, and a suitable climate.

3.3 Organisms of the same type make up a species. Members of a species in a given area make up a population. All the populations in an area are a community. An ecosystem includes all the communities and abiotic factors in an area.

MULTIPLE CHOICE

Choose the letter of the word or phrase that best completes each statement.

1. Glaciers, weather, and water shape the Earth by (a) tectonics; (b) erosion; (c) ice ages; (d) hibernation b
2. The most recent ice age ended about (a) 10,000 years ago; (b) 100,000 years ago; (c) 1 million years ago; (d) 10 million years ago a
3. The decline in the anchovy industry of Peru is blamed on (a) pollution; (b) dormancy; (c) El Niño; (d) economics c
4. Almost all the energy used by living things comes from (a) plants; (b) animals; (c) Earth; (d) the sun d
5. Hibernation enables an animal to save (a) energy; (b) space; (c) time; (d) heat a
6. The type of environment that is suitable for a certain species is its (a) geographical range; (b) habitat; (c) population; (d) community b
7. All the members of a species that live in an area make up a(n) (a) community; (b) habitat; (c) ecosystem; (d) population d
8. A stable ecosystem includes (a) one type of organism; (b) two types of organisms; (c) at least one type of plant and one type of animal; (d) a wide variety of organisms d
9. Habitat destruction can result in a loss of (a) species; (b) air; (c) energy; (d) land a

WORD COMPARISONS

Write the letter of the second word pair that best matches the first pair.

1. Territory: geographical range as (a) time: space; (b) home: job; (c) yard: neighborhood; (d) land: water c
2. Species: population as (a) population: community; (b) ecosystem: community; (c) community: habitat a
3. Hibernation: animals as (a) erosion: land; (b) dormancy: plants; (c) volcanoes: gases; (d) habitat: geographical range b
4. Sun: plants as (a) plants: animals; (b) water: fish; (c) land: Soil; (d) animals: food a
5. Ant: anthill as (a) population: species; (b) individual: population; (c) community: neighborhood; (d) population: ecosystem b

CHAPTER 3 REVIEW

CONCEPT REVIEW Answers on page T33.

Write a complete response to each of the following.

1. Describe the forces that cause change to take place in the lithosphere.
2. List four factors that currently affect Earth's atmosphere. Identify two factors that are caused by humans, and two that are not.
3. What do organisms obtain from the food they eat?
4. Distinguish between territory and geographical range.
5. Why is the geographical range of the mountain lion much smaller than it used to be?

THINK CRITICALLY Answers on page T33.

1. Explain how glaciers are involved in changes in the lithosphere, the hydrosphere, and the atmosphere.
2. Why are animals that eat other animals dependent on energy from the sun?
3. The size of an animal's territory depends more on the type of food the animal eats than on the size of the animal. Why?
4. Sometimes all the members of a species make up a single population. Sometimes a species is made up of many populations. What is the difference between the habitats of the two species? Which species do you think is in greater danger of becoming extinct? Explain your answer.
5. The photograph on page 34 shows fossils of animals called crinoids that thrived in shallow seas 350 million years ago. These fossils were found in limestone in the central plains of North America. What changes in the biosphere can be deduced from these fossils?

Computer Activity Dense tropical rain forests are a type of habitat that is being destroyed in many parts of the world. The table below shows the total area (in thousands of hectares) in selected nations, and the rate at which the rainforests are disappearing. Use a graphing program to construct bar graphs comparing the size of the forests in 1990 and the expected size in the year 2000.

Nation	Area in 1990	Percentage Lost Each Year
Brazil	357,480	2.2
India	36,540	4.1
Ivory Coast	4,458	6.5

WRITE FOR UNDERSTANDING

Use the title of each section of the chapter to create an outline of the chapter's main ideas. Under each title, write a few sentences that summarize the topic.

PORTFOLIO

1. What was your neighborhood like before it was inhabited by humans, and how has it changed? Research the types of wildlife that are native to your area, including plants and animals. Are any extinct or endangered? Prepare a presentation comparing the former habitat and that of the present.
2. How do different types of animals mark and defend their territories? Investigate the behavior of a territorial species of frog, mammal, and bird and compare their territorial activities.

GRAPHIC ANALYSIS Answers on page T33.

Use Figure 3.1 to answer the following.
1. In which direction is the North American plate moving?
2. On how many plates does the continent of South America lie?
3. Why are there more earthquakes on the west coast of the United States than anywhere else in the country?
4. In 1 million years, would you expect the continents of North America and Asia to be closer together or farther apart?

ACTIVITY 3.2

Answers and teaching strategies on page T33.

PROBLEM
What happens when a glacier moves over Earth's surface?

MATERIALS (per group)
- rocks, sand, gravel
- metal pie tin
- flat piece of wood (at least 20 cm by 40 cm)
- marker

HYPOTHESIS
Write a hypothesis that relates to the problem.

PROCEDURE
1. Use the marker to write your group's name on the bottom of a pie tin. Put rocks, sand, and gravel in the pie tin, slightly higher than the top of the sides of the tin.
2. Take the pie tin to the freezer. Pour water into the pie tin almost to the top. Some of the rocks should extend above the water level.
3. Put the pie tin in the freezer, and leave it for 24 hours.
4. Examine the appearance of the piece of wood. Record your observations. Scatter small rocks and sand over the surface of the wood.
5. The next day, remove the pie tin from the freezer. Invert the pie tin on one end of the wood. The rock-scattered wood represents Earth's surface; the ice and rock material in the pie tin represents a glacier.
6. Push the glacier in a straight line along Earth's surface to represent glacial advance. Apply moderate downward pressure to imitate the weight of a glacier. Observe what happens to the rocks on Earth's surface and the glacier as they come in contact. Record your observations.
7. Rescatter the rocks, and repeat Step 6 two more times.
8. Remove all objects from the wood, and note the appearance of the wood's surface. Record your observations and compare the wood to its original condition.

ANALYSIS
1. What happened to objects in the path of the glacier?
2. How was the glacier affected as it moved over Earth's surface? Explain.
3. What happened to the surface of the wood that the glacier passed over?

CONCLUSION
1. How do glaciers affect the surface of Earth?
2. An *erratic* is a huge boulder whose composition is inconsistent with the rocks in the surrounding area. Based on what you have oberved in this activity, write a hypothesis to explain the existence of erratics.

ENVIRONMENTAL PLANNING

A project that uses land and natural resources requires careful, thorough planning. Projects that require planning include wildlife conservation projects, the use of forests and other natural lands, housing and commercial development, road construction, and the restoration of historical sites. Environmental planners are employed by the government (66 percent), nonprofit organizations (19 percent), and private companies (15 percent).

Professional environmental planners design systems that take into account the needs of society, economics, and nature balanced with sound scientific and environmental practices. They conduct research, develop a vision for the future, and oversee the project.

Most careers in environmental science require a college degree and excellent communication skills. Although approximately 30 colleges offer a major in planning, you can enter the field with a degree in other areas. You should, however, take courses in environmental science, economics, and urban studies. Many organizations offer internships or volunteer positions. Experience in environmental planning is almost as important as a college degree.

◀ SCIENTISTS

In 1970, the National Environmental Policy Act was ratified. The act requires that an environmental impact statement (EIS) be issued before the inception of any major project funded by the federal government. An EIS is prepared by a team of scientists who study the area and determine what the environmental impact may be. Biologists study the impact on wildlife. Hydrologists study the flow of water above and below the ground at the project site. Geologists study the soil and rock composition. Most state and local governments now require an EIS for nonfederal projects as well.

POLITICIANS ▶

A planned project must have public support and be responsive to the needs of the local community. Politicians bring the voice of the people they represent to the people who make decisions. Much of the job of environmental planners requires negotiating. Politicians are professional speakers and negotiators who are directly involved in the decision-making process.

◀ COMPANIES AND CONSULTING FIRMS

Environmental planners are employed by many private companies, such as waste management companies, mining companies, the timber industry, and railroads. Planners help these companies obtain permits and comply with government policies.

Many private companies are too small, or their need for planners is too infrequent, to employ full-time planners. Instead, they may turn to private environmental consulting firms. Government agencies occasionally employ private consulting firms as well.

◀ GOVERNMENT PLANNERS

Environmental planners are employed by the government at the federal, state, and local levels. Federal planners design air, water, and waste management programs, as well as military and other federal property development projects. The Housing and Urban Development (HUD) department, as well as other departments, also work with local planners.

State governments employ planners to help set public policy on land use, and to manage natural resources. State planners are also responsible for inspections, permits, and public education.

Local governments in towns and cities have the greatest need for environmental planners. These agencies develop zoning maps that show where and how the land may be used. They also undertake local development projects.

▼ NONPROFIT ORGANIZATIONS

Environmental nonprofit organizations may be involved in neighborhood, urban, or natural resource management issues. Many organizations serve as "watchdog" groups, conducting their own research into the environmental impact of a project. Nonprofit groups such as local public-interest research groups (PIRGs) offer nonprofessional and volunteer positions that do not require a college degree. Such opportunities are an excellent way to gain experience and get involved in environmental planning.

FOR MORE INFORMATION:

American Planning Association (APA)
1776 Massachusetts Avenue, NW
Washington, DC 20036
(202) 872-0611

Partners for Livable Places
1429 21st Street, NW
Washington, DC 20036
(202) 887-5990

*Guide to Graduate Education in
Urban and Regional Planning*
Available from the APA Bookstore
1313 E. 60th Street
Chicago, IL 60637
(312) 955-9100

UNIT 2

ECOLOGICAL INTERACTIONS

CHAPTERS

4 Matter and Energy in the Ecosystem
5 Interactions in the Ecosystem
6 Ecological Balance

This symbol means *house*. It comes from Sumeria, an ancient civilization in the Middle East. The term *ecology* comes from the Greek word meaning house. The study of ecology is the study of "houses," from the nest of a bird, to Earth, the home of all known living things. Humans are very good at changing the environment to meet their needs and at building houses that enable them to live in almost any environment. But in building their houses, people often disturb the homes of other organisms.

All organisms have a place to live, and all change the environment in which they live. Many human societies cause profound changes in the environment. ▶

4

MATTER AND ENERGY IN THE ECOSYSTEM

All ecosystems do two things: they transfer energy and they cycle matter. The energy that powers most ecosystems is sunlight. A few small ecosystems are powered by inorganic molecules. In an ecosystem energy moves in only one direction, from the sun into organisms, then into space as heat. All ecosystems require a continuous input of new energy in order to function.

Unlike energy, matter is recycled in the ecosystem. Atoms of carbon, oxygen, and other elements are used again and again by different organisms. The limits of the nutrient cycles often control the function of the ecosystem.

4.1 ROLES OF LIVING THINGS

Objectives • *Identify* the roles of producers, consumers and decomposers. • *Describe* the concept of the trophic level.

Different living things play different roles in the cycling of matter through the ecosystem. Plants capture sunlight, while some animals eat plants. These animals may be eaten by other organisms. Still other organisms may consume the bodies and wastes of dead organisms. The organisms that play these roles differ widely among ecosystems, but the ways in which they gather food are similar.

Producers, Consumers, and Decomposers

The organisms of most ecosystems gather food in three basic ways: producing, consuming, and decomposing. Energy enters the ecosystem only at the level of the producer. All other organisms are supported by the energy of the producers.

Producers   *Organisms that make their own food from inorganic molecules and energy are called* **producers**. Plants are the most familiar producers. Almost all producers capture energy from the sun and use it to make food through photosynthesis. The reactions of photosynthesis produce sugars from CO_2, water, and sunlight. Nearly all the energy entering the biosphere comes from the sun through photosynthesis.

Plants are the most important producers in terrestrial ecosystems. In aquatic ecosystems, photosynthetic protists and bacteria are the most important producers. A few producers do not rely on sunlight for energy. These producers are bacteria that gather energy from inorganic molecules. Some nonphotosynthetic producers live in harsh environments such as hot springs and near thermal vents on the ocean floor.

Consumers   *Organisms that cannot make their own food are called* **consumers**. All animals are consumers, as are fungi and many protists and bacteria. Consumers gather energy by ingesting other organisms. Consumers use four basic strategies to gather food.

Organisms that eat only plants are called *herbivores* (ER-bih-vors). Because herbivores eat producers, scientists call them primary consumers. Many insects and birds are herbivores, as are grazing animals such as cows, buffalo, and antelope. The bodies of herbivores are adapted to gathering, grinding, and digesting plants or other producers.

Carnivores (KAR-nih-vors) capture and eat herbivores or other carnivores. Carnivores that eat primary consumers are called secondary consumers, and those that eat other carnivores are called tertiary consumers. Lions are carnivores, as are snakes, hawks, and

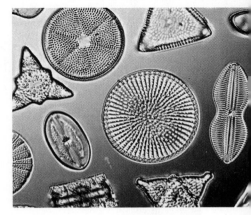

Figure 4.1 Plants are the primary producers in most land ecosystems (top). Diatoms are important producers in the oceans (bottom).

spiders. The bodies of carnivores are adapted to hunting, capturing, and eating prey.

Some consumers, including human beings, are *omnivores* (OM-nih-vors), eating both producers and other consumers. Omnivores act as primary, secondary, or tertiary consumers depending on what they eat. A person who eats a potato acts as a primary consumer, because she eats a producer. If she eats a hamburger, however, the person acts as a secondary consumer because a herbivore is consumed. Animals such as bears and chimpanzees are also omnivores.

Scavengers usually do not hunt living prey, but instead feed on the bodies of dead organisms. They may eat dead plants or feed on the bodies of herbivores, carnivores, or anything else they find. Like omnivores, scavengers act as secondary, tertiary, or higher consumers depending on what they eat. Vultures and hyenas are scavengers, as are many insects. Scavengers start the process where nutrients from dead bodies are returned to the environment.

Decomposers   *Bacteria and fungi that consume the bodies of dead organisms and other organic wastes are called* **decomposers**. They consume a variety of dead organic matter, from the fallen leaves of a tree to the bodies of herbivores and carnivores. Bacteria and fungi also break down the organic matter in animal waste. Decomposers are crucial to the ecosystem because they recycle nutrients from organisms back into the environment. Without decomposers, the producers in an ecosystem would quickly run out of nutrients.

Decomposers complete the cycle of matter in the ecosystem. They do this by converting the organic matter in organisms back into a simple form that producers can use. These nutrients are returned to the soil, where plants can use them to build new organic material. As the plants use the nutrients to grow, the cycle of matter through the ecosystem begins again.

Figure 4.2 The elk (left) is a herbivore. The wolf (center) is a carnivore, and the bear (right) is an omnivore.

Figure 4.3 Scavengers, such as these vultures, feed on the bodies of dead organisms.

Trophic Levels

Scientists call the different feeding levels of organisms in an ecosystem trophic levels. A **trophic** (TROH-fik) **level** *is a layer in the structure of feeding relationships in an ecosystem.* Producers make up the first trophic level, and consumers make up several more trophic levels. The trophic level made up of producers is usually larger than the combined consumer trophic levels.

Producers make up the first trophic level in all ecosystems. Because they make their own food, producers are called *autotrophs* (AHT-oh-TROHFS). Autotrophs are the sole point of entry for new energy into the ecosystem. Think about the word autotroph. Can you explain why scientists use *autotroph* to describe photosynthetic organisms? The prefix *auto* means "self."

Consumers form the second and higher trophic levels in the ecosystem. Because they cannot produce their own food and must obtain nourishment by eating other organisms, consumers are called *heterotrophs*. Primary consumers that eat producers form the second trophic level, and secondary consumers form the third trophic level. Omnivores, scavengers, and decomposers feed at all trophic levels. Most ecosystems have three, four, or five trophic levels. Each trophic level depends completely on the level below it.

SECTION REVIEW

1. List the different groups of organisms in an ecosystem, and explain how each type gathers food.
2. How do autotrophs and heterotrophs differ?
3. **Infer** In most ecosystem the first trophic level contains more organisms than the second trophic level. Can you suggest a reason that explains this pattern?

FIELD ACTIVITY

Explore the community around your school building in groups of two or three. One person should make a list of the organisms you see. Return to the classroom, and classify each of the organisms on your list. Make a table with these headings: Producers, Primary Consumers, Secondary Consumers, Decomposers. Place each of the organisms you observed in one of these categories.

Teaching tips for Field Activity appear on page T38

Word Power

Heterotroph, from the Greek *hetero*, "other or different," and the Greek *trophikos*, "to feed or nourish."

Autotroph means "self-nourisher." Plants and other organisms that make their own food nourish themselves.

1. Lists should include producers, consumers, and decomposers. Producers make food through photosynthesis. Consumers eat producers and other consumers. Decomposers feed on dead producers and consumers.
2. Autotrophs make their own food through photosynthesis. Heterotrophs obtain nourishment by eating other organisms.
3. The second trophic level is smaller because of energy losses between the two levels. The transfer of energy between producers and primary consumers is not 100 percent efficient. A complete discussion of these energy losses appears in Section 4.3

4.2 ECOSYSTEM STRUCTURE

Objectives • *Describe food chains and food webs.* • *Examine the effects of ecosystem structure on population size and pollution.*

The producers and consumers in an ecosystem depend on each other for survival. Producers in the first trophic level produce complex organic molecules that consumers in the second trophic level use to grow and reproduce. Consumers in the third trophic level rely on the second trophic level. The interactions between trophic levels form a chain that links the organisms in an ecosystem.

Food Chains and Food Webs

A series of organisms that transfer food between the trophic levels of an ecosystem is called a **food chain**. All food chains begin with producers, which are usually plants in land ecosystems. The food chain continues to herbivores at the next trophic level, followed by one or more levels of carnivores. The carnivores are consumed by decomposers. An example of a food chain is shown in Figure 4.4.

No ecosystem is simple enough to portray as a single food chain. Most consumers feed on more than one type of food, and some consumers feed at more than one trophic level. *A* **food web** *is a network of food chains representing the feeding relationships among the organisms in an ecosystem.* A food web includes all the food chains in an ecosystem. An example of a simple food web is shown in Figure 4.5. This web does not show decomposers, which feed at all tropic levels.

The interactions of the food web link the organisms in an ecosystem. Changes in the population of one organism can affect many other populations. An example of this linkage is the impact of whaling on the Antarctic ecosystem.

Figure 4.4 This food chain is taken from the food web in Figure 4.5. Where does the marsh grass get the energy it needs?

The marsh grass is photosynthetic. The grass gets its energy from the sun.

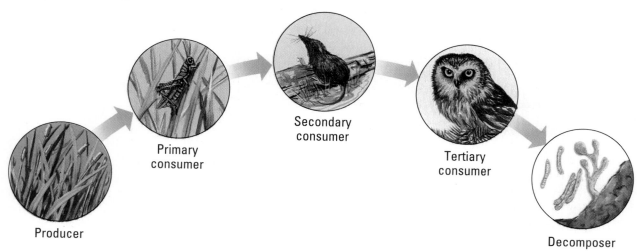

Producer → Primary consumer → Secondary consumer → Tertiary consumer → Decomposer

Figure 4.5 In this simplified food web for a tidal marsh in San Francisco Bay, which organisms are the producers? The food web does not show decomposers.

The marsh grass and water plants are the producers.

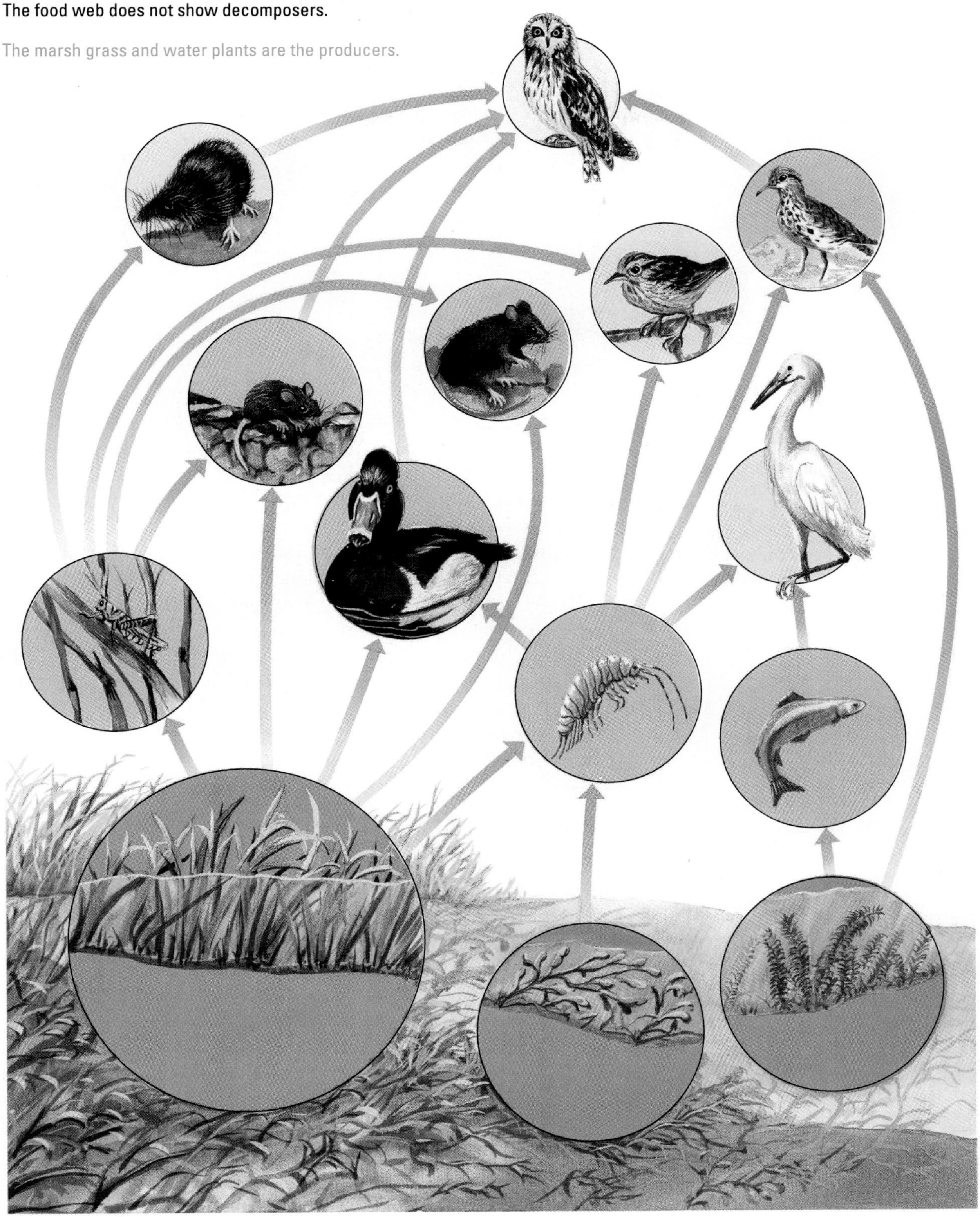

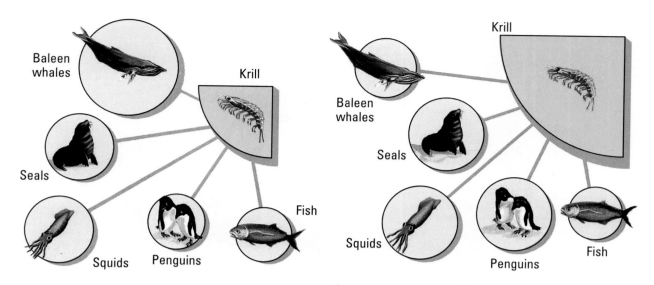

Figure 4.6 The size of the circle around each animal represents the size of its population. When humans destroyed most of the baleen whale population, the population of krill increased. Populations of seals, squids, and penguins increased as they consumed this new food source.

The waters around Antarctica are some of the most productive in the world. Nutrient-rich upwellings of deep ocean water support a huge ecosystem. One of the key animals in the Antarctic food web is krill, a small, shrimplike crustacean. Krill are primary consumers and an important food source for many animals, especially baleen whales such as the blue whale and finback whale. When hunting decreased the number of baleen whales, the population of krill grew much larger because the whales were no longer there to consume it.

The increase in the krill population sent ripples through the food web. The populations of many animals that feed on krill increased, such as seals, squids, and especially penguins. Figure 4.6 illustrates these changes in population size. The example of whales and krill shows how changes in one population can have an impact on an entire food web.

Diversity and Stability

The number of links in the food web varies from ecosystem to ecosystem. An older, more mature ecosystem will often have more species than a young, immature ecosystem. Because a mature ecosystem has more species, its food web will be more complex. Which food web in Figure 4.7 represents a mature ecosystem?

The food web on the right is more complex.

Some ecologists think that a food web with many connections is more stable than one with few connections. A stable food web is more resistant to disturbance by natural disasters or human interference. A deciduous forest is a good example of a stable, mature ecosystem whose food web has many connections. Following a disturbance, deciduous forests usually repair themseleves quickly. A tundra food web, however, has few connections, and changes often. Although many scientists agree that more complex food webs are more stable, this hypothesis is very difficult to test with experiments.

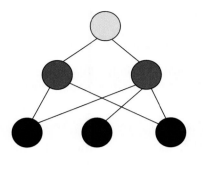
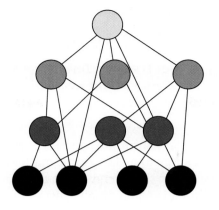

Figure 4.7 These food webs represent two ecosystems. Some ecologists think that webs with many connections are more stable than those with fewer connections.

Biological Magnification

The effects of pollution caused by humans can be magnified in a food web. Recall that a consumer such as an eagle eats organisms from lower trophic levels, such as fish. An eagle will eat many fish in its lifetime. Each fish will also eat many insects. What do you think would happen to the eagle if the insects were contaminated with a pollutant?

The pollutant DDT was actually passed through a food web in this way. DDT, a pesticide, was sprayed on crops to kill insects. Some of the DDT was washed from farmland into streams and rivers by rain. The DDT flowed into lakes and was taken in by the producers in the lake food web. These producers took in small amounts of DDT. But as the producers were eaten by primary consumers, the DDT became concentrated in the bodies of the consumers. At every level in the food web, the DDT was concentrated again because the DDT is ingested but not excreted. As the highest-level consumers, bald eagles had very high concentrations of DDT in their bodies. The DDT caused problems in reproduction, and the population of bald eagles decreased sharply.

The increasing concentration of a pollutant in organisms at higher trophic levels in a food web is called **biological magnification**. Many pollutants can be concentrated in this way, especially metals such as mercury. Biological magnification shows how pollutants taken in by a few organisms can affect the whole food web.

DATELINE 1972

The United States banned the pesticide DDT. In the early 1970s, fewer than 3,000 bald eagles remained in the lower 48 states. Since the banning of DDT, the bald eagle population has rebounded, growing to 12,000 in 1991. Scientists think that the DDT ban and captive breeding programs have been responsible for the bald eagle's success.

The eagle will become contaminated as well.

1. A food chain is a series of organisms that transfers food between the trophic levels in an ecosystem. Each organism is eaten by the organism indicated by the arrow. A food web includes all the food chains in an ecosystem.
2. Biological magnification is the process where pollutants are concentrated in the tissues of organisms at higher trophic levels in a food web. The pollutants are taken in by organisms but are not excreted, so the pollutants concentrate in the organisms' bodies. At high trophic levels, the pollutants have been concentrated through several levels, and concentrations can be very high.
3. The food chain should resemble Figure 4.4, but with grass, mice, snakes, and decomposers in that order. The food web should include the cat, with arrows from the mice and the snakes.

SECTION REVIEW

1. What are food chains and food webs, and how are they related?
2. Explain the process of biological magnification.
3. **Predict** Draw a diagram of a simple food chain containing grass, mice, snakes, and decomposing bacteria. What might happen to the populations of grass, mice, and snakes if a cat entered the chain? The cat feeds on mice and snakes. Redraw the food chain as a food web, and include the cat.

4.3 ENERGY IN THE ECOSYSTEM

Objectives • *Investigate* the movement of energy through an ecosystem. • *Define* ecological pyramid, and explain its relationship to energy in an ecosystem.

Energy from the sun enters an ecosystem when producers use the energy to make organic matter through photosynthesis. Consumers take in this energy when they eat producers or other consumers. But food is scarce in all ecosystems, and without food a population of organisms cannot survive for long. The limits of the energy budget determine the structure and function of the food web.

Energy and Food

ASTRONOMY
L I N K

About 33 percent of the solar energy reaching Earth is reflected back into space by clouds and by Earth's surface. Another 20 percent turns water into water vapor. This water vapor forms clouds and precipitation. The sun powers the movement of water over Earth, as well as the organisms living on its surface.

Producers actually use little of the sunlight that reaches them. Plants absorb less than one percent of the sunlight that reaches Earth. Some plants manage to store over 30 percent of the energy they capture, while most plants store less than this. But a huge amount of sunlight reaches Earth every day, and photosynthetic organisms make a lot of food with it. Photosynthetic organisms make a staggering 170 billion metric tons of food each year.

The energy captured by producers is used to make cells in both producers and consumers. *The total amount of organic matter present in a trophic level is called* **biomass** (BY-oh-MASS). The biomass in each trophic level is the amount of energy—in the form of food—available to the next trophic level.

Most of the energy that enters through organisms in a trophic level does not become biomass. The energy is lost through the activities of the organisms. Energy is used to generate heat and to power motion. This energy cannot be used in the next trophic level. Only energy used to make biomass remains available—and even some of this is lost. Many organisms produce organic material that is very difficult to digest, such as fibers, shells, bones, and hooves. Energy used to produce these structures is often not available to the next trophic level.

When all of the energy losses are added together, only about 10 percent of the energy entering one trophic level forms biomass in the next trophic level. This pattern is called the *10 percent law.* Figure 4.8 shows where energy is lost between producers and primary consumers.

The 10 percent law is the main reason that most food chains have five or less links. Owls, for example, are not preyed upon by a still higher level of carnivores. The biomass of the owl population is not large enough to support another level of consumers. Because 90 percent of the food chain's energy is lost at each level, the amount of available energy decreases quickly.

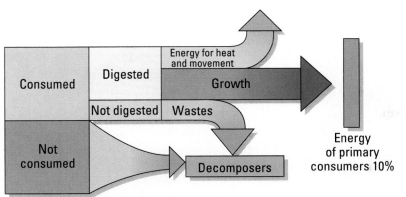

Energy for heat and movement

Consumed

Digested

Growth

Not digested | Wastes

Not consumed

Decomposers

Energy of primary consumers 10%

Energy of producers 100%

Ecological Pyramids

Ecologists represent the relative amounts of energy in an ecosystem in an ecological pyramid. *An* **ecological pyramid** *is a diagram that shows the relative amounts of energy in different trophic levels in an ecosystem.* The pyramid is divided into sections, each section representing one trophic level. An ecological pyramid can show energy, biomass, or the number of organisms in a food web.

The ecological pyramid in Figure 4.9 is an energy pyramid. The base of the pyramid represents the first trophic level of the ecosystem, the producers. The second level of the pyramid represents the second trophic level, the primary consumers. Notice that only about 10 percent of the energy in the first trophic level is present in the second level. This pattern is repeated between the second and third levels. How much of the energy present in the producers appears in the third trophic level?

More food is available lower on the food chain because the 90 percent energy loss between producers and consumers does not happen. The grain that a cow eats contains about ten times the energy of the cow itself.

One percent of the energy of the producers appears in the third trophic level.

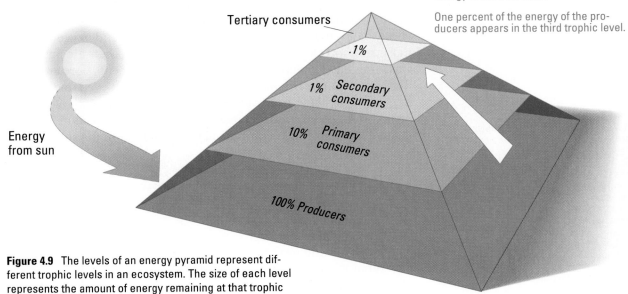

Tertiary consumers

.1%

1% Secondary consumers

10% Primary consumers

100% Producers

Energy from sun

Figure 4.9 The levels of an energy pyramid represent different trophic levels in an ecosystem. The size of each level represents the amount of energy remaining at that trophic level. Where does all the energy initially come from?

All the energy in most ecosystems comes from the sun.

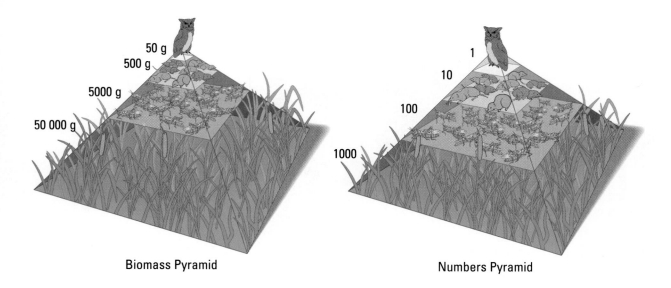

| Biomass Pyramid | Numbers Pyramid |

Figure 4.10 In a pyramid of biomass and a pyramid of numbers, biomass and numbers decrease at higher trophic levels.

Ecological pyramids can show biomass and numbers as well as energy, as shown in Figure 4.10. Pyramids of biomass show the weight of organic matter in each trophic level. The combined weight of all the producers forms the base of the pyramid, while the weights of the consumers form the higher levels. Pyramids of biomass usually follow the same 10 percent pattern as that of energy pyramids. The biomass in one level is 90 percent less than the one beneath it.

In many ecosystems, the number of organisms changes from one trophic level to another. There are countless plants of grass on an African savanna, but the number of antelope and other grazers is much smaller. The pride of lions that preys on the grazers may contain fewer than ten individuals. Pyramids of numbers often follow the 10 percent law, but many do not.

Energy moves between trophic levels in the form of food. But food also contains matter. Carbon, hydrogen, nitrogen, and oxygen are the most common elements in food, although many others are present in small amounts. Molecules composed of these elements store energy as it moves from one trophic level to another. Without even one of these important elements, food cannot be produced. The growth of producers in most ecosystems is limited by the lack of one or more of these elements, not by the amount of energy coming from the sun.

1. About 10 percent of the energy in a trophic level appears in the next trophic level.
2. An ecological pyramid is a diagram that shows the relative amounts of energy, biomass, or numbers of organisms in a food chain. The pyramid demonstrates the inefficiency of the transmission of energy between trophic levels in an ecosystem.
3. Energy is lost in the following ways: Some of the biomass is not consumed, some is not digested, some is used to make heat and power movements. All of this energy is ultimately radiated back into space.

SECTION REVIEW

1. How much of the energy that appears in one trophic level will appear in the next?
2. What is an ecological pyramid?
3. **Infer** Where is energy lost between trophic levels? Where does this energy ultimately go?

Food for the World

Is there a solution to world hunger?

The United Nations estimates that 460 million people in the world do not have an adequate daily diet. Many of the hungry are children. About 100 million children under the age of 5 suffer from malnutrition. And worldwide, more than 230 million children under age 15 are undernourished because they do not get enough to eat each day. Yet in many countries, people eat far more than their bodies need.

Wheat, rice, and corn supply nearly half of the world's

food energy. Much of this grain is directly consumed by humans. However, one-third of all of the grain produced is fed to livestock. And eating consumers is much less efficient than eating producers. Even though meat is an excellent source of protein, it takes 9 kg of vegetable protein to produce 0.5 kg of beef or 2 kg of chicken.

Other factors contribute to world hunger. Short-sighted farming techniques can cause the spread of deserts—a process known as desertification. As the desert grows, the amount of fertile land for growing food decreases. Poor soil management may decrease soil fertility. Once soil is depleted of its nutrients, it can no longer support plant growth. The inbreeding of crop plants has weakened the resistance of plants to insects and disease. Many inbred plant species are useful only in countries that can afford pesticides and herbicides.

Politics plays an important role in world hunger. Often, food never even reaches the tables of families in developing countries because the food grown there is exported. Also, food relief supplies are not always distributed to the people who need them.

Solutions to ending world hunger are as varied as the problems. Desertification can be controlled through replanting and irrigation. Using farming strategies that replenish soil used for growing crops increases soil fertility. Introducing varieties of plants that are more resistant to drought, insects, and disease ensures a higher crop yield without using expensive pesticides. In the United States the livestock industry converts rough forage into high-quality protein. Livestock are often grazed in arid regions and many other areas where corn and cereal grains could never grow.

By creating small, self-sufficient farms that use little water and machinery, people in developing countries could decrease their dependence on unfair government distribution. People in developed countries can eat lower on the food chain. All people need to become a part of the solution to end world hunger.

DECISIONS

1. List four causes of world hunger.
2. Describe a solution for each of the causes of world hunger that you listed.

4.4 CHEMICAL CYCLES

Objectives • *Describe* the chemical composition of the human body.
• *Explain* the water cycle, the carbon cycle, and the nitrogen cycle.

Table 4.1
Elements of the Human Body

Element	Percent Weight of Human Body
Oxygen	65.0
Carbon	18.5
Hydrogen	9.5
Nitrogen	3.5
Calcium	1.5
Phosphorus	1.0
Potassium	0.4
Sulfur	0.3
Chlorine	0.2
Sodium	0.2
Magnesium	0.10
Trace Elements	Less than 0.01

The chemistry of life is based on common elements. About 96 percent of your body is made up of just four elements: oxygen, carbon, hydrogen, and nitrogen. About 77 percent of Earth's atmosphere is nitrogen, and 21 percent is oxygen. Carbon is also present in the atmosphere, as well as in rocks and in biomass. Elements in the human body are shown in Table 4.1.

Even though these elements are common on Earth, organisms cannot always use them. The elements must be in a chemical form that cells can use, and getting an element in a usable form may not be a simple process. Nitrogen is a good example. Although nitrogen makes up most of Earth's atmosphere, a lack of its usable forms limits plant growth in many ecosystems. The absence of an element such as potassium can also limit growth in an ecosystem.

Unlike energy, elements move through the ecosystem in cycles. Matter cycles repeatedly through the ecosystem, moving from the environment to organisms and back to the environment. Matter cycles are naturally balanced. The amount of matter that enters and leaves each cycle is relatively small.

The Water Cycle

More than 90 percent of Earth's water is locked beneath its surface, either in crustal rocks or deep in the interior. This water does not normally take part in the water cycle. It can, however, be released by volcanoes and other geological processes. Water released in this way formed Earth's oceans, but the amount released today is small.

Water moves between the ocean, the atmosphere, and the land. Living things also take part in the cycle. You can begin tracing the water cycle with the evaporation of water from the surface of the ocean. **Evaporation** (eh-VAP-uh-RAY-shun) *is the movement of water into the atmosphere as it changes from a liquid to a gas.* Evaporation requires energy, and this energy comes from the sun. About 20 percent of the sunlight reaching the Earth evaporates water.

Follow the water cycle shown in Figure 4.11 as you read the next two paragraphs. Evaporating water forms clouds when it condenses in the atmosphere. Much of the water vapor then falls back into the ocean as precipitation. But some of the clouds are blown over land, and the precipitation falls onto the land. This water eventually returns to the ocean through runoff and groundwater. An average water molecule stays in the atmosphere for about two weeks before it falls as precipitation, and it takes a bit less than 4,000 years to go through the whole cycle if it falls over land.

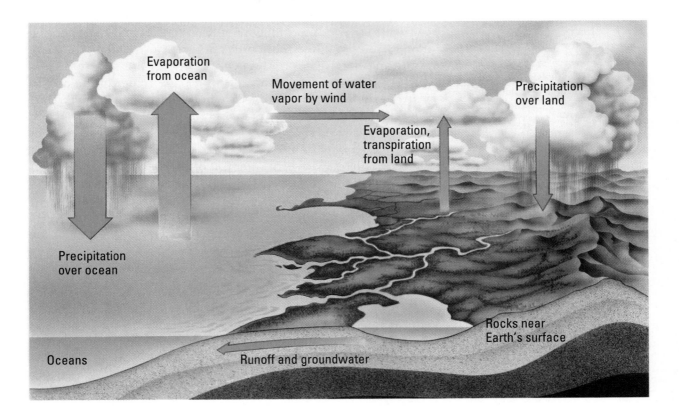

Movement of water vapor by wind

Evaporation from ocean

Precipitation over land

Evaporation, transpiration from land

Precipitation over ocean

Rocks near Earth's surface

Oceans

Runoff and groundwater

Water can also enter the atmosphere through a process called transpiration. **Transpiration** (trans-peh-RAY-shun) *is the evaporation of water from the leaves of plants.* Transpiration plays an important part in plant circulation. In ecosystems such as tropical rain forests, the amount of water entering the atmosphere through plants can be large enough to affect the climate in the surrounding area.

Figure 4.11 In this diagram of the water cycle, the amount of moving water is represented by the width of the arrows. Most of Earth's surface water is stored in the oceans.

The Carbon Cycle

Scientists think that the atmosphere of very young Earth was much like the atmosphere of Mars and Venus today, or about 95 percent carbon dioxide (CO_2.) However, the action of living things removed CO_2 from the atmosphere and released oxygen. The amount of CO_2 in the atmosphere fell while the amount of oxygen rose. Today, the atmosphere is only 0.04 percent CO_2. Living things have played an important role in the formation of Earth's atmosphere.

Living things are still the most important part of the carbon cycle. The reactions of photosynthesis and respiration could not occur without carbon. Look at the chemical equations below for photosynthesis and respiration. Notice that each reaction uses the products of the other:

Photosynthesis: $H_2O + CO_2 + energy \longrightarrow C_6H_{12}O_6 + O_2$

Respiration: $C_6H_{12}O_6 + O_2 \longrightarrow CO_2 + H_2O + energy$

BIOLOGY LINK

Plants use transpiration to move water through their tissues. Water evaporating from leaf cells pulls water from the surrounding cells, which in turn pull water from the cells close to them. This pull is relayed down to the roots of the plant. As a result, water moves up the plant stem. An average maple tree on a summer day will lose 200 L of water per hour through transpiration.

DATELINE

The Industrial Revolution begins. Coal and other fossil fuels are burned to power the industrial age. In the next 250 years, the amount of carbon dioxide in the atmosphere will increase by over 20 percent from the burning of fossil fuels. Other pollutants cause health problems and acid rain.

Plants use CO_2 and sunlight to make starches and sugars during photosynthesis. When these nutrients are consumed by the plant or any another organism, the CO_2 and energy are released again. The biological reactions in organisms are the center of the carbon cycle. The amount of carbon tied up in organisms at any given time is usually larger than the amount of carbon in Earth's atmosphere. The carbon cycle is shown in Figure 4.12.

Two other important sources of carbon are the ocean and rocks. The ocean holds a very large amount of CO_2 because CO_2 dissolves easily in water. Carbon is also stored in rocks. Substances such as coal, oil, and limestone are formed from the bodies of dead organisms. Because the bodies of these organisms never decomposed entirely, the carbon in them was never released. Almost all of the carbon on Earth is stored in rocks.

The Nitrogen Cycle

The nitrogen cycle is very important to living things. Organisms require nitrogen in order to make amino acids, the building blocks of proteins. Nitrogen is common in the atmosphere, but most living things cannot use nitrogen gas in their cells. The nitrogen must be in a more reactive chemical form.

Figure 4.12 In this diagram of the carbon cycle, the amount of moving carbon is represented by the width of the arrows. Most of Earth's carbon is stored in rocks near the surface.

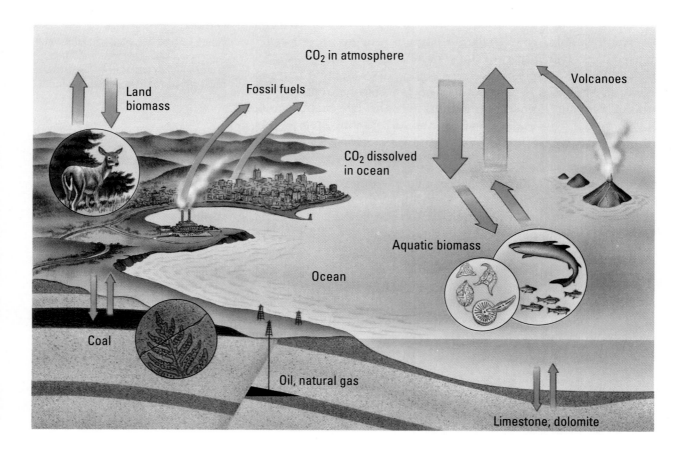

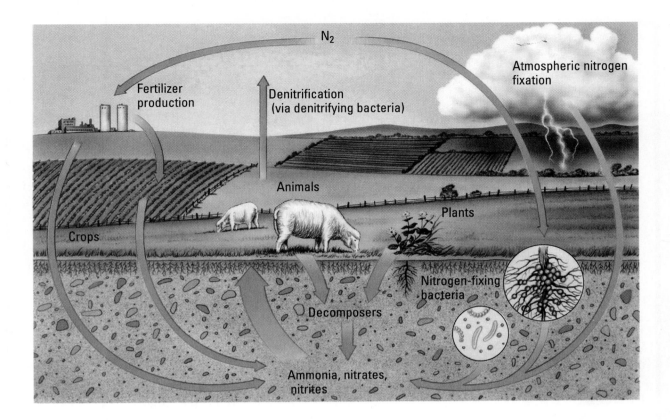

Labels in figure:
N₂
Fertilizer production
Denitrification (via denitrifying bacteria)
Atmospheric nitrogen fixation
Animals
Plants
Crops
Nitrogen-fixing bacteria
Decomposers
Ammonia, nitrates, nitrites

Figure 4.13 Most of the nitrogen in the nitrogen cycle is stored in organic compounds. All nitrogen originally came from the atmosphere.

Only some types of bacteria can use nitrogen from the atmosphere. Such bacteria, called nitrogen-fixing bacteria, produce ammonia (NH_3), a form of nitrogen used by plants. Nitrogen-fixing bacteria live both in the soil and in the roots of legumes. **Legumes** (LEG-yooms) *are plants such as peanuts and clover that have colonies of nitrogen-fixing bacteria in nodules on their roots.* But most ammonia is consumed by more bacteria. These bacteria produce compounds called *nitrites* and *nitrates*, which are compounds of nitrogen and oxygen.

Nitrate is the most common source of nitrogen used by plants. Animals get the nitrogen they need from the proteins in the plants they consume. Decomposers return this nitrogen to the soil in the form of ammonia, and the cycle starts again. Some nitrogen is removed from the soil by still other bacteria, but the amount lost in this way is small.

SECTION REVIEW

1. What are the four most common elements in the human body?
2. **Compare** How do transpiration and evaporation differ?
3. **Think Critically** Humans are releasing large amounts of carbon dioxide into the air by burning fossil fuels like coal and oil. What effect might this carbon have on the CO_2 cycle?

1. The four most common elements in the human body are oxygen, carbon, hydrogen, and nitrogen.
2. Transpiration is the evaporation of water from the leaves of plants, while evaporation is the formation of water vapor from water.
3. Students may suggest that increased levels of CO_2 in the atmosphere will increase plant growth, or may increase the amount of CO_2 stored in ocean water. This topic is discussed in detail in Chapter 22.

Answers and teaching
strategies on page T38.

Plants and the Water Cycle

PROBLEM
What is the role of plants in the water cycle?

MATERIALS
- 4 large clear plastic or glass cups
- 2 15-cm squares of wax paper
- 2 strips of cobalt chloride paper (blue)
- paper clip
- petroleum jelly
- 2 geranium plant leaves with stems
- tape

HYPOTHESIS
Water vapor is released from the surface of leaves and enters the atmosphere.

PROCEDURE

1. Stick a small piece of tape on two of the cups. Label one of them *A* and the other *B*.
2. Fill cups *A* and *B* with water, and apply petroleum jelly to their rims.
3. Straighten the paper clip, and use one end of it to poke a hole in the center of each square of wax paper.
4. Insert a geranium leaf stem through the hole in each wax paper square. Apply petroleum jelly around each stem where it emerges from the wax paper. This makes an airtight seal.
5. Apply a coat of petroleum jelly to both surfaces of one of the leaves.
6. Position the uncoated leaf combination directly over cup *A*, and gently press down on the wax paper around the rims so the wax paper is held in place by the petroleum jelly. The stem should be in the water.
7. Position the coated plant leaf combination directly over cup *B*. As in Step 6, gently press down around the rim and be sure the stem is in the water (see the figure).
8. Tape a piece of cobalt chloride paper to the inside of each of the two other cups.

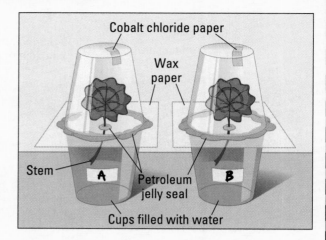

Labels: Cobalt chloride paper · Wax paper · Stem · Petroleum jelly seal · Cups filled with water · A · B

9. Apply petroleum jelly around the rims of these cups.
10. Invert one of these cups over cup *A* and the other over cup *B*. Gently press them together. Do not allow the leaf to touch the cobalt chloride paper.
11. Observe both setups for 10 minutes. Record your observations each minute in a data table, paying particular attention to the color of the cobalt chloride paper.
12. Leave the setups undisturbed for 24 hours and then make your final observations.

ANALYSIS
1. What is the purpose of coating the leaf in setup *B* with petroleum jelly?
2. Which setup is the control?
3. Did the color of either piece of cobalt chloride paper change? What does this indicate?
4. What changes did you observe after 24 hours? Explain.
5. Were you able to confirm the hypothesis?

CONCLUSION
1. How are green plants involved in the water cycle?
2. What is the plant process you observed in this experiment, and how might it affect local climates?

CHAPTER 4 REVIEW

KEY TERMS

producer 4.1
consumer 4.1
decomposer 4.1
trophic level 4.1

food chain 4.2
food web 4.2
biological
   magnification 4.2

biomass 4.3
ecological
   pyramid 4.3
evaporation 4.4

transpiration 4.4
legume 4.4

CHAPTER SUMMARY

4.1 All ecosystems transfer energy and cycle matter. Organisms that make food with sunlight or chemicals are called producers. Organisms that eat other organisms are called consumers. Organisms that break down dead organic matter are called decomposers. Trophic levels are layers in the structure of feeding relations in a food web.

4.2 A food chain is a series of organisms that transfers food between the trophic levels of an ecosystem. A food web includes all the food chains in an ecosystem. Population changes or pollutants that affect one population in a food web may affect other populations in the web.

4.3 The total amount of organic matter present in a trophic level is its biomass. Ninety percent of the energy in one trophic level is lost to the environment; 10 percent appears in the next trophic level. Ecological pyramids represent the amount of energy, biomass, and numbers of organisms in trophic levels.

4.4 Unlike energy, matter moves through the ecosystem in cycles. Water moves between the ocean, the atmosphere, and the land. Carbon moves through the atmosphere, the ocean, rocks, and organisms. Nitrogen is common in the atmosphere but rare in usable forms. Lack of nitrogen limits growth in many ecosystems.

MULTIPLE CHOICE

Choose the letter of the word or phrase that best completes each statement.

1. Organisms that make their own food with sunlight or chemical energy are called (a) producers; (b) consumers; (c) decomposers; (d) scavengers. a

2. Organisms in the lowest trophic level of an ecosystem are always (a) herbivores; (b) carnivores; (c) heterotrophs; (d) autotrophs. d

3. A network of all of the feeding relationships in an ecosystem is called a(n) (a) food chain; (b) energy chain; (c) food web; (d) energy web. c

4. The population that was not affected by the increase in the krill population was (a) clams; (b) seals; (c) penguins; (d) squids. a

5. The pesticide that damaged the bald eagle population was (a) nitrates; (b) DDT; (c) arsenic; (d) malathion. b

6. The total amount of the organic matter in a trophic level is called the (a) bioload; (b) food load; (c) biomass; (d) food mass. c

7. The percentage of energy in one trophic level that appears in the next in the average ecosystem is (a) 10 percent; (b) 20 percent; (c) 30 percent; (d) 40 percent. a

8. The element that is not one of the four most common in your body is (a) nitrogen; (b) hydrogen; (c) oxygen; (d) sodium. d

9. Transpiration is the evaporation of water from (a) the ocean; (b) leaves; (c) lakes and ponds; (d) rivers. b

10. Plants that have nitrogen-fixing bacteria in their roots are called (a) denitrifiers; (b) ammonias; (c) nitrifiers; (d) legumes. d

CHAPTER 4 REVIEW

TRUE/FALSE Answers on page T38.

Write true *if the statement is true. If the statement is false, change the underlined word or phrase to make it true.*

1. <u>Herbivores</u> eat only meat. f, carnivores
2. Decomposers feed at <u>one</u> trophic level. f, many
3. Some scientists think that a food web with many connections is <u>more</u> stable than one with few connections. t
4. Biological magnification <u>decreased</u> the amount of DDT in organisms higher in the food web. f, increased

5. The amount of biomass in the first trophic level is <u>larger</u> than the amount in the second trophic level. t
6. In most ecosystems, there are more individuals in the trophic level <u>above</u> a given level. f, below
7. <u>Carbon</u> is the most common element in the human body. f, oxygen
8. Nitrogen is returned to the atmosphere by bacteria called <u>denitrifying bacteria</u>. t

CONCEPT REVIEW Answers on page T38.

Write a complete response to each of the following.

1. How do producers and consumers differ in the way they gather food?
2. Explain how the reduction in the baleen whale population affected the populations of other organisms in the Antarctic food web.
3. How much energy is lost between trophic lev-

els in an ecosystem? How is this energy lost?

4. Would the world food supply last longer if people acted as primary consumers or secondary consumers? Explain your reasoning.
5. Explain how nitrogen can make up almost 80 percent of the atmosphere and still limit plant growth in many ecosystems.

THINK CRITICALLY Answers on page T38.

1. Many places on the ocean floor are so deep that sunlight cannot penetrate. Because there is no sunlight in these places, there can be no photosynthesis. But the deep ocean floor still supports an ecosystem. How is this possible?
2. Do you agree with scientists who think that complex food webs are more stable than simple ones? Use what you know about food webs to answer this question.

3. Some scientists think the climate of Earth is getting warmer. How would warmer temperatures affect the evaporation of water from the ocean?

Computer Activity Use a graphing program to graph the amount of energy present in the trophic levels of a food chain with four members. What percentage of the energy in the first trophic level appears in the fourth trophic level?

WRITE CREATIVELY

Suppose you are a cheetah prowling across the African savanna. What would you see? How many plants, herbivores, and other cheetahs would you see? How is your body adapted to hunting and capturing prey?

PORTFOLIO

1. Make a poster of the food web in your community. Use your list of organisms from the Field Activity on p. 55.
2. Many communities suffer from water short-

ages. Visit a local water company and collect any information they have on water conservation. Read the information, and report to the class on water-saving techniques.

Use Figure 4.12 to answer the following.
1. What human activities form parts of the carbon cycle?
2. How does carbon in organisms leave the carbon cycle?
3. What is the most important source of carbon entering the atmosphere? What are the other sources?

ACTIVITY 4.2

Answers and teaching strategies on page T38.

PROBLEM
Do different kinds of decomposers grow better on different types of food?

MATERIALS
- 5 Petri dishes with lids
- blotting paper
- hand lens
- small amount of each of the following organic materials: bread (one slice), Roquefort cheese, dill pickle, orange wedge, grapes
- wax pencil
- scissors

HYPOTHESIS
Write a hypothesis that pertains to the problem.

PROCEDURE
1. Mark each Petri dish with your group name and the numbers 1 through 5.
2. Line the bottoms of the Petri dishes with moist blotting paper.
3. Moisten (don't soak) the slice of bread. Tear off some pieces of bread, and place them in Petri dish 1.
4. Place some Roquefort cheese in Petri dish 2.
5. Use the scissors to carefully cut the dill pickle to fit inside a Petri dish. Place the pieces in Petri dish 3.
6. Use the scissors to carefully cut the orange wedge to fit inside a Petri dish. Place a few pieces in Petri dish 4.
7. Cut a few grapes in half and place them in Petri dish 5.
8. Expose the uncovered Petri dishes to the air for 24 hours.
9. After 24 hours of exposure, cover the Petri dishes with the lids and store in a cool, dark place. You may stack the Petri dishes to save space.
10. Observe the Petri dishes each day or every other day for 1 to 2 weeks. **Caution:** *Do not remove the lids from the Petri dishes when you make your observations. The dishes may contain potentially harmful organisms.* In a data table, record the following: (a) date of observation, (b) number of Petri dish, (c) appearance of Petri dish contents to the unaided eye, (d) appearance of Petri dish contents using the hand lens.

ANALYSIS
1. How many different kinds of decomposers did you observe? What physical characteristics distinguished one kind of decomposer from another?
2. Did you find that one kind of decomposer can grow on different types of organic material? Describe your evidence.
3. What evidence did you find that organic material was being decomposed?

CONCLUSION
1. Did you find any evidence that different kinds of organisms grow better on one or another kind of food? Explain.
2. Based on your observations, what is the role of decomposers in the food web?
3. How would an ecosystem be different if no decomposers were present?

CHAPTER 5

INTERACTIONS IN THE ECOSYSTEM

5.1 Habitats and Niches
5.2 Evolution and Adaptation
5.3 Populations

An ecosystem is a network of living and non-living things. Organisms are connected by food webs and by their common needs. All organisms need water, food, and living space. Yet each species has evolved its own way of gathering resources from the environment.

Any discussion of an organism's role in an ecosystem must center on evolution. The principle of evolution ties together biology and the physical world, just as ecology ties together the interactions between living things and their environment. Ecology is the study of how organisms and populations are adapted to their environments. Thus, the study of ecosystems is also the study of evolution.

5.1 HABITATS AND NICHES

Objectives • *Describe* the concept of the niche. • *Examine* how interactions between a species and its environment define the species' niche.

Ecosystems can be large places. They may cover many square kilometers and contain many different types of organisms. The environment in one part of an ecosystem is different from the environment in another part. The conditions near a stream may be very different from those on a dry hill above the stream.

The organisms living in each part of this ecosystem differ from each other. Each organism is adapted to the conditions in the part of the environment in which it lives. Recall from Chapter 3 that the place within an ecosystem where an organism lives is called its habitat. The habitat of a rainbow trout, for example, is a stream or river, while the habitat of a buffalo is a field in a grassland. Habitats can be small or large, depending on the size of the organism and how much the organism travels.

Niches

Every organism is adapted to life in its habitat. For example, each organism has special ways of gathering food, reproducing, and avoiding predators. The actions of an organism define its role in the ecosystem. *The role of an organism in the ecosystem is called its* **niche** (NICH). A niche is more than an organism's habitat; it is also what the organism does within its habitat.

A niche includes both biotic and abiotic factors. Some biotic factors that can help define a niche are food sources and predators. Each species needs a specific type of food, such as insects or a species of plant. At the same time, most organisms are also hunted by other organisms. Temperature, amount of sunlight and water, and time of day or night are abiotic factors. All the biotic and abiotic factors taken together define the organism's niche.

All members of a species are adapted to the same niche. The niche to which a species is adapted is unique to that species. No two species can share the same niche. Two species can, however, occupy niches that are very similar. For example, the niches of different species of *Anolis* lizards in the tropics vary only in the size of the insects they eat. Lizards with large jaws eat large insects, and those with small jaws eat small insects. The different species can live side by side because they occupy different niches.

If two species try to share the same niche, they will compete for resources. If two lizard species eat the same size of insect, they will compete for the available insects in places where they live together. If one lizard species is better at catching the insects, the other species will not get enough food. The second species will have to move to

Figure 5.1 Different species of anoles feed on different sizes of insects.

another area or the population will die out. *The extinction of a population due to direct competition with another species for a resource is called* **competitive exclusion**. Competitive exclusion occurs when one species that tries to use the same niche as another species is excluded from that niche by competition.

In many ecosystems, the activity of one species can help define a species' niche. Two species of barnacles living on the coast of Scotland have very similar niches. Both species live on rocks in the surf zone of the ocean shore. One barnacle species is *Chthamalus stellatus* (species A). The other species is *Balanus balanoides* (species B). Look at Figure 5.3 as you read about the habitats and niches of these two organisms.

Species B lives on lower rocks usually covered by water, except during low tide. Species A occurs on higher rocks that are usually exposed to the air. Species B survives in lower zones because it is vulnerable to drying out. Species A is more resistant to drying out, so it can survive higher up on the rocks.

American scientist J. H. Connell performed an experiment to study how one barnacle species affects the niche of another. He removed all of species B from a small area of the shore, and then observed the effect of the removal. He found that species A began to grow on the lower rocks. Connell hypothesized that species A could live on all parts of the rocky shore, but that species B drove out A wherever B could survive. The A population was limited to the higher rocks by B, even though A could live on all the rocks in the absence of B.

Connell realized that the niche of one species could affect the niche of another. For example, the presence of one species might limit the niche of another, as in the case of the barnacles. Connell called the theoretical niche of an organism its *fundamental niche*. The niche that the organism actually used was called its *realized niche*. Other species are one of many factors that define a species' niche.

Figure 5.2 Both of the barnacle species in J. H. Connell's experiments are shown in this photograph. *Chthamalus* (species A) are the large, ridged barnacles. *Balanus* (species B) are the smaller, smooth barnacles.

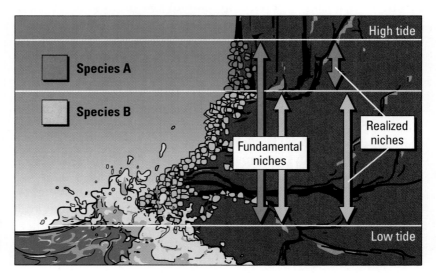

Figure 5.3 The distribution of two species of barnacles on the Scottish coast is shown here. Species A occurs on rocks usually exposed to air, and species B occurs on rocks usually covered by water. The presence of species B keeps species A from spreading downward.

Figure 5.4 This sea star is an example of a keystone predator.

Niche Diversity

Niche diversity is often determined by the abiotic factors in the habitat. In a marsh, for example, there are many organisms, but overall diversity is low because the physical conditions of the marsh do not change much from one place to another. In a desert, however, there are fewer organisms, but they are more diverse. Great differences in abiotic factors such as temperature and moisture form many niches occupied by a variety of organisms.

A **predator** (PRED-ut-or) *is an organism that actively hunts other organisms.* Predators can play an important role in increasing the niche diversity in an ecosystem. Predators are important because they decrease the population size of their prey species. If a predator reduces the population of one species, more resources will become available for another species. The action of the predator, therefore, creates another niche.

American ecologist Robert Paine performed an experiment showing how predators help to form niches. Paine removed the dominant predator from several tidepools on the coast of Washington state, shown in Figure 5.4. The number of mussels increased until they "outcompeted" many of the other species in the tidepools. Without the sea stars, the number of species in the tidepools dropped from 15 to 8. The removal of the sea stars halved the number of species that could survive. *A predator that causes a large increase in the diversity of its habitat is called a* **keystone predator**.

BIOLOGY LINK

Predators help maintain diversity in many ecosystems. The Great Barrier Reef is one example. A species of sea star called the crown of thorns lives and feeds on the corals that make up the reef. In the past, the crown of thorns was rare because it was eaten by many species of fish. But fishing by humans has removed most of the sea star's predators. The crown of thorns is now common, and these sea stars destroy large stretches of the reef every year. The destruction of the reef results in lost habitat for many species, and therefore lower diversity.

SECTION REVIEW

1. How is a niche different from a habitat?
2. What is competitive exclusion? How is it related to the concept of the niche?
3. **Infer** What might happen to an ecosystem if all the carnivores were removed? Explain your answer.

1. A habitat is the place where a population lives, and a niche is a species' role in the habitat.
2. Competitve exclusion is the driving out of one species from a niche that two species are trying to occupy. Competitive exclusion accounts for the observation that each species has a unique niche.
3. The diversity at all trophic levels would decrease because herbivore populations would no longer be controlled by predators.

5.2 EVOLUTION AND ADAPTATION

Objectives • *Explain* how a species adapts to its niche.
• *Describe* convergent evolution and coevolution, and relate each to the concept of niche.

Ecosystems change over time. Mountains rise and erode, rivers change course, and climate factors such as temperature and rainfall may vary dramatically. A change in the environment will affect the niches of the organisms in that environment. A species may occupy a niche successfully, but if that niche disappears the species may become extinct. One way populations respond to this changing environment is by evolving. **Evolution** (EV-uh-LOO-shun) *is a change in a population of organisms over time.*

Evolving to the Niche

Populations of organisms evolve by adapting to niches in the environment. They can also evolve to avoid competition with another species. Species divide available resources to avoid competition. An example of the evolution of species into different yet similar niches is shown in Figure 5.5.

Figure 5.5 shows five species of birds called warblers. The warblers live in forests of the northeastern United States. All five species feed on insects in the branches of spruce trees. Although the five species seem to compete with each other for food, each species looks for food in a slightly different part of the tree. The niches overlap a little, but are different enough to allow the five species to coexist.

Figure 5.5 These five warbler species all eat insects in spruce trees. Each species gathers food from a slightly different area of the tree. Although the areas overlap slightly, they are different enough so that competition between the species is avoided.

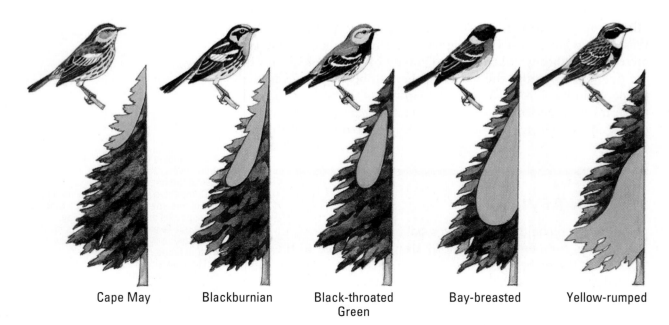

Cape May   Blackburnian   Black-throated Green   Bay-breasted   Yellow-rumped

Each species of warbler has evolved into a narrow niche. Ecologists call an organism with a small niche a *specialized species*. The giant panda is another example of a specialized species. It feeds only on the leaves of one kind of plant, called bamboo. Specialized species are often vulnerable to extinction because they cannot respond to changes in the environment. Pandas are well adapted to eating bamboo. If all the bamboo is destroyed, however, the pandas will have no food and the species will die out.

Ecologists call a species with a wide niche a *generalized species*. A generalized species has several alternate food sources and is more able to adapt to changes in the environment. Generalized species such as mice and cockroaches are often more successful in surviving the effects of human activity because they can alter their behaviors to fit environmental changes.

Convergent Evolution

Similar ecosystems often have similar niches, which places like demands on organisms. Organisms then evolve to meet these demands. Because the niches in the two ecosystems are alike, organisms that evolve to occupy the niches may also be alike.

The development of similar adaptations in two species with similar niches is called **convergent evolution**. The wings of birds and bats are an example of convergent evolution. Birds and mammals are different types of animals, and the bird and bat evolved flight independently. However, the wings of these two animals are very similar. The bird and the bat evolved similar wings because the demands of flying through air are the same for both organisms.

Another example of convergent evolution is shown in Figure 5.6. Both of these animals evolved from ancestors that lived on land. The dolphin is a mammal, while the other animal, an ichthyosaur (IK-thee-oh-SOR), is an extinct reptile from the Jurassic period. The animals share adaptations such as a streamlined shape and fins used in swimming. The animals have adapted to the demands of living in the water in similar ways.

The distinction between generalized and specialized species is an important one. Specialized species are adapted to narrow niches and therefore cannot change their behavior to adapt to environmental changes caused by humans. The effects of rainforest burning and other types of habitat destruction are especially severe for specialized species. Efforts to preserve biodiversity must recognize that generalized species can tolerate more habitat disturbance than specialized ones.

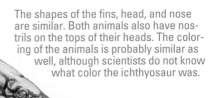

The shapes of the fins, head, and nose are similar. Both animals also have nostrils on the tops of their heads. The coloring of the animals is probably similar as well, although scientists do not know what color the ichthyosaur was.

Figure 5.6 The dolphin and the ichthyosaur share many adaptations to living in the water, such as a streamlined shape. Can you identify other adaptations that the two animals share?

Coevolution

Other species are an important part of an organism's environment. Recall that a keystone predator can make a community more diverse. Species also evolve to limit competition with similar species. Sometimes the interaction between species becomes even closer. Organisms that live closely together and interact may have evolutionary responses to one another. *Species that interact closely may adapt to one another through a process called* **coevolution** (KOH-EV-uh-LOO-shun).

Coevolution can occur between predator and prey species and between species that cooperate. Plants and caterpillars are an example of coevolution between predator and prey. Many plants have evolved poisonous chemicals that prevent insects from eating them. Some caterpillars have evolved the ability to resist these poisons. They can feed on plants that other insects cannot eat. These caterpillars often become specialized and feed only on the poisonous plants. The plant and caterpillar have coevolved because one species evolved in response to the other.

Figure 5.7 The acacia tree and the ants that live on it have coevolved. Neither species can survive without the other.

Species can also evolve to their mutual benefit. Several species of acacia tree that grow in Central and South America have coevolved with insects. These trees have large, hollow thorns that provide a nesting site for stinging ants. The hollow thorns protect the ant colony, and the acacia tree provides the ants with food and a place to build their nest. The ants are totally dependent on the acacia tree. They can nest nowhere else, and the acacia is their only source of food.

The acacia tree also benefits from the ant colony it supports. The ants attack any animal landing on the tree, killing it or driving it away. The ants are active all day and all night, protecting the tree. The ants even clear away the vegetation surrounding the tree to ensure that the tree will get the sunlight it needs. Experiments have shown that the tree cannot grow properly without the ants. The acacia and the ants have coevolved to the point where one cannot survive without the other.

1. Species evolve to occupy different niches to avoid competing for resources. Competition may lead to competitive exclusion.
2. Convergent evolution is the evolution of similar adaptations in species with similar ecological roles. It happens because species respond to the demands of like niches in a like way.
3. The ant colony would die if the acacia it lived on was destroyed. In general, a species cannot survive if its habitat is destroyed because the niche it occupies disappears.

SECTION REVIEW

1. Why do species such as the warblers in Figure 5.5 evolve to avoid competition with other species?
2. Explain convergent evolution and give one example. Why does convergent evolution happen?
3. **Predict** What would happen to the ant colony living on an acacia tree if that tree was chopped down? What does your answer imply about the effect of destroying an organism's habitat?

Accidental Tourists

How do introduced species affect a habitat?

1. New species might be introduced to control other introduced species, to meet certain human needs, or by accident.
2. The mussels could be transported all over the country by boats and over land.

In 1859, two pairs of European rabbits were introduced to a ranch in Australia. The rabbits flourished and reproduced wildly because no natural predators were present in their new area. In less than 100 years, the population of rabbits increased to more than 1 billion.

Ever since humans began trading with each other, they have been introducing species to new habitats. Sometimes new species are introduced on purpose and sometimes they arrive accidentally. The impact of an introduced species depends on the stability of the ecosystem.

Often the solution to an introduced species that is unmanageable is to introduce another species. The prickly pear cactus was an introduced species that spread and covered thousands of hectares of Australian pastureland and rangeland. To control the invasion of the prickly pear, a species of cactus moth from South America was introduced. The caterpillar of the cactus moth feeds on the prickly pear shoots and destroys the plant. The cactus moth was able to control the prickly pear population explosion within a few years.

Since the 1880s, ships have filled ballast tanks with water for balance and stability. The water carried in these tanks

is released and refilled when a ship reaches a new port. Many foreign organisms are deposited into new habitats in the ballast water. In 1988, the zebra mussel was found in the Great Lakes. This type of mussel is native to the Caspian Sea. It is believed that the zebra mussel traveled from the Caspian Sea to England or the Baltic Sea before arriving in the United States. Within 2 years, the number of zebra mussels had increased dramatically in Lake Erie.

Zebra mussels can survive exposure to air for several days while being transported over land to invade new aquatic habitats. The zebra mussel has already spread to the fresh water of the Appalachian Mountains.

Many of the species that people think are native to the United States were actually introduced. Some examples appear in the table to the right.

Species Introduced into the United States

Organism	Place of Origin
Kentucky bluegrass	England
Horse	Europe
Killer bees	Africa
Eucalyptus tree	Australia
Peanut	Africa
Water hyacinth	South America
Dandelion	Europe
Starling	England
Carp	England

DECISIONS

1. **Infer** Why might people introduce a new species to a habitat?
2. How might zebra mussels become common in all freshwater lakes in the United States?

5.3 POPULATIONS

Objectives • *Explain* how populations of organisms grow. • *Describe* the factors that limit the growth of a population. • *Identify* the shapes of growth curves that represent populations of different organisms.

A species evolves to fit its niche. Yet the biotic and abiotic factors that make up a niche change over time. Food may be plentiful in spring but scarce during winter, for example. These changes affect the number of individuals the niche can support. The size of a population will therefore change as its niche changes.

Population Growth

THINK CRITICALLY

Malthus's observations are an important part of Darwin's theory of evolution. Malthus stated that more offspring are born than can survive. If this is true, which offspring would you expect to survive? How would this survival pattern affect the next generation?

Students should suggest that the organisms best adapted to the environment will survive. The next generation would then share these traits.

In 1798, English economist Thomas Malthus made an observation about the human population. He stated that the human population can quickly grow past the environment's ability to support it. Malthus thought that humans suffered from famine and disease when the population became too large. A young English naturalist named Charles Darwin was impressed by Malthus's observation. Darwin is best known for his theory of evolution. Darwin wrote in his book *On the Origin of Species*, "There is no exception to the rule that every organic being naturally increases at so high a rate, that, if not destroyed, the Earth would soon be covered by the progeny [offspring] of a single pair."

The idea that organisms produce more offspring than can survive was important to Darwin. It played an important part in his theory of evolution. Darwin illustrated his point with an example, which appears in Figure 5.8. His example showed that one pair of elephants could produce more than 20 million elephants in less than 750 years if the elephants were not limited by food or other resources. And if they kept

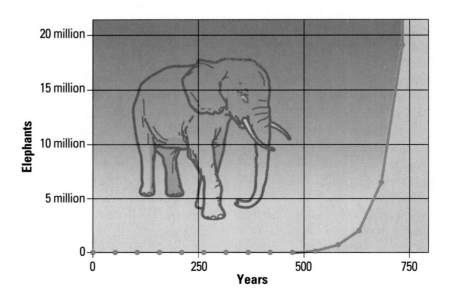

Figure 5.8 Two elephants can quickly produce a large population if conditions are ideal. Elephants reproduce very slowly; populations of most other species would increase much faster.

producing, the world would soon be covered with elephants.

The world is not covered with elephants or any other organism because populations cannot increase forever. All populations have the ability to grow very quickly, however, if they have a perfect environment. *Population growth in which the rate of growth in each generation is a multiple of the previous generation is called* **exponential** (EK-spoh-NEN-chul) **growth**.

In the laboratory, populations can be made to show exponential growth, and some natural populations show it as well. In reality, however, conditions are never perfect. Resources are always limited. A population can grow exponentially, but not for long.

Carrying Capacity

As a population grows, it takes more from its habitat. Resources such as food and living space become scarce. As resources become scarce, individuals begin to compete for them because there is no longer enough to go around. The death rate in the population rises because those who cannot compete die. The birth rate decreases, for producing offspring requires a lot of hard-to-find resources. The growth of the population slows. Finally, the population will stop growing altogether because the number of births and the number of deaths becomes equal. Individuals will be born and die, but the total number of individuals will not change much.

The number of individuals that can be supported by an ecosystem is called the **carrying capacity** *for that species*. The growth of a population toward its carrying capacity is shown in Figure 5.9. The curve represents the change in the size of a population of fruit flies over time. The population starts out small, and then increases rapidly. During this time, the population is growing

Figure 5.9 A population of fruit flies shows an S-shaped growth curve. Early population growth is exponential, but growth then slows and finally reaches zero at the carrying capacity.

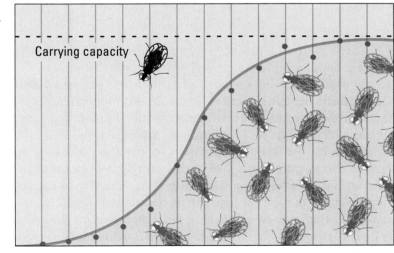

Carrying capacity

Number of flies

Days

exponentially. As the size of the population approaches carrying capacity, the growth rate slows. The population stops growing when it reaches carrying capacity. The growth curve of a population where the birth and death rates become equal is called an *S-shaped curve*.

Limiting Factors

Populations do not grow forever. They stop growing when they reach their carrying capacity. Natural disasters, such as earthquakes and hurricanes, can also cause large changes in population size. The forces that slow the growth in a population are called *limiting factors*. Figure 5.10 shows many of the limiting factors that can affect a population.

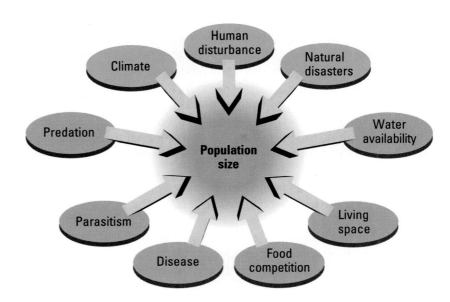

DATELINE 1992

In the summer of 1992, Hurricane Andrew devastated much of southern Florida. The hurricane destroyed thousands of trees and disrupted many ecosystems. Hurricane Andrew was a density-independent factor because it destroyed trees and other organisms regardless of population size.

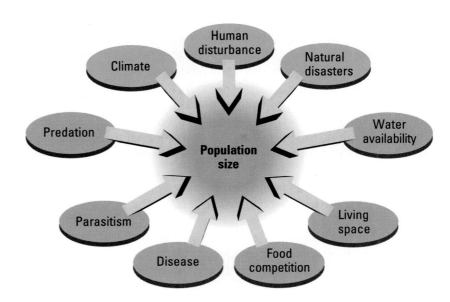

Figure 5.10 All of these factors can influence the size of a population. Factors in purple are density-dependent. Those in green are density-independent.

Cooperative Learning
Have students form groups of two or three. Each group should review the results of the Field Activity on p. 81. Instruct students to divide their lists of limiting factors into density-dependent and density-independent factors. One student should record each list. Compile two lists on the board, one for each kind of factor. Lead a discussion about difficulties students may have had in classifying some factors.

There are two kinds of limiting factors. Some limiting factors affect a population more strongly as the population grows larger. *Limiting factors that are dependent on population size are called* **density-dependent limiting factors**. Some density-dependent factors are lack of food, predation, and disease. As the population grows, each of these factors acts more strongly to limit growth.

Some factors limit a population by the same amount regardless of the population's size. A hurricane, for example, might destroy half of a population of palm trees. The size of the population does not matter because the hurricane would affect any population in the same way. *A limiting factor that affects the same percentage of a population regardless of its size is called a* **density-independent limiting factor**. Natural disasters such as hurricanes and fires are

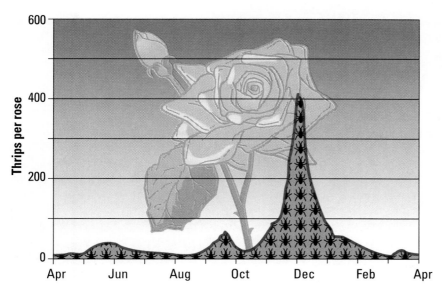

Figure 5.11 Insects called thrips show a boom-and-bust growth curve. Thrips grow on roses. The population of thrips per rose grows very quickly when conditions are favorable; then it falls quickly.

density-independent limiting factors. Habitat damage caused by humans is also density-independent.

Populations controlled by density-dependent factors show an S-shaped growth curve. Populations controlled by density-independent factors show a curve called a boom-and-bust curve. A boom-and-bust curve represents a population whose size grows exponentially and then collapses. Such populations are usually adapted to take advantage of density-independent factors that occur regularly, such as warm temperatures in summer. Many insect populations are controlled in this way, including the one in Figure 5.11.

The Human Population

The growth curve of the human population is an exponential one. The exponential growth of the human population has been caused by many factors, including advances in agriculture, technology, and medicine. No population of organisms can grow exponentially forever. The growth of the human population will level off as resources become more scarce. The human habitat—Earth—already shows signs of strain caused by the size of the population.

Multicultural Perspective
Inform students that the human population is growing fastest in developing nations. Many of these countries suffer from periodic drought and famine due to overpopulation. Developed nations such as the United States often provide relief in the form of food and medicine. But these well-intentioned efforts can sometimes backfire. The United States included powdered milk in relief shipments for years because it was a compact, nutritious food source. But many people who received the shipments could not digest milk, so the powdered milk was used as a whitewash for houses. This example shows the importance of sensitivity to the needs of other cultures.

SECTION REVIEW

1. What is exponential growth? Under what conditions do populations grow exponentially?
2. **Interpret** Draw a graph of an S-shaped growth curve. Label carrying capacity on the graph, and show the region where the population shows exponential growth.
3. What is the difference between density-dependent and density-independent limiting factors?

1. Exponential growth exists when the rate of growth of the population in one generation is a multiple of the last generation. Conditions must be ideal for exponential growth to occur in a population.
2. Curves should look like the one in Figure 5.9.
3. Density-dependent factors limit a population more severely as the population grows larger. Density-independent factors affect a population in the same way regardless of size.

Answers and teaching
strategies on page T42.

Yeast Population Density

PROBLEM
How does the population density of a yeast cell culture change over time?

MATERIALS (per group)
- 5 empty baby food jars with lids
- 100-mL graduated cylinder
- 10% molasses solution
- yeast solution
- 2 medicine droppers
- 5 glass microscope slides
- 5 coverslips
- microscope
- pencil
- graph paper

HYPOTHESIS
After reading the entire activity, write a hypothesis that pertains to the problem.

PROCEDURE
Day 1
1. Label each baby food jar with the names of the people in your group. Number the jars 1 to 5. Add 10 mL of the molasses solution to each of the jars.
2. Stir the yeast solution with the medicine dropper. Transfer ten drops of the yeast solution to each jar before the solution has a chance to settle. Cover each jar and shake gently to mix the solutions.
3. Use a clean dropper to transfer one drop of the solution from jar 1 to a microscope slide. Cover the solution with a coverslip.
4. Observe the slide under the microscope at high power. Count the number of yeast individuals in five different fields of view. Buds count as individual cells.
5. Record each of the five counts in a table. Calculate an average of the five counts. Record this number in the table as well.
6. Place jars 2, 3, 4, and 5 in a warm, dark place where they will not be disturbed.

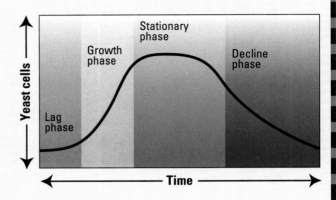

Days 3, 6, 9, and 12
7. Repeat steps 3 and 4 with jar 2 on day 3. Observe jar 3 on day 6, jar 4 on day 9, and jar 5 on day 12. Be sure to record five counts for each jar and to calculate an average. Record these numbers in your data table.
8. Use the graph paper to graph the populations of yeast in the jars. One axis should be yeast cells, the other time. Be sure to record which jar each count comes from.

ANALYSIS
1. Sketch a single yeast cell.
2. Study your graph of the yeast cell population. When did the yeast population grow fastest? Did it ever decline?
3. How did the density of the population of yeast cells change over time? Explain.

CONCLUSION
1. The figure on this page names several different stages in the growth of a yeast cell population. Label these stages on your own graph if they occur. If they do not occur, suggest reasons why your curve was different.
2. Why does the number of yeast cells change over time? Write a paragraph discussing the forces that may have caused the changes in the yeast cell population.

CHAPTER 5 REVIEW

KEY TERMS

niche 5.1
competitive exclusion 5.1
predator 5.1

keystone predator 5.1
evolution 5.2
convergent evolution 5.2

coevolution 5.2
exponential growth 5.3
carrying capacity 5.3

density-dependent limiting factor 5.3
density-independent limiting factor 5.3

CHAPTER SUMMARY

5.1 The area in which a species lives is its habitat, and its role in that habitat is its niche. The niche is influenced by biotic and abiotic factors such as predators and sunlight. The niche of a species is unique to that species.

5.2 Species may evolve to avoid competition with other species for food and other resources. The niche of one organism can influence the niche of another. Convergent evolution is a change in which different species occupying similar niches evolve in similar ways. When species that interact very closely adapt to one another, the change is called coevolution.

5.3 The population growth of organisms is controlled by limiting factors. Limiting factors can be density-dependent or density-independent. Without these limiting factors, the population of a given organism would, in time, cover Earth. The carrying capacity of a species is the maximum number that an ecosystem can sustain, given the limiting factors.

MULTIPLE CHOICE

Choose the letter of the word or phrase that best completes each statement.

1. The role of an organism in an ecosystem is called its (a) habitat; (b) sleeping habits; (c) niche; (d) species. c

2. Temperature, sunlight, and water are examples of (a) biotic factors; (b) abiotic factors; (c) food sources; (d) mineral sources. b

3. When two species interact so closely that they adapt to each other, the interaction is called (a) symbiotic evolution; (b) coevolution; (c) covergent evolution; (d) generalized evolution. b

4. Birds and bats have developed similar wings through a process called (a) specialization; (b) predation; (c) biodiversity; (d) convergent evolution. d

5. To fit its niche, a species (a) evolves; (b) reproduces; (c) competes; (d) regresses. a

6. The carrying capacity for a species is the maximum number (a) born; (b) sustained; (c) eaten; (d) changing. b

7. Population growth is limited by density-dependent factors such as (a) climate; (b) earthquakes and floods; (c) biotic and abiotic factors; (d) predation and disease. d

8. Climate changes and earthquakes are (a) expressed by S-shaped curves; (b) density-independent limiting factors; (c) influenced by exponential growth; (d) factors of carrying capacity. b

9. Keystone predators affect a habitat's (a) food chain; (b) competitive exclusion; (c) fundamental niche; (d) diversity. d

10. As resources become scarce because of population growth, the growth (a) levels off; (b) is represented by a boom-and-bust curve; (c) becomes exponential; (d) increases. a

CHAPTER 5 REVIEW

WORD COMPARISONS

Write the letter of the second word pair that best matches the first pair.

1. Habitat: niche as (a) address: occupation; (b) land: desert; (c) people: work; (d) house: neighborhood. a

2. Keystone predator: diversity as (a) land: desert; (b) food: population growth; (c) environment: ecosystem; (d) ant: acacia tree. b

3. Dolphin: ichthyosaur as (a) predator: prey; (b) convergent evolution: coevolution; (c) ant: acacia tree; (d) bird wing: bat wing. d

4. S-shaped curve: food competition as (a) population: exponential growth; (b) boom-and-bust curve: climate; (c) limiting factors: population; (d) agriculture: food. b

5. Agriculture: exponential growth as (a) tree: forest; (b) organism: evolution;.(c) termite colony: infestation; (d) heat: expansion. d

CONCEPT REVIEW   Answers on page T42.

Write a complete response to each of the following.

1. Explain how the niche of one species might influence the niche of another.

2. Why are the animals in Figure 5.6 similar?

3. Describe the difference between a specialized species and a generalized species. Which species would be more tolerant to change? Why?

4. List two examples of biotic factors and two examples of abiotic factors that can limit or increase the size of a species' population.

5. What do S-shaped curves represent in graphs of population growth?

THINK CRITICALLY   Answe on page T42.

1. If two different species ate exactly the same kind of food in the same location, what would you expect to happen over time?

2. Describe how predation can be an important factor in the long-term survival of a species' population.

3. Why would you expect evolution to take place more rapidly on land than at the bottom of the ocean?

4. Suppose a construction company was to dam a small river. Consider what changes might take place in the regions upstream and downstream from the dam. How might the population growth of species be affected? Why?

WRITE FOR UNDERSTANDING

Think of land mammals that returned to the oceans and have become what we know today as whales, dolphins, and seals. Summarize the adaptations these species have to aquatic niches. Why did these adaptations evolve? How are the challenges of living on land different than those of living in the water? How are the challenges similar?

PORTFOLIO

Construct a collage of density-dependent limiting factors on human population. Use pictures and graphs from newspapers and magazines, and also work with short articles or captions. Organize your collage so that different types of density dependent factors occur together.

GRAPHIC ANALYSIS Answers on page T42.

Use the figure to answer the following.
1. What does this graph show?
2. When is the fruit fly population growing most quickly? What is the population size at this point compared to the carrying capacity?
3. Does the growth rate ever reach zero in the graph? If so, where does this occur?
4. Why does the growth rate of the population slow?

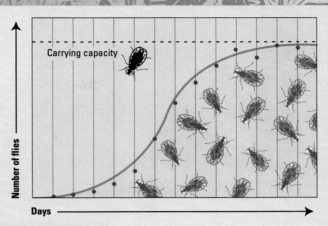

Carrying capacity

Number of flies

Days

ACTIVITY 5.2

Answers and teaching strategies on page T42.

PROBLEM
How can human activities affect a deer population over time?

MATERIALS
• graph paper

INFERENCE
Write an inference that relates to the problem.

PROCEDURE
1. In 1906, the U.S. Forest Service began protecting a herd of deer on a 300 000 hectare range on Arizona's Kaibab Plateau. In previous years, the Kaibab forest area had been overgrazed by cattle, sheep, and horses. Graph the Forest Service's data. Plot the year along the *x*-axis and the population size along the *y*-axis.
2. In 1906, the Forest Service estimated the carrying capacity of the range to be about 30,000 deer. Draw a straight horizontal line across your graph beginning at the 30,000-deer level. Label this line *Carrying capacity*.

ANALYSIS
What was the relationship of the deer herd to the carrying capacity of the range in 1915? 1920? 1924?

CONCLUSION
1. Describe the effects of the following actions taken by the Forest Service:
   a. 1907: Hunting of deer was banned. Also, the Forest Service began a 32-year campaign to exterminate natural predators of the deer. Thousands of predators were killed.
   b. 1920: Seeing that the range was deteriorating rapidly, the Forest Service reduced the number of livestock grazing permits.
   c. 1924: The deer population was on the brink of starvation.

   Deer hunting was allowed again. Deer shot by hunters in autumn represented about one-tenth the number that had been born the previous spring.
2. What do you think the Forest Service learned between 1905 and 1939?

Deer Population, 1905-1939

Year	Population	Year	Population
1905	4,000	1927	37,000
1910	9,000	1928	35,000
1915	25,000	1929	30,000
1920	65,000	1930	25,000
1924	100,000	1931	20,000
1925	60,000	1935	18,000
1926	40,000	1939	10,000

Ecosystems exist in a state of balance. The organisms in an ecosystem work together like the different parts of a machine, capturing energy and using it to cycle matter. Each organism plays a part in keeping the whole ecosystem functioning. The interactions among populations and abiotic factors maintain the balance.

Ecosystems change slowly if they are not disturbed. Yet disturbance, such as fires, storms, or landslides, are facts of life in all ecosystems. Scientists think that the balance in most ecosystems is dynamic, or in a constant state of change. Even though change occurs continuously, the ecosystem remains in balance.

6.1 RELATIONSHIPS IN THE ECOSYSTEM

Objectives • *Explain* the relationship between the population sizes of predator and prey. • *Define* symbiosis and **state** the effects of symbiotic relationships on populations.

The relationships among organisms in a community are complex. Each population of one species interacts with many others, and with abiotic factors as well. A change in any of these relationships can lead to a change in the population. This change can lead to further changes throughout the food web. One common relationship between species is the relationship of predator and prey.

Predators and Prey

All organisms need food and all consumers must eat other organisms to get it. Consumers that actively hunt other organisms are called *predators*. The organisms upon which a predator feeds are called *prey*. A praying mantis that eats a dragonfly is a predator. The dragonfly is the prey. The praying mantis itself is prey to other organisms such as snakes and birds. These predators are, in turn, prey to larger carnivores.

The sizes of predator and prey populations are closely linked. A large prey population can support more predators than a small prey population. If a prey population grows or shrinks, the number of predators the community can support changes as well. An example of this linkage is shown in Figure 6.1.

The snowshoe hare is the prey the lynx eats most often. Even though there are always more hares than lynxes, the number of hares changes greatly from year to year. The number of lynxes also

The example of the lynx and snowshoe hare is a good topic for class discussion. Tell students to read the text and study the diagram, then lead a discussion about the graph. Point out to students that the graph has two vertical scales. The one on the left is for hares; the one on the right is for lynxes. Ask students what the graph would look like if only one scale were used. Answer: The population curve for hares would be much higher than the curve for lynxes. Remind students that the hare is usually the sole prey of the lynx. Discuss the significance of the fluctuations in the two populations, and emphasize that changes in one population are linked to the other.

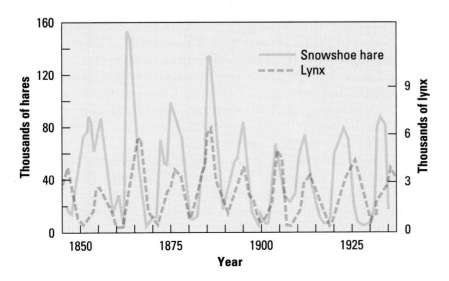

Figure 6.1 This graph shows the sizes of the lynx and snowshoe hare populations in northern Canada between 1845 and 1935. Both populations show cycles. The size of the lynx population and the size of the hare population are interconnected.

Figure 6.2 The lynx generally feeds only on the snowshoe hare. The population sizes of these two animals are closely related.

changes. If you look closely at Figure 6.1, you may observe a pattern. Increases in the hare population are usually followed by increases in the lynx population after one or two years. The increasing number of prey animals allows the predator population to grow as well, because there is more food for the predators. A decline in the number of hares is also followed by a decline in the number of lynxes, again after a delay of one or two years. Can you explain this pattern?

The lynx and hare populations rise and fall about once every ten years. In general, large herbivores, such as the hare, muskrat, and large birds, have peaks in their population sizes every ten years. Small herbivores, such as mice and lemmings, have population cycles similar to that of the lynx. The populations cycle once every four years. Larger animals have longer cycles because they live longer and reproduce more slowly than smaller animals.

Many predators have population cycles that match those of their prey. Predators, such as the Arctic fox, that eat herbivores with four-year cycles also have four-year cycles. Predators that eat herbivores with ten-year cycles also have ten-year cycles. The population of the colored fox cycles every ten years in some places and every four years elsewhere, depending on which herbivore the fox eats. The changing population size of the prey species controls the population size of the predator species.

Parasitism

Some organisms do not kill the prey they feed on. **Parasitism** (PAYR-uh-SIT-IZ-um) *is a relationship in which one organism feeds on the tissues or body fluids of another*. The organism on which a parasite feeds is called the *host*. A parasite is harmful to its host and may even be fatal. Most parasites, however, do not kill their hosts. Fleas are parasites, as are ticks, lice, and a variety of worms, protists, and other organisms.

Many herbivores do not kill the plants they consume, but herbivores are not considered parasites. A true parasite is adapted to living on or in the body of its host. A parasite depends on its host for many functions. Many parasites cannot perform functions that the host provides for them. A tapeworm, for example, has no sensory organs and cannot move by itself. Tapeworms live in the intestines of mammals. The tapeworm does not need to move or use senses because it lives inside the body of its host. It has special adaptations for living in its environment.

The population size of a parasite is closely related to the population size of its host. A large host population can support more parasites than a small host population. Parasite populations are also affected by the density of the host population. Parasites thrive in crowded host populations because the parasite can find new hosts easily. Parasites are a density-dependent limiting factor because parasites are more successful in dense host populations.

Symbiosis

A relationship where two species live together closely is called **symbiosis** (sim-by-OH-sis). Parasitism is one example of a symbiotic relationship. Parasitism harms one organism and benefits the other. Some symbiotic relationships do not harm either organism.

A symbiotic relationship that benefits one species and neither helps nor harms the other is called *commensalism* (ku-MEN-sul-ɪz-um). Barnacles living on the skin of a whale, such as those in Figure 6.3, are one example of commensalism. The barnacles do not harm or help the whale. But the barnacles benefit from the constant movement of food-carrying water past the swimming whale.

A symbiotic relationship in which both species benefit is called *mutualism* (MYOO-choo-ul-ɪz-um). The ants and acacia trees discussed in Chapter 5 are one example of a mutualistic relationship. Another example is the relationship between flowers and the insects that pollinate them. The flower provides the insect with food in the form of nectar, and in return, the insect fertilizes the flower.

The yucca plant and yucca moth in Figure 6.4 have coevolved to the point where one cannot survive without the other. The yucca moth crawls inside the yucca flower to lay its eggs. The moth then gathers a ball of pollen from the plant and carries it to another plant. The moth places the pollen ball in a special part of the yucca flower to pollinate it. In return, the yucca plant provides food for developing yucca moth caterpillars. The yucca plant and yucca moth are an example of a mutualisitic relationship.

Figure 6.3 These barnacles have hitched a ride on the back of a whale. The barnacles do not help or harm the whale, but the barnacles benefit. This relationship is an example of commensalism.

Figure 6.4 The Mojave yucca plant and the yucca moth have a mutualistic relationship. Both species benefit from their interaction.

1. Predator and prey population sizes are linked because the prey provides food for the predator. Changes in the prey population will affect the number of predators that the prey population can support.
2. Herbivores often do not kill the plants they feed on, but they are not parasites because they lack the other characteristics of parasites. Parasites live on or in the body of the host, are relatively small, and may have special adaptations to take advantage of the host.
3. Definitions should resemble those in the text. All types of symbiosis are similar in that they involve a close interaction between two (or sometimes more) species. The types differ depending on which species benefits. In parasitism, the parasite benefits, while the host is harmed. In commensalism, one species benefits while the other is unaffected. In mutualism, both species benefit from the relationship.

SECTION REVIEW

1. What processes link the sizes of predator and prey populations?
2. Why are herbivores not considered to be parasites?
3. **Compare and Contrast** Write definitions of the three types of symbiosis. How are the three relationships different? How are they similar?

6.2 ECOLOGICAL SUCCESSION

Objectives • *Describe* the process of primary and secondary succession. • *Illustrate* the evolution of many species from a single ancestor during the process of island succession.

Organisms affect the environments in which they live. Plants, for example, help form soil by breaking down rocks and making organic matter. The changes a species causes in its environment may not be helpful to that species. The environment may change so much that the species' niche disappears. Old niches are replaced by new niches to which new species are adapted. A species can literally sow the seeds of its own destruction.

Other forces also change the environment. A forest formed slowly over hundreds of years can be destroyed in minutes by fire. Change is a fact of life in all ecosystems, and living things have evolved in response to change. As an environment changes, the community living in that environment changes as well. In many cases, different communities follow one another in a definite pattern.

Primary Succession

Imagine you are standing on the beach during a volcanic eruption. The shore grows as a black and orange river of molten rock flows slowly into the sea. The lava hisses and gives off steam as it cools. After the eruption has ended and the steam has cleared, a new shoreline is visible, one made of bare rock. Organisms move into this lifeless habitat almost immediately. These first organisms are followed by others. *The sequence of communities forming in an originally lifeless habitat is called* **primary succession** (suk-SESH-un).

Primary succession occurs in new habitats without life, such as the cooled lava field in the example above, or the bare rock exposed by a retreating glacier. Primary succession is an orderly process. It follows the same general pattern in most ecosystems. The first step in primary succession is the formation of soil from exposed rocks.

On land, exposed rocks are first colonized by organisms called lichens. *A* **lichen** (LY-kun) *is a fungus and an alga living in a mutualistic relationship.* Unlike most organisms, lichens can live on bare rock. Lichens secrete acids that break down the rock and form organic material by photosynthesis. Rocks are also broken down by weathering caused by wind, rain, and frost. The action of lichens and weathering form soil. Scientists call the lichen community a *pioneer community* because it is the first community to colonize a new habitat.

Once soil has formed, grasses and other small plants begin to grow from seeds carried to the habitat by wind or animals. These

Figure 6.5 A lichen is an example of a symbiotic relationship between an alga and a fungus. Lichens are often a major part of a pioneer community during primary succession.

Lichens, mosses

Grasses, shrubs

Heath mat

Jack pine, black spruce, aspen

Fir, birch, white spruce

Pioneer community ———————————————————————→ Climax community

plants continue the process of soil formation. In time, the plants grow dense enough that lichens cannot get enough light. The lichens disappear. The lichen community is replaced by the grass community.

The grass community survives for many generations and makes the soil deeper and more fertile. Eventually, the soil is deep enough to allow the growth of non-woody plants with deep roots. These plants are taller than the grasses and crowd them out when competing for sunlight. As the shrub community grows, the soil continues to deepen and become richer. The grass and shrub communities are usually not diverse. These communities are unstable. Small disturbances may cause drastic changes in the community.

Pines or other trees with shallow roots invade when the soil is deep enough. As these trees move in, the community changes again. Shrubs are replaced by trees and plants found on the forest floor. The soil continues to deepen. Finally, saplings of broadleaf trees take root. The pine forest is replaced by a hardwood forest. The hardwood forest is the last step in primary succession. If this forest is not disturbed, there will be no more change in the habitat. *A community that does not undergo further succession is called a* **climax community**. Climax communities are usually diverse and stable, with many species of plants and other organisms.

Secondary Succession

Primary succession occurs only on freshly exposed rock or in places where a severe disturbance has destroyed the community and the soil. However, most disturbances are not this drastic. A fire, for example, kills many plants but leaves the soil in place. Living things are quick to colonize clear patches created by these smaller disturbances.

Figure 6.6 This diagram shows the process of primary succession as it occurred on Isle Royale in Lake Superior. One community gave way to the next until a climax community was established.

Teaching tips for Field Activity appear on page T46.

FIELD ACTIVITY

Secondary succession often occurs after human disturbance. Find an abandoned farm field or a vacant lot near your school, and arrange a field trip to study the area. When you arrive, study the plants that have colonized the disturbed area. Try to answer the following questions. How tall are the plants? Are they grasses and weeds, shrubs, or trees? How does this plant community differ from undisturbed communities in the surrounding area? After you have completed your study, use what you know about secondary succession to analyze your findings.

Figure 6.7 Secondary succession has begun in this area. The original community was destroyed by a forest fire, and the new plants are moving in. The process of secondary succession will eventually restore the climax community.

BIOLOGY
L I N K

Many communities are adapted to occasional fires, including the forests in Yellowstone National Park. Humans controlled these fires for many years because they thought the fires where harmful. Some of the communities in the park became unbalanced, and some species crowded out others. Eventually, the park adopted a "let it burn" policy and allowed forest fires to burn without fighting them. Unfortunately, the absence of fires for many years allowed dead plants to accumulate, and some fires raged out of control.

Figure 6.8 This lake is filling quickly with plant material and other sediments. When the process of aquatic succession is complete, the lake will be replaced by dry land.

Succession that occurs where a community has been cleared by a disturbance that does not destroy the soil is called **secondary succession**. Fires, storms, and human activity are common causes of secondary succession.

Secondary succession resembles the later stages of primary succession. Fast-growing grasses and non-woody plants are the first plants to colonize the area, followed by larger shrubs. Fast-growing trees such as pines then crowd out the shrub community, followed finally by slow-growing hardwood trees. Eventually, a climax community forms again, and the process of succession is complete.

Ecologists have recently realized that many habitats never develop climax communities. Habitats that are frequently disturbed do not last for the several hundred years needed to complete the process of succession. Grasslands are a good example of this type of habitat. Frequent fires continually disrupt the grassland. The fires kill the seedlings of shrubs and trees trying to gain a foothold. As a result, succession in this habitat is held at the grass community level. Disruption is crucial to maintaining balance in these communities.

Aquatic Succession

The process of succession also occurs in aquatic habitats. Imagine a clear mountain lake just formed by a retreating glacier. The lake is much like barren rock; the water is very low in nutrients and supports few organisms. As time passes, reeds and other water plants begin to grow in the thin sediments near the shore of the lake, supporting other organisms. Organic matter begins to collect in the lake.

As the lake begins to fill with sediment, the water becomes richer in nutrients. More organisms move in, and water plants begin to cover the surface of the lake. After a long period of time, the lake fills with sediment and becomes a marsh. Land plants begin to colonize the marsh. Finally, the lake becomes a fertile meadow covered with land plants. The meadow may even undergo land succession and turn into a forest.

Island Succession

Islands undergo succession in much the same way as land on the continents. New islands can form quickly through volcanic eruptions. Living things are quick to colonize this new land. Seagulls are observed nesting on some islands before the volcanic activity stops.

Islands are isolated by the water that surrounds them. Any organism found on an island must have ancestors that were carried there by water, wind, or by other organisms. These ancestors may have arrived on the island by chance alone. Many islands therefore have large bird populations, because birds can reach islands much more easily than land animals.

The rare organism that arrives on a new island and can find a mate is often faced with an opportunity. There are many unfilled niches on the island, because the organisms that would fill the niches on the mainland have no way of getting to the island. In this situation, the offspring of a few organisms can evolve to fill several niches, because there is no competition. Populations of organisms adapt to their new niches, and several new species form. The offspring of a few ancestors can adapt to several different niches.

Figure 6.9 These species of finches evolved from common ancestors on Indefatigable Island in the Galapagos.

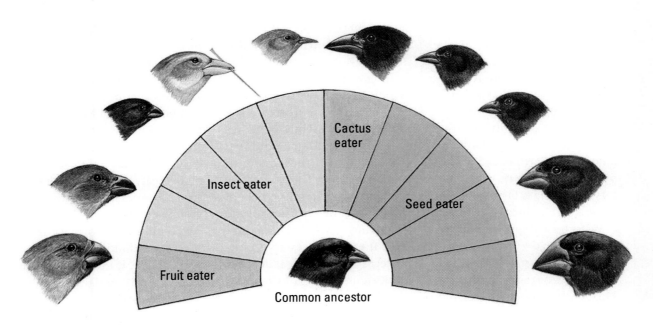

Cactus eater

Insect eater

Seed eater

Fruit eater

Common ancestor

SECTION REVIEW

1. How does primary succession differ from secondary succession?
2. What is a climax community?
3. **Predict** Suppose humans put out all the fires in a large area of grassland over a period of 100 years. What would happen to the grassland community?

1. Primary succession occurs in an environment that is very low in nutrients. Secondary succession occurs after a disturbance destroys a community but leaves soil unharmed.
2. A climax community is a community that does not change in nature with the passage of time. Climax communities are stable and diverse.
3. If all fires were stopped, shrubs and trees from other communities would invade the grassland.

One of Each Organism

How can scientists identify all the species in the world?

1. ATBI will obtain a reasonably accurate picture of plant and animal diversity over the next 50 years.
2. It is computerized, cooperative, and comprehensive instead of individual and biased.

Scientists have described 300,000 different types of flowering plants, 47,000 vertebrates, and over a million other species. Over 1.4 million species of organisms living on Earth have names. This may seem like quite a list. However, it probably accounts for less than 15 percent of the actual number of species, which is thought to range between 8 and 100 million.

Surveying all of these organisms may seem impossible. But that is the goal of the world's first All Taxa Biodiversity Inventory, or ATBI. Actually, the job is so large that scientists have a more realistic goal of gaining a reasonably accurate representation of the plants and animals on Earth over the next 50 years. Currently, the inventory of species is biased because it concentrates mostly on larger, easy-to-locate species. For example, only 69,000 species of fungi have been described, out of an estimated 1.5 million. Most of the insects that live in the canopy of tropical rain forests remain unknown. The number of identified species of bacteria in the world is 4,000, yet studies show that just 1 g of forest soil may contain over 5,000 different species!

The ATBI project must move quickly because species are being destroyed at a rapid rate. In tropical rain forests, the number of species is reduced by almost 1 percent every year, and 20 percent of all species on Earth may disappear within the next 30 years. A species survey could help governments determine which areas to conserve and which species to protect. Also, some of the presently unidentified species could be potential sources of medicines, crops, or other products.

The overwhelming task of identifying the creatures of the world must be undertaken carefully. It will be necessary to survey ecosystems in great detail in a selected number of sites, and in less detail over a wider geographic range. There are several differences between this biological survey and surveys done in the past. Usually, scientists specialized in collecting only one species, such as beetles or fungi. They would ignore other species that shared the habitat of the focus organism. In ATBI, every species in an area will be cataloged. For example, the insects, bacteria, fungi, and worms that live on the body of a bird will be as important to identify as the bird. The other organisms that share the nest and tree of the bird will also be cataloged.

A staggering amount of data will be generated by ATBI. The project will store the information in huge computer databases. By connecting separate biodiversity databases with networks, species information from around the world can be shared. By combining information on species distribution, vegetation, and climate, it may be possible to find new populations of endangered species.

ATBI will be more than a list of species. It will help humans further their understanding of the complex biosphere.

DECISIONS

1. What is the purpose of ATBI?
2. How is ATBI different from earlier inventories of species?

6.3 BALANCE IN THE ECOSYSTEM

Objectives • *Examine* the concept of ecosystem balance, and explain how humans affect that balance. • *Explain* that disturbance is a natural part of all ecosystems, but that disturbances trigger changes in ecosystems.

All the elements of an ecosystem are connected. The interaction between predator and prey demonstrates how the population of one species can affect the population of another. The processes of succession show how organisms can change their environments. Through these interactions and others like them, the biotic and abiotic parts of an ecosystem exchange matter and energy.

All processes in an ecosystem link together into a complex system. The food web is the heart of this system. Succession, evolution, changing climate, and other factors also play important roles. Like the human body, the ecosystem has different parts that perform different functions, each crucial to the survival of the whole.

All natural ecosystems are stable. They maintain a state of balance, called *equilibrium* (EE-kwi-LIB-ree-um). If ecosystems are not balanced, they do not survive. An ecosystem gets this stability from the maze of interactions that link its parts. A disruption in one part of the system, such as a temperature change to a colder climate, is counteracted by changes in other parts of the system, such as the evolution of adaptations to cold weather. The disrupted ecosystem returns to a state of equilibrium.

Major disruptions cause dynamic changes as the ecosystem adjusts to the new conditions. Some disruptions can destroy whole ecosystems. But a new ecosystem will develop to replace the one destroyed. The rapid evolution of mammals after the extinction of the dinosaurs is an example of one ecosystem replacing another. The general rule is: Species and whole ecosystems evolve and may die out, but new species can evolve to replace them.

DATELINE 1972

In 1972 , a scientist named James Lovelock first published the controversial Gaia hypothesis. Lovelock proposed that Earth is actually one giant living organism. Most scientists do not agree with Lovelock. Lovelock's idea did focus scientific attention on the interaction between different parts of the world's ecosystems. The concept of Earth as a single, integrated system is now central to environmental science.

Figure 6.10 A large comet or asteroid hit Earth 66 million years ago. Some scientists think this event caused the extinction of the dinosaurs, while other scientists disagree. Did a comet kill the dinosaurs, or were other factors such as a changing climate responsible? People may never know for certain.

Scientists do not understand every detail of how even simple ecosystems function. They do understand that changes in one part of a system can trigger changes in other parts, like a series of falling dominoes. But scientists cannot always predict how changes in one part of the system will affect another part. Recently, however, a few scientists have tried to apply a new kind of mathematics called *chaos* (KAY-oss) *theory* to the problem of ecosystem function. This field of science is very new, but it has yielded some promising results. Chaos theory suggests that ecosystems may be very sensitive to even small changes, and that the beginning state of an ecosystem is crucial to its later development. Yet scientists are still a long way from understanding exactly how ecosystems function.

At present, species are becoming extinct at the fastest rate since the extinction of the dinosaurs. The cause of these extinctions is human activity. Humans are also placing many other stresses, such as pollution and deforestation, on the global ecosystem. Will people continue to damage the environment without knowledge of the consequences? And how will the consequences affect future generations and the global ecosystem in which they live?

Figure 6.11 This image is called a fractal. It is a visual representation of a mathematical formula. Complex images like this one may be a good representation of the complexity in ecosystems.

Word Power

Chaos, from the Greek *chaos*, a disordered state of matter and energy that existed before the universe began.

1. The study of ecosystems is complex because of the many factors that influence an ecosystem. Organisms influence their own and other populations, and abiotic factors such as climate are important also.
2. The many interactions among the components of an ecosystem make the system stable. Parts of an ecosystem react through these connections to stabilize changes in other parts.
3. Answers will vary. Essays should reflect a knowledge of the content of Section 6.3 and Unit 2 in general. This question is also a good topic for class discussion.

SECTION REVIEW

1. Why is the study of ecosystems so complex?
2. Why is an ecosystem stable? How does it react to a change in one of its parts?
3. **Write Creatively** Write a short essay that answers the two questions at the end of the last paragraph in this section. You may want to discuss the issues with your classmates first.

6.4 LAND BIOMES

Objectives • *Define* the concept of the biome, and name the eight major land biomes. • *Illustrate* where each of the eight major land biomes occurs.

The movement of matter and energy and other principles of ecosystem function are common to all environments on Earth. Yet Earth is a very large and diverse place. Environments range from the ice of Antarctica to the heat and rain of the Amazon. Differences in temperature and rainfall create a vast array of environments on the surface of Earth. Life has adapted to almost all of these environments.

The ecosystems of Earth can be divided into several broad categories. *A major type of ecosystem with distinctive temperature, rainfall, and organisms is called a* **biome** (BY-ohm). Biomes are either terrestrial (on land) or aquatic (in water). On land, the type of biome that occurs in a given area depends on the average temperature and the amount of precipitation the area receives. Aquatic biomes are determined by water depths, nutrients, and nearness to land.

The biome is the largest category scientists use to classify ecosystems. Because each biome is a general category instead of a specific definition, the conditions in a biome may vary from place to place. Smaller ecosystems also have different habitats with different conditions and organisms. Every habitat on Earth is different, and any attempt to classify these habitats is an overgeneralization. But the concept of the biome is useful as a way to talk about certain sets of related habitats.

The terrestrial ecosystems of Earth can be divided into eight major biomes. Two of these biomes—the *desert* and the *tundra*—receive very little water and support a small amount of biomass. Recall that biomass is the total mass of organic material in an ecosystem. Desert, for example, covers 25 percent of Earth's land surface but contains only 1 percent of Earth's biomass. The lack of water in the desert and in the tundra makes plant life scarce in these areas.

Forest biomes contain 75 percent of the earth's biomass. There are three forest biomes: the *coniferous* (ku-NIF-er-us) *forest*, the *deciduous* (dee-SIJ-oo-us) *forest*, and the *rain forest*. Forests receive abundant precipitation. The rain forest alone covers only 6 percent of Earth's land surface, but contains more than 50 percent of all Earth's biomass. The rainforest biome is also the most diverse biome, containing more than 50 percent of Earth's species. The destruction of the rain forests is a serious environmental problem.

The other three land biomes are grasslands. They are the *steppe*, *prairie*, and *savanna*. Grassland biomes cover about 22 percent of Earth's land surface, and contain about 8 percent of Earth's biomass. The grasslands receive less precipitation than the forest

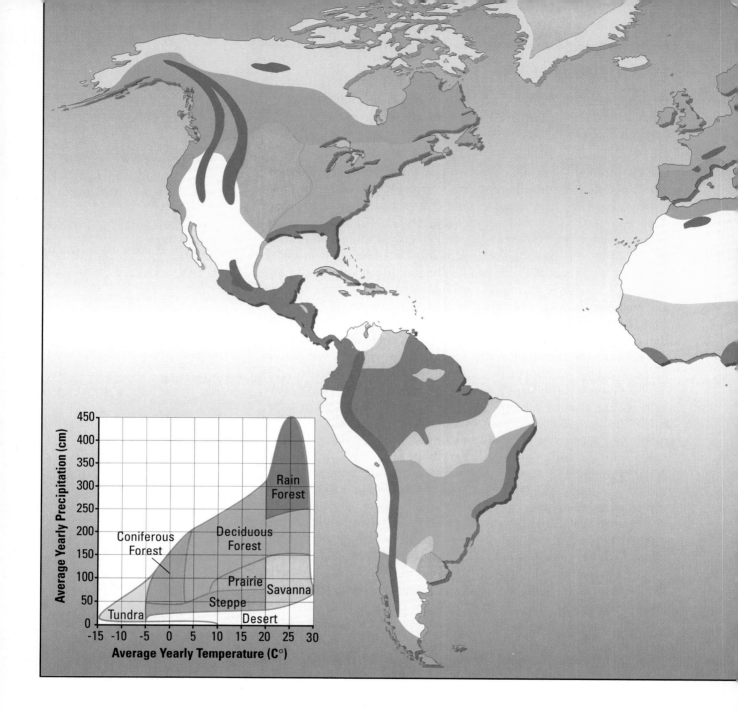

Figure 6.12 This map shows where the major biomes of the world occur. The graph shows the precipitation and temperature usual for each biome.

biomes and may have long dry seasons. Grasslands may be frequently disturbed by fire. Large herds of migrating herbivores are common grassland organisms.

Figure 6.12 shows where each biome occurs on Earth. The areas are color-coded to the key on the right. The graph on the left shows what temperature and precipitation conditions occur in each biome. The areas in the graph are color-coded to the same key as the biome map.

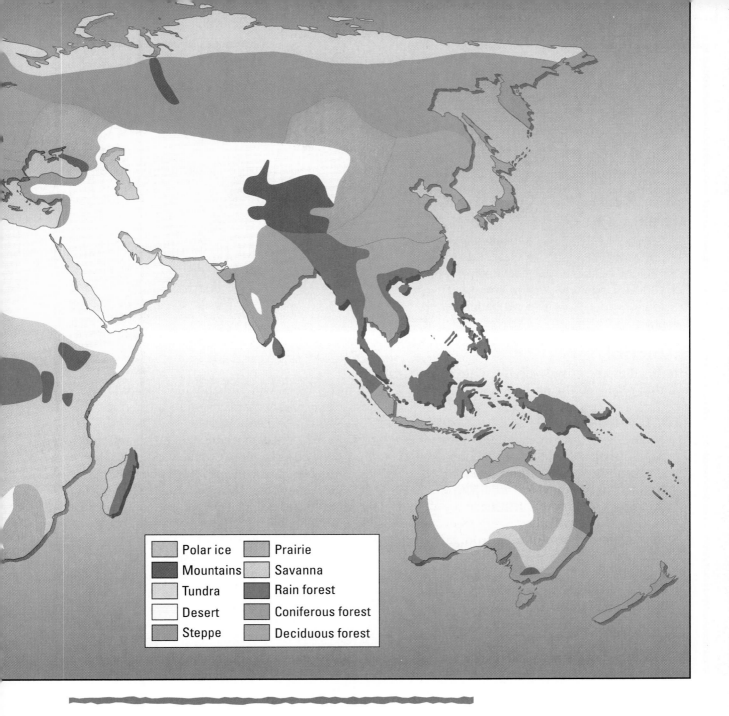

Legend:
- Polar ice
- Mountains
- Tundra
- Desert
- Steppe
- Prairie
- Savanna
- Rain forest
- Coniferous forest
- Deciduous forest

SECTION REVIEW

1. What is a biome? Which biome covers the largest land area?
2. **Interpret** What biome would you expect to find in an area having 312 cm of rain a year and an average annual temperature of 24°C? Use the graph in Figure 6.12 to find the answer.
3. **Relate** Locate the position of the city or town where you live on the biome map. In what biome is your city or town?

1. A biome is a major type of ecosystem with distinctive organisms, precipitation, and temperature. The most common land biome is the desert.
2. An area with these conditions would probably be a rain forest.
3. Answers will vary. Make sure that students locate the correct area on the biome map.

Answers and teaching
strategies on page T46.

Succession in Aged Tap Water

PROBLEM
How does a microscopic community change over time?

MATERIALS (per group)
- paper
- tap water
- 500-mL beaker
- 1000-mL beaker
- soil
- grass
- dropper
- glass slide
- coverslip
- microscope
- pH paper
- leaves

PREDICTION
After reading the entire activity, write a prediction that relates to the problem.

PROCEDURE

1. Make a data table by dividing a sheet of paper into two columns. Label one column *Date* and the other column *Observations*.
2. To make aged tap water, fill a 500-mL beaker with tap water and leave it for 48 hours. This will allow gases to evaporate that might be harmful to microorganisms.
3. After 48 hours, place a 1-cm layer of soil in the bottom of a 1000-mL beaker. Loosely fill the rest of the beaker with a mixture of grasses and leaves.
4. Pour the aged tap water into the 1000-mL beaker.
5. Place the beaker in a cool place overnight.
6. The next day, examine the water in the beaker for signs of living things, such as cloudy water or a strong odor. Fuzzy growths or threads are evidence that molds are growing. A greenish tint in the water shows that algae are present.
7. Use a dropper to remove some of the water. Place a drop of it on a glass slide, and put a coverslip over it.
8. Place the slide under the microscope. Start with low power, and focus on some debris.

The debris will probably have bacteria and other microorganisms on or around it. Switch to high power.

9. Record the date in the data table, and note your observations. Count or estimate the number of organisms under one field of view. Estimate the approximate sizes of the organisms. (*Hint*: The diameter of the field of view under high power of most microscopes is 0.4 mm.) Try to identify some of the organisms you see, using reference sources. Also measure and record the pH of the water.
10. Repeat steps 6–9 each day for two weeks.

ANALYSIS
1. How did the numbers and types of organisms change over the two weeks you made observations?
2. Why might certain populations have disappeared after some time?
3. What is the relationship between pH and the number of organisms that were present in the community?

CONCLUSION
Did you see any evidence of ecological succession? If so, describe it.

KEY TERMS

parasitism 6.1	lichen 6.2	biome 6.4
symbiosis 6.1	climax community 6.2	
primary succession 6.2	secondary succession 6.2	

CHAPTER SUMMARY

6.1 Species interact with the other species in their habitats. All consumers must eat other organisms, and these organisms try to avoid being eaten. Symbiotic relationships between species are called parasitism, commensalism, and mutualism.

6.2 In the process of primary succession, bare rocks are colonized by a series of communities, ending with the climax community. Secondary succession occurs when the plant community in an area is removed, but the soil remains. Island succession is affected by which plants and animals manage to travel to the island.

6.3 Ecosystems exist in a state of equilibrium. If an ecosystem goes out of balance, it will adjust to regain the balanced state. Some disturbances may destroy whole ecosystems. The activity of humans is causing large disturbances in the ecosystems of Earth.

6.4 The surface of Earth is very diverse. Conditions of precipitation and temperature differ from place to place. The general categories of ecosystems are called biomes. There are eight major land biomes: desert, tundra, steppe, prairie, savanna, deciduous forest, coniferous forest, and rain forest.

MULTIPLE CHOICE

Choose the letter of the word or phrase that best completes each statement.

1. An organism that actively hunts other organisms is a(n) (a) herbivore; (b) insect; (c) predator; (d) prey. c

2. A relationship between species in which one species benefits and the other is harmed is called (a) parasitism; (b) commensalism; (c) mutualism; (d) symbiosis. a

3. A relationship between species where both species benefit is called (a) parasitism; (b) commensalism; (c) mutualism; (d) symbiosis. c

4. An example of an organism from a pioneer community is (a) lichen; (b) white spruce; (c) heath mat; (d) grass. a

5. Secondary succession occurs in an area where the community has been destroyed and the soil has been (a) removed; (b) destroyed; (c) compressed; (d) preserved. d

6. Birds are common in island communities because they can (a) eat different foods; (b) fly; (c) swim and walk; (d) adapt to new conditions. b

7. If an ecosystem is disturbed, goes out of balance, and cannot return to a state of equilibrium, the species living there will (a) freeze; (b) find new resources; (c) move; (d) become extinct. d

8. The kind of biome that will develop in an area is determined by temperature and (a) pressure; (b) precipitation; (c) average wind speed; (d) types of animals present. b

9. A land biome that is not a grassland is the (a) savanna; (b) prairie; (c) tundra; (d) steppe. c

10. The land biome that covers the largest percentage of land is the (a) desert; (b) tundra; (c) steppe; (d) savanna. a

CHAPTER 6 REVIEW

TRUE/FALSE

Write true *if the statement is true. If the statement is false, change the underlined word or phrase to make it true.*

1. The population of the snowshoe hares in Figure 6.1 was usually <u>larger</u> than the population of lynxes. t
2. In a commensal relationship, one species is <u>harmed</u> while the other benefits. f, not harmed
3. Parasites are usually <u>larger</u> than their host organisms. f, smaller
4. A lichen is one organism usually found in a <u>climax</u> community. f, pioneer
5. <u>Secondary succession</u> often happens after human disturbance. t
6. The finches on Indefatigable Island adapted to fit several different <u>niches</u>. t
7. <u>Grassland</u> biomes contain the largest percentage of Earth's biomass. f, forest
8. Desert and tundra biomes have different temperatures, but the amount of precipitation each receives is <u>nearly equal</u>. t

CONCEPT REVIEW Answers on page T46.

Write a complete response for each of the following.

1. How are predators different from parasites? What do these two groups have in common?
2. Use the example of the yucca plant and the yucca moth to describe the concept of mutualism.
3. Explain the process of primary succession. How does one community help establish the community that follows it?
4. How does the evolution of finch species on Indefatigable Island support the idea of competitive exclusion introduced in Chapter 5?
5. Deserts usually have mineral-rich soil and cover a large part of Earth's surface. Why do deserts support only 1 percent of Earth's biomass?

THINK CRITICALLY Answers on page T46.

1. Suppose an unusually severe winter killed most of the snowshoe hare population in an area of northern Canada. How would the lynx population be affected?
2. The yucca plant and the yucca moth cannot survive without each other. How could a relationship like this evolve? Assume that both organisms had ancestors that were not dependent on one another.
3. What might happen to the finches on Indefatigable Island if humans introduced seed-eating mice to the island?
4. Why are temperature and rainfall so important in determining which biome will develop in an area? What other factors might also be involved?

Computer Activity Write a computer program that performs the function of the graph in Figure 6.12. The program should ask for the average annual temperature and precipitation for an area and then output the predicted biome for that area based on these two pieces of information. Use the data in the graph in Figure 6.12 when writing your program.

WRITING CREATIVELY

Imagine you are a scientist studying a new volcanic island that has just formed far out at sea. Describe the process of primary succession on the island. Which organisms arrive first? Describe how each species travels to the new island. How do species evolve once they settle on the island?

PORTFOLIO

Make a videotape, a photographic diary, or a series of sketches showing the plants and other organisms around your school and home. Write a short essay discussing how these organisms fit into the biome in which you live.

....

GRAPHIC ANALYSIS Answers on page T46

Use Figure 6.12 to answer the following.
1. Which biome covers most of Florida?
2. Which continent has most of the world's rain forests?
3. Where are most deserts located?
4. Where are most coniferous forests located?

ACTIVITY 6.2

Answers and teaching strategies on page T46.

PROBLEM

If a grass and clover lawn is not cut, which plant is likely to dominate?

MATERIALS

- 3 paper cups
- enough soil to fill the cups
- grass seeds
- clover seeds
- metric ruler
- 3 sheets of paper
- water
- graduated cylinder

PREDICTION

After reading the entire activity, write a prediction that relates to the problem.

PROCEDURE

1. Label the paper cups *A*, *B*, and *C*. Fill each cup a few centimeters from the top with soil.
2. Sprinkle some grass seeds on the soil in Cup *A*. Sprinkle clover seeds on the soil in Cup *B*. Sprinkle both grass and clover seeds on the soil in Cup *C*.
3. Place the cups in a well-lit area. Water the cups each day. Pour the same amount of water in each cup, and do not overwater.

4. Allow the plants to grow until one type of plant in Cup *C* crowds out and clearly dominates the other. *Note: This step will probably take 2–3 weeks.*
5. Label three separate sheets of paper *A*, *B*, and *C*. Pull four grass plants from Cup *A*, four clover plants from Cup *B*, and two grass and two clover plants from Cup *C*. Place the uprooted plants on the appropriate sheet of paper. Pull the plants gently from the soil by the base so that the roots do not break off.
6. Measure the number and length of the root on each plant that was pulled. Also measure the color and number of leaves on each plant. Record the measurements in a data table.

ANALYSIS

1. How did the measurements of the grass plants grown alone compare to those of the grass plants that were grown with clover?
2. How did the measurements of the clover plants grown alone compare to those of the clover plants that were grown with grass?

CONCLUSION

1. How did the grass and clover plants compete? What was the outcome of their competition?

WILDLIFE MANAGEMENT

Today, people who choose a career in wildlife management examine the populations, behaviors, mortality factors, ecology, and habits of animals in nature. A wildlife biologist may determine the economic value of wildlife and the positive and negative effects of humans on species' habitats. Some wildlife biologists use research results to develop habitat protection programs and curb local animal diseases. A person with a position in wildlife management can also administer all of these programs and have little contact with the animal populations themselves. At times, wildlife managers are also public relations experts, explaining their department's or company's position on certain environmental issues that affect the local community.

A career in wildlife management may seem like a contemporary job choice. But a rough form of wildlife management was practiced by early Native Americans when they burned tracts of land to support grazing animals. Officially, wildlife management dates back to the early 1900s when the National Wildlife Refuge System was created in an effort to save waterfowl on Pelican Island in Florida. Before government intervention, people killed great numbers of pelicans to recover their feathers, which were used in the fashion industry. The island became a protected area, and the waterfowl were saved from extinction.

Although careers in wildlife management can require diverse backgrounds, some jobs are very specialized. A person who is a wildlife biologist for a logging company may spend an entire career studying how the local owl population is affected by a company's logging practices. A professor who teaches wildlife biology may spend much of his or her career doing research and applying findings to local animal populations.

To break into the public sector (70 percent), private sector (15 percent), nonprofit sector (7 percent), or education sector (8 percent), you will benefit most from a diverse background in science that emphasizes the study of ecosystems. You will also need strong computer, communications, and administration skills.

Most careers in wildlife management require both a bachelor's and an advanced degree. However there are also some positions available for technicians who have a two-year associate's degree. Though these careers are not highly paid, they are considered prime jobs in wildlife management because a person can venture out into the fields or backwoods and get real hands-on experience.

Breaking into the field of wildlife management can be difficult, but volunteering for local agencies while you are still in school can open doors. Also, taking a position with a federal, state, or local government in a related area, with the long-range goal of transferring to a particular division, can also work as a successful career path.

PUBLIC SECTOR ▶

Most wildlife managers are employed by the federal government, typically in the Department of Agriculture's Forest Service or in the Department of the Interior's Fish and Wildlife Service. However, state and local governments generally provide the most challenging opportunities, including the implementation of endangered species recovery programs.

There is also great interest in local governments because of increased concern in maintaining urban ecological environments, particularly wetlands areas.

▲ NONPROFIT SECTOR

Although nonprofit positions make up a relatively small number of wildlife management posts, the positions are important. The most notable non-profit agencies include the National Audubon Society, the Sierra Club, Greenpeace, and the National Wildlife Federation. In addition, many opportunities exist in the large number of local nonprofit groups around the nation.

▼ EDUCATION SECTOR

Teaching wildlife management can be a very satis-fying career choice that fulfills several functions: educating students about current environmental methods and procedures, carrying out valuable field studies and research, and increasing public awareness about local and global ecological issues.

▲ PRIVATE SECTOR

There are high-paying positions in the private sector, usually as special-interest environment-alists for logging companies, land developers, and public utilities. These jobs tend to be one-of-a-kind and require a grasp of a variety of skills beyond traditional biology. Scientists trained in ecology also work as consultants for private firms.

FOR MORE INFORMATION:

National Wildlife Federation
(Regular publications include
the annual *Conservation Directory*
and the bimonthly *National
Wildlife Magazine*)
1400 16th Street NW
Washington, DC 20036
(202) 797-6800

U.S. Fish and Wildlife Service
U.S. Department of the Interior
Washington, DC 20240
(202) 208-5634

The Wildlife Society
(Publications include *Journal of
Wildlife Management*, Wildlife
Society Bulletin, and *Wildlifer*)
5410 Grosvenor Lane, Suite 200
Bethesda, MD 20814
(301) 897-9770

UNIT 3

BIOMES

This symbol means *snake*. It is the name of a month in an early Mayan calendar. The Maya formed a great civilization in Central America over 1000 years ago. They built cities in the rain forest, the most diverse biome on Earth. The snake and other rainforest organisms are an important part of Mayan culture. People live in almost all of the biomes on Earth. The characteristics of each biome greatly influence the lives of its inhabitants.

Today the ruins of this Mayan city and many others like it are scattered throughout the jungles of Central America. The culture of the Maya reflects the characteristics of the rainforest biome in which it arose.

108

7

DESERT AND TUNDRA BIOMES

For many months, the only apparent motion across the barren landscape is caused by dry winds and lone, scurrying insects. Colors are practically nonexistent, and the land looks lifeless. Suddenly, in just a few days' time, the land explodes into a bright field of wildflowers. Then, almost as suddenly as it began, the season is over, and the long period of waiting begins again.

This scene is played out year after year in two of the harshest land biomes. In the desert, the brief appearance of color and activity occurs after rare downpours of heavy rain. In the icy tundra, the abundant display of life occurs during the short, cool summers of 24-hour days.

7.1 DESERTS

Objectives • *Describe* the characteristics of a desert. • *Explain* how desert organisms are adapted to live in their environment.

What do you think of when you hear the word *desert*? You may imagine a scene with camels trekking across hot, barren sands. Perhaps you think of a scene with tall, spiny cacti and balls of tumbleweed rolling by. From just these two scenes, you can see that not all deserts are alike. Deserts in different parts of the world have different characteristics and are home to different organisms. All deserts have one thing in common, however. They all receive very little rain during the course of a year.

Desert soils tend to be rich in minerals but poor in organic material. *Rainwater moving through soil carries minerals deeper into the soil in a process called* **leaching**. Because deserts do not receive much rainfall, there is very little leaching of the soil. As a result, the upper layers of desert soil are rich in minerals. The dryness of a desert prevents many plants from living there. The lack of rainfall also slows the decay of organic material. Because decayed organic matter is an important part of topsoil, deserts do not have much topsoil.

Loose, dry desert soil is easily blown away by wind. *As the loose soil is removed, a lower layer of soil called* **pavement** *becomes exposed.* The pavement is the desert floor. The desert floor is made mostly of hard-baked sand, bare rock particles, or both.

In the United States, deserts can be divided into two main types: cool deserts and hot deserts. Cool deserts are located on the eastern side of the western mountains, such as the Sierra Nevada and the Rocky Mountains. Hot deserts are located in the southwest, particularly Arizona, New Mexico, and western Texas. The hot deserts also extend into Mexico.

SOCIAL STUDIES LINK

Irrigation of desert soils has enabled some nations to turn deserts into croplands. In the Middle East, for example, irrigation projects have turned the Golan Heights into citrus orchards. Such projects require careful planning and management to avoid draining water resources and accumulating salts in the soil.

Figure 7.1 The cool deserts of North America are dominated by sagebrush (left). Cacti are a dominant plant of North American hot deserts.

Desert Climate

Deserts rarely get more than 25 cm of precipitation in any single year. The lack of precipitation in a desert determines the kinds of plants that can live in the region. Because plants are at the base of the food web, the types of plants determine the types of animals in the area as well. The lack of precipitation, therefore, is the limiting factor of the desert biome.

How much precipitation does a desert get? Although the exact amount varies from place to place and from year to year, most deserts receive less than 10 cm of rain each year. Most of the rain in the desert falls during a few short thunderstorms, followed by long dry periods. Because the desert pavement tends to be dry and compacted, the rain that falls on the desert usually runs off rather than being absorbed into the ground.

Temperatures vary greatly in the desert. Moisture in the atmosphere has a stabilizing effect on the temperature in a region. Moisture acts as a blanket over the ground, absorbing heat during the day and holding in the warmth at night. Because desert air contains very little moisture, temperatures can rise and fall dramatically during a 24-hour period.

Desert Organisms

Organisms that live in the desert are adapted to survive two challenges: lack of water and extreme temperatures. Some of the adaptations that enable organisms to live in the desert involve physical structures. Other adaptations involve behaviors. Although the challenge of living in the desert may seem great, deserts are actually species-rich, complex ecosystems.

Desert Plants Plants that live in the desert must be able to absorb scarce water from the ground. They must also prevent the

Figure 7.2 Although not related to the cactus, the aloe plant (left) has similar adaptations to the desert. The mesquite tree (right) has very deep roots that draw water from underground sources.

loss of water from their tissues. The spines of a cactus are a familiar adaptation for preventing water loss. Cactus spines are actually the leaves of the plant. The spines reduce the loss of water by reducing the surface area from which water can escape.

Cacti are also able to store water in their tissues. *Plants such as cacti, which have thick, water-filled tissues, are called* **succulents** (SUK-yu-luhnts). The stored water in succulents enables the plants to survive long dry periods. Because cacti contain stored water, they are an attractive source of both food and water for desert animals. The spines of the cactus help protect the plant from being eaten by most animals.

Although cacti are native only to the American continents, deserts elsewhere also have succulents. Aloe vera is a succulent native to Africa. Cacti and aloe are not related, but both types of plants have similar adaptations of succulent tissues protected by spines.

Adaptations to the dryness of a desert can also be seen in the roots of desert plants. Some desert plants have very shallow roots that grow over a wide area. These roots maximize the amount of rain the plant can absorb during the infrequent rainstorms. Other desert plants, such as the mesquite tree in Figure 7.2, have roots that extend very deeply into the ground, drawing water from as deep as 20 m.

Desert Animals   The desert is home to many types of animals, including insects, reptiles, birds, and mammals. Most desert animals get the water they need from their foods. Like plants, desert animals face the challenge of reducing water loss.

All insects and reptiles have an outer coating that reduces water loss. The shells of insects and the scales of reptiles originally evolved when these animals first adapted to life on land instead of the sea. The protective coverings make insects and reptiles well equipped to survive the dryness of a desert.

Most desert animals also have adaptations that enable them to survive the heat. Rodents, including the kangaroo rat, are common desert mammals. Desert rodents spend their days in underground burrows where they are protected from the heat of the sun. They come out of their burrows to seek food at night. *Animals that are active at night and sleep during the day are called* **nocturnal** (nok-TERN-ul) *animals*. Many of the animals in the desert are nocturnal.

Figure 7.3 The long ears of the fennec help release heat from the mammal's body.

SECTION REVIEW

1. What is meant by the pavement of a desert?
2. Explain why desert soil tends to be rich in minerals but poor in organic material.
3. **Infer** Why are midday temperatures in the summer generally higher in deserts than in forests?

1. Pavement is the hard desert floor that remains after the soil is removed.
2. The lack of rain slows leaching but also slows the growth and decay of organic matter.
3. Forests have moister air, which helps absorb midday heat. Also, there is little shade in the desert.

7.2 FORMATION OF DESERTS

Objective • *Illustrate* the processes that cause deserts to form.

There are deserts on every continent of Earth except Antarctica. Most deserts lie within two broad belts known as desert belts on either side of the equator. The deserts of the northern belt are near the Tropic of Cancer (23°N), and the southern desert belt is near the Tropic of Capricorn (23°S).

Natural Desert Formation

Air over the equator receives the most direct radiation from the sun. This direct radiation raises temperatures and causes rapid evaporation of water from the surface. The high rate of evaporation causes the air over the equator to be very moist. This moisture returns to Earth in frequent rainstorms, causing the region near the equator to be very wet. The wet region between the Tropic of Cancer and the Tropic of Capricorn is commonly called the *tropics*. Once the moisture in the air has fallen as rain, the air becomes quite dry and flows toward Earth's poles. As it does, the air becomes cooler and heavier. Beyond the tropics, the dry, denser air sinks back to Earth's surface. These dry winds result in the formation of deserts.

The exact locations of deserts within the desert belts are determined, in part, by local geographic features, such as mountain ranges. The deserts of the United States are an example. In the United States, most winds move from west to east. As winds move

Figure 7.4 Deserts form as dry air sinks to the surface beyond the tropics. The rainshadow effect of mountain ranges also contributes to desert formation.

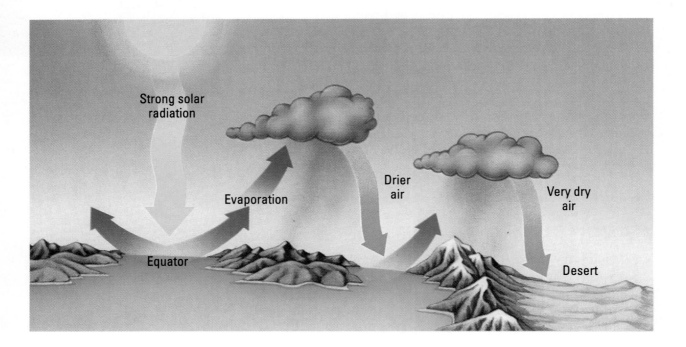

Figure 7.5 The Sahel region bordering the Sahara Desert was once a productive cropland. A natural drought and poor management have turned the area into a desert that can no longer support agriculture. Food must now be brought in from elsewhere.

across the western part of the country, they force warm, moist air up and over the Sierra Nevada. As the air rises above the mountains, it cools and drops most of its moisture as precipitation.

When cool, dry air reaches the eastern side of the mountains, it picks up moisture that may be in the soil. As a result, the soil becomes very dry and a desert begins to form. This process is called the *rainshadow effect*.

Desertification

Deserts are often bordered by regions that are dry, but not as dry as a desert. These areas, called *semiarid* (SEM-ee-AYR-ud) regions, support communities of grasses and shrubs. Human activities, especially raising livestock, have caused many semiarid regions to become deserts. *The process of changing semiarid land into desert as a result of human activity is called* **desertification** (dih-ZERT-uh-fuh-KAY-shun).

Desertification can begin when too many animals graze on too little land. The animals eat all the grasses and pound the soil with their hooves. Without plants, the topsoil erodes quickly. The bare land reflects more of the sun's heat. This process changes weather patterns and drives away rain clouds. Without rain or topsoil, the area becomes a desert. Desertification has occurred on every continent except Antarctica, and is especially severe in the United States, Africa, China, central Asia, western South America, and Australia. About 6 million hectares of land become desert each year. This is an area about the size of the state of Maine.

Teaching tips for Field Activity appear on page T51.

FIELD ACTIVITY

Temperature on Earth's surface depends on the angle of the sun's rays. Test this by making two solar collectors. Keep one held at a right angle to the sun, the other held at a wider angle. Construct the solar collectors by lining two shoeboxes with foil and taping a thermometer to the bottom of each one. Measure the rise in temperature in both boxes every 5 minutes for 30 minutes. Which one warmed up faster?

SECTION REVIEW

1. How do semiarid regions differ from deserts?
2. Explain the role of mountains in the formation of deserts.
3. **Deduce** Why do you think a farmer would try to raise more livestock than the land can support, considering the end result?

1. They receive more rain and support more plants.
2. They cause air masses to rise and cool, dropping rain. The dry air picks up moisture, forming a desert on the leeward side.
3. Short-term needs can override long-term consequences. Also, farmers may not understand the process.

7.3 TUNDRA

Objectives • *Describe* why the characteristics of the tundra make it a fragile ecosystem. • *Compare* the characteristics of tundra organisms with those of their relatives in warmer climates.

DATELINE 1974

After several years of planning, construction began on the Alaska oil pipeline, which transports oil 1285 km south from the North Slope of Alaska. The pipeline was completed three years later. Because oil must be kept warm in order to flow, the pipeline was constructed above the ground to protect the permafrost from melting. To avoid interfering with the migration of caribou and other animals, the pipeline includes 400 raised sections for animal crossings.

Use a globe to explain why the tilt of the Earth causes land north of the Arctic Circle to have continuous daylight during summer and continuous darkness during winter.

The tundra is a cold, windy, dry region. The tundra is located in the Northern Hemisphere just south of the polar ice caps in Alaska, Canada, Greenland, Iceland, Norway, and Asia. In the Southern Hemisphere, the region that would be the tundra is covered by oceans.

The tundra is one of the largest biomes, making up almost 10 percent of Earth's surface. However, fewer types of organisms live in the tundra than in any other biome. The lack of biodiversity makes tundra ecosystems very fragile and unstable.

Tundra Climate

Like the desert, the tundra receives little precipitation. In fact, the tundra receives less than 25 cm of precipitation each year. The main difference between deserts and tundra is temperature. In the tundra, air temperature rarely reaches above 10°C, even in summer. Because temperatures in the tundra are below freezing almost all year, most precipitation falls as ice and snow. Temperature, therefore, is the limiting factor in the tundra.

Summer days are long and cool in the tundra. Because of the low temperatures, only the top layer, or active zone, of soil thaws during the summer months. The active zone may be as thin as 8 cm in some areas. Beneath the active zone, the soil never thaws. *The frozen soil below the active zone is called* **permafrost**. A dense mat of mosses, grasses, and other plant life covers the active zone during summer. This mat keeps the ground insulated and prevents the permafrost from melting. Therefore, any disruption of the plants in the active zone can affect the permafrost.

Because of the short growing season and low temperatures, tundra vegetation does not recover from disruption as quickly as does vegetation in other biomes. Tracks from wagons that crossed the tundra 100 years ago are still visible in some areas.

The tundra receives a small amount of rainfall in summer. Rain that falls during the summer months cannot drain through the permafrost. Instead, the water collects at the surface, forming bogs, marshes, ponds, and small streams. These areas serve as the breeding grounds for insects such as mosquitoes and black flies. These insects are an important link in the food web of the tundra. The permafrost is therefore an important factor in the stability of a tundra ecosystem.

Figure 7.6 Summers in the tundra are short and cool. The brief growing period supports a year-round community, as well as a seasonal community of migrating animals, such as the caribou (inset).

Tundra Organisms

In spite of the cold climate and the lack of rainfall, some plants do grow in the tundra. The summer growing season lasts only about 60 days. The most common tundra plants are mosses, shrubs, grasses, and miniature treelike shrubs.

Tundra Plants   The ground is warmed by radiant energy from the sun. Tundra plants tend to be small and grow close to the ground to get this warmth. The roots of tundra plants grow very close to the ground's surface because they cannot penetrate the permafrost. Trees that grow in the tundra such as willow and birch are much smaller than their relatives in warmer climates. In fact, tundra trees are usually less than 1m tall and are more like shrubs than trees. These plants are dwarfed by the short growing season and by the limited space for roots to grow.

Tundra Animals   Many of the animals that live in the tundra are seasonal visitors. *Long-distance seasonal travel is called* **migration**. Several species of birds, for example, migrate to the tundra during their breeding season. There are fewer predators in the tundra, which makes it a safer place than most to raise young. There are also fewer competitors for food in the tundra. Migratory birds of the tundra feed mostly on the abundant flies and mosquitoes that breed in the bogs and ponds during summer. The birds, in turn, serve as a food source for migratory predators such as the Arctic wolf.

The caribou, a close relative of the reindeer, is a large migratory mammal of the tundra. The adaptations that enable caribou to live in their environment are common among tundra mammals. Like

Word Power
Migrate, from the Latin *migrare*, "to move or change", from the Indo-European *meigw-*, "to change location."

Figure 7.7 The Arctic hare (left) is adapted to live in the tundra. The jackrabbit (right) is a desert dweller. What differences can you see in the adaptations of these two animals to their environments?

The Arctic hare has shorter ears, shorter limbs, and a more compact body. Students may also notice that the coat colors match their environment.

many mammals of the tundra, caribou have a thick coat. The hairs of their coat are filled with air. The air acts as insulation, reducing the loss of body heat. Caribou also have wide hooves to help them move easily through snow or on the muddy ground in warmer months.

Huge herds of thousands of caribou thunder across the tundra every year in search of food. The caribou feed on lichens that grow on rocky surfaces. As you learned in Chapter 6, *lichens* are plantlike organisms that are made up of a fungus and an alga. Lichens grow very slowly and are very sensitive to air pollution. In recent years, the sizes of the caribou herds have dropped quite a bit. This decline may be due, in part, to the loss of lichens as a result of pollution. Caribou and other migratory animals are also threatened by structures that interfere with their migratory routes. The instinctive behaviors that enable these animals to follow the correct path year after year tend to be very inflexible.

Some of the mammals in the tundra are year-round residents. The Arctic fox hunts migratory birds during summer and stores them to eat during the long winter. Musk oxen, polar bears, and wolverines are other permanent members of the tundra community.

SECTION REVIEW

1. Lichens are plantlike organisms made of a fungus and an alga; they are producers in the tundra.
2. They lack the biodiversity that makes other ecosystems more stable.
3. Water would drain from the bogs, insects would have no place to breed, birds would have no insects to eat, and so on.

1. What are lichens? What is their ecological role in the tundra?
2. **Infer** Many mammals of the tundra have brown coats during part of the year and white coats the rest of the year. Why is this change of color an adaptation to the environment?
3. **Analyze** You have read that permafrost is an important abiotic factor in the tundra. Describe how the melting of permafrost could affect the tundra food web.

Oil in the Tundra

Will oil exploration affect the tundra biome?

1. The tundra is often thought of as wasteland, less valuable than other areas. It's not in anyone's backyard.
2. Accept all well-defined answers.

In 1968, oil geologists found what they were searching for—a large oil deposit on the North Slope of Alaska. The deposit contained 10 to 20 billion barrels of oil, making the Alaskan oil deposit the biggest oil field in the United States. A problem arose in transporting the oil from north of the Arctic Circle to port cities farther south for shipment. The solution was to build a pipeline across the Alaskan wilderness.

In 1977, the pipeline was completed at a cost of $10 billion. The cost was shared by eight oil companies that formed the Alyeska Pipeline Service Company. The pipeline is routed from Prudhoe Bay in northern Alaska to the port of Valdez at Prince William Sound. At Valdez, the oil is loaded onto oil tankers.

Although it is the largest oil reserve in the United States, it is a small percentage of the oil consumed in the United States each year. If the pipeline were the sole source of oil for the United States, it would only be enough to last three years. At its current flow rate of about 2 million barrels per day, the Alaskan oil should last about 25 years.

The tundra supports a variety of organisms, such as musk oxen, caribou, Kodiak bears, and migrating birds. Vegetation in the tundra is limited. If the scarce vegetation is destroyed, it takes decades to grow back. Due to the moderate tundra resources, the food web is very simple. A minor disruption in the food web could severely impact Arctic life. The pipeline route could block the annual migration of caribou herds. This disturbance could lead to overgrazing that might demolish the food supply of many tundra animals.

To minimize the amount of damage to the topsoil, trucks carrying heavy equipment across the tundra were equipped with rolligons instead of regular tires. Rolligons are wide tires with no tread. An impact that was not consid-

ered was that the roads built during the pipeline construction, improved tundra access for hunters and tourists.

Before construction of the pipeline, it was argued that the pipe might leak. The leaking hot oil might melt the permafrost. Efforts were made to design a pipeline that could withstand the extreme temperature variations of the tundra, which can drop as low as −50°C (−58°F) in winter and climb to 35°C (95°F) in summer. However, within the first three years after construction, the pipeline cracked twice. One rupture released over 5,000 barrels of crude oil onto the tundra and into local rivers.

DECISIONS

1. Why do you think anyone looked for oil in the Alaskan tundra?
2. Do you think the pipeline should have been built? Why?

Climatograms

PROBLEM

How are climatograms constructed and interpreted?

MATERIALS

- graph paper
- pencil

PREDICTION

Write a prediction about the advantage of using climatograms instead of tables to analyze data.

PROCEDURE

1. Climatograms are graphs that summarize the measurements of temperature and precipitation in an area. Study the climatogram for a deciduous forest.
2. Climatic data for four cities are given in the table. Using graph paper, construct a climatogram for each city.

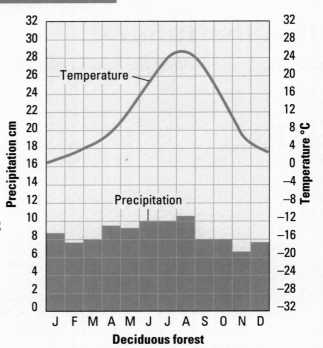
Deciduous forest

3. How are the climates of the two desert cities different?
4. How are the climates of the two tundra cities different?

ANALYSIS

1. Which cities are located in desert biomes? How can you tell?
2. Which cities are located in tundra biomes? How can you tell?

CONCLUSION

What are the advantages of constructing climatograms compared to studying the same data from tables?

Climates of Four Cities

City 1	J	F	M	A	M	J	J	A	S	O	N	D
T (°C)	-26	-28	-26	-20	-8	0	4	3	-2	-10	-18	-24
P (cm)	0.5	0.5	0.5	0.5	0.5	1	2	2	1.5	1	0.5	0.5
City 2	J	F	M	A	M	J	J	A	S	O	N	D
T (°C)	-1	2	6	8	12	16	20	14	14	10	4	0
P (cm)	3	3	2	1	1	1	0.5	0.5	0.5	1	1	2
City 3	J	F	M	A	M	J	J	A	S	O	N	D
T (°C)	24	25	26	28	31	32	31	30	31	29	27	25
P (cm)	1	0.5	1	0.5	0.3	0.3	0	0.3	0.3	0.3	0.3	0.3
City 4	J	F	M	A	M	J	J	A	S	O	N	D
T (°C)	-23	-23	-21	-14	-4	2	5	5	1	-4	-10	-17
P (cm)	1	1	2	2	2	1	2	3	3	3	3	1

KEY TERMS

leaching 7.1

pavement 7.1

succulent 7.1

nocturnal 7.1

desertification 7.2

permafrost 7.3

migration 7.3

CHAPTER SUMMARY

7.1 All deserts receive very little annual rainfall. Desert soils are rich in minerals but lack organic materials and topsoil. Desert climates have a wide temperature variation, due to low atmospheric moisture. The desert ecosystem is rich with plants and animals that have adapted to the lack of water and severe temperatures.

7.2 Desert formation may occur naturally or as a result of human activity. Natural causes are global air movement driven by solar heating and geo-graphic features, such as mountains. Human activities, such as raising livestock, also produce deserts by the process of desertification.

7.3 Cold temperatures distinguish the tundra from deserts. Located in the Northern Hemisphere, the tundra is large in surface area but low in biodiversity. The tundra's permafrost layer is a key feature of the tundra. Few plants have adapted to the harsh climate, and many of the tundra's animal inhabitants are migratory.

MULTIPLE CHOICE

Choose the letter of the word or phrase that best completes each statement.

1. The common characteristic of all deserts is (a) hot temperatures; (b) low annual rainfall; (c) simple ecosystems; (d) mineral-poor soil. b

2. The rainshadow effect causes (a) desertification; (b) leaching; (c) natural desert formation; (d) increased precipitation. c

3. The main difference between deserts and the tundra is (a) amount of precipitation; (b) moisture content of the air; (c) limited topsoil; (d) temperature. d

4. Leaching (a) is common in desert climates; (b) increases the mineral content of the soil; (c) is unrelated to the amount of rainfall; (d) washes minerals from the topsoil. d

5. Desertification is caused by (a) human activity; (b) solar heating patterns; (c) leaching of the soil; (d) temperature variations. a

6. Adaptations to desert life do not include (a) long limbs and ears; (b) a waterproof covering; (c) a large, compact body; (d) an ability to store water. c

7. The spines of desert plants (a) provide protection; (b) increase surface area; (c) store water; (d) are unique to the cacti of the Western Hemisphere. a

8. The limiting factor in the tundra is (a) rainfall; (b) temperature; (c) sunlight; (d) soil nutrients. b

9. Migratory birds in the tundra feed mostly on (a) seeds; (b) small rodents; (c) lichens; (d) flies and mosquitoes. d

10. Tundra ecosystems are considered to be fragile because of (a) the low humidity; (b) low biodiversity; (c) low economic value; (d) low latitude. b

11. The Trans-Alaska Pipeline was built above ground to prevent (a) the migration of caribou and other animals; (b) damage to the fragile tundra topsoil; (c) melting of the permafrost; (d) tourists and other travelers from crossing. c

12. Compared to the desert fennec in Figure 7.3, you might expect the Arctic fox to have (a) longer legs; (b) shorter ears; (c) shorter fur; (d) larger eyes. b

CHAPTER 7 REVIEW

WORD COMPARISONS

Write the letter of the second word pair that best matches the first pair.

1. Desert: pavement as (a) tundra: cement; (b) pavement: city; (c) tundra: permafrost; (d) tundra: desert. c
2. Desert belt: tropics as (a) middle latitude: low latitude; (b) hot: cool; (c) wet: dry; (d) east: west. a
3. Precipitation: desert as (a) rain: tropics; (b) warmth: tundra; (c) desert: heat; (d) mountains: rain shadow. b
4. Cool deserts: sagebrush as (a) lichens: tundra; (b) hot deserts: dwarf trees; (c) tundra: migration; (d) hot deserts: cacti. d
5. Cactus: the Americas as (a) aloe: Africa; (b) Arctic hare: jackrabbit; (c) mesquite: dwarf birch; (d) tundra: willow. a

CONCEPT REVIEW Answers on page T51.

Write a complete response to each of the following.

1. Explain why desert soils tend to be rich in minerals but poor in topsoil.
2. How does the behavior of desert rodents aid their survival?
3. How are reptiles and insects adapted to life in the desert? Why do these animals have such adaptations?
4. Desert plants may have very deep root systems or very shallow root systems. Describe the advantage of each.
5. Describe the process of desertification.

THINK CRITICALLY Answers on page T51.

1. List three potential problems that could arise from drilling for oil in the tundra.
2. Deserts tend to be hotter during the day and cooler at night than other areas with similar latitude. Explain why this is true.
3. Describe two ways in which the permafrost layer affects tundra ecosystems. How might the ecosystems be affected if the permafrost were to melt?
4. Many scientists predict that the temperature of the Earth could rise as a result of the greenhouse effect. How might an increase in temperature affect the deserts and tundras of the world?

WRITE FOR UNDERSTANDING

Suppose a government leader in a small, semiarid nation is planning to convert unused land into farmland for cattle grazing. Write a letter to this person explaining the risks of such farming in semiarid regions, and long-term factors that must be considered.

PORTFOLIO

1. In 1991, the United States and other members of the United Nations participated in Operation Desert Storm in the deserts near the Persian Gulf. Conduct library research about the problems faced by soldiers fighting in the desert environment. Make a presentation of your findings to the class.
2. There are several communities of people who live in the tundra of Alaska and Canada. Locate a high school in a tundra region, and contact the school about establishing pen pals. From your pen pal, find out how living in the tundra affects the daily lives of teenagers in their community.

GRAPHIC ANALYSIS Answers on page T51.

Use the figure to answer the following.

1. According to the map, in which parts of North America is the risk of desertification highest?
2. Why is the risk of desertification lower in most of Canada and Mexico than in the United States?
3. Why do you think there are no deserts in the eastern United States, even though it is within the desert belt? Explain your answer.

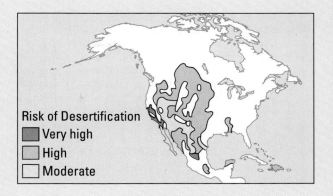

Risk of Desertification
- ▨ Very high
- ▨ High
- ▢ Moderate

ACTIVITY 7.2

Answers and teaching strategies on page T51.

PROBLEM
How can off-road vehicles affect a desert food web?

MATERIALS
- 4 sheets of white construction paper
- reference sources

PREDICTION
Predict how the use of off-road vehicles could affect the desert ecosystem.

PROCEDURE
1. The organisms shown in the table are producers, or primary or secondary consumers. They are part of a food web in a California desert. You probably know something about the niche of some of the organisms. Use reference sources to find out more about those that are unfamiliar to you.
2. On construction paper, draw a food web involving at least ten of the desert organisms.
3. The desert habitat of these organisms has become a popular site for driving off-road vehicles. Choose a species of (a) producer, (b) primary consumer, and (c) secondary consumer that you think would be directly affected by off-road vehicles. Draw three new food webs. In each new food web, show how the original food web would be different if one of the three populations you chose was destroyed.

Organisms of a Desert Ecosystem	
Kangaroo rat	Wildflower (seeds)
Sidewinder	Raven
Pocket mouse	Sagebrush
Kit fox	Desert bighorn sheep
Coyote	Roadrunner
Antelope jackrabbit	Insects
Mule deer	Flatland desert lizard
Bobcat	Desert tortoise

ANALYSIS
Describe how two different populations would be affected when (a) one population of producer was destroyed, (b) one population of primary consumer was destroyed, and (c) one population of secondary consumer was destroyed.

CONCLUSION
1. How can off-road vehicles affect the food web in a desert ecosystem?
2. What limits, if any, should be placed on off-road vehicles in desert ecosystems?

Have you ever stood on a lawn, looked at the short blades of grass, and thought, "It's just grass"? It is simple and green, and sometimes it turns brown and looks ugly. As simple as grass seems, this grass and grasses like it feed billions of organisms all over the world. The bread on your sandwich and the cereal in your breakfast bowl are made from grasses. All grains are grasses. Cattle and sheep eat grass. Prairie dogs and billions of insects eat grass. Grasses can survive temperatures as cold as −25°C and as hot as 70°C. Grass fires can burn hundreds of acres. Still, grasses survive and are the most widely distributed flowering plant in the world. Is this really "just grass"?

8.1 GRASSLANDS

Objectives • *Describe* the characteristics of grasslands.
• *Identify* where grasslands are located.

A **grassland** *is an ecosystem in which there is too much water to form a desert, but not enough water to support a forest.* Grasslands begin at the edges of the desert biome and stretch across the land to the forest biome. Grasslands exist in Africa, central Asia, South America, and Australia. Scientists think that at some time in Earth's history, grasslands covered nearly half the land. In the United States, grasslands stretch from the Rocky Mountains in the west to the forests in the east, and from Canada to Mexico.

Grassland Climate

The climate of grasslands is a little wetter than the climate of deserts. Recall from Chapter 7 that many deserts are located in the rain shadows of mountain ranges. In rain shadows, dry air blows across the land and drops very little or no rain. As the dry air blows, it absorbs the water that evaporates from the land and becomes moist again. Eventually, there is enough moisture for more rain to fall.

The **desert–grassland boundary** *is the area between deserts and grasslands where increased rainfall enables some grasses to grow.* Because rainfall is an abiotic factor affecting both deserts and grasslands, long-term changes in climate patterns can change the desert–grassland boundary. The grassland can become desert or the desert can become grassland. If the climate becomes too dry, the grasslands will no longer sustain the organisms that usually grow there.

Grassland Organisms

Although many kinds of organisms live in the grasslands, grasses are the most common. One reason grasses are common is that most of the mass of a grass plant is underground. For example, one rye plant, which may grow as high as 2 m, can spread up to 600 km of roots. With most of the mass protected underground, grasses are not as limited by factors such as rain and fires as trees or shrubs.

Rainfall is the most significant limiting factor in the grasslands, as shown in Figure 8.1. Without enough rain, forests cannot develop. However, many scientists have determined that natural grass fires, ignited by lightning, also play an important role in the development of grasslands.

Scientists think that if it were not for grass fires, forests might have overgrown many areas of the grassland long ago. Grass fires destroy trees and saplings where most of the mass

Figure 8.1 Abiotic factors such as rainfall and grass fires are important to the development of grasslands. Wildfires can be ignited by lightning. Prescribed burns are started by people to manage the growth of trees and other woody plants in valuable grassland areas.

Figure 8.2 The bison of the North American prairies once numbered in the millions. They helped maintain conditions ideal for grass growth by keeping all vegetation to heights beneficial for grasses but damaging to other plants.

is above the ground, but they leave grasses unharmed. Grass fires also burn away the layer of dead grass that accumulates during the year. Once the dead grasses have burned off, more water and air are able to reach the soil and the new growth of grasses.

Grass fires are useful in helping release valuable nutrients and minerals from the soil. Grasses may use these nutrients more efficiently after fires. The germination of many grass seeds is also aided by fires. Some grass seeds depend on the heat from fire and the moisture from water to dig into the soil.

Grasses are abundant in grassland areas because of biotic factors as well as abiotic factors. Grazing animals, such as the bison in Figure 8.2, and burrowing animals help maintain grasslands with their activities above and below the ground. Grazing animals act as natural lawn mowers, keeping the vegetation of grasslands close to the ground. When kept this low, tree saplings and shrubs become too damaged to grow well. With most of their growth below ground level, the grasses remain unharmed. Animals such as earthworms, prairie dogs, and insects, which aerate the soil by making tunnels and digging, also live below ground. When the soil is aerated, grasses can grow more successfully because nutrients and water can reach their roots more quickly.

The amount of rain a grassland area receives also affects the sizes and textures of the grasses, as shown in Figure 8.3. Grasses that grow in the drier areas of grasslands are low to the ground and have thin, fine leaves. In the wetter regions of the grasslands, grasses such as bamboo may grow as high as 3 m and have thick, coarse leaves.

The trees and shrubs in grasslands often grow near ponds, lakes, streams, and springs. Some trees and shrubs are *drought-resistant*. This adaptation helps these trees and shrubs survive in the dry grasslands, despite small amounts of rain.

Figure 8.3 Sizes and textures of grasses are related to the amount of rain. The drier the climate, the shorter and finer the grasses. The coarse texture of grasses in wetter climates helps the grasses to lose water, and prevents them from rotting in the warm and wet rainy season.

The biotic and abiotic factors in an ecosystem determine particular characteristics for specific areas of the grasslands. For example, trees and shrubs may not grow around a grassland pond because of a large population of grazing animals. Also, wide areas may have no grass growth because of shallow soil. If rain were the only source of water for the grasslands, there would be an obvious absence of trees and shrubs. However, because many of the grassland areas of the world are cultivated, irrigation becomes an important source of water. The water for irrigation may be pumped from aquifers below the ground, or it may be diverted from nearby streams. Sometimes, the water source may be several kilometers away.

Although the *amount* of rain is important to grassland ecosystems, *when* it rains is also important. Some grasslands experience cycles of heavy rain followed by long periods of little or no rain, called *rainy seasons* and *drought seasons*. The rainy season and drought season determine, in part, the kinds of organisms that live in the grasslands. In grasslands where months may go by without rain, many plants and trees have adapted and become drought-resistant.

Grasslands around the world vary by climate and types of organisms. Although scientists do not always agree about how to classify grasslands, one method is to divide the grasslands into three different biomes. These three biomes, shown in Figure 8.4, are called the *steppe*, *prairie*, and *savanna*.

Figures 8.4 The steppes (left), are located at the edges of deserts. Tall-grass prairie gayfeathers (center) grow in the wetter eastern region of the U.S. prairie. The animals of Africa's savanna (right) are very diverse.

Teaching tips for Field Activity appear on page T55.

1. Grasslands are located between deserts and forests. Grasslands begin where a desert climate becomes wetter and end where there is sufficient water to support tree growth.
2. Rainfall, fires, and seasonal climate are abiotic factors. Biotic factors include grazing and burrowing animals.
3. Shorter, fine-bladed grasses have less surface area from which to lose moisture, and are adapted to drier climates. Broadleaf grasses with deeper roots are adapted to wetter climates.

SECTION REVIEW

1. Where are grasslands located in relation to deserts and forests?
2. **Identify** some biotic and abiotic factors affecting the growth of grasslands.
3. **Think Critically** Suggest reasons for the relationship between grass size and texture and climate.

Natural Chaos

Can chaos theory explain patterns in nature?

Suppose you were conducting an experiment on grass and fertilizers. You plant plots of grass seeds and fertilize each plot with different amounts of nitrogen. After 2 years, your data show that the grass given the highest amount of nitrogen has the greatest amount of mass above the ground. What would you predict would happen during the third year? You would probably predict that the plants with high nitrogen had reached a balanced state and that they would continue to produce the greatest amount of aboveground mass. But what if the population of the high-nitrogen plants fell to almost zero during the third year? Would you think your experiment was a failure?

This is exactly what happened during an experiment by two ecologists at the University of Minnesota. But instead of throwing out the experiment as a failure, the results were interpreted as a result of chaotic dynamics. Chaotic dynamics is described by chaos theory, which states that in a dynamic system randomness can result when increasing energy forces the system to a certain point.

In the grass-growth experiment, the energy force was nitrogen. The plots of grass with lower levels of nitrogen produced about the same amount of

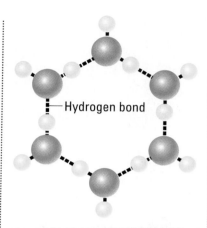

Hydrogen bond

aboveground plant matter each year. However, the plots with great amounts of nitrogen were pushed to the point of chaos.

Chaos depends on the initial conditions of a system. Tiny differences in the initial conditions of a system can magnify into giant differences later on. For the plants in nitrogen-rich soil, the tiny difference that was magnified was the small increase in growth rate. The great amount of plant matter left a heavy layer of litter on the ground when the plants died in winter. The litter layer prevented sunlight from reaching the next shoots during the following spring, causing the population crash.

Chaos is evident in many natural systems. The formation of snowflakes illustrates chaos. If you were to examine several snowflakes, you would observe that their patterns never repeat. Though water molecules are held in a characteristic hexagonal arrangement when water becomes ice, the patterns of the snowflakes always differ.

Chaos theory is causing many ecologists to look at nature in a new way. The idea of balance in an ecosystem has changed to reflect the fact that ecosystems are dynamic, not frozen in one state. Within natural systems, there will always be randomness that has unpredictable results.

Chaotic systems may look as though they are random, but there is actually an underlying, long-term order. The goal of scientists who study these systems is to research what controls natural patterns. The variables that upset nature's balance fit this pattern.

DECISIONS

1. How does chaos theory explain the results of the grass-growth experiment?
2. Discuss how chaos theory explains one of the following: weather, flowing water, development of an embryo.

8.2 STEPPES AND PRAIRIES

Objectives • *Compare* and contrast a steppe and a prairie.
• *Describe* the importance of steppes and prairies in agriculture.

Steppes are similar to deserts in many ways. **Steppes** *are grasslands of short bunchgrasses that get less than 50 cm of rain a year.* Rainfall is very low and plant life is sparse. Because of such similarities, some scientists consider steppes to be deserts rather than grasslands. In the United States, steppes are located at the western and south-western edges of the grasslands. Large areas of steppes exist within the wetter areas of the deserts of the Southwest and the Great Basin. Steppes are also located within drier areas of the prairies.

Prairies make up most of the grasslands in the United States. **Prairies** *are grasslands characterized by rolling hills, plains, and sod-form-ing grasses.* In the United States, the prairies are often called the Great Plains. The Russian steppes in central Eurasia and the veldt in South Africa are local names for prairies in those locations. The prairies in Argentina are known as the pampas. Whatever name they are given, the prairies of the world are large, fertile areas where the human population gets most of its food. Because breads and cereals come from grains grown on the prairies, the prairies are sometimes called "breadbaskets."

Steppe and Prairie Climates

To distinguish between steppe and desert, scientists define a desert as a region that gets less than 25 cm of rain a year. Most of the rain on the steppes evaporates very quickly or reaches only the upper 25 cm of soil. High winds and high temperatures across the steppes are responsible for rapid evaporation. Throughout the year, tem-peratures on the steppes can fall to –5°C or rise as high as 30°C.

The amount of rain in the prairies is about 50 to 75 cm a year. Occasionally, however, prairies get up to twice that much rain in a year, as in the U.S. Midwest during 1993. The rain often comes in thunderstorms during the rainy seasons.

Steppe and Prairie Organisms

Soil in the prairie can hold water very well. The absorbent soil structure is influenced by the organisms that live in the prairie. Most of the grasses of the prairie have roots that form a mat in the soil. The mat of soil and roots is called *sod*. *Grasses that form a mat of soil and roots are called* **sod-forming grasses**. Lawns are an exam-ple of sod-forming grasses. The roots of the sod-forming grasses hold the soil together. When the soil is held together, it does not dry out very quickly, and it does not blow away in strong winds. *As*

Word Power
Prairie, from the Latin *pratum*, "meadow."

Figure 8.5 Vast fields of wheat and other cereal grains now grow in large areas of the world's grasslands. The native grasses that once thrived have been replaced because of the human need for food and space.

Figure 8.6 The dandelion, which is native to Europe, disperses its seeds with the aid of wind. Many grassland plants use this seed dispersal method to take advantage of strong winds.

the roots of the grasses die, they form a layer of organic matter called **humus** (HYOO-mus). The humus helps hold water and provides nutrients and food for grasses and other organisms to grow.

Steppes are sometimes referred to as short-grass prairies. The grasses of the steppes are mostly bunchgrasses. **Bunchgrasses** *are short, fine-bladed grasses that grow in a clump.* Clumping helps save water by holding the water in a small root area, under the shade of the grass. The short, fine blades of the bunchgrasses prevent them from losing moisture in the dry climate. The roots of the steppe grasses may grow only as deep as 50 cm. At that shallow depth, the roots can absorb as much of the scarce rainwater as possible before it evaporates.

Animals of the steppes and prairies have adapted to the changing conditions of these grasslands by migrating, hibernating, or burrowing underground. The grasses and small shrubs have also adapted by using the energy of the wind, as shown in Figure 8.6. The wind carries their seeds and pollen over wide areas of land. With the aid of the wind, grasses can cover large areas rapidly. However, when one area of the prairie or steppe gets very dry or cold, the grasses cannot grow very well.

In colder areas, many of the animals that graze on the grass hibernate to save energy. Others migrate to other areas in search of more food and warmer temperatures. During hot periods, many small animals, like the prairie dogs in Figure 8.7, remain in their burrows to keep from overheating. A cluster of prairie dog burrows, known as towns, can be as large as several hundred square kilometers. Except during winter, the cooler nights are ideal times for burrowing animals to come aboveground to eat. Many of these animals eat at night or in the early or late parts of the day.

The steppe and prairie grasses are only lightly damaged by the feeding habits of migrating grazers because these animals move from place to place. But poor farming and ranching practices can cause extensive damage to the grasses of the steppes and prairies.

Figure 8.7 Prairie dogs aerate the soil of the prairies with their underground network of tunnels, called towns. Around the turn of the century, a prairie dog town was discovered in Texas that covered an area of 64 000 km². An estimated 400 million prairie dogs were thought to live there.

Figure 8.8 As a result of overgrazing, poor farming practices, and a series of terrible droughts, one of the worst environmental disasters in U.S. history occurred. From 1934 to 1938, strong winds stripped the unprotected soil from parts of Oklahoma, Texas, New Mexico, Kansas, and Colorado, an area known as the "Dust Bowl."

One harmful practice is concentrating the feeding of sheep and cattle in small areas. When grazing animals eat too much in one place, they destroy most of the grass in a process called overgrazing. Some farmers and ranchers replace native grasses with grasses that are poorly adapted to the area. The grasses may not survive, making it harder for the land to support as many animals as it did before. The grass roots that hold the soil together die, and the loose soil is blown away. You may recognize this as the first step toward desertification. Since the time of the "Dust Bowl" (see Figure 8.8), American farmers have developed many grazing and growing techniques that help to assure a reduced impact on these ecosystems.

Many nations are replacing the generalized species of the grasslands with species specialized for agriculture. The different grasses and animals have been replaced by huge herds of grazing cattle and sheep. Wide fields of grains such as wheat and corn have also been planted. Armadillos, bison, deer, wolves, and bears were all once very common in the grasslands of the United States, but they have been partially replaced because of human demand for space and food. Without a better understanding of steppe and prairie ecosystems, agriculture can damage these delicate and essential areas.

THINK CRITICALLY

Although agriculture in the grasslands of the world feeds millions of people, millions die annually from starvation. Do you think that more land should be developed into agricultural land? Discuss some reasons for existing problems and predict problems the world might face in the future.

Answers will vary. However, the discussion should include desertification due to low rainfall and overgrazing. Distribution of food may also be discussed, though not covered at this point. Future problems might include lack of water, lack of soil, lack of space, and population increase.

SECTION REVIEW

1. Why are prairies called the breadbaskets of the world?
2. How does the activity of burrowing animals benefit the prairie?
3. **Apply** Name some ways in which steppes and prairies are damaged and desertification develops.

1. The prairies are called breadbaskets because they are the principal farmland for wheat and other grains.
2. Burrowing animals benefit the soil by loosening and aerating it. They also add fertilizer in the form of droppings.
3. Overgrazing and planting of poorly adapted plants weaken soil structure. Because the soil can no longer support vegetation, it is easily eroded by wind and water.

8.3 SAVANNAS

Objectives • *Define savannas, and state where they are located.*
• *Explain how savannas can support a wide range of organisms*

The **savannas** *are tropical grasslands ranging from dry scrubland to wet, open woodland.* Savannas occur in Asia, from India to Southeast Asia; and in Africa, from the Sahara and Kalahari deserts to the southern tip of Africa. The *llanos* of Venezuela and the *campos* of Brazil are regions of savanna in South America.

Savanna Climate

Rainy seasons and long periods of drought are typical of savannas. The amount of rain in a savanna can be as high as 150 cm a year, but most of it falls heavily during thunderstorms in the short rainy season. In Africa, the rainy season usually lasts from January to April. During the rest of the year, the savanna may be very dry. The extreme climate demands a wide range of adaptations in the organisms of the savanna.

Savanna Organisms

In order to survive, the grasses, shrubs, and trees of the savanna must be resistant to drought, fires, and grazing animals. Many plants of the savanna grow runners. **Runners** *are long horizontal stems above or below the ground.* Runners are used by some plants to reproduce; they spread quickly and can extend for several meters. When a fire occurs, the runners are protected underground.

Savanna grasses grow in tufts. **Tufts** *are large clumps of tall, coarse grasses.* The savanna trees and shrubs have thorns or sharp leaves to keep them from being eaten by grazing animals, such as gazelles. Another adaptation of savanna plants is the ability to grow rapidly. This adaptation enables the plants to recover quickly from the damage caused by fire and animals. Growing quickly also gives the plants a better chance to use the water of the rainy season.

Figures 8.9 Runners (right) keep a vital link in the food chain alive despite extreme conditions of drought, heat, and fire. Pampas grasses (left) are an example of tufts. Tufts are very durable and resistant to the grazing of large herbivores.

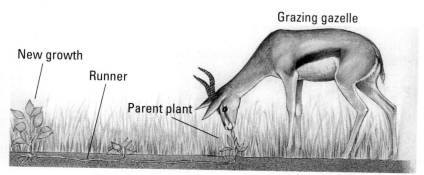

New growth

Runner

Parent plant

Grazing gazelle

Figure 8.10 Vertical feeding patterns minimize the competition for food among the herbivores of the savanna. Vertical feeding patterns occur among the open woodland and the grasses of the open plain. The dik-dik (foreground, far left) eats grasses and leaves from small shrubs. The wart hog (drinking from stream) eats roots, grasses, and leaves from small shrubs. Rhinoceroses eat grasses and small shrubs. However, they also eat leaves from large shrubs and the lower branches of small trees. The elephant and giraffe are capable of reaching high into tall trees where they obtain the leaves and small branches for their diets. Elephants also uproot tough grasses and trees, which they may completely strip of bark and branches, for food.

Animals must take advantage of the short rainy season. Many of the insects, rodents, and larger animals, such as giraffes and antelopes, reproduce during the rainy season when food is more abundant. As in the prairie, many of the larger animals migrate to areas of the savanna where rain has fallen. Elephants, for example, may travel 80 km or more to find water.

The concentration of animal populations in smaller areas around streams and watering holes is also influenced by the rainy season of the savanna. Because of this concentration, some animals have adapted to make use of the available food in what is called a vertical feeding pattern, shown in Figure 8.10. *In a* **vertical feeding pattern**, *animals eat vegetation at different heights.* Vertical feeding patterns enable animals with different eating habits to feed in the same area without competing for food. The pattern allows more animals to live on limited resources because the animals can occupy smaller, more specific niches.

ARCHAEOLOGY LINK

Scientists think that an important step in the evolution of humans occurred when human ancestors left the trees of the forest and began to live on the grasslands. On the grasslands, a human ancestor called *Homo habilis* began to develop tools to aid in hunting and food gathering.

SECTION REVIEW

1. What is the purpose of growing runners?
2. How have plants adapted to savanna life?
3. Make a list of ways animals have adapted to the extreme conditions of savannas for eating and reproducing.
4. **Hypothesize** What could happen to the migrating animals in a savanna if they were fenced in a large wildlife park for protection?

1. Runners are a form of reproduction.
2. Plants grow very quickly to take advantage of the rainy season and recover from damage by fire and animals. Also, plants usually have sharp leaves or thorns that discourage grazers.
3. Lists should include migration to follow vegetation, and the synchronizing of breeding and rainy seasons.
4. The animals might not be able to follow their migration routes and would run out of food. Overcrowding could also result in disease and habitat stresses.

Answers and teaching strategies on page T55.

Seed Dispersal

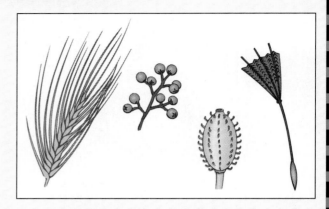

PROBLEM

How are the seeds of plants in a grassland biome adapted for dispersal?

MATERIALS (per group)

- reference sources
- collecting bag
- paper
- glue

INFERENCE

The seeds of grassland plants that fall beneath the parent plant probably could not compete for nutrients and water. Therefore, the seeds of successful plants usually have some adaptation that enables dispersal.

PROCEDURE

1. Use reference sources to find out how seeds from four of the following plants are adapted to be dispersed: milkweed, Russian thistle, dandelion, ragweed, cocklebur, shepherd's purse, goose grass, scarlet pimpernel, knotweed, wisteria, yellow oxalis, chickweed, annual bluegrass, and black mustard.
2. Reproduce the data table below on a separate piece of paper. Include eight rows.
3. Take the collecting bag to an area designated by your instructor.
4. Collect about 12 different types of seeds per group. Look for seeds similar to those shown in the figure or seeds that have obvious

adaptations for dispersal. *Note: You may obtain seeds from live weeds, but do not disturb the ecosystem any more than necessary. Do not remove seeds from trees or cultivated plants that may be in the area.*

5. In the classroom, check for seeds that may have become attached to your clothes. Add those seeds to your collection.
6. Separate 8 seeds from those collected by your group that are most clearly adapted for dispersal.
7. Glue each of the 8 seeds to the empty area in the left-hand column of the data table. In the middle column, classify each seed according to the general way it is dispersed (wind, water, animal, etc.). In the right-hand column, describe the observable adaptations of the seed that allow it to be dispersed.

ANALYSIS

1. Which four types of seeds did you choose to research in Step 1? How is each type of seed dispersed?
2. Did any seeds become attached to your clothing? Describe how the seeds were able to stay attached to you.
3. Were there any seeds that could be dispersed by more than one method? Explain.

CONCLUSION

1. Into which categories did you classify the seeds you collected? Describe how seeds in each category are dispersed.
2. What human activities help to disperse seeds?

Seed	Type of Dispersal	Adaptations

CHAPTER 8 REVIEW

KEY TERMS

grasslands 8.1	steppe 8.2	bunchgrasses 8.2	vertical feeding
desert–grassland	sod-forming	savanna 8.3	pattern 8.3
boundary 8.1	grasses 8.2	runner 8.3	
prairie 8.2	humus 8.2	tuft 8.3	

CHAPTER SUMMARY

8.1. Grasslands are ecosystems in which the climate is too wet to be a desert, but too dry to support a forest. Biotic and abiotic factors such as rainfall, grass fires, and grazing animals help maintain the growth of grasslands. Most of the biomass of grasses is below the ground. Grasslands are an important source of food for humans and other populations. Many of the world's grasslands are cultivated.

8.2. Steppes are considered by many scientists to be either a part of the desert biome or a short-grass prairie. Most steppe grasses are short bunch-grasses. Most prairie grasses are sod-forming.

Many organisms have adapted to wide climate changes by living underground or by migrating. The diversity of organisms has been reduced because of human need for food and space.

8.3. Savannas are tropical grasslands where rain is heavy during a short part of the year. Rainy and drought seasons are major influences, demanding that organisms grow quickly or migrate. Because they have thorns or grow runners, many trees, shrubs, and grasses are resistant to drought, fires, and grazing animals. The concentration of many animals in small areas has resulted in vertical feeding patterns.

MULTIPLE CHOICE

Choose the letter of the word or phrase that best completes each statement.

1. Fires in grasslands are necessary to prevent the growth of (a) plants; (b) trees; (c) migrating animals; (d) runners. b

2. The main difference between deserts and steppes is the (a) grass fire frequency; (b) vegetation density; (c) annual rainfall; (d) animal population. c

3. Grasses of the prairies use the wind to (a) reproduce; (b) start grass fires; (c) keep their leaves dry; (d) carry away dead grass. a

4. The largest limiting factor for the growth of forests is (a) grasslands; (b) rainfall; (c) grass fires; (d) soil structure. b

5. One way of telling if you are in a wet grassland is by the (a) forest of trees; (b) short, fine-bladed grasses; (c) tall, coarse-bladed grasses; (d) presence of animals. c

6. Soil aeration is caused by (a) grazing animals; (b) tree roots; (c) earthworms; (d) fertilizers. c

7. An adaptation that helps trees survive in dry grasslands is (a) having most of their mass below the ground; (b) having shallow roots; (c) growing rapidly; (d) being drought-resistant. d

8. Most grasses of the prairies (a) are bunch-grasses; (b) are sod-forming grasses; (c) grow in tufts; (d) grow in clumps. b

9. Savannas do not exist in the United States because (a) they have been destroyed by overgrazing; (b) they are only in Africa; (c) they exist only in the tropics; (d) it is too dry. c

10. A vertical feeding pattern is (a) a separation of animal habitats; (b) the amount of food predators eat; (c) a way for animals to avoid competition; (d) the time of day animals eat. c

TRUE/FALSE

Write true *if the statement is true. If the statement is false, change the underlined words to make it true.*

1. Wetter areas of the <u>desert</u> can be considered steppes. t
2. The grazing habits of bison in North America were very <u>damaging</u> to prairie grasslands. f, beneficial
3. Soil aeration helps the soil <u>hold water</u>. t
4. Steppes can also be called <u>short-grass prairies</u>. t
5. Sharp leaves on the trees of the savanna protect them from <u>drought</u>. f, grazing animals
6. Many animals reproduce during the rainy season because there is more <u>space</u> f, food
7. Large herbivores migrate to find <u>food and water</u>. t
8. Because savanna plants grow <u>quickly</u>, they can recover well from fire damage. t

CONCEPT REVIEW Answers on page T55.

Write a complete response for each of the following.

1. List four factors that influence the development of grasslands. Identify two as biotic and two as abiotic.
2. Describe the importance of soil aeration to healthy plant growth.
3. Compare and contrast the effects of migrating grazers with herded grazers on grasslands.
4. What factors contributed to the Dust Bowl of the 1930s?
5. Distinguish between the characteristics of a typical grass for a steppe, prairie, and savanna.

THINK CRITICALLY Answers on page T55.

1. Besides protection from fire, why might runners be a valuable adaptation for grasses growing around a watering hole?
2. Suggest some of the risks involved in replacing generalized species with specialized species.
3. When soil structure collapses, the soil may be removed by high winds. Deduce how the soil may be affected by rainfall and water flow if the soil structure is no longer absorbent.
4. Grasses grow tall and fast during the rainy seasons in prairies and savannas. During the drought season, the aboveground mass of the grasses dies. Discuss a possible role of grass fires in connection with this dead layer of grass.

Computer Activity The average annual increase in the world's human population is about 1.8 percent. Currently, there are about 5.3 billion people on Earth. In 1991, it was estimated that there were about 1.5 billion hectares of land used for crops. The area of land on Earth is about 14.5 billion hectares. Use a graphing program to make a line graph that compares human population growth and an appropriate increase in area of land used for crops. Assume that all crops are consumed by humans and each human has an equal share of food. How long would it take before the entire Earth would need to be cultivated to feed the human population?

WRITE CREATIVELY

Apply the concept of a vertical feeding pattern to the human population, and think of some alternative eating habits people may try to ensure that everyone gets enough food to eat. Write a story about a human society that uses this vertical feeding pattern.

PORTFOLIO

1. Find two typical grassland scenes from steppes, prairies, or savannas. Choose a scene from the 1800s and a current scene. Make a poster that compares the two scenes. Try to identify the changes, if any, that have occurred, and note the changes on the poster. Draw the poster, or use illustrations or photographs from books and magazines.
2. How have human societies adapted to living in a savanna? Choose a society from Africa, India, or South America that lives in the savanna. Prepare a presentation on an average day in the life of a teenager in the society you choose.

GRAPHIC ANALYSIS Answers on page T55.

Use Figure 8.10 to answer the following.

1. Which animals would do best finding food during the first few months after a small grass fire? Why?
2. Which animals would do best after a 5-year period in which there were no large grass fires? Why?
3. For two of the animals, list adaptations that enable the animals to fit into the vertical feeding pattern.

ACTIVITY 8.2

Answers and teaching strategies on page T55.

PROBLEM
How do species interact in a grassland ecosystem?

MATERIALS (per group)
- graph paper
- large jar with a lid
- gravel, rocks, and soil
- pinch of grass seeds
- pinch of clover seeds
- 12 mung bean seeds
- 5 of each animal: cricket, mealworm, land isopod, earthworm
- water
- colored pencils

HYPOTHESIS
Write a hypothesis about the food relationships that exist in your grassland ecosystem.

PROCEDURE
1. Place rocks and gravel in the bottom of the container. Then add a few centimeters of soil, and plant the seeds. Water lightly. Put a lid on the container, and place the ecosystem in indirect sunlight for 1 week. You may wish to place the jar outside in case of accidents.
2. Place the animals in the jar, and place the lid lightly on top. Observe the ecosystem for a few minutes every day for 3 to 4 weeks.
3. In a data table, record any increase or decrease in the number of organisms. Record any other changes you observe.
4. Graph each population on a separate sheet of graph paper. Use a different color to distinguish between each of the 4 populations. Compare population changes by comparing the curves.

ANALYSIS
1. Describe any population changes you observed over the 3 to 4 weeks. What might have caused the changes?
2. What relationships did you observe between different species in Step 4?

CONCLUSION
Do your observations support or refute your hypothesis? Explain.

The forests hold more life than any other place on Earth. Forests cover 30 percent of Earth's land surface, yet hold 75 percent of its biomass. While rain forest covers only 6 percent of Earth's land surface, it holds almost 40 percent of land biomass and is home to 70 to 90 percent of Earth's species. The rain forests are the most complex and diverse ecosystems on the planet. The forest biomes are crucial to humans. Wood is the most common building material on Earth. Wood products, such as paper, are equally important. Many of Earth's forests have been harvested to meet the demand for wood, resulting in widespread ecosystem destruction.

9.1 CONIFEROUS FORESTS

Objectives • *Describe* the characteristics of the coniferous forest.
• *Explain* adaptations that enable organisms to survive in coniferous forests.

The coniferous forest biome is located far from the equator and is generally limited to the Northern Hemisphere. The summers in this biome are warm, lasting 2 to 5 months. As winter approaches, daylight gets shorter. Temperatures drop quickly. The winters are long and very cold. Precipitation falls as rain during summer and as snow during winter. Coniferous forests receive 40 to 200 cm of precipitation a year. The plants of the coniferous forest are adapted to the well-defined seasons and to heavy snowfall.

Coniferous means cone-bearing. *Coniferous trees, or* **conifers** (KOHN-ih-fers), *are trees that produce seed cones.* The cones hold the seeds of the tree. Conifers share several other features, as you can see in Figure 9.1. Conifers share an unusual type of leaf called a needle. These leaves are long and thin and covered in a thick, waxy substance. The needles help the trees conserve water. Most conifers are also *evergreen*, meaning they do not lose all their leaves at a given time each year. Conifers lose and replace their leaves slowly throughout the year. The needles of conifers help the trees shed snow during winter.

Species of pine, hemlock, fir, spruce, and cedar are common in coniferous forests. Some broad-leafed trees, such as aspen and larch, are also present. Coniferous forests are not diverse, and most contain only a few species of trees. The trees often grow in dense stands that prevent sunlight from reaching the forest floor. The soil is poor and acidic because conifer needles are acidic and decompose slowly. The lack of sunlight and poor soil prevent most plants from growing on the forest floor. Ferns, lichens, and sphagnum moss are organisms that do grow on the forest floor.

Figure 9.1 Conifers produce cones (left) to hold their seeds. Conifer needles (center) have several adaptations that enable them to conserve water. The shape of conifer trees (right) helps them avoid damage from heavy snowfall.

Figure 9.2 Coniferous forests cover wide belts of the northern continents. Snow is common in this biome, and the growing season is short.

Figure 9.3 The blue jay and the moose are animals from the coniferous forest. The jay survives the long winter by eating seeds. The moose eats bark, young tree branches, and any other plants it can find.

The heavy winter snow that falls in most coniferous forests is important to the ecosystem. The snow acts like an insulating blanket, trapping heat and preventing the ground from freezing solid during the cold winter. This insulating effect protects the roots of the forest trees. Small animals such as mice that would freeze to death above the snow can also survive underneath the ground.

Many animals in the coniferous forest are adapted to the cold winters, and to life in the conifers. Most small herbivores are seed eaters, such as mice, squirrels, jays, and other rodents and birds. Insects are common during summer.

Larger herbivores, such as moose, elk, beaver, and snowshoe hares, feed on plants and bark. These herbivores are pursued by predators, such as grizzly bears, wolves, and lynxes. All these animals have adaptations that enable them to survive the long winters. Many species migrate, while some hibernate or live under the snow. All have thick body coverings to protect them from the cold.

Vast stretches of coniferous forest cover the northern parts of the former Soviet Union and North America. Because of the harsh climate, these forests have been relatively free from human disturbance. However, the growing need for wood has led to tree harvesting. The governments of the republics of the former Soviet Union are selling the rights to large stretches of forest to domestic and foreign companies. The new governments need money quickly, and selling the rights to the forests is one of the few ways they have of getting it.

1. Coniferous means "cone-bearing."
2. The trees have needles and a triangular shape that enable them to shed snow and conserve water. Animals have thick fur to shield them from cold.
3. The waxy covering on conifer needles makes them resistant to decomposition. The low temperatures during most of the year also slow the action of decomposers.

SECTION REVIEW

1. What does the word coniferous mean?
2. List several adaptations that enable organisms in coniferous forests to live through the harsh winter.
3. **Deduce** Conifer needles decompose slowly on the forest floor. Suggest two reasons explaining this slow rate of decomposition.

The Spotted Owl

Should old-growth forests be harvested?

1. The collapse of the timber industry was unavoidable because the industry was based on an unsustainable yield of trees.
2. Responses will vary but should reflect an understanding of the issues involved. Suggestions should also involve the ideas of sustainable yield and tree farming.

The Pacific Northwest is one of the few regions in the United States that still contains areas of undisturbed forest. These native coniferous forests are called old-growth forests. Old-growth coniferous forests are rich and diverse, containing many species found nowhere else on Earth. One of these species is a small owl called the spotted owl.

The spotted owl has been at the center of a bitter battle between environmentalists and members of industry for over ten years. The problem of the spotted owl is a complex one, involving politics, economics, and science. The issue began with the Endangered Species Act.

The Endangered Species Act was passed in 1973. It requires the government to protect the habitat of species that are threatened or in danger of becoming extinct. The spotted owl is a threatened species whose numbers have dropped sharply as a result of the logging of old-growth forests. The owl's remaining old-growth habitats are protected.

Now consider the economics of logging. For many years, the timber industry cut many more trees than the forests could regenerate. Harvests of such large size could not continue forever, or all of the forests would disappear. In the 1970s,

the forests on privately owned lands did begin to disappear.

The unsustainable tree harvest was the center of the economy in Oregon and in some parts of Washington state. When the supply of trees began to drop, the timber industry lost the trees that fed the sawmills—and powered the economy. The Pacific Northwest was faced with a serious economic recession.

The timber industry searched for new sources of logs. One place it found them was in national forests protected by the U.S. Forest Service and by the Endangered Species Act. Politicians in Washington, DC, were able to suspend laws and gain the timber industry special access to the timber on public land. The heavy harvest continued.

Environmentalists raised an outcry about the harvest of old-growth forests. One law that the environmentalists used in their attempt to stop the cutting was the Endangered Species Act. If

the environmentalists could show that harvesting old-growth forests threatened a protected species, the harvest would be illegal. The spotted owl was one species environmentalists used for this purpose.

The status of old-growth forests is still hotly debated. Many people think that jobs and owls are the only issues in the debate. But the spotted owl is not the cause of lost employment in the timber industry. The loss of jobs results from increased automation, increased exports, and from the fact that huge log harvests could not continue forever.

DECISIONS

1. What factor in the timber industry made its collapse unavoidable?
2. State several ideas that could help satisfy both sides in the debate over old-growth forests.

9.2 DECIDUOUS FORESTS

Objectives • *Identify* the characteristics of the deciduous forest.
• *Describe* the organisms that inhabit the deciduous forests.

Word Power

Deciduous, from the Latin *deciduus*, "to fall off."

BIOLOGY LINK

Chlorophyll is a green pigment that traps light in plants. Most plants also have other pigments in smaller amounts. In summer, leaves have a large amount of chlorophyll, and they appear green. But as autumn approaches, leaves stop making chlorophyll. As the remaining chlorophyll breaks down, the other pigments show through and give leaves their beautiful fall colors.

Forests also grow at lower latitudes than the coniferous forest. These latitudes are called the temperate zone. The forests in the temperate zone are made up largely of deciduous trees. *A* **deciduous** (dee-SIJH-oo-us) **tree** *is a tree that sheds its leaves during a particular season of the year*. These trees are the basis of deciduous forest biomes. They form niches used by many other organisms.

Temperature varies greatly in deciduous forests. Temperatures in summer can be as high as 30°C, while in the winter they can fall to −30°C. Precipitation falls as rain or snow, depending on the temperature and season. Deciduous forests receive 50 to 300 cm of precipitation a year. Precipitation falls fairly regularly throughout the year.

Deciduous trees are adapted to the highly variable climate of the temperate zone. The growing season lasts about 6 months. During the growing season, a tree grows quickly and produces and stores large amounts of food. In autumn, the shortening daylight and cooling temperatures trigger changes in the tree. The tree sheds its leaves and becomes dormant. The loss of leaves is an adaptation that enables a tree to conserve water during the cold winter months. Photosynthesis stops, and the tree no longer makes food. The tree survives winter by consuming food stored in its trunk, branches, and roots. The tree grows new leaves in spring. Photosynthesis begins again in preparation for the next winter.

Maple, oak, beech, ash, hickory, and birch are examples of deciduous trees. The inhabitants of deciduous forests are more diverse than those in coniferous forests. The forest has several distinct layers, and each layer has its own group of plant species. Figures 9.4 and 9.5 show deciduous forests.

Figure 9.4 The leaves of deciduous trees often change colors before they fall. These trees will soon lose their leaves and enter a state of dormancy for the winter.

Figure 9.5 Deciduous forests were once common across Europe and North America. Humans have disturbed almost all of this biome, although many of the trees have been replanted.

The highest layer of a deciduous forest is called the *canopy* (kan-uh-PEE). The canopy is made up of the upper branches and leaves of tall trees. The canopy captures most of the sun's direct light, but some filters down to the forest's lower levels. Beneath the *canopy* is the understory. The *understory* is made up of trees that are younger and smaller than those of the canopy. A layer of shrubs grows beneath the understory, while mosses, ferns, and other plants grow on the forest floor.

The leaves that fall from forest trees enrich the soil. The leaves decay quickly during the warm, humid summer months. As you recall from Chapter 8, the decaying leaves that fall in a deciduous forest produce a deep, rich layer of soil called humus. The humus and fallen leaves are home to many insects and other invertebrates that feed on the abundant organic matter.

Because the deciduous forest produces abundant food and has many different habitats, it supports a diverse community of animals and other organisms. Fungi and other decomposers, along with insects and invertebrates, are common in the leaf litter and on fallen trees. These organisms are preyed upon by birds, mice, and small mammals. Herbivorous mammals such as deer are also present. Reptiles and amphibians are common in warmer forests. Predators such as wolves, mountain lions, and foxes fill the higher trophic levels in this ecosystem. Eagles, owls, and other predatory birds are also present.

The deciduous forest has been changed drastically by human activity. This biome once stretched across Europe and Asia and covered the United States from the Mississippi to the Atlantic. Today, very little of the original deciduous forest still stands worldwide. In the United States, only 1 hectare in each thousand remains undisturbed. The loss of forest in Europe is equally severe.

Teaching tips for Field Activity appear on page T59.

FIELD ACTIVITY

In Chapter 6, you determined which biome you live in. What kinds of trees would you expect to find in your biome? Take a tree survey from around your school, or organize a field trip to a forest in your area. Gather samples of dead leaves and any seeds you find. Note which tree each sample comes from, and make sketches of the trees showing the tree's shape and the texture of its bark. *(Do not take living samples from the trees.)* Use a field guide to identify the tree species each sample comes from. Did you find the types of trees you expected? See if you can identify at least one species that has been introduced to your area by humans.

Figure 9.6 The earthworm (left) is common in the leaf litter of the deciduous forest. The fox (center) and the deer (right) are common mammals found in the deciduous forest.

Two factors have driven the human consumption of the deciduous forest. The first is rich soil. The humus in deciduous forest soil makes it deep and fertile, and the soil makes excellent farmland if the trees above it are cleared. Many forests were cleared to provide land for fruit trees and other crops. The second reason for the consumption of the deciduous forest is the trees themselves. Deciduous trees generally have harder wood than conifers, making the wood a better building material. The wood is also used for making paper products and as fuel.

Some of the world's deciduous forests have been replanted. But a forest ecosystem is not just a group of trees. The ecosystem does not simply reappear when new trees are planted. The forest ecosystem regenerates slowly because the many species that were dependent on the trees have disappeared from the area. These species must migrate back into the ecosystem or new species must adapt to empty niches. Also, the tree and plant diversity in most replanted forests is very low, meaning that many niches are no longer present. The community comes back very slowly, if at all. A discussion of the deciduous forest may therefore be more of a history lesson as well as an ecology lesson.

1. Deciduous comes from a Latin word meaning "to fall off." Deciduous trees are so named because they shed their leaves in the fall.
2. Deciduous soil is more fertile because of the large input of organic matter from falling leaves, and from the rapid decay of this organic matter.
3. The point is that almost all of the deciduous forest biome has been destroyed or disturbed by human activity. And even though some forests have been replanted, the ecosystems that once existed there do not just reappear when the trees grow back. Deciduous forests therefore existed more in the past than they do in the present.

SECTION REVIEW

1. From what adaptation does a deciduous tree get its name? Where does the word *deciduous* come from?
2. Why is the soil of a deciduous forest more fertile than that of a coniferous forest?
3. **Integrate** Read the last sentence in this section. What point is being made?

Year of the Fires

Did let-it-burn backfire?

1. The 10 A.M. policy aims to put out all fires. The let-it-burn policy is more in accordance with the ecology of forest ecosystems.
2. Controlled burnings or allowing earlier fires to burn could have controlled the 1988 fires.

During 1988, approximately 60,000 wildfires burned almost 2.4 million hectares (6 million acres) of forest in the United States. The largest fire in Yellowstone National Park's history covered nearly 400 000 hectares (1 million acres). Alaskan fires in the tundra and spruce forests destroyed over 890 000 hectares (2 million acres). There were 10,000 blazes in California alone. Fighting the fires cost more than $580 million and ten lives. A combination of factors helped cause the fires. Dry ground conditions, little summer precipitation, and the 1963 "let-it-burn" policy were responsible.

Previous to 1963, the U.S. Forest Service applied what was called the "10:00 A.M. policy" to forest fires. Any fire that broke out was to be under control by 10:00 A.M. the following day. This policy was based on theories about forest management in the plantation forests of Europe. However, ecologists established that burning is essential for the preservation of many natural forest communities. For example, the cones of the jack pine and lodgepole pine will not release seeds unless they are exposed to the intense heat of a forest fire. Fires also help deer, elk, and other animals by allowing new vegetation to grow on the cleared soil.

Understanding the role that fire plays in the natural forest ecosystem led to the establishment of the natural-burn, or let-it-burn, policy. The policy allows natural fires to burn unless they threaten people, property, or endangered species. The policy seemed to be in the best interest of the forest ecosystem. The problem was that nature had not been allowed to take its course for almost 100 years.

During the years of fire prevention, the forest floor had accumulated undergrowth and dead wood. The litter on the forest floor was thick and dry. It was the hope of the U.S. Forest Service that natural fires would burn themselves out or that precipitation would dampen the fires before they got out of control. This proved to be true—until 1988.

In the summer of 1988, dry weather turned the forest floor into kindling. All it took was a spark, which was supplied by lightning and a careless cigarette smoker in Yellowstone National Park. When the fires began, the park officials thought that rain and the structure of the park would tame the fires. But the rain never came, and winds blew the flames over natural barriers. Thousands of fire fighters had to be called in to help stop the enormous fire that raged out of control.

After the fires of 1988, the let-it-burn policy was under debate. However, the policy still stands. In many forests, small controlled fires are deliberately set in order to clear away the underbrush. By using controlled burning, disastrous fires like those of 1988 can be avoided.

DECISIONS

1. Compare the "10:00 A.M. policy" for forest management and the "let-it-burn" policy.
2. How could the disastrous fires of 1988 have been avoided?

9.3 RAIN FORESTS

Objectives • *Describe* the characteristics of the tropical zone and of the rain forest. • *Illustrate* the complexity and diversity of the rain-forest ecosystem.

The *tropical zone* is located at latitudes near the equator. Because the tropical zone is near the equator, it receives direct rays from the sun during most of the year. As a result, temperatures in the tropical zone average about 25°C all year long. The wide temperature ranges between summer and winter in the temperate latitudes are absent in the tropical zone. The growing season can last 12 months. Precipitation falls as rain except on the tops of high mountains. The amount of precipitation varies from 100 to 450 cm a year. Rain may fall during all months of the year, or there may be a wet season followed by a dry season.

Rainforest Structure

The constant warmth and abundant rain in the tropical zone have given rise to the rain forest. It is the most diverse and productive biome on Earth. *A* **rain forest** *is a biome with a dense canopy of evergreen, broadleaf trees supported by at least 200 cm of rain each year*. Rain forests contain 70 to 90 percent of all the species on Earth. Though they cover only 6 percent of Earth's land surface, rain forests hold 40 percent of Earth's land biomass. The rain forest is a great theater of life, a dramatic expression of evolutionary possibility unrivaled by any other biome.

Trees are the basis of the rain forest. Thousands of species of cyprus, balsa, teak, mahogany, and other trees grow in this biome. The trees in a rain forest are amazingly diverse. For example, British ecologist Peter Ashton found 700 species of trees in just 10 hectares of tropical rain forest in Borneo. Many of these trees reach

Figure 9.7 The rain forest is the most productive and diverse biome on Earth. Rainforest trees can grow to be 60 m tall.

Labels in figure:
Bright light
Emergent trees
Filtered light
Upper canopy
Lower canopy
Dense shade
Understory
Shallow roots

Figure 9.8 The rain forest has several different levels, and each supports its own community. The amount of sunlight available to plants decreases quickly beneath the canopy.

heights of 50 or 60 m, where their leafy tops form a dense canopy. The canopy captures over 99 percent of the light falling on the forest. The 1 percent of sunlight that filters through supports several other levels of vegetation, as shown in Figure 9.8. Vegetation on the forest floor is sparse because there is not enough sunlight to support many plants.

The rain forest as an ecosystem contains as many nutrients as, or more nutrients than, other biomes. But almost all these nutrients exist in living organisms at any one time. The topsoil is therefore thin and poor, with 99.9 percent of the available nutrients in the top 5 cm of soil. Rainforest tree trunks widen at their bases. Ridges of wood called *buttresses* make the trunks seem even wider. The buttresses support the trees, as the tree roots must be shallow to take advantage of the thin topsoil.

The dead organic matter that enriches the soil in other biomes does not last in the rain forest. Fallen trees and other organic matter are decomposed and recycled in days or weeks instead of years. The warm temperatures and constant moisture of the rain forest are ideal conditions for decomposers such as insects, fungi, and bacteria. Life is efficient in the rain forest. Nutrients that fall to the forest floor are quickly recycled and lifted back up into the trees.

Most of the activity in the rain forest occurs in the trees. The canopy and other levels of vegetation support countless species. Each species occupies a niche in the trees. Many organisms live their whole life without ever touching the ground. If you walked through a rain forest, most of the organisms around you would be over your head. The rain forest can be compared to a lake in which different organisms have adapted to the conditions in different water levels.

THINK CRITICALLY

What do you think would happen to the communities in a rain forest if the forest was logged and the topsoil removed? Would the forest ever return to its undisturbed state? Give reasons for your answers.

The communities would be completely destroyed. The forest would take thousands of years to regenerate, if it regenerated at all.

Cooperative Learning
The biological diversity of the rain forest is an important concept. Have students illustrate the diversity of the rain forest by creating a rainforest portrait. Divide the class into several groups. Assign each group to one category of organism, such as trees, other plants, insects, mammals, and amphibians. Have students search magazines and books for examples of organisms from their category, and prepare sketches and short descriptions of each one. Have students combine their research into one large poster. Beginning with the trees, have them draw pictures of their organisms in the appropriate places on the poster, accompanied by short descriptions. When all groups have added their organisms to the rain forest portrait, post it in the classroom.

Organisms and Diversity

The amazing animal diversity in the rain forest is caused by two factors. The first is the diversity of rainforest plants. Each species of tree or plant provides niches for specialized pollinators and herbivores. High plant diversity leads to high animal diversity. The second factor is the wide variety of habitats that exist in the different forest levels. Conditions high in the canopy are different than conditions lower down, and different communities evolve to occupy each habitat.

Habitats in the rain forest vary from tree to tree and from one part of a tree to another. The result is a complex, three-dimensional mosaic of habitats with a tremendous variety of organisms. The food webs that join these organisms are complex, with many species and many connections.

Five rainforest organisms are shown on this page. Each organism appears in the area it would if this page were a cross section of a forest. The tapir at lower left is from the forest floor, and the organisms across the top of the page are from the canopy. Remember that these photographs show only five of the millions of species that inhabit the Earth's rain forests.

Scientists are not sure how many species may live in the rain forest. American biologist E. O. Wilson found 43 species of ants on a single rainforest tree. British ecologist Terry Erwin estimates there may be over 50 million species of insects on Earth, mostly in rain forests. There are millions more species of animals, plants, bacteria, and fungi. Although scientists do not know how many species there are, the more they look, the more they find.

Figure 9.9 The tapir (bottom) lives on the rainforest floor. The margay (center left) is a cat that hunts on the forest floor and in lower branches. The beetle (top left), the toucan (top center) and the howler monkey (top right) all live in the rainforest canopy.

Deforestation

For a long time, difficult conditions kept most nonnative peoples out of the rain forest. But now, as a result of human activity, the rainforest biome is changing. In 1950, over 10 percent of Earth's land surface was covered by rain forests. Rain forests now cover

6 percent, and the area is decreasing. *The destruction of forest as a result of human activity is called* **deforestation**.

The force behind the destruction of the rain forests is the human population's need for space and wood. Most rain forests are in developing countries. Many of these countries are faced with rapid population growth. Rainforest trees are logged for export and burned to make farmland, grazing land, and living space for people.

Recall that the rainforest ecosystem is a vertical one, with many organisms in habitats far above the ground. When the trees in a rain forest are destroyed, the habitats in the canopy and in lower levels of vegetation are destroyed as well. When these habitats are gone, the animals that have evolved to live in them become extinct. Scientists do not know how many species are lost to loggers and bulldozers every day, but if a single tree can hold 43 species of ants, the total may be huge.

If an area of rain forest is burned, it may be able to regenerate after several hundred years if there is more rain forest around it. The diversity in the regenerated forest will still be low, however, because an ecosystem as complex as a rain forest cannot just reappear. But if the forest is destroyed in large tracts or if the fragile soil is bulldozed, the rain forest cannot regenerate. The area that once held a lush forest will grow only weeds. The many organisms that inhabited the forest will be gone forever.

> ## BIOLOGY
> ### L I N K
>
> Rain forests fix huge amounts of carbon through photosynthesis. When these forests are destroyed, the carbon dioxide they would have removed from the atmosphere remains. Deforestation may account for as much as 25 percent of the annual rise in atmospheric carbon dioxide. Carbon dioxide is a *greenhouse gas*, and large increases may cause *global warming*. You can learn about greenhouse gases and global warming in Chapter 22.

SECTION REVIEW

1. Why do rainforest trees have buttresses?
2. What two factors make the animal community in the rain forest diverse?
3. **Hypothesize** Plants on the floor of a rain forest often have very large leaves. Propose a hypothesis explaining this observation.

1. Rainforest trees have buttresses for support. The roots of the trees do not support them well because they are very shallow, in order to maximize exposure to the thin soil.
2. Animal diversity is caused by the high plant diversity and the stratification of the canopy and lower levels of vegetation.
3. The plants have large leaves because very little sunlight reaches the forest floor. Large leaves have a large surface area, so they capture more of the scarce sunlight than smaller leaves.

Answers and teaching
strategies on page T59.

The Water-Holding Capacity of Conifer Needles

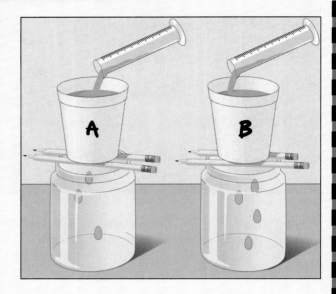

PROBLEM

How do conifer needles affect the water-holding capacity of a forest's soil?

MATERIALS (per group)

- 2 plastic foam cups
- marking pen
- garden soil (1 cup)
- soil containing dead conifer needles (1 cup)
- 4 pencils
- 2 jars (without lids)
- graduated cylinder
- paper towels
- tap water

HYPOTHESIS

Write a hypothesis that is related to the problem.

PROCEDURE

1. Use the marking pen to label one plastic foam cup *A*. Label the other cup *B*.
2. Poke four small holes in the bottom of each cup. Mark a line around each cup that is 2 cm from the top.
3. Pack cup *A* tightly to the line with plain garden soil. Pack cup *B* tightly to the line with soil containing dead conifer needles.
4. Place 2 pencils across the rim of each jar. Balance cup *A* and cup *B* on the pencils as shown in the figure.
5. Use the graduated cylinder to pour 100 mL of water into each cup. Let the water drain through the holes.
6. After the water has stopped draining, measure the amount of water in each jar by pouring the water back into the graduated cylinder. Discard this water after recording your measurements.
7. Make two stacks of paper towels with three towels in each stack. Dump the wet soil from cup *A* onto one stack and the wet soil from cup *B* onto the other stack. Move the soil around on each stack of paper towels so that they absorb as much of the moisture as possible.
8. Put the soil back into the plastic foam cups and compare the wetness of the two stacks of paper towels. Record this subjective measure of moisture.

ANALYSIS

1. In which biome will you find soil like that in cup *B*?
2. Did the jar under the plain soil or the one under the conifer needle soil contain more water after water was poured through the cups?
3. Which stack of paper towels got wetter after wet soil from each cup was dumped on them?

CONCLUSION

1. How do dead conifer needles affect the water-holding capacity of soil?
2. Relate your observations of the effect of conifer needles on the soil to the conditions in the coniferous forest biome. How do the needles affect the biome?
3. Did your observations support your hypothesis? Explain.

CHAPTER 9 REVIEW

KEY TERMS

conifer 9.1	deciduous tree 9.2	rain forest 9.3	deforestation 9.3

CHAPTER SUMMARY

9.1 Coniferous forests are located in northern latitudes on the continents of North America, Europe, and Asia. Temperatures are warm in the short summers and very cold in the long winters. Evergreen trees called conifers are the principal components of this biome. Conifers have several adaptations that enable them to survive winter. Coniferous forest organisms are also adapted to surviving the long winter.

9.2 Deciduous forests are located in the temperate zones. Deciduous forest trees lose their leaves in fall and enter a state of dormancy that lasts through winter. The falling leaves produce a thick, fertile soil called humus. The deciduous forest has been extensively altered by human activity. Very little of this biome remains in its undisturbed state today.

9.3 Rain forests are located in the tropical zone. The rain forest is the most productive and diverse biome on Earth. The growing season lasts all year, temperatures are always warm, and rainfall is abundant. The soil in rain forests is thin and poor because most of the nutrients in the ecosystem exist in organisms at any one time. The large diversity of tree species and many levels of vegetation in the rain forest give rise to diverse communities of other organisms. Human activity is destroying the rain forests, and severely damaged rain forests may regenerate slowly or not at all.

MULTIPLE CHOICE

Choose the letter of the word or phrase that best completes each statement.

1. The forest biome receiving the most annual precipitation is the (a) deciduous forest; (b) coniferous forest; (c) rain forest; (d) steppe forest. c

2. A tree that sheds its leaves at a particular time of the year is (a) deciduous; (b) evergreen; (c) coniferous; (d) tropical. a

3. Conifers have needles and enclose their seeds in (a) cones; (b) pods; (c) sacks; (d) root nodules. a

4. An adaptation that does not help organisms survive the long winter in the coniferous forest is (a) migration; (b) hibernation; (c) thick fur; (d) bright colors. d

5. Falling leaves in the deciduous forest produce a thick, rich soil called (a) pumice; (b) humus ; (c) peat; (d) loess. b

6. Human activity has disturbed all of the deciduous forest in the U.S. except for 1 acre in (a) 10; (b) 50; (c) 100; (d) 1000. d

7. The biome with the most diverse communities of organisms is the (a) deciduous forest; (b) rain forest; (c) coniferous forest; (d) prairie. b

8. The layer of leaves that blocks most of the sunlight from reaching the ground in the rain forest is called the (a) shrub level; (b) understory; (c) canopy; (d) humus. c

9. Most of the nutrients in the rainforest ecosystem are in the (a) organisms; (b) topsoil; (c) air; (d) groundwater. a

10. A rain forest from which all trees and soil are removed will regenerate (a) in 10 years; (b) in 50 years; (c) in 100 years; (d) never. d

CHAPTER 9 REVIEW

WORD COMPARISONS

Write the letter of the second word pair that best matches the first word pair.

1. Evergreen: coniferous as (a) deciduous: humus; (b) deciduous: consumer;(c) leaf-shedding: deciduous; (d) rainfall: deciduous. c

2. Coniferous forest: low diversity as (a) rain forest: high diversity; (b) rain forest: low diversity; (c) deciduous forest: high diversity; (d) deciduous forest: low diversity. a

3. Plant diversity: animal diversity as (a) rain: precipitation; (b) photosynthesis: carbon dioxide; (c) sunlight: forest floor; (d) different habitats: diversity. d

4. Deforestation: population growth as (a) tree: forest; (b) deciduous tree: humus; (c) forest floor: sunlight; (d) loss of diversity: deforestation d

CONCEPT REVIEW Answers on page T59.

Write a complete response to each of the following.

1. Describe some of the adaptations that enable organisms to survive winter in the coniferous forest. To what conditions are all coniferous forest organisms adapted?

2. Why do deciduous trees shed their leaves? How do these leaves affect the rest of the ecosystem?

3. Where are most of the nutrients in a rainforest ecosystem at any one time? How does the soil in the rain forest reflect this distribution?

4. What two factors lead to high animal diversity in the rain forest?

5. How has human activity affected the three forest biomes?

THINK CRITICALLY Answers on page T59.

1. The days in the coniferous forest are much longer in summer than winter. Why?

2. Why have deciduous forests been disturbed by human activity?

3. Illustrate the vertical structure of the rain forest by drawing a diagram. Include the canopy, the understory, forest floor plants, soil, and rainforest trees.

4. Contrast the diversity of organisms in the three forest biomes. Which biome is most diverse? Which is least diverse?

5. **Computer Activity** Rain forests covered 10 percent of Earth's land surface in 1950. That number dropped to 6 percent in 1993. Suppose the rain forests disappear completely by the year 2015. Use a graphing program to show the loss of rain forests.

WRITE FOR UNDERSTANDING Answers on page T59.

The size and shape of plant leaves are discussed several times in this chapter. Write a short essay explaining how the characteristics of conifer, deciduous, and rainforest plant leaves are adapted to their environments. Your essay should include information on leaf shape, size, and other adaptations.

PORTFOLIO

Reread "The Spotted Owl" on page 141. What are your feelings about this complex issue? Write a letter to your congressperson expressing your feelings and suggesting ways in which everyone can use the old-growth forests.

GRAPHIC ANALYSIS Answers on page T59.

1. This figure shows the movement of rainwater through a rain forest and over deforested land. What percentage of rainwater is transpired from the forest and from deforested land?
2. What percentage of rainwater is absorbed by the soil in each case?
3. What percentage of rainwater leaves each area as runoff?
4. What effect do you think the increased runoff and decreased transpiration have on the soil of the deforested region?

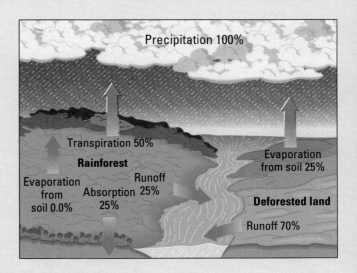

Precipitation 100%

Transpiration 50%

Rainforest

Evaporation from soil 0.0%

Runoff 25%

Absorption 25%

Evaporation from soil 25%

Deforested land

Runoff 70%

ACTIVITY 9.2

Answers and teaching strategies on page T59.

PROBLEM
On which side of a tree do lichens grow most abundantly?

MATERIALS (per group)
- reference sources
- construction paper
- glue or tape
- meter stick
- hand lens (tripod type)
- compass

PREDICTION
Write a prediction that is related to the problem.

PROCEDURE

1. Use reference sources to find out as much as you can about lichen. Be able to identify crustose lichen, foliose lichen, and fruticose lichen.
2. Read the procedures and make a data table to record the data you will collect. Then make a frame out of construction paper that measures 1 m by 10 cm.
3. Go to an area designated by your teacher.
4. Locate a tree that has lichen on its bark. Examine the lichen with the hand lens,

and record your observations in the data table. *Note: Lichens develop slowly so do not disturb them.*

5. Use the compass to find north. Curl the narrow sides of the paper frame around the north side of the lowest part of the tree. Only north-facing bark should be inside the frame.
6. Estimate the percentage of bark area inside the frame that is covered with lichen. Repeat for the east, south, and west sides of the tree. Record your estimates in the data table.
7. Repeat steps 4 through 6 for three other trees.

ANALYSIS

1. What types of lichens did you find attached to trees in the area?
2. Why was it important to examine areas of bark at the same height?

CONCLUSION

1. Did lichens cover more of one side of trees than others? Explain.
2. How would you improve the procedures of this activity if you were a scientist with more time and resources?

S ince the dawn of civilization, people have settled and thrived by the banks of the world's freshwater supplies. Rivers, lakes, and swamps gave people water for drinking, cooking, and bathing. As societies grew, waterways were put to work transporting goods and irrigating farms. In addition to traditional uses, rivers now help supply electrical energy and cool nuclear reactors. But precious freshwater supplies are also important to the other organisms in the biosphere. Are people putting too many demands on the world's supply of fresh water? An understanding of freshwater ecosystems is crucial if these valuable habitats are to be preserved.

10.1 AQUATIC BIOMES

Objective •*Describe* the factors that characterize the various types of aquatic biomes.

All the biomes you have read about so far have had one thing in common. They are all land, or terrestrial, biomes. But land covers less than 30 percent of Earth's surface. With water covering so much of Earth, it is not surprising that many of Earth's organisms live in aquatic habitats. An *aquatic* (uh-KWAHT-ik) *habitat* is one in which the organisms live in or on water. Aquatic biomes are not grouped geographically the way land biomes are, and it is difficult to show them on a map. Aquatic biomes and their ecosystems are scattered and are often determined by depth rather than location.

The characteristics used to describe aquatic biomes are different from those used to describe land biomes. Recall that temperature and rainfall are important factors in distinguishing one land biome from another. While these factors do have some effect, the temperature in large bodies of water is more stable than the temperature on land. Also, rainfall has less effect on many aquatic biomes than on land biomes because the organisms are already underwater. For aquatic biomes, two of the most important factors are the amount of dissolved salts in the water and the depth of the water. The rate of flow and the amount of dissolved oxygen in the water are also important factors in determining the types of organisms that live in an aquatic ecosystem.

Salinity

Aquatic biomes can be divided into two main groups, based on the amount of dissolved minerals in the water: saltwater and freshwater. Although all bodies of water contain some dissolved salts and other minerals, ocean water has a good deal more than the water in most lakes, ponds, and streams. *The amount of dissolved salts in a sample of water is called* **salinity** (suh-LIN-ih-tee).

Salinity is measured in parts per thousand, or the number of units of salt in a thousand units of water. The salinity of ocean water is about 30 parts per thousand. The salinity of fresh water is 0.5 parts per thousand or less. Water that is more saline than fresh water, but less saline than ocean water, is called brackish water. Brackish water is common in areas such as river deltas and coastal marshes, where fresh water meets the ocean.

The water in most lakes, ponds, and rivers is fresh water. There are, however, some exceptions. Some lakes, such as the Great Salt Lake in Utah and Mono Lake in California, are more saline than the ocean. Such lakes are called hypersaline lakes, and they may be as salty as 40 parts per thousand.

If natural water sources are not available, you can grow pondwater organisms by making a grass infusion. Combine some soil, grass clippings, and leaves in a jar of water. Allow to sit for 1 to 2 weeks at room temperature. Students may need assistance using a microscope if they have not had a course in biology or life science.

PHYSICS LINK

Salty water is denser and heavier than fresh water. The salinity of water can be tested using a tool called a hydrometer. A hydrometer measures the density of water by testing its buoyancy, or how much mass can float on the water. Because it is denser, salt water has more buoyancy than fresh water.

Figure 10.1 In deep bodies of water, only the photic zone is well sunlit. In shallow water, sunlight reaches to the benthic zone.

DATELINE 1977

The first deep-sea research submarine, called *Alvin*, was launched from the Woods Hole Oceanographic Institute in Massachusetts. The mission was to seek and study deep cracks in the ocean floor where the tectonic plates are spreading apart. Researchers were surprised to find an ecosystem deep on the ocean floor that did not use energy from the sun. Instead, the base of the food web was bacteria that use energy from the chemicals that ooze through the cracks.

Word Power

Aphotic from the Greek a-, "without," and *phos*, "light."

1. Sunlight penetrates the photic zone but does not reach the aphotic zone.
2. Salinity is determined by the density, and therefore the buoyancy, of the water. It is measured in parts per thousand.
3. The fish would die because they are adapted to a different type of habitat.

Depth

Water depth is directly related to the amount of sunlight that reaches the bottom of the body of water. The amount of sunlight is important in determining the types and amounts of plants that can grow on the bottom. As the producers in the ecosystem, plants form the base of the food web.

Bodies of water can be divided into depth zones, shown in Figure 10.1. *The top layer of water that receives enough sunlight for photosynthesis to occur is called the* **photic** (FOHT-ik) **zone.** The depth of the photic zone depends on how clear or cloudy the water is. In the open ocean, the photic zone is about 100 m deep. Although sunlight reaches the bottom of the photic zone, the amount of light available decreases steadily as the depth increases. Below the photic zone is the *aphotic zone*. Sunlight never reaches the aphotic zone. Only the ocean and very deep lakes have aphotic zones.

The floor of a body of water is called the **benthic zone.** The benthic zones of shallow ponds, streams, and coastal areas have a variety of organisms. Snails, mussels, catfish, and turtles are common freshwater benthic animals. In shallow waters, sunlight reaches the benthic zone, which can therefore support plant life. In contrast, the benthic zone of the open ocean is far below the photic zone.

SECTION REVIEW

1. What characteristic distinguishes the photic zone from the aphotic zone?
2. How is salinity determined and measured?
3. **Predict** Suppose a friend wants to set up an aquarium and discovers that saltwater fish are more attractive, but a freshwater aquarium is easier to maintain. Your friend decides to set up a freshwater aquarium but buys some saltwater fish to place in it. Predict what the result of this decision would be, and why.

10.2 STANDING-WATER ECOSYSTEMS

Objectives •*Identify* the characteristics of different types of standing-water ecosystems. •*Explain* the value of wetlands and the reasons for their decline.

Freshwater biomes can be divided into two main types—standing-water ecosystems and flowing-water ecosystems. Lakes and ponds are the most common types of standing-water ecosystems. Standing-water ecosystems also include many types of wetlands, such as bogs, prairie potholes, swamps, and freshwater marshes. Table 10.1 shows some of the characteristics of different standing-water ecosystems.

Although there is no net flow of water in and out of most standing-water ecosystems, there is usually a characteristic flow of water circulating through the system. This flow helps to distribute warmth, oxygen, and nutrients throughout the system.

Table 10.1   Types of Standing-Water Ecosystems

	Abiotic Factors	Biotic Factors
Lake	Deepest type of standing water; may have an aphotic zone; usually fed by underground aquifers.	Main producers are floating algae in the photic zone and benthic plants along the shoreline; complex food webs.
Pond	Light reaches benthic zone; fed mostly by rainfall; may be seasonal.	Main producers are plants and algae that grow on the bottom; food web usually simpler than lakes.
Marsh	Very shallow water with land occasionally exposed; soil is saturated; water is often free of oxygen; may be freshwater, saltwater, or brackish; often tidal; Florida Everglades is the largest freshwater marsh in the United States.	Plants have roots under water, but leaves are above the water (emergent); mostly grasses, cattails, and rushes; ducks, waterfowl, and benthic animals are common.
Swamp	Land is soaked with water because of poor drainage; usually along low streambeds and flat land; mangrove swamps are salty and found along coastlines.	Dominated by large trees and shrubs; plants are adapted to grow in muddy, oxygen-poor soil; cypress trees common in the south, willow and dogwood common in the north.
Bog	Inland wetland with little inflow or outflow; soil is acidic; decay is slow; also called a fen or moor.	Sphagnum moss is the dominant organism; partly decayed moss accumulates as peat.

Standing-Water Organisms

Many standing-water ecosystems have several levels of habitat. Organisms that live in the upper levels of water are different from those are that live in the middle and bottom levels. The upper levels of the water are warmer and better sunlit than the lower levels.

The top level of a standing-water ecosystem supports the plankton community. *Plankton* is a general term for microorganisms that float on the surface of the water. Most plankton are about the size of dust particles. There are two main types of plankton: phytoplankton and zooplankton. *Plankton that carry out photosynthesis are called* **phytoplankton** (FYT-oh-PLANK-tun). Although they are usually too small to see without a microscope, phytoplankton are the main producers in most aquatic biomes. In the ocean and in lakes that are too deep for plants to grow on the bottom, phytoplankton are particularly important. Why do you think this is true?

Plankton that do not carry out photosynthesis are called **zooplankton** (ZOH-oh-PLANK-tun). Zooplankton include microscopic animals and protozoans. Because zooplankton are unable to carry out photosynthesis, they are consumers in the ecosystem. Zooplankton feed on phytoplankton. Small fish feed on plankton and insects on the surface of the water. Larger fish feed on smaller fish, and so on. As you can see, plankton are an essential part of the aquatic food web.

The benthic community of a standing-water ecosystem is quite different from the community at the surface. Many benthic organisms are scavengers, feeding on the remains of other organisms. This is particularly true of deep lakes, where sunlight does not reach the benthic zone. The benthic community depends on a steady rain of organic material that drifts down from the top. The decomposers of standing-water ecosystems are also members of the benthic community.

Wetlands

There is no single definition for wetlands that all scientists and government officials agree upon. As the name suggests, wetlands are found where water and land come together. *In general,* **wetlands** *are ecosystems in which the roots of plants are submerged under water at least part of the year*. Marshes, swamps, and bogs are just a few of the many types of wetlands. Wetland soils are soaked with water and are very low in dissolved oxygen. The water in most types of wetlands is standing water that may be fresh or brackish. However, there are also wetlands with flowing water and salt water.

Wetlands are a very important part of the biosphere that have not, until recently, been fully appreciated by most people. Wetlands act as filters, detoxifying chemicals in the water that passes through them. Wetlands are so efficient in this process that they can be used as part of treatment systems for waste water. Wetlands are also important breeding, feeding, and resting grounds for waterfowl,

Figure 10.2 Although they are rarely larger than pieces of dust, plankton form the base of the food web in freshwater and saltwater ecosystems.

Without plants growing from the bottom, phytoplankton are the only producers in the food web.

Multicultural Perspective

Papyrus is a common grass in the wetlands of northern Africa and the Middle East. Egyptians first used papyrus to make a paper-like writing material as early as 3000 B.C. Papyrus was the most commonly used writing surface in the eastern Mediterranean area for 4,000 years.

Figure 10.3 Wetlands serve many purposes in the environment. They purify water, recharge aquifers, provide a breeding ground for many animals, and protect the surrounding land from floods.

such as ducks and geese, and other animals. Wetlands along the banks of rivers act as flood protection regions. And the water that seeps into the ground under wetlands contributes to the refilling of aquifers.

Wetlands are being destroyed by human activity in the United States and other parts of the world at an alarming rate. There are several reasons for the disappearance of the wetlands. Many people do not find wetlands as attractive as other natural habitats. They are often breeding grounds for mosquitoes. Wetlands may give off an unpleasant odor, due to the methane, or "swamp gas," released by the organisms in the muddy, oxygen-free soil.

Because wetlands are often found in coastal areas, the land they occupy may be very valuable for other uses. People like to own and develop property with a waterfront view. In addition, many wetlands have been used as landfill sites, helping solve garbage-disposal and land-shortage problems at the same time. The lack of respect that people have traditionally held for wetlands can be seen in the Swamp Lands Act passed by Congress in 1849. This policy encouraged the filling and draining of wetlands. Since that time, more than half the wetlands in the U.S. have been destroyed. The fact that there is no universal definition of a wetland has contributed to their decline. How can you make laws that protect wetlands if you cannot even define what a wetland is?

The Florida Everglades

The history of the Florida Everglades shows how difficult it is to manage and protect a wetland area. The Everglades were once a swampy marsh that spanned 160 km from Lake Okeechobee to the tip of Florida. Water flowed slowly in a wide sheet across the whole region, varying in depth from a few centimeters to 2 m. The region has a wet season from May through October, followed by a dry season. Many areas that are under water during the wet season are exposed during the dry season. Natural fires occur during the dry season, burning off dried plant material that grew during the wet season.

BIOLOGY
L I N K

Swamps and marshes in which the water contains no oxygen are often home to a type of bacteria called methanogens. These anaerobic bacteria release the gas methane, also known as swamp gas. Methanogens also live in the digestive tracts of many mammals, helping break down plant material that would otherwise be indigestible. The methane released contributes to digestive gas.

Word Power
Everglades, from the Middle English *glad*, "a bright, smooth place."

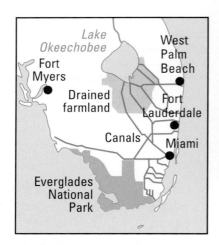

Figure 10.4 The Florida Everglades were originally formed by a slow-moving sheet of water that flowed south from Lake Okeechobee. Drainage canals converted much of the swamp to farmland and changed the flow of water through the park.

Figure 10.5 Alligators form holes in the mud by swinging their powerful tails. Fish and other organisms survive the dry season by living in the gator holes.

The Everglades is home to a huge number of organisms. These organisms are adapted to the annual cycle of growth, drought, and fire. Alligators scoop out large depressions in the ground, forming pools called gator holes. During the dry season, fish, turtles, and other aquatic animals survive by living in the water that remains in the gator holes. Birds build nests on the exposed land and feed on the animals trapped in the gator holes. Without the gator hole, neither the fish nor the birds would survive.

To create farmland, water from Lake Okeechobee was channeled, and much of the wetland was drained. The areas south of the lake became farmlands with a maze of canals. To save the wetland, Everglades National Park was established in 1947. But without the water from the lake, the ecosystem was in danger. In 1967, a canal was dug to bring water from the lake to the park. Soon, flooding became a problem. The water came too fast and in too narrow a stream. The gator holes were flooded, bird and alligator nests were flooded, and birds could no longer feed on the fish in the gator holes. Between 1962 and 1981, bird populations dropped by 50 percent. The alligator population declined as well.

In 1983, park officials and the state of Florida launched a "Save Our Everglades" campaign. Since then, 100,000 acres have been returned to the wetland. The flow of water has also been adjusted to provide a more natural water supply. Although the Everglades is still an endangered habitat, there is now hope for short-term recovery and long-term survival.

SECTION REVIEW

1. Where would you be likely to find benthic organisms in an aquatic ecosystem?
2. What is the difference between the role of phytoplankton and the role of zooplankton in an aquatic food web?
3. **Infer** The number of migratory birds in the tundra during the summer has been declining in recent years. How might public attitudes toward wetlands be contributing to this decline?

1. Benthic organisms live on the bottom.
2. Lack of appreciation for wetlands has contributed to their destruction. Because wetlands are important to migratory birds, the loss of wetlands could reduce the number of birds that reach the tundra.
3. Phytoplankton are producers; zooplankton are primary consumers.

10.3 FLOWING-WATER ECOSYSTEMS

Objective •*Describe* how abiotic factors of gravity, erosion, and sedimentation affect stream ecosystems.

Flowing freshwater environments have many names: rivers, streams, creeks, and brooks all refer to water that flows over land. To most people, the different names suggest bodies of water of different sizes. To a scientist, however, all aboveground bodies of flowing fresh water are called streams. Recall that fresh water can also flow underground through aquifers. Even though they are under the ground, there is some life in aquifers. Some aquifers contain fish and other animals. In these cases, the aquifers are the animals' habitats.

Stream Organisms

Organisms that live in flowing-water habitats are adapted to the rate of the water's movement. Some organisms such as insect larvae have hooks that enable them to grab hold of plants. Others have suckers that anchor them to rocks. One type of animal that has adapted to life in freshwater streams is the fish of the salmon and trout families. Salmon and related fish breed and grow in freshwater streams but spend their adult lives in the oceans. When the fish mature and are ready to breed, they swim upstream and return to the very same spot in which they hatched. Research has shown that salmon find the stream and the breeding spot by "smelling" tiny amounts of chemicals in the water.

Stream Flow

Most streams begin at high altitude, often from the runoff of melting snow on the tops of mountains. Gravity causes streams to flow downhill. Because inland areas usually have higher altitudes than coastal areas, streams usually flow toward the ocean. The place where the stream begins is the source, or head, of the stream. Water near the source is called headwater. Headwaters in the mountains are often cold and contain large amounts of dissolved oxygen that can support a variety of organisms. But these headwaters tend to flow too rapidly for most organisms to live in the water.

As the slope of the land becomes more gentle, the stream slows down. As the flow of water slows, small particles of minerals, sand, and organic material that were picked up by the flowing water begin to settle. *Small particles that settle to the bottom of a body of water are called* **sediments**. Sediments accumulate on the bottom of the streambed and provide a place for plant roots to grow. The plant growth further slows the flow of water, allowing the water to be warmed by the sun. Phytoplankton multiply in the warmer water, and soon there is enough food to support populations of consumers.

Figure 10.6 When they are ready to breed, salmon swim upstream and return to the very spot where they hatched. Research has shown that salmon use their keen sense of smell to locate the specific stream.

CHEMISTRY LINK

According to the laws of chemistry, gases such as oxygen dissolve more readily in cold water than in warm water. This law explains why sodas lose their fizz quickly at room temperature, and why air bubbles appear in water when it is heated. Because of this law, colder water usually contains more dissolved oxygen and can support more animal life than warmer water can.

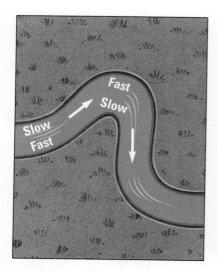
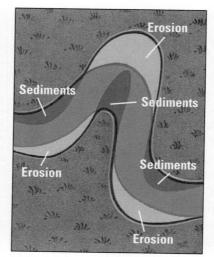

Figure 10.7 Erosion along the fast-flowing outer edge, and sedimentation along the slow-flowing inner edge, result in the winding, or meandering, of a stream.

The processes of sedimentation and erosion cause the course of a stream to change naturally over time. Use Figure 10.7 to follow the steps of this process. As a stream curves, or meanders, the water flowing along the inside of the curve slows down. At the same time, the water on the outside of the curve speeds up. Sediments accumulate along the inner edge because of the slowed flow. The increased flow on the outer edge, however, increases the rate of erosion along the banks of the stream. The curve in the stream gradually becomes more pronounced. As a stream becomes older, it becomes more and more curved.

The flow of many streams has been changed dramatically by human activities. Some streams have been dammed to create reservoirs. These reservoirs help provide water and hydroelectric energy for the growing needs of human societies. Because salmon must return to the place where they hatched in order to breed, any change in the course of a stream presents a serious threat to the fish. Changing the course of a stream damages or destroys the delicate habitats of other organisms as well. Areas that were once streambeds become the bottoms of deep lakes. Organisms that are adapted to live in the stream would probably not survive in a lake.

THINK CRITICALLY

Floodplains are areas along the sides of rivers where the river overflows during floods. Floodplains tend to contain very fertile soils that are good for growing crops. Why do you think this is true? What is the main risk of farming along a floodplain?

The sediments that are deposited on the floodplain make the soil fertile. The risk is that the river could flood again, destroying crops, as occurred along the Mississippi in 1993.

1. Sediments settle when the flow slows down.
2. The water flows too fast in headwaters.
3. Headwaters are colder, and colder water can hold more oxygen.

SECTION REVIEW

1. What condition encourages sediments to settle out of the flowing water in a stream?
2. Why are there fewer organisms in the headwater of a stream than further downstream?
3. **Apply** The headwaters of a stream often contain more dissolved oxygen than the water hundreds of kilometers downstream. Why is this true?

Human Impact on the Nile River Delta

How are humans changing Egypt's only water source?

The 6695 km Nile River is the longest river in the world. The yearly flooding and the constant flow of the river sustained civilization along Egypt's only river for thousands of years. In 1968, the Aswan High Dam was built to create hydroelectricity and to irrigate farmland. This construction has modified the natural flow of the river.

The ancient Greek historian Herodotus said of the Nile River Delta over 2,000 years ago, "In the part called the Delta, it seems to me that if…the Nile no longer floods it, then, for all time to come, the Egyptians will suffer." The natural flow of a river is important for maintaining the ecosystem of a river basin.

Flowing rivers carry sediments which are deposited at the mouth of the river, forming deltas and wetlands. Sediments are also distributed along the floodplain of the river when the river overflows its banks. The Nile River drainage system has been modified so that almost all the water is diverted by channels. The flow of the river is now controlled by the amount of water released by the Aswan High Dam.

Before the construction of the Aswan High Dam, the Nile River deposited about 124 million metric tons of sediments onto the delta each year. Also, an average of 9.5 million metric tons of sediment were deposited onto the floodplains each year. Now sediments are no longer transported to the delta or to the floodplains. The result has been widespread erosion of the shoreline and an influx of salt water from the Mediterranean Sea into coastal low-lying areas.

Flood deposits once fertilized the floodplain. Now, farmland depends on manufactured fertilizers or crop management for fertile soil. The salt content of agricultural soil has also increased. Flooding used to flush out the evaporated salts that collected in the soil.

River deposits also carried nutrients for organisms that lived in the river or the delta. The loss of nutrient-rich water has decreased the fish populations and the increase in polluted waste water draining into the lagoons threatens the natural habitat of migrating birds.

In most places, the building of a dam does not have such a major impact on the river drainage system. However, the Nile River is unique because it is the single source of fresh water for an entire area. As increasing populations created the need for more food and energy, the building of the dam seemed logical. But the long-term complications of human intervention into a natural system are becoming evident.

DECISIONS

1. Why is the Nile River drainage system a unique situation?
2. Do you think Egypt was better off before or after the Aswan High Dam was constructed? Why?

Answers and teaching
strategies on page T63.

Deposition of Sediments in a Meandering Stream

PROBLEM

What causes a stream's meanders to become larger over time?

Assumption 1: A fast-moving stream erodes its banks quickly.

Assumption 2: A slow-moving stream deposits sediment quickly.

MATERIALS (per group)

- stream table (see figure)
- metric ruler
- beaker
- clock with second hand
- graduated cylinder

HYPOTHESIS

Write a hypothesis that is related to the problem.

PROCEDURE

1. Set up a stream table that looks like the one in the figure. Be sure that the sand is wet, piled deeply enough, and contoured according to the sketch. The sand should be about 3-cm deep at the thickest part of the layer.
2. With your finger, cut a meandering streambed through the sand that has the shape of the one in the figure. The streambed should be cut almost to the bottom of the sand.
3. Make fine adjustments to the sand, if necessary, so that the slopes of opposite banks are about equal.
4. Determine the size of the curves by measuring distances y and z shown on the figure. Record all the measurements in a data table.
5. Set up a siphon with a long piece of rubber hose so that the water flows from container *A* into the upper river reservoir and then down the streambed. Half the groups in the class should adjust the rate of water flow to about 4 mL/s. The other groups should adjust the rate to about 8 mL/s. *Hint*:

Measure the flow rate using the clock. Intercept and measure the water draining into Container B with a graduated cylinder.

6. Allow the water to flow down the streambed for 20 min. Observe and compare the flow rate of water near the outside and inside bank. You will need to continuously refill container A and drain container B. Turn off the water, but leave the sand in place.
7. Compare the slopes of the inside and outside banks at the center of each curve. Repeat Step 4.

ANALYSIS

1. Was the flow rate of water fastest near the outside or the inside bank?
2. How did the slopes of the inside and the outside banks change relative to each other after water flowed down the stream?
3. How did the size of the meanders change after water flowed down the stream?
4. Compare your group's data with the data of a group that used a different water-flow rate. How do your results differ?

CONCLUSION

How do erosion and sedimentation cause the meanders of a stream to become larger?

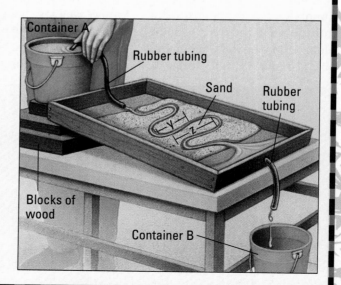

CHAPTER 10 REVIEW

KEY TERMS

CHAPTER SUMMARY

10.1 Many of Earth's habitats are under water and are called aquatic habitats. Salinity, depth, rate of flow, and amount of dissolved oxygen are factors that determine the types of organisms that live in different aquatic biomes.

10.2 Standing-water ecosystems include lakes, ponds, marshes, swamps, and bogs. Phytoplankton are often the main producers in deep standing water. Wetlands are habitats where water and land come together. Wetlands are a very important part of the biosphere that are particularly in danger from human activities.

10.3 All bodies of flowing fresh water are considered streams. Stream organisms are adapted to the rate of flow in the stream. The course of a stream changes naturally over time, but stream-diversion projects have changed or destroyed many stream habitats. Stream-diversion projects provide water and energy for growing human populations.

MULTIPLE CHOICE

Choose the letter of the word or phrase that best completes each statement.

1. To be considered fresh water, water must contain salt in a concentration (a) more than 30 parts per thousand; (b) less than 0.5 parts per million; (c) more than 40 parts per million; (d) less than 0.5 parts per thousand. d

2. Brackish water is common in (a) lakes; (b) oceans; (c) coastal marshes; (d) aquifers. c

3. Sunlight reaches the benthic zone in (a) ponds; (b) deep lakes; (c) oceans; (d) vents in the ocean floor. a

4. Organisms that live in the benthic zone of deep lakes are often (a) producers; (b) plants; (c) scavengers; (d) plankton. c

5. A type of standing-water habitat in which the soil is acidic and decay is slow is called a (a) bog; (b) swamp; (c) marsh; (d) pond. a

6. Cypress trees are adapted to living in (a) stream beds; (b) swamps; (c) the northern U.S.; (d) bogs. b

7. Phytoplankton are (a) consumers; (b) decomposers; (c) producers; (d) scavengers. c

8. Wetlands (a) are easy to define; (b) have traditionally been protected by laws; (c) are nonproductive areas that could be better used for other purposes; (d) are important breeding grounds. d

9. Sediments tend to accumulate (a) in slow-moving parts of a stream; (b) on the outer edge of a curve in a stream; (c) in fast-moving parts of a stream; (d) near the beginning of the stream. a

10. Streams always flow (a) south; (b) toward the ocean; (c) downhill; (d) toward the poles of Earth. c

11. Levees and dams are *beneficial* to farmlands because they (a) prevent stream sediments from being deposited on the fields; (b) protect the fields from floods; (c) provide a source of irrigation; (d) help refill aquifers. b

12. Levees and dams are *harmful* to farm lands because they (a) prevent stream sediments from being deposited on the fields; (b) protect the fields from floods; (c) provide a source of irrigation; (d) help refill aquifers. a

CHAPTER 10 REVIEW

TRUE/FALSE Answers on page T63.

Write true if the statement is true. If the statement is false, change the underlined word to make it true.

1. Organisms that live on the bottom of aquatic habitats are <u>benthic</u> organisms. t
2. <u>Zooplankton</u> are the main producers in deep-water ecosystems. f, phytoplankton
3. Salinity is measured in parts per <u>million</u>. f, thousand
4. Sunlight always reaches through the <u>photic</u> zone. t
5. Wetlands contribute to the <u>depletion</u> of aquifers. f, refilling
6. Methane is produced in swamps by <u>benthic animals</u>. f, bacteria
7. The course of a stream can change over time as a result of sedimentation and <u>erosion</u>. t
8. The Swamp Lands Act <u>encouraged</u> the draining and filling of wetlands. t

CONCEPT REVIEW Answers on page T63.

Write a complete response to each of the following.

1. Explain how the construction of the Aswan High Dam affected the ecosystem in the Nile River.
2. List four abiotic factors that determine the types of organisms in aquatic ecosystems.
3. Compare and contrast the characteristics of a swamp and a lake.
4. How does depth affect the food web of a lake ecosystem?
5. Describe four beneficial functions of wetlands.

THINK CRITICALLY Answers on page T63.

1. Why do you think the food webs in lakes are generally more complex than the food webs in small ponds?
2. Why does the reproductive behavior of salmon make the fish vulnerable to changes in habitat?
3. Certain farming and irrigation practices increase the amount of sediments that are carried by streams. How might these practices affect the ecosystem in the stream?
4. Fish that are adapted to live in cold water may not survive in warmer water. Why does temperature affect the ability of an animal to survive in the water?
5. Suppose advances in technology made it very easy to make fresh water out of seawater. How might this affect the impact of human activity on freshwater ecosystems?

WRITE CREATIVELY

Imagine you are a drop of water that has just melted from a snow-capped mountaintop. Write a short story about the experiences you have on your journey down the stream to the ocean.

PORTFOLIO

1. Where does your tap water come from? Investigate the source of tap water in your community. Include projects such as dams and aqueducts that were built to help deliver water. What was the impact of this construction on the natural ecosystems?
2. Research the complex ecosystem of the Florida Everglades. Create visual presentations of the ecosystem dynamics and relationships among organisms in the Everglades. Include the changes that have occurred in the ecosystem during the past 50 years.

GRAPHIC ANALYSIS Answers on page T63.

Use the figure to answer the following.

1. Many rivers have been dammed to provide clean water for people. According to the graph, did the percentage of people with clean water worldwide increase or decrease between 1970 and 1980?
2. Was the change in percentage greater in rural areas or in urban areas?
3. Although the information in the graph is accurate, the worldwide supply of clean drinking water actually increased during the 1970s. Give two reasons that would explain the apparent contradiction.

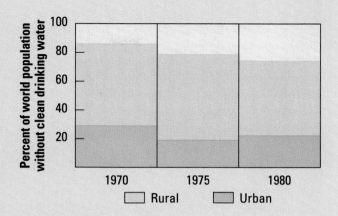

ACTIVITY 10.2

Answers and teaching strategies on page T63.

PROBLEM
To what kind of environment are tardigrades adapted?

MATERIALS (per group)
- depression slide
- spatula
- 2 cryptobiotic tardigrades
- dropper
- coverslip
- dissecting microscope
- distilled water

HYPOTHESIS
After reading the entire activity, write a hypothesis that is related to the problem.

PROCEDURE

1. Use a spatula to place two cryptobiotic tardigrades on a depression slide. View them under a dissecting microscope. Look for signs of life. Describe their appearance and sketch what you see.
2. Add three drops of distilled water to the tardigrades on the slide, and put a coverslip on the slide. **Caution:** *handle glass slides and coverslips carefully.*

3. Observe the tardigrades in water. Note any changes you observe in the tardigrades' appearance and behavior. Sketch the appearance of the tardigrades in water.
4. Take off the coverslip. Leave the slide undisturbed overnight so that the water will evaporate.
5. The next day after all the water has evaporated, observe the tardigrades again under the microscope. Describe them, and make a sketch of what you see.

ANALYSIS

1. Describe what the tardigrades looked like when they were in the cryptobiotic state.
2. How did the tardigrades change when water was added?
3. What happened to the tardigrades when the water dried up?

CONCLUSION

1. Where did you hypothesize the tardigrades live? What evidence did you obtain in this activity to support your hypothesis?
2. Under what conditions would the changes that you observed be advantageous to the survival of the organism?

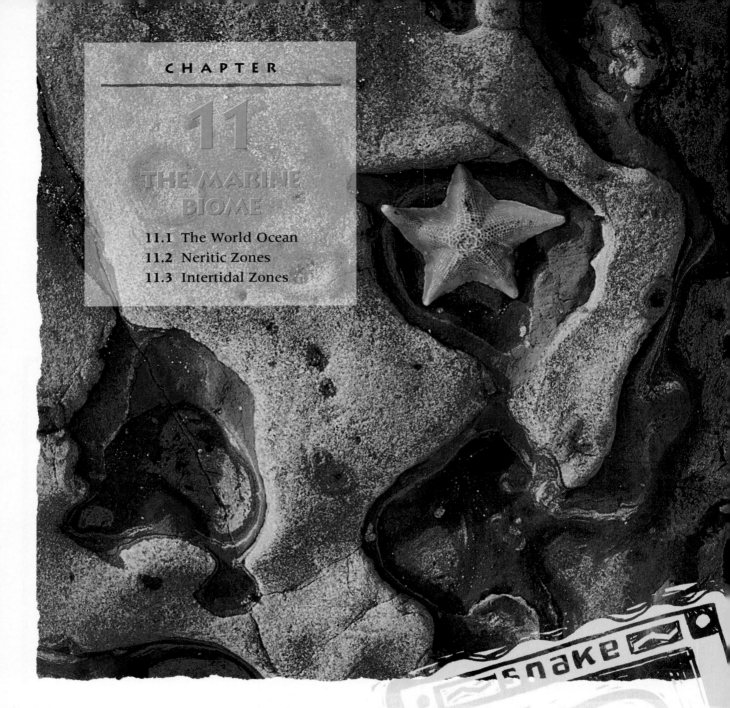

CHAPTER

11

THE MARINE BIOME

11.1 The World Ocean

11.2 Neritic Zones

11.3 Intertidal Zones

If you stand on a beach, the ocean may appear to be infinitely huge. It would seem, from its vastness, that the ocean is too big to be affected by the activities of the organisms on the relatively small patches of land. Yet the impact of human activities can be found from the open seas to the calm tide pools along the ocean's shores.

Oceans have been called the lungs of Earth, cycling carbon dioxide and oxygen constantly. The ocean also serves as a buffer that modifies temperature changes. In addition, oceans are home to many organisms. Without a healthy ocean, Earth may not have the stability to support its complex web of life.

11.1 THE WORLD OCEAN

Objectives • *Locate* the major ocean zones based on their relationship to the shore. • *Describe* the flow of water through the world ocean and the characteristics of ocean water in different parts of the world.

All the water between the continents on Earth's surface can be thought of as one big ocean. Although people have given names to separate oceans, such as the Atlantic and Pacific, all the oceans of the world are connected and therefore make up one large body of water. Because this body of water, called the world ocean, is interconnected, it can be thought of as one large biome with many ecosystems and habitats.

The world ocean can be divided into zones both horizontally and vertically. You are already familiar with the vertical zones. The photic, aphotic, and benthic zones that apply to large lakes also apply to the ocean. In addition to the depth zones, oceans can also be divided into zones based on distance from the shore. These zones, called the oceanic, neritic, and intertidal zones, are shown in Figure 11.1

DATELINE 1985

Rainbow Warrior, a ship belonging to Greenpeace, was bombed and sunk off the coast of New Zealand. One crew member was killed. Greenpeace is one of the largest environmental groups in the world, with a membership of more than 2.5 million people. *Rainbow Warrior* was on its way to French Polynesia to protest nuclear testing in delicate marine habitats.

The Oceanic Zone

The open ocean, or **oceanic zone***, is by far the largest zone in the ocean, or marine biome, making up more than 90 percent of the surface area of the world ocean.* The oceanic zone is very deep, ranging from 500 m along continental slopes to as deep as 11 000 m below the surface. Sunlight does not penetrate very deeply into the oceanic zone.

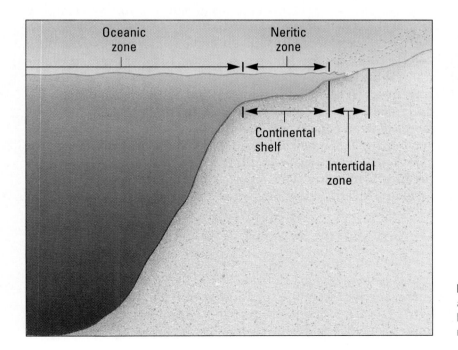

Figure 11.1 The oceanic zone is mostly aphotic, but the neritic zone, which lies above the continental shelf, is mostly photic.

Figure 11.2 Fishes that live in deep ocean habitats (left) have many unique adaptations to their environments. The deep-sea angler fish has a glowing "lure" that attracts prey. Baleen wales, such as the humpback whale (right) feed entirely on plankton, especially a small species of shrimp called krill.

The photic zone accounts for a layer less than 100 m from the surface of the open ocean. Therefore, the only producers of the open ocean ecosystem are phytoplankton. It may seem that microscopic plankton are too small to support much life. But each year, the phytoplankton in the world ocean produce about 1.6 billion tons of organic carbon, the basic material of living tissue that forms the base of the food web. Within the photic zone, zooplankton feed on phytoplankton, and small fishes feed on both types of plankton. Plankton are a major food source for many larger animals of the oceanic zone as well. Baleen whales, such as the humpback whale in Figure 11.2, feed exclusively on plankton, despite their enormous size.

The aphotic zone of the open ocean can be thought of as the desert of the marine biome in terms of biomass. Just as the lack of rain in the desert limits the number and types of organisms that live there, the absence of sunlight limits the diversity of the deep ocean. But organisms in the desert have adapted through evolution to thrive in an otherwise hostile environment. In a similar way, the deep ocean has organisms that have adapted to the cold, dark, deep waters. Many organisms in the deep ocean feed on pieces of dead organic material that drift down from the surface. *Tiny pieces of dead organic material that are food for organisms at the base of an aquatic food web are called* **detritus** (dee-TRY-tus). Benthic organisms in many types of aquatic habitats feed on detritus, including invertebrates such as clams, worms, and sponges.

Ocean Water

Although all the oceans of the world are connected, not all ocean waters have the same characteristics. Differences in the amount of energy received from the sun cause oceans in different parts of the world to vary in temperature, salinity, and density. Water near Earth's equator receives stronger radiation from the sun than water

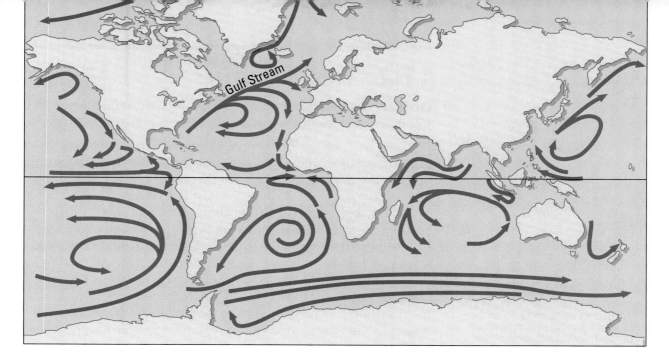

Gulf Stream

Figure 11.3 The major currents of the world are driven by energy from winds. Warm currents are shown in red. Cold currents are shown in blue. The Gulf Stream carries warm water north along the eastern coast of the United States.

elsewhere. This increased radiation causes the water to be warmer and evaporate more rapidly in the tropics. As a result of the evaporation, the water in the ocean near the equator tends to be more saline and have a higher mineral content than average.

Near the poles, the ocean is fed by melting glaciers and polar ice caps. Because the frozen water is fresh, not salty, the water near the poles is less salty than the rest of the ocean. But cold water is denser than warm water. Therefore, water near the poles is denser than water elsewhere.

The water in the ocean flows in characteristic patterns called *ocean currents*. Although ocean currents vary somewhat during the year and from one year to the next, certain patterns are quite stable. Ocean currents are driven mostly by winds. Water currents flow through the ocean in large masses. One mass of water can be very different from an adjacent mass. Fish and other ocean organisms travel within specific water masses, following the pattern of currents over large distances.

SECTION REVIEW

1. What is detritus made of, and why is it important to deep-sea organisms?
2. Why does the oceanic zone have no plants? What are the producers of the open ocean?
3. **Synthesize** Compare the map in Figure 11.3 to the one in Figure 1.8 on p. 10. What type of winds drive the Gulf Stream current?

1. Detritus is made of dead organic material and is a major food source for deep-sea organisms.
2. There are no plants because sunlight cannot reach the ocean floor. The producers are phytoplankton.
3. The Gulf Stream is driven by westerlies.

11.2 NERITIC ZONES

Objectives • *Describe* the factors that define a neritic zone.
• *Compare* and contrast two types of neritic zone ecosystems.

The edges of continents do not drop suddenly into the ocean. Instead, the major landmasses are surrounded by an area of relatively shallow water. *The shallow border that surrounds the continents is called the* **continental shelf**. The continental shelf is the area between the shore and about 500 m below the surface of the water. The width of the continental shelf varies among the different continents and coasts.

The region between the continental shelf and the surface of the water is called the **neritic** (nee-RIHT-ihk) **zone**. Because the continental shelf is usually shallow enough to be within the photic zone, the waters in the neritic zone receive enough sunlight for photosynthesis to occur. Although the neritic zone accounts for only about 8 percent of the ocean, these shallow, warmer waters are the most productive part of the ocean. Two types of very productive neritic ecosystems are reefs and estuaries.

Coral Reefs

A **reef** *is a natural structure built on a continental shelf.* The structures are made from products of the reef organisms. Coral reefs are found in warm, tropical waters. Kelp reefs, also called kelp beds, are common in colder waters.

Coral reefs can be thought of as the tropical rain forests of the marine biome. Coral reefs are not only productive ecosystems, as are rain forests, but are also home to a huge variety of organisms. The coral reef ecosystem is extremely important to both the ocean organisms and the human populations living near the reef. Coral reefs are the breeding and feeding grounds for many economically important types of fish. In fact, one-third of all ocean fish live on or depend on coral reefs. The reef itself protects the shoreline from erosion. Like the species of the rain forests, many coral reef organisms may have medicinal value that has not yet been identified. And like the rain forests, the delicate coral reef ecosystems of the world are vulnerable to human activities.

The ecology of the coral reef is a unique and fragile system. The reef itself is made of the calcium carbonate skeletons of millions of tiny corals. Only the top layer of the reef is alive. Corals depend on a symbiotic relationship with a form of alga that lives inside the tissues of the coral. The algae carry out photosynthesis and provide corals with food. Like all photosynthetic organisms, the algae that live inside corals require an adequate amount of sunlight. Because of the algae's need for sunlight, coral reefs cannot grow below a certain depth.

The area from the shore to the point at which the ocean floor is no longer in the photic zone is also called the littoral zone. The difference between the neritic zone and the littoral zone is the continental shelf that may exist below the photic zone. The neritic zone includes the aphotic portion of the continental shelf, if any, while the littoral zone does not.

Figure 11.4 Coral reefs are made of the skeletons of millions of tiny corals. Corals belong in the group of animals called Cnidarians, which also includes jellyfish and sea anemones.

Human activities can harm coral reefs in many ways. The reef is often blasted with dynamite to make harbors and shipping channels. The coral itself is often harvested and sold for jewelry. Many of the bright, colorful fishes that inhabit coral reefs are popular for use in home aquariums. The methods used to collect the fish, however, can damage the reefs.

Water pollution is also a major cause of coral reef damage. Toxic chemicals can kill the corals and other organisms that live on the reef. Silt, sand, and topsoil that wash into the water make it cloudy and reduce the amount of light available for photosynthesis. The condition of a coral reef can be an indicator of water quality. When the corals begin to die rapidly, it is a sign that there is something wrong with the quality of the water.

Estuaries

An **estuary** (ES-tyoo-ayr-ee) *is a region of water in which a freshwater source, usually the mouth of a river, meets salt water from the ocean.* Estuaries are partly enclosed but are still subject to the rise and fall of ocean tides. The water in estuaries is usually brackish but the salinity varies with the depth, time of year, rate of flow, and tide. Many marine organisms, including fish and benthic animals, lay their eggs in the calm, warmer waters of estuaries. The newly hatched young are then swept into the ocean by the flow of the water. Although estuaries are not as productive as coral reefs, they are much more productive than the open ocean.

Neritic Zone Productivity

Many factors contribute to neritic zone productivity. The fact that sunlight can reach the benthic zone of the continental shelf is the most important factor. The availability of sunlight allows photo-

HEALTH
L I N K

Competition for food and space is intense on densely populated coral reefs. To protect themselves, many reef animals secrete chemicals that are toxic to other organisms. Some of these chemicals include antibiotics and hormones that may be useful to people. For example, one species of reef sponge produces a chemical that may help reduce the pain and swelling of arthritis. Medical researchers are studying many reef organisms for new sources of medicines.

Word **Power**
Estuary, from the Latin *aestus*, "tide."

Figure 11.6 Reefs are more productive than farmland but less productive than rain forests. How does the productivity of a reef compare to that of an estuary?

Reefs are slightly more productive than estuaries.

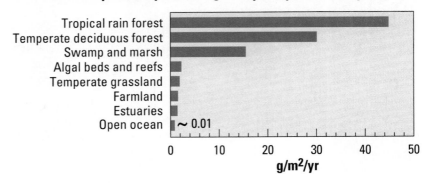

Productivity of ecosystems in grams per square meter per year

Tropical rain forest
Temperate deciduous forest
Swamp and marsh
Algal beds and reefs
Temperate grassland
Farmland
Estuaries
Open ocean ~ 0.01

0   10   20   30   40   50
g/m²/yr

THINK CRITICALLY

Based on the information in the graph in Figure 11.6, do you think the open ocean contributes significantly to the overall productivity of the biosphere? Why or why not?

Yes, because of its enormous size. See graph page 181.

Figure 11.7 As coral reefs grow larger, less oxygen and fewer nutrients from the ocean are carried by the surf to the corals closest to land. Eventually, a channel forms between the reef and the land, creating a barrier reef.

synthesis to take place throughout the zone. Waters in neritic zones also tend to be high in mineral nutrients. The nutrients are washed into the water from the shore, either in rain runoff or in the streams that feed into the ocean. Tides also play a role in the productivity of neritic ecosystems. The tide washes a fresh supply of nutrients and oxygen over the zone and carries away wastes. Figure 11.6 compares the productivity of neritic ecosystems with that of other aquatic and land ecosystems.

The effects of tides on coral reefs can be seen in the way the reefs develop over time. When a reef first forms, it grows just off the shore of the land. Such reefs are called fringe reefs. As the reef ages, it grows farther and farther out onto the continental shelf. As it grows, water from the ocean tides has to travel a longer distance to reach that part of the reef closest to land. Along the way, nutrients and oxygen are used up by the corals and other organisms. Eventually, the water that reaches the reef along the shore is so low in oxygen and nutrients that it cannot support the live corals. Corals nearest the shore begin to die, and a channel forms between the land and the reef. Reefs that are separated from the shore by a channel are called barrier reefs. The barrier reef surrounding the island of Bora Bora in French Polynesia can be seen in Figure 11.7. The Great Barrier Reef of Australia is the largest coral reef in the world.

SECTION REVIEW

1. Where in the ocean does the neritic zone begin and end?
2. Continental shelves have been called the breadbaskets of the ocean. Explain this statement.
3. **Infer** Some types of ecosystems recover from damage more quickly than others. Would you expect coral reefs to recover quickly from the types of damage described in this section? Why or why not?

1. The neritic zone begins at the end of the intertidal zone and ends at the edge of the continental shelf.
2. Continental shelves are responsible for much of the productivity that feeds the entire ocean.
3. Students should recognize that coral reefs, made of so many tiny skeletons, grow very slowly and therefore recover slowly from damage.

11.3 INTERTIDAL ZONES

Objectives • *Explain* the processes that contribute to the formation of salt marshes and mangrove swamps. • *List* several human activities that damage intertidal habitats.

The intertidal zone is located along the shoreline of the world ocean. *The* **intertidal** (in-ter-TI-duhl) **zone** *alternates between periods of exposure and periods of submersion twice each day.* Organisms in the intertidal zone must be able to survive both exposed and submerged conditions. These organisms must also be able to withstand the constant pounding of the surf. Some organisms attach themselves to the rocks. Others burrow into the sand.

Because intertidal zones occur where the water meets the land, they are often surrounded by wetlands, such as tidal salt marshes and mangrove swamps. Like other types of wetlands, salt marshes and mangrove swamps are vulnerable to human activity.

Salt Marshes

Salt marshes are flat, muddy wetlands that often surround estuaries, bays, and lagoons. Most salt marshes are influenced by tides. The mud flats of tidal salt marshes are exposed during dry periods and low tides, but submerged during wet periods and high tides. Salt marshes are a common form of wetland along the coast of the United States, especially the east coast and the Gulf of Mexico.

Many of the environmental roles of wetlands described in Chapter 10 also apply to coastal salt marshes. One of the most important functions of salt marshes is their role in supporting migratory bird populations. Migratory birds use salt marshes for feeding and resting during their long journeys. Salt marshes are also essential in supporting the ocean ecosystem. Abundant plant life, especially grasses, grow on the salt marsh. As the plants die, detritus washes into the surrounding estuary or other shallow waters. Recall that many marine animals breed in these waters. The plant material becomes food for the animals that breed, hatch, or grow in the water. Many of these animals then move out to sea or become food for ocean animals.

Salt marshes form when streams flow into the calm waters of an estuary or other shallow, neritic waters. The slowing of the water causes sediments, picked up by the stream, to be deposited at the mouth of the stream. The sediments build up over time, forming a delta. *The weight of the accumulated sediments causes the delta to sink under the water in a process called* **subsidence** (sub-SID-enz). To remain stable, there must be a balance between the rate of sediment deposition and the rate of subsidence in a salt marsh. Sometimes, the course of the stream may change as a result of

Cooperative Learning
Tidepools can form in the intertidal zone. In their learning groups, have students research the organisms that live in tidepools and how they are adapted to life in the intertidal zone.

Figure 11.8 Most migratory birds that summer in the tundra and other cold regions rely on coastal salt marshes to rest and feed during their journey.

these two factors. The Mississippi River delta undergoes a 5000-year cycle of sediment accumulation, subsidence, and change in the river's course. With every change in course, the Mississippi delta changes shape. The salt marshes of the Mississippi River delta account for 40 percent of the coastal wetlands of the United States.

Mangrove Swamps

Mangrove swamps are a type of coastal wetland that occurs only in warm climates. The plants in a mangrove swamp are killed by frost. Therefore, mangrove swamps can only exist in areas that do not freeze for more than one or two days each year. The dominant plant life in a mangrove swamp is the mangrove, a woody plant that can be either a tree or a shrub. There are about 800 species of mangroves worldwide, of which only 10 live in the United States. The red mangrove is the most common U.S. type.

The water in mangrove swamps typically has very little dissolved oxygen. Mangroves are adapted to the low oxygen by having roots that emerge from the water. Some species have roots that grow up from the bottom of the plant, with tips that stick out above the water. Other species have roots that grow from high up on the tree's trunk. The roots make the plant appear to be up on stilts. These elaborate root structures trap sediments, causing soil to accumulate behind the plants. This soil enables other plants to grow. In some parts of the world, such as Southeast Asia, mangrove swamps can develop into extensive mangrove forests.

Mangrove swamps and forests support complex ecosystems full of organisms with unique adaptations. Like many ecosystems worldwide, some species that live in the mangrove swamps are endangered due to loss of habitat. In the Philippines, for example, the 5000 km² of mangrove swamps that existed in the 1920s have been reduced to less than 1400 km² today. The swamps are destroyed for many reasons. One major reason is the creation of culture ponds used for raising commercial fish and shrimp. Other reasons for mangrove swamp destruction include coastal building construction and waste dumping.

Figure 11.9 The tangled, stiltlike roots of the red mangrove trap sediments that accumulate as mud behind the trees. Other swamp plants then take root in the mud, causing the growth of mangrove forests.

Multicultural Perspective
Mangrove swamps are an important part of the economy of Indonesia, where fish have been farmed in the swamps since the 1400s. The Nypa swamp palm grows in the mangrove swamps of the Malay Peninsula. Local people use the trees to supply fruit, sugar, vinegar, and alcohol.

1. Salt marshes are exposed during low tides and submerged during high tides.
2. 25%. They would be found in warm coastal areas.
3. The containment has reduced the amount of sediments carried by the river. Much of the delta is sinking from the loss of sedimentation to offset subsidence.

SECTION REVIEW

1. Why are salt marshes considered part of the intertidal zone?
2. What percentage of the world's mangrove species live in the United States? In what parts of the country would you expect to find them?
3. **Apply** Much of the Mississippi River has been contained by levees, dikes, and other flood-control structures. How do you think this change has affected the river's delta?

Real Estate versus Salt Marshes

Should salt marshes be drained for development?

1. Answers will vary but should be supported by information from the essay.
2. Students should site possible damage to oceans and migratory bird populations, as well as possible economic benefit from jobs and sale of real estate.

A salt marsh may not look like a very inviting area. However, these muddy, grassy, areas are among the most biologically productive environments on Earth. The salt marshes of Georgia, for example, produce seven times as much organic matter as a field of wheat.

At the base of the salt-marsh food web is the grass *Spartina*. Bacteria and fungi feed on the dead plants. Crabs, snails, clams, worms, and birds also inhabit the salt marsh, eating the animals that eat the dead plants.

Land adjoining water has attracted humans for centuries because of the access to ocean transport and resources. Coastal land is beautiful, and it offers many enjoyable activities. To meet the human need for more coastal land, salt marshes are often drained for development. Should salt marshes continue to be drained to meet the growing needs of human populations?

Supporting Points

• The land along coastal regions is desirable property for recreation and housing. People enjoy living and vacationing near the water.
• Salt-marsh sites are crucial areas for industries and nuclear power plants. The land is located near water for shipping. Also, the water is convenient

for cooling pipes.
• Housing, recreational, and industrial development of marsh areas helps the economy by providing employment for millions of people.
• Real estate along coastal areas generates money. In some areas of the United States, 1 m^2 of former salt marsh may sell for as much as $10,000.
• New salt marshes could be constructed on less valuable land. The salt-marsh species could be relocated to alternative habitats because they have a high tolerance for changes in temperature, salinity, and sediment composition.

Opposing Points

• Salt-marsh habitats support many different species of organisms including several en-

dangered birds.
• The restoration or formation of salt marshes on alternative sites is often unsuccessful. The ecology of the salt marsh is not understood well enough to be reproduced artificially.
• Salt marshes are vital sources of protein for humans because many fish, crabs, oysters, and clams breed and live in the marshes. The draining of the marshes would affect all the people who depend on the productivity of the salt marsh for their livelihood.
• Salt marshes and their adjoining waters are natural flood-control areas. These zones also block damaging waves, protecting developments built along coasts.
• Salt marshes filter pollutants from coastal waters. It is estimated that the filtering capacity of 1 acre of marsh is equal to the capacity of a waste-treatment plant.

DECISIONS

1. Do you think salt marshes should be converted to real estate property? Explain your reasoning.
2. If a hotel were built on land that was formerly a salt marsh, how might the ecology of the area change? How might the economy of the area change?

Answers and teaching strategies on page T67.

Saltwater Concentration and Brine Shrimp Survival

PROBLEM
At what concentration of salt can brine shrimp hatch and survive?

MATERIALS (per group)

- marking pen
- 5 plastic cups
- 250-mL beaker
- salt
- metric measuring spoons
- brine shrimp eggs
- cotton balls
- shoebox
- plastic wrap
- glass stirring rod
- dropper
- Petri dish
- hand lens or dissecting microscope
- dry yeast

PREDICTION
Write a prediction that is related to the problem.

PROCEDURE

1. Copy the data table onto a separate sheet of paper.
2. Use the marking pen to label each cup with a different letter, A through E.
3. Pour 250 mL of water into each cup.
4. Use the measuring spoons to add 1 mL of salt to cup A, 2 mL of salt to cup B, 5 mL of salt to cup C, and 10 mL of salt to cup D. Do not add any salt to cup E. Stir the water in each cup.
5. Put a dry cotton ball into the container of brine shrimp eggs so that the eggs stick to the cotton. Dip the cotton ball into cup A, and swirl the cotton around so the eggs transfer to the water.
6. Repeat step 5 for cups B through E. Use a dry cotton ball each time.
7. Cover each cup with plastic wrap, and store them in the shoebox. Put the shoebox in a safe place where the temperature will remain stable.
8. The next day, gently stir the eggs in cup A to spread them throughout the cup. Remove a dropperful, and squirt the contents into the Petri dish.
9. Observe the contents of the Petri dish with the hand lens or microscope. Count and record the number of eggs and the number of hatched shrimp.
10. Add a small amount of dry yeast to the cup if brine shrimp have hatched.
11. Repeat steps 8–10 each day for the next 3 days for cups A through E.

ANALYSIS

1. In which cups did brine shrimp eggs hatch? In which cup did the greatest number hatch?
2. Were physical differences noticeable between brine shrimp raised in different salt concentrations? Explain.
3. In which cup did brine shrimp survive the longest time?

CONCLUSION
Based on your data, make an inference about the natural habitats of brine shrimp.

Cup	Amount Salt Added	Number of Brine Shrimp in Sample							
		First Day		Second Day		Third Day		Fourth Day	
		Eggs	Shrimp	Eggs	Shrimp	Eggs	Shrimp	Eggs	Shrimp
A	1 mL								
B	2 mL								
C	5 mL								
D	10 mL								
E	none								

KEY TERMS

oceanic zone 11.1	continental shelf 11.2	reef 11.2	intertidal zone 11.3
detritus 11.1	neritic zone 11.2	estuary 11.2	subsidence 11.3

CHAPTER SUMMARY

11.1 Scientists divide the ocean into zones horizontally and vertically. The vertical photic, aphotic, and benthic zones that apply to deep lakes also apply to oceans. The oceanic zone, or open ocean, makes up more than 90 percent of the surface of the world ocean. Water flows in large masses through the currents of the ocean, driven by energy from winds.

11.2 The neritic zone of the ocean lies between the shore and the edge of the continental shelf and accounts for about 8 percent of the world ocean. Reefs and estuaries are two types of ecosytems in the neritic zone. Neritic zones are more productive per square meter than is the open ocean because of the penetration of sunlight to the benthic zone.

11.3 The intertidal zone of the ocean is located along the shoreline and alternates between periods of exposure and periods of submersion. Salt marshes are a type of coastal wetland that exists in the intertidal zone in temperate regions. Salt marshes are common along the shores of estuaries. Mangrove swamps are coastal wetlands found in the intertidal zone of tropical regions. Mangrove swamps contain woody mangrove trees and shrubs.

MULTIPLE CHOICE

Choose the letter of the word or phrase that best completes each statement.

1. The oceanic zone is (a) mostly aphotic; (b) mostly photic; (c) mostly benthic; (d) mostly photic or aphotic, depending on the distance from shore. a

2. The main producers of the open ocean are (a) ocean plants; (b) symbiotic algae; (c) phytoplankton; (d) zooplankton. c

3. In terms of diversity, deep ocean habitats are similar to (a) rain forests; (b) deserts; (c) grasslands; (d) coral reefs. b

4. Ocean currents are driven by (a) wind energy; (b) gravity; (c) temperature differences; (d) density differences. a

5. The location of the neritic zone is determined by (a) water temperature; (b) the amount of sunlight; (c) productivity of the ecosystem; (d) the location of the continental shelf. d

6. Coral reefs are made of (a) sodium chloride; (b) calcium carbonate; (c) rock; (d) silica. b

7. Topsoil that washes onto a coral reef (a) makes the water less fertile; (b) is used as food for reef organisms; (c) helps protect the reef from the surf; (d) makes the water cloudier. d

8. The water in estuaries is usually (a) very salty; (b) as salty as the ocean; (c) brackish; (d) fresh water. c

9. Compared to a temperate deciduous forest of the same size, a swamp is about (a) twice as productive; (b) half as productive; (c) one-third as productive; (d) three times as productive. b

10. Sediment accumulation contributes to the formation of (a) salt marshes; (b) mangrove forests; (c) both salt marshes and mangrove forests; (d) neither salt marshes nor mangrove forests. c

11. You would be most likely to find a mangrove swamp along the shores of (a) Florida; (b) southern Argentina; (c) the Great Lakes; (d) Japan. a

WORD COMPARISONS

Write the letter of the second word pair that best matches the first pair.

1. Mangrove swamp: tropical water as (a) kelp reef: temperate water; (b) salt marsh: temperate water; (c) estuary: fresh water; (d) rain forest: land biomes. b

2. Sunlight: oceanic zone as (a) rain: desert; (b) sunlight: desert; (c) temperature: climate; (d) saltiness: estuary. a

3. Salt marsh: intertidal zone as (a) mangrove: neritic zone; (b) wetland: oceanic zone; (c) reef: intertidal zone; (d) estuary: neritic zone. d

4. Mangrove: swamp as (a) coral: reef; (b) sand: beach; (c) mud flat: salt marsh; (d) estuary: salt marsh. a

5. Wind: ocean currents as (a) heat: growth; (b) reefs: erosion; (c) sunlight: photosynthesis; (d) energy: light. c

CONCEPT REVIEW   Answers on page T67.

Write a complete response for each of the following.

1. Explain how topsoil erosion from nearby farmlands could affect a coral reef.

2. What factors contribute to the high productivity of neritic ecosystems? What is the effect of each of these factors?

3. What human activities result in the destruction of salt marshes? What are the benefits of these activities to humans?

4. How might building construction on temperate salt marshes affect the tundra ecosystem?

THINK CRITICALLY   Answers on page T67.

1. Many scientists predict that the level of water in the world ocean will rise as a result of global warming. How do you think a rise in sea level would affect the coral reefs of the world?

2. An island in the tropics routinely dumped sewage into the ocean several hundred meters offshore. After about 10 years, the coastline began to crumble, and large buildings along the shore washed into the ocean. What might have been the connection between the sewage and the collapse of the coastline?

3. Green peas help attract the colorful fish that live on coral reefs. Many areas now prohibit tourists from feeding peas to the fish. How might feeding peas to the fish affect the ecosystem?

WRITE FOR UNDERSTANDING

Suppose you read in the newspaper that the owner of a tropical resort is planning to dynamite the coral reef surrounding the resort in order to make a port for cruise ships to dock. Write a letter to the owner of the resort expressing your opinion of the plan.

PORTFOLIO

1. Compare the coral reef communities of at least two different regions of the world. What are the roles of the various organisms that occupy the reefs? What factors, if any, threaten the survival of the reefs you chose?

2. Greenpeace is a large citizens' action group. Research the various issues that the organization has been involved in. Decide whether you agree or disagree with their actions and present a persuasive report expressing your opinion.

Use the figure to answer the following.
1. Compare the graph on the right to the graph on p. 174. How can you explain the difference in open ocean productivity shown on the two graphs?
2. What can you deduce from the two graphs regarding the relative amount of farmland compared to deciduous forests worldwide? How did you reach this conclusion?
3. How would you expect the quantities shown on this graph to change during the next 10 years? Explain your answer.

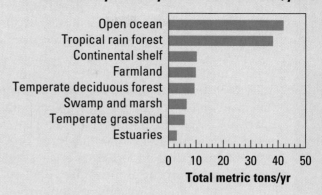

Productivity of ecosystems in metric tons/yr

ACTIVITY 11.2

PROBLEM
How is the metabolic rate of clams affected by water temperature?

MATERIALS (per group)
- biology references
- aged tap water
- salt
- balance
- 500-mL beaker
- 1-L beaker
- 2 jars
- pan of ice
- 2 thermometers
- food coloring
- 2 live clams

HYPOTHESIS
Write a hypothesis that is related to the problem.

PROCEDURE
1. Use reference sources to find out how clams obtain food.
2. To make seawater, add 35 g of salt to 1 L of aged tap water. Stir.
3. Add 500 mL of the seawater to each jar. Place a clam in each one. **Caution:** *Handle live animals with care and respect.* Place one of the jars in the pan of ice for 10 minutes.
4. After 10 minutes, measure the temperature of the water in each jar, and record the

data. Remove the jar from the pan.
5. Place a drop of food coloring next to the clam, about 1 cm away from the side of the shell that is pointed. Have your partner do the same for the other clam.
6. Each partner should look for colored water being forced out from the shell of the clam. A third partner should record the time that it takes for each clam to expel the colored water.

ANALYSIS
1. What was the temperature of the uncooled water? How long did it take for the clam to take in and expel the food coloring?
2. What was the temperature of the water that was cooled? How long did it take for the clam to take in and expel the food coloring at this temperature?

CONCLUSION
1. Did the results of this experiment support or refute your hypothesis? Explain.
2. How do you think the metabolic rates of clams at the bottom of shallow water compare to those of clams at the bottom of deeper water? Explain.

FORESTRY MANAGEMENT

In the past, a job in forestry management was a rather narrow profession, restricted to overseeing national and state parks or managing timberlands. Today, this job description has shifted dramatically, and the emphasis of forestry management is on integrating the uses of the forest. Forestry has become a diverse, specialized profession.

Forests cover about one third of the land in the United States. Those who choose a career in forestry management still care for our state and national parks, as well as privately owned timberlands. Foresters have also moved into the cities, caring for urban forests and wetland environments. They plan and supervise the growing, harvesting, and protecting of trees. They may concentrate on a particular segment of the forest, such as protecting the forest from fire or disease; studying insects; or specializing in forest economics, forest genetics, or hydrology. Foresters are also an integrated part of maintaining the rain forests, as well as supervising harvesting operations in developing nations.

About 45 percent of foresters today work for private-sector companies whose products are lumber, paper, and office supplies, pulpwood, and timber equipment and materials. About 26 percent of those in forestry management are employed by the federal government, where they balance forest preservation and commercial interests. These federal employees are members of the Forest Service, the Bureau of Land Management, the Soil Conservation Service, the National Park Service, the Bureau of Indian Affairs, and the Army Corps of Engineers. Government employees at the state and local level comprise about 17 percent of foresters. This is the fastest growing segment of forestry management. Ten percent of those in forestry management are educators, and about 2 percent are consulting foresters.

The best pathway to a career in forestry management blends education with experience. Most foresters obtain a bachelor's degree from one of the 45 colleges accredited by the Society of American Foresters. Students in these programs must hold at least one study position in field forestry. Students should also participate in other, similar positions whenever possible.

For students who seriously want to pursue a career in forestry management, graduate schools will open doors and allow them to focus on a chosen area. Many schools specialize in one particular application of forestry, such as economics, recreation, forestry ecology, or plant biology. Students are encouraged to talk with those already in the profession to learn about the best colleges and graduate schools in their special-interest areas.

A well-rounded education for a career in forestry management should also include a solid grasp of both oral and written communication, economics, political science, management and accounting skills, and a working knowledge of computer systems.

To obtain most full-time positions, seasonal or part-time experience is necessary. To get experience, volunteer for local forestry and environmental programs whenever possible. In addition to experience, you will acquire new, diverse skills while establishing valuable contacts.

FORESTRY CONSULTANTS ▶

Sometimes acting as brokers, forestry consultants manage timber sales for public and private agencies. They develop forest management plans for privately owned lands. And they supervise planting, spraying, and harvesting for smaller companies and agencies that do not have their own forestry specialists. Forestry consultants are also hired by municipalities when planning departments need forestry statements and inventories.

▲ NATURAL RESOURCE MANAGERS

In either the public or the private sector, natural resource managers have the responsibility of balancing forest preservation with the need to make some forestlands available for public use and sale. Natural resource managers ensure that the forest areas they oversee are environmentally healthy, growing and harvesting the optimum number of trees. They also make sure that an adequate percentage of the lands they oversee is set aside for preservation and public use.

URBAN FORESTERS ▼

One of the most rapidly growing jobs in forestry management, urban foresters and arborists work at the local level caring for trees and forests in their communities, which add beauty and enhance the quality of life in an area. Because trees play such a fundamental role in an ecosystem, urban foresters also help protect the air and water quality of their communities. Since mixed-use forests in urban areas cover more land than all of the forests managed by the Forest Service, Urban foresters have a big task.

FORESTRY TECHNICIANS ▲

Although not at the top of the pay scale in forestry management, forestry technicians perform the hands-on business of forestry management. They work as log scalers, timber cruisers, fire dispatchers, recreation area custodians, tree maintenance staff members, and research aides, spending the majority of their time out in the field.

FOR MORE INFORMATION:

American Forestry Association
(Regular publications include
the monthly magazine *American Forestry*)
P.O. Box 2000
Washington, DC 20013
(202) 667–3300

Opportunities in Forestry Careers, Christopher M. Wille.
Details how to become a forestry professional.
Published by VGM Career Horizons
4255 Touhy Avenue
Lincolnwood, IL 60646

Society of American Foresters
(Publications include
Journal of Forestry and Forest Science)
5400 Grosvenor Lane
Bethesda, MD 20814
(301) 897–8720

UNIT 4

PEOPLE IN THE GLOBAL ECOSYSTEM

CHAPTERS

12 People and Their Needs
13 Human Population
14 Feeding the World

ልጅ This word means *child*. It comes from Ethiopia. Currently, the human population is growing faster than at any other time in human history. The human population grew from 500 million in 1650 to about 5.5 billion in 1992. The sharp rise in population is due to advances in technology, agriculture, and medicine. The demand on Earth for natural resources has increased along with the population; this increased demand is a central cause of many environmental problems.

One thing that all families share is a line of descent ▶ from one generation to the next. The size of different generations is one factor determining the growth of a population. Population growth has a strong effect on the environment.

184

CHAPTER

12

PEOPLE AND THEIR NEEDS

12.1 A Portrait of Earth
12.2 Human Societies
12.3 Sustainable Development

In the 1600s, British philosopher John Locke wrote that people must be "emancipated from the bonds of nature," and that "the negation of nature is the way toward happiness." Locke's words express the attitude held by industrial societies, toward nature. In this view, the natural world is something to be conquered and consumed for the benefit of humans. People are seen as being separate from the natural world.

Most cultures do not share Locke's view of Earth. Many indigenous peoples view Earth as a living being. According to this viewpoint, people are a part of nature and just one of Earth's many interconnected communities.

12.1 A PORTRAIT OF EARTH

Objectives • *Describe* Earth as a network of systems and connections.
• *Explain* how Earth is closed with respect to matter, and open with respect to energy.

The first part of this textbook discusses how Earth functions. The lithosphere, hydrosphere, and atmosphere are the abiotic parts of the planet. Parts of these three spheres come together and form the biosphere, the zone that contains living things. The science of ecology studies the interactions between nonliving and living things in the biosphere. The interactions between living and nonliving factors gives rise to distinct ecosystems, called biomes. An understanding of these concepts, explained in Part 1, enables one to paint a portrait of Earth and how it functions.

Section 12.1 summarizes many of the concepts that appear in the first part of this text. If students have questions about the content of this section, refer them to the appropriate chapter in Part 1. The content in Part 1 is meant to serve as a reference when teaching Part 2. Use Part 1 to expand the class discussion on topics presented in Part 2.

Systems and Connections

The portrait of Earth outlined in Part I is one of *systems* and *connections*. There are many kinds of systems on Earth. One system is plate tectonics, the movement of the plates of Earth's crust over the mantle. Another system is ocean circulation, or the movement of water from one part of the ocean to another. Climate is determined largely by the interaction between the ocean, air, and land. Ecosystems are affected by all of these systems. Each system has its own interactions and is governed by the physical laws of energy and matter.

The connection between ecosystems and abiotic systems such as climate is very close. The characteristics of living things in each biome are determined largely by the temperature and precipitation in that biome. Other systems, such as ocean circulation and plate tectonics, are also linked to the world ecosystem. The movements of continents can change ocean basins and thus change the circulation of seawater. This change in circulation can lead to a change in climate and, therefore, to a change in the ecosystem

THINK CRITICALLY

Do you think that cutting down trees in a rain forest could affect the rainfall in a rainforest region? Explain your answer.

Yes. Transpiration from trees plays an important part in cloud formation in many rain forests. Removal of the trees results in a drier climate.

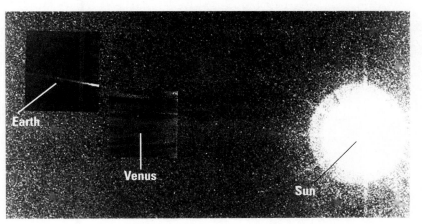

Figure 12.1 This group of photographs was taken by the Voyager 1 spacecraft from the edge of the solar system. Earth, like Venus, is a small planet circling an average star.

affected by the climate change. All the systems on Earth—from a community of insects and birds high in a rainforest tree to the movement of the continents—are connected.

Another way to think about Earth is in terms of matter and energy. Earth is a closed system with respect to matter. Only tiny amounts of matter leave or join Earth as it journeys through space. The planet is open, however, with respect to energy. Earth receives a huge amount of energy from the sun, and this energy eventually radiates back into space as heat. Some energy is reflected immediately by clouds and by the surface. However, the energy that is absorbed powers many of the planet's systems. The movement of ocean currents, the formation of clouds, and the growth of plants and animals are all powered by energy from the sun.

Connected systems of energy and matter form the portrait of Earth. The planet is made of various elements of matter. Energy from the sun moves this matter, organizing it and rearranging it through systems such as weather and ecosystems. Each system affects every other system because matter does not enter or leave Earth. Systems are connected through biotic and abiotic interactions. Every nonliving and living thing—including every human being—is a part of these systems.

Viewing Earth

As human societies have changed over thousands of years, ways of viewing Earth have changed as well. The perception of Earth as a living being is a view held by people in many cultures. However, in modern industrial society, humans are often seen as being apart from nature. Nature is something to be controlled and consumed.

Figure 12.2 This illustration shows the portrait of Earth. Earth is an open system with respect to energy, and a closed system with respect to matter. Energy from the sun powers cycles of matter on Earth.

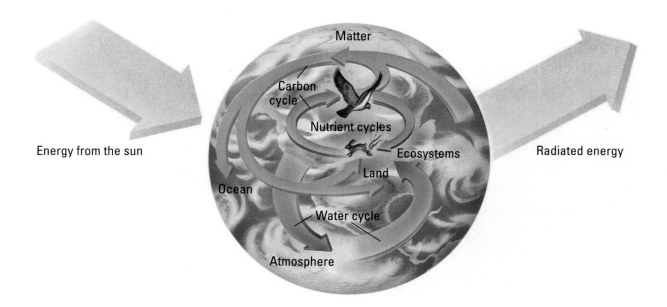

Energy from the sun

Radiated energy

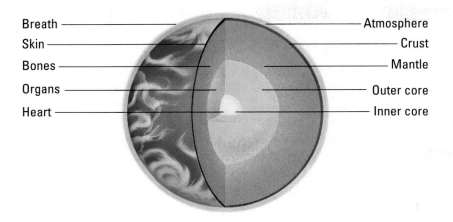

Breath — Atmosphere
Skin — Crust
Bones — Mantle
Organs — Outer core
Heart — Inner core

Figure 12.3 The Native-American view of Earth's structure and the scientific view are similar. Scientists have recently begun to notice the many parallels between the views of indigenous peoples and the emerging field of environmental science.

Many people view Earth as existing for human use. People are separate from the systems that govern the rest of the biosphere.

The modern industrial view does not match the portrait of Earth. Like any other population of organisms, humans are part of Earth's systems. The principles that govern lynx and hare populations in an ecosystem govern the human population as well. Scientists are now beginning to study these connections among systems.

In 1972, British scientist James Lovelock proposed a hypothesis called the Gaia hypothesis. *The* **Gaia** (GY-uh) **hypothesis** (hy-PAH-thih-sus) *states that Earth is a single, living organism that regulates itself to maintain life.* Lovelock's hypothesis reflected a view of Earth that many cultures have held for thousands of years. By proposing it as a scientific hypothesis, however, Lovelock introduced the idea of Earth as a living being into the minds of Western thinkers.

At first the Gaia hypothesis was not well received by most scientists. The difference between an organism and a planet was too great. But the Gaia hypothesis had a strong impact on the way scientists looked at the world. They began to look at the bigger picture and form connections between different systems of the biosphere. While the Gaia hypothesis may not be a proven scientific theory, its effect has been very important. Scientists are beginning to step back and view the portrait of Earth as a whole.

SECTION REVIEW

1. How could species in the rainforest canopy be affected by a moving continent?
2. Describe how Earth is a closed system with respect to matter, and an open system with respect to energy.
3. **Analyze** What is the Gaia hypothesis? Do you agree with it? Give reasons for your answers.

1. The organisms could be affected by a change in climate, such as decreased rainfall. A change in climate could be caused by a change in ocean currents, which could be caused by the shifting of a continent.
2. Earth is closed with respect to matter because essentially no matter enters or leaves Earth. It is open with respect to energy because large amounts of energy enter Earth from the sun and large amounts return to space.
3. The Gaia hypothesis is a theory proposed by Dr. James Lovelock. The theory states that Earth is a single, living organism. Student responses will vary, but conclusions should be supported with facts and logical reasoning.

12.2 HUMAN SOCIETIES

Objectives • *Identify* hunter–gatherer, agricultural, and industrial societies. • *Describe* how the impact of humans on the environment has increased over time.

Figure 12.4 This bushwoman is from the Kalahari Desert in South Africa. Almost all hunter–gatherer societies are threatened by the expansion of industrial societies.

Human beings have lived on Earth for a long time. Fully modern *Homo sapiens* first evolved from ancestral humans about 100,000 years ago. Scientists know very little about these early people, called Cro-Magnons. All that remain of the Cro-Magnons are a few bones, artifacts such as tools and jewelry, and haunting cave paintings such as those at Lascaux, in France. These humans were as intelligent as modern humans. Their tools are intricate and finely made, and the cave paintings and other art show they had an artistic and spiritual sense.

Since the time of the Cro-Magnons, people have devised many different ways of solving the problems of survival. These strategies for living on Earth can be divided into three main categories: hunter–gatherer, agricultural, and industrial. These are broad categories, and no human society fits perfectly into any one of them. However, the categories do describe three general ways of dealing with the problems of survival.

Hunter–Gatherer Societies

A **hunter–gatherer society** *is a society in which people gather natural food, hunt, and are nomadic.* Nomadic people do not settle permanently in one place. Hunter–gatherers usually do not plant crops. They gather naturally occurring plant food and hunt wild animals. Many hunter–gatherer cultures have lasted into modern times, although most have been destroyed or are threatened by modern civilization.

Hunter–gatherer cultures have a small impact on the environment because their population density is low. Hunter–gatherers take advantage of the resources they find and then move on. Their low population density allows the environment time to regenerate. A hunter–gatherer society lives within the ability of the land to sustain it. It can survive indefinitely unless it is disturbed from outside.

Agricultural Societies

Between 10,000 and 20,000 years ago, peoples from Southeast Asia and Africa developed a new strategy for living. They began to plant crops and raise animals for food. Farming caused two changes in the way the people lived their lives. The first was that many people stopped roaming and settled permanently. The second was that people began to divide the work among members of society.

One important invention during the rise of agriculture was the plow. The plow enabled people to plant more land and grow more food. The plow and the domestication of animals caused a large increase in the food supply. The human population began to grow.

Because farming produced a relatively large amount of food, some people did not have to farm at all. They began to form cities and to engage in crafts and manufacturing. The concept of trade developed to control the movement of food into the city and finished goods out of the city. *A society in which crops are grown and people have specialized roles is called an* **agricultural society**. Figure 12.5 shows some places where agriculture began and the locations of some early civilizations. Agricultural societies are not "better" than other societies. They simply deal with the problems of survival in a different manner.

The new agricultural societies harmed the environment. Increasing populations caused more environmental damage. Increased logging, overgrazing, and poor farming practices also led to the loss of soil and vegetation because the agricultural societies did not move often. The environment had little chance to regenerate. The loss of vegetation often led to changing rainfall patterns, and fertile land turned into desert.

Industrial Societies

Another strategy for dealing with the problems of survival arose in the 1700s. In England and later in the rest of Europe and the United States, the production of goods switched from skilled craftspeople to machines. Coal-fired steam engines powered factories that mass-produced clothes and other products. The demand for energy and raw materials increased. Machines became common on farms as well, and food production increased greatly. *A society in which the production of food and other products is performed by machines, demanding large amounts of energy and resources, is called an* **industrial society**.

DATELINE 1600 B.C.

The Babylonian Empire fell to invading armies. The empire had been weakened after overgrazing, poor farming methods, and excessive timber cutting caused soil erosion and the formation of deserts on once-fertile land. The lack of food and wood helped weaken the empire to a point where it could be conquered by armies of the Hittites.

✿ Multicultural Perspective
Many crops were developed and cultivated by the Maya and other civilizations in the Americas. Corn, potatoes, tomatoes, squash, chocolate, avocados, and peppers are just a few of these crops. Today, corn is one of the world's most important food crops. It is a food staple in regions of North America, South America, and Africa.

Figure 12.5 Agriculture first appeared 10,000 to 20,000 years ago. This new strategy for meeting the needs of people arose in many different cultures and made use of many different crops.

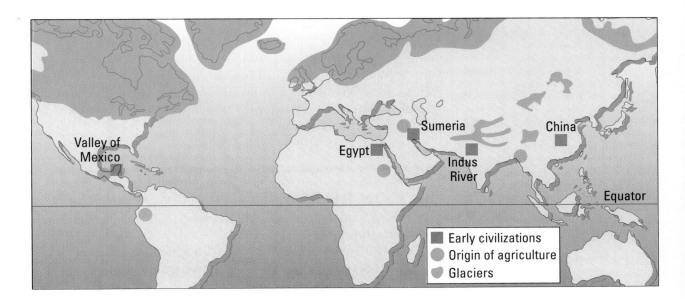

Table 12.1   Characteristics of Human Societies

	Hunter–Gatherer	Agricultural	Industrial
Lifestyle	Mostly nomadic	Permanently settled	Often permanently settled
Technology	Simple tools and weapons.	The plow and agriculture. Cities allow the advance of technology, simple machines.	Mass production based on large amounts of energy and materials. Advanced technology, biotechnology, nuclear weapons.
Resource use	Use sustained by the environment.	Some overuse of soil, forest, other resources. Sometimes sustainable.	Overuse of soil, forest, mineral resources. Not sustainable.
Environmental knowledge	Intimate knowledge of the environment.	Knowledge of the environment, farm organisms.	Generally little or no environmental knowledge.
Health	Healthy lives, well fed, low disease rates. High infant mortality, short lifespan.	Healthy, usually well fed, diseases common in cities.	Pollution is health threat. Stress-related illnesses are common. Medical advances increase lifespan.
Environmental impact	Use of fire causes some environmental damage.	Overgrazing, poor farming methods, timber cutting cause widespread damage.	Damage caused by industry, large population, high energy use. Global ecosystem threatened.
Energy use	Small energy use; fuel is wood.	Larger energy use. Fuel is wood, wind, water, animal power, some coal.	Very large energy use. Fuel is fossil fuels, hydroelectric, nuclear, and other.

The rise of industry was accompanied by advances in other areas. Scientists began to breed plant varieties to increase crop yield. Advances in medicine helped people live longer. Because of the increased food supply and better medical care, the human population began to grow very quickly.

Increases in production, energy use, and the human population led to severe environmental damage. This damage continues today. Pollution of the air, land, and water is a widespread problem. Raw materials are running out, and the actions of human beings are affecting the composition of the atmosphere and the global climate. The environmental damage caused by industrial societies is a principal theme of this book.

1. The plow increased agricultural production.
2. Answers should come from Table 12.1. Some differences are technological advances, permanent settlements, and the pronounced division of labor in the society.
3. The most important reason is lower population density. Less people cause less damage. Industrial societies also cause more damage because they pollute and consume large amounts of raw materials.

SECTION REVIEW

1. What technological advance increased food production in all agricultural societies?
2. How do an industrial society and an agricultural society differ?
3. **Infer** Give three reasons why hunter–gatherer societies generally cause less environmental damage than industrial societies.

Conflict for a Tribal People

What is the future for the Wayana Indians?

Imagine that you stand among the rainforest trees along the edge of the Maroni River in French Guiana in South America. You see a dugout canoe. The male passengers wear *kalimbe*, a traditional red loincloth drawn between the legs and fastened at the waist. The women wear *weyu*, an apron of the same brilliant red color. This is the dress of the Wayana tribal people. But you notice something odd about the scene. The canoe is propelled by an outboard motor!

The Wayana population once numbered in the thousands. Their numbers dwindled to about 500 after outsiders exposed the native people to tuberculosis, measles, pneumonia, and other diseases. Increased medical care for the Wayana from the French government halted the spread of the deadly diseases. Their numbers climbed to almost 1,000. However, another invader now threatens the Wayana—the breakdown of traditional life from increasing exposure to the outside world.

The Wayana people are skilled at living in the rain forest. They gather wild berries, nuts, grubs, and eggs. They farm small plots of land and hunt for iguanas and other animals. Their knowledge of the rain forest is essential for survival. For this reason, many Wayana men become employed as guides by exploration teams searching for minerals and other natural resources. Money earned from guiding explorers enables the Wayana to buy modern conveniences, such as outboard motors, guns, radios, clothing, toys, and kitchenware. This infiltration is changing the traditional lifestyle.

The introduction of rum has brought alcoholism to many Wayana families. Alcohol is not new to the tribal people. The Wayana have a traditional brew called *kasili* made from manioc root. Kasili is a very mild drink, but rum is much stronger. The Wayana are accustomed to the mild effect of kasili, but they are not used to the effects of the strong rum they get from river traders.

The effects of the outside world may be even more devastating to Wayana youth. Since 1971, tourists have been allowed to visit two Wayana villages. The tourists visiting the villages treat the tribal people like zoo animals, having them pose for photographs and giving them treats such as candy and cigarettes. The effect on the Wayana is degrading. This demeaning of their cultural ways is witnessed by tribal youth, who are increasingly taking on Western habits, such as wearing clothes, listening to rock music, and

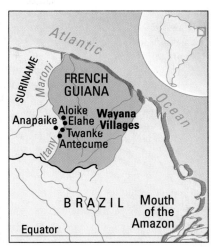

smoking cigarettes. Even children as young as age 5 will puff a cigarette if one is available.

The conflict between the tribal ways and the modern world deeply distresses young people. After a celebration that combined the two worlds, an 18-year-old Wayana youth tried to kill himself. He said that he could no longer cope with the problems confronting him. Suicide is new to the Wayana. During the same year that the young man attempted suicide, three other Wayana youths succeeded in ending their confused lives.

DECISIONS

1. Describe three ways that modern culture has infiltrated the Wayana people.
2. What do you think is the future for the Wayana people? Why?

193

12.3 SUSTAINABLE DEVELOPMENT

Objectives • *Define the frontier ethic and the sustainable development ethic.* • *Describe the differences between a renewable and a nonrenewable resource.*

The concept of a *resource* is common in industrial societies. Oil and coal are resources, as are minerals and trees. Books and people are also resources. But what exactly is a resource? The dictionary defines a resource as "something that lies ready for use". The idea of a resource is therefore a part of industrial culture, and the assumptions behind this term help illustrate the way in which industrial societies view the world. Viewing Earth as a pile of resources that lie ready for use by humans has led to many of the environmental problems that challenge the world today.

The Frontier Ethic

An *ethic* is a set of standards or rules, that serves as a guideline for determining what is right and what is wrong. Every society has a system of ethics; they are the rules by which the society operates. *The system of ethics in the modern industrial society is the* **frontier ethic***, which is based on the view that humans are separate from nature.* The frontier ethic has three rules:
- Resources are unlimited and meant for human consumption.
- Humans are separate from nature and do not obey natural laws.
- Human success is measured in terms of control over the natural world.

The first two rules of the frontier ethic are false in view of the portrait of Earth. Resources are not unlimited because Earth is not infinitely large. In addition, the consumption of resources has an impact on other organisms. Humans are also animals, and they are a part of nature. A population of human animals obeys the same laws as any other population. It has a carrying capacity and is affected by limiting factors. Humans are a part of nature's systems and connections.

The third rule of the frontier ethic is a statement of values. Success is defined differently by each person. Yet another look at the portrait of Earth reveals that viewing human control over nature as success may be dangerous. This view ignores what scientists know about how Earth functions. In response, many people are now forming a new ethic. This new set of rules better reflects the way Earth functions.

The Sustainable Development Ethic

The new ethic of the environment is called sustainable development. *The* **sustainable development ethic** *is an ethic that meets the current needs of society without limiting the ability of future generations to*

Word Power

Ethics, from the Greek *ethos*, "disposition" or "character."

FIELD ACTIVITY

Form groups of two or three. Take a notebook and pencil and look for evidence of the frontier ethic around your school, outside your school, or in your home. Make a list of ten observations that seem to support one of the three basic rules of the frontier ethic. When each group has finished its list, each student should write a short essay stating what an ethic is, what the frontier ethic is, and how the frontier ethic appears in his or her life.

You may wish to repeat this activity with the sustainable development ethic. A comparison of student observations will then be an excellent review for these two concepts.

Figure 12.6 These oil wells were damaged in the Persian Gulf War. Damage like this led to massive pollution of the air, land, and ocean. Conflicts over resources and the hunger of industrial societies for raw materials and energy have made scenes like this more and more common.

meet their needs. It relies on reducing demand, recycling, conservation, and the wise use of resources. Like the frontier ethic, the sustainable development ethic can be summarized in three basic components:

- Resources are limited and are not all meant for human consumption.
- Humans are part of nature and obey natural laws.
- Human success is living in harmony with the natural world.

The rules of the sustainable development ethic contrast with the rules of the frontier ethic that currently governs industrial societies. Sustainable development is an ethic that can help ensure that the human future on this planet is a pleasant one. This ethic reflects the way Earth functions.

All materials used to build societies are limited. But some materials, such as wood, animals, and plants, can regenerate fairly quickly. Other materials, such as minerals and oil, regenerate very slowly, if at all. A resource that regenerates quickly is called a *renewable resource*. A resource that does not regenerate quickly is called a *nonrenewable resource*. Industrial societies are based on the use of nonrenewable resources. They cannot continue to grow or survive forever. The ethic of sustainable development is based on the use of renewable resources and on conservation. A society based on the sustainable development ethic should be able to survive indefinitely.

SECTION REVIEW

1. What is the frontier ethic?
2. How does the sustainable development ethic differ from the frontier ethic?
3. **Apply** List ten ways you can implement sustainable development in your life.

Answers and teaching
strategies on page T72.

A Nonrenewable Resource

PROBLEM
Will the world's zinc reserves run out?

MATERIALS (per group)
- reference sources
- 152 paper clips
- watch or clock with a second hand

PREDICTION
Read the entire activity, then write a sentence
that predicts the outcome of the experiment.

PROCEDURE
1. Use reference sources to find out about
   industrial uses for zinc.
2. Copy the data table on a separate sheet of
   paper. Add rows as needed.
3. Each person in the group will play a different role in this model.
   a. The Zinc Reserves person gets 120
      of the paper clips and places them in a
      pile. This pile represents zinc that can be
      economically recovered from Earth.
   b. The Natural Processes person gets
      32 paper clips. These represent metals
      or metal compounds in the ground
      that will form new ores, adding to
      the Zinc Reserves.
   c. The World Need person will acquire
      paper clips throughout the model from
      the Zinc Reserves person to represent
      ore that has been mined.
   d. The Timekeeper will announce the time

every 15 seconds throughout the
model.
4. When the first 15 seconds have passed,
   Natural Processes adds a paper clip to
   Zinc Reserves' pile. Natural Processes
   will continue to do this every 15 seconds throughout the model.
5. At the end of the first minute, World Need
   removes 1 paper clip from Zinc Reserves.
   At the end of each succeeding minute,
   World Need will double, so remove twice
   as many paper clips as were removed in
   the preceding minute. The model is over
   when Zinc Reserves can no longer meet
   World Need.
6. As the model proceeds, record the
   world status during each minute in the
   data table. Each minute represents five
   years into the future. Each paper clip
   represents 2 million metric tons of zinc.
7. Plot Zinc Reserves and World Need over
   the next 50 years on a graph.

ANALYSIS
1. What are some of the industrial uses
   for zinc?
2. How is the world's need for zinc
   increasing? How much zinc will be
   needed in 15 years? In 30 years?

CONCLUSION
Can the world's zinc reserves run out? If
you answer no, explain why not. If you
answer yes, state when, and describe the
possible effects.

World Status of Zinc

Minutes Elapsed	Zinc Reserves at Start of Minute	Input from Natural Processes	World Need	Zinc Reserves at End of Minute
1	120	+4	−1	123

CHAPTER 12 REVIEW

KEY TERMS

Gaia hypothesis 12.1
hunter–gatherer
   society 12.2

agricultural
   society 12.2

industrial society 12.2

frontier ethic 12.3
sustainable develop-
   ment ethic 12.3

CHAPTER SUMMARY

12.1 The portrait of Earth is one of systems and connections. All the systems on Earth are connected to all others, and almost all systems are powered by the sun. Earth is an open system with respect to energy and a closed system with respect to matter. The one-way flow of energy drives cycles of matter on Earth's surface. The Gaia hypothesis states that Earth is a single living being.

12.2 Modern humans first evolved on Earth 100,000 years ago. Humans have developed many strategies for dealing with the challenge of survival. These strategies can be placed in three categories: hunter–gatherer, agricultural, and industrial. The environmental damage that each of these strategies causes is related directly to population density and resource use. The total amount of damage has increased over time.

12.3 Societies use ethics to determine what is right and what is wrong. Modern industrial societies have a frontier ethic. In the frontier ethic, resources are thought to be unlimited, and people are seen as being separate from nature. The frontier ethic does not reflect the way Earth functions. A new ethic called sustainable development is on the rise. This ethic reflects a society that can last indefinitely.

MULTIPLE CHOICE

Choose the letter of the word or phrase that best completes each statement.

1. Earth is an open system with respect to
   (a) matter; (b) energy; (c) information;
   (d) people. b
2. Earth is a closed system with respect to (a) matter; (b) energy; (c) information; (d) people. a
3. The Gaia hypothesis states that Earth is a
   (a) nonliving planet; (b) nonliving planet with living parts; (c) nonliving being;
   (d) living being. d
4. Modern humans have lived on Earth for about (a) 1000 years; (b) 10,000 years;
   (c) 100,000 years; (d) 1 million years. c
5. Hunter–gatherer societies are often (a) nomadic; (b) semipermanent; (c) permanent;
   (d) very dense. a

6. An early invention that helped raise food production in agricultural societies was
   (a) mass production; (b) gunpowder;
   (c) sustainable development; (d) the plow. d
7. Industrial societies were made possible by inventions such as the steam engine and
   (a) mass production; (b) gunpowder;
   (c) sustainable development; (d) the plow. a
8. A renewable resource is one that regenerates (a) slowly; (b) not at all; (c) quickly;
   (d) without human action. c
9. A nonrenewable resource is one that regenerates (a) only after human action;
   (b) slowly or not at all; (c) quickly; (d) without human action. b
10. An ethic is a set of rules in a society that determines (a) right and wrong; (b) holidays;
    (c) economic function; (d) government. a

CHAPTER 12 REVIEW

TRUE/FALSE

Write true *if the statement is true. If the statement is false, change the underlined word to make it true.*

1. Almost no <u>energy</u> enters or leaves Earth. f, matter
2. The Gaia hypothesis states that Earth is a <u>nonliving being</u>. f, living being
3. The major source of energy in hunter–gatherer societies is <u>wood</u>. t
4. <u>Industrial</u> societies use more energy per person than any other society. t
5. Agricultural societies often cause <u>more</u> damage to the environment than hunter–gatherer societies. t
6. People in hunter–gatherer societies are generally <u>less healthy</u> than people in agricultural societies. f, as or more healthy
7. The <u>sustainable development</u> ethic holds that humans are separate from nature and immune to nature's laws. f, frontier
8. Oil is an example of a <u>renewable</u> resource. f, nonrenewable

CONCEPT REVIEW Answers on page T72

Write a complete response for each of the following.

1. What is the Gaia hypothesis?
2. Which factor is most important in determining the amount of environmental damage caused by a society?
3. Which inventions led to the formation of industrial societies?
4. What environmental factors contributed to the fall of the Babylonian Empire?
5. Write a short essay in which you define the following terms: ethic, frontier ethic, sustainable development ethic. Use your own words as you describe each term.

THINK CRITICALLY Answers on page T72

1. Do you think the Gaia hypothesis is valid? Give reasons explaining your answer.
2. The human population has grown much more quickly during the last 200 years than at any other time in human history. List some reasons for this sudden increase in the growth rate.
3. What do you think will happen to the culture of the Wayana Indians if industrial societies continue to disturb it?
4. Write a paragraph stating the similarities and differences between renewable and nonrenewable resources.

WRITE CREATIVELY

Reread the short essay you wrote in response to Question 5 in the Concept Review section. Then write a longer essay expressing how you feel about the concept of ethics, and how ethics relate to you personally. Do the ethics of a society always reflect the personal ethics of the people in the society? How can people work to change a prevailing view with which they disagree?

PORTFOLIO

1. Take photographs of five objects or activities that embody the ethic of sustainable development.
2. Use pencils, paint, computer drawing programs, videotape, or other media to create your own portrait of Earth. Emphasize the systems and connections on Earth in your portrait. How do people fit into your portrait?

GRAPHIC ANALYSIS Answers on page T72

Use Figure 12.5 to answer the following.

1. In what area did most agriculture and early civilizations arise?
2. Why did no civilizations appear in the far north of Europe or North America?
3. Do the origins of agriculture and early civilizations seem to be related? How?
4. Did agriculture tend to arise near water, or in the center of continents away from water? Can you explain this pattern?
5. Humans first evolved in Africa. How do you think humans traveled to the Americas?

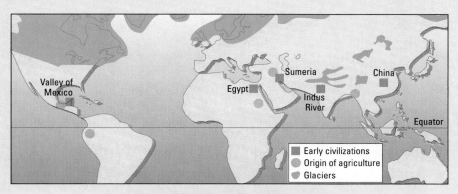

Valley of Mexico
Egypt
Sumeria
Indus River
China
Equator

■ Early civilizations
● Origin of agriculture
● Glaciers

ACTIVITY 12.2

Answers and teaching strategies on page T72.

PROBLEM

How does the availability of food affect a population?

MATERIALS (per group)

- scissors
- Petri dish with lid
- paper towel
- dropper
- fresh green leaf
- cotton-tip swab
- 5 aphids

INFERENCE

Read the entire activity, then write an inference that is related to the problem.

PROCEDURE

1. Cut a piece of paper towel to fit the bottom of the Petri dish, and place it there.
2. Use the dropper to moisten the paper towel with water. Place a green leaf in the Petri dish.
3. Take the Petri dish and its lid outside to an area designated by your instructor. Find a plant that has aphids on it. Use the cotton-tip swab to transfer five aphids to the Petri dish. Cover it and return to the classroom. *Note: Aphids suck juices from plant stems and leaves. Look for aphids on both sides of the leaves.*
4. Each day for the next 2 weeks, lift the lid and count the number of living aphids. Be sure to check both sides of the leaf. Record the number of aphids each day. Make a graph to show any population changes over the 2 weeks.

ANALYSIS

1. Did the number of aphids change from day to day during the 2 weeks? What caused the changes?
2. What might the aphids and the leaf represent? How did changes in the aphid population affect the population later on?

CONCLUSION

What inference did you make at the beginning of this activity? Do your observations support it? Explain.

CHAPTER

13

HUMAN POPULATION

Much attention is currently given to the question of human population growth. In 1650, only about 500 million people inhabited Earth. Today, there are over 5.5 billion people living on this planet, and that number increases by about 80 million every year. Many of the environmental problems discussed in this book can be traced indirectly to this population increase. Scientists predict that if current trends continue, the human population could be 8 billion by 2017, and perhaps 12 billion by 2100. How will such a large population impact Earth's ability to provide the resources necessary for the continuation of the human species?

13.1 HISTORY OF THE HUMAN POPULATION

Objective • *Describe* the major events that have affected the rate of human population growth throughout history.

The issue of overpopulation has been a subject of concern for at least four centuries. In the 1500s, English statesman Thomas More portrayed the ideal state in his book *Utopia*. In More's ideal state, population is kept constant, crops are controlled, and food is distributed at public markets and in common dining halls. Robert Wallace, an eighteenth century English writer, argued that even if a perfect society could be established, Earth would be "unable to support its numerous inhabitants."

Some of the most well known ideas about population growth in the past two centuries were proposed by British economist Thomas Malthus. In his first published book, written in 1798, Malthus stated that population growth was not always desirable. Malthus pointed out that populations tend to increase geometrically (1, 2, 4, 8, 16. . .) whereas the food supply tends to increase arithmetically (1, 2, 3, 4, 5. . .). The human population, therefore, has the potential to increase at a much faster rate than the food supply. Malthus believed that the tendency of the human population to outgrow its resources led to such conditions as famine, war, and other human suffering.

Increases in Growth Rate

Scientists estimate that the first modern humans evolved on Earth approximately one-half million years ago. Scientists can only guess about population size and growth during the early stages of human history. However, there is some agreement that during this time, the population consisted of hunter–gatherers who lived in small families or tribal groups.

When humans roamed the forests and plains as hunter–gatherers, populations grew slowly. Starvation, predation, and disease kept the death rate fairly high, and the infant death rate was very high as well. About 20,000 years ago, some people began to establish permanent settlements. Evidence suggests that although these people did not cultivate food, they did store the food they gathered. Food storage reduced starvation and the death rate. As a result, the relationship between birth and death rates changed.

Agriculture A second period of major population growth occurred around 8000 B.C. This period of history was marked by the agricultural revolution. *During the* **agricultural revolution**, *hunter–gatherers began to develop farming skills and techniques, and*

BIOLOGY LINK

In 1838, the ideas of Malthus greatly impressed a young naturalist named Charles Darwin who had recently returned from a sailing trip around the world. Malthus's idea that populations tend to outgrow their resources became a major point in Darwin's theory of evolution by natural selection. According to Darwin's theory, organisms produce many more offspring than can survive. Within the population there are a variety of traits. Those individuals with the most favorable traits are the ones that survive and pass their traits to their offspring. Over many generations, favorable traits accumulate in the population, resulting in evolution.

Cooperative Learning
Have students work in small groups to conduct research on the evolutionary history of humans. Have students create a visual that identifies the different hominid species, their characteristics, and when they lived. Have students predict the types of societies in which members of each hominid group lived.

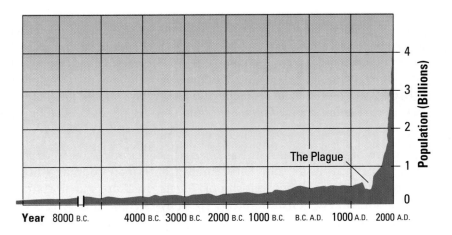

Figure 13.1 The human population grew slowly and irregularly for thousands of years. The growth rate has been geometric since the industrial revolution.

FIELD ACTIVITY

What was the population of your city, town, or community 50 years ago? 100 years ago? Use library or town hall resources to find out the history of population change in your town or the nearest large city. What factors accounted for the changes?

Teaching tips for Field Activity appear on page T76.

Multicultural Perspective
Point out to students that although most hunter–gather societies evolved into agricultural and industrial societies, some peoples still live as hunter-gatherers. Locations of such societies include the Kalahari of Africa and the Guayami of Panama. Some anthropologists consider peoples living in such societies to be an endangered species.

learned to domesticate animals. As agriculture became a dominant means of obtaining food, the nomadic hunter–gatherer societies were gradually replaced by small farm communities, each with its own social structure. Farming provided an increased food supply, which led to an increase in the size of the human population.

Shortly after the start of the agricultural revolution, the human population grew to nearly 5 million. Food availability accounted for much of the growth. In addition, social structure caused a general rise in the standard of living. These changes reduced mortality rates and increased life expectancy.

Industry   The third major period of population growth has occurred during the past 300 years. This period of history, marked by the industrial revolution, has included a number of events that favor population growth. Technological advancements have improved food production and distribution, reduced the length of the work day, and provided people with safer work environments. In addition to a greater availability of goods and materials, there have been major advances in the areas of health care and medicine.

Health Care   The development of the germ theory of disease occurred at about the same time as the industrial revolution. *The* **germ theory** *of disease identified bacteria and other microorganisms* (MY-kro-OR-guhn-izuhms) *as the agents responsible for many diseases.* Before the development of the germ theory, people did not recognize the connection between health and hygiene. The germ theory resulted in improved hygiene, sterile surgery, better methods of waste disposal, and water treatment. These developments reduced the death rate, particularly among infants and children.

The biomedical revolution of the twentieth century has also resulted in an increase in population growth. During this revolution, death rates continue to decrease as health and hygiene improve. The discovery of antibiotics and vaccines has wiped out or controlled many life-threatening diseases. At the same time, birth rates have increased due to better prenatal care.

Declines in Growth Rate

Throughout most of human history, the human population has been increasing. However, population growth has not always been steady and uninterrupted. If you look at the growth curve in Figure 13.1, you will observe a sharp decline in population growth during the mid-fourteenth century. This decline is a result of the bubonic plague, or Black Death, that struck much of Europe and Asia. The plague may have killed more people than any other single disease. So devastating was the plague that within several years it claimed the lives of more than 25 percent of the adult population of Central Europe and Asia. The population of England was reduced by about 50 percent between 1348 and 1379. In addition to the plague, worldwide outbreaks of cholera, typhus, malaria, yellow fever, and smallpox claimed hundreds of thousands of lives. The more densely populated cities became, the more quickly diseases spread.

Figure 13.2 The death and despair brought on by the bubonic plague were common themes in the art of the middle ages.

Famine Famine can also devastate human populations. The Irish Potato Famine of the 1840s resulted in the death of more than one million people. At this time, the potato was a main food staple in Ireland. A disease called potato blight destroyed the potato crop, resulting in severe starvation. A famine in China during 1877–1888 was responsible for more than 9 million deaths.

War Wars have a destructive affect on human populations. Combat can claim many lives in a short time period. Other factors that reduce populations, such as disease, famine, and environmental destruction, are also the results of military activities. Cutting off food supplies is a common tactic among warring groups. Examples of wars that have taken enormous tolls on human life include the Thirty Years' War (1618–1648), when about one-third of the inhabitants of Germany and Bohemia were killed. Historically, many lives have also been lost in tribal and civil wars throughout Africa, India, China, South America, and the United States. World War I claimed an estimated 10 million lives, while nearly 17 million people died as a result of World War II.

Discuss the effects that military devices and weaponry (chemical, biological, and nuclear) have on combatants, civilians, and future generations. You may wish to have students research the effects of such weaponry as it relates to Hiroshima, Nagasaki, Viet Nam, and the Persian Gulf War of 1991.

SECTION REVIEW

1. What changes in human society occurred during the agricultural revolution?
2. What are some factors that can result in a decline in human populations?
3. **Analyze** If the human population increased arithmetically instead of geometrically, would the potential for an overpopulation problem still exist? Explain your answer.

1. People developed farming skills and domesticated animals.
2. Responses should include famine, war, and disease.
3. The human population would still outgrow its resources over time, but the amount of time it would take for this to occur would be longer.

13.2 GROWTH AND CHANGING NEEDS

Objectives • *Compare* and *contrast* population growth trends in developing and industrialized nations. • *Infer* reasons why emigration is higher in developing nations than in industrialized nations.

Overpopulation is one of the most serious problems facing people. Scientists argue that overpopulation threatens the continued existence of humans on Earth. In addition, they suggest that many of the most significant environmental problems we now face may never be resolved unless worldwide population growth trends are not only slowed, but reversed.

Measuring Growth Rate

Determining the rate of population growth is helpful for scientists, urban planners, and others who have to anticipate the needs of the population of the future. Growth rates are determined by subtracting the death rate (number of deaths per one thousand people) from the birth rate (number of births per one thousand people). For example, in 1989 the birth rate in Egypt was 38 births per 1,000 people. The death rate was 9 deaths per 1,000 people. Thus, the population grew at a rate of 29 persons per 1,000 people, or 2.9 percent (2.9 persons per 100 people).

The doubling time of a population indicates how long it will take, at the present rate of growth, before a particular population doubles its size. The populations of some cities and countries have doubled in 10 years or less. The population of Mexico City doubled between 1960 and 1970, and doubled again by 1980. The populations of entire countries, such as Peru, Kenya, Syria, Iran, and Guatemala, are currently doubling in less than 30 years.

Doubling time can be used to illustrate the negative potential of uncontrolled population growth. For example, consider the need to double housing, food supplies, jobs, education, water, energy, and

SOCIAL STUDIES LINK

Most governments conduct a survey called a census every few years to determine the size of the population. Censuses were conducted by the First Emperor of China during his reign from 259-210 B.C. A census is conducted by the U.S. government every ten years to determine the age, sex, employment, and other data about the population. The information is used to determine such things as the number of representatives for each state in the House of Representatives.

Table 13.1 Doubling Time of the Human Population

Year	Approximate population size	Doubling time (in years)
8000 B.C.	5 million	1,500
1550 A.D.	500 million	200
1850	1 billion	80
1930	2 billion	45
1975	4 billion	36
2017 (projected)	8 billion	42

health facilities, just to maintain the present standard of living. Then consider the challenge of attempting to improve that standard of living in the same time period.

When measuring the growth rate of a specific population, births and deaths are not the only factors to be considered. Immigration and emigration can also affect the size of a population. Immigration is the movement of individuals into an area, while emigration is movement out of an area. When determining the size of the human population in a specific area such as a city or nation, the factors of immigration and emigration must be considered. When studying the size of the entire population of Earth, however, these factors do not apply. Humans cannot leave the planet, nor can newcomers arrive from elsewhere.

Demography

When scientists, planners, and policy makers study populations, they need to know not only how many people there are, but also what types of people make up the population. By including such information in their studies, scientists can determine how the population is changing. Are people becoming older, richer, or better educated? Are they having more children? Are there more women than men? These questions can be answered by demographic studies. *The science of the changing vital statistics in a human population is called* **demography** (de-MAH-gruh-fee). Figure 13.3 shows the demographic statistics of population ages in three nations: one growing quickly (Mexico), one growing slowly (United States), and one that is not growing at all (Sweden). Notice how much younger

Have students think about and discuss why the U.S. government may want to know about the age, sex, and employment of the population, and how this information might be used.

Word Power

Demography from the Greek *demos*, "the people," and *graphein* "to write."

Figure 13.3 These charts show the percentage of the population in each age group of three nations: one growing rapidly (Mexico), one growing slowly (U.S.), and one that is not growing at all (Sweden). The darkly shaded areas show people in their child-bearing years.

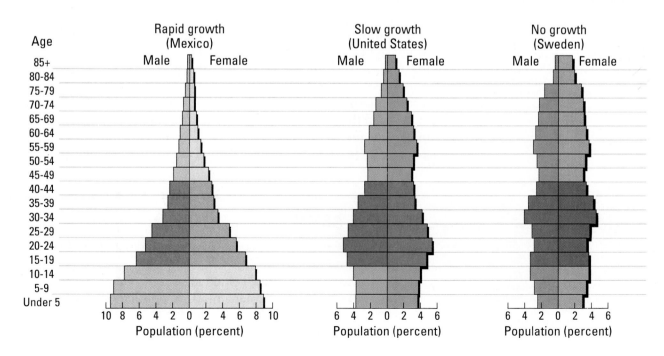

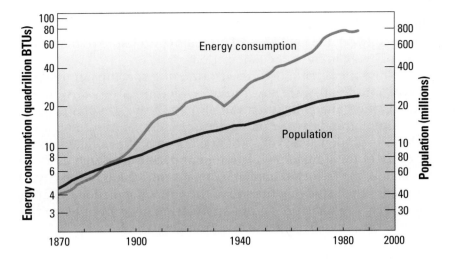

Figure 13.4 During the 1900s, the energy consumption of the United States grew faster than the population. What do you think was the reason for the drop in energy use in the 1930s? [the Depression]

the population of Mexico is compared to Sweden. The information in these graphs is much more useful than a simple number showing population size. With the additional information, plans can be made to accommodate the future needs for child care, care for the elderly, and other groups.

Changing Needs

It is not difficult to understand that a society with more people has greater needs than a society with fewer people. However, population size is not the only factor that determines the needs of a society. Changes in technology, lifestyles, and standards of living all affect the needs and consumption rates of a population. Notice the change in energy use during the past 150 years in the United States, as shown in Figure 13.5. The energy use far outpaced the population growth. Much of this change in usage was due to the increased industrialization and modernization of the American lifestyle. Industrial societies generally use more resources than underdeveloped societies. As more nations of the world develop into industrialized nations, their needs can be expected to increase faster than the population increases. Ironically, it is the least developed nations of the world that are expected to experience the greatest increase in population during the coming decades.

Discuss with students how the trend toward "western" tastes and lifestyles has impacted the emigration of peoples from developing nations to industrialized nations, as well as how such tastes exemplify the frontier mentality in terms of wastefulness. You may wish to have students conduct research on the immigration of the "Boat People" of Viet Nam to the United States, as well as the mass immigration of Chinese and Haitian peoples to the United States in 1993. Have students identify the risks these people take in trying to immigrate illegally into countries such as the United States, and compare how each group was received.

SECTION REVIEW

1. List four types of information that may be included in demographic studies.
2. What factors are considered when measuring population growth?
3. **Calculate** What is the percentage of population growth in a region if the number of people per 10,000 individuals increases by 330 each year?

1. Information about age, sex, family size, employment, and education are mentioned in the text. Students may volunteer other responses.
2. Birth rate, death rate, and doubling time
3. 3.3 percent

The Great City of Copán

How can a thriving city be reduced to ruins?

1. Poor farming practices depleted and destroyed resources needed to support the growing urban population, as is occurring today.
2. People today could learn the danger of unsustainable farming.

As you stand on a mountaintop in western Honduras overlooking more than 200 km² of green valley, you are amazed at the beauty and complexity of the acropolis, or raised portion, of the city of Copán. The main group of buildings includes elaborate pyramids, platforms, and plazas decorated with stone figures portraying the great rulers of the city. Extending from the main group are stucco buildings and streets. Surrounding the town, houses with red tile roofs dot the fields of crops.

As you descend from the summit to enter the city, you notice that much of the forest was removed to make room for farmland. Although farming occupies most of the area around the great city, many of the people look hungry. Closer observation of the soil and crops reveals poor, infertile soil. Although the soil near a river should be fertile, poor farming techniques have depleted the nutrients.

A diversity of activity takes place in the rural area surrounding Copán. Some households manufacture pottery. Other people are woodworkers or stoneworkers. However, most of the households are empty and abandoned.

As you enter the outskirts of the city, you encounter suburban Copán. This elite residential zone contains a large decorated palace. Other buildings vary in function from shrines to kitchens to dormitories.

You notice few people walking the streets of Copán, as you head toward the main group of buildings. At the ceremonial center you climb the steps to view the field used for ball games. Ball games once attracted crowds of thousands, but the field now stands empty. The great city of Copán is dying, but why?

You meet an elderly man on the street and ask him what has become of Copán. The man tells you that Copán once had a population of about 20,000. However, as the population increased, disease spread. The surrounding farmland had one bad year after another and could no longer grow enough food. People became hungry and sick. Most residents fled or died.

The processes that brought about the demise of Copán are a familiar story in many parts of the world today. However, to visit Copán, you would have to travel back in time. The great city of Copán existed during the Mayan empire and died out

more than 1,000 years ago. If you went to Copán today, you would find only ruins.

Knowledge of the ruins of Copán was brought to western scientists in 1839 by an American traveler and his English companion. For 150 years, people wondered what happened to the city of Copán. From the ruins and analysis of skeletons and old pollen deposits, archaeologists have pieced together a story similar to the one you just read. The ancient city died from the same misuse of land and overpopulation that are occurring around the world today.

DECISIONS

1. Compare and contrast the problems in Copán to the problems in the urban centers of many developing countries.
2. What lessons could the people of today learn from Copán?

207

13.3 CHALLENGES OF OVERPOPULATION

Objectives • **Relate** *how overpopulation affects natural resources, energy demands, and biodiversity.* • **Hypothesize** *how the availability of resources affects population growth.*

Figure 13.5 The problems of overcrowding can be seen in urban centers throughout the world. In 1970, about 37 percent of the human population lived in cities. This number is expected to climb to more than 60 percent by the year 2025.

DATELINE 1878

Ellen Richards, a chemistry instructor at the Women's Laboratory at the Massachusetts Institute of Technology, accepted a position at the newly formed Department of Sanitary Engineering. There, she developed the first system for the treatment of waste water. Her system, which improved the quality of public water supplies, helped reduce the threat of deadly diseases such as cholera, typhoid fever, and dysentery.

Rapid population growth directly affects the global ecosystem. An increase in population places a greater demand on the space needed to sustain large numbers of people. Population growth also places a greater demand on resources, such as minerals, fuels, and food. As humans take up more space on the surface of Earth, there is less land available for the planet's other inhabitants. It is very difficult to convince people to give up the land and other resources they need to survive for the sake of saving wildlife. As you have read throughout this text, however, all life on Earth is interconnected. Many scientists feel that the human species is conducting a gigantic experiment in overpopulation. How many more species can the planet lose before Earth is no longer a healthy place for humans?

Human health problems can be directly tied to overpopulation. The more crowding there is in a given area, the more contacts people make with other people. For example, people who live in crowded cities are exposed to more illnesses than people in remote areas. Diseases related to malnutrition, poor hygiene, and a lack of medical facilities are also problems associated with overpopulation.

Overpopulation also causes the harmful things that people do to the environment to be magnified. For example, exhaust fumes from one car do not pose a serious threat to the environment, but those of several million cars do. Clearing a tract of land to build a house may not seem harmful in an area with several kilometers of undisturbed grassland or forest. But building a house on the last available tract of land within an ecosystem may have a serious environmental impact, destroying the homes and breeding grounds for several species.

Controlling Population Size

It may seem obvious that controlling the birth rate is the answer to the problems of overpopulation. However, empowering people to control the number of children they have is not easy; convincing them that they *should* have fewer children is even more difficult. Forcing people to limit the size of their families is a step that most people find unethical and unacceptable.

Large-scale efforts are underway in many underdeveloped and developing countries to educate people and provide effective methods of birth control. There are many factors, however, that contribute to people's continuing desire to have children. In many religions, any effort to prevent pregnancy, other than avoiding sexual activity, is considered unacceptable. Also, many people feel that children are a source of pride and joy, and without them their lives would have little meaning. In many societies, the number of children in a family is considered a sign of strength and manliness in the father. It is very difficult for education efforts to change such basic cultural beliefs.

There are also many people who feel that population sizes should not be controlled. In several nations, such as Japan, Singapore, and parts of Europe, the birth rate has fallen below the rate of replacement, or fewer than two children are born for every two adults. Such nations face special challenges due to an aging and declining population. A decrease in military strength due to fewer soldiers, and a decrease in the number of working taxpayers threatens to weaken the economic strength of these nations. The governments of some nations now offer financial support and tax advantages to encourage couples to have more children.

Figure 13.6 The government of China strongly encourages couples to have only one child by promising better housing, longer vacations, and an extra month's pay each year to single-child families. Those who have an unapproved pregnancy can expect pay cuts, reprimands, and strong pressure to have an abortion.

Is Technology the Answer?

Many of the advances of modern technology have the potential to increase the resources available to humans. New sources of renewable energy, new strains of crops developed through genetic engineering, and other scientific breakthroughs could help relieve many of the problems of overpopulation. Will these solutions be adequate to meet the challenges that lie ahead?

There have been other episodes in the history of the human population when technological changes have increased the carrying capacity of Earth. The agricultural and industrial revolutions both increased the number of people that an area can support. It is likely that future developments in science will increase the number of people that can occupy the planet. Such developments often encourage spurts of population growth. However, most scientists feel that there is a limit to the number of people that can live on Earth. Many think that the limit will be reached sometime in the near future.

> **THINK CRITICALLY**
>
> How do you think people in the United States would feel about the government limiting the number of children a family could have? Would people feel differently if the limit was one child, two children, or ten children? Explain your answer.

1. Contact with more people and a reduction in food, hygiene, and medical care all contribute to poor health.
2. Answers will vary, but may include that pollution produced by people in one area can be carried in air or water to other areas, and people in overpopulated areas often seek the resources of less populated areas.
3. An increase in resources tends to increase the birth rate and decrease the death rate, both factors leading to an increase in population.

SECTION REVIEW

1. How can overpopulation affect human health?
2. How might overpopulation in one area affect ecosystems in other areas?
3. **Hypothesize** What effect does increasing the resources in an area have on the population in that area?

Answers and teaching
strategies on page T76.

Modeling Disease Transmission

PROBLEM
How are diseases transmitted?

MATERIALS (per student)
- wax pencil
- empty baby food jar
- safety goggles
- rubber gloves
- dropper
- stock solution
- phenol red indicator
- lab apron

HYPOTHESIS
After reading through the activity, write a hypothesis that explains how disease moves through a population.

PROCEDURE
1. Write your name on the empty baby food jar with the wax pencil.
2. Transfer to your jar three droppersful of the stock solution provided by your teacher.
   Caution: *Wear goggles, gloves, and apron when handling solutions. Do not let skin or clothing come into contact with solutions.*
3. Take one dropperful of solution from the jar of a classmate, and empty it into your own jar. Gently swirl the mixture.
4. Record the other student's name. This person represents your first "partner."
5. Exchange a dropperful of solution with two other students, and record their names.
6. Add one dropperful of phenol red to your jar, and record the color of your solution.
7. You can tell by the color of your solution if you were infected of not. A red solution means you were infected; a yellow solution means you were not. Inform your teacher if you were infected, and provide the names of your partners. Your teacher will write the names of all infected persons and their partners on the chalkboard.
8. After the whole class has completed the experiment and collected all data, work together and deduce who was the original source of infection (there was only one infected source). Then trace the routes of the transmission of the disease.

ANALYSIS
1. Draw a diagram that traces the disease transmission in your class.
2. Were you infected? If so, who infected you? How many people did you infect?
3. What is the maximum number of infected persons after two rounds of exchanging fluids? What is the maximum after three rounds?
4. Phenol turns yellow in acidic solutions and red in basic solutions. Which represented the infectious microbe in this model, the acidic or the basic solution?

CONCLUSION
1. Using the data you gathered as a class, write a paragraph stating your conclusion including your observation.
2. Suppose you had exchanged fluids with six partners instead of only three. What would have happened to your chances of becoming infected?

CHAPTER 13 REVIEW

KEY TERMS

agricultural
  revolution 13.1

germ theory 13.1
demography 13.3

CHAPTER SUMMARY

13.1 The human population has grown at various rates throughout history. The agricultural revolution, the germ theory of disease, and modern developments in medicine have contributed to a very rapid population growth. Disease, famine, and war are factors that cause the human population to decline.

13.2 As the human population increases in size, the need for resources also increases. The percent growth rate of the human population can be determined by subtracting the number of deaths from the number of births and dividing by 100.

Immigration into an area, and emigration out of an area can affect the growth rate of the population in a specific area. Demographic studies help planners to anticipate the future needs of a society.

13.3 Efforts to reduce the growth rate of the human population are difficult to implement. Social and religious beliefs about family size and birth control vary from culture to culture. Technological advances that increase the carrying capacity of Earth by increasing available resources are often followed by spurts in population growth.

MULTIPLE CHOICE

Choose the letter of the word or phrase that best completes each statement.

1. Of the following, the factor most likely to result in a decrease in the size of a specific population is (a) improved medical care; (b) increased food availability; (c) famine; (d) industrialization. c

2. The agricultural revolution took place approximately (a) 20,000 years ago; (b) 10,000 years ago; (c) 300 years ago; (d) during the past 100 years. b

3. The germ theory of disease established that many diseases are caused by (a) microorganisms; (b) water; (c) poor nutrition; (d) overpopulation. a

4. A dramatic decline in the population of Europe in the 1300s was caused by the (a) potato famine; (b) bubonic plague; (c) Thirty Years' War; (d) outbreak of cholera. b

5. A nation with a population that is not increasing is (a) Peru; (b) Guatemala; (c) Sweden; (d) Kenya. c

6. When calculating global population growth, the death rate is (a) added to the birth rate; (b) subtracted from life expectancy; (c) multiplied by 100; (d) subtracted from the birth rate. d

7. At present, the growth patterns of the human population are best described as (a) above carrying capacity; (b) exponential; (c) arithmetic; (d) stable. b

8. The greatest growth of human populations today is occurring in (a) industrial societies; (b) tribal societies; (c) developing nations; (d) hunter–gatherer societies. c

9. Problems associated with a declining population size include (a) increased famine; (b) decreased health care; (c) loss of habitat; (d) weakened economic strength. d

10. The change in energy consumption in the United States during the past 100 years is due to (a) population growth; (b) modernization; (c) both population growth and modernization; (d) neither population growth nor modernization. c

TRUE/FALSE

Write true *if the statement is true. If the statement is false, change the underlined word to make it true.*

1. The person who compared the growth of the human population to its resources was Thomas <u>Moore</u>. f; Malthus
2. The life expectancy of people in industrial societies has <u>increased</u> over time. t
3. A population that shows growth of 24 persons per 1000 has a population growth of <u>24%</u>. f; 2.4%
4. The population of Mexico City has doubled in the past <u>20</u> years. f; 10
5. The increase in modern machinery tends to <u>decrease</u> the energy needs of a society. f; increases
6. The period of the twentieth century marked by huge advances in medicine is sometimes called the <u>biomedical</u> revolution. t

CONCEPT REVIEW Answers on page T76.

Write a complete response to each of the following.

1. How did the discovery of the germ theory of disease impact society?
2. Describe three factors that can cause a population size to decrease.
3. Why have infant death rates decreased in the past 50 years?
4. Explain the concept of doubling time.
5. Why does an increased number of people affect the availability of resources?

THINK CRITICALLY Answers on page T76.

1. Why is the growth rate of the human population difficult to control?
2. Describe three ways that a growing human population affects other organisms.
3. Some scientists consider the hunter–gatherer societies that exist today to be endangered species. How would people living as hunter–gatherers be similar to species of other organisms that are considered endangered?

Computer Activity (Use a spreadsheet program to solve the following problem.) Population A and Population B both start with 100 people. With each generation, Population A grows by 2 percent, while Population B grows by 5 percent. How many generations will it take for each population to double?

WRITE CREATIVELY

Write a fictional story that describes the life of a hunter–gatherer living 10,000 years ago in a society that is just beginning to establish its first permanent settlement.

PORTFOLIO

1. The People's Republic of China is one of the few nations in the world that limits family size. Research the changes that have occurred in Chinese society as a result of the one-child-per-family rule. Make a presentation of your findings, including how people in China feel about the rule.
2. There are organizations that enable people in the United States to sponsor a needy child in various parts of the world. Research one such organization and find out how much it costs to sponsor a child, and how the money is used to help the children and their communities.

Use Figure 13.3 on page 205 to answer the following.

1. Which of the three nations has the highest percentage of children under the age of 15? What does this imply about the amount of money needed for schools and children's services?
2. In which nation would you expect to find the largest population of elderly people?
3. What can you infer about the life expectancy of men compared to women in the three nations shown?
4. In which nation would you expect to find the greatest percentage of children ten years from now? Explain your answer.

ACTIVITY 13.2

Answers and teaching strategies on page T76.

PROBLEM

What happens when too many people are crowded into a living space, and what are the advantages of careful community planning?

MATERIALS

meter stick or metric tape measure

PREDICTION

After reading through the activity, predict how you will feel when restricted to a small area.

PROCEDURE

1. Measure the length and width of your classroom. Calculate the area of the room using this formula: length (m) × width (m) = area (m²)
2. Count the number of people in the class. Then calculate the population density (number of people per square meter) using this formula:

$$\frac{\text{number of people}}{\text{area (meters}^2)} = \text{population density (people/m}^2)$$

3. Your teacher will draw an imaginary line dividing the classroom in half. Then all students will move to one half of the room. Determine the new population density.
4. Observe your classmates in this restricted environment: note how people talk, sit or stand, what they say, and how the area looks.
5. Again the teacher will draw an imaginary line, this time dividing the classroom into fourths. Repeat steps 3 and 4.

ANALYSIS

1. After you finish recording your calculations and observations, comment on the behavior of the class members as the available living space got smaller and smaller.
2. Discuss how and why some individual behaviors change as the density increases.

CONCLUSION

1. What conclusions can you draw from the data you gathered? Does increased population density adversely affect a community?
2. Record how you felt as the classroom got smaller and more crowded.

Population Density Data Table

Classroom Size	Length (m)	Width (m)	Area (m²)	Population Density (people/m²)
Full				
Half				
Fourth				

CHAPTER

14

FEEDING THE WORLD

Y ou have probably seen horrifying images on television and in news magazines of starving children in developing nations. You may have seen hungry people in the United States waiting in lines at soup kitchens and shelters for a hot meal. Perhaps you or someone you know has been in such a situation.

Yet during the past 40 years, world food production has increased faster than the rate of population growth. The real reason for hunger is often not the amount of food available. Instead, it is the unequal distribution of food around the world and within individual nations that can result in starvation and other social crises.

14.1 HUMAN NUTRITION

Objectives • **List** *the major groups of nutrients and the amount of energy provided by each type.*

Like all organisms on Earth, humans need energy to carry out their life processes, which include growth, movement, and tissue repair. Humans are omnivores, or animals that can consume either plants or animals for food. Dietary habits vary a great deal from one society to another. Because all humans belong to one species, all have the same basic nutritional needs. In addition to the energy required for life processes, people also need a blend of other substances, or nutrients, to maintain good health.

Nutrients

Nutrients can be divided into two main groups: macronutrients and micronutrients. *Macro*nutrients (MAK-roh-NOO-tree-unts) provide the body with energy. *Micro*nutrients (MYK-roh-NOO-tree-unts) provide the body with small amounts of chemicals needed in biochemical reactions.

Energy provided by macronutrients is measured in units called kilocalories (kcal). One kilocalorie provides enough energy to raise the temperature of 1 kilogram of water 1 degree Celsius. In nutritional information for consumers, kilocalories are commonly referred to simply as Calories. The number of Calories contained in a food indicates how much energy the food provides. The three types of macronutrients are carbohydrates, proteins, and fats.

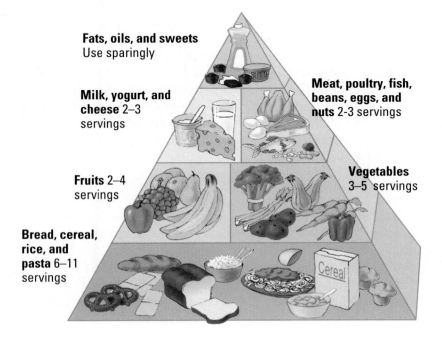

Fats, oils, and sweets
Use sparingly

Milk, yogurt, and cheese 2–3 servings

Meat, poultry, fish, beans, eggs, and nuts 2-3 servings

Fruits 2–4 servings

Vegetables 3–5 servings

Bread, cereal, rice, and pasta 6–11 servings

Figure 14.1 According to the nutritional guidelines of the U.S. Food and Drug Administration, a healthful diet contains many more servings of plant products than animal products each day.

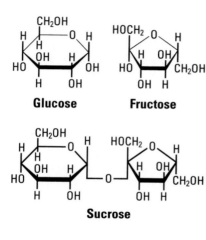

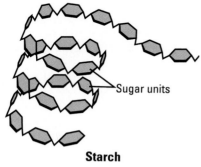

Figure 14.2 Simple sugars like glucose and fructose contain one carbon ring. Double sugars like sucrose contain two. Starches are made up of long chains of simple sugars.

Discuss the role of fiber from fruits, vegetables, grains, and beans in the diet. Made of cellulose, plant fibers cannot be broken down or absorbed by the digestive system. Fiber is important, however, in removing residues from the digestive system. Certain types of fibers have been shown to reduce the risk of heart disease and cancers of the digestive system.

Carbohydrates   *A* **carbohydrate** *is a compound made up of carbon, hydrogen, and oxygen in approximately a 1:2:1 ratio.* There are two main types of carbohydrates that can be used as an energy source by humans. Sugars are small, simple carbohydrates that can be absorbed by the body relatively quickly, providing almost immediate energy. Starches are larger, more complex carbohydrates that provide the body with steadier, longer-lasting energy. Regardless of the source, taste, or complexity, all carbohydrates provide the body with about 4 kcal per gram. Foods that are high in carbohydrates include fruits, vegetables, bread, and grains such as wheat, corn, rice, and oats.

Protein   *A* **protein** *is a large compound made of amino acids that provides the body with the construction materials for making blood, muscle, and other tissues.* Amino acids are small organic molecules that contain nitrogen. Without nitrogen, proteins cannot be made by any organism, either plant or animal. Recall from Chapter 5 that the cycling of nitrogen through an ecosystem is an essential function of the biosphere. Like carbohydrates, each gram of protein provides the body with about 4 kcal. Proteins provide energy and make up most body tissues, including muscles, blood, skin, and enzymes.

All the proteins in the human body are made up of 20 different amino acids arranged in an almost infinite number of ways. The ability of the body to make millions of different proteins from the same 20 amino acids is similar to the way the English language contains millions of words all made from the same 26 letters. Of the 20 amino acids, the human body can make 12. The remaining 8 amino acids must be obtained from foods. *The eight amino acids that must be obtained from foods are called* **essential amino acids**.

Foods that come from animals, including meats, eggs, and dairy products, are high-protein foods with all the essential amino acids. Grains, such as wheat, rice, and corn, and legumes, such as peas, beans, and peanuts, are foods from plants that are also good sources of protein. Unfortunately, plant proteins are usually not complete, lacking one or more of the essential amino acids. To obtain all the essential amino acids, people who do not eat meat must combine proteins from different types of plants. By eating meals that include both grains and legumes, a vegetarian can get all the protein needed for good health.

Fats   Fats belong to a group of organic compounds called lipids. *A* **lipid** *contains three long chains of fatty acids and is a main component of all cell membranes.* Because all organisms are made of cells and all cells have membranes made of lipids, all foods contain some lipids. Solid lipids, such as butter and lard, are commonly called fats. Liquid lipids are called oils, but they are also considered to be fats for nutritional purposes. Whether solid or liquid, fats contain 9 kcal per gram. Notice that per gram, fats provide more than twice the amount of energy as carbohydrates and proteins.

O   H H H H H   H H H   H H H H H H H H H
‖ | | | | | | | | | | | | | | | | |
C—C—C—C—C—C=C—C—C=C—C—C—C—C—C—C—C—C—C—H
HO | | | | | | | | | |
    H H H   H   H H H H H H

Linoleic Acid (unsaturated)

O   H H H H H H H H H H H H H H H H H
‖ | | | | | | | | | | | | | | | | |
C—C—C—C—C—C—C—C—C—C—C—C—C—C—C—C—C—C—H
HO | | | | | | | | | | | | | | | | |
    H H H H H H H H H H H H H H H H H

Palmitic Acid (saturated)

Figure 14.3 Unsaturated fats contain double bonds between the carbon atoms, reducing the number of places for hydrogen to bond. Saturated fats contain only single bonds and have the maximum amount of hydrogen atoms.

Fats may be saturated or unsaturated. A *saturated fat* contains the maximum number of hydrogen atoms on the fatty acid chains. In an *unsaturated fat*, some of the hydrogen is missing. A monosaturated fat contains only one double carbon bond. A polyunsaturated fat, such as the palmitic acid shown in Figure 14.3, contains more than one double carbon bond. Naturally occuring fats contain saturated, monounsaturated, and polyunsaturated fats in varying amounts. Food labels often show the amounts of each type of fat in the food.

Most animal fats are highly saturated, while most plant oils are highly unsaturated. You can tell how saturated a fat is by how firm it is at room temperature. The more saturated the fat, the more firm it is. Margarine manufacturers often *hydrogenate* liquid vegetable oils by adding more hydrogen, giving the margarine the firm texture of butter. In recent years, nutritional research has shown that saturated fats contribute to the risk of heart disease. While a high-fat diet in general presents many health risks, saturated fats appear to be more involved in the development of heart disease than are unsaturated fats.

Vitamins and Minerals   Vitamins and minerals are micronutrients. Although they do not provide energy directly, vitamins and minerals play key roles in the biochemical reactions that release energy. All the micronutrients that humans need can be obtained from plants, although meats and other animal products are good sources as well. Fruits, vegetables, and breads made from whole grains are particularly good sources of vitamins and minerals.

Many of the micronutrients that occur naturally in plant foods are removed by improper processing, cooking, or storage. Proper handling is very important to preserve the vitamin and mineral content of most foods. Plants grown on soil that is low in certain minerals may also have reduced nutritional value.

Nutritional Deficiency

According to the Food and Agriculture Organization (FAO) of the United Nations, an average human adult requires about 2500 kcal per day. People who receive less than 90 percent of their energy

A FIELD ACTIVITY

How healthful is healthful? Go to the supermarket and compare the nutritional information labels on two similar products, one regular and one "healthy." For example, you can compare a regular frozen turkey dinner with one sold as a healthful dinner. You can compare cookies, ice creams, or other foods for which there is a "healthy" counterpart on the market. Compare the fat content in the two products as well as sodium (salt), protein, vitamins, serving size, and cost per serving. Evaluate the advantage, if any, in buying the more healthful product.

Figure 14.4 When there is not enough food to eat, it is the children who suffer the most.

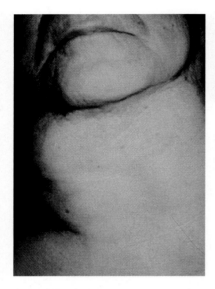

Figure 14.5 A goiter is a swelling of the thyroid gland that results from a shortage of iodine in the diet. Because iodine is common in seafoods, goiters are most common in inland areas.

HEALTH
L I N K

For many years, people in Japan considered whole-grain brown rice to be peasant food, while members of the rich upper class ate only polished white rice. People did not realize that most of the nutrients in rice are contained in the parts that are removed during polishing. As a result, nutritional deficiencies were more common among the rich than among the poor.

1. Undernourishment is a shortage of energy. Malnutrition is a shortage of a particular nutrient and may not accompany undernourishment.
2. They should be the same.
3. Getting enough food does not necessarily guarantee getting enough of each nutrient.

needs are considered undernourished. Those who receive less than 80 percent are seriously undernourished. Children who are seriously undernourished often suffer from permanently stunted growth and mental retardation. In 1980, there were an estimated 730 million undernourished people in developing nations. In developing nations, one out of every four children dies of a disease related to poor diet, which works out to an average of one child dying every 2 seconds.

Although lack of energy is a serious nutritional problem, many people who receive enough energy lack one or more of the other nutrients. **Malnutrition** *is the lack of a specific type of nutrient in the diet.* Malnutrition can also result from an inability to absorb or use a particular nutrient. Vitamin deficiency is a type of malnutrition that occurs in all nations of the world, and it may even affect those who have an adequate supply of food. Scurvy, beri beri, and rickets are vitamin-deficiency diseases that result from a lack of vitamins C, B_1 (thiamine), and D.

Kwashiorkor (KWAH-shee-OR-kor) is a deficiency disease caused by too little protein in an otherwise adequate diet. This condition occurs when people live on diets of starchy, low-protein foods. Children with kwashiorkor develop a characteristic "flag" of red hair, a bloated belly, become unresponsive, and catch infectious diseases easily. Marasmus, a related condition, occurs when the diet is lacking in both protein and calories.

SECTION REVIEW

1. Explain the difference between being undernourished and having malnutrition.
2. Which contains more calories, a food that is two-thirds protein and one-third carbohydrate, or a food that is one-third protein and two-thirds carbohydrate?
3. **Analyze** About 90 percent of the people in the U.S. have enough to eat. Why do you think vitamin supplements and vitamin-fortified foods are so popular?

Measuring the Energy in Food

PROBLEM
How is the energy in food measured?

MATERIALS (per group)
- ring stand
- test-tube clamp
- test tube
- paper clip
- fireproof pad
- matches
- thermometer
- safety goggles
- laboratory apron
- metric ruler
- cork stopper (at least 4-cm base diameter.)
- 4 food samples (such as nuts, dried beans, cereals, potato chips, and sharp cheese)
- heat-resistant gloves
- triple-beam balance
- 100-mL graduated cylinder

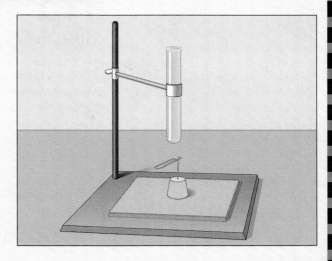

PREDICTION
After reading through the activity, predict which of the food samples will give off the most energy.

PROCEDURE

1. Set up the ring stand, test-tube clamp, test tube, and fireproof pad as shown.
2. Make a food platform for the calorimeter by bending the outer end of the paper clip straight down so it is at a right angle to the rest of the clip. Insert the free end of the clip into the middle of the narrow end of the cork stopper (see figure).
3. Adjust the height of the test tube so that the space between the food platform and the bottom of the test tube is 2 cm.
4. Measure exactly 15 mL of water into the test tube. Record the mass of the water in the correct place in the data table. *Note: 1 mL of water has a mass of 1 g.*
5. Measure and record the temperature of the water in the test tube. Remove the thermometer from the test tube after you record the temperature.
6. Select a food sample and measure its mass. Record the mass in the data table.

7. Place the food sample on the paper clip. Quickly ignite the food sample with a match, and place the platform under the test tube. **Caution:** *Wear safety goggles. Use care when using matches.* Allow the food to burn completely.
8. Measure and record the temperature of the water in the test tube. **Caution:** *Do not touch the test tube; it may be hot.*
9. Determine the change in mass of the food sample.
10. Determine the change in temperature of the water.
11. Repeat steps 3–10 using three other food samples.

ANALYSIS:
Use the formula to find the calories per food sample. *Note: The specific heat of water is 1 kcal per kilogram degree Celsius.*

Calories per food sample = Change in water temperature × Mass of water × Specific heat of water × $\frac{1\ kg}{1000\ g}$

CONCLUSION
1. Which of your food samples contained the most energy?
2. How do your results compare with your predictions? As a class, discuss what you learned about the foods you tested.

14.2 WORLD FOOD SUPPLY

Objective • *Explain the effects of economics on the production of food.*

Food supplies worldwide have increased a great deal during the past 40 years. Not only is there more food being produced, but there is more food available per person than at any point in history. Why, then, are there so many starving people? Part of the reason is that much of the food increase has been accomplished through advances in agricultural practices and improvements in crop plants. The main reason, however, is that food is traded as a commodity whose price is driven by economic factors.

The Green Revolution

The **Green Revolution** *began in the mid-1960s with the development of new strains of wheat and rice, the two main foods of the world.* The new varieties are more responsive to the use of fertilizers and irrigation than are older plant varieties. Given adequate water and fertilization, the new crops have better resistance to disease, grow faster, and can adapt to a wide variety of climates. The new "miracle" plants can increase crop yields as much as four times the normal yield. Green Revolution farming also uses modern farming methods and machinery to plant, maintain, and harvest the crops efficiently. The Green Revolution has resulted in a large increase in food production without a large increase in the amount of farmland.

Green Revolution farming, though intended to help underfed nations feed themselves, is often not available to the people who need it the most. Many farmers in developing nations do not have the water necessary to maintain the new crops. These farmers rarely have the money to buy fertilizers, and they do not own modern machinery. Even if they did have the machines, few could afford the fuel to run them. Farmers in the developed nations can take full advantage of Green Revolution farming, producing huge crops. These large crops increase the world's supply of grains, which drives down the price of grains on the market. Poorer farmers who cannot use the new methods find that the price they receive for their crops is even lower than it used to be.

Cash Crops

In developing nations, many farmers or landowners cannot generate the income they need to maintain their farms by growing food to feed the local people. The people are often too poor to pay much for food, and the foods they eat tend to be low-priced grains. Instead, many farmers have chosen to grow crops that can be exported to other nations for higher prices. *A* **cash crop** *is a crop grown for the*

Figure 14.6 When regular wheat is given extra water and fertilizers, it grows too tall, falls over, and cannot be harvested.

purpose of export sale. For example, many farmers in African nations grow cash crops that are exported to Europe to feed livestock.

In many developing nations, as much as 85 percent of the farmland is owned by less than 5 percent of the people. Often, the income from the sale of cash crops is used to buy weapons and support political leaders that help the landowners. Although much of the hunger in the world results from natural causes, especially drought and overpopulation, the role of governments and profit-driven land management cannot be ignored.

Food from the Water

Food crops grown on land provide a large portion of the world's food supply, but not all of it. Fish and other sea animals provide much of the animal protein consumed by people around the world and 40 percent of the animal protein supply in developing nations. As much as 200 billion metric tons of biomass grow naturally in the oceans each year, which is at least as much as plant production on land.

The FAO estimates that the oceans of the world can provide about 100 million metric tons of food per year without damaging the marine biome. The commercial harvest of fish reached 100 million metric tons in 1989. Since then, the harvest has continued to increase, in part because of new fishing techniques. The fact that the ocean harvest is now exceeding the safety limits is beginning to affect the fishing industry. Quantities of fish of various species are beginning to drop. Commercial fishers are catching fewer fish per boat, and the fish are often small and immature. About 40 of the 280 species of fish harvested commercially are now in danger.

An alternative to fishing in the open oceans for food is to raise fish in confined pools. *Commercial production of fish in a controlled, maintained environment is called* **aquaculture**. Fish can be raised in either fresh water or salt water, in coastal swamps or inland ponds, in small areas or on a large scale. Aquaculture produces about 85 percent of the mollusks, mostly clams and oysters, eaten in the United States. Rainbow trout are also raised successfully in aquaculture. In China, India, Thailand, and Vietnam, fish are raised on algae grown in waste-water ponds.

Figure 14.7 Aquaculture has provided food for people in many nations of Southeast Asia for centuries. This technique is now becoming an important source of food for the U.S. and China.

SECTION REVIEW

1. What occurred during the Green Revolution?
2. How does the growing of cash crops help individual farmers?
3. **Apply** Do you think aquaculture is damaging to the environment? Why or why not? (Hint: Review sections of Chapters 10 and 11.)

1. New strains of grains and machinery-based farming techniques were developed.
2. They can be sold for more money, increasing the farmer's income.
3. Aquaculture in coastal areas could alter or damage wetlands and intertidal ecosystems.

Rainforest Land Use

Should livestock be raised on rainforest land?

1. Answers will vary, but should be supported by facts from the feature.
2. Richer soils are better able to support grazing over longer time periods.

I f you lived in one of the developing nations of the world that contains rainforests, you might understand the importance of biodiversity. If you were poor or hungry, however, you might want to help yourself or your family by sacrificing rainforest land to support cattle grazing.

There are about 1.28 billion cattle on Earth. Each animal eats approximately 900 lbs of vegetation each month. Both the cattle and the cattle feed need area to grow. Almost one-quarter of the land on our planet is used as either grazing land for cattle or as farmland for growing feed grain. Much of this grazing land, however, is not suitable for farming.

The land devoted to growing cattle feed is found not only in the major beef-eating nations. Millions of acres of land in developing nations are used to grow grain that is exported for use as livestock feed. In Ethiopia, some of the available agricultural land produces seed for export as animal feed. In 1984, when thousands of Ethiopians died daily from starvation, agricultural land in that country was still being used to grow livestock feed for export.

Exporting beef and cattle feed is an important source of income for many developing countries. Much of the beef is exported to industrialized nations for fast and frozen foods,

luncheon meats, and other meat products.

To make space to grow feed and raise cattle, some developing nations have cleared millions of acres of land. Most developing nations are near the equator and contain much of the world's tropical rain forests.

About 150,000 square kilometers of rainforest land (an area the size of Illinois or Florida) are cleared each year. Much of the land is cleared in order to meet consumer demand for meat, food crops, and timber. To increase exports, some governments have even given special tax advantages for clearing large areas of rain forest.

After the land is cleared, however, the farms and ranches that replace the rain forests do not remain productive. Unlike some other biomes, which have a thick layer of nutrient-rich soil, most of the nutrients in rain forests are in the living organisms. After the rain forest is cleared, there are few nutrients left in the soil to support plant growth. In addition, overgrazing of livestock can degrade pasture land. This makes it even harder to grow the grass that the cattle eat.

Due to the low soil fertility and the impact of grazing on the land, ranches in tropical re-

gions cannot support as many animals per hectare as ranches in other areas. In fact, the tropical ranches are often ten times less efficient than American and European ranches. For the first few years, each hectare will feed one cow. After five or ten years each animal needs five to seven hectares.

When the ranch is no longer profitable, some ranchers leave the land for new pastures, which have been more recently stripped of trees. After the ranchers leave, weeds and grasses grow in the nutrient-poor soil. The unique rainforest ecosystem that once covered the region will probably never grow back.

DECISIONS

1. Suggest ways that the needs of people and the rainforest can be met without the destruction of the forest.
2. How does the soil quality in a biome affect cattle-ranching?

14.3 MODERN FARMING TECHNIQUES

Objective • *Describe* how farming techniques have changed during the past 50 years.

As you learned in the last section, the Green Revolution changed the way commercial farming is conducted. In addition to the development of improved varieties of grains, the techniques and machines of modern farming have also changed. Modern farming techniques have some advantages and disadvantages in feeding the world.

Historically, agriculture was a very labor-intensive occupation. The jobs of preparing the soil, planting seed, maintaining crops, and harvesting were all done by humans and their animals. To grow more crops, the farmer needed to cultivate more land, which required more labor. Farmers grew a variety of crops, rotating the use of land. Occasionally farmers allowed the land to lie fallow, growing no crops, in order to restore the fertility of the soil.

In the middle of the twentieth century, agriculture in the developed nations of the world, especially the United States, began to change. Large pieces of equipment that use fossil fuels replaced human-powered tools. In 1950, less than half a barrel of oil was used to produce a ton of grain. By 1985, this quantity had doubled. During the same period, the use of chemical fertilizers and pesticides became widespread. Many smaller family farms could not afford the machinery and equipment needed to compete with the larger commercial farms. As a result, many were sold to large *agribusiness* corporations. Today, more than two-thirds of the food produced in the U.S. comes from fewer than 50 agribusiness corporations. Some of the same corporations also produce 75 percent of the pesticides and other chemicals used by the industry.

DATELINE 1972

The U.S. secretary of agriculture called upon American farmers to help "feed the world," predicting an unlimited international market for U.S. grains. Farmers were encouraged to drain wetlands and plant on every available inch of land. The price of farmland went up, and farmers invested in modern machinery. The result was a huge increase in production, which was not met with the expected demand. In the late 1970s, matters became worse when the U.S. refused to sell grain to the U.S.S.R. because of its invasion of Afghanistan. Surpluses piled up, and grain prices fell. Many farmers, now heavily in debt, were forced out of business.

DATELINE 1982

By 1982, the surplus of grain was so large that the Reagan administration offered farmers money *not* to grow any crops. During the same year, billions of dollars were cut from food-assistance programs for the poor, dropping millions of people from food stamps and other programs. The poverty level and number of hungry people in the U.S. were larger in 1982 than they had been in 20 years. Hunger in the U.S. is not caused by lack of food, but by lack of money among the poor.

Figure 14.8 When grain elevators are full, the excess grain is stored outside, where it can be destroyed by birds, rodents, and wet weather.

Figure 14.9 The routine, scheduled dusting of crops with pesticides, whether pests are present or not, has contributed to the development of pesticide-resistant insects.

The widespread use of pesticides has altered ecosystems in many harmful ways. One problem with the use of pesticides is an increase in resistant insects and other pests. In 1992, many of the crops in California were destroyed by an infestation of white flies. Because the white flies had evolved to be resistant to insecticides, growers were unable to protect their crops from the pest.

Many farms that used to grow a variety of crops shifted toward growing only one or two crops that commanded the highest prices. This technique, called *monoculture* farming, can cause several problems. By growing large numbers of genetically identical crops, the plants are more vulnerable to disease. Also, the soil becomes depleted of the mineral nutrients needed to grow the monoculture crop. Eventually, the ability of the soil to produce a healthy crop is reduced.

The Green Revolution produced new varieties of grains. However, some of the newer, higher-yielding grains were not well adapted to local conditions. Scientists are now looking at traditional grains as alternative crops in some areas. For example, the grain quinoa was once so important to the Incas of South America that they called it the "mother grain." Quinoa is very high in protein, has a good balance of amino acids, and grows well in mountainous areas. It can be made into flour for baking, breakfast cereal, beverages, and livestock feed. Quinoa may hold promise for improving the diets of people in poor mountainous regions of Southeast Asia, Africa, and the Himalayas.

SECTION REVIEW

1. Describe what is meant by monoculture farming, and why it can be a problem.
2. Why have many American farmers gone out of business since the early 1980s?
3. **Infer** Many of the lesser-known plants of the world are in danger of extinction. How might this affect food supplies of the future?

14.4 SUSTAINABLE AGRICULTURE

Objective • *Describe the basic components of sustainable agriculture, and explain why they are desirable.*

Modern agriculture is driven by economics and by international trade. The need to remain competitive in the global market has resulted in soil erosion, deforestation, desertification, hunger, war, and environmental damage on a global scale. As the population of the world increases, as discussed in Chapter 13, it is becoming clear that people will have to find a way to produce food without destroying the environment. To do so, many people in the U.S. and around the world are working toward developing sustainable agriculture. *Also called regenerative farming,* **sustainable agriculture** *is based on crop rotation, reduced soil erosion, pest management, and a minimal use of soil additives.*

Crop rotation means changing the type of crop grown in an area on a regular cycle. The cycle for crop rotation is usually 1 to 6 years. Crop rotation helps prevent soil from becoming depleted in mineral nutrients, especially nitrogen. As you have learned, nitrogen is necessary for plants to make proteins. Most plants extract nitrogen from the soil. The bacteria on the roots of some plants, however, especially legumes, can convert the nitrogen in the air to a usable form. Soils in which such plants grow become rich in nitrogen. By alternating legumes with other crops, farmers can avoid the use of synthetic nitrogen fertilizers. Nitrogen-fixing crops can also be used as a cover crop. Cover crops are nonfood plants that are grown between growing seasons. Cover crops not only restore nitrogen to the soil, they also help reduce one of the other major problems of modern agriculture: erosion.

Reducing Erosion

Erosion is a natural process by which soil is lost, transported, and reformed. When the soil that is being eroded and removed is valuable topsoil, the natural process becomes a disaster. Wind and flowing water will carry away loose pieces of topsoil that are not held down by plants. Because topsoil contains the organic and mineral nutrients needed to make the farmland fertile, the erosion of topsoil can make a field useless for agriculture.

Erosion can be reduced by careful irrigation and soil management. In traditional irrigation systems, water floods the fields and then drains off, carrying valuable topsoil away. Irrigation systems that deliver small quantities of water directly to the roots of plants reduce the erosion of soil by flowing water.

Since the 1800s, heavy tilling has been part of traditional agriculture. Tilling is the process of turning the soil so that lower

SOCIAL STUDIES LINK

In 1959, Chairman Mao Tse Tung brought all farming in China under the control of the government. The government set schedules for planting, standardized crops, and ordered the planting of all land, regardless of its condition. The poorly managed plan resulted in the greatest famine in world history, which claimed about 30 million lives between 1959 and 1961. After the death of Mao Tse Tung in 1976, farms were returned to family control. The family farms now produce 50-percent more crops and require about one-fifth the amount of labor as the government-controlled farms. Less than 3 percent of the population is now underfed, compared to 10 percent in the United States.

Figure 14.10 In an integrated pest management system, natural predators such as ladybud beetles are used to combat insect pests. The predators would be killed by traditional pesticide use.

layers are brought to the surface. Extensive tilling destroys weeds and other pests, brings fresh nutrients to the surface, improves drainage, and aerates the soil. Unfortunately, this process also wastes water, uses energy, and increases soil erosion. Farmers are now finding that reducing tillage sometimes increases crop yields.

Pest Management

A new approach to managing pests, called integrated pest management, or IPM, is being used successfully in many areas. IPM can reduce the use of pesticides by as much as 90 percent. Many IPM systems make use of the natural predators of pest organisms. Wasps, ladybug beetles, and a variety of viruses and bacteria are the natural enemies of many insect pests. Farmers in the United States have increased their use of IPM and reduced their use of pesticides over the last five years.

One of the most successful IPMs is now in use in Indonesia. There, farmers were routinely spraying their crops with insecticides on a regular basis. An insect called the brown planthopper developed a resistance to insecticides and was destroying the nation's rice crop. In 1986, the president banned 56 of the 57 insecticides commonly used and launched a program to educate farmers about the dangers of pesticides. By reducing the use of insecticides so dramatically, the natural insect predators of the planthopper were able to combat the pest. Farmers using the IPM system are now enjoying higher crop yields than their neighbors using traditional methods.

1. By softening and loosening the top layers of soil, it is more easily carried away by water and wind.
2. Crop rotation maintains the fertility of a field but prevents the farmer from growing the most profitable crop year after year.
3. Sustainable agriculture reduces or eliminates the use of chemical fertilizers and pesticides, relying on organic methods instead.

SECTION REVIEW

1. Explain the role of tilling in soil erosion.
2. Describe how crop rotation benefits a field. What might be a disadvantage of crop rotation?
3. **Apply** Why do you think sustainable agriculture is sometimes called regenerative farming?

CHAPTER 14 REVIEW

KEY TERMS

carbohydrate 14.1
protein 14.1
essential amino acid 14.1

lipid 14.1
malnutrition 14.1
Green Revolution 14.2

cash crop 14.2
aquaculture 14.2
sustainable agriculture 14.4

CHAPTER SUMMARY

14.1 Humans need to consume enough energy, or Calories, to carry out life processes, as well as a blend of other nutrients to maintain good health. Carbohydrates, protein, and fat are macronutrients that provide energy. Vitamins and minerals are micronutrients needed for biochemical reactions. Nutritional deficiencies result from too little of a particular type of nutrient in the diet.

14.2 The world's food supply has been increasing faster than the population, but the economics and politics of food distribution often prevent food from reaching hungry people. The Green Revolution of the 1960s increased the productivity of modern farms, but did not help the poorer farmers of the world who cannot compete with the machinery

and high-yield grains used in developed nations. Cash crops are often grown for export because they command higher prices. Aquaculture of seafood can contributes to the food supply.

14.3 Modern farming is based on the use of machinery, chemical fertilizers, pesticides, and monoculture crops. Each of these practices has some problems, including environmental degradation.

14.4 Sustainable agriculture, or regenerative farming, is based on practices that enable fields to produce crops without damaging the soil. Sustainable farming practices include crop rotation, reduction of erosion, and integrated pest management.

MULTIPLE CHOICE

Choose the letter of the word or phrase that best completes each statement.

1. The kilocalories in a food indicates the amount of (a) protein; (b) carbohydrates; (c) healthfulness; (d) energy. d

2. Energy in foods is provided by (a) vitamins; (b) minerals; (c) macronutrients; (d) micronutrients. c

3. Nitrogen is a component of all (a) proteins; (b) carbohydrates; (c) fats; (d) vitamins. a

4. The nutrient that provides the greatest amount of energy per gram is (a) fat; (b) vitamins; (c) protein; (d) carbohydrate. a

5. The Green Revolution occurred during the (a) Middle Ages; (b) nineteenth century; (c) the 1960s; (d) the 1980s. c

6. A cash crop is a crop intended for (a) animal feed; (b) export; (c) protecting the soil

between growing seasons; (d) local use. b

7. In some developing nations, the percent of animal protein that comes from fish can be as high as (a) 10 percent; (b) 20 percent; (c) 40 percent; (d) 80 percent. d

8. To help restore nitrogen to the soil, fields should occasionally be planted with (a) cash crops; (b) grains; (c) legumes; (d) weeds. c

9. Quinoa is a (a) type of wheat; (b) historical food of the Incas; (c) plant native to Asia; (d) type of cover crop. b

10. The effects of tilling include (a) reduced soil drainage; (b) improved crop production; (c) reduced need for energy input; (d) increased soil erosion. d

11. An IPM is used to (a) control pests; (b) aerate soil; (c) improve soil nutrients; (d) reduce erosion. a

CHAPTER 14 REVIEW

TRUE/FALSE

Write true *if the statement is true. If the statement is false, change the underlined word to make it true.*

1. A saturated fat contains <u>more</u> hydrogen than an unsaturated fat. t
2. The essential amino acids are those that <u>can</u> be made by the body. f; cannot
3. Compared to protein, carbohydrates contain <u>fewer</u> calories per gram. f; the same
4. The use of pesticides tends to <u>decrease</u> the number of resistant pests. f; increase
5. Tilling of soil has the effect of <u>increasing</u> soil aeration. t
6. A monoculture crop contains a <u>variety</u> of species. f; only one
7. Agribusiness corporations produce more than <u>two-thirds</u> of the food in the U.S. t

CONCEPT REVIEW Answers on page T80.

Write a complete response to each of the following

1. Explain how the Green Revolution caused hardship for some farmers.
2. Describe the difference in structure between a saturated and an unsaturated fat.
3. Explain the benefits and problems associated with heavy tilling of farm soil.
4. What are cover crops, and why are they grown?

THINK CRITICALLY Answers on page T80.

1. What might be the economic value of paying farmers not to grow crops? Who would benefit from such a policy?
2. If you were the owner of a small farm in a developing nation, would you grow food for people or animal feed for export? Would your answer be the same if you could receive three times the price for the animal feed? Explain your answer.
3. Describe the principle behind crop rotation and its benefit to farmers. Can you think of any drawbacks to crop rotation?
4. Abraham Lincoln once said, "You cannot escape the responsibility of tomorrow by evading it today." How can this idea be applied to the world's food situation?

WRITE CREATIVELY

In the Charles Dickens novel *The Prince and the Pauper*, two boys, one rich and one poor, trade lifestyles. Write a similar short story about a teenager from the United States who trades places with a teenager from a developing nation. Be sure to include the perspective of both characters.

PORTFOLIO

1. There have been many famines that have affected the progress of human civilization. Choose a major famine in human history and research the causes and effects of the famine. Make a poster or other visual representation showing the flow of events leading up to and following the famine.
2. There are hunger relief centers, such as soup kitchens and shelters, in the United States. Visit one of these establishments, and talk with some of the people, including workers at the facility. Determine what factors contributed to the situations the people are now facing. Write a magazine-style article about your findings.

GRAPHIC ANALYSIS Answers on page T80.

Use the figure to answer the following.

1. During which year did the greatest percentage increases in insecticide-resistant species occur?
2. Why do you think there was relatively little change between 1943 and 1957?
3. Between 1961 and 1965, the amount of DDT needed to kill a tobacco budworm increased from 0.13 mg to 16.51 mg. How does this relate to the graph?

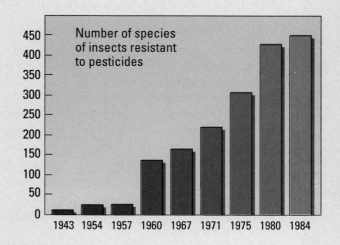

Number of species of insects resistant to pesticides

ACTIVITY 14.2

Answers and teaching strategies on page T80.

PROBLEM
Which foods contain more protein than others?

MATERIALS (per groups of 2 or 3)
- 5 test tubes
- test-tube rack
- Biuret's solution
- small amount of each of these 5 foods:
  cooked egg white
  potato
  tuna fish packed in water
  mashed lima beans
  white bread

PREDICTION
After reading through the activity, predict which food sample will contain the most and the least protein.

PROCEDURE
Biuret's solution is light blue. When combined with protein, it turns purple.

1. Label five test tubes *A* through *E*, and place them in the test tube rack.
2. Place a small sample of these foods in the test tubes: tube *A*, cooked egg white; tube *B*, potato; tube *C*, tuna fish packed in water; tube *D*, mashed lima beans; tube *E*, white bread.
3. Add 5 mL of Biuret's solution to each test tube. **Caution:** *If you get any of the Biuret's solution on your skin or clothes, immediately wash off the area with water.*
4. Wait several minutes, then observe the color of the Biuret's solution in the test tubes. Record your observations.
5. Rank the food samples with numbers from 1 (most protein) to 5 (least protein).

ANALYSIS
1. How did your results compare with your prediction?
2. Can you make a generalization about the amount of protein in animal products compared to plant products based on your results? Why or why not?
3. Why was there no control test tube in this experiment?

CONCLUSION
Based on your observations, which of the foods that you tested would you send to the starving people of a war-ravaged area? Discuss this issue as a class.

ENVIRONMENTAL EDUCATION

Environmental education is a growing field with many diverse applications. It encompasses classroom teaching at all grade levels; outdoor education at zoos, parks, and nature centers; print and electronic environmental journalism; public information in industry and government; and environmental education to raise public awareness. Best described as a blend of disciplines, environmental education brings together people of varied backgrounds: those who are strong in science education, those who are at ease in the public spotlight as information officers and community affairs managers, and those who blend strong journalism talents with science backgrounds. The one common thread that unites all these people is the drive to inform the public to understand and protect the world of nature.

About 60 percent of environmental educators are in the public sector as teachers in our school systems and colleges, environmental educators for state and local agencies, and interpretive rangers in our national parks. Approximately 10 percent are in the private sector, serving as community affairs managers, public information officers, trainers and workshop leaders, and journalists. The remaining 30 percent work in the nonprofit sector for organizations dedicated to educating the public on environmental issues. Groups such as the Sierra Club, Greenpeace, and the National Wildlife Federation, along with many local grass-roots organizations, do much to spread information and create public awareness.

What is the best type of background for an environmental educator? People often disagree about this topic. Some think that obtaining a degree in education and developing strong communication skills are more important than science and technical knowledge. Others maintain that students should primarily concentrate on science classes and acquiring technical knowledge, and let education and communication skills come later. Most likely, a combination of education and technical experience will get you jobs in environmental education. As a student, you can volunteer for local groups and causes whenever possible. This experience will look good on a resume, and will help you make many valuable contacts.

COMMUNITY AFFAIRS MANAGERS ▶

Working in the private sector, community affairs managers serve as links between their companies and the public. They listen and respond to public complaints, and meet with representatives of environmental organizations to help deal with environmental issues. Community affairs managers are also responsible for educating the public about steps their companies are taking to help the environment and lessen the negative impact their companies may have on the community.

◄ ENVIRONMENTAL JOURNALISTS

Environmental journalists are public educators at-large, spreading information, in print or electronically, about the latest issues in the field. They report on new techniques that are saving the environment, which companies are taking active steps to correct past mistakes, and which companies are playing a positive role in helping preserve our fragile ecosystems. Many journalists get their start by volunteering. Whether reporting for the school paper or writing an article for a private group or organization, volunteering opens doors and gives new journalists valuable experience.

ENVIRONMENTAL STUDIES EDUCATORS ►

Teachers of environmental studies are responsible for educating students about their interrelationship with the environment, while instilling in students a love of nature. At the elementary and secondary level, these teachers give students some of their first experiences of how humans affect their environment, and what students can do in their communities to improve their relationship with the natural world. At the college level, environmental educators teach those who will become the caretakers of the future.

INTERPRETIVE NATURALISTS ▼

Interpretive naturalists have one of the most desirable jobs in environmental education. Working at the hubs of public education in state and national parks, as well as in the community, these naturalists lead groups, conduct lectures, and distribute a wealth of information about their particular areas. They raise public awareness, which helps preserve the environment. They also serve as guides for visitors to these areas, sharing their knowledge and encouraging public appreciation.

FOR MORE INFORMATION:

National Association of Professional Environmental Educators
P.O. Box 06 8352
Chicago, IL 60611
(312) 661–1700

North American Association for Environmental Education
(Sponsors annual conferences and workshops, lists internships and job opportunities, and publishes *The Environmental Communicator bimonthly*)
P.O. Box 400
Troy, OH 45373

Outdoor Writers Association of America
2017 Cato Avenue, Suite 101
State College, PA 16801
(814) 234–1011

UNIT 5

ENERGY RESOURCES

CHAPTERS

15 Organic Fuels
16 Nuclear Energy
17 Solar and Alternative Energies

火 This symbol means *fire*. It comes from China. Fire was the first form of energy used by people. They used it for light, heat, and cooking. Today, in addition to basic needs, people use energy for transportation and processing information. This energy comes from many sources. Fuels such as wood, coal, and oil are common around the world. Nuclear fuels are an important and controversial source of energy. Solar energy and other alternative sources will become common in the future.

Cooking food is one of the oldest and most important ▶ uses that people have for energy. Pollution produced by burning fuels is a serious environmental problem. Alternative energy sources, such as solar, wind, and water, can help reduce this pollution.

232

CHAPTER

15

ORGANIC FUELS

What would your life be like without electricity? Of course, there would be no electric lights, televisions, stereo systems, or video games. There would also be no movie theaters or amusement parks. Most large home appliances, such as dishwashers, washing machines, and refrigerators, would also not exist. People have come to take for granted the conveniences and pleasures that electricity can provide. Where does the electricity come from? Although electricity can be generated from many types of fuels, most electricity is produced by burning organic fuels. Much of the oil pumped by off-shore drilling is used to produce electricity.

15.1 THE NEED FOR ENERGY

Objectives • *Explain* how changes in human societies have changed the demand for energy. • *Describe* the structure of organic fuels.

Heat, light, and electricity are three forms of energy with which you are probably familiar. Other forms of energy include mechanical energy, chemical energy, and nuclear energy. Together, these forms of energy meet the energy needs of the people on Earth.

One of the laws of physics states that energy cannot be created or destroyed. Energy can, however, be changed from one form to another. The storage, transfer, and conversion of energy are the driving forces behind all life on Earth. For example, the energy in the food you eat once came from the sun. First, the energy is converted to chemical energy that is stored in plant material. When you eat food, the energy stored in the plant or animal tissues is converted to heat, mechanical energy, and the chemical energy used to carry out life processes. Food is a form of fuel that your body uses for energy. *A* **fuel** *is any substance from which energy can be obtained.*

Except for lightning, electricity is not a form of energy that is common in nature. Electricity is generated by the conversion of other forms of energy. To produce electricity, fuel must first be converted to mechanical energy, which turns giant machines called turbines. This is usually accomplished by using the original fuel to boil water, which produces steam. The pressure of the steam provides mechanical energy that rotates the turbines. The turning of the turbines generates electricity. Much of the energy needed by today's society is used to generate electricity. But the conversion of energy from one form to another is never 100 percent efficient. Some energy is lost during the conversion, usually in the form of heat, light, or both.

Changing Energy Needs

The energy needs of most nations of the world have changed over time. Hunter–gatherer societies had very limited energy requirements. People used energy only for light, heat, and cooking. Wood adequately met these needs. Later, as agricultural societies emerged, some energy demands changed. For example, domesticated animals such as horses, mules, and oxen became the power sources for plows and other farm equipment.

Following the Industrial Revolution in the late eighteenth century, societies that had been based largely on agriculture turned to industry to meet the needs of their growing populations. Tasks that used to be done by people and animals were taken over by machines. For example, farm equipment such as the horse-drawn plow gave

Figure 15.1 The manufacture and operation of machinery have greatly increased the need for energy in agriculture.

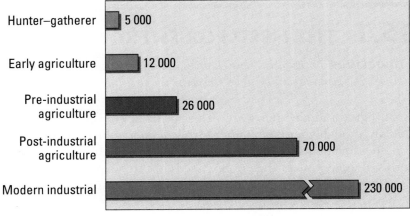

Figure 15.2 The need and uses for energy have changed over time as societies developed from agricultural to industrial cultures.

Kilocalories per person per day

Hunter–gatherer — 5 000
Early agriculture — 12 000
Pre-industrial agriculture — 26 000
Post-industrial agriculture — 70 000
Modern industrial — 230 000

You may wish to have students pool their data and develop a class graphic.

Additional teaching tips are on page T85.

way to tractors and harvesters. Manufacturing these machines required large amounts of iron, steel, and other materials produced in factories. Both the factories producing such equipment and the use of the equipment itself required large amounts of fuel.

Factories that produce the clothing, furniture, and building materials needed by a growing population also increase fuel consumption. Even more fuel is required to distribute and market these products. As societies have developed, their energy demands have both changed and increased.

Fuels from Organisms

Fuels made from organisms are organic fuels. Organic fuels contain carbon-based molecules that were formed by living things. In addition to carbon, organic fuels also contain hydrogen. *A compound composed only of carbon and hydrogen is called a* **hydrocarbon**. Methane is a simple hydrocarbon. As shown in Figure 15.3, the formula for methane is CH_4. Ethane is a hydrocarbon with the chemical formula C_2H_6. Octane is an eight-carbon hydrocarbon with the formula C_8H_{18}.

Notice that octane can have two different arrangements of carbon. Because of the branched arrangement of the bonds, iso-octane contains more energy than regular octane. You may recognize the word *octane* as being an important component of gasoline. It is actually iso-octane that is the desirable ingredient. The rating number of gasoline that appears on the pumps is derived from a complex formula based on the amount of energy contained in the gasoline compared to the energy of pure iso-octane.

With the exception of single-carbon methane, all hydrocarbon molecules contain carbon atoms bonded to each other in a chain. The chain may be straight, branched, or arranged in a ring. In nature, only the biological activities that take place within the cells of organisms can cause carbon to form such chains. Because these

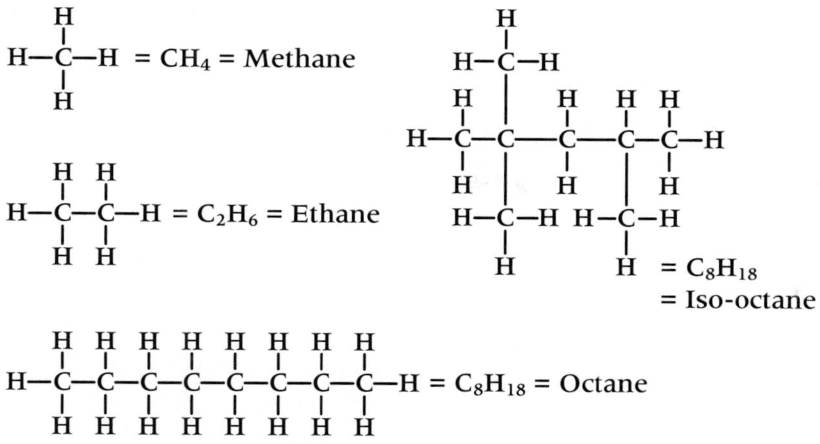

Figure 15.3 Hydrocarbons contain only carbon (C) and hydrogen (H). The carbons may be arranged in a straight chain, branched, or in a ring structure.

molecules must come from organisms, the study of hydrocarbons and related chemicals is known as organic chemistry.

In addition to hydrocarbons, many organic fuels contain other chemicals, such as sulfur or lead compounds. These other chemicals are considered to be impurities in the fuel. Some of these impurities, such as lead in gasoline, improve the ability of the fuel to provide usable energy. Unfortunately, impurities also contribute to the pollution released when the fuels are burned.

Fossil Fuels

Like the organisms of today, ancient organisms required energy to carry out their life processes. The energy was provided by the sun and converted to stored chemical energy by plants. This energy was then used by the plants themselves or passed on to animals that ate the plants. When these organisms died, the energy remained stored in their cells.

The energy stored within the cells of organisms that died millions of years ago is used today as fuel. *Fuels derived from the remains of organisms that lived long ago are called* **fossil fuels**. Fossils are the remains or traces of living things. Fossil fuels are one category of organic fuel. There are three kinds of fossil fuels: coal, petroleum, and natural gas.

Cooperative Learning
Have students keep a journal for one week that details all the ways they use energy. Working in groups of three to five, they should combine their journal entries into a group log. Challenge students to identify ways they can reduce the amount of energy they use without eliminating any of the activities on their list. Have a student or pair of students from each group explain their energy-saving alternatives to the class.

SECTION REVIEW

1. What is a fuel?
2. How can you recognize a hydrocarbon from its molecular structure?
3. **Apply** Make a list of four activities in your daily life that can be accomplished with or without tools that require energy. Example: you can open a can manually or you can use an electric can opener.

1. A fuel is a substance from which energy can be obtained.
2. Hydrocarbons contain only carbon and hydrogen.
3. Responses will vary.

Figure 15.4 Peat (top) is not coal, but it is the first stage of coal formation. Lignite (center) gives off little smoke, but less heat than other forms of coal. Anthracite (bottom) is the purest and hottest-burning form of coal. It is also the least common and most expensive.

Students may benefit from a review of Chapter 1, in which the formation of igneous, sedimentary, and metamorphic rock is discussed.

15.2 COAL

Objectives • *List the stages of coal formation and describe the characterisitics of each stage.* • *Locate the major coal deposits on a map of the United States.*

Millions of years ago, many parts of Earth that are now dry land were covered by swamps. These areas had a warm, humid climate that was ideal for plant growth. As these plants died, their remains accumulated and, in time, were covered by sediments. Over millions of years, layer upon layer of sediment covered the plant remains. The heat and pressure produced by the weight of these sediments caused chemical changes to occur within the plant matter. At the same time, water was forced out. These processes changed the plant material into a solid rock called coal.

Coal formation occurs in stages. Each stage produces a material with distinct physical and chemical properties. You can see the locations of major coal deposits in the United States in Figure 15.5.

Peat

Plant materials become compressed, forming a compacted mass of twigs, leaves, and branches called peat. **Peat** *is a brittle, brown plant material containing a great deal of water and a low percentage of carbon.* Peat is not a form of coal, but its formation is the first stage in the formation of coal. Peat resembles wood and is usually located at or near Earth's surface. Peat burns very quickly. It also gives off a large amount of smoke because of its high percentage of water and impurities.

Lignite

The second stage in coal formation is lignite. Over millions of years, layers of sediments are deposited on top of beds of peat. The heat and pressure caused by the weight of these sediments compress the peat, changing it to lignite. **Lignite** (LIG-nyt) *is a soft, brown coal composed of about 40 percent carbon.* Lignite burns quickly and gives off very little smoke. Unlike peat, most lignite is located below Earth's surface and must be mined.

Bituminous Coal

Over time, heat and pressure change lignite into a purer form of coal called bituminous coal. **Bituminous** (by-TOO-mih-nus) **coal** *is a soft coal located deep in Earth's crust.* Deep shafts are used to take miners down into the ground to remove this coal. Bituminous coal is the most abundant type of coal mined in the United States.

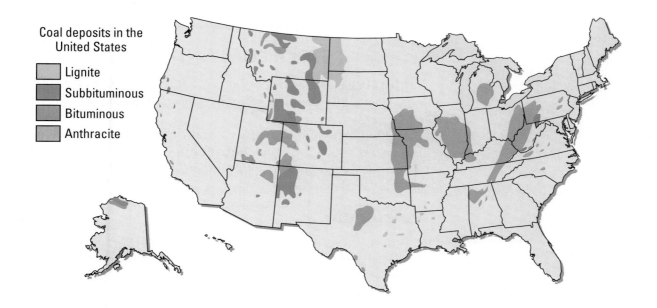

Coal deposits in the
United States

- Lignite
- Subbituminous
- Bituminous
- Anthracite

Bituminous coal has less water and fewer impurities than lignite. It also has a higher carbon content and burns hotter and with less smoke than peat or lignite. Bituminous coal is the main fuel used in industry, and it is used by many power plants to produce electricity. In addition, many homes are heated with bituminous coal.

Figure 15.5 Bituminous coal is the most common form of coal in the United States. Subbituminous coal is a stage of coal formation that occurs between lignite and bituminous forms.

Anthracite Coal

As more sediments are added to the upper layers of rock, greater pressure and heat are exerted on the bituminous coal. *Extreme pressure and heat change the sedimentary bituminous coal into a metamorphic rock called* **anthracite** (AN-thruh-cyt) **coal**, *or hard coal.* Anthracite coal has a shiny black color, and it is located deeper in the ground than any of the other forms of coal.

Anthracite coal has less water and fewer impurities than any other form of coal. It also burns the hottest and has the highest carbon content of all forms of coal. These characteristics make anthracite coal clean-burning and almost smokeless. Anthracite coal is most often used to heat homes and is considered the best form of coal because it burns cleanly. However, because anthracite coal is less abundant and located deeper in the ground than other forms of coal, it is also more expensive.

GEOLOGY LINK

Coal that is subjected to an extreme increase in heat and pressure turns into diamonds. Diamonds are made of pure carbon. Diamonds are mined from deep beneath Earth's surface. Many diamond mines are located in South Africa. The hardest mineral known, diamonds are used in cutting and drilling tools.

SECTION REVIEW

1. What is the most common type of coal in the United States?
2. Why is anthracite coal the most expensive type of coal?
3. **Infer** Explain why peat is not considered to be a fossil fuel.

1. Bituminous coal.
2. It is rare and releases the most heat when burned.
3. It is formed from modern organisms that died recently, rather than millions of years ago.

15.3 PETROLEUM AND NATURAL GAS

Objectives • ***Describe*** *the processes of petroleum formation and extraction.* • ***List*** *several uses for petroleum and natural gas.*

Each kind of fossil fuel occurs naturally in a different state of matter. Coal is a solid fossil fuel. **Petroleum** (puh-TRO-lee-um), *which is also called crude oil, is a liquid fossil fuel.* Fossil fuel in the gaseous state is called *natural gas.*

Petroleum

As you have read, coal is a fossil fuel formed from the remains of plants that lived in swamps. Petroleum is a liquid fossil fuel. Scientists think that petroleum formed from the remains of plankton and other microscopic protists, plants, and animals living in shallow seas millions of years ago. The remains of these organisms settled on the ocean floor and were covered by sediments. Over millions of years, the pressure and heat produced by the sediments converted the remains of these organisms into a syrupy liquid called petroleum.

As petroleum formed, it seeped into pores and cracks of sedimentary rocks. When the petroleum became covered by nonporous rock such as shale, pools of petroleum became trapped below the surface. Other substances, such as water and natural gas, also collected in the pools of petroleum.

A great deal of pressure can build up in an oil pool trapped deep in the ground. When a well is drilled into this pool, the pressure forces the oil to shoot upward, forming a gusher. Where there is little or no pressure, oil must be pumped to the surface.

Petroleum is one of the world's most important resources. The petroleum pumped from a well is separated, or refined, to make a variety of products. Gasoline and jet fuels come from petroleum. The

Word Power

Petroleum, from the Latin, *petra* , "rock," and *oleum*, "oil."

DATELINE 1859

The first commercial oil well was drilled and opened for business on August 27, 1859, in Titusville, Pennsylvania, by Edwin L. Drake. The construction of the well marked the beginning of the so-called age of petroleum.

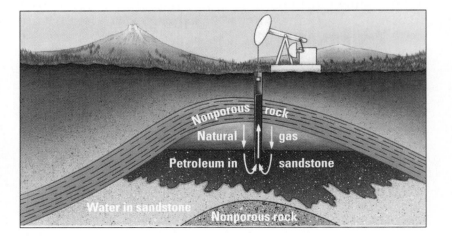

Figure 15.6 Petroleum and natural gas are trapped below the surface between layers of nonporous rock, such as shale. The pressure of the rocks above the pool of oil forces the oil to the surface once the pool has been tapped.

diesel fuel used by trucks, ships, and trains is also a petroleum product. Fuel oil is used to heat homes and to produce electricity in generating plants. In addition to fuel, petroleum is also used to make non-fuel products. Grease and other lubricants used to reduce friction are petroleum by-products. The asphalt used to pave roads, synthetic fabrics such as nylon and polyester, as well as many forms of plastics are also made from petroleum.

Because petroleum takes millions of years to form, it is not a renewable resource. As worldwide populations increase, so does the demand for petroleum. Each day, industrialized nations are becoming more and more dependent on petroleum to meet the energy needs of their people.

Natural Gas

Natural gas is a mixture of gases. These gases include methane, ethane, propane, and small amounts of hydrogen sulfide, carbon dioxide, nitrogen, and helium. The composition of natural gas varies according to its source.

More than 2,000 years ago, the Chinese used bamboo poles to pipe natural gas to areas where they evaporated seawater to recover the salt. The people of Italy made commercial use of natural gas in 1802 when they began burning the gas to light the streets of Genoa. Today, natural gas is used in industry in the same way as coal or oil. In many homes and businesses, natural gas is used instead of coal or oil for heating because it burns cleaner than these other fuels. Common household appliances that can use natural gas as a fuel include gas stoves, water heaters, and clothes dryers. Because the natural gas does not have to be converted to electricity first, appliances that use natural gas instead of electricity are more energy-efficient and less expensive to use.

Natural gas forms in much the same way as petroleum. Natural gas is located in regions that produce petroleum or coal. The same well frequently produces both natural gas and oil. In fact, natural gas is sometimes viewed as a waste, or by-product, of petroleum drilling. Petroleum processing plants, such as the one in Figure 15.7, can sometimes be seen burning off the natural gas.

Figure 15.7 Natural gas is sometimes burned off as a by-product of petroleum drilling and processing.

SECTION REVIEW

1. List five different products made from petroleum. Include fuels and other products in your list.
2. Why is using natural gas as a fuel for cooking more efficient than using electricity?
3. **Compare and Contrast** Compare and contrast the formation of petroleum and the formation of coal.

1. Gasoline, diesel and jet fuel, heating oil, plastic, synthetic fabrics.
2. Electricity has to be converted from another source, and energy is always lost in the process.
3. Coal is made from plant material only. Petroleum is made from plants, animals, and protists. Both result from the action of heat and pressure over millons of years.

Public versus Private Transportation

Which type of transportation is better?

On a typical weekday morning in Los Angeles, 3.3 million commuters jam the roads. Of all these daily travelers, 3 percent commute by train or bus. Seven out of 10 cars on the road contain only one passenger. Elsewhere in the United States, this scene is repeated as 144 million cars take to the streets each day throughout the year.

Each year, an average American will travel about 9,000 miles by car. To accommodate automobile travel, the United States has paved over 3 million miles of land. One-quarter of all the energy consumed in this country is used for transportation; three-quarters of the energy used for transportation goes to fueling highway vehicles.

The increasing use of the car has caused a decline in public transportation. City public transit use has declined by more than 50 percent since the early 1970s. However, the impact of cars on the environment has led some people to reconsider public transportation. Tax money funds the building and maintenance of roads, trains, and buses. Because this money is limited, governments and citizens must decide if the money should be spent on public or private transportation projects.

Points Supporting Private Transportation

• Twenty-two percent of American workers depend on the automobile industry for a living. Funding public transportation projects could cost many of these people their jobs.
• Most roads in the United States are already built. Because the taxpayers have already paid for the roads, they should be able to use them.
• Public transportation is not time-efficient. Buses and trains make many stops, and if a person has to transfer, it may take a long time to reach a destination.
• People have to adjust to the schedule of a public transportation system. In today's busy, complicated world, a person has to be able to move about as needed.

Points Supporting Public Transportation

• Automobile exhaust is a major source of carbon monoxide, sulfur oxides, and other pollutants that affect human health.
• Cars release a large amount of carbon dioxide, which may lead to global warming. Global warming will affect the climate of the entire planet.
• Fossil fuels are a limited resource. A bus is 1.5 times more fuel-efficient as a car because it

can carry more passengers. If people use public transportation, fossil-fuel reserves will last longer. Also, the amount of fossil fuels shipped will be reduced, resulting in fewer oil spills.
• Each year, over 50,000 people are killed and over a million people are injured in the United States in car accidents. Using public transit would reduce the number of vehicles on the road, which would lower the accident rate.

DECISIONS

1. Do you think tax money should be spent to build roads for automobiles or to improve public transit? Explain your reasoning.
2. How would better public transportation affect the area where you live?

15.4 OTHER ORGANIC FUELS

Objectives • **Describe** *some of the problems associated with the use of fossil fuels.* • **Compare** *biomass fuels to fossil fuels, and give an example of a bioconversion technique.*

There are many problems associated with the increasing use of fossil fuels. To help resolve some of the problems, scientists are looking into developing fuels from other organic sources. Alternative fuels can solve some, but not all, of the problems of using fossil fuels.

Problems with Fossil Fuels

Most of the problems associated with the use of fossil fuels fall into two general categories: availability and pollution. The availability problem stems from the fact that fossil fuels are not renewable. All the coal, oil, and natural gas that will ever be available to humans is already formed. To reach these resources, people have to keep looking deeper beneath Earth's surface and exploring farther into natural areas. The proposal to search for oil in the Alaska tundra was examined in Chapter 7. California and other coastal states are constantly addressing the question of whether or not to explore for oil offshore. Wherever exploration for fossil fuels takes place, the risk of environmental damage is great. Oil spills and other forms of widespread habitat alteration are possible results of exploring for fossil fuels.

An alternative to seeking new fossil fuel sources is to depend on the large deposits of oil that are already known to exist. Unfortunately for many nations, oil deposits are not always located in the same country that needs the fuel. In 1991, Operation Desert Storm, also known as the Persian Gulf War, reminded many Americans of the need to reduce their dependence on imported oil.

DATELINE 1973

OPEC, the Organization for Petroleum Exporting Countries, put an oil embargo into effect. An embargo is a government order to stop ships from entering or leaving a port. The embargo disrupted the shipping of oil to many countries throughout the world, resulting in massive oil shortages and long lines at gas stations. The oil shortages led many nations to analyze their energy consumption and begin searching for alternative fuels to meet their needs.

Figure 15.8 Seeking, drilling, and transporting fossil fuels can result in accidents that damage the air, water, and land.

Pollution of various kinds, especially air pollution, is produced by the use of fossil fuels. When fossil fuels are burned, they release carbon dioxide. As a result of the increased use of fossil fuels since the Industrial Revolution, the amount of carbon dioxide in the atmosphere has increased by more than 20 percent. Many scientists, as well as other citizens, think that this increase in carbon dioxide could raise the temperature of Earth through a process called the greenhouse effect. You will read more about the greenhouse effect in Chapter 22.

Obtaining fossil fuels can also be dangerous. Because natural gas is extremely combustible, obtaining natural gas is hazardous. The danger created by natural gas combustion also exists when mining for other fossil fuels. For example, coal miners can die of suffocation by natural gas. At other times, miners perish from explosions of natural gas and coal dust.

Biomass Fuels

Have you ever used wood to make a fire? Wood is an example of a biomass fuel. *A **biomass fuel** is a fuel formed from the products of living organisms.* Other biomass fuels include garbage, methane, and alcohol. Unlike fossil fuels, biomass fuels are a renewable resource. They can be grown specifically for use as fuels in large quantities.

Recall that in a food pyramid, lower-level organisms are the energy source for the next-higher-level organisms. The amount of energy available at any given level depends on the mass of the organisms. The total mass of organisms at a given trophic level is the biomass of that level. The amount of biomass at an energy level determines the amount of energy available.

Wood Many people in the United States who once used wood for fuel now use other fuels as their energy source. However, in developing nations where fuel is too expensive or unavailable, people still rely on wood as a fuel source. In some parts of the world, people spend a great deal of time searching for the wood necessary to meet their energy needs.

Using wood for fuel has advantages and disadvantages. Wood gives off a great deal of smoke that is high in carbon dioxide. Also, obtaining wood can be damaging to natural forests. Trees grown specifically for use as fuel could help reduce this problem.

Garbage The materials you throw away are collectively called garbage. Much of the garbage produced in homes is composed largely of organic materials, such as paper and food scraps. About two-thirds of the material in garbage can be burned. Some cities in the United States are now burning garbage to produce electricity. In this process, heat produced from burning garbage is used to change water into steam. The steam turns the turbines that generate electricity.

Multicultural Perspective
In most developing nations, wood serves as the primary source of fuel. People in India, parts of South America, and the Sahel region of Africa all rely on wood as their primary energy source. As a result of extensive deforestation activities, each of these regions is experiencing a shortage of wood.

MATHEMATICS
L I N K

Scientists estimate that 2 metric tons of garbage produce an amount of energy equal to 1 metric ton of coal. In Paris, France, about 1.7 million metric tons of garbage are burned each year for the production of heat and electricity. How much coal is conserved by this use of garbage?

.875 million metric tons of coal

Figure 15.9 Burning garbage for fuel helps provide energy and reduce the problem of solid waste disposal. Garbage dumps also produce methane, which can be used like natural gas.

Methane People have long known that swamp gas is produced in swamps from decaying plants. Swamp gas is a naturally produced form of methane. Recall that methane is a hydrocarbon and is a main component of natural gas. Decaying garbage in dumps also produces methane. Today, methane is being removed from swamps and garbage dumps for use as a fuel. The methane is used the same way as natural gas.

Alcohol *The conversion of organic materials into fuels is called* **bioconversion** (BY-oh-cun-VER-zhun). One example of bioconversion is the use of plants to make alcohol. Sugarcane and corn are two plants that can be used to make alcohol through bioconversion.

An alcohol is a hydrocarbon in which one of the hydrogens is replaced with a hydroxyl, or oxygen-hydrogen group, as shown below:

```
              H   H                           H   H
              |   |                           |   |
Ethane    H – C – C – H        Ethanol    H – C – C – OH
              |   |                           |   |
              H   H                           H   H
```

The alcohol called ethanol, or ethyl alcohol, is made by yeast through the process of fermentation. Alcohol is a liquid biomass fuel that burns clean and costs little to produce. In Brazil, more than 2 million cars are fueled by ethyl alcohol. Other cars in that country are fueled by a gasoline-alcohol mixture called *gasohol*. Gasohol is a mixture of four parts gasoline to one part alcohol. Manufacturers are now producing car engines that run on alcohol made from sunflower or peanut plants.

THINK CRITICALLY

Propane is a hydrocarbon with a chain of 3 carbon atoms. Draw the chemical structure of the alcohol propanol. Isopropyl alcohol has the same formula as propanol, but the hydroxyl group is attached to the middle carbon. Draw the structure for isopropyl alcohol.

```
Propanol              H   H   H
                      |   |   |
                  H – C – C – C – OH
                      |   |   |
                      H   H   H

Isopropyl             H   H   H
                      |   |   |
alcohol           H – C – C – C – H
                      |   |   |
                      H   OH  H
```

SECTION REVIEW

1. What is bioconversion?
2. Name three types of plants that can be used as biomass fuels.
3. **Infer** What are the two ways that using garbage as fuel helps the environment?

1. Bioconversion is the conversion of organic material into fuel.
2. Corn, sugarcane, wood
3. It provides an inexpensive fuel source and helps eliminate garbage accumulation problems.

Answers and teaching
strategies on page T85.

Supply and Demand of Crude Oil

PROBLEM
So far, about one-quarter of the world's petroleum reserves have been consumed. How long will the supply of oil continue to meet the demand?

MATERIALS (per group)
- graph paper
- pencils, 3 different colors

PREDICTION
Read the entire activity, then write a prediction that is related to the problem.

PROCEDURE
1. Study the information in the data table. Some of the information is the result of analyzing trends. Trends are general movements or directions that have happened in the past. The information is also based on oil reserves known to exist and thought to exist.
2. Using the Oil Production table, make a line graph of the information showing world oil production. Use a whole sheet of graph paper. Plot time along the x-axis, and billions of barrels of crude oil on the y-axis. Connect the data points. Label this line "World Oil Supply."
3. On the same graph that you plotted world oil production, plot the information for U.S. oil production from the same table. Connect the data points using a different colored pencil. Label this line "U.S. Oil Supply."
4. Oil consumption in the United States is currently about 6 billion barrels of oil per year, and has been increasing at a rate of approximately 5 percent each year. Construct a table to show what U.S. oil consumption would be each year between now and the year 2050, based on the expected 5 percent per year increase.

Oil Production

Year	World Oil Production (x 10^9 barrels)	U.S. Oil Production (x 10^9 barrels)
1900	1	0
1925	1	6
1950	4	2.3
1975	18	3.2
2000	37	1.6
2025	19	0.4
2050	9	0.1

5. Use your table to plot data points on the graph showing your projected consumption of oil in the United States between now and 2050. Use a third colored pencil to connect these points. Label this line "U.S. Oil Demand."

ANALYSIS
1. How do current U.S. oil production and world oil production compare in terms of volume?
2. When did U.S. oil production peak? Do you think U.S. demand for oil peaked in the same year? Explain.
3. If the U.S. demand for oil is 6 billion barrels this year, how will it be supplied?
4. If demand continues to increase at 5 percent per year, approximately how much oil will have to be imported into the United States annually in 5 years?

CONCLUSION
1. Do you think the world supply of oil will be able to meet the U.S. demand when you are 30 years old? When you are 50?
2. Two-thirds of the world's oil reserves are in the Middle East. What is your opinion regarding U.S. dependence on foreign oil? What are the alternatives?

CHAPTER 15 REVIEW

KEY TERMS

fuel 15.1
hydrocarbon 15.1
fossil fuel 15.1

peat 15.2
lignite 15.2
bituminous coal 15.2

anthracite coal 15.2
petroleum 15.3
biomass fuel 15.4

bioconversion 15.4

CHAPTER SUMMARY

15.1 Energy can take many forms, including heat, light, electrical, mechanical, chemical, and nuclear energy. The rise of agriculture and the Industrial Revolution increased the energy needs of many human societies. Organic fuels contain hydrocarbon molecules. Fossil fuels are organic fuels formed from the dead tissues of organisms that lived millions of years ago. Coal, petroleum, and natural gas are fossil fuels.

15.2 Coal is a solid fossil fuel made from the remains of plants that lived millions of years ago. Coal forms in several stages: peat, lignite, bituminous coal, and anthracite coal. Heat and pressure force out water, forming coal that is higher in carbon and burns more cleanly.

15.3 Petroleum is a liquid fossil fuel formed from the remains of plants, animals, and protists. Petroleum is used to make heating oil, gasoline, and other liquid fuels. It is also used to make plastics and synthetic fabrics. Natural gas is a fossil fuel made of a mixture of gases, including methane, ethane, and propane. Appliances that use natural gas are more efficient than those that use electricity.

15.4 The use of fossil fuels is associated with many problems, including lack of availability, pollution, and habitat disruption. Biomass fuels, made from organic materials, can help solve some of these problems. Biomass fuels include wood, garbage, methane, and alcohol.

MULTIPLE CHOICE

Choose the letter of the word or phrase that best completes each statement.

1. The first stage in the formation of coal is (a) lignite; (b) peat; (c) anthracite coal; (d) bituminous coal. b
2. Crude oil is another name for (a) alcohol; (b) methane; (c) peat; (d) petroleum. d
3. The burning of garbage to produce electricity is an example of (a) bioconversion; (b) fossil fuels; (c) hydrocarbon; (d) refining. a
4. Compounds that contain only carbon and hydrogen are (a) fuels; (b) fossil fuels; (c) organic fuels; (d) hydrocarbons. d
5. The type of society that has the greatest energy needs is the (a) hunting society; (b) gathering society; (c) industrial society; (d) agricultural society. c
6. The type of coal that is located deepest in Earth's crust is (a) peat; (b) lignite; (c) bituminous coal; (d) anthracite coal. d
7. Of the following, the only example of a biomass fuel is (a) coal; (b) petroleum; (c) wood; (d) natural gas. c
8. The process by which plant sugars are converted to alcohol is called (a) fermentation; (b) bioconversion; (c) purification; (d) distillation. a
9. Biomass fuels are better for the environment than fossil fuels because they (a) do not release carbon dioxide; (b) are renewable resources; (c) are buried beneath the surface; (d) are not products of living things. b
10. The most abundant form of coal in the United States is (a) peat; (b) lignite; (c) anthracite coal; (d) bituminous coal. d

WORD COMPARISONS

Write the letter of the second word pair that best matches the first pair.

1. Coal: fossil fuel as (a) petroleum: crude oil; (b) peat: coal; (c) methane: natural gas; (d) alcohol: biomass fuel. d
2. Crude oil: petroleum as (a) brown coal: lignite; (b) corn: alcohol; (c) gasoline: alcohol; (d) alcohol: gasohol. a
3. Methane: natural gas as (a) petroleum: crude oil; (b) carbon: anthracite coal; (c) petroleum: plastic; (d) sugar: corn. b
4. Petroleum: plastics as a) alcohol: gasoline; (b) coal: carbon; (c) garbage: electricity; (d) industry: fuels. c
5. Mines: coal as (a) petroleum: refineries; (b) corn: alcohol; (c) land: agriculture; (d) wells: petroleum. d

CONCEPT REVIEW Answers on page T85.

Write a complete response for each of the following.

1. Why are coal, oil, and natural gas referred to as fossil fuels?
2. How do biomass fuels differ from fossil fuels?
3. Explain why the making of alcohol for use as a fuel is an example of bioconversion.
4. What chemical properties are shared by coal, oil, and natural gas?
5. Why do societies based on industry have greater fuel needs than societies based on hunting and gathering or agriculture?

THINK CRITICALLY Answers on page T85.

1. How might an increase in the use of biomass fuels benefit an agricultural society?
2. If you were to search for fossil-fuel deposits, what information would you try to find out to help you decide where to look?
3. What environmental risks are associated with offshore oil exploration?
4. Explain why biomass fuels are considered renewable and fossil fuels are considered nonrenewable, when both types of fuel are formed from living things.
5. How does the use of fuels such as alcohol, gasohol, and methane help conserve fossil fuels? Why is conserving fossil fuels important?

WRITE FOR UNDERSTANDING

Identify the topic of each paragraph in Section 15.1. Write a sentence that summarizes the topic of each paragraph. Organize the topics into a summary of the section.

PORTFOLIO

1. Research the locations of petroleum and natural gas deposits in the United States. Combine this information with Figure 15.5 to identify the locations of the major deposits of all types of fossil fuels in the United States. Create a visual representation of the information you collect.
2. Conduct library research to find out what kinds of synthetic fuels are being developed in the laboratory. Determine the uses of each fuel and the benefits and drawbacks associated with the use of synthetic fuels. Present your findings in a written or an oral report.

GRAPHIC ANALYSIS Answers on page T85.

Use the figure to answer the following.

1. During which decade did the quantity of coal surpass the quantity of wood used as a fuel?
2. What event occurred in the 1970s that affected the use of petroleum? What was the effect of this event on coal consumption?
3. Why does the line representing natural gas not appear at the far left side of the graph?

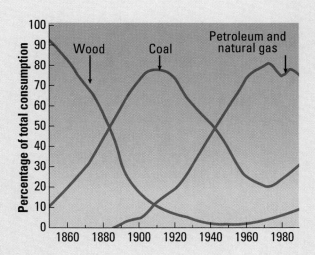

ACTIVITY 15.2

Answers and teaching strategies on page T85.

PROBLEM
What is the effect of coal mining on the environment?

MATERIALS (per group)
- 3 jars or beakers
- masking tape or labels
- marking pen
- cloth rag
- hammer
- pyrite
- sulfur coal
- water
- blue litmus paper

PREDICTION
Read the entire activity, then write a prediction that is related to the problem.

PROCEDURE

1. Make a data table on a separate sheet of paper to record your observations.
2. Label the 3 jars *Pyrite*, *Coal*, and *Water*. Also label the jars with your name or your group's name.
3. Wrap some pyrite in the cloth. Crush the pyrite with a hammer. Place the crushed pyrite in its jar.
   Caution: *Wear safety goggles. Be careful when using the hammer.*
4. Repeat Step 3, using coal instead of pyrite.
5. Drip tap water over the pyrite and coal until they are submerged in the jars. Pour tap water in the last jar.
6. Set the jars in the sun or a warm place for 3 days.
7. After 3 days, test the water in each jar with blue litmus paper. Record any changes in the color of the paper.

ANALYSIS
1. What source of water in a natural environment might the water in the jars represent?
2. Which jar was the control?
3. Which jar(s) contained water that changed the color of the litmus paper after 3 days?
4. What type of substance, if any, formed in the jars?

CONCLUSION
What effect did you predict mining coal might have on the environment?

Nuclear energy comes directly from atoms. In the most common process, atoms of a heavy element such as uranium are split. A small amount of matter in the atom is converted to energy by the reaction. Atomic reactions release a large amount of energy. This energy can be used to generate electricity.

Many places in the world depend on nuclear energy for power. France, for example, gets 60 to 70 percent of its energy from nuclear power. There are about 500 nuclear power plants in operation around the world. Questions about cost, safety, and waste disposal have cast doubt on the future of this energy source.

16.1 ATOMS AND RADIOACTIVITY

Objectives • *Describe* the structure of the atom and the atomic nucleus. • *Explain* how unstable nuclei become stable by releasing radiation.

All matter is made up of atoms. All atoms are made up of just three major kinds of particles. These particles are *protons, electrons,* and *neutrons*. Figure 16.1 shows an atom of the element helium. Notice that the protons and neutrons occur together in the middle of the atom. *This cluster of protons and neutrons in the center of an atom is called the* **nucleus** (NOO-klee-us). The nucleus is orbited by the electrons of the atom. Atoms usually contain the same number of protons and electrons.

Atoms and Isotopes

The basic properties of an atom are determined by the number of protons in its nucleus. All atoms of the same element have the same number of protons in their nuclei. The number of protons in an atom is called the *atomic number* of the element. For example, oxygen has 8 protons, and its atomic number is 8. The atomic number of uranium is 92. Uranium has 92 protons.

The atoms of most elements have neutrons as well as protons and electrons. The number of protons and the number of neutrons make up the atomic mass of an atom. The *atomic mass unit (amu)* is the unit of mass for the atom. Oxygen has an atomic mass of 16. You know that oxygen has 8 protons. Because the atomic mass is equal to the number of protons plus the number of neutrons, oxygen must also have 8 neutrons.

Individual atoms of the same element may have different atomic masses. The atomic masses vary because the number of neutrons in the atoms' nuclei varies. For example, all atoms of the element uranium have 92 protons. Yet some atoms of uranium have 146 neutrons, while others have 143 neutrons. *Atoms of the same element that have different atomic masses are called* **isotopes** (EYE-soh-tohps). Most atoms of uranium contain 146 neutrons and have a mass of 238 amu. This form of uranium is commonly called U-238. Another form, called U-235, has an atomic mass of 235 amu. U-238 and U-235 are isotopes of uranium.

Radioactivity

Some isotopes of atoms are unstable. Unstable atoms sometimes change the number of protons or neutrons in their nuclei in order to become stable. When atoms decay, they emit particles and energy from their nuclei. Atoms that decay in this way are called radioactive atoms. Marie Curie, a Nobel Prize-winning physicist and chemist, was the first person to use the word *radioactive* to describe an element.

Word **Power**
Nucleus, from the Latin *nuculeus*, "small nut" or "kernel."

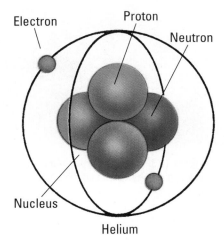

Figure 16.1 A helium atom contains two protons and two neutrons in its nucleus. The nucleus is orbited by two electrons.

Multicultural Perspective
Marie Sklodowska Curie was born in Poland in 1867. Curie left Poland at age 24 and traveled to Paris, where she studied science. Her doctoral thesis was on a strange new discovery she called radioactivity. Marie married a French physicist named Pierre Curie in 1894. The Curies worked in difficult conditions, with little money and only basic equipment. The Curies discovered the elements polonium (named after Marie's native Poland) and radium, and they shared the Noble Prize in Physics in 1903. Marie Curie won another Nobel Prize, this time in Chemistry, in 1911. She died in 1934 after a long series of illnesses caused by exposure to radiation.

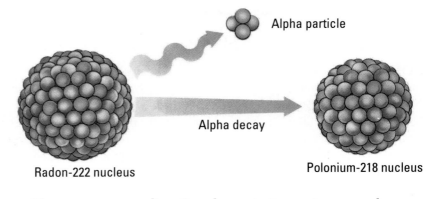

Figure 16.2 Atoms of radon decay into atoms of polonium by releasing an alpha particle. The radioactive decay of radon gas is the largest single source of radiation in many homes in the United States.

Alpha particle

Alpha decay

Radon-222 nucleus

Polonium-218 nucleus

Figure 16.3 Radiation produced by this uranium ore has exposed the photographic film.

1.The difference is the number of neutrons in the nucleus. The identity of an atom is determined by the number of protons in its nucleus. The number of neutrons can vary in atoms of the same element. One isotope is usually more common than the others, and the less common isotopes are often radioactive.
2. Alpha particles are made up of two protons and two neutrons. Beta particles are high-speed electrons. Gamma rays are a form of electromagnetic radiation.
3. The half-life of an element is the amount of time it takes half of a sample of the element to undergo radioactive decay. After one half-life, half of the original sample will remain. The other half will have decayed into atoms of other elements, radiation, and energy.

There are many radioactive elements. In most cases, only certain isotopes of an element are radioactive. For example, the most common isotope of hydrogen, H-1, is not radioactive. However, H-2 and H-3 are radioactive.

Two kinds of particles given off by radioactive atoms are *alpha* (AL-fuh) *particles* and *beta* (BAY-tuh) *particles*. Alpha particles are large particles made up of two protons and two neutrons. Beta particles are high-speed electrons. Radioactive elements also give off energy in the form of *gamma* (GA-muh) *rays*. Gamma rays are a form of electromagnetic radiation. *The alpha particles, beta particles, and gamma rays given off in the decaying of unstable nuclei are called* **radiation**.

An atom that emits alpha particles loses protons and neutrons. This changes its atomic number and its atomic mass. The atomic number of an atom determines which element it is. Thus, when an atom loses an alpha particle, it becomes a different element. This process is called *radioactive decay*.

Uranium has many isotopes. Some of these isotopes are more stable than others. For example, U-238 is the most stable form of uranium. U-235 is unstable. As it decays, uranium-235 changes into thorium-234. But thorium-234 is also unstable. Through a series of decays, the atoms that began as U-235 change to a stable form of lead. The process by which uranium changes to lead takes place over billions of years. *The amount of time in which half the atoms in a sample of a radioactive element decay is called the isotope's* **half-life**. The radioactive decay of other isotopes can occur much more quickly.

SECTION REVIEW

1. What is the difference between two isotopes of an element?
2. Name and describe the three kinds of radiation emitted by radioactive elements.
3. **Explain** What is the half-life of a radioactive sample? Explain the meaning of the term half-life.

16.2 REACTIONS AND REACTORS

Objectives • **Illustrate** *the fission chain reactions that power nuclear reactors and breeder reactors.* • **Diagram** *the structure and function of a nuclear reactor.*

Energy is required to hold the protons and neutrons in an atom's nucleus together. Scientists have discovered ways to release the energy inside an atom. One way to release this energy is by splitting the nucleus of the atom apart. *A reaction in which the nucleus of a large atom is split into smaller nuclei is called* **nuclear fission** (NOO-klee-er FIZH-un). When an atom is broken apart through nuclear fission, it emits large amounts of energy. This energy can be used to generate electricity.

Nuclear Fission

Uranium-235 is the atom used most commonly in fission reactions. An atom of U-235 splits when its nucleus is struck by a neutron. When U-235 splits, it releases energy and forms two new nuclei, called daughter nuclei. These daughter nuclei are often the elements barium or krypton, although there are several hundred possible nuclei that can form in the fission of U-235. Many of these daughter nuclei are radioactive.

The steps in the fission of a U-235 atom are shown in Figure 16.4. To begin the reaction, a neutron is fired into the nucleus of the atom. The neutron strikes the nucleus, which splits, forming two daughter nuclei. The reaction also releases energy and several more neutrons. These neutrons can strike other U-235 nuclei, causing those nuclei to split and release more energy and more neutrons. This continuous action of neutrons splitting atomic nuclei is called a *chain reaction*.

The concept of the fission chain reaction can be difficult to grasp. Diagram a chain reaction on the board, and use the diagram to lead a class discussion. Point out that a uranium nucleus struck by one neutron releases several neutrons. If some of these neutrons are not absorbed by control rods, the chain reaction will cause more fission every second. The increasing number of fissions in the chain reaction is the reason that malfunctioning reactor cores melt down. This increase also causes nuclear bombs to explode.

Figure 16.4 Atoms of uranium-235 undergo a chain reaction in a nuclear reactor. The fission of one atom of U-235 releases several neutrons. These neutrons trigger the fission of several more atoms of U-235.

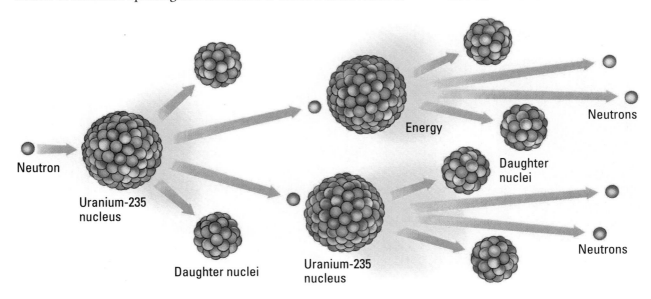

Neutron

Uranium-235 nucleus

Daughter nuclei

Uranium-235 nucleus

Energy

Daughter nuclei

Neutrons

Neutrons

When an atom of U-235 splits, the resulting elements have less mass than the original element. For example, the combined weight of a barium atom and a krypton atom is 221.14 amu. The original uranium atom had a mass of 235 amu. Some of the mass in the original nuclei is missing from the daughter nuclei. The neutrons emitted in the fission reaction contained some of this missing mass. The rest of the mass was converted into energy.

Nuclear Reactors

Electricity is produced from nuclear fuel in much the same way as electricity is produced from fossil fuels. However, in the case of nuclear reactors, heat is produced through the fission of nuclear material instead of the burning of fossil fuels. Nuclear fuel is usually about 97 percent U-238 and 3 percent U-235. The U-238 does not take part in the nuclear reaction.

The fission of U-235 takes place inside a *nuclear reactor vessel*. This vessel can be as tall as 20 m, with steel walls at least 15 to 30 cm thick. The walls are surrounded by a large shield that keeps neutrons and other radiation from escaping from the reactor. The reactor is housed inside a thick concrete container. The fuel for the reactor consists of long rods filled with uranium oxide pellets. These fuel rods contain the fissionable U-235.

The fuel rods are positioned vertically in the center of the reactor so that water can circulate between them. The water performs two functions. It acts as a coolant and slows the movement of the neutrons released during the chain reaction. U-235 will split only when it captures slow-moving neutrons.

The speed of the chain reaction is regulated by *control rods*. Control rods are made of cadmium, boron, or other materials that absorb neutrons. Lowering the control rods into the reactor allows

Figure 16.5 A nuclear power plant generates heat that is used to produce electricity. Waste heat leaves the plant through the cooling tower.

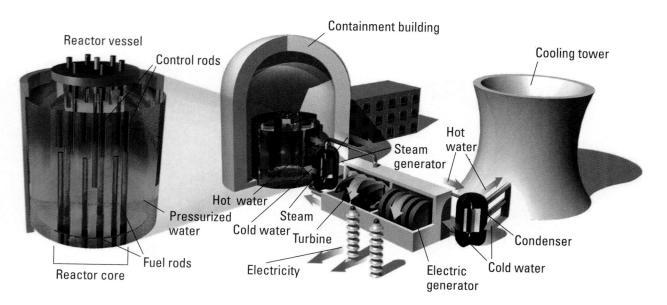

the rods to absorb more neutrons, thus slowing the chain reaction. Raising the rods results in the absorption of fewer neutrons, and the speed of the chain reaction increases.

Raising or lowering the control rods also regulates the amount of heat produced. The temperature of the water circulating within the reactor may reach temperatures above 275°C. This hot water moves inside pipes to a heat exchanger, where it heats water for steam. The steam is then used to turn turbines connected to electric generators.

Breeder Reactors

Some nuclear reactors are designed to produce new fuel as they produce energy. In this process, more fuel may be produced than is used. This is important because fissionable fuel is not very plentiful. A reactor that generates fuel as it works is called a *breeder reactor*.

Plutonium (Pu-239) is used as the fissionable fuel in a breeder reactor. The Pu-239 core is surrounded with non-fissionable U-238. Fast-moving neutrons trigger the chain reaction in plutonium. In a breeder reactor, liquid sodium is used as a coolant. Water cannot be used as a coolant because it would slow down the speed of the neutrons, which keeps the chain reaction going.

Figure 16.6 shows how plutonium is made in a breeder reactor. During the reaction, the U-238 captures a free neutron from the plutonium core and changes to a very unstable isotope, U-239. The U-239 changes to Pu-239, which can be used in the reactor. For every four atoms of plutonium used in the reactor, five new atoms of plutonium are formed from the U-238. A breeder reactor not only produces heat energy, it also manufactures more nuclear fuel.

Figure 16.6 A breeder reactor produces more fuel than it consumes. Neutrons from the fission in a nuclear reactor change stable atoms of uranium-238 into unstable plutonium-239. Plutonium-239 can then be used as a nuclear fuel. This reaction is also used to produce plutonium for nuclear bombs.

Neutron — Uranium-238 → Uranium-239 (Beta decay) → Neptunium-239 (Beta decay) → Plutonium-239

1. In a U-235 fission chain reaction, atoms struck by neutrons split and release daughter nuclei, energy, and neutrons. The released neutrons, in turn, strike other U-235 nuclei.
2. The control rods absorb some of the neutrons released by the chain reaction of U-235.
3. The number of neutrons in the core of the reactor would increase. The reaction would run faster, producing more and more heat, until the core melted from the heat of its own reactions.

SECTION REVIEW

1. Describe what happens in the fission chain reaction of U-235.
2. What function do the control rods perform in a nuclear reactor?
3. **Predict** What would happen to the nuclear fuel in a reactor if the water-cooling system and control rods stopped working?

16.3 RADIOACTIVE WASTE

Objectives • *Define radioactive waste, and explain the dangers that arise from it.* • *State the problems involved in the safe disposal of radioactive wastes.*

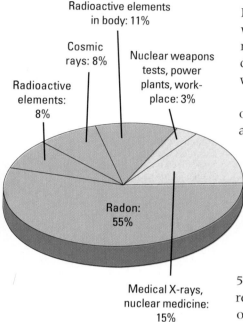

Radioactive elements in body: 11%

Cosmic rays: 8%

Nuclear weapons tests, power plants, workplace: 3%

Radioactive elements: 8%

Radon: 55%

Medical X-rays, nuclear medicine: 15%

■ Natural sources
□ Human produced

Figure 16.7 This graph shows the sources of annual radiation exposure of an average person in the United States. Over half the radiation comes from decaying radon gas. Radon gas comes from decaying uranium atoms in Earth's crust. Average exposure (per person per year) is about 0.5 rems, although the actual amount varies widely.

Nuclear power plants, like most other power plants, produce wastes. But the wastes produced by nuclear power plants are radioactive. About 1.4 metric tons of radioactive wastes are produced by a typical nuclear fission plant in one year. Some of these wastes are more radioactive, and more dangerous, than others.

Excessive radiation is unhealthy for living things. The amount of exposure determines the extent of damage. Large doses of radiation can cause severe skin burns and other health problems—even death. Radiation also causes changes in DNA, leading to cancer and genetic mutations. Even small doses over a long period of time can increase a person's risk of cancer.

Radiation exposure is measured in rems. Most people receive about 0.5 rems a year from natural and human-made sources of radiation. Figure 16.7 shows where an average person is exposed to radiation. During a medical X-ray, a patient is exposed to 0.1 to 1 rem. Until recently, a yearly exposure of up to 5 rems was thought to be safe. Recent findings have shown that 5 rems may not be safe. Radiation exposure varies widely, depending on where a person lives and where he or she works. The amount of radiation produced by a nuclear power plant accident or a nuclear bomb explosion can be enormous.

Types of Waste

Radioactive wastes that emit large amounts of radiation are called **high-level wastes**. High-level waste materials include used uranium fuel rods, control rods, and the water used to cool and control the chain reactions. The vessel that surrounds the fuel rods is also radioactive. These wastes are very dangerous to handle and may also be poisonous.

Medium-level and low-level wastes *are not as radioactive as high-level wastes, although a much larger volume of these wastes is generated.* Medium-level and low-level wastes can be anything from the mine wastes scattered around a uranium mine to the contaminated protective clothes of a power plant worker. Low-level radioactive wastes are also produced by hospitals and laboratories. The damage to people's health that these wastes cause is not as obvious as the damage caused by high-level wastes. Because they are more common, however, medium-and low-level wastes may pose a greater risk to human health.

Waste Disposal

Radioactive wastes are very difficult to dispose of safely. The contaminants may have long half-lives, taking thousands of years to decay. Low-level wastes are dangerous for about 300 years. High-level wastes may be dangerous for tens of thousands of years. Plutonium-239, for example, is a waste product of nuclear reactors and the key ingredient in nuclear bombs. Pu-239 has a half-life of 24,000 years. Plutonium waste will remain dangerous for 192,000 years. Plutonium is also a deadly poison, even in minute amounts.

The long half-lives of elements in radioactive wastes pose a serious disposal problem. Wastes must be sealed in containers that will not corrode for thousands of years. The U.S. government has decided to seal the wastes in thick blocks of glass. The site where wastes are stored must be geologically stable. An earthquake or volcano could spill the stored wastes, so the chance of geologic activity must be low. The wastes must also be stored deep under the ground. The cost of this disposal method is very high.

Almost all the high-level radioactive wastes in the world have not been disposed of permanently. They sit in storage tanks outside nuclear power and weapons plants. In many cases, these tanks have begun to leak, contaminating the groundwater and releasing radioactive wastes into the environment. These wastes must be permanently removed before the contamination gets worse. The government predicts that the cleanup of 17 of the most contaminated nuclear weapons sites in the United States could cost $100 billion.

Medium-level and low-level wastes also pose disposal problems. Low-level wastes are often buried or enclosed in concrete and dropped into the ocean. These methods of disposal expose the environment to contamination. Most medium-level wastes have not been disposed of permanently. A permanent disposal site for medium-level wastes presents many of the same problems as does a site for high-level wastes.

Figure 16.8 This is the Hanford Reservation nuclear weapons facility in Washington state. Large amounts of radioactive wastes have been released into the environment at Hanford. The Columbia River (foreground) has been contaminated several times. The last reactor at Hanford was shut down in 1988. Cleanup at the site has begun.

Identifying a Waste Site

How can people in the future be warned?

Some radioactive wastes give off dangerous levels of radiation for tens of thousands of years. For example, it takes 192,000 years for 1 kg of plutonium-239 to decay to a safe level. Radioactive wastes are buried under the ground in permanent storage sites in the northwestern and southwestern United States. These permanent storage sites will remain dangerously radioactive for many generations.

Imagine the world 10,000 years from now. How will people know that an area is contaminated with hazardous radioactive wastes? How will people be warned of the danger buried below the ground? This task was set before a panel of science, engineering, art, and humanities experts. They concluded that the site must convey a clear message to a culture that may have a different written language, number system, no

knowledge of radioactivity, and no information about the history of the location.

If large structures were erected at the site, would it attract rather than distract people from the sight?

The panel decided to avoid large structures that might attract attention to the area. They chose to scatter small stone and glass markers throughout the contaminated area. Since the markers lie flat on the ground, it is hoped that they will alert people who may travel directly into the area without drawing attention to the site.

What should the markers say? How can you communicate to a culture that may be very different from the society that placed the markers? In the world today, there are many different languages. Symbols,

however, can communicate information without words. For the nuclear waste-site markers, several ideas for symbols were presented. A drawing of atomic fission would convey the message to a culture with scientific knowledge. A skull and crossbones has conveyed danger for much of recent history, so it may still be used as a danger sign. The current symbol of a circle with a slanted slash may also be recognizable to future people.

Will the message engraved on the plaques be an adequate warning? We will never know.

DECISIONS

1. If you were on the panel, describe how you think the site should be identified.
2. Do you think people today should be concerned about the hazards radioactive wastes could pose in the distant future? Why?

Radiation   **Poison**   **"Don't drill"**

Symbols associated in pairs by meaning

ACTIVITY 16.1

Answers and teaching strategies on page T89.

Disposal of Nuclear Waste

PROBLEM
What problems are encountered when storing nuclear waste?

MATERIALS (per group)
- 4 sodium hydroxide pellets
- 4 jars with lids
- phenolphthalein solution
- water
- plastic wrap
- twist-tie
- aluminum foil
- modeling clay
- tweezers
- safety goggles
- tap water
- medicine dropper

INFERENCE
Read the entire activity, then write an inference that is related to the problem.

PROCEDURE

1. You are a scientist who tests nuclear waste storage containers that will be used underground. The sodium hydroxide pellets represent solid nuclear waste that will be radioactive for thousands of years.
   Caution: *Do not touch sodium hydroxide pellets with your bare hands. Use the tweezers and wear safety goggles.*
2. Copy the data table onto a separate sheet of paper.
3. Fill each jar about three-quarters full with water. Use the medicine dropper to add four drops of phenolphthalein solution to each jar.
4. Use the tweezers to put one sodium hydroxide pellet in one of the jars. Observe any changes in the water. This jar is your control. Be sure to label all jars.
5. Handling the pellet with tweezers, wrap one of the remaining pellets tightly in the aluminum foil. Try to make it water tight. Wrap another pellet in plastic wrap, and tie it securely with the twist-tie. It should be water tight as well. Insert the last pellet into the clay. Bend the clay around the pellet to make a watertight seal.
6. Gently drop each wrapped pellet into one of the three remaining jars. This action represents soaking nuclear waste storage containers in groundwater. Screw the lids on the jars.
7. Observe the jars for 3 days. Look for signs of leaks. Record the information in the data table.

ANALYSIS
1. What happened when you put a sodium hydroxide pellet into the water of the control jar?
2. Did any of the wrapped pellets show signs of leakage? If so, which type of wrapping was used and on which day was the leak noticed?
3. Compare your data with that of other groups in your class. Which material would make the best storage container? Which, if any, material would make a storage container with an acceptable risk against leakage?

CONCLUSION
What did you infer at the beginning of this activity regarding the problems associated with storing nuclear waste? Did your observations support the inference? Explain.

Table 16.1

Storage Container	Observations		
	Day 1	Day 2	Day 3
Control			
Aluminum			
Plastic			
Clay			

Figure 16.9 A steam explosion blew the roof off the Chernobyl reactor building. This mutated pine tree grows 500 m from the damaged plant.

MATHEMATICS
L I N K

When the accident occurred, people living near the Chernobyl reactor received a radiation dose of between 20 and 100 rems. This exposure level is 400 to 2000 percent of the level considered safe by the U.S. government. Exposure of this level causes nausea, vomiting, and a greatly increased risk of cancer. About one out of ten of these people will probably die of cancer caused by Chernobyl radiation.

1. High-level radioactive wastes remain dangerous for thousands of years due to long half-lives. Medium-level and low-level wastes are generated in large volume.
3. 55 percent of the average person's radiation exposure is due to radon gas decay.
3. The cause of the Chernobyl accident was human error. This cause cannot be eliminated because humans must be involved in the building and running of nuclear power plants.

Safety and Cost

The danger that radioactive contamination creates for the environment makes safety at nuclear power plants very important. If the cooling and control systems in a reactor core fail, the chain reaction can no longer be controlled. The core will grow hotter, causing the fuel rods and even the reactor vessel to melt. *The process by which a nuclear chain reaction goes out of control and melts the reactor core is called a* **meltdown**. A full meltdown would release huge amounts of radiation into the environment.

Nuclear power plants are built to avoid meltdowns and to contain them if they occur. In April 1986, however, the core of the Chernobyl nuclear power plant in Ukraine did melt down. The plant's control rods were made of graphite. The graphite began to burn, and fire spread radioactivity over a vast area. About 50 people were killed immediately, and 116,000 people had to permanently leave their homes. Scientists think that Chernobyl radiation may cause as many as 15,000 cases of cancer.

The Chernobyl plant was old and lacked many of the safety features built into newer plants. The accident itself was caused by human error. The severity of this accident and the problems with radioactive waste disposal have led many people to question the wisdom of using nuclear power. Nuclear power plants are also very expensive because the required safety measures are very costly.

SECTION REVIEW

1. What makes radioactive waste difficult to dispose of?
2. What percentage of the average person's radiation exposure is due to radon gas?
3. **Analyze** What was the cause of the Chernobyl nuclear accident? Is there any way that this factor can be eliminated?

CHAPTER 16 REVIEW

KEY TERMS

nucleus 16.1

isotope 16.1

radiation 16.1

half-life 16.1

nuclear fission 16.2

high-level waste 16.3

medium-level and
  low-level wastes 16.3

meltdown 16.3

CHAPTER SUMMARY

16.1 The nucleus of an atom is made up of protons and neutrons. The number of protons in the nucleus determines the identity of an atom. Atoms of the same element with different numbers of neutrons are called isotopes. Unstable isotopes emit radiation when they decay to stable atoms. The half-life of a radioactive element is the amount of time it takes for half of a sample of the element to undergo radioactive decay.

16.2 The reaction used to generate energy in a nuclear power plant is called nuclear fission. Uranium-235 is the most common fuel in nuclear power plants. U-235 atoms are split by free neutrons. The fission of a U-235 nucleus generates more free neutrons, maintaining a fission chain reaction. Nuclear power plants use the heat generated by fission to boil water and drive steam generators. Breeder reactors make more nuclear fuel than they consume.

16.3 Nuclear power plants produce radioactive wastes. Radiation is harmful to living things. High-level wastes stay dangerous for many thousands of years. Medium-level and low-level wastes are dangerous for hundreds of years and are produced in large amounts. A safe, inexpensive, and effective way to dispose of radioactive wastes has not yet been found. The Chernobyl nuclear accident released large amounts of radiation into the environment.

MULTIPLE CHOICE

Choose the letter of the word or phrase that best completes each statement.

1. Protons and neutrons are found together in the part of the atom called the (a) alpha particle; (b) electron; (c) nucleus; (d) isotope. c

2. Two atoms of the same element with different atomic masses are called (a) isotopes; (b) nuclei; (c) electrons; (d) neutrons. a

3. One kind of radiation not released by radioactive decay is (a) alpha particles; (b) free protons; (c) beta particles; (d) gamma rays. b

4. The fuel most commonly used in fission reactions is (a) Np-239; (b) U-238; (c) U-235; (d) Pu-239. c

5. Devices that absorb neutrons and are used to control the speed of a fission reactor are called (a) reactor vessels; (b) fuel rods; (c) containment buildings; (d) control rods. d

6. The fuel used in a breeder reactor is (a) Np-239; (b) U-238; (c) U-235; (d) Pu-239. d

7. Each year, an average person in the United States is exposed to a radiation level of (a) 5 rems; (b) 0.5 rems; (c) 50 rems; (d) 500 rems. b

8. Pu-239 has a half-life of (a) 24 years; (b) 240 years; (c) 2,400 years; (d) 24,000 years. d

9. Losing control of the fission reaction in a reactor core may result in a (a) cooldown; (b) meltdown; (c) draindown; (d) cooling tower. b

10. The number of people forced to evacuate because of the Chernobyl accident was (a) 1,160; (b) 11,600; (c) 116,000; (d) 1,160,000. c

CHAPTER 16 REVIEW

TRUE/FALSE

Write true *if the statement is true. If the statement is false, change the underlined word or phrase to make it true.*

1. All isotopes of an element contain the same number of <u>neutrons</u>. f, protons
2. <u>Beta particles</u> contain two protons and two neutrons. f, alpha particles
3. A fission chain reaction begins when an atom of U-235 is struck by a <u>neutron</u>. t
4. In a fission reaction, some of the mass of the original atom is converted to <u>energy</u>. t
5. In a breeder reactor, the fission reaction of <u>Np-239</u> produces neutrons that change U-238 into Pu-239. f, Pu-239
6. Radon gas is responsible for <u>25 percent</u> of the radiation in most U.S. homes. f, 55 percent
7. Plutonium must be stored for <u>192,000 years</u> before it is safe. t
8. The cleanup of the 17 most polluted nuclear weapons facilities in the United States will cost <u>$100 billion</u>. t

CONCEPT REVIEW   Answers on page T89.

Write a complete response for each of the following.

1. Describe how an unstable nucleus of radon-222 decays into the element polonium-218. By what amount does the atomic mass change? How does this change take place?
2. Write a paragraph summarizing the events in a fission chain reaction.
3. What function do the control rods serve in a nuclear reactor?
4. Are there sources of radioactive waste other than nuclear power plants? Name some of these sources.
5. Explain how the half-life of a radioactive element determines how long it will be dangerous to living things.

THINK CRITICALLY   Answers on page T89.

1. An atom of radon-222 releases an alpha particle when it decays into polonium-218. Must the radon atom also emit a beta particle? Explain your answer.
2. Fission bombs work by assembling a large mass of pure uranium-235, or another unstable isotope. This mass, called a critical mass, then undergoes a spontaneous chain reaction and explodes. Why did the reactor core of the Chernobyl nuclear plant melt down instead of exploding like a fission bomb?
3. **Computer Activity** Use a computer graphing program to graph the decay of 1 kg of plutonium over 200,000 years. How did you calculate the numbers for your graph?

WRITE CREATIVELY

Write an essay stating your position on the use of nuclear power. If you think using nuclear power is a good idea, suggest ways to solve the disposal and safety problems caused by radioac- tivity. If you think nuclear power is a bad idea, suggest other energy sources that would replace the energy now supplied by nuclear reactors. Ex- plain how you made your decision.

PORTFOLIO

Use balls of colored clay to build a model of a ura- nium-235 nucleus. Use more clay to build models of daughter nuclei and the other parts of a fission reaction. Mount and label your model.

GRAPHIC ANALYSIS   Answers on page T89.

Use the figure to answer the following.

1. Which state gets the largest percentage of its energy from nuclear power?
2. Do any of the states on this graph get less than half of their energy from nuclear power?
3. Where are these states located? Is there a pattern to the distribution of the states that rely heavily on nuclear energy?
4. Would you expect this graph to show the same states if it graphed the total amount of energy produced by each state instead of a percentage? Why or why not?

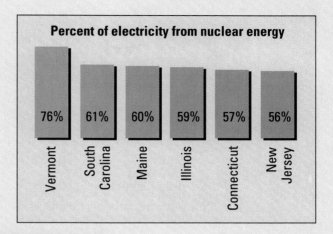

Percent of electricity from nuclear energy

76%	61%	60%	59%	57%	56%
Vermont	South Carolina	Maine	Illinois	Connecticut	New Jersey

ACTIVITY 16.2

Answers and teaching strategies on page T89.

PROBLEM

How can you model the reactions that occur in a nuclear reactor?

MATERIALS (per group)

- 15 dominoes
- stopwatch
- ruler

INFERENCE

Read the entire activity, then write an inference that is related to the problem.

PROCEDURE

1. Stand 15 dominoes in a single straight row. The distance between them should be about half their height. Knock over the first domino. Measure and record the time it takes for all the dominoes to fall.
2. Repeat Step 1 two more times. Average the three times.
3. Arrange the dominoes in four rows. The distance between rows should be about half their height. Arrange them so that each domino in the first three rows will knock over two others. The row closest to you should have only one domino. The second row should have two dominoes. The third row should have four dominoes, and the fourth row should have eight dominoes. Knock over the first domino. Measure and record the time it takes for all the dominoes to fall.
4. Repeat Step 3 two more times. Average the three times.
5. Set up the dominoes again, as in Step 3. This time, hold a ruler on edge between the third and fourth rows. Knock over the first domino. Observe what happens.

ANALYSIS

1. How did the average falling times compare when the dominoes were arranged in single file and in four rows?
2. What type of reaction is represented by the falling dominoes arranged in single file? In four rows?
3. When the dominoes were arranged in four rows, what did your finger striking the first domino represent? What did the ruler represent?

CONCLUSION

Describe how dominoes can be used to model the reaction in a nuclear reactor. Discuss the strengths and limitations of the model.

CHAPTER 17

SOLAR AND ALTERNATIVE ENERGY

People have always been fascinated by the power of the sun. In ancient Greek mythology, the character Icarus perished because he ignored warnings not to fly too close to the sun. People have long been aware of the role of the sun in growing plants and providing warmth and light. In recent years, the sun has taken on a new role in human society. Using the energy produced by the sun, people are discovering a new source of clean, renewable energy that will last as long as Earth itself. Combined with other renewable energy sources such as water and wind, people are finding alternatives to the use of fossil fuels.

17.1 SOLAR ENERGY

Objectives • *Explain* the importance of the sun in supplying energy to Earth. • *Describe* how solar energy can be used to heat buildings and generate electricity.

The sun is the source of almost all the energy on Earth's surface. *Energy from the sun, or* **solar energy**, *is absorbed by plants and used as fuel by virtually all organisms.* Because fossil fuels contain energy from the remains of organisms, they also contain energy from the sun.

Solar energy does more than provide energy for the organisms on Earth. The source of energy that drives the water cycle is the sun. The flow of streams on Earth's surface is part of the water cycle. Fast-moving rivers are often used to generate electricity. Since the water in the rivers results from the sun-driven water cycle, the energy produced by the flow of rivers can be traced to the sun. The sun also produces uneven warming of Earth's surface. These temperature differences cause winds to blow. Therefore, wind energy is also driven by energy from the sun.

The Sun as Fuel

The sun obtains its energy through thermonuclear (THER-moh-NOO-klee-ur) fusion. In this process, high temperatures in the sun's core cause hydrogen nuclei to fuse, forming helium nuclei. As each helium nucleus forms, a loss of mass occurs. This lost mass is converted to the heat and light energy of the sun.

Earth receives only about one 2-billionth of the energy produced by the sun. Much of the solar energy that reaches Earth is in the form of visible light and infrared radiation. Recall that energy cannot be created or destroyed. It can, however, be changed in form. When light energy from the sun strikes certain objects, the energy in the light is absorbed by these objects. As substances absorb light energy, the energy is changed to heat, or thermal energy. Solar energy can be harnessed and used to generate heat and electricity. In many places, solar energy is replacing nuclear, biomass, and fossil fuels as an energy source.

The use of solar energy has many advantages. It is free, clean, and nonpolluting. Although you must buy the equipment for capturing and storing solar energy, the cost may be recovered by the savings in fuel bills over many years.

One drawback to solar energy systems is that the energy source is not constant. There is limited sunlight on cloudy or rainy days, and no sunlight at night. However, solar energy collected during the day can be stored. Another drawback to solar energy is that devices for harnessing and storing solar energy are not very

FIELD ACTIVITY

Take a hand lens and a thin sheet of paper to a paved area on a sunny day. Place the paper on the pavement, and hold it down with a small rock. Hold the hand lens above the paper at an angle that focuses the sun's rays as sharply as possible onto the paper. **Caution:** *Have a container of water handy in case the paper catches fire.* Do not do this activity in a grassy area. Observe what happens. Based on your observations, what conclusions can you make about the energy in sunlight?

Solar energy includes heat that can be focused and used. Additional teaching tips on page T93.

efficient. The size and cost of the equipment may outweigh the benefits. But as technology progresses, the use of solar energy is becoming more cost-effective.

Passive Solar Energy

If the energy of sunlight is used directly as a source of light or heat, the energy use is described as passive. *In **passive solar heating**, the sun's energy is collected, stored, and distributed naturally in an enclosed dwelling.* You have experienced passive solar heating if you have ever walked through a greenhouse or gotten inside an enclosed car on a sunny day. Passive solar energy is not used to produce electricity. But it can reduce the need for electricity by providing an alternative source of heat. Passive solar energy therefore helps reduce the use of fossil and nuclear fuels.

Passive solar heating of homes is mostly accomplished through well-planned building design and construction. In North America, houses that make optimum use of passive solar heating have large windows that all face south. South-facing windows can gather the greatest amount of the sun's energy for the longest number of day-light hours. In addition, these homes contain building materials and furnishings that best absorb solar energy. Examples of such materials are stone, brick, and concrete.

Buildings that make use of passive solar energy often have glass-enclosed areas. A glass-enclosed area functions much like a greenhouse. The area generally has walls and floors made from dark-colored, light-absorbing materials such as concrete and brick.

Notice the large, dark, water-filled barrels in the glass enclosure

Discuss with students how the color of materials and the substances that materials are made of affect the light-absorbing abilities of different objects.

THINK CRITICALLY

If a home is located in the Southern Hemisphere, in which direction would windows have to face to make use of passive solar energy? Why?

In the Southern Hemisphere, north-facing windows would absorb the most heat because this is the direction that receives the most sunlight.

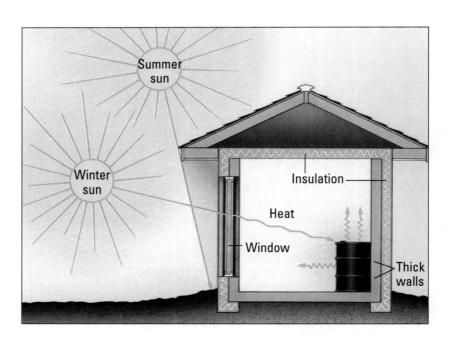

Figure 17.1 A house with passive solar heating has large windows that face south. In winter, when the sun is low in the sky, sunlight warms the barrels of water. The barrels release heat after the sun goes down. In summer, the roof shades the windows.

in Figure 17.1. These barrels are used as energy-absorbing and storage structures. During the day, the barrels absorb energy, and the water inside becomes heated. At night, when temperatures become cooler, the heat energy in the water is returned to the air in the room. To get the greatest benefit from passive solar heating, good insulation is needed to prevent the escape of the captured energy from the house. Thick, heavy curtains or shutters also help prevent heat from escaping from a room when there is no sunlight.

In existing homes, passive solar energy may not be practical as a primary energy source. Such homes may require costly renovations or major construction to obtain the greatest benefit from solar heating. However, when new homes are built, passive solar heating should be considered. The University of Saskatchewan in Canada built a house using passive solar heating. After one year, the house saved $1,350 in fuel bills compared to an average house.

Active Solar Energy

An active solar energy system has a greater capacity for storing and distributing energy than a passive system. *An* **active solar heating system** *uses devices to collect, store, and circulate heat produced from solar energy.* In a passive system, the building itself and its position act as the system. An active system, however, uses tubes, tanks, fluids, pumps, fans, and other devices to collect and distribute energy. These pieces of equipment release the sun's energy to the system long after the sun has set.

Buildings that use active solar energy gather the sun's energy by using *solar collectors*. Most solar collectors are mounted on the roofs of houses or buildings where they can capture a maximum amount of the sun's energy. Placement of the collector on roofs also saves space on the ground.

Most solar collectors use a flat-plate collector. The flat-plate collector is a large, flat box. The base is made of a black metal plate that covers a layer of insulation. Tubes filled with fluid run across the top of the metal. The fluid inside the tube is usually water, but air or antifreeze may also be used.

Cooperative Learning
Challenge students working in groups to research how active solar systems can be used for cooling purposes. Have students gather data about these systems and present their data to the class in some type of visual format.

Figure 17.2 The Solar One facility in the Mojave Desert of California uses hundreds of mirrors focused on a single collector.

Figure 17.3 Flat-plate collectors began to appear on rooftops all across the United States in the early 1980s, when the federal government offered tax incentives to homeowners who installed the energy-saving devices.

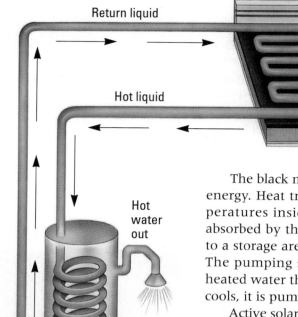

Flat–plate collector

Return liquid

Hot liquid

Hot water out

Cold water in

Pump

Figure 17.4 A house with an active solar heating system has flat-plate collectors on the roof. Heat is absorbed by liquid in tubes. The liquid is pumped into the house. The hot liquid from the collectors can be used to heat water, as shown, or to heat a room.

The black metal plate in a flat-plate solar collector absorbs solar energy. Heat trapped in the collector by the glass can cause temperatures inside the collector to rise up to 200°C. The heat is absorbed by the fluid in the tubes. Heated water is then pumped to a storage area, usually located in the basement of the building. The pumping system, which requires electricity, circulates the heated water throughout the building when needed. As the water cools, it is pumped back to the collector for reheating.

Active solar energy systems are being successfully used in many parts of the world. In areas where other fuel sources are scarce or too expensive, solar energy is a cost-effective heat source. For example, many people in Israel, India, Japan, and the West Indies use active solar heating.

Solar energy can be used to produce the steam needed to rotate the turbines that generate electricity. Scientists and engineers working in the Mojave Desert near Barstow, California, used more than 1,000 giant mirrors to concentrate the sun's rays at one position. Enough heat, at more than 600°C, was obtained to make steam. This steam was used to rotate turbines that generate electricity. This project, called Solar One, is producing enough electricity for a town of 10,000 people.

Photovoltaic Cells

Of all the devices that use solar energy, the solar cell, or photovoltaic cell, is the only one that actually produces electricity. *A* **photovoltaic** (FOH-toh-vahl-TAY-ik) **cell,** or *PV cell, uses thin*

Figure 17.5 A PV cell is made from two thin layers of semiconductor material. When energized by the sun, electrons move from the top layer to the bottom layer, making the top layer positively charged and the bottom layer negatively charged. This difference in charges forces electrons to flow through the circuit.

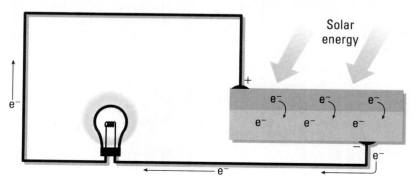

Solar energy

wafers of semiconductor material to produce electricity directly from solar energy. Semiconductors are made of elements such as silicon or selenium that can conduct electricity very quickly when mixed with tiny amounts of other elements. A PV cell is made up of two thin slices of a semiconductor material joined together. One slice is positively charged; the other is negatively charged. Sunlight striking the cell causes electrons on the negative side to move to the positive side. This movement of electrons results in an electric current.

PV cells are commonly used today. For example, you may use a solar-powered calculator or wear a solar-powered watch that uses PV cells. PV cells are convenient to use because they are lightweight and produce no wastes or pollutants. They also have no moving parts, nor do they consume any materials, so they last a relatively long time. Combined with rechargeable batteries, PV cells can have even more uses. For example, most space satellites depend on PV cells for their power. PV cells can produce electricity for homes, industry, and some means of transportation. Currently, engineers are trying to develop solar-powered automobiles that will run as efficiently as gas-powered models.

DATELINE 1958

PV cells made their debut in space aboard the Vanguard I space satellite, the second space satellite launched by the United States. Every satellite since the Vanguard I has made use of PV-cell technology.

SECTION REVIEW

1. How does active solar energy differ from passive solar energy?
2. List three electrical devices that currently make use of solar energy to operate.
3. How can solar-powered automobiles help reduce pollution?
4. **Evaluate** Suppose a classmate suggested that PV cells could be used to power street lights. Do you agree or disagree? Explain.

1. Passive systems rely on the position of the home and the locations of windows and materials. Active systems make use of devices to collect and distribute heat, and they are more efficient.
2. Calculators, watches, and space satellites.
3. Because they do not rely on fossil fuels as their source of energy, solar-powered vehicles reduce pollution and conserve fossil fuels.
4. Because street lights are only used at night, they would require rechargeable batteries to be used at night.

Answers and teaching
strategies on page T93.

Storing Solar Energy

PROBLEM
Which materials store solar energy best?

MATERIALS (per group)
- 5 thermometers
- 5 250-mL beakers
- 3 sheets of newspaper
- large black cardboard box with lid
- stopwatch or clock
- wax marking pencil
- salt
- sand
- water at room temperature

PREDICTION
After reading the entire activity, predict which of the materials tested will store the most solar energy.

PROCEDURE

1. Using the wax marking pencil, label the five beakers *Sand, Salt, Water, Paper,* and *Air*.
2. Mark each beaker about seven-eighths of the way up from the bottom.
3. Pour sand up to the mark on the first beaker. Pour salt to the mark on the second beaker, and water to the mark on the third. In the fourth beaker, stuff crumpled news-paper up to the mark. Leave the fifth beaker empty.
4. On a separate sheet of paper, copy the data table shown.
5. Place a thermometer in each beaker, and record the starting temperature of each beaker in the data table.
6. Place all beakers inside the black box, and cover the box with the lid. Put the covered box in direct sunlight for 30 minutes. After the time has elapsed, record the temperatures from each beaker in the data table.
7. In a shaded area, remove the beakers from the box, and note the temperature changes after 5 min, 10 min, and 30 min. Record all temperatures in the data table.
8. Follow your teacher's instructions for disposal of all materials.

ANALYSIS

1. In which beaker did the temperature rise the most after being heated for 30 min? In which did it rise the least?
2. Rank the materials tested from the one that increased the most in temperature to the one that increased the least.
3. In which beaker did the temperature drop the fastest? In which did it drop the slowest?

CONCLUSION

1. From your test results, which substance has the best heat-storing capacity?
2. From the results of your investigation, explain why certain materials are used for the construction of solar panels on new homes.

	Sand	Salt	Water	Paper	Air
Room temperature					
After 30 min in sun					
5 min after removal from sun					
10 min after removal from sun					
30 min after removal from sun					

17.2 HYDROELECTRIC ENERGY

Objectives • *Describe* two ways that moving water can be used to produce electricity. • *Discuss* the benefits and drawbacks of producing electricity through the use of hydroelectric power.

In the mid-nineteenth century, the work of English chemist and physicist Michael Faraday led to the invention of the electrical generator. Faraday showed that moving a wire through a magnetic field caused electricity to flow through a wire. Turbines generate electricity by moving wire coils through a strong magnetic field.

The kinetic energy of flowing water can be used to produce electricity. *Electricity that is produced from the energy of moving water is called* **hydroelectric power**. Moving water is a nonpolluting energy source that is readily available in many areas. Producing electricity using hydroelectric power is also less expensive than using fossil or nuclear fuels.

Energy from Flowing Streams

People have made use of the energy released by moving water for centuries. For example, waterwheels positioned on fast-moving rivers have been used for hundreds of years to grind grains. In the late 1800s, turbines were invented that could produce electricity from flowing water. By 1925, 40 percent of the world's electricity was generated by flowing water. Today, huge dams are built across waterways to generate electricity.

To generate electricity, water behind a dam is directed at the blades of huge turbines. When water pushes against the turbine blades, the energy in the moving water is transferred to the turbine, causing it to turn. The motion of the spinning turbine is transferred to coils of wire located within generators. The coils spin through a magnetic field, producing electricity.

In addition to their use in producing hydroelectric energy, dams benefit society in several ways. Because dams control the flow of water, they are important in flood control. By controlling the flow of water, dams also determine the speed at which water flows. This can help in the navigation of boats. Lakes created behind dams often serve as recreation areas for fishing, boating, and swimming. Dams also create reservoirs that store water for irrigation and for home use in towns and cities.

Figure 17.7 Dams and reservoirs provide many benefits to society, including recreation, flood control, and a reliable supply of fresh water.

Figure 17.8 The rotation of turbines converts mechanical energy into electrical energy. In the case of a hydroelectric plant, the mechanical energy is supplied by flowing water. In other systems, high-pressure steam may be used to provide the mechanical energy that rotates the turbines.

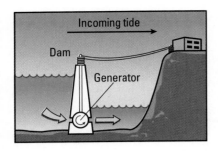

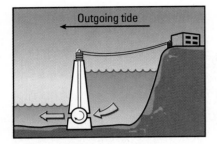

Figure 17.9 The turbines in the generator of a tidal energy system must be able to turn either way, according to the direction of the water flow. Tidal energy systems are effective only in places where the tide flows through an inlet, estuary, or other narrow opening.

Although dams have many benefits, they can also harm the environment. By altering water depth and flow, dams can alter the natural plant life of streams. Altering the plant life also alters the animal life. The rising and falling water level, both upstream and downstream from a dam, affects the food chain. There may also be flooding of the land behind the dam, leading to both shoreline erosion and a change in shoreline ecosystems.

Dams containing turbines pose a problem for fish living in the stream. Fishes may be caught in the blades of the turbine. Dams also interfere with the reproductive processes of some fish species. For example, adult salmon return to the stream where they were born to spawn. Dams create a barrier that prevents salmon from fulfilling their reproductive cycle.

By reducing water depth, dams tend to lower the temperature of water downstream. Changes in temperature can upset the balance of an ecosystem by making it unsuitable for the organisms that are adapted to living in the water. This problem is made worse when cool water from behind the dam is released through the dam. The cool water mixes with the warmer water downstream, resulting in rapid changes in temperature.

Energy from Tides

The tides of the ocean contain huge amounts of energy. Like the energy in streams, the energy in tides can be converted to electricity by rotating turbines inside dams. The turbines in a tidal generator must be able to turn in both directions, depending on the direction of the tide.

So far, the use of tidal electrical generators is limited. Plans exist for the construction of a generator in Nova Scotia, Canada, that could produce as much electricity as 250 nuclear reactors. But there are serious environmental consequences to be considered. The project could damage wetlands surrounding the generator, and the community on the ocean floor near the generator could also be affected. Scientists are also studying the possibility of harnessing the energy in ocean waves. So far, no device has been invented that can convert wave energy to electricity efficiently.

SECTION REVIEW

1. What is hydroelectric power?
2. How might the formation of a reservoir behind a dam affect the environment?
3. **Justify** Do you think the benefits of generating hydroelectric power by using dams outweigh the drawbacks? Give reasons to support your response.

The Ocean Resource

Is seawater the answer?

1. Students may question whether the system changes water temperatures nearby, thus affecting the ecosystem.
2. Accept all well explained answers.

Imagine using the same substance to make electricity, to air-condition buildings, raise lobsters, grow carrots, and produce fresh water. What substance on Earth could be this useful? The substance is seawater, and at Keahole Point, Hawaii, seawater is being used to do all of these things.

The machinery at Keahole is fairly simple. Pipes plunge into the ocean at several different depths. Some pipes collect cold deep-ocean water. Other pipes collect warmer surface water. The water flows into a 13 m tall tower, called an ocean thermal energy conversion system, or OTEC.

First, the warm water enters a vacuum chamber that causes the water to boil and change to a vapor. The vapor turns a generator, producing about 260 kilowatts of electricity. Compared to a nuclear reactor, which generates 1100 megawatts of electricity, an OTEC plant produces a small amount of power. But OTEC fuel is free, limitless, and creates no pollution.

Cool water flows through pipes in the system to condense the vapor into fresh water. The fresh water could be used for drinking or for irrigation. The piped cool water then continues its journey for further use elsewhere.

One possible application for the piped cold water is air conditioning. The 10°C water passes through the heat exchangers, cooling several buildings. The Keahole site saves $1,300 each month in electrical bills by using the cold water. A plan is in place to air condition a nearby airport in the near future.

Next, the water is transported to a garden. The cool pipes cause water vapor in the humid air to condense and drip onto the soil. Vegetables and fruits grow larger and sweeter than in a conventional garden as a result of the cooler temperatures and steady water supply. Note that it is not the seawater itself that is used for irrigation. It is the vapor in the air condensing on the cold pipes that provides the fresh water.

The water has now been warmed to about 13°C. In its final stop before returning to the ocean, the water is pumped

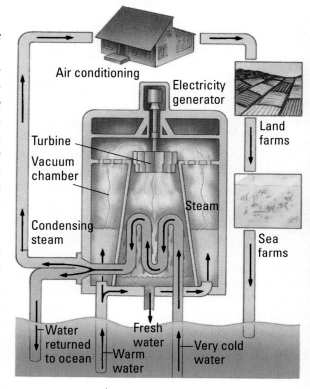

Air conditioning

Electricity generator

Turbine

Vacuum chamber

Condensing steam

Steam

Land farms

Sea farms

Water returned to ocean

Fresh water

Warm water

Very cold water

into many small aquaculture businesses. The nutrient-rich, pure ocean water nourishes seaweed, lobster, and fish farming. Finally, the water is returned to the ocean.

DECISIONS

1. Do you think there are environmental problems caused by the OTEC system described? Explain.

2. Choose another energy source besides seawater. Compare the advantages and disadvantages of seawater and the energy source you choose.

17.3 WIND ENERGY

Objectives • *Relate* the energy of sunlight to the formation of air currents and winds. • *Explain* how the energy in wind can be used to produce electricity.

In ancient times, Egyptians used wind to move their sailing ships. Babylonians used windmills to pump water to irrigate their land. Windmills are still in use today. They are used to grind grains, pump water, and generate electricity. *Windmills that are used to generate electricity are called wind turbine generators, or* **aerogenerators** (AYR-oh-GEN-er-ay-ters).

The use of wind power to generate electricity has many of the same advantages and disadvantages as the use of solar power. Like solar power, wind power is free, unlimited, and nonpolluting. Unfortunately, wind power is not constant or steady, and elaborate storage devices are needed to make wind power available during periods when there is no wind.

Today's windmills are constructed of strong, lightweight materials. Vanes of aerogenerators are connected to coils of wire. Winds blowing against the aerogenerator vanes cause the vanes to spin. As the vanes are turned by the wind, electricity is produced by a generator similar to the generator at a hydroelectric plant.

There are two different types of aerogenerators commonly in use. In traditional aerogenerators, the vanes turn on a horizontal axis. The vanes are shaped like the propeller of an airplane. This shape allows the vanes to turn at great speeds and generate large amounts of electricity. Aerogenerators with two or three very long vanes have proven to be the most efficient.

The other type of aerogenerator turns on a vertical axis and is shaped like an upside-down eggbeater. First patented in 1927 by G.J.M. Darrieus of France, the Darrieus rotor can produce electricity at lower wind speeds than is required by the traditional type.

Figure 17.10 People have been using wind power to provide energy for hundreds of years. Windmills have traditionally been used to pump water and grind grains.

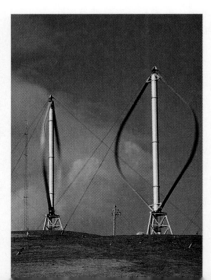

Figure 17.11 Traditional aerogenerators (left) can produce large amounts of electricity, but require high wind conditions. The Darrieus rotor (right) cannot produce as much electricity, but it can operate effectively under calmer wind conditions.

Figure 17.12 Wind farms require large amounts of land. Fortunately, the high-wind conditions that make a location attractive for a wind farm often make the area undesirable for development.

Wind farms are sites where many aerogenerators are placed together. Wind farms are located in open areas where wind conditions are favorable. Favorable conditions include steady winds of at least 15 mph every day. One such place is Altamont Pass near San Francisco. There are more than 7,000 wind aerogenerators in this area. There are four other large wind farms in California. Together, they produce more than 1500 megawatts of electricity—the equivalent of three large nuclear reactors. The wind farms of California account for 95 percent of the total wind energy production in the United States, and 75 percent of the world's production.

Wind energy is not without its problems. As you have learned, winds are not always steady or strong enough. Wind farms take up a lot of land, which means that they must be located far from heavily populated areas where the price of land is high. They may also interfere with radio and television reception. Birds may be severely injured when they fly into the spinning vanes of the aerogenerators. This is a particular concern in California, where the wind farms are located near sensitive habitats of the endangered California condor. Some people consider aerogenerators to be ugly, disturbing the look of the otherwise natural landscape. In addition, the current cost of constructing towers and generators is fairly high.

LITERATURE LINK

Cervantes' epic tale *Don Quixote* makes extensive use of windmills as part of its story line. Read the story of Don Quixote, and write a report that explains the importance of windmills to the plot.

SECTION REVIEW

1. What is an aerogenerator?
2. List several benefits and drawbacks to using wind as a source for producing electricity.
3. **Analyze** Do you think it is likely that aerogenerators could be used to produce electricity in the region where you live? Explain your response.

1. A device that produces electricity from wind energy.
2. Benefits: Wind does not pollute and is free. Drawbacks: Wind farms threaten birds, are ugly, can interfere with radio and television reception, and may not be viable where winds are not strong and steady.
3. Answers will vary, depending on location. Accept all logical responses.

17.4 GEOTHERMAL ENERGY AND NUCLEAR FUSION

Objectives • *Describe* how geothermal energy is used.
• *Explain* how nuclear fusion could be a valuable source of energy in the future.

The most important source of Earth's energy is the sun, but it is not the only source. Earth itself generates heat energy deep within its crust by the decay of radioactive elements. Imagine the energy that could be made available if people could use the energy of the planet itself. Perhaps even more attractive would be the possibility of reproducing the reactions that release energy in the sun. Geothermal energy makes use of the energy inside Earth. Nuclear fusion, the process that produces the sun's energy, may be the answer to the energy needs of the future.

Geothermal Energy

The heat energy generated within Earth is called **geothermal energy**. Geothermal energy is generated by the decay of radioactive elements deep beneath the ground. As these elements decay, they give off energy in the form of heat. Temperatures rise about 30°C with every kilometer of depth.

Enough heat is present deep within Earth to melt rock. This molten rock is called *magma*. The lava that flows from volcanoes is magma that has reached the surface. Rocks closer to the surface are also heated by geothermal energy. Water that collects near the heated rocks is heated and may be changed to steam. Cracks in the rocks allow steam, hot water, and heat to escape to the surface. Geysers, steam vents, hot springs, and bubbling mud are heated by geothermal energy.

Geothermal energy is used in some regions where the source of the energy is near the surface. In both ancient and modern times, steam baths have been common in areas where steam and hot water come to the surface naturally. In 1904 in Laradello, Italy, an engine driven by natural steam was connected to an electric generator. This was the first attempt to produce electricity from Earth's heat. Today, Laradello produces more than 390 megawatts of electricity in this way.

Worldwide, at least 20 nations are using geothermal energy to heat homes. Most of Iceland obtains its energy from geothermal energy. About 65 percent of the homes in Iceland are heated using geothermal energy. Fresh vegetables are grown in heated greenhouses during the long winter. In addition to using

Figure 17.13 Energy from radioactive decay inside Earth heats the water that flows underground in certain areas, resulting in hot springs and geysers.

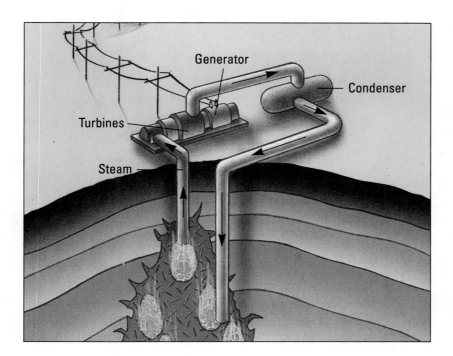

Figure 17.14 Hot rocks below the surface heat water pumped into the ground in pipes. The heat turns the water to steam, which turns the turbines.

geothermal energy for home heating, some areas in New Zealand, Japan, and China are experimenting with the production of electricity from geothermal energy. In the United States, some parts of California and Hawaii also use geothermal energy to generate electricity.

There are several methods used to extract usable energy from geothermal sources. One method that is commonly used involves hot-rock zones. Hot-rock zones are areas where the bedrock is heated by magma deeper below the surface. A simplified diagram of a hot-rock extraction system is shown in Figure 17.14. Explosives are used to break up a portion of the bedrock. Cool water is pumped into the area of hot, broken rocks. The water turns to steam, forming a steam reservoir underground. The steam is then extracted through additional pipes and used to rotate turbines that produce eletricity.

Using geothermal energy to produce electricity has both advantages and disadvantages. Most areas do not have enough concentrated geothermal heat to be worth the cost of extraction. Suitable geothermal areas are not always easy to locate. In some areas that have adequate geothermal energy sources, the air is naturally polluted by toxic hydrogen sulfide gas that is given off along with the heat. Mineral wastes, salts, and toxic metals are also abundant in geothermal areas. These waste products tend to corrode the pipes and boilers that carry the steam and water heated by geothermal energy. Another problem with geothermal energy is the lack of an adequate water supply for the production of steam. It is often too expensive to pipe water over long distances for use in the production of electricity.

Multicultural Perspective
Have students research which areas of the world use each of the alternative energy sources discussed. Ask them to present their findings visually, using an outline map of the world.

Figure 17.15 In nuclear fusion, two deuterium nuclei fuse to become a helium-3 nucleus.

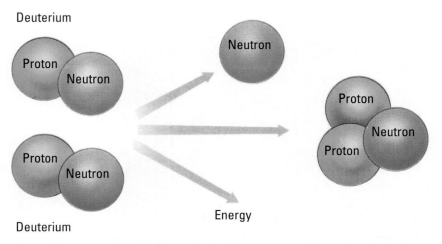

Deuterium

Neutron

Proton

Neutron

Proton

Proton

Neutron

Proton

Neutron

Energy

Deuterium

Nuclear Fusion

Perhaps one of the most promising new sources of energy for the future is nuclear fusion. **Nuclear fusion** (NOO-klee-er FYOO-zhun) *occurs when two atomic nuclei fuse to become one larger nucleus.* Do not confuse nuclear fusion with nuclear fission, in which nuclei are split. Nuclear fusion is the source of the energy given off by the sun. Although nuclear fusion reactions can produce enormous amounts of virtually unlimited energy, people have not yet learned how to harness the energy and use it efficiently.

The fuel for nuclear fusion reactions is usually deuterium, the heavy isotope of hydrogen. Deuterium is fairly common in seawater, and is therefore abundant in nature. In nuclear fusion, the deuterium nuclei are subjected to enormous pressure and temperature, supplied either by a magnetic field or by laser beams, until the nuclei collapse into a single nucleus. So far, however, the devices needed to create the necessary pressure and temperature for a working plant have not been built.

In theory, nuclear fusion has many advantages over most other energy sources. Much less radioactive waste is produced by fusion than by traditional nuclear energy. Also, the fuel is more easily obtained. Unfortunately, technology will have to overcome many roadblocks before nuclear fusion can become a source of usable energy.

1. The nuclei of two atoms fuse to become one nucleus. The extra mass is converted to energy.
2. The heat could be used to make steam that rotates turbines, producing electricity.
3. Answers will vary, depending on location. Accept all logical responses.

SECTION REVIEW

1. Describe what occurs during the process of nuclear fusion.
2. How can geothermal energy be used to provide usable energy for people?
3. Analyze Could geothermal energy be used as a source of energy in the region where you live? Explain.

CHAPTER 17 REVIEW

KEY TERMS

solar energy 17.1
passive solar heating 17.1
active solar heating 17.1

photovoltaic (PV) cell 17.1
hydroelectric power 17.2
aerogenerator 17.3

geothermal energy 17.4
nuclear fusion 17.4

CHAPTER SUMMARY

17.1 Solar energy, the energy of the sun, is the main source of energy on Earth. Solar energy can be used to heat homes either passively or actively. Photovoltaic (PV) cells convert the sun's energy to electricity. In the future, solar energy may provide the best alternative to the use of fossil, biomass, and nuclear fuels.

17.2 Electricity produced from the energy of flowing water is called hydroelectric power. Hydroelectric power makes use of dams containing turbines to generate electricity. Hydroelectric power is renewable and nonpolluting, but does threaten some parts of the environment.

17.3 Aerogenerators are devices that use the energy of wind to produce electricity. Aerogenerators may be clustered in areas called wind farms. Wind is a renewable, nonpolluting energy source, but it is not a practical source of energy in all parts of the world.

17.4 Geothermal energy is the energy produced by heat deep within Earth's crust. Geothermal energy has limited use because it is not available in many places. Nuclear fusion is a potential source of huge amounts of energy, but devices for releasing the energy do not yet exist.

MULTIPLE CHOICE

Choose the letter of the word or phrase that best completes each statement.

1. Of the following, the energy source that can be used in the greatest number of areas is (a) geothermal energy; (b) wind energy; (c) hydroelectric power; (d) solar energy. d

2. Aerogenerators are used to produce electricity from (a) wind; (b) moving water; (c) the sun; (d) heat inside Earth. a

3. Photovoltaic cells convert the energy of the sun to (a) heat; (b) light; (c) electricity; (d) fuel. c

4. The production of electricity from moving water is called (a) solar energy; (b) wind energy; (c) hydroelectric power; (d) geothermal energy. c

5. Iceland is a country that makes extensive use of (a) solar energy; (b) nuclear energy; (c) fossil fuels; (d) geothermal energy. d

6. A characteristic common to all the alternative energy sources discussed in this chapter is that they (a) can be produced anywhere; (b) do not use fossil fuels; (c) are nonrenewable; (d) must be used along with fossil fuels. b

7. The sun is not involved in providing the energy in (a) wind energy; (b) hydroelectric energy; (c) solar energy; (d) geothermal energy. d

8. Photovoltaic cells are used to provide the energy for all of the following except (a) passive solar heating systems; (b) space satellites; (c) calculators; (d) wristwatches. a

9. Nuclear fusion (a) produces no wastes; (b) uses fuels that are difficult to obtain; (c) is not yet available; (d) is an inexpensive energy source. c

10. The tubes in a solar collector are filled with (a) metal; (b) solid; (c) fluid; (d) insulation. c

11. A resource that is *not* supplied by the ocean thermal energy conversion system described on page 273 is (a) heat; (b) fresh water; (c) electricity; (d) air conditioning. a

CHAPTER 17 REVIEW

WORD COMPARISONS

Write the letter of the second word pair that best matches the first pair.

1. Hydroelectric power: moving water as (a) solar energy: light; (b) wind energy: moving air; (c) heat: geothermal energy; (d) solar cells: electricity. b
2. Windows: passive solar heating as (a) PV cells: active solar heating; (b) PV cells: flat-plate collectors; (c) flat-plate collector: active solar heating; (d) solar energy: sun. c
3. Nuclear fusion: nuclear fission as (a) addition: division; (b) subtraction: multiplication; (c) division: multiplication; (d) subtraction: addition. a
4. Dams: hydroelectric power as (a) solar collectors: passive solar heating; (b) solar collectors: electricity; (c) solar collectors: active solar energy; (d) aerogenerators: geothermal energy. c
5. Magma: geothermal energy as (a) PV cells: active solar energy; (b) wind: air; (c) fusion: solar energy; (d) water: dams. c

CONCEPT REVIEW Answers on page T93.

Write a complete response for each of the following.

1. What are some advantages of using solar energy instead of fossil fuels?
2. Discuss how geothermal energy, solar energy, wind energy, and hydroelectric power conserve fossil fuels and reduce pollution.
3. How is the movement of air currents different from the movement of wind?
4. Why is the sun considered a renewable resource?
5. What factors limit the use of geothermal energy?

THINK CRITICALLY Answers on page T93.

1. If you were going to use one of the alternative energy sources mentioned in this chapter to heat your home, which would you use? Explain your choice.
2. Explain how the sun is involved in the availability of solar energy, wind energy, and hydroelectric power.
3. Deep ocean vents give off heat produced by geothermal energy. Do you think it is possible and practical to harness the energy given off by these vents for use in home heating systems? Why or why not?
4. Explain the benefits and drawbacks of hydroelectric power to people, other organisms, and the environment.
5. Explain how generators are used to produce electricity from moving water and wind.

WRITE FOR UNDERSTANDING

Suppose your utility company is planning to build a wind farm on the outskirts of town. Write a letter to your local newspaper supporting or opposing the construction. Defend your point of view.

PORTFOLIO

1. Find out what types of energy sources are used in your community. If possible, make a videotape of sites using alternative energy sources.
2. Conduct library research to find information on other methods people of the past or present have used to meet their energy needs. Make a poster that summarizes your findings.

Use Figure 17.4 to answer the following.

1. Look at the diagram of active solar heating. Does the liquid that flows through the collector need to be replaced when the shower is used? Why or why not?
2. If the house using this system was in Argentina, which direction should the collectors face?
3. If this active solar heating system was to be used to heat a room, how would this diagram be different? On a separate piece of paper, sketch a diagram of the system.

ACTIVITY 17.2

Answers and teaching strategies on page T93.

PROBLEM
How does the design of a windmill affect its ability to harness wind?

MATERIALS (per group)
- hand drill
- hammer
- scrap wood
- bolt
- washer
- 3 nuts
- 3 or 4 foil pie tins
- crayon
- thread spool
- scissors
- protractor
- electric fan (1 per class)

HYPOTHESIS
After reading the entire activity, write a hypothesis that explains how the design of a windmill affects its ability to use wind power to do work.

PROCEDURE

1. Break up into groups of three or four students. One person per group makes the handle of the windmill by drilling a small hole through a piece of scrap wood.
2. Each group makes windmill blades of its own design. Use the pie tins for the blades, and experiment with different shapes, lengths, and number of blades. *Note: When constructing the blades, think about the best lengths combined with the best angles.* Measure and record the angle of the blades with a protractor.
3. Fasten the windmill blades to a thread spool with the long bolt. Secure the blades, spool, and handle with the washers, nuts, and bolts

as shown in the figure. Fasten the bolts lightly so that the blades can rotate freely.
4. With a crayon, make a mark at the edge of one of the blades. This mark will help you count the number of times the windmill turns per minute.
5. While holding the windmill 1 m away from an electric fan, count the number of revolutions the windmill makes in 1 min.
6. One person from each group makes a table with these headings: *Number of Blades, Diameter of Windmill (cm), Angle of Blades,* and *Turns in 1 min.*

ANALYSIS
1. What factors have the greatest effect on the speed of the windmill?
2. Why do you think many new windmills have only two blades?

CONCLUSION
Based on the findings of your group, what windmill design is the most effective at harnessing wind power?

HAZARDOUS WASTE MANAGEMENT

In one of the most rapidly growing areas of the environmental sciences, hazardous waste managers are on the cutting edge of environmental technology. Because toxic waste has become a common problem, a huge industry and profession have arisen. Their focus is twofold. They are involved in the handling and cleanup of hazardous waste sites already recognized as environmentally toxic, and they are responsible of preventing future hazardous waste problems.

Hazardous waste managers perform the following functions:
- Analyze hazardous wastes.
- Monitor proper handling of wastes.
- Supervise disposal facilities and techniques.
- Clean up toxic spills and contaminated areas.
- Issue permits for the creation, transportation, and disposal of wastes.
- Limit the use of toxic substances whenever possible.
- Provide information to the public about specific problems and remedies.

Hazardous waste management has been positively affected by the passage and amendment of two laws: the Resource Conservation and Recovery Act (RCRA) and the Comprehensive Environmental Response, Compensation, and Liability Act (better known as Superfund). These two acts provide money for the cleanup of already existing hazardous waste sites, and they prevent waste dumping as well. Because of the extent of the hazardous waste problem in the United States, there will probably be a great demand for professionals in this field for at least the next 30 years.

An undergraduate degree in biology, chemistry, engineering, or health technology is fundamental if you want a job in hazardous waste management, but many better-paying jobs require graduate degrees. Liberal arts and environmental science majors should enroll in engineering and core science classes. Courses in public policy, economics, statistics, toxicology, and hydrology are also helpful. Although previous experience is important, many hazardous waste companies are more concerned with the level of education of their employees. The education level of principal employees is made public in the company's portfolio, and is instrumental in gaining contracts.

Many hazardous wastes managers recommend that students participate in community meetings. Many local issues are decided at this level of government, and input from students and volunteers is valuable. Students benefit from internships and volunteer work, which add to their experience, skills, and contacts.

CHEMICAL ENGINEERS ▶

At a hazardous waste site, chemical engineers test and analyze samples to determine what toxic substances are present, and what damage has been done to the soil, water, and air of the affected ecosystem. They then recommend corrective action and develop a plan for separating and disposing of the pollutants. They also recommend substitutes that can be used instead of toxic pollutants.

HOUSEHOLD HAZARDOUS WASTE COORDINATORS ►

An important new role in environmental careers, hazardous waste coordinators work in local governments to educate the public about common household hazardous wastes. They inform the community about the best methods of disposal and offer suggestions as to what substitutes can be safely used in the home instead of toxic ones. They also coordinate grass-roots efforts to collect and dispose of household toxic pollutants in their communities.

HAZARDOUS MATERIALS SPECIALISTS ▼

These professionals are experts in identifying hazardous wastes at an affected site. They are responsible for handling, transporting, and disposing of toxic substances. Hazardous materials specialists may work on a large or small scale. Some are called upon to assess damage at a huge hazardous site such as Love Canal. Others may evaluate the impact on the environment of chemicals used by local unregulated businesses.

◄ HAZARDOUS WASTE LAWYERS

These lawyers, working together with other specialists in the field, determine the financial cost of damages to hazardous waste sites. They prepare court cases and may represent the companies responsible for dumping the hazardous materials. They may also represent the people and communities that are directly affected by a hazardous spill or accident. Besides working with court cases, hazardous waste lawyers also work with lawmakers, helping write and assess new laws and regulations that affect business and industry.

The government has begun to clean up hazardous waste pollution by identifying a National Priority List of 1245 sites that are severely polluted. The demand for hazardous waste lawyers will probably increase as the government tries to determine who is at fault and who should pay for the cleanup.

FOR MORE INFORMATION:

American Chemical Society
(Publishes more than 20 periodicals, including the weekly *Chemical & Engineering News* and the monthly *Environmental Science and Technology*; student memberships available)
1155 16th Street NW
Washington, DC 20036
(202) 872-4600

Citizens' Clearinghouse for Hazardous Wastes
P.O. Box 6806
Falls Church, VA 22040
(703) 237-2249

Hazardous Materials Control Research Institute
(Publishes monthly newsletter, *FOCUS*)
7237-A Hanover Parkway
Greenbelt, MD 20770
(301) 982-9500

UNIT 6

RESOURCES IN THE BIOSPHERE

CHAPTERS

This symbol means *gold*. It comes from ancient Egypt. Gold is one of many metals valuable to people. Metals and all other resources come from Earth. For thousands of years people have dug mines, built irrigation systems, and otherwise gathered and manipulated resources. The search for resources that Earth provides and the use of these resources have lead to pollution problems on land, in the water, and in the atmosphere.

The pyramids at Giza were constructed nearly 5,000 ▶ years ago on land near the Nile River. Ancient Egyptian civilization was dependent on the Nile for water and transportation, and for the rich soils it left after flooding each year.

284

CHAPTER

18

MINERALS AND SOILS

Stone Age, Bronze Age, and Iron Age refer to time periods in many human cultures when technological breakthroughs influenced the course of human history. Stone, bronze, and iron are all made of minerals. The Iron Age began about 4,000 years ago in some cultures. Today's technology is still deeply rooted in the use of minerals.

R. Neil Sampson, an expert in agriculture, once wrote, "We stand only six inches away from desolation, for that is the thickness of the topsoil layer upon which the entire life of the planet depends." The food that every land organism needs comes from the soil. However, soil mismanagement threatens this six-inch lifeline.

18.1 MINERALS AND THEIR USES

Objectives • *Describe* minerals and *identify* some of their characteristics. • *List* several ways that minerals are used.

Humans and other organisms use nutrients contained in food to carry out their life processes. For example, human bodies use iron, a nutrient found in meat and grains, to help blood carry oxygen from the lungs to every cell of the body. Many of the nutrients needed for daily life are made of substances that are also important for science and industry. Those substances are called *minerals.*

Characteristics of Minerals

To be defined as a mineral, a substance must possess specific characteristics. *A* **mineral** *is an inorganic, naturally occurring, solid material with a definite chemical composition, and with its atoms arranged in specific patterns.* Do you think coal can be considered a mineral?

Minerals may be either elements or compounds. Elements are substances that are made up of one type of atom. For example, gold (Au) is a mineral that is made up of one kind of atom. A piece of quartz (SiO_2) is an example of a compound mineral, containing the two elements silicon (Si) and oxygen (O).

Minerals make up the rocks of the lithosphere, and a single rock is rarely composed of only one mineral. Often, minerals that form under similar conditions occur together. For example, the granite shown in Figure 18.2 is made of quartz, feldspar, and biotite minerals. Feldspar and biotite contain silicon and oxygen, as does quartz. However, feldspar also contains such elements as calcium, potassium, or sodium. Biotite contains iron and magnesium.

Often minerals are contained in rocks. *Rocks that contain large amounts of economically desirable minerals are called* **ores.** Metals such as iron seldom exist as a pure mineral. Usually iron is combined with less desirable minerals in ores such as hematite.

Figure 18.1 This family in Japan is enjoying a healthy meal of rice and fish. The nutrients in the rice come from the minerals in soil. The fish also provides valuable nutrients.

No. Coal cannot be considered a mineral because it is formed from organic material.

Figure 18.2 Granite (left) and hematite (right) are rocks that are made of minerals. The pink feldspar and black biotite minerals grew together, along with clear quartz, forming granite. Hematite is an ore that is processed to obtain iron.

Figure 18.3 The sand that is found on beaches or in streams is used to make the microprocessors that go into powerful computers.

Table 18.1 Some Minerals and Their Common Uses

Mineral	Uses
Copper	Electrical wiring, water pipes
Aluminum	Packaging for food and beverages, airplanes
Lead	Car batteries, paint
Gypsum	Concrete, wallboards
Iron	Automobiles, construction
Silicon	Windows, microprocessors
Gold	Electronics, aerospace, jewelry
Silver	Photography, jewelry
Sulfur	Batteries

Uses of Metals and Nonmetals

Most metals, including iron, lead, and aluminum, occur naturally as metallic ores. These ores must be refined and heated in order to extract the desired metal. The process of heating and refining an ore to separate the valuable mineral is called *smelting*.

Metals have several properties that make them important in technology and industry. Metals are *ductile* (DUK-til), or able to be pulled and stretched into wires. They are also *malleable* (MAL-ee-uh-bul), or able to be hammered and shaped without breaking. These two properties make metals ideal for construction and other industries. Another property of metals is that they are good *conductors,* materials that allow electricity and heat to flow through them. This additional property makes metals such as copper and gold especially important for use in electronic devices.

Nonmetallic ores are also useful. Nonmetallic minerals such as sulfur, gypsum, and halite (common table salt) are valuable resources. Sulfur is used to make sulfuric acid, the acid in car batteries. Gypsum may be used in concrete for construction. Table 18.1 shows other minerals and their common uses.

EARTH SCIENCE
L I N K

Every mineral has distinct properties. These properties are like fingerprints that can be used to identify the mineral. Some mineral properties are color, hardness, cleavage, and fracture. Cleavage and fracture refer to the way a mineral breaks apart. Other mineral properties are luster, crystal shape, and streak. Luster refers to the way a mineral reflects light from its surface. Streak is the color of the mineral's powder.

Figure 18.4 The use of minerals in the United States is enormous compared to that of other nations with larger populations. Because the United States is an industrial nation, the need for mineral resources is great.

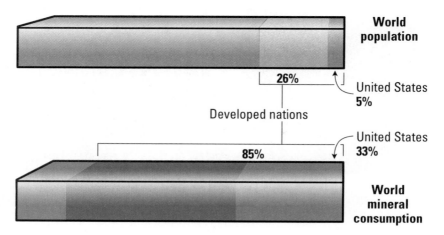

World population

26% ← United States 5%

Developed nations

United States 33%

85%

World mineral consumption

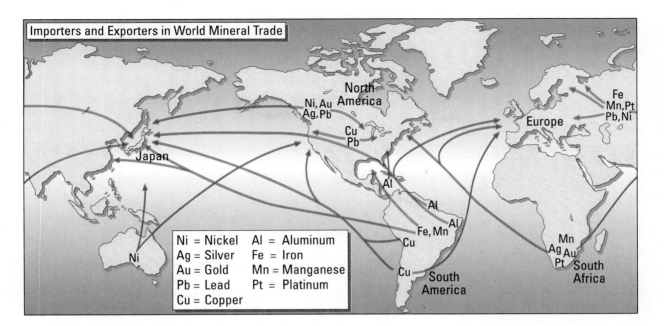

Importers and Exporters in World Mineral Trade

Ni = Nickel   Al = Aluminum
Ag = Silver   Fe = Iron
Au = Gold   Mn = Manganese
Pb = Lead   Pt = Platinum
Cu = Copper

Minerals in International Trade

Metals and other minerals are crucial to economic and technological development. Industry and agriculture rely heavily on minerals for machinery and building materials. If key minerals such as iron or aluminum were unavailable, the industries that form the basis of industrial societies would be crippled. To prevent this, some nations store 3- to 5-year reserves of scarce minerals.

The unequal natural distribution of minerals, such as those shown in Figure 18.5, adds to an interdependence among the global community. Some minerals occur only in specific areas of the world. The political, environmental, and economic stability of nations in these areas is vital on a local level and on an international level. Nations that depend on resources from unstable regions are vulnerable to the changes in those regions.

In 1971, poor management and sabotage of copper mines in Chile resulted in decreased production of copper. Copper mines were deliberately destroyed because of land use disputes and disagreements over wages for miners. The decreased production of copper forced the government of Chile to decrease payments of debts owed to the United States.

Figure 18.5 The human dependence on minerals connects the nations of the world in a global import and export system.

SECTION REVIEW

1. What is a mineral?
2. **Identify** five minerals and list the ways they may be used.
3. **Compare** How does the amount of mineral resources used by the United States compare with that of all other nations?

1. A mineral is a solid, inorganic material that occurs naturally; it has a definite chemical composition and atoms arranged in a particular order.
2. Answers may vary; examples are gypsum—concrete; copper—electronics; iron—cars.
3. Although only 5 percent of the world population inhabits the United States, the United States is responsible for 30 percent of the world's mineral use.

18.2 OBTAINING MINERALS

Objectives • ***Describe*** *methods for extracting minerals.*
• ***Identify*** and ***explain*** *ways in which extraction methods may affect the environment.*

Figure 18.6 Studies of core samples give earth scientists an idea of where to look for minerals. By tracing sediments back to their source, scientists can determine where the minerals in the sediments originated.

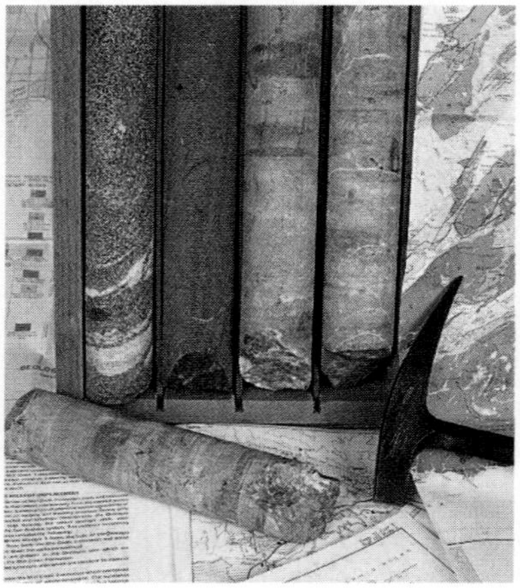

People who study Earth and earth processes, such as earthquakes and volcanoes, are called earth scientists. These scientists use their knowledge of minerals and earth processes to determine where minerals of economic or scientific value are located. Drill core samples, satellite imagery, and aerial photography are useful aids for locating minerals.

Mining and the Environment

Depending on their location, different methods are used to extract minerals. Those minerals at or near the surface are often removed by surface mining. Minerals located deep below the surface are extracted by subsurface mining. Minerals may also be removed by a method called dredging.

Surface Mining In surface mining, layers of rock, soil, and vegetation are removed to uncover mineral deposits. A common method of surface mining, shown in Figure 18.8, is called *open pit mining.* In open-pit mining, large machines are used to dig ore from huge holes in the ground. Bulldozers and power shovels gather the ore for processing. Large deposits of discarded materials, called *tailings,* are left near the mines in heaps known as *spoil piles.* Tailings often contain toxic substances in the form of heavy metals such as lead and copper. Heavy metals are poisonous to living things.

Multicultural Perspective
Indigenous people who had been displaced by colonization and mineral exploration in North America, South America, and Australia are now using legal means to regain their homelands. The Inuits of Canada, Yanomami of Brazil, and Aborigines of Australia have all recently regained land rights in areas they historically called home. The courts in these nations have granted ownership, but with conditions. In some areas, mineral and oil exploration is still the right of the government. Also, there is constant debate between environmentalists and representatives of mining industries over land use.

Figure 18.7 A pick and shovel are no longer enough to extract the minerals needed by technology and industry today. Giant power shovels are used to dig out the mineral deposits held in Earth's crust.

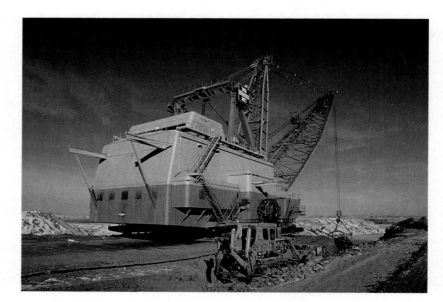

Figure 18.8 Open-pit mines are dug in order to extract mineral ores. Open-pit mining can form deep depressions where hills once stood.

Tailings in spoil piles can be eroded by wind and running water. Winds may carry dust and harmful particles, such as lead, arsenic, and sulfur. Rainwater may leach through spoil piles and pollute groundwater, or carry toxic materials into fields or streams. Open-pit mines often fill with water that becomes polluted. In time, this process affects the groundwater in the area.

Subsurface Mining   In subsurface mining, shown in Figure 18.9, a shaft is dug into the crust. When the mineral deposit is reached, explosives are used to expose the minerals. Machinery is then lowered into the shaft to loosen the mineral deposits and bring them to the surface.

Subsurface mining creates less environmental damage than surface mining, but it is more dangerous to the workers. Walls, ceilings, and underground chambers and tunnels may collapse, trapping miners. Miners are also in danger of explosions of natural gas and dust in the mines. In addition, dust inhaled over long periods of time can cause life-threatening lung diseases.

Figure 18.9 Subsurface mining requires a complex network of tunnels and shafts to remove the minerals from deep deposits.

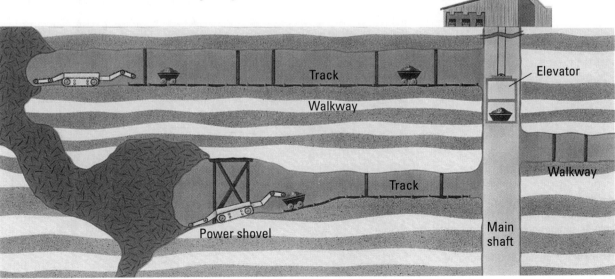

Track

Walkway

Elevator

Track

Walkway

Power shovel

Main shaft

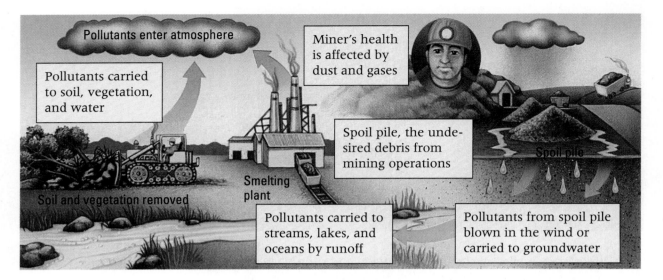

Pollutants enter atmosphere

Pollutants carried to soil, vegetation, and water

Miner's health is affected by dust and gases

Spoil pile, the undesired debris from mining operations

Spoil pile

Soil and vegetation removed

Smelting plant

Pollutants carried to streams, lakes, and oceans by runoff

Pollutants from spoil pile blown in the wind or carried to groundwater

Figure 18.10 The extraction and processing of minerals for use in industry and agriculture can have harmful effects on the environment.

THINK CRITICALLY

Trends in research and development are improving the ways minerals are extracted. These trends also aim to reduce mining costs. A large part of these research and development costs is in the use of automated machinery. Predict what trends will take place in employment, resource supplies, and resource demands.

Answers will vary. Accept all reasonable responses. Answers should include a shift from employment in mines to research and development, miner safety, a greater supply of minerals, and a more rapid depletion of minerals.

Dredging   Dredging involves scraping or vacuuming desirable minerals from ocean floors, lakes, and stream beds. Dredging is used to obtain sand and gravel for construction. Dredging is also used to clear away the sand and silt that accumulate at harbor mouths or behind dams.

Many people are concerned about the dredging of the sea floor. They feel that removing organisms and nutrients may alter complex aquatic food webs. They also question the effects dredging may have on currents, coral reefs, and beaches.

Other environmental damage caused by mineral extraction is caused by smelting and heap leaching processes. Recall that smelting is the removal of desirable minerals from ore. Smelting generates about 8 percent of the world sulfur dioxide emissions. Sulfur dioxide is one of the chemicals that causes acid precipitation, which is discussed in Chapter 22. Smelting also emits large volumes of arsenic and lead into the atmosphere. These toxic metals contribute

Figure 18.11 Dredging may disturb the food chains in certain ecosystems. Dredgers scrape sediments and minerals from stream beds and ocean floors, possibly removing nutrients needed by organisms.

Figure 18.12 A pile of used cars is far from worthless. The energy it takes to recycle the metal in dumps and junkyards is far less than the amount of energy it takes to process new metal materials. Recycling this metal reduces the demand for new material.

to the formation of large areas where plant and animal life cannot live. For example, a smelting plant in Canada is surrounded by about 10 000 hectares of dead landscape.

Heap leaching, a process used to extract gold, involves the use of cyanide, a poisonous chemical sprayed over piles of ore. The cyanide dissolves gold and leaches it from the crushed ore. The gold is then collected from the cyanide liquid. Cyanide collection ponds can contaminate groundwater and are responsible for the deaths of thousands of birds every year.

Mineral Conservation

Some experts warn that about 15 important minerals may soon be depleted. Such minerals include gold, silver, mercury, and sulfur. The depletion of these minerals could have severe consequences unless effective resource management is applied.

Plans for mineral resource management and conservation have been suggested and implemented by concerned groups in government, industry, and in communities. These plans include recycling, substitution, and reuse. In *recycling,* waste materials are treated and used to make more products. *Substitution* uses an abundant material, instead of a less plentiful one, to make products. *Reuse* is using the same product over and over again.

SECTION REVIEW

1. What is substitution?
2. List three methods that are used to extract minerals. Describe how each method is carried out.
3. **Infer** How can recycling reduce pollution?

Cooperative Learning
Have students work in groups of three to five to prepare lists of materials that are typically discarded after one use, or when broken. Have each student make a list of ten items. Then have the groups combine their lists to form a group list. Items should not be listed more than once. Have students compare lists between groups. As a class, discuss how the amounts of these "throwaway" materials can be reduced.

1. It is the use of a more plentiful material instead of a scarce material for manufacturing.
2. Open pit mining involves removal of soil and vegetation, then extraction of minerals from deep pits. Subsurface mining involves a complex network of shafts and tunnels dug underground. Explosives are used to loosen mineral deposits. Later, machinery is lowered to remove minerals and bring them to the surface. Dredging is the scraping or vacuuming of minerals from ocean floors or stream beds.
3. Recycling and the reuse of minerals decreases the demand for extracting new materials. Extraction methods often involve machinery that requires oil and gas to operate. Exhaust from the machinery is reduced. Refining steps require less energy. There is less pollution from factories involved in refining. Environmental impacts from the chemicals leached out of spoil piles are reduced. Accept all reasonable responses.

HISTORICAL NOTEBOOK

Out of the Ground and Into the Soil

How did an iron plow change history?

1. An iron plow capable of digging in hard-to-work soils enabled farmers to plow more land for crops. More crops were capable of sustaining more people. People may have had to organize and perform different functions within growing agricultural centers. This may have been the beginning of urban centers.

2. China was probably isolated, politically and culturally, and many other nations may have been unaware of what was occurring there. Trade may have developed slowly.

Native-American tools made from iron meteorites have been found in several archeological study sites. These findings suggest that iron was a desirable metal to humans for thousands of years. However, the wide-scale use of iron tools only became possible after the iron could be separated from its ore. Iron has such a high melting point that it cannot be smelted using the heat from a wood or coal fire alone. The fire must be supplied with blasts of air to get the temperature high enough.

About 1500 B.C., the first primitive blast furnaces were developed by the Hittites, who lived in what is now central Turkey. The Hittites carefully protected their secrets of iron-working for many years because they could make superior weapons with iron. After the overthrow of the Hittite government around 1100 B.C., their knowledge of ironworking spread throughout the world. The Iron Age began.

During the Iron Age, much of the world used the strong metal to produce weapons and war materials, such as swords and armor. For this reason, when they think of the Iron Age, most people think of knights in armor carrying heavy iron swords.

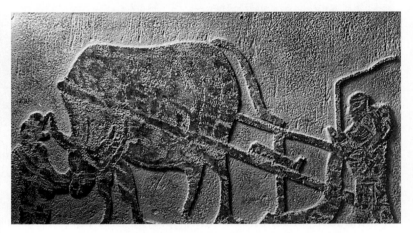

However, the most important impact iron had on civilization was probably off the battlefield and on the farm fields of China.

By the sixth century B.C., China was smelting iron and turning it into plows. The solid iron plows replaced plows made of less durable wood. This small change in the material used for plows later led to an agricultural revolution in Europe. However, the revolution did not occur until 2,000 years later, when the iron plow was introduced to Europe from China.

In the seventeenth century, after the Chinese had perfected the iron plow, Dutch sailors brought the iron plows to Holland and England. Since the Chinese plow was successful on wet, boggy land as well as on fertile, soft soil, its use spread quickly. From England and Holland the iron plow spread to Scotland, France,

and America. The advanced tool meant greater food production. Increased food production supported the growth of cities.

The advantages of the iron plow are obvious. The hardness and durability of the blade made it possible to plow in heavier soils. Land composed of heavy or waterlogged soil could now be cultivated. This meant that the farmer could cultivate in any type of soil, in various weather conditions, and during more seasons.

DECISIONS

1. **Describe** how replacing the material used to make one type of tool may have changed the history of humankind.

2. **Infer** why the iron plow took so long to spread from China to other parts of the world.

18.3 SOIL AND ITS FORMATION

Objectives • *Describe* the relationship between climate and soil formation. • *Identify* different soil types and how they influence soil characteristics.

Soil is home for many organisms. Some of these organisms, such as earthworms, aerate the soil and contribute to its formation. All organisms that live in the soil are vital to the energy and nutrient cycles of Earth.

Soil Formation

Wherever rock is exposed to changing conditions, either at or near Earth's surface, it will break down, or weather, into smaller and smaller fragments. The weathering of exposed rock may occur mechanically or chemically. An example of mechanical weathering is the pounding of waves on a sea cliff. An example of chemical weathering is the rusting of iron-containing minerals, such as biotite, in granite.

The igneous, metamorphic, and sedimentary rock of the lithosphere that may exist as mountains, cliffs, or low-lying plains is called **bedrock**. As the solid bedrock weathers, it supplies the material needed to build soil. *An area of bedrock that is the source of an area of soil is called the soil's* **parent rock**.

The exposed outer layers of a rock are the most unprotected and easily weathered layers. It is the outer layer that begins to change in structure, with cracks and holes beginning to develop, as in Figure 18.14. With time and further weathering, cracks and holes reach deeper and deeper into the bedrock, and the outer layer becomes broken into smaller mineral particles. **Soil** *is a mixture of mineral particles, air, water, bedrock, and living and decaying organisms*. Hundreds to thousands of years may be required to form just 10 cm of soil.

The organic activity of plants and animals can also influence the weathering and structure of soil and bedrock. Burrowing animals and plant roots mechanically break down bedrock and aerate the soil. Many soil organisms aerate enough for water and air to reach

Word Power

Granite, from the Greek *granum,* "seed," or "grain."

Figure 18.14 Not all soils form at the same rate, but all are formed from bedrock. The hard bedrock begins to weather because of temperature changes and moisture (left). Holes and cracks develop deeper in the rock as the layer above weathers into smaller and smaller pieces (center). Layers of small particles sit on top of larger particles, which in turn sit on the original bedrock (right).

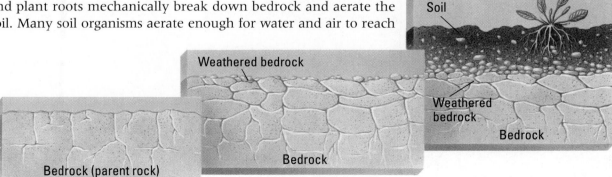

Soil

Weathered bedrock

Bedrock

Weathered bedrock

Bedrock

Bedrock (parent rock)

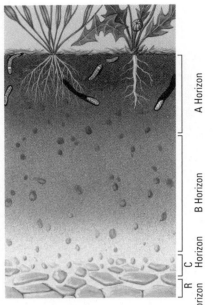

A Horizon

B Horizon

C Horizon

R Horizon

Figure 18.15 A mature soil profile contains layers commonly known as topsoil, subsoil, and bedrock. However, soil scientists may divide layers further into horizons to describe them in greater detail.

Figure 18.16 Particle size and mixture determine, in part, whether or not plants will grow in an area of soil. The sand particles (left) enable soil to drain well but dry out quickly. Clay particles (center) are flat and trap water, preventing water drainage. Loam soil (right) contains a mixture of particle sizes that provides good drainage and moisture for plant roots.

deeper into the soil. Water and air carry with them agents of chemical weathering, such as carbon dioxide and oxygen. When soil organisms die, they again contribute to the soil by becoming the organic material of humus.

As weathering progresses, distinct layers of weathered bedrock become apparent. These layers, shown in Figure 18.15, form what are known as the A, B, C, and R horizons in a mature soil profile. A **soil profile** *is a vertical cross section of soil from the ground surface down to the bedrock.* The A horizon in a soil profile is commonly known as the topsoil. The B horizon is often called the subsoil. However, the C horizon is a layer of partially weathered bedrock. The R horizon is the bedrock.

Composition and Characteristics of Soil

Although there are thousands of different types of soil, the simplest separation of soils is into three major soil textures, based on the sizes of the particles within them. It should be noted, however, that the mixture of the particles is equally important to the classification of soil. The three major soil textures, shown in Figure 18.16, are sandy, clay, and loam.

In *sandy soils*, most of the mineral grains vary in size from 0.05 to 2.0 mm. Soil that contains a high number of clay-sized grains (smaller than 0.002 mm each) are called *clay soils*. Mineral grains between 0.002 and 0.05 mm in diameter are called *silt*. Soils containing roughly equal amounts of sand, clay, and silt particles are called *loam soils*.

The sizes and amounts of mineral particles, or grains, in the soil determine some characteristics of the soil. Sandy soil has good drainage and good aeration, but it does not store water very well. This characteristic makes sandy soil unsuitable for many plants. Clay soils, however, hold water very well, but they do not drain well and do not contain much space for air. Clay soils are also unlikely to sustain many plants. Loam soils, on the other hand, with their even mixture of different particle sizes, are ideal for many plants. The even mixture enables loam soils to hold water and air.

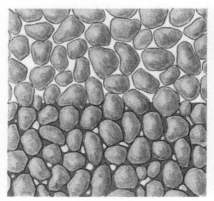
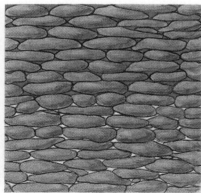

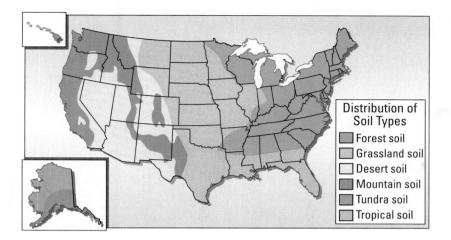

Figure 18.17 This map shows a simplified distribution of different soil types throughout the United States. There are over 20,000 different types of soil in the United States alone.

Distribution of Soil Types
- Forest soil
- Grassland soil
- Desert soil
- Mountain soil
- Tundra soil
- Tropical soil

The Interaction Between Soil and Climate

Because climate affects the rate of weathering, climate is one of the most important factors in the formation of soil. In the desert and tundra, for example, the soil profile may be only a few centimeters thick because there is less water to break down the bedrock. Soil particles in these biomes are generally larger in size because strong winds and infrequent rainfall only remove the smaller, lighter particles from the thin layer of soil.

Grasslands may have a thicker soil profile because of greater precipitation. Also, the weathering of the bedrock underlying grasslands may occur at a faster rate because of the activity of more plants and burrowing animals. The soils of the midwestern United States got a head start in forming because they began as rock fragments carried by glaciers.

The high amount of rainfall on tropical soils results in thick soil profiles. However, the structure of these soils is very fragile because the high rainfall quickly leaches nutrients and small clay particles into the subsoil. An accumulation of nutrients and clay particles occurs in the subsoil. But because of the large amounts of clay in the subsoil, subsoil does not drain well and is not well aerated. For these reasons, accumulated nutrients in soils are usually unavailable for plant roots. The fertility of tropical soils is maintained by the rapid decay of a constant fall of organic matter from trees and native vegetation.

Figure 18.18 The fertile soils along a floodplain are often used for agriculture. These soils may form without the influence of local climate.

1. A soil profile is a cross section of soil from the ground surface to the hard bedrock.
2. Soil is weathered bedrock. Rainfall acts to mechanically and chemically weather bedrock. Higher amounts of rain should develop more soil.
3. As water flows through the soil, it carries the smaller particles with it. Usually, these smaller particles are the clay particles and nutrients that are washed out of the upper layers of soil. The decaying matter from trees does not accumulate because there are no trees.

SECTION REVIEW

1. What is a soil profile?
2. How are climate and soil thickness related?
3. **Think Critically** How is the fertility of a tropical rain forest influenced by the removal of native vegetation for space to grow grain crops?

Answers and teaching strategies on page T98.

Looking for Life in Soil

PROBLEM
Are there living organisms in soil?

MATERIALS (per group)

- safety goggles
- ring stand
- Bunsen burner
- tongs
- sugar
- methylene blue solution
- graduated cylinder
- 3 test tubes with stoppers and a rack
- wax pencil
- balance
- garden soil
- wire gauze
- crucible

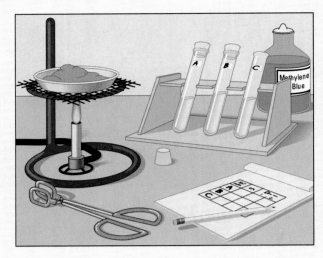

INFERENCE
Read the entire activity, then write an inference about what gases would be given off by living organisms in a stoppered test tube.

PROCEDURE

Test Tube	Contents	Observations	
		Day 1	Day 2
A			
B			
C			

1. Copy the data table onto a separate sheet of paper. Label three test tubes *A*, *B*, and *C*.
2. Transfer 1 g of the soil to a crucible. Set the wire gauze and crucible on the ring stand, and heat the soil in the crucible over a Bunsen burner for 10 minutes.
   Caution: *Be careful around the Bunsen burner. Tie back long hair and wear safety goggles. Use tongs to move the hot crucible.*
3. Transfer 1 g of unheated soil to test tube *A*. Add 1 g of sugar and 10 mL of methylene blue solution. *Note: Methylene blue solution is an indicator of carbon dioxide (CO$_2$).*
   Caution: *Methylene blue may stain.*
4. To test tube *B*, transfer the heated soil from the crucible, 1 g of sugar, and 10 mL of methylene blue solution.
5. To test tube *C*, transfer 1 g of sugar and 10 mL of methylene blue solution.
6. Observe the liquid in each test tube. In the *Day 1* column of the data table, describe the colors using the terms *blue*, *light blue*, and *colorless*.
7. Put a stopper in each test tube and shake them well. Return them to the test-tube rack and leave them over night.
8. The next day, observe the test tubes again. Do not shake them. Record your observations in the *Day 2* column using the same terms as before.

ANALYSIS

1. What was the purpose of heating the soil that was placed into test tube *B*?
2. Carbon dioxide causes methylene blue solution to change to light blue or colorless. What color changes did you observe in each test tube on Day 1? Day 2? What do these color changes indicate?
3. Was your inference accurate? Support your answer with data.

CONCLUSION
Does soil contain any living organisms? What evidence do you have to support your answer? Explain your conclusions.

18.4 SOIL MISMANAGEMENT

Objectives • *Identify* causes of soil mismanagement.
• *Predict* possible outcomes from such mismanagement.

Fragile soil structures may be abused by the simple act of planting something other than what is naturally suited for the region. Care must be taken to maintain the connection between soil and life. The human population is straining the connection through lack of information and careful planning.

Symptoms of Soil Mismanagement

Every year that passes brings some news of the symptoms of poor land management and planning. In 1992 and 1993, the United Nations sent men and women into Somalia to help get food to starving people. Many in the United Nations and International Red Cross claimed that long-term drought was responsible for the famine. However, studies show that the major cause is most likely soil erosion. In the mid-1980s, the head of Kenya's agricultural ministry stated that the widespread famine in areas such as Ethiopia, Chad, and Somalia was closely related to the absence of soil conservation programs.

Another symptom of soil mismanagement is the fact that nearly one billion dollars a year are spent on clearing sediment from streams and lakes in the United States. The sediment comes from hills and mountains where protective vegetation has been removed, allowing wind and water to carry away exposed soil. Fortunately, goals are being redirected from plans to clean up damages to methods for preventing damages. Some methods for controlling soil erosion are discussed in Chapter 19.

A FIELD ACTIVITY

Road cuts or small cliffs are ideal places to find soil profiles. Use a small hand trowel to lightly cut away the surface layer of loose debris and expose a fresh soil face. Step back to see if any color differences are noticeable. If different layers are noticeable, examine the soil closely and try to identify the composition of the soil. Determine what soil layers are represented. Sketch the soil profile and label the layers. **Caution:** *Be sure to watch for traffic and have a partner with you at all times.*

Teaching tips for Field Activity appear on page T98.

Figure 18.19 Here are a few examples of how soil is poisoned, compacted, and stripped of its protective vegetation.

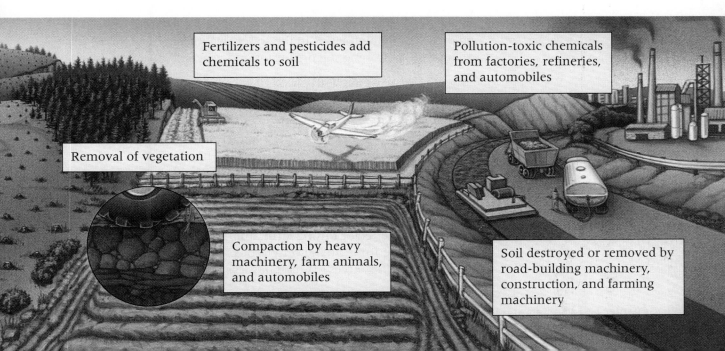

Fertilizers and pesticides add chemicals to soil

Pollution-toxic chemicals from factories, refineries, and automobiles

Removal of vegetation

Compaction by heavy machinery, farm animals, and automobiles

Soil destroyed or removed by road-building machinery, construction, and farming machinery

Figure 18.20 Vegetation protects soil from erosion. Here, soil erosion has removed all but what was held by the roots of a few scattered trees and shrubs.

DATELINE 1991

In 1991, the National Resources Defense Council presented a report on the use of insecticides. The report stated that farmers could reduce their use of insecticides by 80 percent. This reduction could be accomplished by using already existing methods of insect control. Methods include rotating crops, or planting different crops during different seasons, and planting insect-resistant crops. Another method is using predator insects that kill insect pests but do not feed on food crops.

Causes of Soil Mismanagement

The removal of vegetation is widespread due to mining, construction, and agriculture. These industries remove vegetation to make access easier to minerals, to clear space for housing and buildings, or to plant crops that have immediate economic value. Human needs drive these industries.

Political needs also contribute to soil mismanagement. In the case of Ethiopia and Somalia, government officials desired to have mostly nomadic peoples settle down permanently. Nutrient-poor soils in Ethiopia and Somalia are naturally unable to sustain millions of people over long periods of time. The previously nomadic people had rarely worked the same area of soil for more than a year. Keeping these nomads in one area quickly depleted the soils within two or three years.

Overgrazing and deforestation are results of poor agriculture practices that lead to soil mismanagement. Pesticides, fertilizers, and irrigation also contribute to soil deterioration. Poisons may be added to the soil when gardeners and farmers use chemical fertilizers and pesticides to increase productivity. These chemicals can accumulate to dangerously high levels in the soil. Irrigation can recirculate salts to topsoils, poisoning soil organisms and vegetation.

1. Compaction is the squeezing or pressing together of soil particles.
2. Causes involving poisoning, removal of vegetation, and compaction are all acceptable. Poisoning kills vegetation and soil organisms that maintain soil health. Removal of vegetation displaces the roots that hold soil. Compaction forces water to run off in heavy streams that wash away soil.
3. Answers may vary, but should include the food chain, land use, fertilizers and pesticides, processing, and soil mismanagement.

SECTION REVIEW

1. What is compaction?
2. Identify three major causes of soil abuse and describe how each results in soil loss.
3. **Think Critically** Compare the energy and mineral resource requirements for raising farm animals, such as cattle and pigs, and those for growing only crops. Which do you think uses the most resources? Which has less environmental impact?

KEY TERMS

mineral 18.1	bedrock 18.3	soil 18.3
ore 18.1	parent rock 18.3	soil profile 18.3

CHAPTER SUMMARY

18.1 A mineral is a solid, inorganic, naturally occurring material with a definite chemical composition and a specifically arranged pattern of atoms. Minerals are used in a wide variety of ways, depending on the properties of the mineral. The availability of minerals influences technology and economics.

18.2 The processes that form Earth's crust determine the location of minerals. Methods such as satellite imagery, field study, and aerial photography are used to find minerals. Methods such as open-pit mining, surface mining, and dredging are used to extract minerals from the crust. Methods for extracting and processing can have serious environmental impacts.

18.3 Soil is formed by the weathering of rock. The soil profile from surface to bedrock consists of horizons. Topsoil and subsoil are common names for these horizons. Soil is composed of rock fragments, minerals, and organic matter. The size of grains and the mixture of grains and organic matter determine soil characteristics. Three major soil types are clay, sandy, and loam. Soil organisms and vegetation are vital to healthy soil.

18.4 Removal of vegetation leaves the soil unprotected. Soil structure will break down because of a decrease in organic matter generated by vegetation and associated organisms. Chemicals and pollution can poison the organisms that help support soil structure. Topsoil may be removed for mining, construction, or agriculture.

MULTIPLE CHOICE

Choose the letter of the word or phrase that best completes each statement.

1. Minerals are solid, inorganic substances that (a) are made by machines; (b) are found only on Earth; (c) exist naturally; (d) are made of iron. c

2. Some metals are very important in electronics because they are (a) conductors; (b) inexpensive; (c) magnetic; (d) strong. a

3. The United States is a major producer of (a) copper; (b) diamonds; (c) aluminum; (d) mercury. a

4. Mineral deposits in streams may be extracted by (a) open-pit mining; (b) satellite imagery; (c) dredging; (d) leaching. c

5. The environmental impact of mineral extraction can be reduced by (a) 15 percent; (b) using clean minerals; (c) recycling; (d) getting minerals from the ocean floor. c

6. The fertile layer of a soil profile is the (a) subsoil; (b) topsoil; (c) bedrock; (d) rooting layer. b

7. Soils with a high percentage of clay are (a) ideal for growing crops; (b) able to drain rapidly; (c) full of large grains of sand; (d) able to hold water for too long a time. d

8. The bedrock from which an area of soil may have formed is called the soil's (a) B horizon; (b) mineral deposit; (c) parent rock; (d) A horizon. c

9. Fertilizers and pesticides can lead to soil mismanagement by (a) poisoning soil organisms; (b) taking minerals from the soil; (c) feeding plant roots; (d) forming holes in the soil. a

10. Soils form over periods of (a) 20-25 years; (b) 10 years; (c) hundreds to thousands of years; (d) 50 years. c

TRUE/FALSE

Write true *if the statement is true. If the statement is false, change the underlined word to make it true.*

1. Hematite is an ore that is a source of <u>iron</u>. t
2. Nonmetals are minerals that are <u>widely</u> used. t
3. Metals can be called minerals because metals are <u>ductile and malleable</u>. f, solid, inorganic, and naturally occurring
4. <u>Subsurface mining</u> uses open-pit mines to obtain minerals. f, surface mining
5. <u>Parent rock</u> is the rock from which soils form. t
6. The <u>subsoil</u> in a mature soil profile is the most fertile layer of soil. f, topsoil
7. <u>Loam</u> is a type of soil with an even mixture of differently sized particles. t
8. Grasslands have <u>thicker</u> soil profiles than deserts and tundras. t

CONCEPT REVIEW   Answers on page T98.

Write a complete response for each of the following.

1. Describe three ways in which minerals may be conserved.
2. Distinguish between chemical and mechanical weathering.
3. Name the three types of soil, and describe the characteristics of each type.
4. How is climate related to soil formation?
5. How does agriculture contribute to soil abuse?

THINK CRITICALLY   Answers on page T98.

1. Compare the fertility of soil in a grassland to that in a rain forest. Which soil is more fertile? Why?
2. How does political stability affect the trade of minerals?
3. If you were to build an environmentally sound house, what would you use as building material? Where would you get your building material? Would you damage anything to obtain this material?
4. What would happen to the agriculture on a river delta if the river were dammed?
5. Can soil be considered a renewable or non-renewable resource? Explain your answer.

WRITE CREATIVELY

You are traveling through the galaxy in your personal spacecraft when your sensors indicate the presence of life on a nearby planet. You land and discover a planet where all the humanlike inhabitants live underground. The conditions above the ground are unhealthy. The air is very dry and full of sand and dust. Imagine interviewing the inhabitants to find out what happened on this dusty planet. The humanlike inhabitants also have many questions to ask you. They wonder about the planet from which you come. After learning about your planet, these inhabitants request your aid in making their planet's surface livable again. If you were to assist the planet's inhabitants, consider the issues you would need to face. Write a story about this adventure.

PORTFOLIO

Collect magazine and newspaper articles on mining and soil issues. Organize these articles by date, into categories on changing methods in farming and mining, and environmental impacts. Try to determine trends in employment, productivity, and resource availability.

Use Figure 18.5 to answer the following.

1. Where are the major natural resources of copper located?
2. What metals does North America import from South Africa?
3. How does Japan's economy depend on global political stability?
4. What minerals does the Commonwealth of Independent States (the former Soviet Union) supply to Japan and Europe?
5. Why do you think the United States imports additional copper from South America?
6. What pattern in the world mineral trade describes where minerals are most consumed?
7. How might government relations between South Africa and the United States be influenced?

ACTIVITY 18.2

Answers and teaching strategies on page T98.

PROBLEM

How do earthworms change soil?

MATERIALS (per group)

- 3 types of soil
- 1-L jar
- water
- partly decayed leaves (humus)
- apple peelings
- construction paper
- rubber band or tape
- shovel or trowel

HYPOTHESIS

Read the entire activity, then write a hypothesis that is related to the problem.

PROCEDURE

1. Add three different types of soil to the jar, one layer at a time. Each layer should fill about one-quarter of the jar. Sprinkle some water in the jar to make the soil moist but not wet.
2. Add partly decayed leaves and some apple peelings. Sprinkle a little more water inside.
3. Wrap a sheet of construction paper around the jar. Hold the paper in place with a rubber band or piece of tape.
4. Obtain a few shovelfuls of damp soil. Look in the soil for three earthworms. Return to class with the earthworms. Place the earthworms in the jar, and store it in a cool place. *Note: Handle the earthworms with care.*
5. The next day, take out the jar and remove the construction paper. Record your observations in a data table. If the soil is dry, add a little water. After making your observations, wrap the jar as before, and return it to its storage place.
6. Repeat Step 5 every day for a week.

ANALYSIS

1. What happened to the partly decayed leaves and apple peelings?
2. What happened to the layers of soil?
3. What three types of soil did you use?
4. How might the soil type affect earthworm activity?
5. What would you predict would happen if no water was added to the jar?

CONCLUSION

What was the effect of earthworms on soil? Describe how specific earthworm behaviors caused this effect.

CHAPTER
19
LAND POLLUTION

On March 22, 1987, the towed barge *Mobro* left from Long Island City, New York. On board were 2800 metric tons of garbage being carried to a landfill in Moorehead, North Carolina. When the barge arrived in North Carolina, its cargo was rejected. Similar rejections occurred in Florida, Alabama, Mississippi, Louisiana, Texas, Mexico, Belize, and the Bahamas. The repeated rejection became national news. For five months, the "garbage barge" searched for a port to accept its ripening cargo. Finally, an incinerator in Brooklyn, New York, accepted the garbage. The displaced garbage points to one of the many problems associated with land pollution: Space is running out.

19.1 SOLID WASTES

Objectives • *List examples of solid wastes, and **identify** their sources.* • ***Identify** past and present methods used to dispose of solid wastes.*

Garbage, trash, refuse, junk, scrap, and sewage are all examples of waste materials that need to be disposed of in a way that does not pollute the land. Collectively, these materials are called solid wastes. *In 1976, the U.S. Congress defined* **solid wastes** *as all garbage, refuse, and sludge products from agriculture, forestry, mining, and municipalities.*

Garbage Disposal in the Past

Early peoples were hunter–gatherers who followed game animals from place to place. Garbage disposal was not a problem in these societies. They simply left their garbage where it fell and moved on. Later, some hunter–gatherers began to develop agriculture and build small cities. As cities grew, refuse disposal became a problem.

As early as 500 B.C., the city of Athens, Greece, passed laws that resulted in the first garbage dump. Garbage could no longer be thrown into the streets. Instead, all garbage had to be placed in locations not closer than 1.6 km from the city walls. Despite this ruling, the rest of Europe continued depositing garbage into the streets.

In 1892, outbreaks of typhoid and cholera forced New York City officials to establish better sanitary conditions. By 1900, garbage was collected from the streets, loaded onto barges, and dumped into the ocean. This method of garbage removal continued for some time, until swimmers in Atlantic City, New Jersey, observed mattresses and dead animals floating past them.

To solve the problem of the polluted waters, the first landfills were established. About 70 percent of today's garbage is dumped in landfills. *A* **landfill** *is a site where wastes are disposed of by burying them.*

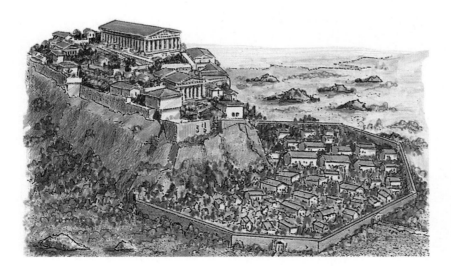

Figure 19.1 Perhaps the first garbage dump in Europe was developed in Greece in 500 B.C. City leaders in Athens declared that the dumping of refuse within city walls was illegal. Garbage had to be dumped at least 1.6 km outside the city walls.

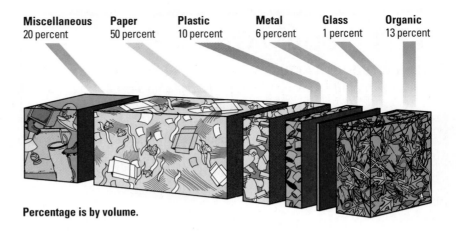

Miscellaneous	Paper	Plastic	Metal	Glass	Organic
20 percent	50 percent	10 percent	6 percent	1 percent	13 percent

Percentage is by volume.

Figure 19.2 Waste created by most communities consists largely of paper and paper products such as newspapers and packaging materials. Other solid wastes include food remains, plastics, glass, metals, textiles, yard wastes, leather, and rubber.

The Landfill Problem

Today, hunter–gatherers have been replaced by people who work in industry and offices. Cities have grown larger. More food and goods are brought into the cities each day to meet the needs of the increasing population. In turn, larger and larger amounts of wastes are produced. The graph in Figure 19.2 shows the contents of city wastes in landfills.

As populations grow and more garbage is produced, a major problem arises: Where will all the garbage be placed? For many years, open dumping in landfills was the cheapest and most convenient way to dispose of garbage. A land site was chosen, and truckloads of garbage were deposited there each day. But open dumping was stopped because it supported large populations of rats, flies, cockroaches, and other unwanted organisms. Foul odors given off by open landfills invaded areas close to the dumps.

In addition, rainfall over the open landfills carried pollutants from the garbage into the soil. Some of these pollutants were

Teaching tips for Field Activity appear on page T102.

FIELD ACTIVITY

Conduct research on the use of pesticides by the growers who supply your supermarket with produce. There are references in libraries regarding pesticide use. Make a list of pesticides and their related health risks.

Figure 19.3 Open landfills are no longer legal in most of the United States. They are breeding grounds for many harmful diseases. This open landfill in the Philippines, called Smoky Mountain, is home to more than 20,000 people. These people live and work here but suffer greatly from poverty and health problems.

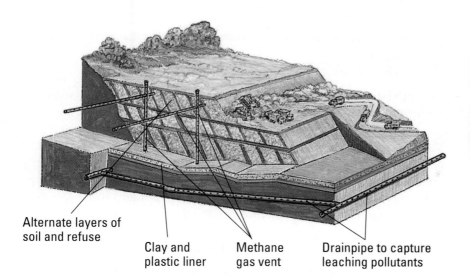

Alternate layers of
soil and refuse

Clay and
plastic liner

Methane
gas vent

Drainpipe to capture
leaching pollutants

leached into groundwater systems. Because of these problems, this method of garbage disposal is now illegal in many states.

Many communities today use *sanitary landfills* for refuse disposal. In a sanitary landfill, wastes are spread in layers about 3 m deep and compacted by bulldozers. About 15 cm of soil is then spread on top of the refuse and compacted. The process is repeated daily until the mountain of garbage reaches a designated height. The landfill is closed and a final layer of soil, about 60 cm thick, is placed over the entire area. Grass and trees are planted in the soil. The site may be reserved for use in the future.

Sanitary landfills are not as harmless as they may seem. Decomposition of some wastes produces methane gas. Methane is highly flammable and explodes easily. To keep methane gas from building up in the landfill, ventilation pipes are placed into the ground. These ventilation pipes enable methane to slowly escape from the landfill. At some landfills, the methane is collected and sold for profit.

Another problem associated with sanitary landfills is the leaching of toxic substances. To avoid leaching, new landfills must place a double liner around the landfill area. However, liners sometimes tear from uneven land settling. To reduce liner tear, liners are constructed of layers of clay and a thick plastic sheet. This construction enable the liner to flex during uneven land settling.

SECTION REVIEW

1. What are solid wastes?
2. What are some ways that people have disposed of solid wastes?
3. **Infer** How might placing a landfill near an aquatic ecosystem be harmful to the organisms living in the water?

1. Solid wastes are garbage, refuse, and sludge produced as a result of agricultural, mining, commercial, and residential activities.
2. Disposal methods include open dumping, landfills, and ocean dumping.
3. As water seeps into the soil of a landfill, harmful substances may be leached into the groundwater and carried into an aquatic ecosystem. These substances could be toxic to some or all of the organisms living there, killing them or altering food chains in such a way as to kill some species.

19.2 HAZARDOUS WASTES

Objectives • *Identify* problems associated with hazardous wastes.
• *Classify* hazardous wastes according to their characteristics.

The emergence of industrial and technological society has brought great advances in science and medicine, and a significant impact on global ecosystems. Technology makes bigger, better, and stronger materials for today's world. However, the use, storage, and disposal of these materials can have widespread effects.

Effects of Hazardous Materials

Solid, liquid, or gaseous wastes that are potentially harmful to humans and the environment, even in low concentrations, are called **hazardous wastes**. The problems of hazardous wastes are well illustrated by the example of the Love Canal community in New York. Homes in Love Canal were built next to an old chemical waste dump. An elementary school and playground were built on top of the dump.

Many cases of birth defects and cancer-related illnesses were reported by residents of the Love Canal community. However, it was not until after the steel containers that held the hazardous wastes rusted through, leaking chemicals to the surface, that the government was forced to take action. More than 1,000 families were evacuated and relocated at the government's expense. The cleanup efforts and relocation policies cost more than $190 million. Now, the government has declared the area safe for the former residents to move back. Would you move back?

Similar situations have occurred in other parts of the world. In Bhopal, India, more than 3,600 people died and another 200,000 were injured when a toxic gas escaped from a storage tank.

Figure 19.6 Farmers are vulnerable to health risks because of their constant contact with dangerous pesticides. The townspeople of Bhopal (bottom) protest possible out-of-court agreements between their government and Union Carbide, the company responsible for 3,600 deaths in Bhopal.

Figure 19.7 In the late 1970s, a serious problem arose in Love Canal. How could a community, school, and playground be built over a toxic chemical dump?

The accident left more than 2,500 people with permanent disabilities to their eyes, lungs, and reproductive systems. The company responsible agreed to pay $470 million to the people of Bhopal as compensation.

The number of other dangerous incidents involving hazardous wastes is staggering. Table 19.1 lists only some of these incidents. The table does not show the impact on other organisms.

Discuss the concept of compensation with students. People's lives have changed because of health problems due to accidents involving hazardous materials, such as the one in Bhopal, India. Ask if people can truly be compensated for their pain and suffering. You may wish to point out to students that such issues are one concern of the branch of the legal profession known as environmental law.

Table 19.1 Accidents Involving Hazardous Wastes

Location	Year	Nature of Damage
Minamata, Japan	1959	By 1983, 300 people killed from mercury discharged into waterways
Detroit, Michigan	1966	Nuclear breeder core meltdown
Flixborough, UK	1974	22 dead in chemical plant explosion
Seveso, Italy	1976	190 injured in dioxin leak
Love Canal, New York	1970s	Toxic waste dump responsible for high rates of birth defects and illnesses
Elizabeth, New Jersey	1979	30 people injured when explosion produced toxic smoke over city
Three Mile Island near Harrisburg, Pennsylvania	1979	Partial nuclear core meltdown
Woburn, Massachusetts	1979	15 dead from leukemia associated with nearby toxic waste dump
Chernobyl, Ukraine	1986	Explosion and fire released huge amounts of radiation
Hagersville, Ontario	1990	Tire fire lasting 17 days produced toxic smoke over city

Word Power

Hazardous, from the French, *hasard*, "game of dice," and the Latin -*ous*, "full of."

The Minamata, Japan, event illustrates the connection between land and water pollution. The Chernobyl, Ukraine, incident connects air and land pollution. Both events are detailed in Chapters 21 and 16, respectively.

Classification of Hazardous Materials

Problems associated with hazardous wastes have become a global concern. In the United States, this concern has prompted the Environmental Protection Agency (EPA) to classify hazardous wastes. Categorizing hazardous wastes helps determine specific methods for disposal.

Reactive Wastes Wastes that can explode are called reactive wastes. Certain chemicals are so unstable that they will explode when handled incorrectly or mixed with other substances. Gunpowder and the metal sodium are examples of reactive substances.

Corrosive Wastes Wastes that can eat through steel and many other materials are called corrosive wastes. Such chemicals eat through clothing and burn the skin. Battery acid and the lye used in drain-cleaning solutions are examples of corrosive wastes.

Figure 19.8 Toxic wastes are a growing concern in today's society. The directions for proper use and disposal of such materials must be followed carefully.

Because few containers can hold corrosive wastes for long periods of time, storing and transporting these substances is a problem. Materials engineers are constantly in search of suitable containers.

Ignitable Wastes   Substances that can burst into flames at relatively low temperatures are called ignitable. Ignitable wastes present an immediate danger from smoke and fire. They can also spread toxic fumes over a wide area. Refuse associated with paint thinners, oils, and some cleaning fluids are examples of ignitable wastes.

Toxic Wastes   Chemicals that are poisonous to people are called toxic, causing health problems such as birth defects or cancer. Wastes from chemicals such as arsenic, cyanide, mercury, and some pesticides are classified as toxic wastes.

Radioactive Wastes   Radiation given off by radioactive wastes can harm people and other organisms. Radiation burns the skin and destroys body cells and tissues. While some radioactive materials take a relatively short time to decay, others may take hundreds of thousands of years to decay.

Radioactive wastes are produced in the mining of radioactive materials such as uranium. Protective clothing, tools, and equipment used in nuclear power plants, as well as mining and processing ores, can also give off radiation. Most radioactive materials used in agricultural, medical, and scientific research give off radiation as well.

Medical Wastes   Old medicines, medicine containers, lab equipment, and lab specimens are referred to as medical wastes. Used syringes, blood vials, and tissue samples are also medical wastes. Some medical wastes may be considered toxic wastes.

Hazardous Home Wastes

Many households are warehouses of hazardous chemicals. Examples are ammonia, bleaches, toilet bowl cleaners, drain cleaners, oven cleaners, disinfectants, furniture polish, outdated medicines, paints, oils, and pesticides. Proper use and disposal of these substances should be practiced at all times. All of these materials have become common necessities in households of industrial nations. However, natural and less hazardous products are beginning to replace these materials on supermarket shelves.

1. Hazardous wastes are solid, liquid, or gaseous wastes that are potentially harmful to humans and the environment, even in low concentrations.
2. Toxic wastes
3. Likely responses will be paints, oils, pesticides, antifreeze. Accept all logical responses.

SECTION REVIEW

1. What are hazardous wastes?
2. **Classify** In what category of hazardous wastes are substances containing mercury or cyanide classified?
3. **Apply** Name five products in your home that contain hazardous materials and therefore require careful disposal.

The Wismut Mines

How did mining operations change people's lives?

1. Arsenic, lead, iron, cadmium, sulfuric acid, and radium.
2. Summary should include legal action, research on effects of exposure, possible increase in death rates and disease, lack of access to countryside, and constant threat of poisoning from local environment.

Kumpels sterben früher is German for "miners die young." This saying illustrates the local wisdom for the residents of Oberrothenbach, a region in eastern Germany. The wisdom is based in fact, as area residents witnessed the death of thousands of workers from the secret Wismut uranium mines and uranium-processing factories. The common cause of miner death was either a deterioration of lung tissue or lung cancer. During the secret Soviet operation that began after World War II and continued until the end of the Cold War, more than 20,000 workers died. This death rate is more than double the death rate in other industrial nations.

Although the Wismut operation is now abandoned, the results will affect many people for years to come. During the history of Wismut, about 450,000 people worked in the mines and the factories. The employees were exposed to high levels of radon, radioactive dust, arsenic, lead, and other poisons. It is estimated that the additional death toll in surviving miners from lung cancer and other related diseases, such as kidney disease and other types of cancer, will be 10,000 to 15,000 deaths.

Epidemiologists, doctors who study the factors involved in the occurrence of diseases in a population, plan to study living former employees to determine whether they show an increased rate of any specific diseases. Participants in the study will have their health checked for the rest of their lives. Researchers hope that the Wismut data will provide information on the combined effects of exposure to low-level radiation and toxic chemicals.

Loss of life caused by direct exposure to radiation and toxic chemicals is just one legacy left behind by Wismut. The other is contamination of the soil and toxic lake dumps. In the city of Oberrothenbach, a barbed-wire fence surrounds the lake. The fence was installed in the 1980s after residents complained that their animals were dying from drinking the water. In 1990, a cover placed over the shore of the lake reduced the blowing of sand containing toxic chemicals and radium. Residents used to stay indoors because blowing sand caused painful burning in the nose and throat. Analysis of the lake contents revealed that it contains about 21,000 metric tons of arsenic. This would be enough to kill every person in Europe. The waters also hold lead, iron, cadmium, sulfuric acid, low-level radioactive material such as radium, and other poisons.

These problems are not isolated to the area around Oberrothenbach. Many more people may be affected. About 450 million metric tons of toxic chemicals and radioactive waste are spread over 1250 km² of Germany .

DECISIONS

1. List the toxic substances in the lake near Wismut mines.
2. Summarize how the wastes of uranium mining and processing may affect an area for many years.

311

19.3 TOPSOIL EROSION

Objectives • *Identify* ways in which soil is lost. • *Describe* the methods used in agriculture to prevent soil erosion.

Like water and a number of minerals, soil is cycled in the environment. While mechanical and chemical weathering form new soil, natural forces carry away soil in a process called *erosion*. The major causes of erosion are wind and running water.

Soil Loss and Desertification

If managed carelessly, soil may become unsuitable for planting crops and sustaining livestock. Activities such as overgrazing, deforestation, and poor irrigation and cultivation practices cause soil loss and desertification. These activities damage land by disturbing the balance between living organisms and soil.

The process of desertification is most visible in dry regions that border on deserts. It is estimated that about 30 percent of Earth's land has undergone desertification. Worldwide, about 6 million hectares are lost to desertification each year. In the United States, parts of Arizona, Colorado, California, and the High Plains region of Texas are at risk.

A report issued by the U.S. Department of Agriculture estimates that soil loss from erosion threatens one-third of all farmland in the United States. It is also estimated that about 2.5 billion metric tons of topsoil in the United States are washed away by water each year. The volume of topsoil lost as a result of wind erosion is estimated to be about 1.5 billion metric tons. Soil erosion is not limited to the United States. Table 19.2 shows the topsoil erosion rates for selected regions of the world.

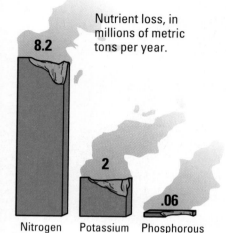

Nutrient loss, in millions of metric tons per year.

8.2 — Nitrogen
2 — Potassium
.06 — Phosphorous

Figure 19.9 Along with the 4 billion metric tons of topsoil lost annually from the United States, about 10 million metric tons of soil nutrients are also lost. Nitrogen, phosphorus, and potassium are the nutrients most needed by plant life. It is estimated that about $5 billion are spent annually to replace these valuable nutrients.

Table 19.2   Topsoil Erosion Rate in Selected Regions

Region	Erosion Rate, in Metric Tons/Hectare/Year	Causes
United States	18	Wind and water
China	43	Water
Belgium (central)	10–25	Water
Ethiopia: (Gondor region)	20	Water
Salvador–Acelhuate Basin	19–190	Water
Guatemala (mountain region)	200–3600	Water
Thailand (Chao River Basin)	21	Water
Venezuela and Columbia (Orinoco River Basin)	18	Water

Soil Conservation and Land Management

American farmers and ranchers, in cooperation with state and local governments, have developed many less destructive agricultural methods. But methods such as contour farming and terracing may be time-consuming. Also, efforts to use protective methods may be slowed because the cost of using them is higher than the cost of using traditional methods. Other soil protection methods include strip-cropping and shelter belts.

Strip-cropping Farmland is plowed so that plowed strips are separated by planted strips. Having at least part of the land covered by vegetation reduces soil loss. Different strips may be planted with crops that have overlapping growing seasons.

Contour Farming Contour farming is a method of plowing along a slope instead of across it. The furrows between rows of crops collect water, preventing heavy soil erosion. Contour farming is often used together with strip–cropping where farmland is sloped.

Terracing In terracing, a series of platforms called terraces are built into the slope of a hill. Each terrace is separated from the next by a vertical step. Terracing is effective on steep slopes and slows water flow, enabling water to soak into the soil.

Shelter Belts Rows of trees may be planted along the outer edges of a field. These rows of trees are called windbreaks or *shelter belts*. Shelter belts help reduce erosion by slowing down the wind.

Figure 19.10 Some proper land management techniques, such as contour farming and strip-cropping (left) and terracing (right), are becoming more widespread in agriculture. The costs for such methods may be greater in the short term, but far less expensive in the long term.

SECTION REVIEW

1. What is strip-cropping?
2. What types of practices lead to desertification?
3. **Predict** How will the loss of major water resources in the High Plains region of Texas change the way agriculture is managed?

1. Strip-cropping involves planting different crops or crops with different growing seasons in alternating strips.
2. Cultivation, overgrazing, deforestation, and irrigation
3. Loss of water resources could lead to changes in the types of crops grown. It may lead to more conservative uses of water, or finding another water resource. Some agricultural activities would have to move. Crop prices could increase.

19.4 CONTROLLING LAND POLLUTION

Objectives • *Identify* and **explain** *four methods for reducing the volume of wastes.* • **Discuss** *the benefits and drawbacks of various forms of waste disposal.*

EARTH SCIENCE
L I N K

There are plans to bury radioactive and toxic wastes in the ocean crust around subduction zones. Subduction zones are a major part of the lithologic cycle where crust is melted. Some scientists think that the depths to which ocean crust sinks, the time involved for the crust to sink, and the heat involved to melt rocks make subduction zones very reasonable areas for depositing wastes.

The best way to eliminate wastes is not to produce them in the first place. Excess packaging makes a great deal of waste materials. Placing limits on the amounts and types of materials used in packaging can significantly reduce waste.

Disposal of the Disposable Society

Disposable items make up about one-quarter of all wastes placed in landfills. By substituting reusable or recyclable goods for disposable items, the volume of waste can be diminished. Cloth handkerchiefs, napkins, and towels can be used instead of paper ones. Reusable plastic or china plates can replace paper plates, and cloth diapers can be substituted for disposable ones. Repairing a broken appliance instead of discarding it will keep the appliance out of a landfill.

Recycling programs are another way of reducing refuse. Paper, metal, glass, and plastics are sorted from garbage and collected regularly. Not only is this recycled material kept out of landfills, it also serves as a source of revenue. For example, many newspapers and book publishers use recycled paper.

Some materials are naturally recycled. For example, plant cuttings, including grass clippings, leaves, and branches, are biodegradable. **Biodegradable** (BY-oh-dih-GRAY-duh-bul) *substances decompose easily and enrich the soil.* Plant wastes and food wastes may be collected to make a *compost pile*. The result is a sort of human–made humus. Many communities and industries are experimenting with producing and marketing compost material.

Figure 19.11 The world's largest compost producer is located in the Netherlands, in Wijister. On average, this facility collects about 1.1 million metric tons of refuse a year. After composting, about 110 000 metric tons of human-made humus are available for sale.

Figure 19.12 Controlled incinerators are used to destroy hazardous materials such as medical and toxic wastes. The method is considered the most efficient form of disposal for dangerous materials, but the ashes that are left behind pose another disposal problem.

Disposing of Hazardous Wastes

Is there a safe method for disposing of hazardous wastes? Many people think that no safe method of hazardous waste disposal exists. However, new technologies have been developed to combat the safety problem.

Waste Exchange   Many hazardous waste materials can be used in the production of other products or materials. When a company has waste material for disposal, they notify a waste-exchange agency. The agency then notifies other companies that have some use for the waste. The first company avoids the cost of waste disposal and may make a profit by selling the waste. The second company may purchase the materials it needs, at a reduced price.

Deep-well Injection   The petroleum industry uses deep-well injection to dispose of liquid hazardous wastes. In this process, liquid wastes are pumped into deep porous rocks through lined pipes. The rocks are located well below drinking-water aquifers.

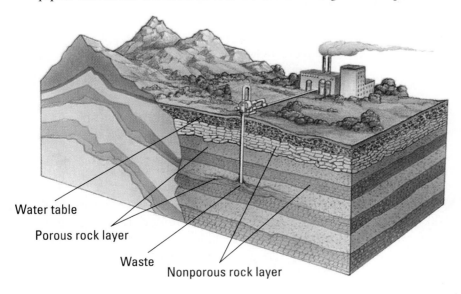

Water table

Porous rock layer

Waste

Nonporous rock layer

Figure 19.13 The disposal of hazardous wastes from petroleum refinement is done through the use of deep-well injection. As long as careful site inspection for the well is made, problems with disposal are minimal.

Secure Chemical Landfill   A landfill constructed in an area of nonporous bedrock is considered to be secure. The nonporous bedrock prevents the leaching of pollutants into groundwater. Pipes are installed in the landfill containment area to monitor and collect any leached materials that may accumulate. Finally, the top of the landfill is covered with a layer of clay to keep out water.

Controlled Incineration   The burning of wastes at extremely high temperatures is called controlled incineration. At temperatures between 542°C and 1662°C, complete burning takes place, destroying most nonmetallic hazardous wastes. Some people consider controlled incineration to be the best method of hazardous waste disposal. However, it is also the most expensive.

Chemical and Biological Treatment Plants   Some hazardous wastes can be made harmless by treatment plants. Certain chemical or biological reactions can neutralize hazardous wastes. Once they are contained, they can be disposed of more safely.

Radioactive Waste Disposal   Radioactive wastes also need a proper method of disposal. At present, radioactive wastes are placed in water. The water, along with the waste, is sealed in stainless steel tanks. These tanks are then encased in concrete. The tanks are then placed into concrete vaults located deep underground.

Legislation

Environmental disasters have made the public more aware of potential dangers to global ecosystems. When the EPA was established in 1970, its job was to carry out federal laws designed to protect the environment. Some of the major laws passed to protect and restore the land environment are listed in Table 19.3.

To protect communities from the dangers of hazardous wastes, Congress passed a law, nicknamed Superfund. The official name of this law is the Comprehensive Environmental Response, Compensation, and Liability Act of 1980 (CERCLA). The obligations of CERCLA are listed below.

- Cleaning up hazardous waste dumps.
- Making polluters pay for cleanups.
- Developing a national priorities list (NPL), a list of sites presenting the most serious threat to health and the environment.
- Taking emergency actions in areas where there are spills or accidental releases of hazardous wastes.
- Encouraging research for the reduction, treatment, and disposal of hazardous wastes.

The EPA was authorized $1.6 billion for a 5-year period to fulfill the Superfund obligations. In 1986, an amendment to the original law allocated the spending of $9 billion. This amount of money is still not enough. More money will be needed to decrease the production of hazardous wastes.

Table 19.3 Federal Environmental Protection Legislation

Year	Legislation
1969	National Environmental Policy Act
1972	Ocean Dumping Act (Marine Protection, Research, and Sanctuaries Act)
1972	Environmental Pesticide Control Act
1973	Endangered Species Act
1976	Toxic Substances Control Act
1976	Resource Conservation and Recovery Act
1977	Surface Mining Control and Reclamation Act
1980	Comprehensive Environmental Response, Compensation, and Liability Act (Superfund)
1980	Low-Level Radioactive Waste Policy Act
1982	Nuclear Waste Policy Act
1984	Hazardous and Solid Waste Amendments
1985	Food Security Act
1986	Emergency Response and Community Right-to-Know Act
1986	Superfund Amendments and Reauthorization Act

Cooperative Learning
Divide the class into groups of three to five students. Ask groups to compile a list of environmental agencies in the community. Have them write to some of these agencies, requesting information. Have them design programs for disposing of solid or hazardous wastes. They may develop diagrams and step-by-step instructions.

Foreign governments are joining in and also helping stop environmental pollution. For example, the governments of France and Denmark are giving grants to industries to research and use cleaner methods of technology. Industries throughout the world are looking for ways to reduce hazardous wastes.

The high cost of disposal and the lack of availablity of convenient disposal sites have driven many American and European cities to ship their wastes to other nations, often developing nations. This practice is a sensitive political issue. Toxic wastes from the United States have ended up in West Africa and Zimbabwe.

In some cases, where the contents of garbage ships are known, finding a place to dump toxic cargo is not easy. In 1986, the *Khian Sea* left from a controlled incinerator in Philadelphia loaded with ashes containing toxic dioxin, mercury, and arsenic. After 2 years, constant rejections, and name and registration changes, the *Khian Sea* showed up in Singapore—without its deadly cargo.

SECTION REVIEW

1. What is a secure chemical landfill?
2. In what ways can controlled incineration affect the environment?
3. **Infer** Why do you think hazardous wastes from the United States end up in developing nations?

1. A secure chemical landfill is a covered landfill constructed in an area of nonporous bedrock so that toxic chemicals cannot leach into the environment.
2. The ashes may still contain dangerous levels of toxic materials. Burning can release harmful materials into the air.
3. Dumping costs are inexpensive, and officials are not told the contents of the wastes. Local people do not have the means to determine what the contents are.

Pollution and Plant Growth

PROBLEM

How is plant growth affected when the water source is polluted?

MATERIALS (per group)

- wax pencil
- 4 plastic Petri dishes with lids
- 40 radish seeds (approx.)
- 10 mL of 5% detergent solution
- 10 mL of 5% salt solution
- 10 mL of 5% oil solution
- tape
- water
- potting soil mix

HYPOTHESIZE

After reading through the entire activity, hypothesize how the different pollutants in each water sample will affect plant growth.

PROCEDURE

Preparations

1. Be sure the Petri dishes are clean. Using the wax pencil, label the Petri dishes as shown in the figure. Write your initials on the lids of the Petri dishes.
2. Lightly fill each Petri dish with potting soil. Pour 10 mL of tap water into the control dish. Then pour 10 mL of each of the solutions into the corresponding Petri dishes.
3. Place 10 radish seeds in each dish, lightly scattering the seeds over the soil.
4. Cover and tape the lid on each Petri dish. Store the dishes according to your teacher's instructions. *Note: Keep lids sealed so the water will not evaporate.*

Days 2, 3, and 4

1. Make observations about what has occurred thus far in the Petri dishes. Copy the data table, and record the percentage of seeds that have germinated. If 3 out of 10 seeds have germinated, the percentage is 30 percent. *Note: Do not throw the seeds away.*
2. Record your observations of the plant growth in your notebooks. Answer the following questions: Are the roots, stems, or leaves visible? Have the leaves unfolded? What color are the leaves? Are the root hairs visible?
3. Observe the seeds again for 2 more days. Record your observations.

Day/Hour	Percent Germinated in			
	Control	Oil	Detergent	Salt
2				
3				
4				

ANALYSIS

1. In which Petri dish did the seedlings seem to grow the best? Why do you think this is so?
2. Was your hypothesis correct? Describe how your data supports or disproves your hypothesis.

CONCLUSION

1. Write a paragraph describing the effects that polluted water has on crops.
2. Write another paragraph that describes how plants flourish with clean, pure water.

CHAPTER 19 REVIEW

KEY TERMS

solid waste 19.1

landfill 19.1

hazardous waste 19.2

biodegradable 19.4

CHAPTER SUMMARY

19.1 Wastes produced as a result of municipal, agricultural, industrial, and mining activities are considered solid wastes. Past and present methods of solid waste disposal include open dumping, landfills, sanitary landfills, and ocean dumping. Today, open dumping is limited in the United States, and ocean dumping is no longer used because of negative environmental impacts.

19.2 Hazardous wastes are solid, liquid, or gaseous wastes that are potentially harmful to humans and the environment, even in low concentrations. The EPA classifies hazardous wastes into several categories. These categories are reactive wastes, corrosive wastes, ignitable wastes, toxic wastes, and radioactive wastes.

19.3 Cultivation, irrigation, deforestation, and overgrazing lead to soil loss and desertification in many parts of the world. Desertification is most visible in regions that border deserts. Strip-cropping and contour farming are examples of ways to control soil loss and desertification.

19.4 The best method for controlling land pollution is reducing wastes by recycling, reusing, and reducing products. The disposal of hazardous wastes is a greater problem than the disposal of solid wastes. Ideas such as controlled incineration, deep-well injection, and waste exchange are examples of improving methods. Several laws help protect the environment from solid and hazardous wastes.

MULTIPLE CHOICE

Choose the letter of the word or phrase that best completes each statement.

1. The type of waste in most landfills is (a) toxic waste; (b) radioactive waste; (c) solid waste; (d) compost. c

2. Waste products that are easily broken down by nature are (a) hazardous wastes; (b) biodegradable; (c) toxic wastes; (d) pesticides. b

3. Overgrazing and poor cultivation can lead to (a) deforestation; (b) incineration; (c) irrigation; (d) desertification. d

4. Substances containing mercury would be classified as (a) radioactive wastes; (b) corrosive wastes; (c) toxic wastes; (d) medical wastes. c

5. Legislation designed to help identify and clean up hazardous areas is the (a) Superfund; (b) NIMBY; (c) Love Canal Act; (d) Clean Land Act. a

6. Substances that can eat through metals and other containers are classified as (a) ignitable wastes; (b) toxic wastes; (c) radioactive wastes; (d) corrosive wastes. d

7. Ocean dumping is a source of pollution for (a) land environments only; (b) air environments only; (c) water environments only; (d) land and water environments. d

8. Wastes that explode easily are classified as (a) ignitable wastes; (b) reactive wastes; (c) toxic wastes; (d) corrosive wastes. b

9. The process in which grass clippings and other plant material are returned to the environment for recycling is called (a) desertification; (b) deforestation; (c) composting; (d) waste exchange. c

10. All of the following are methods for disposal of hazardous wastes except (a) deep-well injection; (b) controlled incineration; (c) waste exchange; (d) sanitary landfills. d

CHAPTER 19 REVIEW

WORD COMPARISONS

Write the letter of the second word pair that best matches the first pair.

1. Cyanide: toxic waste as (a) compost: grass clippings; (b) radioactivity: radiation; (c) sodium: reactive waste; (d) trash: hazardous waste. c

2. Irrigation: desertification as (a) composting: recycling; (b) clear-cutting: deforestation; (c) open dumping: landfills; (d) deep-well injection: incineration. b

3. Leaching: landfills as (a) corrosion: acids; (b) air: water; (c) flames: incineration; (d) heat: incineration. a

4. Syringes: medical waste as (a) fuel rods: radioactive waste; (b) trees: deforestation; (c) disinfectants: home; (d) dumping: landfills. a

5. Deep-well injection: petroleum wastes as (a) chemicals: landfills; (b) concrete vaults: radioactive wastes; (c) legislation: EPA; (d) chemical wastes: Love Canal. b

CONCEPT REVIEW Answers on page T102.

Write a complete response for each of the following.

1. How are radioactive wastes disposed of?
2. How does a sanitary landfill differ from a secure chemical landfill?
3. How does composting help soil?
4. What methods can be used to reduce the amount of garbage produced by people?
5. Why is ocean dumping harmful to both aquatic and land ecosystems?

THINK CRITICALLY Answers on page T102.

1. What characteristics of radioactive wastes make their disposal especially difficult?
2. What are the benefits of incineration?
3. Would you live in an area that was once a disposal site for chemical wastes? Explain.
4. Why must care be used in the storage of substances such as kerosene and gasoline?

Computer Activity Use a graphing program to generate a line graph that compares topsoil loss for China and the United States over the next 20 years. Assume the erosion rates in Table 19.2 will remain constant. Also assume that there is an average of 5000 metric tons of topsoil per hectare in both China and the United States. The area of China is 960 million hectares. The area of the United States is 940 million hectares. How many metric tons of topsoil per hectare of land will be left in each nation?

WRITE FOR UNDERSTANDING

Identify the topic sentence for each paragraph in Section 19.2. Organize the sentences into a summary of the section. You may need to add sentences to make your summary clear.

PORTFOLIO

1. Interview someone from your local fire department about the proper methods of disposal for at least three types of hazardous wastes that are common in your home.
2. Begin a scrapbook of newspaper and maga-zine articles related to illegal dumping and land pollution. After a month, review the articles you have collected. Prepare a map summarizing the type of dumping or polluting involved, with locations and dates.

Use Figure 19.13 to answer the following questions.

1. What type of waste disposal is shown in the diagram?
2. What would happen if the wastes were pumped above the layer of nonporous rock?
3. What types of wastes are disposed of using this method?
4. How does nonporous rock differ from porous rock?
5. Why is it important to dispose of wastes well below the water table?
6. What geologic features do you think a site inspection would need to study?

ACTIVITY 19.2

Answers and teaching strategies on page T102.

PROBLEM

How does plant cover affect the erosion of soil by rainwater?

MATERIALS

- watering can
- 2 wide-mouthed jars with lids
- ice pick or nail
- large dish or roasting pan
- water
- topsoil
- fresh grass clippings

PREDICT

After reading through the activity, write a prediction about how ground cover affects the erosion of topsoil by rainwater.

PROCEDURE

1. Place the two jars at least 10 cm apart in the middle of the roasting pan.
2. Use the ice pick or nail to poke 10–15 holes in both jar lids. **Caution:** *Be careful when using the ice pick or nail.*
3. Fill both jar lids with lightly packed topsoil. Cover the soil in one jar lid with the grass clippings. Balance the soil-filled lids on the mouths of the jars.
4. Use the watering can to sprinkle the jars from a height of about one meter. Sprinkle about 2 L of water onto the jars. This water simulates rainwater.
5. As you sprinkle the water, observe the following and record your data in a data table. How much soil splashed from each lid? What color is the water that collects in the pan from each jar? How much water collected in each jar? What color is this water? How much time did it take for the water to soak through the soil?

ANALYSIS

1. From which lid was more soil removed by the water?
2. How did the color of the water in the two jars compare?
3. How long did it take for the water to soak through each soil sample?

CONCLUSION

1. Did the covering of grass clippings change the way the water affected the topsoil? Describe any differences that occurred.
2. How would the covering of grass clippings affect the sample over time? Which sample would last longer?
3. What do your findings suggest about the erosion of bare topsoil in a farm field or deforested area? What recommendations would you make to minimize erosion?

GOLD

"Water, water, everywhere, nor any drop to drink." This famous line from Samuel Taylor Coleridge's poem, *The Rime of the Ancient Mariner*, describes a situation in which people on a boat, surrounded by water, have no water to drink. The problem is that the boat is sailing in the ocean—a body of salt water.

Many people throughout the world use water as if it were in endless supply. However, recall that only about 3 percent of Earth's water is fresh water. Only a very small part of this fresh water is available for use by all of Earth's organisms. An even smaller fraction of this fresh water is *potable*, or safe for drinking.

20.1 USES FOR WATER

Objectives • *Describe* the ways in which people use water.
• *Explain* why water conservation is important. • *Infer* ways in which water can be conserved.

Water should be used wisely. Sometimes, nature reminds people of just how important a resource fresh water is and how its availability is limited. For example, regions that normally receive a sufficient amount of precipitation to meet their needs may sometimes suffer periods of drought. Also, many people live in areas of deserts and rely on water from distant sources.

Natural disasters such as floods and earthquakes can leave entire communities without any fresh water for long periods of time. Earthquakes can destroy underground water pipes, leaving people without water for days or even weeks. Floods, such as the one that occurred along the Mississippi River in 1993, can mix sewage and sediments with drinking water, making the water *unpotable*.

Residential Use

The average person in the United States uses about 300 L of water daily. Most of this water is used for personal hygiene and home cleaning. Only a very small amount of the 300 L is used for drinking and cooking. Table 20.1 lists estimates for the amounts of water used each day in the average U.S. household for various activities. Water is also used outside the home for gardening, landscaping, car washing, and recreational activities. A lawn sprinkler uses as much as 40 L of water every minute. Depending on its size, a home swimming pool may require from hundreds to many thousands of liters of water to fill. More water must also be added to the pool throughout the season.

Figure 20.1 People stood in long lines at water trucks, their only supply of fresh water during the devastating Mississippi River flood of 1993 (top). The 1989 Loma Prieta earthquake, near San Francisco, disrupted the flow of fresh water to homes (bottom).

Table 20.1   Estimated U.S. Household Water Use

Activity	Daily Consumption
Brushing teeth	19–39 L (faucets running)
Shaving	39–58 L (faucets running)
Washing hands and face	4–8 L (faucets running)
Showering	75–80 L (faucets running)
Tub bathing	96–116 L (full tub)
Machine dishwashing	56–60 L (full cycle)
Dishwashing (in sink)	75–80 L (faucets running)
Clothes washing	115–120 L (full cycle)
Toilet flushing	20–30 L (per flush)

Industrial Use

Of the water used by people, about 44 percent of all fresh water is used by industry. Water is used to transport goods and dispose of wastes. Water is also used as a power source and as a coolant.

Industries use enormous amounts of water in the mining and refining of natural resources. Manufacturing the raw materials needed to make other products requires large quantities of water. For example, it takes more than 15 000 L of water to manufacture the steel needed to make one home washing machine. Producing synthetic materials, such as the rayon used in the carpet industry, requires even larger amounts of water.

Access to water is a factor many businesses must consider as part of their short-term and long-term plans. The availability of water can affect where a company will locate. In turn, where a company locates can strongly affect the economy in the region. Also, the company's presence may generate other job opportunities in the area, because the community will need public services, such as health care.

Agricultural Use

The farming industry is the single largest user of water in the United States. As shown in Figure 20.2, almost half of all freshwater use is by agriculture. Most of this water, more than 200 billion L each day, is used for the irrigation of farmland. **Irrigation** *is the process of bringing water to an area for use in growing crops.*

Irrigation practices increase crop yield. However, increased crop yields are not without cost. Many people think the tax dollars spent on research and development related to irrigation systems could be more wisely spent. Others question the use of scarce water supplies to grow crops in an area that is not suitable for farmland.

Several types of irrigation systems are presently in use. The type of system depends on cost, the crop to be irrigated, the slope of the land, and the source of water being used. Four common methods of irrigation are flood irrigation, furrow irrigation, overhead irrigation, and subirrigation.

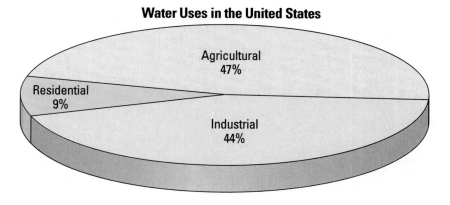

Water Uses in the United States

Agricultural 47%

Residential 9%

Industrial 44%

Figure 20.2 The United States drains over 1 trillion L of water a day from various water sources. About 75 percent is from surface waters such as lakes and streams. The other 25 percent is from groundwater in aquifers. About 500 billion L of the water drained is either consumed or lost to evaporation.

Flood Irrigation   Flood irrigation is the flooding of an area of land that is flat. This method is commonly used because it is inexpensive. However, it is very wasteful because much of the water drains into soil not occupied by plants. Also, more than 50 percent of the water is lost to evaporation.

Furrow Irrigation   Furrow irrigation releases water into furrows, or ditches, dug between rows of crops. Furrow irrigation is also used in flat areas, but it is more efficient than flood irrigation because water is deposited closer to plants. However, mineral salts accumulate quickly, and the evaporation rate is high.

Overhead Irrigation   Sprinkler systems are the most common form of overhead irrigation. Sprinkler systems are useful on flat ground and uneven slopes. The efficiency of sprinkler systems decreases if strong winds blow the water away from its target.

Drip, or trickle, irrigation is an overhead irrigation method developed and commonly used in Israel. This system uses tubing to deliver small quantities of water directly to the root system of plants. Drip irrigation is expensive, but it is very efficient. This method may be used where slopes are irregular or where the water supply is low.

Figure 20.4   Drip, or trickle, irrigation (right) and sprinklers (left) are overhead irrigation methods used in areas with irregular slopes or low water supplies. Drip irrigation is very efficient but expensive. Sprinklers are also efficient, but they are not very useful when strong winds blow the water away from crops.

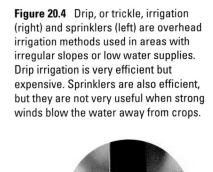

Figure 20.5 The runoff from melting snow and ice in the Sierra Nevada Mountains that naturally flows into Mono Lake is being diverted to Los Angeles, about 650 km away. The result has been the drying up of Mono Lake and an increase in the concentration of salt in the water.

Subirrigation In a subirrigation system, water is introduced naturally or artificially beneath the soil. This system helps develop an artificial underground water source. Subirrigation is most effective in places where underground water sources are near the surface.

Effects of Water Use on Ecosystems

Often, human needs for water alter or destroy the habitats of other living things. The building of dams, draining of swamps, changing of stream courses, or removal of water from natural sources can all adversely affect wildlife. One example is illustrated by the case of Mono Lake in California.

Mono Lake is a saltwater lake fed by streams that carry meltwater rich in dissolved minerals from surrounding mountains. Mono Lake has no outlet. As water evaporates, salts are left behind. Algae, brine shrimps, and brine flies are the major organisms in the lake. They are food for California gulls and migratory birds such as grebes, phalaropes, and plovers.

In the 1940s, Los Angeles began diverting the meltwater that fed Mono Lake to other areas. The water-diversion project resulted in a major drop in the water level of the lake. The drop in water level has increased the salt concentration of the water. Some scientists predict that if this trend continues, the salt concentration in the lake will become so high that the lake will be unable to support the organisms now living in the water. How might this affect the gulls and migratory birds of the region?

Likely responses will include that the food chain will be altered, forcing the gulls and migratory birds to seek food from other areas or else die.

1. Irrigation is the process of bringing water to an area for use in growing crops. The four main methods are flood irrigation, furrow irrigation, overhead irrigation, and subirrigation.
2. The three main consumer categories are agricultural, industrial, and residential. Specific examples will vary. Accept all logical examples.
3. Likely responses will include not keeping water running while brushing teeth, doing dishes, or shaving; taking showers instead of baths; only running a dishwasher when it is full; and placing a brick in a toilet tank to reduce the amount of water needed to fill the tank. Accept all logical responses.

SECTION REVIEW

1. Define irrigation, and name the four main methods of irrigation.
2. Use Figure 20.2 to identify the three main consumers of water. Give two examples of how each of these consumers uses water.
3. **Infer** Review the ways that water is used in the home. Use the information in Table 20.1 to make five specific recommendations to reduce the amount of water use in the home.

20.2 WATER RESOURCES

Objectives • *Explain* ways in which fresh water is naturally stored as a resource. • *Predict* the effects of the depletion of an aquifer and the damming of rivers in ecosystems that rely on these water sources.

Water is stored for human use by dams and in reservoirs. The water from rivers and rain runoff captured by dams may be used to meet water needs, to generate electricity, or both. The water in reservoirs comes from rain runoff, streams, and underground sources.

Surface Water

Surface water is water above the ground in streams, lakes, and ponds. Some sources of surface water are rainfall and the water from melting snow, glaciers, and ice sheets. The water resulting from rainfall and melting ice travels along the ground as runoff. Runoff is the water that does not seep into the ground, but instead flows down a slope over land. If the land is not developed with concrete and asphalt, the runoff carves shallow grooves in the ground called *rills*.

If the flow is continuous, the rills deepen and connect, forming streams. These streams flow and connect to form larger streams. The water in these larger streams is then deposited into lakes, ponds, or oceans.

A body of surface water may exist a great distance away from its source. For example, the Rio Grande originates from snow in the Rocky Mountains. Its mouth is located 3033 km away.

Surface water can also come from underground aquifers. If a stream channel intersects the aquifer, the water in the aquifer can flow into the stream channel. Water in aquifers that cross geological faults can flow to the surface as springs. Ponds, lakes, and bogs can form where depressions cross an aquifer.

Word Power
Aquifer, from the Latin *aqua*, "water," and *-fer*, "bearing" or "carrying."

Figure 20.6 The runoff from rainfall and melting snow in the Rocky Mountains is the source for the Colorado River, which brings water to California, Nevada, and Arizona. Runoff from the Rocky Mountains is also the source for the Rio Grande, which brings water to Texas and Mexico.

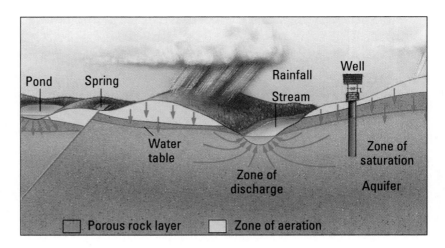

Figure 20.7 Slow-filling aquifers are fed by surface waters that seep into the ground through a zone of aeration. This groundwater may later leave the aquifer through a zone of discharge, or through wells that are used to pump water out of the aquifer for human use.

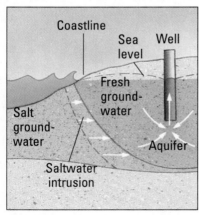

Figure 20.8 Subsidence (above) and saltwater intrusion (below) can result from overdraft of the groundwater in aquifers. The water pressure within the aquifer can no longer support the weight of overlying structures or hold the salt water out of freshwater aquifers.

Aquifers

The water that does not flow as runoff seeps down through the spaces between soil particles. Water that fills the spaces between soil particles is called *soil water*. If the layer of bedrock beneath the soil is porous or full of cracks, called joints, the water is able to seep into the bedrock. Water within porous or jointed bedrock is called *groundwater*.

Over long periods of time, groundwater collects and saturates the layer of bedrock. *The top of the saturated layer of rocks is called the* **water table**. Look at Figure 20.7. Locate the *zone of saturation*. The zone of saturation is the saturated rock layer beneath the water table. An aquifer is another name for the zone of saturation.

Recall from Chapter 1 that an aquifer is a layer of porous rock that contains water. This layer is filled by the water seeping through overlying soil. The area where water enters an aquifer is called the *zone of aeration*. The place where groundwater leaves the aquifer and becomes surface water is called the *zone of discharge*.

The water in an aquifer does not move at a constant rate. It may move only a few centimeters a year or not at all. The rate at which water moves depends on the amount of precipitation or meltwater feeding the aquifer, the amount of open space, or porosity, of the rocks, and the slope of the aquifer.

Water Resource Problems

As the human population grows, there are increasing demands on freshwater resources. *When a body of water is drained faster than it is filled, it is called* **overdraft**. Overdraft can lead to some very serious problems.

Two problems associated with overdraft are subsidence and saltwater intrusion. Examples of subsidence and saltwater intrusion are shown in Figure 20.8. Water pressure from the water within aquifers helps support structures on top of the aquifers. The water pressure also helps keep salt water out of aquifers that are located in coastal areas. When this fresh water is removed, the bedrock may be weakened. The overlying structure may sink, or subside.

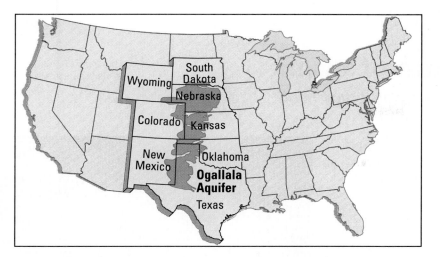

Figure 20.9 At one time, the Ogallala Aquifer is estimated to have held about 2000 km³ of water. It is the largest known aquifer in the world. However, many scientists predict that the Ogallala Aquifer will run dry in about 40 years. The aquifer is being depleted very rapidly as a result of overdraft. The shaded area shows the underground extent of the Ogallala Aquifer relative to the surface.

Overdraft in coastal aquifers can cause another problem. Salt water from the ocean will begin to intrude into the freshwater aquifers, contaminating the fresh water.

Overdraft in coastal regions can also lead to subsidence over large areas. The San Joaquin Valley in California stretches nearly 400 km. The heavy agricultural activity in the valley has used huge amounts of water from local groundwater sources. Overdraft has caused a subsidence of up to 4 m in some areas.

The Ogallala Aquifer is another example of groundwater overdraft. As shown in Figure 20.9, the Ogallala Aquifer, the largest aquifer in the world, is located beneath parts of Texas, Colorado, Nebraska, Oklahoma, Kansas, Wyoming, South Dakota, and New Mexico. These High Plains states depend heavily on the Ogallala Aquifer for water, much of which is used for agriculture. However, because of the dry climate of the High Plains region, overdraft is occurring in the aquifer. Scientists estimate that the water remaining in the aquifer will last only about 40 more years.

The decrease of freshwater resources due to human activity is a serious concern for all organisms on Earth. Contamination of water supplies has led to the development of water-treatment projects. Also, the search for additional water resources has led to the development of ways to remove salt from water in the oceans and saline lakes.

SECTION REVIEW

1. What causes overdraft?
2. Water in the Ogallala Aquifer may be as old as a million years. This water is often called "fossil water." Why might people refer to this water as fossil water?
3. **Predict** What will happen to organisms in a bay when a nutrient-rich stream that enters the bay is dammed?

1. Overdraft is caused by the removal of water from a body of water faster than the body of water is filled.
2. Fossils are the preserved remains of living things. Discoveries of fossil organisms from millions of years ago have been made. Therefore, people often apply the word "fossil" to very old things.
3. Responses will vary but are likely to include a breakdown in the food chain because the organisms that live off the nutrients from the river will decrease in number.

The Great Dam of China

Is the Three Gorges Project Worth the Energy?

1. Humans built the Grand Canal 1,300 years ago. In the 1980s, a dam was built at Yichang.
2. Answers will vary.

Originating in the steep slopes of the mountains of Tibet, the Yangtze River begins its 4,800-km trek to the Yellow Sea. The Yangtze River, also known in Chinese as the Chang Jiang, or "long river," is the longest river in Asia and the third longest river in the world. The Yangtze cuts through the steep mountainous landscape, forming spectacular gorges. The Yangtze River also serves practical purposes for China.

Alteration of the Yangtze River began over 1,300 years ago. A canal was built that connected the Yangtze River with the Huang He to the north. It took 3 million people to build the Grand Canal. Its completion connected trading routes that extended from the city of Luoyang, southeast to the coastal city of Hangzhou.

In the early 1980s, the Yangtze River was changed again, when a dam was built upriver at Yichang. The Gezhouba Dam, shown in the photo, regulates seasonal fluctuations of water levels and creates hydroelectric power.

Now, the Chinese government is beginning its greatest project since the building of the Great Wall of China—construction of the world's largest hydroelectric project on the Yangtze River. The Three Gorges Dam

will reach a height of about 200 m. It will stretch nearly 2 km across one of the river's three gorges. The dam will submerge the famous Three River Gorges and create a 560-km² lake. The Three Gorges Dam will not be the highest dam in the world, nor will it be the largest reservoir. But it will produce the greatest hydroelectric output of any dam on Earth. Its rated electric capacity is 17 680 megawatts, which is almost three times greater than the largest hydroelectric project in the United States.

Although the dam has great potential for producing electric power, it also affects the area in various ways. About 1.2 million people are being forced to move from their homes to make way for the dam. Thus far, only several hundred people have relocated. Besides humans, the dam will also displace or destroy many animals and plants that live in the area of the dam site.

Another concern of opponents to the project is that the dam will eventually turn into a giant mud puddle. The Yangtze

carries millions of tons of sediment in its flow each year. The dam will cause the water to slow down and drop silt on the bottom of the reservoir. The buildup of silt may gradually turn the lake into a grand pool of mud.

Dam opponents have not been able to halt the preparatory building of roads and a bridge to the future dam site. However, the major project may be stopped for another reason—cost. The estimated cost of the project is $10 billion. The economy of China is not financially prepared to fund the project. If the Three Gorges Dam cannot attract foreign lenders and investors to help pay for the project, it will be cancelled.

DECISIONS

1. Explain how humans have changed the Yangtze River.
2. Do you think the Three Gorges Dam should be built? Explain your reasoning.

20.3 WATER TREATMENT

Objectives • *Explain* why fresh water in many parts of the world is not potable. • *Trace* the sequence of events involved in the purification of water.

In the United States and many other developed nations, water is treated in order to remove impurities. Safety checks monitor the quality of water to ensure it is safe to drink. This is not the case in many of the developing nations. For example, tap water is not considered safe to drink in much of South America, Mexico, China, and parts of Africa.

A large supply of fresh water is essential to a nation's development. Many areas of the world do not have a large supply of natural fresh water. These areas may not be able to support their human populations or the populations of other organisms.

Removing Salts

To increase their supply of fresh water, some nations seek alternative sources. They may look to the seas, saline lakes, or oceans for water. Few organisms can meet their water needs with ocean water. Penguins can tolerate the high concentration of salt in ocean water because they have special glands that remove the salts. But most organisms do not have such adaptations.

The process by which salts are removed from water is called **desalination**. Desalination can be used to obtain fresh water for drinking, cooking, and irrigation. Desalination can also be used to remove salt from agricultural waste water. For example, high concentrations of salt in the waters of the Colorado River were killing crops in Mexico. The salts were leaching into the water as a result of the irrigation of farmland. To solve this problem, the United States built a desalination plant near Yuma, Arizona. The plant produces water with a lower salt content, which is returned to the river for use by Mexican farmers.

Three of the most common methods of desalination are distillation, reverse osmosis, and freezing. These methods may be very expensive, however. The cost of obtaining fresh water through these methods may be as much as four times greater than the cost of getting fresh water from traditional sources, such as lakes and streams.

Distillation In distillation, salt water is heated to boiling. Water is evaporated, but the salt remains. The water vapor is cooled, and liquid fresh water is collected.

Reverse Osmosis In reverse osmosis, salt water is forced through a strainer that traps the salt and lets the fresh water pass. The strainer is a thin membrane with tiny pores. The pores are large enough for water to pass through but too small for the salt.

DATELINE *1993*

In December of 1993, the Environmental Protection Agency issued a warning for residents of Washington D.C., and nearby suburbs of Virginia and Maryland to avoid drinking water straight from the tap. The EPA told people to boil their water. It was feared that the tap water was contaminated with the parasite cryptosporidium. Cryptosporidium was responsible for thousands of illnesses in Milwaukee earlier that year. No illnesses were reported in the Washington D.C. area. A week later, EPA tests showed water samples were healthy, and the warning was removed.

Figure 20.10 The salt removed from seawater also provides valuable nutrients and minerals for food and industrial uses.

Figure 20.11 These steps are used in many typical water-treatment plants around the world. Treatment plants remove sediments and harmful microorganisms from the water, making it safe for human use.

Freezing   In the freezing method, salt water is frozen. As it freezes, it separates, forming ice and a brine slush. The ice is free of almost all salt and can be melted to obtain fresh water. A desalination plant in Wrightsville Beach, North Carolina, obtains almost 1 million L of fresh water each day using the freezing process.

Water Purification

The treatment of fresh water for the removal of minerals may sometimes be combined with the treatment of water for purification. Water purification removes harmful chemicals and microorganisms that make the water unpotable. Water purification involves several processes: sedimentation, filtration, aeration, and sterilization. Similar processes are used in waste water treatment, which is discussed in Chapter 21. Refer to Figure 20.11 as you read about each process.

Sedimentation and Filtration   In many water-treatment plants, screens are used to trap and remove debris that floats or is suspended in water. Once screened, the water is put into a settling tank, where it is allowed to stand undisturbed. As the water stands, particles suspended in the water settle to the bottom as sediment.

Some particles in the water are so fine they do not settle out but remain in the water. Often, chemicals called *coagulants* are added to the water to aid the settling process. The coagulant causes

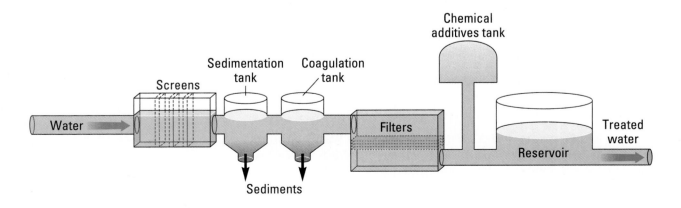

the fine particles to clump together. These heavier particle masses settle to the bottom of the tank. Together, sedimentation and coagulation remove most suspended particles, including bacteria, from the water. After the water is drained away, the sediment is removed from the settling tank.

Water drained from the settling tank is then ready for filtering. The water is passed through a 1-m-thick layer of fine sand. The sand filters out many of the particles that were not removed by sedimentation.

Aeration and Sterilization   Water that has been cleaned and filtered may still have undesirable qualities. For example, dissolved gases in water may give it an unpleasant taste or odor. In addition, harmful bacteria may still be present. Taste, odor, and bacteria are treated through aeration and sterilization.

The exposure of water to air and sunlight is called **aeration**. Aeration is achieved by spraying the water into the air or by allowing it to flow as a waterfall. During aeration, bacteria that aid in purification enter the water. These bacteria break down organic matter still present in the water. At the same time, oxygen, a powerful purifying agent, mixes with the water.

The harmful bacteria and microorganisms left behind by the previous processes are killed through sterilization. Sterilization can occur through the use of extreme heat or chemicals. The chemicals most often used in water sterilization are chlorine and ozone.

Chlorine is a very powerful purifier. It can be produced and stored easily. It destroys microorganisms and removes unwanted odors, colors, and tastes. Often, chlorine adds a distinctive smell to drinking water. The drinking water may smell like the water in most swimming pools.

Ozone is also a strong purifying agent and sterilizes water more rapidly than chlorine. The use of ozone, however, is limited because it is more expensive and more difficult to use than chlorine. Ozone must be refrigerated and can only be stored for a short amount of time.

At high concentrations, both chlorine and ozone are dangerous to most organisms. However, very little chlorine and ozone are needed to purify large volumes of water. Some studies show that the use of chlorine may produce other harmful chemicals.

Teaching tips for Field Activity appear on page T106.

FIELD ACTIVITY

Obtain a water sample from a local pond or stream. Study the sample for color and clarity. Use the following steps to experiment with your water sample. Record and sketch your observations after each step. First, examine a small amount of the water with a microscope. Then pour another small amount of the sample through a piece of filter paper, and collect the water that passes through the paper. Examine a small amount of this new sample with a microscope. Compare your observations of the water samples. Describe what effects, if any, filtering had on color and clarity. Also, what effect did filtering have on objects you may have seen under the microscope? **Caution:** *wash hands after handling water that may contain microorganisms.*

SECTION REVIEW

1. What is aeration?
2. **Compare and Contrast** In what ways are the processes of screening, filtration, and sedimentation similar? How are these processes different?
3. **Infer** What types of methods may be needed to analyze water to make sure it is free of microorganisms?

1. A process in which water is moved through air to expose it to oxygen and sunlight.
2. All three processes remove particles from liquids. The manner in which particles are separated from the liquid differ. For example, screening and filtration separate particles based primarily on size. Sedimentation separates particles based largely upon mass.
3. Likely responses will include light or electron microscopy techniques.

Answers and teaching strategies on page T106.

Desalinating Seawater

PROBLEM

How can seawater be changed to fresh water?

MATERIALS (per group)

- 500-mL beaker
- metric measuring spoons
- 1000-mL flask
- glycerine
- glass tubing (fire polished) bent at right angle
- 1-hole rubber stopper
- rubber tubing
- pan of ice
- silver nitrate solution
- hot plate
- sodium chloride standards (prepared)
- cardboard
- coins
- salt
- 2 labelled test tubes with rack

PREDICTION

Write a prediction that is related to the problem.

PROCEDURE

1. To make salt water that has the salinity of seawater, pour 500 mL of tap water into the beaker. Add 18 g of salt with the metric measuring spoon and stir. Transfer about 15 mL of salt water from the beaker to a test tube labelled "seawater." Add silver nitrite solution to the test tube. Allow the test tube to stand for 2 to 3 minutes. Compare the amount of silver chloride precipitate in the test tube to the prepared sodium chloride standards. Record your observations in a data table. **Caution:** *Be sure all glassware used in this activity is clean.*
2. Transfer saltwater solution from beaker to flask. Rinse out the beaker. Set the flask on the hot plate, which should be turned off.
3. Rub some glycerine on both ends of the glass tubing, and construct the setup shown.

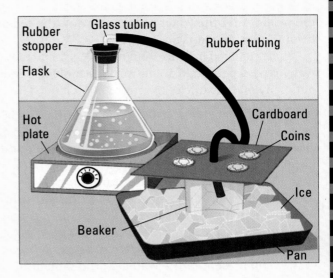

Caution: *Be careful when inserting the glass tubing into the rubber tubing and the glass tubing into the rubber stopper. If there is some difficulty in this step, please ask your instructor for help.*

4. Turn the hot plate on. Let the salt water boil until a small amount remains in the flask.
5. Turn the hot plate off, and let both the flask and the beaker cool before touching them.
6. Transfer 15 mL of water that has collected in the beaker to a second test tube, labelled "desalinated." Repeat silver nitrate procedure from Step 1.

ANALYSIS

1. Why was it important to stopper the flask tightly?
2. How do the amounts of silver chloride precipitate in steps 1 and 6 compare?
3. What caused the change you described in question 2?

CONCLUSION

Imagine you are stranded on an island without fresh drinking water. You have only the following items in your possession: an army mess kit, a small mirror, a coffee cup, a roll of electric tape, and a pen. Describe in words and a sketch how you would obtain fresh drinking water from seawater.

CHAPTER 20 REVIEW

KEY TERMS

irrigation 20.1	overdraft 20.2	aeration 20.3
water table 20.2	desalination 20.3	

CHAPTER SUMMARY

20.1 Fresh water is used in great quantities by agriculture, industry, and households. The availability of fresh water in an area helps determine the type of agriculture and industry the region can support. Water availability is connected to the economy. Agriculture uses the greatest amount of water. Most of the water required for residential needs is used for hygine. Human needs for water can often alter or destroy the ecology of an area.

20.2 Precipitation and meltwater are the sources of fresh water. Water from precipitation and runoff may flow as surface water, forming lakes, ponds, and streams. Water from precipitation and runoff may also flow beneath the ground in porous layers of bedrock. Water-bearing layers of bedrock are called aquifers. Aquifers fill slowly and can be depleted. Results of aquifer depletion are reduced freshwater supplies and subsidence. In costal areas, salt water intrusion may result.

20.3 In the United States, most water used by people is monitored and treated to ensure its potability. Many developing nations do not have water-treatment plants, resulting in the spread of diseases, such as cholera and typhoid, by microorganisms in the water supply. In a water-treatment plant, screening, sedimentation, filtration, aeration, and sterilization are used to improve water quality. The ocean can serve as a source of fresh water after desalination. However, fresh water obtained from desalination methods, such as distillation and reverse osmosis, is very expensive.

MULTIPLE CHOICE

Choose the letter of the word or phrase that best completes each statement.

1. The process by which water is brought to an area for use on crops is called (a) desalination; (b) purification; (c) irrigation; (d) sedimentation. c

2. The largest consumer of water in the United States is (a) agriculture; (b) industry; (c) urban centers; (d) residential areas. a

3. In the home, most water is used for (a) cooking; (b) drinking; (c) personal hygiene; (d) washing dishes. c

4. Water that is fit for use as drinking water is said to be (a) polluted; (b) runoff; (c) contaminated; (d) potable. d

5. The type of irrigation that makes use of sprinkler systems is (a) flood irrigation; (b) drip, or trickle, irrigation; (c) furrow irrigation; (d) overhead irrigation. d

6. The most wasteful and inefficient type of irrigation is (a) flood irrigation; (b) drip, or trickle, irrigation; (c) overhead irrigation; (d) subirrigation. a

7. Many reservoirs are fed by underground water supplies flowing in (a) pipes; (b) aquifers; (c) streams; (d) runoff. b

8. The water-treatment process in which water is forced into the air is called (a) purification; (b) aeration; (c) sedimentation; (d) filtration. b

9. Particles in the water are able to settle out by (a) filtration; (b) aeration; (c) boiling; (d) sedimentation. d

10. Two chemicals used to purify water are (a) bicarbonate and calcium; (b) sulfur and oxygen; (c) fluorine and sodium; (d) ozone and chlorine. d

TRUE/FALSE

Write true *if the statement is true. If the statement is false, change the underlined words to make it true.*

1. Most of the water used in households is for <u>drinking and cooking</u>. t
2. Sprinklers are a method of <u>overhead</u> irrigation. t
3. The most efficient method of irrigation is <u>furrow irrigation</u>. f, drip and trickle irrigation
4. <u>Distillation</u> is the process used by water-treatment plants to kill dangerous microorganisms. f, sterilization
5. Reverse osmosis is a method of <u>aeration</u>. f, desalination
6. <u>Groundwater</u> can be a source of surface water.
7. <u>Subsidence</u> can result when overdraft occurs. t
8. <u>Coagulants</u> are used to add fluorine to water. f, chemical additives tank

CONCEPT REVIEW Answers on page T106.

Write a complete response for each of the following.

1. Explain why water in some countries of the world is not fit for drinking.
2. Why is drip, or trickle, irrigation considered more efficient than flood or furrow irrigation?
3. Why must the zone of aeration for an aquifer be located at a point higher in elevation than the aquifer itself?
4. How are the zones of aeration and discharge similar to the source and mouth of a river?
5. What are some ways in which the construction of reservoirs harm living things?

THINK CRITICALLY Answers on page T106.

1. What can you infer about the properties of salt water based on the fact that freezing and boiling can be used as desalination processes?
2. Explain why icebergs can be used as sources of fresh water.
3. Why must wind be considered when using sprinkler systems but not when using flood or furrow irrigation techniques?
4. If you were the owner of a farm that had land with steep slopes, which irrigation method would you probably use? Why?
5. Why is the Ogallala Aquifer not being replenished today?

WRITE CREATIVELY

Write a story telling of the attempts of a small island nation that is trying to get fresh water. Getting fresh water from the ocean is impossible because there are deadly microorganisms in the water. The small island is located in the southern hemisphere, and the island leaders are thinking of getting water from icebergs. However, the icebergs are located thousands of kilometers away, in Antarctica.

PORTFOLIO

1. Conduct library research to find out about Typhoid Mary. Report your findings in a written or oral presentation.
2. Interview a worker from the water-treatment plant that serves your community.

Find out what microorganisms are especially common in your area and what methods the facility uses to eliminate them from the water supply. If possible, arrange for the worker to speak to your class.

Use the figure to answer the following.

1. In what part of a water-treatment plant does settling take place?
2. What happens to water when it first enters a water-treatment plant?
3. At what stage of the water-treatment process is fluorine likely to be added to the water?
4. What step of the water treatment process is left out of the figure?

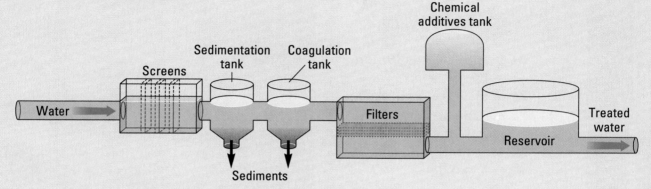

ACTIVITY 20.2

Answers and teaching strategies on page T106.

PROBLEM
How does boiling make water potable?

MATERIALS (per group)
- pond water
- 500-mL beaker
- dropper
- 2 microscope slides and 2 coverslips
- microscope
- hot plate
- tongs

HYPOTHESIS
Write a hypothesis that is related to the problem.

PROCEDURE

1. Obtain 100 mL of pond water in a beaker. Using a dropper, transfer a drop of the pond water to a clean microscope slide. Apply a coverslip.
2. View the drop of pond water under a microscope set at low power. View all parts of the drop. Count the number of living organisms you see. Record this number.

Switch to high power, and record your observations in a data table. **Caution:** *Wash hands after handling pond water.*

3. Place the beaker of pond water on the hot plate. Turn the hot plate on, and bring the water to a full boil. Let the water boil for 10 minutes. **Caution:** *Wear safety goggles.*
4. After 10 minutes, turn the hot plate off. Carefully remove the beaker of water from the hot plate using tongs. Let the water cool to about room temperature.
5. Repeat steps 1 and 2 with the boiled water.

ANALYSIS
1. What did you see in the unboiled pond water with the microscope set at high power? In the boiled pond water?
2. Which sample of pond water had the most living organisms?

CONCLUSION
1. How does boiling water make it potable?
2. Describe three situations when you might have to boil water before drinking it.

CHAPTER

21

WATER POLLUTION

Medical waste litters beaches in New York and New Jersey. In Delaware, health warnings are issued against eating shellfish because of bacteria in the water. Oil slicks near Texas and Alaska discolor beaches and damage ecosystems. Along the coast of California, fish, shorebirds, and sea mammals are threatened.

These are examples of why the ocean ecosystem is strained. Humans and other organisms are threatened by water pollution. The major cause of water pollution is ocean dumping. But water pollution is not limited to the ocean. Pollution is also a problem in lakes, ponds, rivers, and underground water systems.

21.1 THE WATER POLLUTION PROBLEM

Objectives • *Explain* the link between water pollution and human disease. • *Identify* the major types of water pollutants and their sources.

Water pollution is not a new problem. During the nineteenth century, people in England, France, Germany, and the United States often dumped their garbage into convenient waterways. The waterways became choked with wastes. Many rivers became unfit for drinking and bathing due to bacterial contaminations. At the British Parliament building, located on the banks of the River Thames in London, England, the smell from the river became so bad on several occasions that Parliament was forced to close.

As waters all over the world became contaminated, infectious diseases such as cholera (KOL-er-uh), typhoid (TY-foyd), and dysentery (DIS-uhn-TAIR-ee) became more common. For example, an outbreak of typhoid claimed the lives of 90,000 people in Chicago in 1885. In 1892, another outbreak of cholera killed many people in Hamburg, Germany.

Robert Koch, a German doctor, linked the cholera outbreak in Hamburg to contaminated water from the Elb River. People began to realize that contaminated water was a major cause of human disease. As a result, the practice of direct dumping into waterways was banned in the United States and most European countries. Instead, barges were used to dump the garbage farther out to sea. As you can see in Figure 21.1, however, ocean dumping did not solve the problem. Contaminated water is still a major cause of disease in many parts of the world.

Ocean dumping is a common practice in the world today. Garbage that is dumped into the ocean does not simply disappear. It affects the ocean ecosystem and may drift back to shore, where it can become a health risk to humans. Many people are working hard to prevent the world's waterways from becoming a giant sewer system.

Sewage

Water that carries organic wastes from humans and industry is called **sewage**. Sewage comes from toilets, sinks, dishwashers, washing machines, and industrial equipment. In the United States, most sewage is treated before it is dumped. In many developing countries, however, the sewage is not treated. The United States government estimates that the country dumps about 8.9 trillion L of sewage into the ocean each year. Some of this waste is not treated before it is dumped. Much of the waste is from factories and contains toxic chemicals and metals.

BIOLOGY LINK

Robert Koch's work with diseases such as cholera, anthrax, and tuberculosis led him to develop a set of postulates that linked certain pathogens with certain diseases. Koch proved that anthrax and tuberculosis were caused by bacteria. Koch's postulates are still used today by scientists to link a disease with a pathogen.

Figure 21.1 Water pollution has been a problem for a long time. New York began dumping garbage into the Atlantic Ocean in 1900. The garbage often ended up on beaches in New Jersey, as shown in this cartoon. New York stopped ocean dumping in 1933.

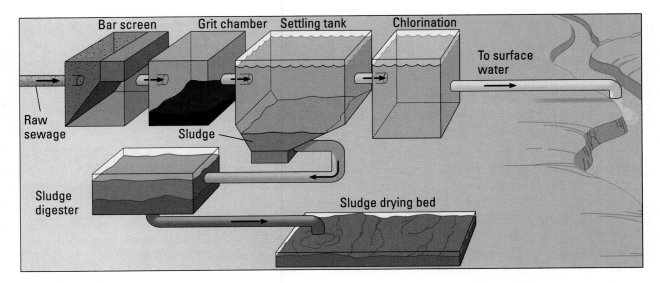

Bar screen   Grit chamber   Settling tank   Chlorination

To surface water

Raw sewage

Sludge

Sludge digester

Sludge drying bed

Figure 21.2 Sewage-treatment plants remove much of the pollution from sewage before it is dumped. Solids are separated out, and liquids are sterilized with chlorine. The dried solids are used as fertilizer or disposed of in landfills.

In urban areas, solid and liquid wastes enter an underground system of interconnected pipes called a sewer system. Older sewer systems may dump untreated sewage directly into surface water. Modern sewer systems are connected to sewage-treatment plants. *A* **sewage-treatment plant** *is a facility that processes raw sewage before the sewage is returned to surface water systems.*

Figure 21.2 diagrams the path of sewage through a treatment plant. Sewage is first passed through screens that filter out plastics, fabrics, and metallic objects. Further processing includes the treatment of solid materials, called sludge, and the addition of bacteria and purifying chemicals. The bacteria break down organic pollutants. Chlorine and other chemicals are used to sanitize and deoderize the treated water. These treatments remove microorganisms and harmful chemicals, but they do nothing to the organic matter in the sewage. This organic matter can lead to an excess of nutrients in the water system receiving the waste, leading to a problem called *eutrophication.*

Sewage-treatment plants filter out most, but not all, of the pollutants in waste. Treatment plants can also break down if they are overloaded or are not properly maintained. In such cases, untreated sewage may be discharged into surface water systems. Water contamination occurred in 1993 in Des Moines, Iowa, after a treatment plant was flooded by the Mississippi River.

Many countries do not have effective sewage treatment. Sewage is a major health threat in these countries and a major source of pollution in rivers and oceans. Pollution from the Mexican city of Tijuana, for example, has forced beach closures in San Diego, California. The pollution also leads to outbreaks of diseases, such as cholera and dysentery. These diseases are treatable and preventable. However, the contaminated water makes disease a chronic problem.

Pathogens

Water pollution and disease are closely linked. Many disease-causing organisms spend part of their life cycle in water. *Parasites, bacteria, and viruses that cause diseases in living things are called* **pathogens** (PATH-uh-jens). Many pathogens enter water systems through infected raw sewage or animal wastes. The pathogens can then infect other organisms that come into contact with the contaminated water.

Pathogens carried by water result in more human illness and death than any other environmental factor. Typhoid and cholera, for example, are bacterial diseases spread by water contaminated by infected human wastes. With improved sewage and sanitation, these diseases have been controlled in most developed nations. However, people in many developing countries in Asia, the Middle East, Africa, and India still suffer from high rates of cholera and typhoid.

Schistosomiasis (SHIS-tuh-soh-MY-uh-sis) is a disease caused by microscopic worms. The worms enter through the skin of people who walk in water contaminated with infected human wastes. Once in the body, the worms attack the liver, urinary bladder, and intestines. Schistosomiasis is most common in Africa, the Middle East, and Egypt. This disease may affect as many as 100 million people in the tropics and causes more than 1 million deaths each year.

Malaria (muh-LAYR-ee-uh) is a disease caused by a *protozoan*. Protozoans are microscopic, animal-like protists. Malaria is usually transmitted to humans by the bite of an infected mosquito. Unlike typhoid, cholera, and schistosomiasis, malaria is not transmitted by contact with contaminated water. But water serves as the breeding ground for the mosquito that transmits the disease. Malaria is common in Africa, East Asia, and Latin America. Worldwide, more than 800 million people are infected with malaria. Of these, one million die each year.

Figure 21.3 These three organisms cause millions of human deaths every year. Water is an important part of the life cycle of the bacterium that causes cholera (left), the worm that causes schistosomiasis (center), and the protozoan that causes malaria (right).

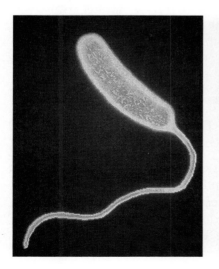

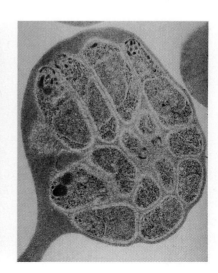

Types of Water Pollution

Sewage is the second largest source of water pollution caused by humans. The largest source of water pollution is runoff from agriculture. Pesticides, fertilizers, and plant and animal wastes may end up in surface water systems as a result of poor agricultural practices. These pollutants can cause many environmental problems. Table 21.1 lists the most common water pollutants and their sources.

Table 21.1   Water Pollutants and Sources

Source	Pathogens	Nutrients	Sediments	Toxic Chemicals
Agriculture	•	•	•	•
Sewage-treatment plants	•	•		•
Industry				•
Urban runoff	•	•	•	
Mining runoff			•	•
Construction runoff		•	•	•

Pathogens, nutrients, and sediments are the most common pollutants in sewage and agricultural wastes. Toxic chemicals are also dangerous pollutants. These range from crude oil and solvents to metallic elements, such as lead and mercury. Nontoxic substances can also pollute. Plastics, for example, are major pollutants. Because they do not break down easily in the environment, plastic items can trap or choke aquatic organisms.

Acids and radioactivity are pollutants that affect the land, water, and air. Acid from industrial air pollution can fall as rain, making lakes acidic and disrupting their ecosystems. You can read more about acid precipitation in Chapter 22. Radioactive substances are very dangerous and can last a long time. Even the waste heat from a power plant can be a pollutant. All these pollutants have one thing in common: they disrupt aquatic ecosystems. Many are also a threat to human health.

1. Sewage is water carrying organic wastes from humans and industry.
2. Definitions should reflect a basic understanding of the four types of pollutants. Definitions should become more detailed as the pollutants are discussed in the chapter.
3. Check student diagrams for logic and accuracy. Diagrams should demonstrate that many pathogens spend parts of their life cycle in water. Water contaminated by wastes from diseased individuals leads to further disease in people who come into contact with the water.

SECTION REVIEW

1. What is sewage?
2. **Organize Data** Make a list of the pollutants that appear in Table 21.1. Write a definition for each pollutant. Update your definitions as you read the rest of this chapter.
3. **Diagram** Create a flowchart or concept map that details the relationship between sewage, contaminated water, pathogens, and humans.

21.2 CHEMICAL POLLUTANTS

Objectives • **Examine** *the sources and effects of inorganic and organic toxic chemicals.* • **Describe** *the process of eutrophication and its effects on lake ecosystems.*

Elements and molecules that are directly harmful to living things are called **toxic chemicals**. Toxic chemicals are either inorganic or organic. *Inorganic chemicals are elements or molecules that are not derived from organisms.* *Organic chemicals are molecules containing atoms of carbon that are derived from organisms.*

Inorganic Chemicals

Inorganic chemicals include acids, salts, heavy metals, and plant nutrients. **Heavy metals** *are metallic elements with high atomic masses.* Examples of dangerous heavy metals are mercury, lead, cadmium, arsenic, nickel, and chromium. Plant nutrients are molecules that do not contain carbon yet are needed for plant growth. Phosphates and nitrates are important plant nutrients.

Acids and heavy metals enter groundwater and surface water systems as a result of seepage, runoff, and direct discharge into lakes, rivers, and streams. Recall that mine tailings often contain high levels of heavy metals, sulfur, or other toxic substances. Rain water may leach through tailings and carry wastes into groundwater and surface water. Heavy metals and acids enter water systems through leaching.

Heavy metal compounds are often by-products of industrial processes such as metal treatment and paint and plastics production. Factories sometimes discharge these materials directly into surface water systems. Metal drums filled with toxic factory wastes can corrode, allowing the waste to seep into groundwater or to

LITERATURE
L I N K

One reference to mercury poisoning occurs in Lewis Carroll's book *Alice's Adventures in Wonderland*. One character in the book is the Mad Hatter, an individual who suffers from Mad Hatter's disease. This disease was common among hat makers in seventeenth-century France. The material used to make hats was softened by soaking it in mercury compounds. Unprotected skin on a worker's hands and arms was in constant contact with the mercury. Mercury poisoning caused tremors, lack of coordination, nerve damage, and even insanity.

Figure 21.4 This toxic waste dump is on land, but it causes water pollution. Corroded drums release toxic waste, which can then be carried to streams and groundwater by rain.

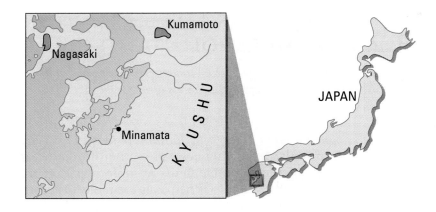

Figure 21.5 Minamata Bay was the site of mercury poisoning in the 1950s. Mercury from a plastics plant contaminated seafood that was eaten by the townspeople.

contaminate streams. These drums are also dumped into the ocean. Unfortunately, ocean water is very corrosive to most metals. The drums corrode quickly and release their contents.

Heavy metals are poisonous. Ingestion of these metals can cause brain, liver, and kidney damage, as well as coma and even death. A devastating case of mercury poisoning occurred in the 1950s in the coastal town of Minamata (min-uh-MAHT-uh) on the Japanese island of Kyushu (KYOO-shoo), shown in Figure 21.5.

The first sign of the problem was strange animal behavior. Birds began to fall out of trees and fly into buildings. Cats developed a strange walk, foamed at the mouth, meowed constantly, and sometimes ran in circles until they died. The problem became worse. Townspeople complained of headaches, dizziness, blurred vision, and numbness in their hands and feet.

Doctors soon discovered that the cause of the symptoms was mercury poisoning. The mercury came from a plastics factory that discharged mercury wastes into the waters of Minamata Bay. The mercury contaminated the fish and shellfish that were the main diet of the townspeople. Over a period of 20 years, 8,000 people suffered paralysis or brain damage, and several hundred people died as a result of mercury poisoning.

Mercury poisoning in Minamata is one example of toxic chemical pollution. There are many others. Pesticides from agriculture are common inorganic pollutants. Acids from burning fossil fuels can accumulate in lakes, disrupting lake ecosystems. Inorganic pollutants can be very toxic, and they may be difficult to clean up once they contaminate an area.

Organic Chemicals

Organic chemicals can also be pollutants. Many of these chemicals come from living things, while others are made in the laboratory. Synthetic organic substances include gasoline, oils, plastics, some pesticides and fertilizers, solvents, and wood preservatives. Some organic chemicals can be poisonous to living things.

Organic chemicals enter surface and groundwater systems in

a number of ways. Wastes from petroleum refineries, chemical factories, and from canning, meat-packing, and food-processing plants are often discharged into sewer systems that empty into lakes or rivers. This discharge contains organic chemicals. Runoff from farmlands contains large amounts of organic pesticides and fertilizers. In time, these pollutants run into rivers and groundwater, and finally into the oceans.

Crude oil is one of the most common and dangerous organic pollutants. Because crude oil is transported along rivers and across oceans in huge amounts, its potential as a pollutant is a major concern. Crude oil often enters surface water systems as a result of spills at drilling sites, or from shipwrecked or damaged oil tankers. Oil may also be flushed into the sea when tanker crews use seawater to rinse out oil tanks.

A major oil spill occurred at an offshore drilling site in Mexico in 1979. An unsealed drill pipe allowed about 440 000 metric tons of crude oil to pour into the Gulf of Mexico. It took almost a year to control the flow of oil. In 1978, the oil tanker *Amoco Cadiz* tore open its hull when it ran aground off the coast of Brittany in France. Its entire cargo—220 000 metric tons of crude oil—was discharged into the Bay of Biscay. The largest oil spill in history occurred during the Persian Gulf War of 1991. Hundreds of thousands of metric tons of oil were spilled into the gulf, although no one knows the total amount.

A metric ton of oil is equal to about 265 gallons of oil. A barrel of oil is equal to 55 gallons, so 1 metric ton of oil is equal to about 4.8 barrels.

The worst oil spill in U.S. history took place in 1989. The oil tanker *Exxon Valdez*, shown in Figure 21.6, ran aground on Bligh Reef in Prince William Sound off the coast of Alaska. About 42 000 metric tons of crude oil gushed into the pristine water of the sound. The ecosystem of the sound was devastated, and thousands of birds, mammals, and other organisms died. Marine biologists predict that the region's ecosystem will be affected for at least another 10 to 15 years.

Figure 21.6 The *Exxon Valdez* ran aground off the coast of Alaska in 1989. The bird in this photograph is one of thousands of animals killed by the resulting oil spill.

Lake Erie: A Success Story

Can pollution damage be undone?

During the 1960s, Lake Erie was not a place where you would want to swim. The lake's surface was covered by large mats of blue-green algae. The water smelled terrible from the dead fish and rotting plants that floated on the water's surface and washed up on the beaches. Oil coated much of the water's surface. The water was cloudy and full of sediments. Most beaches were closed because the water was unsafe.

Besides being ugly and a health hazard, the Lake Erie waters also presented other dangers. Some of the rivers draining into Lake Erie were declared fire hazards. Several rivers actually caught fire.

The problems on Lake Erie were caused by agricultural runoff and wastes from major industrial centers such as Detroit, Michigan; Toledo, Ohio; Buffalo, New York; and Erie, Pennsylvania. Lake Erie is the smallest of the Great Lakes, with an average depth of only 18.3 m. Unable to dilute the wastes that poured into it daily, the lake was dying from chemical pollution and lack of oxygen.

Sewage dumped by cities, waste water from factories, and fertilizers from farming contain phosphorus and nitrogen. These chemicals caused algae to flourish. The large algae blooms depleted the lake of its oxygen. This lack of oxygen resulted in the death of many fish and other organisms.

In the 1970s, the people and governments surrounding Lake Erie decided to clean up the lake. Laws were passed in the United States and Canada to prevent dumping into the lake. Phosphate-containing detergents were banned. Farmers were encouraged to reduce their use of fertilizers. New sewage-treatment plants were built that released 90 percent less organic waste into the water.

Because the amount of pollutants entering the lake was greatly reduced, the lake began to recover. Lake Erie cleansed itself through natural biological and chemical processes. The algae population decreased, and the fish populations grew.

Lake Erie still has problems. Pollutants such as PCBs are still in the lake, although most have settled to the bottom. The lake also has persistent problems with introduced species, such as the lamprey eel and the zebra mussel. Yet if you were to visit Lake Erie today, you would not hesitate to swim in the clean water. You would probably never guess that the lake had once been a giant pool of pollution.

DECISIONS

1. Explain how Lake Erie became polluted. What kinds of pollutants were there? Where did they come from?
2. Why could Lake Erie be considered a success story?

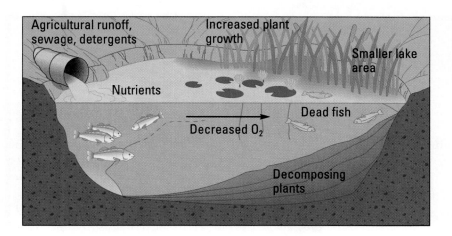

Figure 21.7 Eutrophication occurs in most lakes over time. Plant nutrient pollution can greatly accelerate this process. Large amounts of plant growth change the nature of the lake, leading to the disappearance of the original community.

Labels in figure: Agricultural runoff, sewage, detergents; Increased plant growth; Smaller lake area; Nutrients; Dead fish; Decreased O₂; Decomposing plants

Eutrophication

Plant nutrients, nitrates, and phosphates are all used to fertilize crops. Solid and liquid animal wastes are also a rich source of plant nutrients. Many household detergents contain phosphates as well. These nutrients enter surface water systems as a result of runoff, industrial wastes, and sewage.

While these nutrients are generally not toxic and are good for plant growth, there are times when too many nutrients can cause environmental problems. Large amounts of nitrates and phosphates promote the runaway growth of algae and aquatic plants. In time, open water areas become choked with plant growth. The plants die, resulting in a huge increase in the number of decomposing bacteria. This process lowers the amount of oxygen in the water. Many animal communities die out. *The process by which lakes and ponds are changed by excess plant nutrients is called* **eutrophication** (yoo-TRUHF-uh-KAY-shun).

Scientists estimate that more than 65 percent of the lakes in the United States are affected by eutrophication caused by human activity. One example of the effects of eutrophication is the Chesapeake Bay, the largest estuary in the United States. Rivers carry farm fertilizers, mostly nitrates and phosphates, into Chesapeake Bay. Chemical factories also dump wastes. As a result, many fish, crabs, and other important food populations in the bay are in sharp decline.

DATELINE 1955

Fishermen caught about 9 million kg of blue pike in Lake Erie. This was the largest catch ever. During the next few years, the blue pike fishery collapsed from pollution and overfishing. The blue pike is now extinct in Lake Erie. Fish such as the whitefish and cisco have been driven to extinction in a similar way.

SECTION REVIEW

1. What is eutrophication?
2. Describe the difference between an organic and an inorganic chemical. Give one example of water pollution by each.
3. **Analyze** The *Exxon Valdez* oil spill occurred because of human error. Can the possibility of human error ever be eliminated?

1. Eutrophication is the process by which lakes and ponds receive runoff rich in life-supporting plant nutrients.
2. Organic chemicals are based on carbon atoms. Inorganic chemicals are not based on carbon atoms. Mercury pollution in Minamata Bay is an example of inorganic chemical pollution. The *Exxon Valdez* oil spill is an example of organic chemical pollution.
3. The possibility of human error can never be completely eliminated.

Answers and teaching
strategies on page T110.

Nutrients and Algae Growth

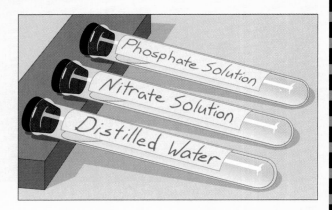

PROBLEM

How do phosphate and nitrate affect the growth of algae?

MATERIALS

- wax marking pencil
- 3 test tubes with screw caps
- distilled water
- 100-mL graduated cylinder
- 100 mL of 0.4% phosphate solution
- 100 mL of 0.4% nitrate solution
- *Chlorella* culture
- dropper
- light source
- pencil
- paper

PREDICTION

After reading through the entire activity, predict which of the solutions will contain the largest amount of the alga *Chlorella* after 6 days: phosphate solution, nitrate solution, or distilled water.

PROCEDURE

Day 1

1. Write your name on all three test tubes with the wax pencil.
2. Measure the volume of a test tube using the graduated cylinder. Then calculate 75 percent of this volume.
3. With the wax pencil, mark the first test tube *Distilled Water*, and fill it three-quarters full with distilled water.
4. Label the second test tube *Nitrate Solution*, and the third test tube *Phosphate Solution*. Fill both of these test tubes three-quarters full with the correct solutions.
5. Gently mix the *Chlorella* culture. Using the dropper, place 10 drops of the culture into each tube. Shake each tube gently to mix the contents.

6. Place the caps tightly on the test tubes, and lay them on their sides in a sunny, well-lighted area such as a windowsill.
   Days 2–6
7. Check the test tubes every day for 5 days. Growth of *Chlorella* can be determined by an increase in the density of the algae, as well as an increase in the darkness of the green color in the tubes. Record any changes in density or color for each tube.

ANALYSIS

1. What were the changes, if any, in the *Distilled Water* test tube? Describe what you observed.
2. Were there any changes in the *Nitrate Solution* test tube? If so, describe them.
3. What occurred in the *Phosphate Solution* test tube? Describe what you observed.
4. Which test tube or tubes showed the most changes in color or density?

CONCLUSION

1. Which solution contained the most algal growth? Which contained the least?
2. Why did the algae grow in the pattern you observed?
3. Write a paragraph applying your findings. What effect would phosphate and nitrate run-off from farms have on a lake? How would organisms in the lake be affected? How could negative effects be prevented?

21.3 RADIOACTIVITY AND THERMAL POLLUTION

Objective • *Explain* the problems of radioactive and thermal water pollution.

Nuclear power plants produce clean energy, but they also produce pollution. Nuclear power plants share the problem of waste heat disposal with other types of power plants. They also produce large amounts of radioactive water and other radioactive wastes. Radioactive wastes come from other sources as well. These radioactive pollutants are very dangerous.

Radioactivity

Recall from Chapter 16 that radioactive elements give off radiation when they decay. Radioactive elements such as uranium-235 and plutonium-239 are used as fuels in nuclear power plants. Radioactive elements are also used in medicine. Uranium mines and nuclear fuel refineries produce radioactive waste. Nuclear weapons detonations and power plant accidents produce the most radioactive waste of all.

Even under the safest operating conditions, tiny amounts of radiation are released into the air and water near a nuclear power plant. These emissions are not dangerous. The wastes produced by nuclear plants are dangerous. These wastes are very difficult to handle and pose a serious disposal problem.

The disposal of radioactive wastes, both solid and liquid, may also result in water pollution. Liquid wastes are placed in steel storage containers. These containers are encased in concrete and buried. Over time, these containers may corrode and break down allowing radioactive material to leak into the soil. The waste may eventually contaminate groundwater.

You may wish to review Chapter 16 with students when teaching this section. Refer students with questions about radioactivity and its harmful effects to Sections 16.1 and 16.3. Section 16.2 can help them identify exactly where radioactive wastes come from. Emphasize that radioactive pollutants can move easily between air, water, and land, and can be a problem in all of these areas.

Figure 21.8 Tailings from uranium and copper mines are sources of metal pollutants. Uranium is mined to produce fuel for nuclear reactors and nuclear bombs.

Such events have occurred at many temporary disposal sites. In 1973, almost 1 million L of radioactive liquid waste leaked into the soil from the Hanford nuclear weapons site near Richland, Washington. Some of this contaminated material made its way into the Columbia River. A study released nearly 21 years after the leakage shows that the radiation contaminated fish and drinking water along the river. The study also states that about 2,100 people were exposed to dangerous levels of radiation.

During the 1950s, the Savannah River Weapons Plant in South Carolina discharged radioactive waste into the Savannah River. This river is a source of drinking water for several southern states, including Georgia, Alabama, and parts of Florida and South Carolina. The Department of Energy is currently studying the possible health effects of this discharge.

Thermal Pollution

Power plants and other industrial facilities give off large amounts of heat, which can pollute water. *A large increase in water temperature due to human activity is called* **thermal pollution**. Thermal pollution usually occurs in lakes, rivers, or shallow bays located near power plants or industrial sites.

Power plants and industrial complexes often use water cooling systems to reduce excess heat. In such a system, cool water from lakes, rivers, or bays is pumped into pipes that lie alongside pipes containing hot water from the plant. Heat is transferred from the hot water to the cool water. Once cooled, the water is returned to the plant. The cool water, now heated, is returned to the water source.

Thermal pollution affects water ecosystems in several ways. The body temperature of fish is determined partially by the environment. Thus, as water temperature increases, so does their body temperature. Increased body temperature increases metabolism, which in turn increases respiration rate and the amount of oxygen the fish need. At the same time, an increase in water temperature decreases the amount of dissolved oxygen the water can hold. The fish suffocate because they cannot get enough oxygen. The increased water temperature is also destructive to developing eggs and young fish.

1. Thermal pollution is pollution caused by an increase in temperature.
2. Nuclear power plants produce large amounts of radioactive water because water is used to cool the reactor core.
3. If a great deal of decomposition is occurring in a given area, enough heat can be generated to raise the temperature of the surroundings to a point where it can harm organisms. Waterways near landfills are often affected in this way.

SECTION REVIEW

1. What is thermal pollution?
2. **Deduce** Nuclear power plants produce large amounts of radioactive water. Why? You may need to refer to Chapter 16.
3. **Predict** Many organic products give off heat as they decompose. Do you think this heat could serve as a source of thermal pollution? Explain.

21.4 CONTROLLING WATER POLLUTION

Objectives • *Identify* government attempts to control water pollution. • *Describe* the problems involved in enforcing laws regarding water pollution.

The first U.S. legislation to address water pollution was the Rivers and Harbors Act of 1898. Yet after a century of concern and laws designed to control it, water pollution is still a problem. Why have many of the laws failed? The reasons are that the laws were often not strong enough, and strong laws were not enforced.

Before 1948, individual states were responsible for enforcing laws governing water pollution. Scientific reports on kinds and amounts of pollution were not accurate. Several sources were often responsible for pollution at different sites along a given waterway, making it difficult to determine who was responsible and who should be punished. In addition, little was known about the effects of pollution on aquatic ecosystems.

The politics of industry was also an important factor in the failure of early water pollution laws. If a factory was charged with violating a law and fined, the factory might threaten to move to a state where laws were less strict. The removal of the factory would cause a large loss of jobs in the surrounding area, harming the economy. Some industries used the threat of moving to avoid fines and to get water pollution laws suspended.

In response to concerns about the environment and political pressure, Congress passed the Federal Water Pollution Control Act in 1972. That legislation, now called the Clean Water Act, was an attempt to set water-quality standards for all states. The Clean Water Act provides a vision of water quality standards and a means of measuring improvement. The Clean Water Act is not, however, a set of laws for enforcement.

Although a number of states has shown some improvement in water quality, there are still many problems with sewage treatment, soil erosion, land-use control, and the removal of toxic chemicals and heavy metals. More recently, cancer-causing agents have been identified in the drinking water in several states. Local, state, and federal laws must be strengthened if water-quality standards are to be met.

Progress has been slow and the results mixed. Phosphates and other pollutants have been greatly reduced in Lake Erie. At the same time, however, the lower Mississippi River is dangerously polluted, and Chesapeake Bay is still threatened by an overload of nutrients and toxic chemicals. It is important to note that the quality of the U.S. water supply has not gotten worse at a time

DATELINE 1969

The Cuyahoga River in Cleveland, Ohio, was so polluted that the river actually caught fire and burned for several days. This incident was a major factor behind the passage of the Clean Water Act of 1972.

Figure 21.9 Most plastics are not toxic, but they are still pollutants. Plastics break down very slowly in the environment. Discarded fishing nets and other plastic objects are a threat to sea animals. You can help solve this problem by disposing of plastics properly.

Teaching tips for Field Activity appear on page T110.

when the population continues to grow. On the whole, the nation is moving toward better water quality. Table 21.2 summarizes water pollution legislation.

Table 21.2 Water Pollution Legislation

Year	Legislation
1898	**Rivers and Harbors Act:** U.S. Army is responsible for protecting navigable waters.
1934	**Fish and Wildlife Coordination Act:** Fish and Wildlife Service and other agencies to determine the impact of proposed projects on fish and wildlife.
1948	**Federal Water Pollution Control Act:** U.S. Army to apply environmental standards when approving water dumping.
1966	**Clean Water Restoration Act:** Authorizes federal assistance for sewage-treatment plant construction.
1970	**Water Quality Act:** Regulates oil pollution from vessels and offshore facilities.
1972	**Clean Water Act:** Establishes four broad national goals addressing the elimination of polluting wastes, better sewage treatment, and a cleanup program.
1972	**Ports and Waterways Safety Act:** Monitors pollution from ships; regulates ship design and safety.
1972	**Marine Protection and Sanctuaries Act:** Regulates ocean dumping and creates sanctuaries for endangered marine species.
1974	**Safe Drinking Water Act:** Establishes minimum safety standards for community water supplies.
1976	**Toxic Substance Control Act:** Regulates the use and disposal of toxic chemicals.
1985	**Clean Water Act Amendment:** Sets a national goal of making all surface waters "fishable and swimmable."
1990	**London Dumping Convention:** Calls for an end to all ocean dumping of industrial wastes, plastics, and tank washing wastes.

SECTION REVIEW

1. What is being done to control water pollution? Are these measures effective?
2. What can you do as an individual to reduce the effects of water pollution?
3. **Justify** You are on the town planning committee. A company that employs 75 percent of the people in your community has been cited for water pollution violations. The company says it will move if it is told to pay the fines. Will you vote to make the company pay? Explain your answer.

1. Laws are passed to regulate pollution and help clean up polluted areas. These laws are difficult to enforce and are not always effective.
2. Responses will vary, but they should reflect any water-quality problems experienced by the school's community.
3. Accept all logical responses that are supported by the text. You may wish to use this question as the basis for a class discussion.

KEY TERMS

sewage 21.1	toxic chemical 21.2	eutrophication 21.2
sewage-treatment plant 21.1	heavy metal 21.2	thermal pollution 21.3
pathogen 21.1		

CHAPTER SUMMARY

21.1 Contaminated water is closely linked to human diseases. In developed countries, sewage is treated to remove pollutants before it is discharged into waterways. Agricultural runoff is the largest source of water pollution; sewage and industry are other major sources.

21.2 Toxic chemicals are molecules or elements that are directly poisonous to living things. Toxic inorganic chemicals include acids, pesticides, and heavy metals such as lead and mercury. Toxic organic chemicals include some pesticides, oil, and oil products. Nutrient pollution can lead to eutrophication in lakes and estuaries.

21.3 Radioactive pollutants last for a long time and can be dangerous in small quantities. Thermal pollution is excess heat from power plants discharged into surface water systems. Thermal pollution can damage aquatic ecosystems.

21.4 The U.S. government has passed laws attempting to regulate water quality for about 100 years. State-controlled legislation failed because different states had different standards. The Clean Water Act was passed in 1972. Laws controlling water pollution have been difficult to enforce, and some laws have not been strong enough.

MULTIPLE CHOICE

Choose the letter of the word or phrase that best completes each statement.

1. Mercury is a pollutant classified as (a) an organic material; (b) a pathogen; (c) a radioactive waste; (d) a heavy metal. d

2. The solid waste produced by a sewage-treatment plant is called (a) sludge; (b) slime; (c) discharge; (d) runoff. a

3. The process by which excess nutrients enter an aquatic ecosystem is called (a) subsidence; (b) eutrophication; (c) thermal pollution; (d) pathogen pollution. b

4. Thermal pollution is caused by excess (a) heat; (b) sewage; (c) inorganic materials; (d) radioactivity. a

5. The pollutants associated with eutrophication are (a) pathogens and inorganic chemicals; (b) nitrates and pathogens; (c) nitrates and phosphates; (d) heavy metals. c

6. Crude oil is a toxic chemical that is (a) a pathogen; (b) inorganic; (c) organic; (d) a heavy metal. c

7. Microorganisms that cause disease are classified as (a) pathogens; (b) inorganic materials; (c) organic materials; (d) thermal pollutants. a

8. The types of pollution that result from nuclear power plants are (a) radioactivity and pathogens; (b) thermal pollution and heavy metals; (c) radioactivity and thermal pollution; (d) thermal pollution and organic materials. c

9. The first step in the sewage-treatment process is the (a) screening of large particles; (b) chlorination; (c) sedimentation; (d) grit chamber. a

10. In 1972, the U.S. government passed an important act called the (a) Rivers and Harbors Act; (b) Clean Water Act; (c) Water Safety Act; (d) Strategic Water Initiative. b

CHAPTER 21 REVIEW

WORD COMPARISONS

Write the letter of the second word pair that best matches the first pair.

1. Cholera: sewage as (a) radioactivity: nuclear power plant; (b) nitrates: phosphates; (c) oil: plastics; (d) laws: enforcement. a
2. Organic: inorganic as (a) nitrates: phosphates; (b) toxic: nontoxic; (c) oil: plastics; (d) lake: estuary. b
3. Radioactivity: thermal pollution as (a) lake: estuary; (b) inorganic: organic; (c) nitrates: eutrophication; (d) oil: plastics. d
4. Mercury: heavy metals as (a) nitrates: phosphates; (b) cholera: pathogens; (c) agriculture: eutrophication; (d) agriculture: food. b
5. Clean Water Act: water standards as (a) nitrates: phosphates; (b) oil production: pollution; (c) Ports and Waterways Safety Act: ship design; (d) nitrates: eutrophication. c

CONCEPT REVIEW Answers on page T110.

Write a complete response for each of the following.

1. Name several sources of radioactivity that may result in water pollution.
2. Why is heat considered a form of pollution?
3. How do organic nutrients from human activity affect aquatic ecosystems?
4. Give examples of inorganic materials that are pollutants.
5. Where do the pathogens in water come from?

THINK CRITICALLY Answers on page T110.

1. Describe the process of sewage treatment. Are all pollutants removed during the process?
2. Suppose you observed a lake with a great deal of plant growth and large numbers of dead fish. Explain what may have caused this problem and what evidence you would look for to support your hypothesis.
3. Shellfish often collect and concentrate pollutants from their surroundings in their bodies. Could this fact have played a role in the mercury poisoning in Minamata Bay?
4. Suggest ways to make the transport of oil safer. Is there any way to transport oil without posing any environmental risk?
5. Explain how the differences in state water pollution standards for industry made state pollution laws difficult to enforce.

WRITE FOR UNDERSTANDING Answers on page T110.

Describe the mercury poisoning of Minamata Bay in your own words. Where did the pollution come from? Explain how the pollution got into the bodies of the people living near the bay. What were the effects of the mercury pollution?

PORTFOLIO

1. Identify and draw or photograph locations in your community where water pollution has occurred or is likely to occur. Create a visual display explaining why the area is at risk of pollution, including captions that explain how the situation could be corrected.
2. Begin a scrapbook of newspaper and magazine articles that cite examples of how people and other living things are being harmed by water pollutants. Group related articles together according to which means of legislation could be used to stop the pollution.

Use Figure 21.2 to answer the following.
1. What is shown in the diagram?
2. Where in the diagram are large solids separated from water by screening?
3. At what stage in the process shown are chemicals added to water to purify the water?
4. What is the material called that collects at the bottom of the tanks?
5. What happens to water that leaves this treatment facility?

ACTIVITY 21.2

Answers and teaching strategies on page T110.

PROBLEM
How does organic material break down and pollute water sources?

MATERIALS
- 3 different water samples (such as dishwater, well water, rainwater, tap water, or pond water)
- 3 test tubes and a rack
- masking tape
- graduated cylinder
- diluted methylene blue dye
- dropper

HYPOTHESIS
After reading through the activity, write a hypothesis about the relationship between the amount of organic matter in water sources and the resulting amount of water pollution.

PROCEDURE

Note: Bacteria act on methylene blue dye and cause it to change from blue to a colorless liquid. The more bacteria a water sample contains, the faster the color of the dye breaks down.
1. Mark three test tubes *A*, *B*, and *C*. Put 5 mL of a different water sample in each tube. *Note: Be sure and choose water samples that contain different amounts of organic material, such as tap water, rainwater, and pond water.*
2. Add 20 drops of diluted methylene blue dye to each of the water samples. Put the test tubes in the test-tube rack, and observe them at 10-minute intervals for 1 hour. Record your observations in the data table.

ANALYSIS
1. In which test tube did the color disappear first?
2. Which water sample contains the greatest amount of organic matter? Which contains the least?
3. Since bacteria use oxygen and do not carry out photosynthesis, which gases would be limited in water that is rich in organic material?

CONCLUSION
1. What are possible sources of organic matter in each positive sample?
2. Hypothesize about the reasons for a lack of organic material in each negative sample.

Appearance of Methylene Blue in Test Tube

Test Tube	Kind of Water	After 10 min	After 20 min	After 30 min	After 40 min	After 50 min	After 60 min
A							
B							
C							

CHAPTER

22

AIR AND NOISE POLLUTION

Imagine you are hiking in the Adirondack Mountains in New York State. You walk through a forest and stop by the edge of a clear lake. No fish jump and break the glassy surface. You notice that there are no plants in the water at all. Suddenly you realize the lake is completely dead. It doesn't hold a single living thing.

Scenes like this one are occurring more and more often across the Northern Hemisphere. The cause of the lake's death was acid precipitation. Acidic pollutants released into the atmosphere by coal-burning power plants fell into the lake as rain and snow. The organisms in the lake died when the lake water became too acidic to support life.

22.1 THE AIR POLLUTION PROBLEM

Objectives • **Describe** *air pollution.* • **Explain** *the historical background of air pollution.* • **Identify** *common air pollutants.*

Air is a mixture of gases, including nitrogen (78 percent), oxygen (21 percent), and small amounts of argon, carbon dioxide, and water vapor. As air moves across Earth's surface, it picks up materials formed by natural events and human activities. Some of these materials are harmful to both living and nonliving things. *Harmful materials that enter the environment are called* **pollutants** (poh-LOOT-unts).

Harmful substances released into the atmosphere are collectively called *air pollution.* Most pollutants entering Earth's atmosphere come from natural sources, such as sand and dust storms, volcanic eruptions, and forest fires. Ocean spray and gases produced by decaying organisms also add pollutants to the air. However, human activity has become a major source of air pollution.

Air pollution caused by human activity is not a new problem. Early Western philosophers complained of air pollution when they described the contaminated air of ancient Rome. Air pollution became a widespread problem during the Industrial Revolution of the 1700s. This period of rapid industrial growth required the burning of huge amounts of coal and wood. The effects of polluted air on human life were devastating. For example, 1500 Londoners died from the effects of coal smoke in 1911. Table 22.1 lists other cases of illness and death caused by air pollution. These deaths were caused by everyday industrial pollution, not by chemical spills or other accidents.

Table 22.1 Air Pollution Disasters

Year	Location	Human Casualties
1880	London, England	1000 dead
1948	Donora, Pennsylvania	6000 ill, 20 dead
1950	Poza Rica, Mexico	322 ill, 22 dead
1952	London, England	3500–4000 dead
1953	New York, New York	250 dead
1956	London, England	900 dead
1957	London, England	700–800 dead
1962	London, England	700 dead
1963	New York, New York	200–400 dead
1965	New York, New York	400 dead
1966	New York, New York	165 dead

Figure 22.1 Air pollutants come from many sources. Coal-burning power plants, automobiles, and livestock are three main sources.

Outdoor Pollutants

Air pollutants are classified as either gases or particulates. *Tiny solids suspended in the atmosphere are called* **particulates** (par-TIK-yu-luts). The most common particulates are pieces of ash, dust, and soot from burning organic matter. Liquid droplets in smoke or smog are particulates. Traces of metals such as lead, iron, and copper are particulates as well. Pesticides, herbicides, and fertilizer dust are common pollutants in rural areas, as is plant pollen. Because of their size, particulates are dangerous to people. The tiny particles are easily inhaled with air and become trapped in the lungs.

Most gaseous pollutants come from a group of chemicals called oxides. **Oxides** (OK-syds) *are compounds of oxygen and another element.* The most common oxides are compounds of oxygen and carbon, sulfur, or nitrogen. These compounds are released when fossil fuels and organic matter are burned, especially in automobiles and coal-burning power plants.

Cities with heavy automobile traffic often develop a condition called photochemical smog. **Photochemical smog** *is a yellow-brown haze formed when sunlight reacts with pollutants produced by cars.* One of the chemicals in photochemical smog is ozone (O_3). Ozone is very corrosive and easily breaks down rubber and some synthetic fibers. In high concentrations ozone is also poisonous to plants and animals. Photochemical smog contains other pollutants as well. One of these pollutants is nitrogen dioxide (NO_2). Nitrogen dioxide is a brown gas that gives photochemical smog its distinctive brown color.

The hydrocarbons are another group of gaseous pollutants. Recall that hydrocarbons are compounds made up mostly of hydrogen and carbon. Methane is the most common hydrocarbon pollutant. It is produced by certain bacteria, livestock, and by rotting plant and animal matter. A related group of pollutants is called the chlorofluorocarbons. **Chlorofluorocarbons** (KLOR-oh-FLUR-oh-KAR-bunz), *or* **CFCs**, *are compounds of carbon, chlorine, and fluorine once used in refrigerators, air conditioners, aerosol cans, and in the production of styrofoam.*

Indoor Pollutants

With so many pollutants in the outside air, you may feel safer staying indoors. However, indoor air is not always cleaner than outdoor air. Air inside buildings often contains high levels of pollutants.

Several factors are responsible for the high levels of indoor air pollutants. Home products such as plastics, insulation, and cleaners give off harmful fumes. Air circulation in buildings is often poor, especially during winter, when buildings are closed up to save energy. The effects of fumes and decreased air circulation are multiplied because most people spend 16 to 18 hours a day indoors. This exposure to pollutants can cause serious health problems.

Table 22.2 Common Indoor Pollutants

Pollutant	Source
Carbon monoxide	Cigarette smoke, stoves and heaters, automobiles
Formaldehyde	Particle board, furniture, carpeting, foam insulation
Paradichlorobenzene	Mothballs
Methyl chloride	Paint thinner
Tetrachloroethylene	Dry-cleaning fluid
Ammonia	Cleaning agents
Hydrocarbons	Solvents, adhesives
Asbestos	Insulation, fireproofing materials
Particulates	Cigarette smoke, pollen, burning wood and coal
Bacteria, fungi	Heating and cooling ducts

DATELINE 1976

Thirty-five American Legion members died mysteriously at a convention in Philadelphia. Doctors discovered that the deaths were caused by a bacterium living in the ventilation system of the hotel. The disease became known as Legionnaires' disease. Legionnaires' disease is curable, and now affects about 125,000 people every year.

The greatest source of indoor air pollution is cigarette smoke. The combination of particulates, gases, and other chemicals contained in cigarette smoke makes it the deadliest of all indoor pollutants. Cigarette smoke is hazardous not only to smokers but to non-smokers as well. Nonsmokers breathe in secondhand, or side-stream, smoke. Secondhand smoke from filtered cigarettes contains higher levels of particulates from burning paper and tobacco than the smoke inhaled by the smoker.

Microorganisms are another kind of indoor air pollutant. Ventilation ducts and vents are often home to bacteria and fungi. Airtight buildings can fill quickly with potentially disease-causing organisms. Table 22.2 lists other common indoor pollutants.

In 1988, the National Council on Radiation Protection and Measurements alerted homeowners to another indoor pollutant, radon gas. **Radon** (RAY-don) *is a colorless, odorless, radioactive gas.* Scientists think that at least half of an average person's yearly radiation exposure comes from radon. Radon forms when a natural, radioactive element called radium breaks down. As radon forms, it enters the soil and becomes a part of soil gases. Radon from soil is drawn into a home through the basement. Long-term exposure to high levels of radon is one cause of lung cancer.

SECTION REVIEW

1. What is a pollutant?
2. **Organic Data** Make a table that lists common outdoor air pollutants and their sources.
3. **Analyze** Suggest ways that you could reduce the amount of air pollutants in your home.

1. A pollutant is any harmful substance that enters the environment.
2. Tables should list all outdoor air pollutants covered in the text. Each pollutant should be matched with its source.
3. Answers will vary. Likely responses may include: eliminating the sources of pollutants, such as solvents, carpeting, and cigarettes; increasing circulation in the home; and using air filtration devices.

22.2 AIR POLLUTION AND LIVING THINGS

Objectives • *Identify the effects of air pollution on human health.*
• *Describe the effects of air pollution on plants and animals.*

Air pollution has been linked to many health problems. Long-term exposure may cause diseases and chronic health problems. Pollutants may also worsen existing medical conditions, especially in children and the elderly.

Carbon monoxide is a dangerous air pollutant. One characteristic of this gas is that it readily binds with hemoglobin in the blood. Hemoglobin is the substance in red blood cells that carries oxygen. Carbon monoxide actually binds to hemoglobin more easily than oxygen does. If carbon monoxide binds to a hemoglobin molecule, the hemoglobin can no longer carry oxygen. The amount of oxygen carried to all the cells of the body is reduced. High concentrations of carbon monoxide stress the heart and can cause headaches, dizziness, and even death.

Ozone and oxides of sulfur and nitrogen can also cause health problems. These gases irritate the eyes and respiratory tract. They cause discomfort and difficulty in breathing. They also may trigger asthma or allergy attacks. Long-term exposure to ozone and oxides can also cause more serious diseases such as bronchitis and emphysema. **Emphysema** (EM-fuh-ZEE-muh) *is a disease in which tiny air sacs in the lungs break down.* More than 1.5 million people suffer from emphysema in the United States. Emphysema is often caused by cigarette smoking.

Particulates in the air have been linked to cancer. **Cancer** *is a disease in which cells grow abnormally and without restraint.* Some forms of cancer are very difficult to treat and can be fatal. Lung cancer is responsible for more than over 100,000 deaths each year in the United States. Most of these lung cancers are caused by cigarette smoking. Cigarette smoke also causes other diseases, such as heart disease.

HEALTH
L I N K

The number one cause of death in the United States is heart disease. Heart disease is responsible for about 750,000 deaths annually. Most scientists agree that the leading cause of heart disease is cigarette smoking.

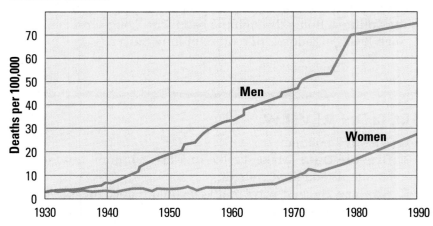

Figure 22.2 This graph shows the increase in the rate of lung cancer deaths since 1930. Cigarette smoking is almost the sole cause of this increase.

Air pollution also affects plants and animals. Ozone and the sulfur oxides are the pollutants most hazardous to plants. These chemicals damage plants directly, causing stems to become brittle and leaves to become spotted. Millions of ponderosa pines have been severely damaged by ozone pollution in the mountains around Los Angeles. Ozone and sulfur oxides damage agricultural crops as well. The United States loses up to $10 billion worth of crops each year because of air pollution.

Animals are also affected by air pollution. The loss of plants in an ecosystem due to pollution can disrupt the ecosystem's food chains and deprive animals of nourishment. Animals also suffer from many of the same pollution-related health problems as humans, including eye and lung irritation, bronchitis, and cancer.

Industrial air pollutants such as lead and zinc can contaminate rangeland. These poisons accumulate on grass and may enter the groundwater. Grazing animals such as cattle and sheep can take in large amounts of these pollutants as they feed and drink. The bones and teeth of these animals become weak. Lameness and weight loss often lead to death in severely poisoned animals.

SECTION REVIEW

1. What is emphysema? What causes this disease? How many people suffer from it?
2. **Organize Data** Make a table that lists air pollutants and the health problems each pollutant causes.
3. **Predict** List the diseases that cigarette smoking causes. How do you think industrial pollution would affect a person who smokes?

1. Emphysema is a lung disease caused by cigarette smoke and other air pollutants. Over 1.5 million people suffer from emphysema.
2. Tables should list all air pollutants covered in the text and the health problems associated with each one.

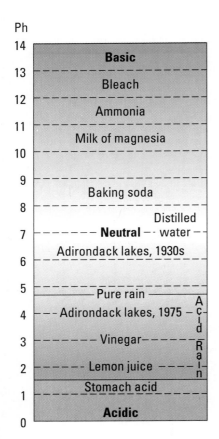

Figure 22.4 This scale shows the pH of many common substances and of acid rain. Notice the large drop in the pH of Adirondack mountain lakes.

Teaching tips for Field Activity appear on page T114.

Teaching tips for Field Activity appear on page T114.

FIELD ACTIVITY

Rain is naturally slightly acidic, but polluted air can increase the acidity dramatically. On a rainy day, uncover Petri dishes at various locations around your school or community. Let rain fall directly into the Petri dishes. Transfer the rain to vials if you won't be returning to class immediately. Record the location where each sample was taken. In class, test the pH of the rain samples. Distilled water has a pH of 7.0. It is neutral. Normal rain has a pH of 5.6. How do your rain samples compare?

22.3 GLOBAL EFFECTS OF AIR POLLUTION

Objectives • *Identify* the effects of acid precipitation and ozone depletion. • *Explain* the greenhouse effect and global warming.

Pollutants harm living things directly. They can also cause far-reaching damage to the global environment. Some forms of pollution can threaten whole ecosystems. Pollution may even change the climate across the entire planet. Three major air pollution problems threatening the global environment are acid precipitation, ozone depletion, and global warming.

Acid Precipitation

Rain or snow that is more acidic than normal precipitation is called **acid precipitation**. Acidity is measured on a scale called the pH scale. A pH of 7 is neutral. A pH less than 7 is acidic, and a pH greater than 7 is basic. Figure 22.4 shows the pH of some common liquids, acid rain, and lakes affected by acid rain.

Normal rain and snow are slightly acidic and have a pH of about 5.6. Water in the atmosphere becomes acidic when it reacts with carbon dioxide, forming a weak acid called carbonic acid. However, water can also form much stronger acids when it reacts with other pollutants in the air. Recall that burning fossil fuels such as coal and gasoline produce oxides of sulfur and nitrogen. Sulfur and nitrogen oxides combine with water in the atmosphere, forming sulfuric acid and nitric acid. Both of these acids are strong, highly corrosive, and can be harmful to living things.

Sulfuric and nitric acids can fall to Earth with rain or snow or even on their own. Much of the acid falls into forests such as those in the Adirondack Mountains in New York. The acids accumulate in mountain lakes, lowering the lakes' pH. In Sweden, for example, 20,000 lakes are too acidic to allow fish to survive. Thousands of other lakes in Norway, Canada, and the northeastern United States are so acidic that they contain no fish or plant life. The absence of producers and other aquatic life disrupts food chains and causes the lake ecosystem to collapse. Some scientists project that half of Quebec's 48,000 lakes will be destroyed by the year 2000.

Acid precipitation also damages trees. In former West Germany, more than 500 000 hectares of forest are dying from the caustic effects of acid rain. Forests are dying across Europe and in the United States and Canada. Acid rain also damages crops and buildings. Although it is impossible to put a dollar value on the destruction of entire lake and forest ecosystems, the economic cost of acid rain is estimated to be more than $5 billion a year in the United States alone.

Assault on the Past

How is acid rain erasing history?

Acid rain, sulfur dioxide, and nitrogen oxides are eroding many works of ancient art and architecture. Acid decomposition is rapidly disintegrating the Parthenon in Athens, Greece; the Colosseum in Rome, Italy; the Taj Mahal near Agra, India; Cleopatra's Needle in New York City; and many other historic monuments and statues around the world.

A striking example of acid decomposition is Cleopatra's Needle, an Egyptian granite tower, or obelisk. The obelisk was carved in Egypt about 1500 B.C. For almost 35 centuries, the monument stood almost unchanged in Egypt. The surface inscriptions remained clear and readable. In 1881, the obelisk was brought to New York City as a gift to the United States. Only a few years after it arrived in the heavily polluted city, it began flaking. Now, a century later, the inscriptions have almost disappeared.

Fossil-fuel combustion is the source of the pollution that is eating away these ancient treasures. The burning of fossil fuels releases sulfur dioxide and nitrogen oxide into the atmosphere. The amounts of these two pollutants released into the air are ten times greater now than before industrialization. Acids formed from oxides of nitrogen and sulfur are very corrosive. These acids break down stone easily.

Limestone and marble are two types of stone widely used in ancient buildings and statues. These materials contain calcium carbonate. When acid rain falls on structures made from these materials, the calcium carbonate changes into gypsum. Gypsum dissolves in water, so it is easily washed away. At the Temple of the Dioscuri in Rome, a light rubbing with a finger removes the white gypsum powder from the surface of the marble blocks.

Statues sheltered from acid rain may also suffer major damage. Dry deposits of sulfur dioxide collect on the surface. Condensation on the surface forms a gypsum crust. This crust falls off in layers or chunks, exposing the stone beneath.

Several attempts to preserve the ailing relics from the past are being made. One approach is to replace statues with plastic models, and move the originals into a museum. Michaelangelo's *David* in Florence was replaced with a plastic copy. The draped maidens, or caryatids, that support the Acropolis in Athens are also plastic copies. The original marble statues are preserved safely in a museum.

But many monuments are too large to copy and store. Archaeologists are trying to clean

them up, and they are studying ways to treat many of the larger structures. They hope to develop methods to slow down the destructive acid corrosion.

DECISIONS

1. List and discuss each of the ways that acid decomposition may destroy stone.
2. Infer why the protection of ancient statues and buildings is important to future generations.

Ozone Depletion

At the surface of Earth, ozone is a corrosive, poisonous gas. But a layer of ozone 20 to 50 km above Earth's surface is vital to life. Ozone in the stratosphere forms a protective layer around Earth. This ozone layer absorbs almost all of the ultraviolet (UV) radiation given off by the sun, preventing it from reaching Earth's surface. UV radiation is very damaging to living things.

Hole in the Sky During the early 1980s, scientists discovered a thin area, or hole, in the ozone layer over the South Pole. Scientists have since found a small but growing hole over the North Pole. Some scientists claimed that holes in the ozone layer are normal and that more holes may exist. Other scientists thought that the ozone holes were early signs of a dangerous problem. Recent data, however, have quieted much of the debate. Most scientists now agree that the problem of ozone depletion is serious. The air over the South Pole now loses half its ozone every spring, and the global ozone layer has thinned by 2 to 3 percent in the last ten years.

Damage to the ozone layer could greatly increase the amount of UV radiation that reaches Earth. In humans, UV radiation can cause sunburn, blindness, and skin cancer. UV radiation can also cause severe crop damage. UV radiation could destroy the microorganisms that form the base of the aquatic food chain, disrupting the ocean ecosystem. Damage to land organisms would be equally severe.

Causes of Ozone Depletion The main cause of ozone depletion is CFC pollution. Recall that CFCs are a kind of hydrocarbon in which atoms of chlorine and fluorine are attached to carbon atoms in place of hydrogen. CFCs, also called freons, have been used as coolants in refrigerators since the 1930s. CFCs were used as coolants in air-conditioning units and as propellants in aerosol sprays beginning in the 1950s. CFCs were also used in the manufacture of styrofoam and other plastic foams.

Figure 22.5 Air conditioners are a major source of CFCs.

Figure 22.6 These satellite data show the South Pole ozone hole since 1979. The hole is growing, and a similar hole has formed over the North Pole.

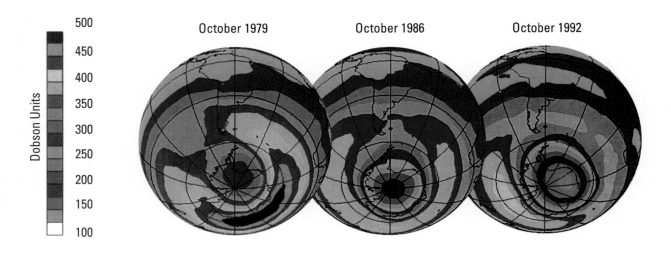

Dobson Units

500
450
400
350
300
250
200
150
100

October 1979   October 1986   October 1992

In the lower atmosphere, CFCs do not react with other compounds; they are *inert*. Because they are inert, they do not break down. They circulate in the atmosphere and eventually rise into the stratosphere. In the stratosphere, CFCs are exposed to UV radiation. UV radiation causes the CFCs to break down, releasing chlorine and fluorine atoms. Both of these kinds of atoms destroy ozone. The chemical reactions in Figure 22.7 show how chlorine is produced and how it destroys ozone.

Word Power

Inert, from the Latin *iners*, "without skill or art; idle."

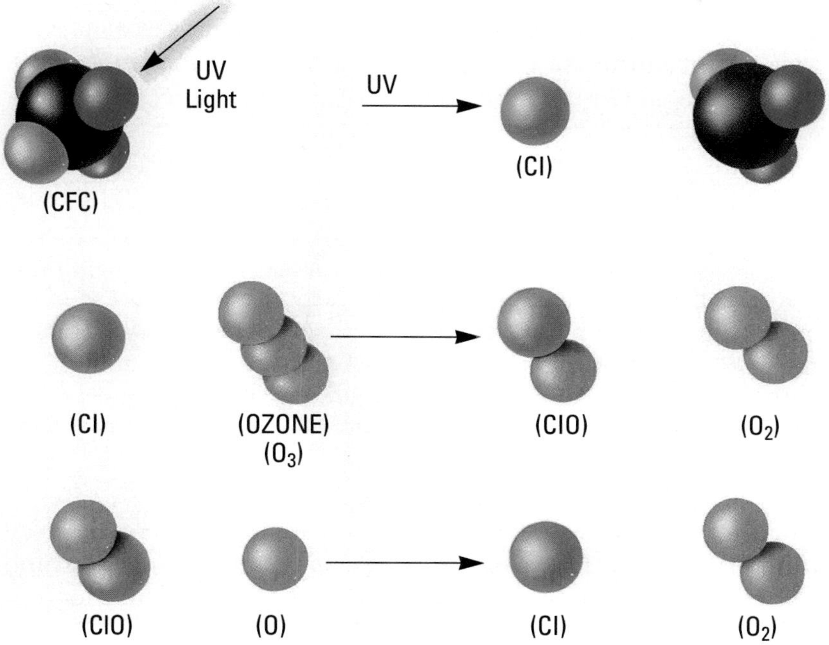

Figure 22.7 These reactions show how chlorine is produced from a CFC by UV radiation, and how the chlorine destroys ozone. Notice that the chlorine atom is regenerated.

Atoms of chlorine and fluorine act as catalysts in the destruction of ozone. Chlorine and fluorine are regenerated easily from chlorine oxide (ClO) and fluorine oxide (FO). The atoms are then free to destroy more ozone. Scientists think that every atom of chlorine or fluorine can destroy thousands of molecules of ozone.

Because CFCs are inert, they stay in the atmosphere for a long time, most of them for several thousand years. Some CFCs may last more than 50,000 years. These long lifetimes mean that most CFC pollution will eventually make it to the stratosphere—and ultimately destroy ozone.

Chlorine atoms are produced by many natural sources. Volcanoes emit large amounts of chlorine into the atmosphere, as do the oceans. Critics of the link between CFCs and ozone depletion have used this fact to argue that human-produced chlorine does not affect the ozone layer. But evidence from long-term experiments in the Swiss Alps has shown that natural sources contribute very little chlorine to the stratosphere. These experiments show that the major source of stratospheric chlorine and fluorine is CFCs produced by people.

THINK CRITICALLY

A catalyst is an atom or molecule that helps a chemical reaction take place. The catalyst is not consumed in the reaction. Explain how chlorine acts as a catalyst in the breakdown of ozone.

Chlorine acts as a catalyst because it takes part in the destruction of ozone and is then regenerated.

DATELINE 1978

In 1978, the United States banned the use of CFCs in many products, such as aerosol spray cans. Denmark, Sweden, Norway, and Canada also banned the use of CFCs. In 1987, 24 nations agreed to reduce the use of CFCs by 50 percent by the end of this century. In 1989, this plan was changed in response to growing evidence that the ozone depletion problem was more serious than first thought. Nations belonging to the United Nations have agreed that CFCs will no longer be used by the year 2000.

Global Warming

Light energy from the sun enters the atmosphere and is absorbed by Earth's surface. Once absorbed, the light energy is changed to heat. Earth radiates this heat energy back into space in the form of infrared radiation.

The Greenhouse Effect Earth's atmosphere acts much like a pane of glass. It allows light energy to enter, but traps some infrared radiation. The buildup of heat energy warms the air in the lower atmosphere. *The trapping of radiated heat by gases in the atmosphere is called the* **greenhouse effect.** Earth's greenhouse effect raises the average global temperature about 35°C. Without the greenhouse effect, life on Earth would probably be impossible.

Some atmospheric gases trap infrared radiation. The atmospheric gases that trap heat are called *greenhouse gases*. The most important natural greenhouse gas is carbon dioxide. Methane, oxides of sulfur and nitrogen, ozone, CFCs, and water vapor are also greenhouse gases. Compared to carbon dioxide, these gases exist in the atmosphere in small amounts. However, they trap heat much better than carbon dioxide does. Methane traps heat 20 times better than CO_2, while nitrogen dioxide (NO_2) is 200 times more efficient. What do you think would happen if the amount of greenhouse gases in the atmosphere increased?

The amounts of carbon dioxide and other greenhouse gases in the atmosphere are rising because of the pollution caused by human activities. The main cause of this pollution is the burning of fossil fuels and other organic compounds. Look at the chemical

Students may suggest that if the amount of greenhouse gases in the atmosphere increased, global temperature would rise.

Figure 22.8 The greenhouse effect is a natural occurrence, although pollution caused by people can make the greenhouse effect stronger.

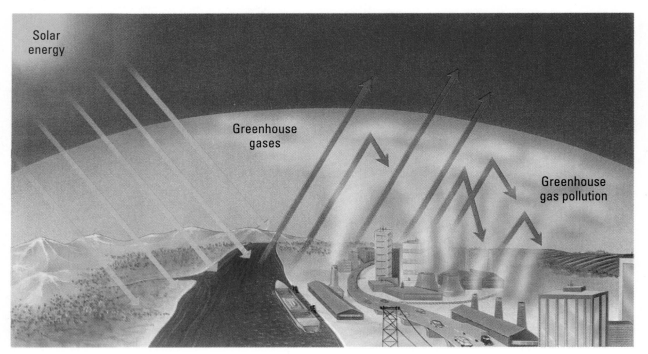

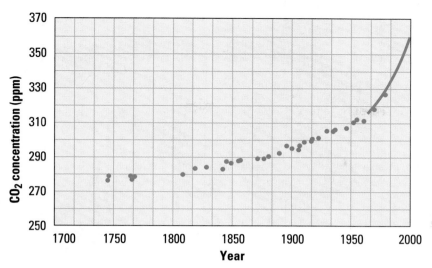

Figure 22.9 This graph shows the increase in CO_2 concentration in the atmosphere since 1750. The dots are ice core data. The solid line is a series of direct measurements.

reaction for the burning of a simple hydrocarbon called octane. Octane is a part of gasoline. Notice that CO_2 is produced:

$$2\ C_8H_{18} + 25\ O_2 \longrightarrow 16\ CO_2 + 18\ H_2O + \text{Energy}$$

Before 1750, the amount of carbon dioxide in the atmosphere was about 280 parts per million (ppm). Today, carbon dioxide levels are about 355 ppm and rising—an increase of over 21 percent. Figure 22.9 shows the increase in CO_2 levels during the last several hundred years.

The data for the graph in Figure 22.9 come from **ice cores**, *long cylinders of ice that are drilled and removed from deep within a sheet of polar ice.* The ice in these cores is filled with small bubbles, which are filled with air. The air has been locked in the bubbles for hundreds or even thousands of years. Scientists collect the air and test it for levels of greenhouse gases.

Figure 22.10 Ice cores like this one are used to study climate as it existed in the past.

Effects of Greenhouse Gas Pollution No one knows for certain what effect greenhouse gases will have on Earth's climate. But most scientists agree that they will have some impact. One thing *is* sure: The potential dangers of greenhouse gas pollution have made global warming a serious political issue. The powerful fossil fuel industry and environmentalists continue to debate the issue.

Greenhouse gas pollution may result in global warming. **Global warming** *is an increase in Earth's average surface temperature caused by an increase in greenhouse gases.* Recall that ice cores can be used to gather samples of the atmosphere as it existed in the past. Scientists now have reliable records of Earth's atmosphere for the last 200,000 years. These records show that another large increase (25 to 30 percent) in atmospheric CO_2 occurred at the end of the last ice age, about 14,000 years ago.

Scientists think that the large CO_2 increase at the end of the last ice age played an important part in changing Earth's climate. Earth's

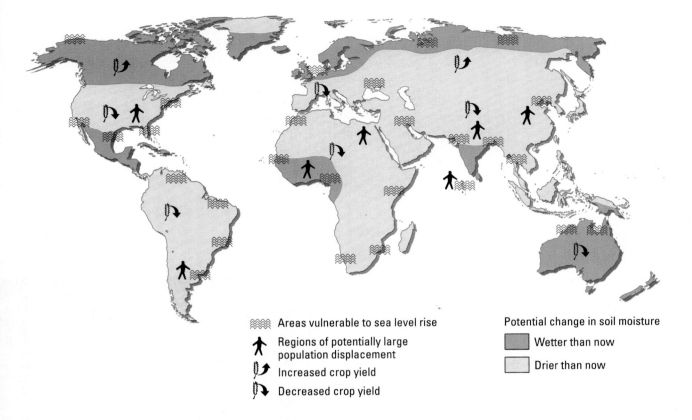

Areas vulnerable to sea level rise

Regions of potentially large population displacement

Increased crop yield

Decreased crop yield

Potential change in soil moisture

Wetter than now

Drier than now

Figure 22.11 If global warming occurs, it will greatly affect the world's climate. This map shows many of the effects global warming may have.

temperature rose by several degrees. Glaciers that covered much of North America melted, and sea levels rose. These climate changes were caused, at least in part, by increased amounts of CO_2 in the atmosphere.

Computer models predict the same kind of climate change in the future. Because of greenhouse gas pollution, computer models project that Earth's temperature will rise by 2°C to 4°C by the year 2050. This increase may not seem large, but it could have disastrous results, as shown in Figure 22.11.

As Earth's temperature rises, the water in the ocean will expand, and ice in the polar caps will begin to melt. The sea level will rise more than 1 m, flooding lowlands, farmland, and coastal cities like New York and Los Angeles. In many areas, salt water from the oceans will enter the groundwater system. In addition, weather patterns will change. How might these changes affect housing, agriculture, transportation, and food production?

1. CFCs are chlorofluorocarbons. They are compounds of chlorine, fluorine, hydrogen, and carbon. CFCs destroy ozone in the stratosphere.
2. Acid precipitation is rain or snow that is more acidic than natural precipitation. It destroys lake and forest ecosystems.
3. Answers will vary, but they should be based on the merits of the evidence presented in the text.

SECTION REVIEW

1. What are CFCs, and why are they harmful?
2. What is acid precipitation, and why is it harmful?
3. **Think Critically** Evaluate the evidence from ice cores and computer models. Do you think global warming will occur?

Answers and teaching
strategies on page T116.

Greenhouse Model

PROBLEM
What causes the greenhouse effect?

MATERIALS (per group)
Labels must be completely removed. Try scrubbing the bottles in warm soapy water.

- 2 2-L plastic soft drink bottles
- scissors
- tape
- 2 thermometers
- 750 g dry potting soil
- clear plastic wrap
- rubber band
- 100-watt light bulb
- ring stand
- graph paper

HYPOTHESIS
After reading the entire activity, write a hypothesis that pertains to the problem.

PROCEDURE
1. Completely remove the labels from two 2-L plastic soft drink bottles. *Note: use the figure to guide you through Steps 2–7.*
2. Using scissors, cut off the top of the bottles where they begin to narrow.
3. Tape the thermometers to the inside of the bottles.
4. Tape small squares of paper directly over the thermometer bulbs.
5. Put about 375 g of dry potting soil into each bottle.
6. Cover one of the bottles with clear plastic wrap. Secure the plastic wrap with a rubber band.
7. Hang a 100-watt light bulb from a ring stand, and position the bottles at equal distances on each side of it. Face the thermometers away from the light bulb. Do not turn the light on yet.
8. Read the thermometers, and record the temperatures. The thermometers should both show the same temperature. If they are different, you will have to add the difference to the thermometer showing the lower temperature.
9. Turn the light on for 25 minutes. Record the temperatures in the bottles every 5 minutes.

ANALYSIS
1. Make a graph of your data. Use a computer graphing program if one is available.
2. Compare how each bottle heated up over time. Explain your results.
3. What was the control of the experiment? The variable?
4. Identify four components of the experimental setup, and explain what parts of Earth each represents.

CONCLUSION
1. Did the results of the experiment support your hypothesis? Explain.
2. Would your results be affected if you used two pieces of plastic wrap instead of one? Test your answer by performing the experiment with two pieces of plastic wrap on one bottle.
3. In what other situations have you observed the greenhouse effect?

22.4 CONTROLLING AIR POLLUTION

Objectives • *Describe* natural processes that help control air pollution. • *Explain* human efforts to control air pollution. • *Identify* federal legislation for curbing air pollution.

Air pollution is a global problem. But government and industry in some nations are beginning to respond and work together to control and reduce air pollution. In addition, natural processes that are at work continue to remove some pollutants from the air.

Natural Air Pollution Controls

Precipitation, such as rain and snow, is the most effective natural method of removing particulates and aerosols from the air. As rain and snow fall, particles in the air stick to the precipitation and are carried to the ground. In addition, many aerosols dissolve in rain and snow. But removing a pollutant from the air often means putting it somewhere else.

Carbon dioxide is removed naturally from the atmosphere in two ways. One way is through biological activity. Plants and some protists remove CO_2 from the air and use it to make sugars and shells. If this organic material is buried, the carbon in it cannot reenter the atmosphere. This carbon from buried organic deposits is the source of fossil fuels.

The water in the ocean can also remove CO_2 from the atmosphere. But the ability of ocean water to hold CO_2 depends on its temperature. The ocean already holds a large amount of CO_2. If seawater temperatures rise because of global warming, the ocean might release even more CO_2, making the problem worse.

Human Air Pollution Controls

Automobiles are a major source of air pollution. Many state governments have set strict emission-control standards for cars and other vehicles. Most cars are equipped with catalytic converters, which remove many pollutants from the exhaust. Today's cars get better gas mileage than in the past and burn unleaded gasoline. But burning gasoline will always produce large amounts of CO_2 and other pollutants.

The only way to end pollution from automobiles is to stop using gasoline as a fuel. California has taken a legislative step in this direction. Beginning in the year 1998, a percentage of cars sold in California must produce zero emissions. This means that these cars must be fueled by electricity or clean fuels instead of gasoline.

Burning hydrogen produces only water, and electric cars produce no emissions. The Federal Government has enacted legisla-

Figure 22.12 This electric car does not burn gasoline and therefore produces no gaseous pollutants.

Table 22.3   Federal Air Pollution Legislation

Year	Legislation
1955	Air Pollution Control and Technical Assistance Act
1963	Clean Air Act
1965	Clean Air Act Amendments
1967	Air Quality Act
1976	Gasoline refineries required to reduce lead.
1977	Clean Air Act Amendments
1978	Use of CFCs banned in the United States.
1980	Acid Precipitation Act
1987	Montreal Protocol
1989	Amendment to Montreal Protocol

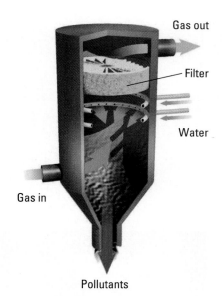

Figure 22.13 This device is called a scrubber. It uses water to remove pollutants from coal smoke. The polluted water still must be disposed of safely.

tion in response to growing concerns about the air pollution problem. Table 22.3 lists federal air pollution legislation since 1955.

Electric power plants that burn fossil fuels are another major source of air pollution. Coal plants use several different techniques to remove pollutants from the exhaust they produce. One device, called a scrubber, is shown in Figure 22.13. These techniques are fairly effective. The emission of most pollutants by coal plants has dropped during the last ten years. But the measures taken are expensive, and not all plants use them. There is also no way to stop the production of large amounts of carbon dioxide.

There is great debate surrounding legislation that requires factories to install and use pollution-control devices. Some people are against the use of such devices because they feel the economic costs are too high. The added costs of pollution control could cause businesses to fail, leading to job losses and financial hardship. Other people think that the importance of protecting and improving air quality outweighs the economic cost of pollution control. Some of these people also argue that the jobs created by pollution control offset those that would be lost.

SECTION REVIEW

1. How have cars been changed to reduce the amount of pollution they produce?
2. Is there any way to produce energy without producing carbon dioxide? Make a list of carbon dioxide-free energy sources. You may wish to refer to Chapter 17, Solar and Alternative Energies.
3. **Analyze** What things can you do as an individual to help reduce air pollution?

1. Answers will vary. Likely responses may include not smoking or not permitting smoking in their personal environments (car, home, etc.); keeping their automobile in good operating condition to reduce the amount of pollutants produced from inefficient burning of fuels; reducing temperatures in the home during cold months to use less fuel; and car pooling or using mass transit instead of adding to the number of cars on the road. Accept all logical suggestions. This is an excellent topic for class discussion.
2. Cars have become smaller and more energy-efficient. They also burn unleaded gasoline and have catalytic converters.
3. Lists may include solar, nuclear, geothermal, tidal, hydroelectric, and wind energy, as well as the burning of pure hydrogen.

22.5 NOISE POLLUTION

Objectives • *Describe* the problem of noise pollution.
• *Explain* measures and legislation for controlling noise pollution.

Although noise is not a particle or a gas, it can be a form of pollution. Loud or high-pitched sounds can harm living things. Noise pollution can cause annoyance, stress, and even hearing damage. Noise pollution can come from airplanes, machines, and even loud concerts.

The unit used to measure sound intensity is the decibel (dB). The softest sounds you can hear are rated at 0 dB. Sounds rated at about 70 to 80 dB are annoying and can lead to hearing loss. Sounds louder than 120 to130 dB can cause physical pain and serious hearing damage.

Besides hearing loss, loud or persistent noise can cause other health problems. Over periods of time, noise can lead to stress and anxiety. Stress can produce harmful changes within the body. Chronic stress causes many health problems. Some of these are constricted blood vessels, vision problems, digestive disorders, and increased blood pressure and heart rate. Doctors have recently discovered that constant noise may also lead to emotional and psychological problems.

Figure 22.14 Rock concerts can be as loud as 120 dB. This sound level is equivalent to the sound of a jet airplane taking off about 65 m away from you.

In 1972, Congress passed the Noise Control Act. This legislation directed the Environmental Protection Agency (EPA) to set standards for maximum noise levels. Industries have also attempted to reduce sources and levels of noise pollution in the workplace. Legislation at the state and local levels has also been enacted to reduce noise pollution.

In addition to legislation, individuals are now encouraged to protect themselves from the effects of noise. People should limit the amount of time they spend in noisy areas, and not listen to music too loudly. People who must work around loud noise should wear earplugs or specially designed earmuffs to reduce the amount of exposure. What other ways can you suggest to reduce or control noise pollution and its effects?

Answers will vary, but should concern avoiding loud, constant noise and wearing protective equipment when necessary.

1. Noise pollution is loud or constant noise in the environment.
2. Answers will vary but will likely include these: by causing hearing problems and by causing stress that brings about a rise in blood pressure or heart rate. Accept all logical responses.
3. Answers will vary but should reflect the idea that such noises could interfere with the ability of a hospitalized patient to rest and relax.

SECTION REVIEW

1. What is noise pollution?
2. What are some ways that long-term exposure to noise can affect people?
3. **Analyze** Why might signs prohibiting the honking of car horns be posted on roads surrounding hospitals?

CHAPTER 22 REVIEW

KEY TERMS

pollutant 22.1	photochemical	radon 22.1	greenhouse effect 22.3
particulate 22.1	smog 22.1	emphysema 22.2	ice core 22.3
oxide 22.1	chlorofluorocarbons	cancer 22.2	global warming 22.3
	(CFCs) 22.1	acid precipitation 22.3	

CHAPTER SUMMARY

22.1 Pollutants are harmful substances that enter the environment. Air pollution may be made of particulates or gases, usually oxides. Air pollution can be present outdoors, such as photochemical smog, or indoors, such as cigarette smoke and radon.

22.2 Air pollution can affect human health and the health of plants and animals. Human health problems range from eye and respiratory tract irritations to emphysema and lung cancer. Air pollution can also damage crops and be passed from contaminated food and water to grazing animals.

22.3 Air pollution can have global as well as local effects. Acid precipitation is rain or snow with a very low pH, resulting from oxides combining with water in the air. Ozone depletion results from the breakdown of ozone molecules in the stratosphere by CFCs. The greenhouse effect, caused by gases such as carbon dioxide in the atmosphere, could lead to global warming.

22.4 Some air pollutants are removed by natural processes such as precipitation and biological activity. Air pollution can be reduced in part by controlling automobile emissions. Some types of legislation to reduce air pollution could cause economic hardship.for certain industries.

22.5 Noise can be considered a type of pollution. Loud or persistent noise can cause stress, hearing loss, and other health problems. The federal government sets limits on allowable noise levels.

MULTIPLE CHOICE

Choose the letter of the word or phrase that best completes each statement.

1. The gas that is most abundant in the air is (a) oxygen; (b) nitrogen; (c) carbon dioxide; (d) argon. b

2. Air pollution first became a widespread problem (a) 100,000 years ago; (b) during the thirteenth century; (c) during the 1700s; (d) about 100 years ago. c

3. Photochemical smog results from automobile pollutants reacting with (a) ozone; (b) carbon dioxide; (c) acid rain; (d) sunlight. d

4. The greatest source of indoor air pollution is (a) smog; (b) radon; (c) cigarette smoke; (d) insulation. c

5. A pollutant that can reduce the amount of oxygen carried by blood is (a) carbon monoxide; (b) carbon dioxide; (c) ozone; (d) sulfur dioxide. a

6. Normal rain has a pH of about (a) 4.0; (b) 5.6; (c) 7.0; (d) 8.4. b

7. Acid rain is mostly a problem (a) in the eastern United States; (b) in Europe; (c) in Asia; (d) throughout the Northern Hemisphere. d

8. The ozone layer absorbs (a) CFCs; (b) ultraviolet light; (c) photochemical smog; (d) chlorine molecules. b

9. Greenhouse gases trap (a) UV radiation; (b) visible spectrum radiation; (c) infrared radiation; (d) carbon dioxide. c

10. Sounds can cause physical pain if they are louder than (a) 10 dB; (b) 50 dB; (c) 80 dB; (d) 120 dB. d

CHAPTER 22 REVIEW

TRUE/FALSE.

Write true *if the statement is true. If the statement is false, change the underlined word or phrase to make it true.*

1. Ash, dust, and liquid droplets in the air are <u>particulates</u>. t
2. All oxides contain <u>carbon</u>. f, oxygen
3. A radioactive type of indoor air pollution is <u>ozone</u>. f, radon
4. Lung cancer is a <u>more</u> common cause of death in the United States than heart disease. f, less
5. Industrial pollutants that contaminate rangeland include <u>heavy</u> metals. t
6. Acid rain can result from the burning of <u>fossil fuels</u>. t
7. Nations belonging to the United Nations have agreed to ban CFCs completely by the year <u>2010</u>. f, 2000
8. The softest sounds that you can hear are rated at <u>0 dB</u>. t

CONCEPT REVIEW   Answers on page T114.

Write a complete response for each of the following.

1. Explain why air pollution is a global problem.
2. How can ice cores be used to analyze changes in air quality?
3. How can the use of gasoline in automobiles cause a decrease in the number of fish in a lake hundreds of miles away?
4. Name two causes of emphysema. Which cause is more easily avoided?
5. Why can one molecule of CFC destroy many molecules of ozone?

THINK CRITICALLY   Answers on page T114.

1. UV light causes the skin to become darker in most people. Why can sun-tanning be a dangerous activity?
2. Why do some people resist government limits on the release of air pollutants?
3. Ozone can be harmful to life, or it can be a protector of life, depending on its location in the atmosphere. Explain why this is true.
4. Compared to the United States, Canada is less industrialized. Why do you think acid precipitation is more serious in Quebec than in most of the United States?

Computer Activity Suppose that the ozone layer contains 1 million molecules of ozone, and that 50 atoms of chlorine are added to it. Each atom catalyzes the destruction of 1000 ozone molecules each day for five days. Use a computer to calculate the amount of ozone remaining after each day. Using a graphing program, display your results.

WRITE CREATIVELY

If the ozone layer was severely damaged, it would affect the way people live. Write a short story that takes place in a future time when the ozone layer has lost its ability to absorb UV radiation.

PORTFOLIO

1. Collect newspaper and magazine articles from the past ten years about the ozone layer, and compare the information in the older articles to more recent ones. What new information has come to light? How has public opinion changed?
2. How can electricity be used to fuel cars? Research the basic design of electric cars, and prepare a video or audio presentation comparing electric cars to gasoline-fueled cars.

GRAPHIC ANALYSIS Answers on page T114.

1. According to the graph, what was the concentration of CO_2 in the atmosphere in 1850? In 1950?
2. What is the percent change of CO_2 concentration between the two years?
3. How was the data obtained?

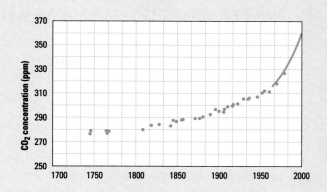

ACTIVITY 22.2

Answers and teaching strategies on page T114.

PROBLEM
How do the number and types of air particulates differ in areas around your school?

MATERIALS (per group)
• masking tape
• 5 microscope slides
• petroleum jelly
• 5 Petri dishes with lids
• binocular microscope or hand lens

HYPOTHESIS
Write a hypothesis that pertains to the problem.

PROCEDURE
1. Make five separate particulate collectors by writing your group name on masking tape labels, and sticking the labels to an end of each slide. Identify one as the *Control*.
2. Smear the center of each slide with a thin layer of petroleum jelly.
3. Place each particulate collector in the bottom half of a Petri dish. Cover the dishes with lids immediately.
4. Remove the particulate collectors from their Petri dishes, and leave them exposed to the air at four locations where particulate levels may differ.

5. Write the locations on the appropriate labels.
6. Keep the control in your classroom, and do not remove it from its covered Petri dish.
7. Retrieve the particulate collectors anywhere between 25 minutes and five days later. Put them in covered Petri dishes.
8. Examine the slides, including your control, with a microscope set at low power or a hand lens. Move the slides around and count the number of particulates that fell on each one. Record these numbers.

ANALYSIS
1. What was the purpose of the control?
2. Identify five particulates that landed in your particulate collectors. Which of these would you classify as pollutants? Explain.
3. Describe the locations you chose. Which location showed the greatest number of air particulates? The least?

CONCLUSION
1. Did the results of your experiment support your hypothesis? Explain.
2. List the possible sources of error in your experiment.

WATER-QUALITY MANAGEMENT

Water-quality management is one of the fastest-growing fields in environmental science today. Those in the field are concerned with monitoring the levels of toxins in water supplies; recognizing the links between air, land, and water pollution; preventing pollutants from reaching groundwater supplies; protecting and sustaining the wetlands; and improving waste-water treatment facilities.

Water-quality management has a wide range of applications. Whether you want to be a scientist, policy maker, planner, engineer, manager, or lawyer, there is a place in water quality management for people with all these skills.

Since 1972 and the passage of the Clean Water Act, the federal government has played an important role in monitoring water quality nationwide. The government has provided financial assistance for the construction of water-treatment plants and mandated that those who dump wastewater into the waterways acquire permits. These permits are issued through the National Pollution Discharge Elimination System (NPDES). The NPDES has created an abundance of job opportunities in water-quality management.

Five areas of employment exist in the water-quality management field:
- Monitoring the supply and quality of drinking water.
- Detecting groundwater toxins and planning corrective action.
- Locating surface water contaminants, such as those in ponds,lakes, streams, and rivers, and attempting to eradicate them.
- Designing and managing waste-water treatment plants. This area employs the greatest number of water-quality professionals.
- Monitoring and protecting wetland areas, in order to preserve these valuable aquatic habitats.

About 45 percent of those in the field are in the public sector, and most of these employees work at the state and local levels. Approximately 50 percent of those in water-quality management work in the private sector as consultants or for companies that install their own water-treatment facilities. The remaining 5 percent are in the nonprofit sector, where many foundations are concerned with legislation that preserves water sources and habitats.

There are positions for people with a two-year degree as water-quality technicians. Those who want to go further and study the impact of certain pollutants on the environment need a bachelor's degree in toxicology, mathematics, organic chemistry, risk assessment, or environmental engineering. The demand for groundwater scientists is growing rapidly. Those with degrees or advanced studies in hydrology, groundwater engineering, biology, and inorganic chemistry will have an easier time getting a job, especially with an extensive background of lab and fieldwork classes.

People currently in the business of water-quality management suggest that students stay current with technology and enhance their knowledge of computer systems as much as possible. They also emphasize the importance of internship programs.

BIOLOGISTS ▶

These scientists study water sources to determine the kinds and amounts of pollution present in a particular area. After they have found the pollutants, they determine the short-term and long-term damage to species that depend on the water supply.

◀ WATER-QUALITY TECHNICIANS

Water-quality technicians work in private or public water-treatment facilities. They collect samples in the field and analyze data in the laboratory. Some water-quality technicians operate complicated machinery, while others are in managerial positions.

HYDROGEOLOGISTS ▶

These people monitor the quantity and quality of groundwater in an area. They develop computer models of groundwater flow and determine whether the groundwater supply has been contaminated. If it has been, they will find the source of the contamination. Hydrogeologists also study groundwater supplies, helping to determine if aquifers are overdrawn.

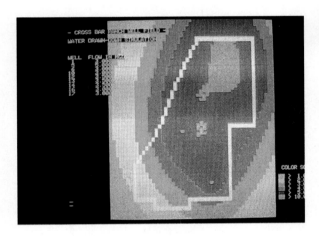

INFORMATION SYSTEMS SPECIALISTS ▲

These people blend a science background with strong computer abilities. They input and analyze data, devise programs that estimate damage in a polluted area or project water quality in the future, and help find solutions for water sources that have been polluted.

FOR MORE INFORMATION:

American Water Resources
(Publishes *Water Resources Bulletin* bimonthly, plus an annual directory)
5410 Grosvenor Lane, Suite 220
Bethesda, MD 20814
(301) 897–8720

National Ground Water Association (Publishes *Water Well Journal* and *The Well Log* monthly; also runs Job Mart, a job-placement service)
6375 Riverside Drive
Dublin, OH 43017
(614) 761–1711

The Center for the Great Lakes
(Publishes *The Great Lakes Directory of Natural Resource Agencies and Organizations*)
35 East Wacker Drive, Suite 1870
Chicago, IL 60601

UNIT 7

MANAGING HUMAN IMPACT

CHAPTERS

एह This symbol means *to protect*. It comes from the ancient language of Sanskrit, first spoken by people in northern India. Elephants have shared the lands of India with humans for thousands of years. Today, elephants and other animals from this area are some of the most endangered on Earth. The protection of species like these is an important step in building a society that is sensitive to the environment. Conserving energy and resources, and recycling waste will also help to make human society more sustainable.

Earth has a limited amount of living space and resources. The growth of the human population leaves fewer resources for other organisms. You can do many things to help protect the remaining ecosystems of our planet. ▶

378

Do the names *Stegosaurus*, *Triceratops*, and *Tyrannosaurus rex* sound familiar? These dinosaurs and many others roamed Earth millions of years ago. All that remains of these dinosaurs are fossils. The dinosaurs were well adapted to their environment. Yet 66 million years ago, the last dinosaurs died.

Today, the lowland gorillas, several species of whale, and countless plants and other organisms are threatened with extinction. Humans are causing the current extinctions. Human activity is destroying many of Earth's habitats. As habitats disappear, the organisms adapted to those habitats also disappear.

23.1 THE LOSS OF BIODIVERSITY

Objectives • *Discuss extinction and how it occurs.* • *Explain habitat destruction and the loss of biodiversity, and how they are related.*

Every organism is adapted to live in a certain habitat. If a habitat is altered or destroyed, the organisms adapted to that habitat must either find a new habitat or die. If a species is generalized, it may be able to occupy another niche. Specialized species almost always die with their habitats. *The disappearance of a species from all or part of the species' geographical range is called* **extinction**.

When the last population of a species dies, some species diversity of the ecosystem is lost. *Recall from Chapter 3 that the variety of species in an ecosystem is known as* **biodiversity**. Because the extinction of a species affects factors such as the flow of energy and matter and the habitats of other organisms, a loss in biodiversity upsets the balance, health, and stability of an ecosystem.

Extinction

Extinctions are a natural part of ecosystem function. All ecosystems change, and species must evolve to keep pace with these changes. Sometimes a species fails to adapt, and it becomes extinct. Other species evolve to fill the empty niche left by the extinct species. Niches can also appear or disappear as the ecosystem changes. Extinction and evolution create a natural cycle in the appearance and disappearance of species.

The rates of species extinction and species appearance are not constant. More than 99 percent of the species that have lived on Earth are extinct today. Figure 23.1 shows the rate of extinction and appearance of animal species since the Cambrian period. Relatively short periods of time in which many species die are called *mass extinctions*.

BIOLOGY
L I N K

Look at the graph in Figure 23.1. You may notice that periods of mass extinction are followed by periods of rapid species evolution. These periods of fast evolution are called *adaptive radiations*. The largest adaptive radiation on the graph occurs at the start of the Cambrian period. In this radiation, almost all the major groups of animals evolved in just a few million years. This event is called the Cambrian explosion. You can read more about the Cambrian explosion in the book *Wonderful Life* by Stephen Jay Gould.

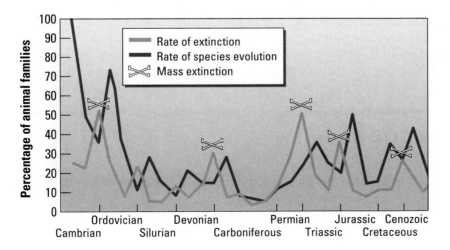

Figure 23.1 The rate of extinction and evolution of animal species has changed over time. Mass extinctions are followed by a high rate of species evolution. This graph covers about 600 million years.

Earth is currently experiencing another mass extinction. This extinction does not follow the pattern of previous extinctions. The activities of one species—humans—are causing the extinction of hundreds or even thousands of other species each year. The number and kind of extinctions occurring today are not natural. The rate of extinction may be the fastest ever. Entire ecosystems are being destroyed instead of just a few species.

Loss of Habitat

Extinctions and the resulting loss of biodiversity often occur when humans destroy the habitat of organisms. *Disturbing the part of an ecosystem that an organism needs to survive is called* **habitat destruction**. Cutting down all the trees in a forest is one form of habitat destruction.

Land development is another form of habitat destruction. Draining swamps for housing complexes, and altering wetlands for use as resorts, marinas, and farmlands, destroy fragile wetland habitats. Changing the course of rivers, through the use of dams that control water flow, can destroy aquatic habitats. Some mining and quarrying practices, overgrazing, and even recreation activities can drive native species away from a habitat.

Native species can also be threatened by other species that are introduced by humans. *Nonnative species introduced to an area by humans are called* **alien species**. The water hyacinth, for example, is an ornamental water plant that was brought into Florida from South America. The plant has invaded about 800 000 hectares of rivers and lakes stretching across the country to California. In many ecosystems, the water hyacinth has "outcompeted" other plants for the resources in the ecosystem. The result has been the disappearance of the native plants and a loss of biodiversity.

Human activity is destroying or altering habitats in all biomes. The rate of biodiversity loss increases every day. Many of the activities that destroy habitat result from people looking for places to live and food to eat. As the human population grows, Earth will continue to lose biodiversity as people alter more habitats. The biosphere has a limited amount of space. As the number of humans increases, the amount of space available to other organisms declines.

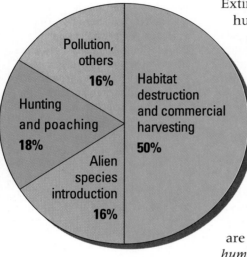

Figure 23.2 Many human activities contribute to the extinction of species. The most serious factor is deforestation and other types of habitat destruction.

1. Extinction is the disappearance of a species from all or part of its geographical range.
2. The current mass extinction has a direct cause, is occurring much more quickly, and involves whole ecosystems instead of groups of species.
3. Concept maps should demonstrate that habitat destruction leads to an increase in the rate of extinction. The increased rate of extinction leads to a loss of biodiversity.

SECTION REVIEW

1. What is extinction?
2. In what ways is the current mass extinction different from those that have come before?
3. **Relate** Prepare a concept map showing the relationship between extinction, biodiversity, and habitat destruction.

23.2 HUMANS AND HABITATS

Objectives • ***Explain*** *the causes of deforestation and its impact on biodiversity.* • ***Investigate*** *the disappearance of the Aral Sea and other examples of aquatic habitat destruction.*

About 150 years ago, rain forests worldwide covered an area larger than the United States. Today, rain forests cover an area half that size. The present rate of destruction is equal to the loss of an area the size of the state of Oregon each year. The rain forest is the most diverse and productive biome on Earth, and the loss of even small areas may result in many extinctions. Deforestation in rain forests and other forests is the most important factor in the loss of biodiversity.

Causes of Deforestation

Several forces lead to deforestation in rain forests. All stem from the fact that most rain forests are in developing countries. Developing countries are usually poor and have populations that are growing rapidly. The rain forest is often used in attempts to solve both of these problems as shown in Figure 23.3.

Population Growth   The growing populations in many developing countries need food and a place to live. Many rain forests are cleared or burned to make farmland. Recall from Chapter 9 that soil in rain forests is nutrient-poor because most of the nutrients are within the plants at any one time. Removing the plants also removes most of the nutrients. Because the soil is poor, conventional farming methods used on cleared land usually fail after several growing seasons. Within a few years, land that once was a habitat for many species becomes barren and unproductive. Habitat destruction of this kind is currently taking place in the Philippines, Southeast Asia, and in many South and Central American nations.

You may wish to review Section 9.3 on rain forests with students while teaching this chapter. It describes the biodiversity and structure of the rain forest in detail. A knowledge of the characteristics of the rain forest will help students understand why habitat destruction in these areas is such a severe threat to biodiversity.

Figure 23.3 Most of the rain forests of the world are being deforested rapidly. The planet will lose 70 to 90 percent of its biodiversity if all of the rain forests are destroyed.

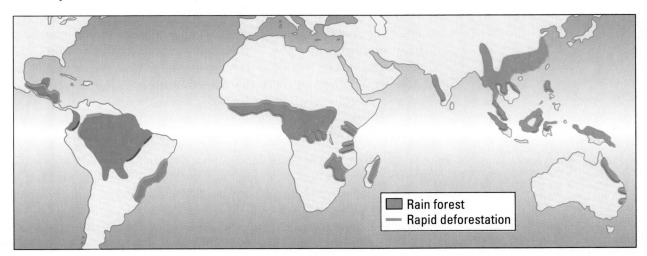

☐ Rain forest
— Rapid deforestation

Figure 23.4 The rain forest that used to grow on this land was cleared to make grazing land for cattle. Almost all the beef grown in this way is exported to developed countries.

Multicultural Perspective
Animals and plants are not the only organisms displaced by habitat destruction. Many indigenous peoples are also displaced by the growth of industrial societies. Several tribes in the Amazon are currently threatened because the forests in which they live are disappearing. A particularly moving account of emotions brought on by the encroachment of industrial societies is a speech delivered by Chief Sealth of the Duwamish League in 1854. The speech can be found in "The Land Is Sacred to Us: Chief Seattle's Lament."

DATELINE 1989

The Convention on International Trade in Endangered Species (CITES) proposed a worldwide ban on the trade of ivory elephant tusks. Although elephants are protected, poachers destroyed half of the world population between 1979 and 1989 to get the valuable ivory. The ban was accepted. The world market for ivory collapsed almost immediately, and poaching has dropped dramatically.

You may wish to review Chapters 10 and 11 with students before teaching this section. These chapters describe the characteristics of aquatic biomes in detail. An understanding of the characteristics of lake and wetland habitats will help students understand the text discussion on the destruction of these habitats.

Demand for Resources Developing nations have resources that developed nations want. For example, Japan and other nations encourage the Philippines, Thailand, Borneo, and Indonesia to strip their forests of wood. The lumber is then sold to the developed nations. Similar deforestation is taking place in the old-growth forests in the United States. Almost all of the old-growth trees cut down in the United States are exported to other countries.

In Central America, the demand for grass-fed beef has led to the clearing of forests for cattle raising. The beef grown on the cleared rainforest land is often sold to industrialized countries, where the demand for beef is high. This large market encourages cash-poor governments to destroy rain forests and raise cattle for export. Beef from cattle raised on former rainforest land is often used to make hamburgers, luncheon meats, and other meat products.

No one knows how much time it will take for the rain forest to regenerate. Scientific estimates range from hundreds to many thousands of years. The rain forest will not regenerate at all if none of it is left; there will be no organisms adapted to rainforest life to fill empty niches. The destruction of all rain forests would result in the loss of 70 to 90 percent of Earth's biodiversity.

Destruction of forest land is also a problem in the deciduous forests of developed nations. In the United States, deforestation has been ongoing since the first European colonists arrived in the Americas. About half of all U.S. forests have been destroyed. The advanced deforestation in developed nations is one reason why these countries rely on developing nations for wood.

Aquatic Habitat Destruction

All land biomes are losing biodiversity through habitat destruction. Aquatic biomes are losing biodiversity as well. Recall from Chapter 11 that coral reefs and wetlands are productive and diverse ecosystems. Both of these ecosystems have been disturbed by human activity. Coral reefs are damaged by water pollution and overfishing. Wetlands are damaged by pollution and development.

Figure 23.5 The Aral Sea has lost two-thirds of its volume and 40 percent of its surface area since 1960. (The map for the year 2000 is a prediction.) Towns such as Kokaral and Muinak were ports in 1960. Today, they are many kilometers away from the lakeshore. Ships have been stranded because of the water loss.

The Everglades The Everglades, a large group of marshes in southern Florida, is habitat for a variety of organisms, including grasses, fish, invertebrates, and migrating birds. Much of the Everglades is prime real estate property that has been developed for recreation and commercial activities. The Everglades and other wetlands have been drained to produce land for farming, housing, and industry. Almost half of all the wetlands in the United States have been destroyed, and an estimated 175 hectares are being destroyed annually. Congress and the government of Florida have begun a project to return at least part of the Everglades to its natural state.

The Aral Sea The Aral Sea is actually a large, saltwater lake in the southern desert of the former Soviet Union, as shown in Figure 23.5. The Aral Sea used to be the fourth largest lake in the world. But the diversion of the two rivers that feed the lake is making the Aral Sea disappear. The rivers were diverted to irrigate crops. In 1960, the lake held more than 1000 km³ of water. Today, it holds less than one-third of this amount, and it may disappear completely by the year 2010.

The amount of habitat loss caused by the disappearance of a 68 000-km² lake is very serious. The loss of biodiversity is serious, as well. The Aral Sea supported an aquatic ecosystem that no longer exists. Its disappearance has also caused problems for the people near the lake. A fishing industry that harvested 48 000 metric tons of fish in 1957 is now gone. Many people have lost jobs that depended on the lake. Salt carried from the exposed lake bed by wind also causes many health problems.

SECTION REVIEW

1. What two problems lead to deforestation in developing countries?
2. Explain the human activity that led to the disappearance of the Aral Sea?
3. **Deduce** What effect might deforestation have on global warming?

1. Deforestation is chiefly the result of the need of growing populations for space and food, and the need for money from developed countries.
2. The two rivers that fed the lake were diverted for agriculture.
3. The removal of large numbers of trees could cause carbon dioxide levels in the atmosphere to increase because the trees would no longer remove the carbon dioxide from the air.

23.3 THE IMPORTANCE OF BIODIVERSITY

Objectives • **State** *the ways that biodiversity benefits humans.* • **Describe** *how the pattern of the current mass extinction differs from that of earlier extinctions.*

If extinction is a natural part of all ecosystems, how can habitat destruction and the loss of biodiversity be undesirable? There are two answers. First, humans benefit directly from high biodiversity. Second, the loss of biodiversity threatens the health of the global ecosystem, and therefore indirectly threatens human health.

Crop Genetics

One direct benefit that biodiversity provides humans is new genetic material for farm plants. Today, about 30 species of plants are grown as crops. Selective crossing of these plants produces higher yields, but it also makes the crops more vulnerable to weather, disease, and insects. All the crops that humans grow for food were originally wild plants. The ancestors of these plants still grow wild in some areas.

The genetic material from wild plant strains can be used to improve the traits of food crops. This crossbreeding can develop crop strains that are more productive, more resistant to climate changes, and more resistant to disease and insects. In 1978, for example, a variety of wild corn was discovered in Mexico. Cross-breeding this corn with local varieties enabled farmers to avoid season-to-season plowing and sowing. Crossbreeding also offered resistance to several viruses that attacked the commercial corn.

Figure 23.6 Humans first grew wheat as a crop about 10,000 years ago. Today, there are about 22,000 varieties of domestic and wild wheat in two species. One species is used to make bread; the other, pasta.

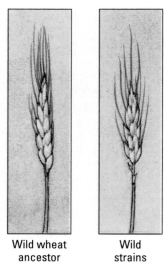

Wild wheat ancestor   Wild strains

Bread

Pasta

Crop plants

Genetic material is a vital resource because it makes the global food supply more flexible. As pathogens and insects evolve strains that resist pesticides, farmers will need new plant varieties that will resist pests. Pests are also less damaging to crops with high genetic variety. New strains of crop plants may also be useful if global warming changes the climate of Earth's agricultural regions.

Habitat destruction threatens many populations of wild crop ancestors. The loss of this genetic material might be a disaster because it could endanger the food supply of major parts of the human population. Several groups are currently working to collect and store the genetic material of crop ancestors before they disappear.

Medicines

Another direct benefit of biodiversity is the use of natural chemicals in medicine. Currently, about 40 percent of all medicines used in the United States comes from plants. Quinine, a malaria drug, comes from the cinchona plant. Digitalis, used in the treatment of heart disease, comes from foxglove. Researchers are also working with leaves of the periwinkle plant and the bark of the Pacific yew. These plants show promise in the treatment of certain types of cancer.

Word Power

Quinine, from the Quechua word *quinaquina*, "cinchona."

Figure 23.7 The cinchona plant (left) is the source of quinine, a drug that fights malaria. Foxglove (center) is the source of the heart medication digitalis. The Pacific yew (right) is the source of a potential anticancer drug called taxol.

No one knows how many more medicines are in the world's rain forests. Drug companies are spending millions of dollars trying to find out. But the species in the forest must escape destruction if they are to be evaluated for medicinal use.

If the rain forests and other habitats are destroyed, a cancer-curing drug may be lost before it can be discovered. The Pacific yew is a rare tree that grows only in old growth forests on the west coast of North America. These forests are threatened by clearcutting and other types of habitat destruction. If the Pacific yew had become extinct before the discovery of the anti-cancer drug in its bark, the world would have lost an important medicine.

Wilderness Areas

Declining biodiversity will have other effects. One is the loss of wilderness areas for recreation. *A **wilderness** is an area where the ecosystem is relatively undisturbed by the activities of humans.* Wilderness areas are important to people. They are a haven from the pollution and hectic life of an industrial society. Many people feel that wilderness areas are vital to their emotional health.

Ecosystem Destruction

The most dangerous characteristic of the current mass extinction may be the pattern of the extinction. In the past, mass extinctions followed a general pattern. Some species died out, while others were affected a little or not at all. The dinosaur extinction, for example, did not affect most species of plants. Many elements of the ecosystem were still in place, and there were opportunities for the surviving species to evolve and occupy empty niches.

The pattern of today's mass extinction is different. When people destroy a habitat, they do not remove just a few species. The whole ecosystem is often destroyed. After this kind of habitat destruction, there are few surviving species and few remaining niches. Biodiversity has already dropped sharply because of habitat destruction, and it continues to decline. No one knows how the loss of diversity will affect the global ecosystem. Ecologists have many more questions than answers.

1. The ancestors have genes that can give cultivated strains beneficial traits. They add flexibility to the world food supply and help avoid the dangers of monoculture.
2. Foxglove, the cinchona plant, and the Pacific yew are three plants mentioned in the text.
3. Earlier mass extinctions involved large numbers of species dying out in a relatively short period of time. Today's extinction is happening even more quickly and has a different pattern than earlier extinctions.

SECTION REVIEW

1. Why are wild ancestors of crop plants important?
2. Name three plants that have yielded important drugs.
3. **Contrast** Write a paragraph comparing other mass extinctions and the one occurring today.

Plant Comebacks

What is the future of native plants?

1. The project has devoted money and habitat to wildflower species.
2. Threatened species provide many benefits. They may provide important food crops, medications, or vital habitats for other organisms.

If you travel on a Texas highway in the spring, you may notice a variety of colorful wildflowers, shrubs, and trees growing on hillsides along the side of the road. Although the vegetation is native to Texas, the plants did not sprout in this habitat naturally. These plants were introduced to the roadsides through the efforts of the Texas Highway Department and other dedicated people.

Before the Texas highway beautification programs began in 1930, many roadsides were dry and barren. To assure the continuation of the program, one percent of all highway construction funds are devoted to landscaping. Also, organizations adopt sections of the road to landscape and maintain. The planting of native vegetation not only improved the landscape, it also ensured the survival of many plants that might have been threatened by habitat destruction.

One wildflower you will not see, however, is the Texas snowbell. The Texas snowbell is a small plant with a delicate flower. This native wildflower is threatened with extinction due to habitat destruction. In an effort to save the Texas snowbell, the plant is being experimentally reintroduced into the Texas ecosystem. The outcome of the experiment is uncertain. The location of the reintroduction site is being kept secret to prevent vandalism of the few remaining plants.

The Texas snowbell is only one of many threatened plant species in the United States. Of the 20,000 native U.S. plant species, about 4,200 are threatened with extinction. In the hope of rescuing as many of the threatened plants as possible, thousands of reintroduction projects are in progress.

Although the botanists and conservationists choose sites with similar conditions to the plant's natural habitat, successful reintroduction is risky. When a native species is reintroduced into the wild, it faces many threats, such as microbes, fungi, insects, herbivores, and competition from other native plant species. In California, a survey of 45 plant reintroduction projects revealed that only 4 were successful, 15 were moderately successful, and 10 were unsuccessful. The data on the remaining projects were not sufficient to draw conclusions.

Several reintroduction victories give the botanists hope. In Oregon, the Malheur wire lettuce was saved from extinction. In the Florida panhandle, 1,300 Apalachicola rosemary plants were transplanted to a new site. Most of the transplants survived, and five new seedlings have poked out of the soil in the new habitat.

DECISIONS

1. Explain how the Texas highway beautification program may have helped preserve native plant species.
2. Why is it important to save threatened plant species?

Teaching tips for Field Activity appear on page T119.

DATELINE 1992

The United Nations Conference on Environmental Development met in Rio de Janeiro, Brazil. The conference, also called the Earth Summit, was attended by over 100 world leaders. One agreement reached at the conference was the Biodiversity Agreement. This agreement encourages wealthier nations to provide money to developing countries for the protection of biodiversity. Former U.S. President George Bush did not attend the Earth Summit. President Bush also refused to sign the Biodiversity Agreement, arguing that it was too vague.

23.4 CONTROLLING HABITAT DESTRUCTION

Objectives • *Describe* the social and economic factors that cause habitat destruction. • *Explain* the Endangered Species Act and how it is applied.

Recall that most rain forests are located in developing nations, and that many of these nations are poor and have rapidly growing populations. Their governments have urgent needs. When faced with overcrowding in cities and serious food shortages, expanding into rainforest land may seem like the only option. The governments can also make much–needed money by selling rainforest products to developed nations. As a result, the rain forests are being destroyed. Developed countries play a part in this destruction. These countries often exhaust their own resources and turn to other countries for raw materials. The demands of wealthy industrial societies cause deforestation by providing a market for rainforest products. Deforestation is a global problem that needs a global solution.

International Efforts

Some progress had been made in international efforts to stop deforestation and other types of habitat destruction. Several groups are working to discover and collect as many organisms as possible before they are destroyed. Seeds from wild crop plants are gathered and stored. *A secure place where seeds, plants, and genetic material are stored is called a* **gene bank**. Gene banks in many parts of the world are working quickly to preserve as much of Earth's biodiversity as possible. The best solution would be to end habitat destruction. But the continued growth of the human population makes this unlikely.

Figure 23.9 Habitat destruction is a problem in all nations. This clearcut is in Washington State.

The Endangered Species Act

The U.S. Congress passed the Endangered Species Act in 1973. This law requires the government to make a list of all species in the United States that are in danger of extinction. The government must also protect the habitat of these species. The Endangered Species Act has stopped many developments that threatened the habitats of endangered species.

The main provisions of the Endangered Species Act are:

- The United States Fish and Wildlife Service must keep a list of all threatened and endangered species.
- Threatened or endangered animals may not be caught or killed.
- Threatened or endangered plants may not be disturbed.
- Threatened or endangered species may not be bought or sold.
- The federal government may not construct any project that jeopardizes endangered species.
- The Fish and Wildlife Service must prepare a species recovery plan for each threatened or endangered species.

The Endangered Species Act has flaws, however. In order to be protected, a species must be on the endangered species list. Getting a species on this list can be difficult. One way around the law is simply to develop an area before it has been studied for endangered species. Another way is to ensure that the developer will create a new habitat for the species. Humans have found the task of reproducing a habitat to be very difficult, however.

A species cannot survive without its habitat. Many ecologists think the Endangered Species Act focuses too much on individual species. They feel the emphasis of laws that protect diversity should be on whole habitats, not on individual species.

One example of the problem of focusing on an individual species is the case of a bird called the clapper rail in California. The clapper rail lives in wetland habitats that are prime real estate for development. In several areas, the developers were allowed to build as long as they created new habitats for the birds. The new habitats did not work, however, because they did not replace the whole wetland ecosystem. The clapper rail disappeared from these areas.

Figure 23.10 The clapper rail is threatened by the development of wetlands in California. Efforts by developers to replace destroyed habitats have failed.

Cooperative Learning
Have students work in small groups to find examples of ten animals or plants that were once indigenous to their state but are now extinct. Have them combine their data in an illustrated table. The table should include information about when the organism became extinct, the organism's habitat, and reasons for the extinction.

SECTION REVIEW

1. Explain how developing and developed countries are both responsible for deforestation.
2. What is a gene bank? Why are gene banks important?
3. **Analyze** Would it ever be possible for a developer to reproduce a whole ecosystem for the clapper rail or any other organism? Explain your answer.

1. Developing countries have growing populations that need food and living space. Developed countries are a market for rainforest products.
2. Gene banks are secure places that store seeds, plants, and genetic material. They preserve the biodiversity of wild crop plants and other plants.
3. Responses will vary but should reflect an understanding of the complexity of all ecosystems. Building a whole ecosystem would be a tremendously difficult task.

Answers and teaching strategies on page T119.

Modeling a Bald Eagle Population

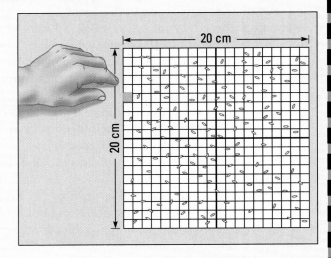

20 cm

20 cm

PROBLEM
How does the environment affect an eagle population?

MATERIALS (per pair of students)
- index card
- red marking pen
- #2 pencil
- 150 uncooked rice grains
- one 20-cm by 20-cm piece of paper
- metric ruler
- scissors
- graph paper
- 6 different colored pencils
- notebook (one per student)

HYPOTHESIZE
After reading through the entire activity, hypothesize how a bald eagle population is affected by biotic factors.

PROCEDURE
1. Work in pairs. On the piece of paper, mark off a 20-cm by 20-cm grid in 1-cm increments. The grid represents a 4-km² lake where the eagles hunt (100 cm² = 1 km²).
2. Cut two 1-cm squares from the index card, then color both sides with the red marker. Use the #2 pencil and label one *F* for female and the other *M* for male.
3. Put the lake grid on a flat surface, and scatter the 150 rice grains over it.
4. Hold the *F* square over the grid about 30 cm, and drop it. Remove all of the rice from under the square. Repeat the process with the *M* square. *Note: This step represents eagles catching fish.*
5. After each hunting expedition, rescatter the remaining rice, and repeat Step 4. After each eagle has hunted four times, total the number of fish caught by each eagle on Day 1.

Make a data table in your notebook and record your data.

6. Repeat steps 4 and 5 nine times (representing the nine remaining days), recording the data in your notebook.
7. An eagle will share its food with its mate, but feeds itself first. If an eagle does not eat three fish per day, it becomes too weak to hunt will die. Be sure to examine the data for each 3-day period. If one eagle dies, continue hunting with only one eagle.
8. Use different colored pencils for the male and the female eagles, and graph the data from your notebook, totaling the number of fish caught by each eagle per day. *Note: On the graph, record the days on the horizontal axis and the number of fish caught on the vertical axis.*

ANALYSIS
1. How might the fish population be affected by the eagles' hunting over time?
2. What effect might a small decrease in the fish population have on the eagle population?
3. What effect, if any, would an increase in the fish population have on the eagle population?

CONCLUSION
Write a paragraph describing the results of your experiment.

CHAPTER 23 REVIEW

KEY TERMS

extinction 23.1	habit destruction 23.1	wilderness 23.3
biodiversity 23.1	alien species 23.1	gene bank 23.4

CHAPTER SUMMARY

23.1 Extinction is the disappearance of a species from some or all of its geographical range. Extinction is a natural part of the functioning of all ecosystems. Earth is currently experiencing a mass extinction due to habitat destruction. Habitat destruction is occurring in all biomes and is linked to the size of the human population.

23.2 The loss of Earth's rain forests would result in a 70 to 90 percent decline in biodiversity. The loss of rain forests is caused by factors linked to the rainforest's location in developing countries. Developed countries contribute to deforestation by providing a market for rainforest products. Many aquatic ecosystems are experiencing habitat destruction. The Aral Sea has lost two-thirds of its volume since 1960.

23.3 Biodiversity is important to humans for several reasons. Wild strains of crop plants can be a valuable genetic resource. Plants and other organisms can provide new medicines to treat a variety of illnesses. The destruction of whole ecosystems may impair the biosphere's ability to regenerate.

23.4 Developed and developing countries are both responsible for deforestation. The pressing needs of people, economic forces, and a lack of international cooperation make controlling deforestation difficult. The Endangered Species Act protects species that are near extinction. Many ecologists think the focus of biodiversity legislation should be on whole habitats, not individual species.

MULTIPLE CHOICE

Choose the letter of the word or phrase that best completes each statement.

1. Most of the loss of biodiversity in ecosystems is caused by (a) pollution; (b) collectors; (c) habitat destruction; (d) hunting. c
2. The medicines digitalis and quinine come from (a) animals; (b) plants; (c) fungi; (d) microorganisms. b
3. Nonnative organisms introduced into an area by humans are called (a) helpful species; (b) alien species; (c) intruding species; (d) indigenous species. b
4. Disturbing an area of an ecosystem where an organism lives is called (a) habitat destruction; (b) loss of biodiversity; (c) extinction; (d) evolution. a
5. The disappearance of a species from all or some of its geographical range is called (a) deforestation; (b) loss of biodiversity; (c) habitat destruction; (d) extinction. d
6. An area that is undisturbed by human activity is a (a) wilderness; (b) state park; (c) national park; (d) forest. a
7. The number of strains of domestic and wild wheat is about (a) 22; (b) 220; (c) 2200; (d) 22,000. d
8. The volume that the Aral Sea has lost since 1960 is (a) one-quarter; (b) one-third; (c) two-thirds; (d) three-quarters. c
9. The amount of biodiversity that will be lost if all rain forests are destroyed is (a) 10 to 30 percent; (b) 70 to 90 percent; (c) 30 to 50 percent; (d) 50 to 70 percent. b
10. The Endangered Species Act has been criticized for its emphasis on protecting (a) species; (b) ecosystems; (c) habitats; (d) biomes. a

WORD COMPARISONS

Write the letter of the second word pair that best matches the first pair.

1. Deforestation: trees as (a) irrigation: Aral Sea; (b) alien species: water hyacinth; (c) dams: salmon; (d) biodiversity: extinction. a

2. Digitalis: plants as (a) parasites: animals; (b) genetic material: wild crop strains; (c) biodiversity: extinction; (d) water hyacinth: alien species. b

3. Biodiversity: extinction as (a) water hyacinth: alien species; (b) dams: salmon; (c) pest resistance: inbreeding (d) genetic material: wild crop strains. c

4. Biodiversity: healthy ecosystem as (a) alien species: water hyacinth; (b) extinction: unhealthy ecosystem; (c) habitat destruction: forests; (d) habitat destruction: biodiversity. b

5. Gene banks: genetic diversity as (a) Endangered Species Act: species; (b) alien species: water hyacinth; (c) cinchona: digitalis; (d) Pacific yew: cancer. a

CONCEPT REVIEW Answers on page T119.

Write a complete response for each of the following.

1. What is a mass extinction? When have mass extinctions occurred?

2. How do developing countries contribute to deforestation?

3. How do developed countries contribute to deforestation?

4. Why has the Aral Sea dried up?

5. What is a gene bank? What is stored there?

THINK CRITICALLY Answers on page T119.

1. Explain how the introduction of a species to an area might result in habitat destruction.

2. Why might the destruction of the rain forests deprive future generations of valuable medicine?

3. Describe the connection between habitat destruction and the loss of biodiversity.

4. Why are wild strains of crop plants important? Will they continue to be important in the future?

5. Why do many ecologists think it is better to protect whole habitats rather than individual species?

WRITE FOR UNDERSTANDING

Write a short essay summarizing the reasons that biodiversity is important. Which reason do you think is most important? Are there any reasons that are not in the text?

PORTFOLIO

1. Conduct library research on one organism that was once common in your area but is now extinct. Prepare an oral report that explains the conditions leading to the extinction of the organism.

2. Make a list of ten endangered organisms. Be sure to include plants and animals.

Survey 100 people to find out which organisms they would most like to save. Analyze your results. Which organisms would people most like to save? Why? Is public opinion a good way to make this decision?

GRAPHIC ANALYSIS

Use Figure 23.1 to answer the following.

1. How are mass extinctions shown on the graph? How many mass extinctions are there, not counting the present one?
2. When was the rate of evolution fastest?
3. Is there a pattern in the peaks in extinction and evolution rates? If so, describe the pattern.
4. Explain why the pattern in extinction and evolution rates exists. How are the two processes related?
5. Find the place on the graph where species' evolution is fastest. Why is evolution fastest at this time?

ACTIVITY 23.2

Answers and teaching strategies on page T119.

PROBLEM

What is the impact of various alternative energy sources on the environment?

MATERIALS (per group)

- newspapers
- scissors
- glue or tape
- paper
- pencil

INFERENCE

After reading through the activity, infer how alternative energy sources affect the environment.

PROCEDURE

1. Working in groups of three, scan the titles of the newspaper articles for an article that interests you about an alternative energy source and how it affects the environment.
2. One member of the group cuts out the article, attaches it to a sheet of paper, and goes through the reference materials provided by your teacher or the library. He or she then puts this information in outline form for the rest of the group. *Note: Discard any newspaper scraps in your recycle bin.*
3. A second member puts the collected information into a written report for the whole group. *Note: Be sure your report answers the questions in the Analysis and Conclusion sections.*
4. The third student prepares an oral report to be given to the entire class. After the oral presentation, other classmates may direct questions to any of the group members.

ANALYSIS

1. What energy source or technology does your article focus on? Is it a renewable or nonrenewable resource?
2. Does the author of the newspaper article seem to be for or against this energy source? Explain.
3. In your opinion, what are the benefits of your chosen energy source? What are the drawbacks?
4. What risks does this energy source present to the environment? Explain.

CONCLUSION

1. Summarize the potential benefits and hazards of your chosen energy source, and its environmental impact. Present your findings in the oral report.
2. After all groups have presented their oral reports, the whole class participates in a discussion of the following question: If the entire United States used nuclear energy as its only energy source, how do you think people would be affected 100 years from now? 1000 years from now?

The rapid growth of the human population has put a strain on the biosphere. Earth has limited resources. An increase in people means an increase in the demand on these resources. When the increasing population is combined with the frontier ethic, the damage to the biosphere can be severe.

Recall from Chapter 12 that the sustainable ethic is based on the idea that resources are limited. Building a sustainable society is a goal that many people share. A sustainable society minimizes waste and maximizes the benefit from each resource. The concepts behind a sustainable society have much in common with natural ecosystems.

24.1 CONSERVATION

Objectives • **Define** conservation, explaining how resources can be conserved. • **Describe** ways of conserving energy.

One basic concept in a sustainable society is conservation. **Conservation** *is a strategy to reduce the use of resources through decreased demand and increased efficiency.* If a resource is to be conserved, less of it must be used. What is used must be used completely, with waste kept to a minimum. Conservation also includes the protection and management of Earth's remaining ecosystems.

Waste Reduction

The frontier ethic has led to a disposable society. In a disposable society, products are used once and then thrown away. Newspapers, food and beverage containers, and the other items in Figure 24.1 are designed for only one use. The amount of waste generated by the use of disposable items is vast. This waste is buried, burned, or dumped into the ocean.

The amount of material and energy that humans waste is unique in the biosphere. No other species uses so many resources as inefficiently as humans. In a normal ecosystem, organisms evolve naturally to a state in which nothing is wasted. Organisms other than humans use resources efficiently. A sustainable society models the other ecosystems on Earth. Waste is minimized, and efficiency will increase.

Figure 24.1 Industrial societies produce many disposable items. These items are used once and then thrown away. Items like these increase the amount of garbage that needs disposal.

Teaching tips for Field Activity appear on page T123.

Conservation can reduce waste in several ways. One way is through source reduction. **Source reduction** *is the lowering of the demand for a resource, resulting in a reduction in the amount of resource needed to satisfy that demand.* Source reduction decreases the amount of a resource taken from the environment in the first place. Habitat destruction and pollution can also be minimized through this type of conservation.

Another way waste can be reduced is by minimizing the amount of material that is thrown away. You and other consumers play a crucial role in reducing garbage. If you buy products that are packaged in reusable or recyclable containers, you are helping reduce waste. Glass, paper, aluminum, and plastics can all be recycled. Separating these items from trash and setting them aside for recycling can also reduce waste. Through the reduction of wastes and decreased demand for resources, a society can become more sustainable.

Conserving Energy

Minimizing the use of energy is another method of conservation. Energy can be conserved by using it more efficiently. For example, most of the energy used in the home is used for heat and hot water. Much of this heat escapes if a house is not well insulated. Checking for drafts and for the proper insulating materials is the first step in reducing such heat loss. Insulated windows also help conserve energy. Keeping the heat down when you are not at home conserves a great deal of energy, as does sleeping with heavy blankets and lowering the thermostat at night.

Hot water can be conserved by taking shorter showers and running washing machines and dishwashers only when full. Washing clothes at lower temperatures reduces the use of hot water and helps keep clothes in better condition for a longer time, reducing the need to replace them. Special devices provide energy savings of up to 60 percent by reducing the flow of water. These devices can also be used in areas that have chronic water shortages, such as California.

Figure 24.2 U.S. energy consumption has risen steadily since 1950. Most of the energy produced in the United States comes from fossil fuels. Nuclear energy and other types of energy, such as hydroelectric and geothermal, make up the balance. A quad is a measure of energy equal to 1×10^{15} BTU, or 2.93×10^{11} kilowatt hours of electricity.

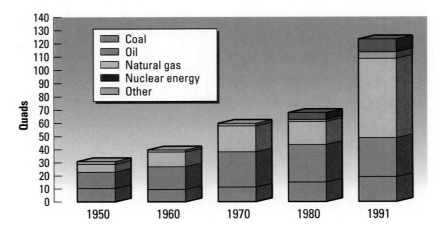

The use of electricity can be limited in other ways. Turning off lights and other electric appliances when not in use saves energy. Fluorescent (floh-RES-unt) bulbs, such as the one in Figure 24.3, which use less energy than incandescent (in-KAN-DES-unt) bulbs, are used in many homes and offices. Unlike incandescent bulbs, which give off much of their energy as heat, fluorescent bulbs produce little heat and generate light more efficiently. In addition, many office buildings, commercial centers, and homes are installing skylights. Skylights allow greater amounts of sunlight to enter a room during daylight hours. The increased sunlight reduces the need for overhead lighting powered by electricity.

Large appliances, such as air conditioners, refrigerators, washing machines, and dishwashers, are now constructed to operate in a more energy-efficient manner. Such appliances have an energy-rating number. When buying an appliance, it is important to know its energy rating. The consumer can use energy-rating numbers as a guide to energy-saving features when buying appliances. Look for the most efficient product when buying.

To conserve gasoline, more people are using mass transportation and car pooling. By traveling in groups, people use less fuel. They also help to lessen air pollution because fewer cars are on the road. Properly tuned car engines also conserve fuel. In October 1993, General Motors asked for volunteers to test its new electric automobiles. Electric motors and more efficient gasoline-powered engines in cars conserve fossil fuels and reduce pollution. Most automobile manufacturers are developing more fuel-efficient engines. In the near future, electric cars and cars fueled by natural gas or hydrogen will very likely become available. Driving these cars will save gasoline and greatly reduce emissions.

Recall from Chapter 17 that solar, hydroelectric, wind, and geothermal energy are being used as alternative forms of energy in some parts of the world. Not only are these forms of energy renewable, they produce little pollution if operated correctly and help cut back on the use of fossil fuels and nuclear energy. The more often these forms of energy are used, the greater the long-term benefits from conservation.

Figure 24.3 A 15-watt fluorescent bulb produces as much light as a 60-watt incandescent bulb. The bulbs also last about ten times as long. Fluorescent bulbs conserve energy and reduce waste.

TECHNOLOGY
LINK

To help improve the efficiency of automobile engines and reduce pollution, the federal government has established standards for manufacturers to produce automobiles according to minimum efficiency requirements. The cars must emit only a low level of pollution. In the late 1980s, a major Japanese automobile manufacturer developed a car called the AXV, which averaged 98 miles to a gallon of gas (37.4 km/L). A high degree of efficiency is an important part of the sustainable ethic.

SECTION REVIEW

1. What is conservation?
2. Identify some methods currently in use that are designed to conserve energy or resources.
3. **Apply** List five specific things you can do in your home to cut back on the amount of garbage you produce and energy you use. Explain how each activity you list saves resources. Compare your list with the lists from other students.

1. Conservation is a strategy to reduce the amount of resources used through decreased demand and increased efficiency.
2. Responses may include the production of less garbage by using nondisposable items, using fluorescent rather than incandescent bulbs, turning off lights when not in use, and driving more energy-efficient automobiles.
3. Responses will vary. Likely responses will be some of the practices discussed in this section or related activities. Accept all logical responses.

Living Sustainably

How can you live a sustainable lifestyle?

"Live simply so that others may simply live." Perhaps you have seen these words on a bumper sticker, or maybe you have heard someone speak them aloud. These words are the essence of living sustainably. It may seem that to have a sustainable lifestyle, you would have to change your life completely. Yet this is not true. You can begin to create a sustainable lifestyle very easily. You can choose a simpler lifestyle by reducing your energy and material consumption.

Probably one of the easiest ways to reduce your energy consumption is to recycle. The amount of energy saved by recycling one glass bottle would light a 100-watt light bulb for 4 hours. Not only does recycling save energy because new bottles need not be manufactured, it saves natural resources and reduces the amount of garbage that must be hauled and dumped into landfills. You can recycle many materials including glass, most plastics, cardboard, white paper, newspaper, aluminum cans, tin cans, grocery bags, and magazines. Many cities have organized curbside pickup for recycling. If this program does not exist in your area, you can take your recyclable materials to recycling centers.

Buying products made from recycled materials is as important as recycling wastes. Some products made from recycled wastes include writing paper, greeting cards, packaging materials, tissue, boxes, and plastic containers. By choosing products made from recycled materials, you have completed the recycling cycle.

Sustainable living also includes your choice for a mode of transportation. Choose to take public transportation, ride a bike, or car-pool as your main method of transportation. Since you may not drive yet or have not been driving for many years, now is the time to develop an environmentally conscious approach to transportation that may establish a lifelong pattern. Alternative transportation will not only save energy, it will also reduce the amount of pollution released into the atmosphere and relieve traffic congestion.

The food you choose to eat can also reduce energy use and material impact on the environment. If you choose to eat foods that are lower on the food chain, you decrease the energy cost of producing the food. You may decide to eat less meat or to eat more foods grown organically.

You probably cannot immediately implement most of the steps outlined above. However, this you can do right now. Look around the area where you are currently sitting. Notice how much energy is being wasted on lights or other appliances that may be running needlessly. Think about the amount of energy being wasted and the amount of pollution being produced to run the unnecessary electrical equipment. What can you do about it? Remember to turn off electrical appliances and lights that are not in use.

DECISIONS

1. Make a list of the actions you will take to live more sustainably. You may include actions that were not discussed above.
2. How can you convince others to live sustainably?

24.2 RECYCLING

Objectives • *List materials that are currently recycled.*
• *Identify the benefits of recycling.*

Recycling is one of the most effective ways of conserving resources.
Recycling *is reducing resource use by collecting usable waste materials and using them to produce new items.* In a natural ecosystem, all matter is recycled. Only energy is added to the system. In industrial societies, almost nothing is recycled. If all materials could be recycled without loss, humans would never need to cut down another tree or dig another iron mine. Many materials cannot be recycled, however, and even those that can are never recycled completely.

Recycling has several benefits, including a reduction in both the amount of waste produced and the resulting disposal problems. Recovered waste is also a good source of limited resources, such as steel and aluminum. Recovering waste materials is often less polluting, cheaper, and more energy-efficient than taking new materials from the environment. Recycling also prevents damage to the environment caused by the gathering of new resources. The fate of solid waste in the United States is shown in Figure 24.4.

Just as in a natural ecosystem, recycling is a crucial part of a sustainable society. Japan currently recycles about half of its waste, the most of any country in the world. The United States does not do nearly as well. In 1990, the United States recycled 2 percent of its plastic, 20 percent of its glass, 29 percent of its paper and cardboard, and 38 percent of its aluminum. A large increase in the amount of recycled materials is an important part of the sustainable ethic.

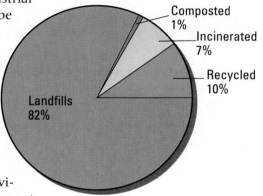

Figure 24.4 Most solid waste from homes and industry is thrown away in the United States. Decreasing the amount of waste is a central part of the sustainable ethic.

Recycling Paper

Paper is one of the easiest materials to recycle. The recycling of a 1.2-m stack of newspaper saves one 12-m Douglas fir tree. Recycling paper requires 75 percent less energy and uses 50 percent less water than producing paper from trees. Making paper from recycled paper also produces less toxic waste because it uses fewer chemicals. Today, about one-third of the newspaper and one-half of the cardboard in the United States is recycled.

Unfortunately, paper cannot be recycled forever. Each time it is recycled, the cellulose fibers in the paper shorten and weaken, reducing the quality of the paper. These fiber particles are sometimes visible in lower-quality recycled papers. To improve the quality, more fresh wood must be added. Recycled paper is used for newsprint, and in cardboard boxes. Higher-quality recycled papers are becoming more common. They are used in books, packaging,

Figure 24.5 Paper is cheap and easy to recycle. Many items (including this book) are now printed on recycled paper.

Figure 24.6 Recycling glass uses half the energy of producing new glass. Recycling aluminum is 95 percent less polluting than producing it from ore.

DATELINE 1973

The OPEC (Organization of Petroleum Exporting Countries) nations caused a steep rise in the price of crude oil. The increased price of energy motivated people to find ways to conserve energy. One way is to add recycled glass to the raw ingredients of new glass. Glass melts at a lower temperature than its raw materials. Adding recycled glass reduces the temperature needed to make new glass, thus saving energy. Manufacturers had always used a small amount of recycled glass when making new glass. Today, manufacturers know they can use up to 80 percent recycled glass when making new glass without affecting its quality.

and other paper products. You can support recycling by buying products made from recycled paper.

Recycling Minerals

Many minerals can be recycled. Glass and several different metals have been recycled for years. Aluminum is the most common metal on Earth, but it is never found in its elemental form. Aluminum must be separated from an ore called bauxite (BOKS-yt). Producing aluminum requires large amounts of energy and water. The use of 900 kg of recycled aluminum saves 3600 kg of bauxite and 700 kg of fossil fuels, which would have been used in the refining process. Eliminating the refining process also decreases water and air pollution. It is estimated that the use of recycled aluminum reduces air pollution, water pollution, and energy use by as much as 95 percent.

In the United States, about 90 percent of all junked cars are recycled. Much of the iron and steel of junked cars and appliances is used to make new appliances and automobiles. Many other metals are also recycled in large quantities. Silver, copper, lead, and zinc are some examples. Silver is recycled from photographic film used by hospitals and health clinics for X-rays. Copper is recycled from car radiators and telephone and utility cables. Almost all the lead in car batteries is recycled, and zinc is obtained from recycled plumbing materials.

One recent addition to the recycling effort is motor oil. The recycling of motor oil protects the environment in several ways. Used motor oil contains toxic elements such as lead, cadmium, arsenic, and benzene. Recycling the oil keeps these toxic substances from polluting both land and water. The EPA estimates that it takes only 3.8 L of used motor oil to contaminate 3.8 million L of fresh water. Used motor oil can be cleaned and reused again and again for the same purpose. It requires two-thirds less energy to clean oil than it does to refine it. Recycled motor oil can also be used as a fuel.

Recycling Plastics

The United States produces about 9 million metric tons of plastic every year. In 1990, only about 2 percent of this plastic was recycled. Recycling plastic is more difficult than recycling other materials. Plastics do not break down in the environment, and many give off toxic fumes if they are incinerated. Most plastics are complex organic molecules that do not break down easily. There are also many different kinds of plastics, most of which cannot be recycled together. Most plastics are also made from petroleum, a limited resource.

The amount of plastic being recycled is increasing. About 20 percent of all plastic soft drink containers are recycled. Most plastics are now coded with a number that indicates the kind of plastic from which the product is made. These numbers can be used to separate plastics into groups that can be recycled together. Recovered plastic can be made into items such as bath tubs, containers, insulation, and building materials.

Many communities now have recycling programs run by local governments. These programs provide containers for sorting discarded paper, aluminum, glass, and plastic. The materials are picked up like garbage and taken to recycling centers. Perhaps your school has a recycling program. If not, you can start one. Aluminum could be collected in the cafeteria, and paper could be collected in each classroom. Recycling is an important part of the sustainable ethic. Using materials more than once cuts down on waste, saves energy, and reduces the demand on the environment for new resources.

HEALTH LINK

The U.S. Food and Drug Administration (FDA) requires that all food containers be sterilized to guard against disease. Because the processing of recycled plastic does not expose the plastic to temperatures high enough for sterilization, recycled plastics are generally not used to produce new food containers.

Cooperative Learning
Have students work in groups to research recycling programs in other countries. Have them find out the following information: what products are being recycled, how much of each product is being recycled, and what percentage of resources/energy each recycling program conserves. Encourage students in each group to combine data from all groups on a world map that includes a key to the information.

SECTION REVIEW

1. What is recycling?
2. List five types of materials that are currently being recycled.
3. **Predict** Plastics are compounds made from carbon and other atoms. Where do you think most plastics come from?

1. Recycling is reducing resource use by collecting wastes and using them to produce new items.
2. Responses may include aluminum, cardboard, paper, plastic, glass, iron and steel, and lead.
3. The raw material for almost all plastics is crude oil.

Recycling Paper

PROBLEM
How is paper recycled?

MATERIALS
- sheet of newspaper
- large mixing bowl
- eggbeater
- water
- liquid laundry starch
- hand lens
- large square pan
- screen
- 4 sheets of blotting paper
- rolling pin
- pencil
- notebook

INFERENCE
After reading through the entire activity, make an inference about how recycling paper could improve the environment.

PROCEDURE
1. Tear a sheet of newspaper into small pieces.
2. In the bowl, mix the newspaper pieces with equal amounts of water and laundry starch (about $1\frac{1}{4}$ cups each).
3. With the eggbeater, beat the newspaper, water, and starch until it becomes cloudy and smooth.
4. *Note: A mixture of paper fibers and water is called a slurry.* Use the hand lens to observe the paper fibers in your slurry. Record your observations in your notebook.
5. Pour the slurry into the square pan, and add enough water so that the slurry is 8 or 9 cm deep. Be sure to mix well so the fibers are evenly distributed.
6. Place the screen in the pan so that it rests evenly on the bottom. Slosh the slurry back and forth over the screen.
7. Lift the screen out of the slurry slowly, but continue to hold it over the pan until much of the liquid has drained off.
8. Place the screen fiber-side-up on a sheet of blotting paper. Cover the top of the screen with another sheet of blotting paper to absorb the remaining water.
9. Repeat Step 8 using two fresh sheets of blotting paper. Then use a rolling pin to squeeze out any excess water.
10. Let your sheet of recycled paper dry between the blotters. If necessary, peel off the blotters when your recycled paper is dry.

ANALYSIS
1. What made it necessary to beat the paper-water-starch mixture until it was cloudy and smooth?
2. Liquid laundry starch acts as a glue. Why is starch needed in this process?
3. Dense paper has many fibers arranged tightly together. Lighter-weight paper has fibers more loosely arranged and is, therefore, less dense. Was your recycled paper more or less dense than the newspaper?
4. How could you make your recycled paper more dense? Less dense?

CONCLUSION
1. Write a paragraph that describes how your recycled paper could be improved. Would you want to read a book that was printed on this type of recycled paper?
2. As a class, discuss the following: Do you think you could you use this process to recycle plastics?

24.3 CONSERVING BIODIVERSITY

Objectives • **Identify** *methods being used to preserve biodiversity, and assess their effectiveness.* • **Relate** *the loss of biodiversity to the growth of the human population.*

As population increases, more and more people move into places where natural ecosystems once flourished. Forests are cut down, wetlands are drained, and land and water ecosystems are changed forever. The demand for resources leads to logging in old-growth forests and oil spills in protected areas. However, people are beginning to realize that something must be done to conserve Earth's biodiversity.

Until recently, scientists and the U.S. government focused their conservation efforts on individual species. If a species was endangered, it was protected and managed in an effort to keep it from becoming extinct. Complicated and expensive attempts were made to save individual species. Sometimes these efforts were successful, as in the case of the California condor. Habitat loss and the pesticide DDT led to a steep decline in the condor population. There were fewer than ten condors in the mid-1980s. All the remaining birds were captured, and a breeding program was started. Breeding was successful, and a few birds have now been introduced back into the wild.

Not all captive breeding programs are successful. In South America, captive herds of vicuna (vy-KOON-uh), a member of the camel family, are doing better in wild preserves than in captivity. Even if captive breeding is successful, reintroducing a species back into the environment may be difficult or impossible because its habitat may no longer exist. Saving a species while allowing the destruction of its habitat is short-sighted. Ecologists now think that conservation efforts should be focused on preserving entire ecosys-

Multicultural Connection
Many of the game preserves in Africa have been severely depleted by poachers. For example, poachers in search of the ivory tusks of elephants killed half the elephants in Africa between 1980 and 1990. The demand for products such as ivory and rhinoceros horn is very high, especially in Asia. Have students conduct library research to find out what the markets are for products taken from endangered species. Students should determine what needs these products satisfy.

Figure 24.8 These California condors were part of a breeding program in San Diego. Many ecologists think that conservation efforts should focus on saving whole ecosystems, not just species threatened by habitat destruction.

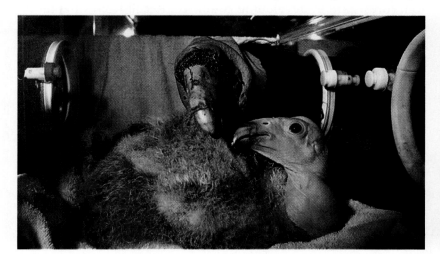

Figure 24.9 The controversial Wildlands Project recommends protecting and restoring large expanses of land in the United States. The project's plan for Florida is shown here. Many people feel the Wildlands Project is too radical. Most ecologists agree, however, that existing preserves are too small and fragmented.

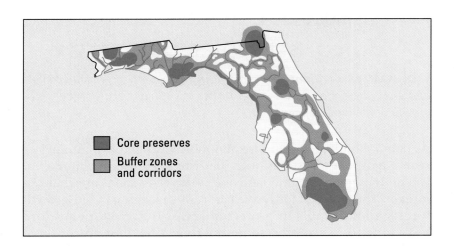

Core preserves

Buffer zones and corridors

tems instead of single species. Protecting an entire ecosystem will ensure that the natural habitats and interactions of many species will be preserved.

The United States has an extensive system of national parks and protected areas. Yet these areas contain just 60 percent of the ecosystems in North America. *A* **preserve** *is an area of land or water set aside for the protection of the ecosystem in that area.* Only 19 percent of the continent's ecosystems are protected in preserves larger than 100 000 hectares (about 20 mi^2.) Ecologists are beginning to realize that these preserves are not large enough. Populations need to be large to survive natural changes in size, and large populations need space. For example, 50 grizzly bears may require 5 million hectares of land. Conservation ecologists are working on plans to enlarge and connect existing preserves into a giant network of natural habitats. Expansion will conflict with the interests of people, however, so expanding the preserves may be difficult.

Unfortunately, the need to protect biodiversity is greatest in countries that are least able to protect it. The destruction of the rain forests is the greatest single threat to biodiversity. But most rain forests are in developing countries. Recall from Chapter 23 that these countries have social and economic problems that make it difficult to view biodiversity as a priority. Education in developing countries is often poor as well, meaning that people are not aware of the biodiversity problem.

SECTION REVIEW

1. Are most preserves in the United States large enough? How large must a preserve be to be effective?
2. What percentage of North American ecosystems is currently represented in U.S. preserves?
3. **Hypothesize** What problems do you think could result if an endangered species were introduced into a nonnative habitat?

CHAPTER 24 REVIEW

KEY TERMS

conservation 24.1   source reduction 24.1   recycling 24.2   preserve 24.3

CHAPTER SUMMARY

24.1 Conservation is a strategy to reduce the use of resources through decreased demand and increased efficiency. Resources must be conserved, and wastes must be reduced, if human societies are to become sustainable. Source reduction is lowering the demand for a resource, thereby reducing the amount taken from the environment. Energy can be conserved by using more efficient appliances, insulating homes, turning down the thermostat, and changing other behaviors that use a lot of energy.

24.2 Recycling is reducing resource dependence by collecting reusable waste materials and making them into new items. Recycling uses less energy and generates less pollution than starting with fresh resources. So recycling eases the demand on the environment for limited resources. Paper, glass, metals, and plastics can all be recycled. Many communities have curbside recycling programs.

24.3 Biodiversity must be conserved, just as other resources are. In the past, conservation efforts often focused on individual species. Ecologists now think conservation efforts should focus on preserving entire ecosystems. The United States has a large network of national parks and preserves. Most ecologists think the preserves are too small and fragmented.

MULTIPLE CHOICE

Choose the letter of the word or phrase that best completes each statement.

1. A strategy to reduce resource use through decreased demand and increased efficiency is (a) source reduction; (b) conservation; (c) recycling; (d) biodiversity. b

2. The lowering of the overall demand for a resource is called (a) source reduction; (b) conservation; (c) recycling; (d) reducing. a

3. Reducing resource use by collecting usable waste materials and using them to produce new items is (a) source reduction; (b) conservation; (c) recycling; (d) reducing. c

4. Natural ecosystems usually waste about (a) 75 percent of their resources; (b) 50 percent of their resources; (c) 25 percent of their resources; (d) none of their resources. c

5. A way that homes cannot be made more energy-efficient is by (a) raising the thermostat setting in cold weather; (b) reducing hot water use; (c) increasing insulation; (d) using fluorescent light bulbs. a

6. The form of waste that is most difficult to recycle is (a) glass; (b) paper; (c) plastics; (d) aluminum. c

7. Japan currently recycles about (a) 10 percent of its waste; (b) 25 percent of its waste; (c) 40 percent of its waste; (d) 50 percent of its waste. d

8. Recycling a 1.2-m stack of newsprint saves (a) one 12-m fir tree; (b) three 12-m fir trees; (c) one 20-m fir tree; (d) three 20-m fir trees. a

9. An area of land or water set aside for the protection of an ecosystem in the area is a (a) state; (b) county; (c) preserve; (d) national park. c

10. In the mid-1980s the number of living California condors was (a) 560; (b) 110; (c) 20; (d) less than 10. d

CHAPTER 24 REVIEW

TRUE/FALSE

Write true *if the statement is true. If the statement is false, change the underlined word or phrase to make it true.*

1. One concern of conservation is <u>increasing</u> the demand for resources. f, decreasing
2. In a disposable society, products are designed to be used <u>once</u> and then discarded. t
3. Faucets that reduce hot water flow can result in energy savings of up to <u>60 percent</u>. t
4. In a natural ecosystem, <u>all</u> matter is recycled. t
5. Recycling paper uses <u>50 percent</u> less energy than producing paper from new trees. f, 75 percent
6. <u>Iron</u> is the most common metal on Earth. f, aluminum
7. The breeding program for the California condor <u>was not successful</u>. f, was successful
8. The Wildlands Project proposes a network of <u>core preserves</u> linked by corridors and buffer zones. t

---

CONCEPT REVIEW   Answers on page T123.

Write a complete response for each of the following.

1. What is source reduction?
2. Describe some ways that you can save energy.
3. Why are plastics more difficult to recycle than other materials?
4. Which metals are commonly recycled?
5. Describe the Wildlands Project in several sentences. Does everyone think that this project is a good idea?

THINK CRITICALLY   Answers on page T123.

1. Describe some differences in the way an industrial society and a natural ecosystem function.
2. How can industrial societies be made to function more like natural ecosystems?
3. Why do you think it takes less energy and produces less pollution when materials are recycled instead of produced new?
4. Why do ecologists think the focus of conservation efforts should be ecosystems and not individual species?

Computer Activity Fifty grizzly bears require about 5 million hectares to live comfortably. How many hectares are needed to support a population of 1,000 bears? Use a computer program to compute your answer.

WRITE CREATIVELY

Write a short story describing life in a sustainable society of the future. Include details about how food and energy are produced, how people move around, and how wastes are disposed of. Include ideas such as source reduction and recycling.

PORTFOLIO

1. Use photographs from newspapers and magazines to build a collage of activities that can make society more sustainable.
2. Build a model of the sustainable city you wrote about in the Write Creatively section. Use whatever materials you need.

Use Figure 24.9 to answer the following.

1. What are the basic areas of the Wildlands Project called? How many of these areas are there in Florida?
2. What is the purpose of the corridors and buffer zones? Why are they important?
3. About what percentage of Florida is covered by the Wildlands Project? Do you think that setting aside this much land is practical?

ACTIVITY 24.2

Answers and teaching strategies on page T123.

PROBLEM
How can you design a model city?

MATERIALS (per group)
- assorted colored marking pens
- large sheet of posterboard
- large assortment of magazines, suitable for cutting

HYPOTHESIS
After reading through the activity, hypothesize about what features should be included in the model city of the future.

PROCEDURE
1. Students work in groups of three. Each group designs a self-contained model city that will house 50,000 people. All basic services are provided, including housing, police, health care, shopping, waste disposal, water, power, and recreation. Include the criteria in the data table below when planning your model city.

Your Model City Must:	Method Used
Recycle all wastes	
Supply all power	
Be completely safe	
Have mass transportation	
Encompass 3 km² of land	
Be pollution-free	

2. Your model city must: Recycle all wastes; supply all power; be completely safe; have mass transportation; encompass 3 km² of land area; be pollution-free.
3. The first student in the group, the Researcher, collects research material about what features should be included in the model city of the future. *Note: You will know if you have enough information if you are able to fill in the data table.*
4. The second student, the Implementer, organizes the library material in a cohesive manner to make a poster, collage, or other visual image of the model city. Use your own drawings or pictures from magazines.
5. The third student, the Presenter, prepares an oral report and delivers it to the class. After the oral presentation, other class members may ask anyone in the group for more information about the group project.

ANALYSIS
1. What did your group choose for a power supply for your model city? Is your power supply pollution-free?
2. How did your model city recycle its wastes? Is this method pollution-free?

CONCLUSION
What do you think is the most important component of your model city of the future? *Note: For one possible answer, refer to the data table.*

CHAPTER
25
PROTECTING THE ENVIRONMENT

Earth is a complex collection of ecosystems, each with structured food webs and energy pyramids. Humans have connected these ecosystems by interacting with them to obtain food, shelter, and energy. Agriculture has carried grassland organisms into rain forests. Construction has placed homes on top of wetlands. Dams have been built across flowing freshwater ecosystems.

Humans have also connected the human population through transportation, trade and commerce, and telecommunications. Humans have come to depend on their relationships with one another and with their environment. In effect, Earth exists as a global ecosystem.

25.1 THE GLOBAL ECOSYSTEM

Objectives • *Describe* the relationship between the environment, human behavior, and human values. • *Describe* the steps involved in decision-making and policy-making.

Chapter 24 discussed concepts that are important in applying a sustainable ethic to natural resources and the organisms that require these resources. Such concepts involve conservation, recycling, and source reduction. While it is essential to understand the theories behind recycling and conservation, it is equally important to understand how such plans can be applied effectively.

Economics and Values

Human behavior as it relates to resources is modeled after economic concepts. Human values as they relate to resources, however, are not easily modeled. Ideal models would reflect religious and cultural variables, as well as economic considerations.

Two main concepts in economics are the ideas of supply and demand. *Supply* is the availability of a resource to be purchased. *Demand* is the amount of a resource that people desire and are willing to purchase. *The relationship between supply and demand and the purchase price for a resource is represented by a* **supply–demand curve.** A supply-demand curve, as shown in Figure 25.1, represents how the price of a resource increases as the demand for that resource increases. The price will also increase if the supply of a source decreases. If the price is too high for a resource, other resources will be sought.

The supply and demand for a resource are controlled by different factors. Supply is merely the availability of a resource. Business or political control can make a resource unavailable, but if there is no resource, there is no supply. Demand, on the other hand, can be affected by values.

DATELINE **1977**

President Jimmy Carter instructed the Council on Environmental Quality and the State Department to study changes in population, resource depletion, pollution, and land management through the year 2000. In 1980, the results of the Global 2000 Report concluded that "If present trends continue, the world in 2000 will be more crowded, more polluted, less stable ecologically, and more vulnerable to disruption than the world we live in now...unless the nations of the world act decisively to alter current trends."

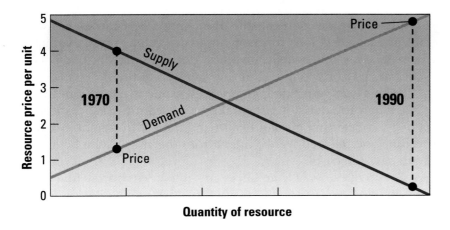

Figure 25.1 How people relate to the use of resources can be represented by a supply–demand curve.

Figure 25.2 Different human values determine how people may view a resource such as gold. Gold may be valued for economic, scientific, or cultural reasons.

At this point in the book, concepts and examples of policy-making, and not a listing of policies at local, federal, and international levels, should be provided as a guide to the next step, which is application. Some questions are left open-ended and nonspecific because it is hoped that if students leave the class with more questions, they will pursue answers related to environmental protection. Even if students may not intend to go into environmental science or related fields, their lives will still be very much affected by the concepts and the policies concerning the environment.

Value development is very complicated. Religion, culture, society, and economics are a few of the things that influence how people form values. For example, in the United States, the consumer society encourages people to buy new and improved products. The result is that people demand more resources.

Some things have no direct economic value. Air, water, food, space, and warmth are basic resources required by all living organisms. Regardless of the supply, the growing human population has demanded, and will continue to increase its demand for, these resources. Unfortunately, people must consider the supply of these resources because human activity not only depletes resources, it can damage them as well.

If the supply–demand curve was applied to current environmental conditions, basic resources would be shown as decreasing, and human demands would be shown as increasing. The price for basic resources would also be shown as increasing. No other resource can replace a basic resource. Money will not replace a basic resource. How would the price be paid?

Decisions for the Global Ecosystem

Each day, every person capable of making a decision makes several. To make decisions, a person has to determine priorities among the risks, costs, and benefits involved. Decisions may include which shoes to wear or when to shut the water off in the shower.

At this level, most people can easily come to a decision. However, when the decision must take into account risks, costs, and benefits concerning human health and the environment, matters become complicated. Who suffers from the risks? Who benefits? Who pays the costs?

Group interests play an important role in environmental decision-making. For example, two groups may argue over the risks, costs, and benefits of controlling toxic waste discharge into streams.

Industries that are forced to place controls in action may complain about their rising costs and the decrease in their profits. Groups not associated with these industries may argue that having less toxic waste in the stream will reduce health risks and health-care costs for the people who use or live near the stream. How are the risks, costs, and benefits evaluated so that a policy can be developed and put into effect?

Making Policies

There are questions involving time and money, and questions concerning whether or not changes need to be made. No one wants to change business or agricultural practices when there is no definite idea of the costs involved or of just how long it will be before a change must absolutely be made.

To regulate practices and activities in respect to their impact on the global ecosystem, policies are developed. *A **policy** is an outline of actions, incentives, penalties, and rules that a company, group, or government follows concerning a particular issue.* Developing an environmental policy involves making decisions based on risk assessment and cost/benefit analysis. Risk assessment and cost/benefit analysis are based on a system of educated estimates and predictions.

*Determining how much risk is acceptable is called **risk assessment***. Scientists conduct laboratory studies, examine historical events, and develop models to determine the relationship between causes and effects. In many cases, assessing the risks involved in using a particular product, technology, or activity is quite difficult. Money for research may be insufficient, and real-life cause-and-effect models for new products and new technology are limited.

Risk assessment can become subjective, however. Independent researchers or research groups must provide definite research results in order to receive funding. Researchers who work with particular industries must provide results that support the efforts of these industries.

Figure 25.3 Today, and certainly in the future, close contact with a potential environmental disaster is almost certain. Here, a residential area stands next to the cooling tower of a nuclear power plant.

THINK CRITICALLY

Much of the information concerning environmental protection is communicated through books, magazines, and scientific journals. How might literacy be related to policy development and enforcement?

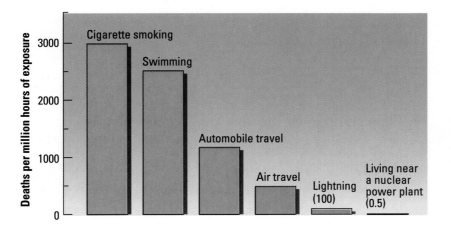

Figure 25.4 Historical research can help scientists and policymakers identify risks. However, where new technology and new activities are more frequent, historical models are rare. The only time to be certain of a risk is after problems occur.

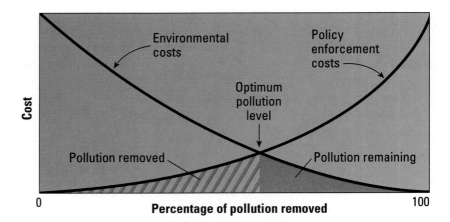

Figure 25.5 This graph shows the costs of controlling pollution compared to environmental costs. A cost/benefit analysis shows that the most favorable pollution level is one that provides a balance between protection costs and health risks.

Labels in figure:
Environmental costs
Policy enforcement costs
Optimum pollution level
Pollution removed
Pollution remaining
Cost
Percentage of pollution removed
0
100

The stronger reader is capable of gathering more information and making more informed decisions.

A **cost/benefit analysis** *is the analysis of social costs versus social benefits.* Cost/benefit analysis is a way of identifying the positive and negative impacts of environmental activities and determining the costs of these impacts. Next, the analysis reflects whether or not the benefits are greater than the costs. The goal is to determine how to increase benefits and reduce costs.

If a cost/benefit analysis is detailed and specific, interest groups may review and challenge the results of the analysis. Each interest group may be able to determine if the list of costs and benefits is complete. For example, economic and environmental harm can result from a policy that does not consider if using strip-cropping is more costly than the loss of soil.

However, many people argue that cost/benefit analysis is not effective for many issues. Critics of cost/benefit analysis maintain that not all things can be given a specific economic value. For example, how much is clean air or a beautiful landscape worth? Others argue that if an object is not given an economic value, its importance at the policy-making table will be reduced. Another drawback to cost/benefit analysis is that costs may be difficult to calculate if costs are shared by a large number of people, as is the case with air pollution.

1. A supply–demand curve is a graphic representation of the relationship between the supply, demand, and the price of a resource.
2. Religion, culture, society, and economics may all influence values through telecommunications, religious activities and ceremonies, advertising, cultural practices, and accessibility to resources.
3. The processes are risk assessment and cost/benefit analysis. Personal and group interests may conflict. Risk assessment may be subjective. Hidden costs may be difficult to identify or calculate.
4. Responses will vary.

SECTION REVIEW

1. What is a supply–demand curve?
2. List four factors that may influence value development, and give examples of how values may be communicated.
3. What processes are involved in policy development and decision-making? What are some problems related to these processes?
4. **Predict** What do you think the competition for basic resources such as food, water, and space will be like in 15 years in the United States?

Taking a Stand

How can you influence politics?

1. Responses will vary.
2. Answers will vary.

You may be disappointed to hear news about the failure of Congress to pass a wetlands protection act or pollution control legislation. Whatever your views on environmental issues, you can make a difference in how your country makes environmental decisions. You can write letters or telephone your congressional representatives and senators. You can join environmental interest groups. You can donate money for the protection of the environment. These personal actions, when multiplied by many concerned citizens, can drive the force of politics in our country.

In the early 1970s, funding for the SST, a supersonic jet, was overturned in Congress. The defeat was largely due to the efforts of citizens and environmental groups. The SST was supported by the president and by many corporations. When it came time to vote on the SST, Senator Clinton Anderson voted against it, although he was a strong supporter of the SST. His explanation was, "This morning my letters and telegrams opposed the SST by a whopping 78 to 8 margin." Letters and messages changed his mind. Letters to elected officials can accumulate until it becomes obvious that if they do not vote a certain way, they are not as likely to be reelected.

Letters do not have to be long or even typed. Recommendations for writing effective letters include the following:
• Address the letter properly:

Senator _____

U.S. Senate
Washington, DC 20510

or

Honorable _____
U.S. House of Representatives
Washington, DC 20510

• Identify the bill by number or describe the issue.
• Be brief. In a page or less, cover only one subject.
• Give reasons for your position. If you do not have time to write a letter, make a phone call. The number for the switchboard at the Capitol building is (202) 224-3121. Make sure you follow the recommendations outlined above.

Concentrating your efforts at the state and local levels is also essential to influence change. Most areas have organizations devoted to environmental issues. Some of these groups are the Sierra Club and the Audubon Society. There is a list of several such organizations on page 431 of this text. If you are not interested in joining the groups active in your area, you can obtain a listing of national and international environmental organizations in the *Conservation Directory* or the *World Directory of Environmental Organizations*, both available at most local libraries.

Become active, and you may influence decisions made by elected officials. Do nothing, and you can guarantee that your opinion will never be heard in Washington. Weigh the costs and benefits.

DECISIONS

1. Find out about an environmental issue or bill being presented in Congress. Write a letter to a member of Congress who supports or opposes the issue.
2. Is the issue one which affects you personally? If so, what is your next step?

25.2 LOCAL POLICIES

Objectives • *Identify* how environmental protection may be carried out at the local level. • *Explain* the reasons why policies may be more effective at the local level.

The words of a single voice must be informed and organized in order to be well heard. These words may be spoken through boycotts, letters, protests, court action, or voting. Personal concerns become community concerns when more people recognize the concern and understand that they all share it.

Many environmental problems are not spontaneous events. Instead, a potentially harmful condition persists, sometimes unnoticed, over an extended period of time during which a health hazard arises. The problem that occurred in Love Canal, New York, is a good example.

Problems related to the health hazard in Love Canal began in 1954. The company responsible for the dump maintains that local officials were aware of potential problems. However, it took until the late 1970s before local residents became aware of the toxic chemical dump under their feet.

Concerned citizens are often the first to vocalize the dangers of harmful environmental conditions. These people may sponsor discussions to enlighten the public about practices they feel influence their health and their environment. These people may choose to challenge existing policies.

In many communities, issues concerning environmental policies may be put on local ballots at election time. Such issues are

Figure 25.6 This map is an example of how local problems can be viewed as national concerns. Recall the crisis of the Ogallala aquifer, and consider how the High Plains states are connected.

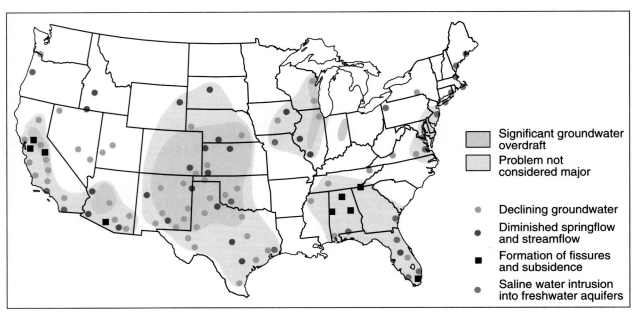

Significant groundwater overdraft

Problem not considered major

● Declining groundwater

● Diminished springflow and streamflow

■ Formation of fissures and subsidence

● Saline water intrusion into freshwater aquifers

often related to pollution, land management, and the quality of health. An example of a concern related to noise pollution is the construction of sound barriers along highways.

Land-management policies at the state and local levels address both land use and land pollution. Land-use policies may require that, before land can be developed, environmental impact studies must be performed. Conducted by ecologists, other scientists, and engineers, these studies predict how a proposed project may affect the biotic and abiotic factors in the environment.

Recall that two goals of recycling are decreasing solid wastes and reducing the need to open new landfills. Most recycling efforts have been started at the state or local level. For example, in 1972, the Oregon state legislature passed the state's first bottle law. The law required a deposit on cans and bottles for beverages such as soft drinks and beer. The bottle law helps reduce litter and increases recycling. By 1987, eight other states enacted similar laws: Connecticut, Delaware, Iowa, Maine, Massachusetts, Michigan, New York, and Vermont.

Recycling is only one of the ways that state and local governments are dealing with environmental issues. Prior to 1972, most environmental concerns were dealt with at the federal level. But since that time, the emphasis for environmental responsibility has been shifted back to local communities and states. This shift in focus is largely the result of a cutback in federal funds to states that do not meet environmental standards set by the federal government.

Many communities are implementing programs or practices designed to reduce energy consumption or provide alternatives to fossil-fuel use. Many utility companies now provide free home energy audits, including literature, to show customers how to reduce their energy use. In addition, the utility companies provide homeowners with energy-saving bulbs and rebates. Some communities are meeting their electrical demands by using alternatives to fossil fuels. In some communities, trash is being burned to generate the steam needed to produce electricity. Several communities in California now require solar hot water systems in all new housing.

If awareness of issues in the global ecosystem does not improve, environmental conditions will only get worse. Solving environmental problems at the state and local levels requires the education of citizens. Once educated, citizens must take action.

Figure 25.7 Residents sign petitions to protest the use of poisonous pesticides.

Word Power

Legislation, from the Latin *lex*, "law," and *latio*, "a proposing."

SECTION REVIEW

1. What is environmental responsibility?
2. List three ways in which local concerns may be communicated.
3. **Infer** Why might local policies be more easily developed and enforced than federal or international policies?

1. Responses will vary.
2. Voting, boycotts, protests, letter campaigns, legal action
3. Often, concerns and values are similar. The urgency of environmental issues may be more visible at the local level. Also, the problem may not seem too big to solve.

25.3 FEDERAL POLICIES

Objectives • **Explain** *the necessity for federal intervention in local environmental issues.* • **Identify** *opposing values and how they complicate policy enforcement.*

Federal policies involve a more complicated decision-making process than local policies. Whereas specific local issues are dealt with by local residents and local policies, federal policies must consider the local issues of many communities and states. Something that benefits one region of a nation may be a disadvantage to another region.

National Quality of Life

Although the responsibility for maintaining environmental quality lies largely with local and state governments, the federal government must intervene on behalf of the people when the actions of one state affect the quality of life in another state. Consider, for example, that a great deal of pollutants enter the Mississippi River at various points within the river's watershed. Because of the flowing nature of water, these pollutants have an impact on all the states located along the river. Resolution of such problems takes place most often in the form of environmental legislation.

The Environmental Protection Agency is responsible for managing and investigating environmental concerns so that effective federal legislation may be developed. Matters dealing with the environment, except those related to nuclear energy, fall under the EPA's control. Nuclear energy is regulated by the Nuclear Regulatory Commission (NRC). The different divisions of the EPA include: The Office of Planning and Management, Office of Enforcement, Office of Air and Waste Management, Office of Water and Hazardous Substances, and the Office of Research and Development.

Teaching tips for Field Activity appear on page T127.

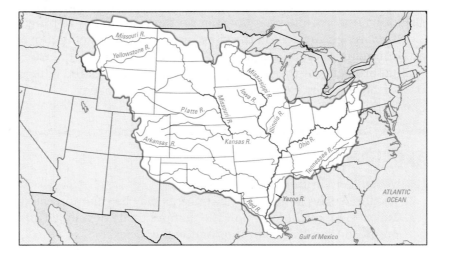

Figure 25.8 Toxic chemicals entering any area of the Mississippi River watershed can have widespread effects that cross many state boundaries.

FIELD ACTIVITY

Keeping in mind that people view environmental risks differently, conduct a poll. Develop a list of five environmental issues. Ask twenty to twenty-five people how they rate the risks of these five environmental issues, from low to high. Try to poll as many people from different backgrounds as possible. Be sure to ask about occupation, educational background, and age. Identify connections, if there are any, between these factors and environmental awareness. Present your findings to your class.

Figure 25.9 Fishing the waters of the Pacific Northwest and The Great Lakes is a way of life for many people in the United States. However, economic survival and concern for threatened fish populations has sparked many disputes among neighboring communities that fish these areas.

Native American Fishing Rights

Trout and salmon populations in the Pacific Northwest and the Great Lakes are seriously threatened. To reduce the threat to endangered fish populations, there are restrictions and bans on commercial fishing for the general public. However, treaties, or agreements, made between Native Americans and the U.S. government in the 1800s prohibit any changes from being made in Native-American fishing rights.

The fishing rights issue has gone to court many times. State and sport-fishing representatives argued that fishing methods had changed and that most fishing areas were stocked with fish from state hatcheries. In 1987, a federal judge ruled that because the treaty was a federal policy, the states had no right to regulate Native-American fishing.

Native-American nations involved in the fishing rights treaties are concerned with environmental issues and the livelihood of their communities. Attempts are being made between these nations and the federal government to develop policies that encourage a sustainable use for the fishing resources. For now, however, the controversies and conflicts continue—and probably will until new agreements are reached that settle these difficult issues.

Cooperative Learning
Have students form groups of three to five. Inform the groups that their common goal is to seek a well-planned solution to a common school problem. They may have a member of the group write down the steps they plan to take to solve this problem. Advise them to be positive and to respect each other's values. Also let them know that no responsible idea, no matter how creative, is worthless. Set a time limit. After time is up, ask students to state, either as a group or by representative, the outcomes of their "summit." How do the questions in problem-solving relate to policy-making?

1. A treaty is an agreement between nations that are concerned with the same issues. It is similar to a policy.
2. Different regions or states may only enforce local policy that supports their own needs, with little concern for the needs of other regions or states.
3. Regarding the way Native Americans have been treated throughout U.S. history, there is a moral question. There are economic concerns for the families of Native Americans and other U.S. citizens. Religious and cultural sensitivity in respect to how Native Americans use natural resources is also a concern.

SECTION REVIEW

1. What is a treaty?
2. Why is it important for the federal government to enforce environmental policies at the local level?
3. **Think Critically** What kinds of value issues may be involved in the fishing-rights dispute?

25.4 INTERNATIONAL POLICIES

Objectives • *Describe* the conflict between developed and developing nations over environmental policy issues. • *Identify* the importance of individuals in policy development at all levels.

Most scientists, environmentalists, and concerned citizens' groups agree that there is a need for international cooperation if a sustainable future is to be achieved. However, while cooperation is desirable, is it possible or even practical on a global scale?

Development and Environmental Protection

At present, there is a widening gap between the economic and political needs and interests of developed nations and those of developing nations. A common view among developing nations is that developed nations have already obtained wealth and consumed much of Earth's resources for their own needs. This comes at a time when developing countries, under pressure to obtain wealth through the sale of their resources, are cautioned by developed countries to conserve and better manage these resources. The argument is that developed nations dominate decision-making and policy-making to benefit themselves within international organizations such as the United Nations. Developing nations feel that such practices widen the economic gap between countries and encourage resentment and mistrust.

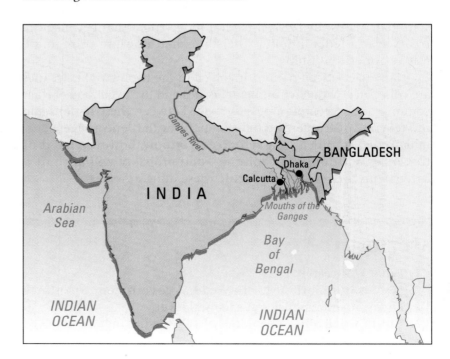

Figure 25.10 Half of India was once covered by forests. Today, in its race to meet economic needs, India has removed all but about 15 percent of its protective forests. Deforestation along the Ganges River has led to greater runoff and, consequently, to massive flooding in Bangladesh, located at the mouth of the Ganges.

Table 25.1 Outcomes of the Earth Summit

Agenda Item	Resolution
The Rio Declaration on Environment and Development	Statement of principle governing worldwide policy on the environment and development.
Agenda 21	Action plan for environmental protection and sustainable development.
Biodiversity Convention	Concerned with the extinction of species; requires signatory nations to inventory and protect endangered species.
Global Warming Convention	Commitment by nations to reduce greenhouse-gas emissions.
Statement on Forest Principles	A statement relative to the protection of the world's forests.

Figure 25.11 Here, on the Rio Grande between Mexico and the United States, Mexican citizens use water filled with runoff from nearby industrial activity for household needs. This is an example of why substantial international policies are needed.

A Global Agenda

In 1992, the United Nations had a meeting of all member nations in Rio de Janeiro. This meeting was called the Earth Summit. The countries attending this meeting addressed such issues as biodiversity, global warming, sustainable development, and relationships between developed and developing nations relating to environmental matters. Although these issues were addressed, many feel that more substantial action must be taken at this level. A summary of the major outcomes of the meeting is presented in Table 25.1.

Hearing a Single Voice

The policies made at local, federal, and international levels may involve scientists, powerful politicians, and business leaders, but those policies usually begin with a single voice. For example, a high school student in the United States became concerned about the number of dolphins captured and killed by fishermen using tuna nets. This student began a writing campaign to heads of corporations that processed tuna products. As public pressure grew and boycotts threatened the tuna industry, several companies changed their fishing practices to reduce the threat to dolphins.

SECTION REVIEW

1. What was the Earth Summit?
2. In what ways are developed nations and developing nations divided over global environmental concerns?
3. **Infer** What is the relationship between environmental protection and economic development?

1. It was a meeting held by the United Nations to develop an outline for global environmental protection policies.
2. There is a conflict of opinion concerning how developed nations may dominate policy-making procedures. Developing nations may require more resources and fewer restrictions on how they use the resources.
3. Responses will vary.

Answers and teaching
strategies on page T127.

Government and the Environment

PROBLEM
How do you communicate your concerns about the environment to your elected government officials?

MATERIALS (per group)
- paper
- pen or pencil
- notebook (one per student)

PREDICTION
After reading through the activity, predict how a group of people polled will respond to a particular question regarding the environment.

PROCEDURE
1. Each group makes a list of four or more environmental issues. *Note: Topics might be local water quality, clear-cutting of timber stands, offshore oil drilling, use of public lands, and disposal of hazardous wastes.*
2. From the list, the group selects one issue that particularly interests all group members. Research the facts on this issue in the library, and put your data in your notebook.
3. Conduct your own opinion poll, with each group member asking ten people outside of the class their position on this issue. Use the data table to record the results of your poll.

Table 25.2

Issue Being Investigated:	
Number of people for:	
Number of people against:	
Number undecided:	

4. As a group, write a letter to send to one of your elected government officials in Washington, DC, stating the results of your environmental poll. *Note: In your letter, be sure to include the facts about the issue that you compiled in your library research. Use a positive tone, and offer practical suggestions for a solution.*
5. From the information in the enrichment feature, select a congressperson to receive your letter. Make a photocopy of your letter, then put it in the mail.
6. If you receive a response, describe the position of the person you contacted. If you do not receive a response, send a copy of your letter to another government official.
7. Have a class discussion summing up what you learned about communicating with people in the government about environmental issues.

ANALYSIS
1. Did your predictions about the results of your poll prove to be correct? Were you surprised by the data you collected?
2. What did you learn about conducting opinion polls that you would do differently next time?

CONCLUSION
1. Considering all the data your group collected, are you happy with the response you received from your government official?
2. From all the data you collected and the people you polled, have you changed or modified your views on your particular environmental issue? Why or why not?

KEY TERMS

policy 25.1   cost/benefit analysis 25.1
risk assessment 25.1   supply–demand curve 25.1

CHAPTER SUMMARY

25.1 While food supplies and living space are decreasing, the human population is increasing. Supply–demand curves show that competition for resources will intensify as more demands are placed on a scarce supply. Decisions and policies are made to regulate the ways supplies are used. They are based on risk assessment and cost/benefit analysis.

25.2 Voting, boycotts, and protests are a few ways in which the voice of the individual may be heard throughout the community. Attitudes need to change to include a complete picture of the global ecosystem. Education and action are the keys to dealing with environmental problems.

25.3 Federal policies must consider the costs and benefits for all members of the country. When states come into conflict over environmental issues, the federal government must intervene. Intervention can be complicated by issues of culture, morals, and economics.

25.4 There are disagreements on how to attain global cooperation. Developing and developed nations have different economic and political attitudes. Current attitudes need to change in order for people to act on ideas developed in international discussions, such as the Earth Summit. The voices and actions of individuals are the most important part of policy-making.

MULTIPLE CHOICE

Choose the letter of the word or phrase that best completes each statement.

1. Earth can be considered a global ecosystem because its organisms (a) live on the same planet; (b) interact closely; (c) use oxygen; (d) gather food in special ways. b

2. Competition for resources will intensify because (a) global temperatures are rising; (b) agriculture is improving; (c) supplies are becoming scarce; (d) technology is advancing. c

3. Risk assessment depends on (a) scientific research; (b) climate; (c) political stability; (d) medicine. a

4. Risk-assessment models are used to (a) control pollution; (b) maintain treaty agreements; (c) reduce population growth; (d) develop policies. d

5. Definitions of risks are (a) objective; (b) persuasive; (c) subjective; (d) destructive. c

6. An argument against cost/benefit analysis is that it requires (a) too much time; (b) placing a monetary value on everything; (c) risk-assessment models; (d) hidden costs. b

7. Developing nations often suffer great environmental destruction because (a) they place little value in the environment; (b) they have so few environmental resources; (c) they are desperate for economic development; (d) they control environmental policy-making. c

8. Boycotting is a way of (a) fishing for tuna; (b) voting; (c) protesting; (d) assessing risks. c

9. In the United States, public perception and professional perception of risk is (a) similar; (b) different; (c) low; (d) high. b

10. Native-American fishing rights are protected by (a) a state judge; (b) senators and congresspersons; (c) cultural practices; (d) federal treaties. d

WORD COMPARISONS

Write the letter of the second word pair that best matches the first pair.

1. Supply: demand as (a) basic resource: human population; (b) food: eating; (c) ice: water; (d) benefit: cost. a
2. Value: demand as (a) food: human population; (b) voting: policy; (c) religion: culture; (d) television: popular media. b
3. Individual: policy as (a) voting: democracy; (b) federal: international; (c) pollution: environment; (d) cars: pollution. a
4. Environmental responsibility: sustainable resource as (a) frontier ethic: human population; (b) water use: depletion; (c) air travel: risk; (d) exercise: endurance. d
5. Earth Summit: global agenda as (a) local policy: federal policy; (b) math class: math; (c) school: telecommunications; (d) federal policy: Earth Summit. b

CONCEPT REVIEW Answers on page T127.

Write a complete response for each of the following.

1. What is meant by the terms *supply* and *demand*?
2. How is price related to demand?
3. What are the factors that can make risk assessment difficult?
4. List three drawbacks in identifying costs for a cost/benefit analysis.
5. Explain the connections that make Earth a global ecosystem.

THINK CRITICALLY Answers on page T127.

1. When two or more organisms compete for the same resource, such as food, what will happen?
2. What costs and benefits may be hidden or difficult to estimate in some agricultural or mining practices?
3. If you were in charge of the budgeting office of the EPA, what environmental issues would you make sure received federal funding? On what criteria would you base your funding?
4. What does the expression, "Think globally, act locally" mean? How does it apply to the way you think and act?
5. At the personal level, what may be the largest obstacles to acting in the name of environmental protection?

WRITE FOR UNDERSTANDING

Use your outline to apply a step-by-step procedure for the use of insecticides in and around your home. Recall relevant concepts from previous chapters, such as ecosystem balance, hazardous wastes, and water pollution.

PORTFOLIO

Collect photographs, illustrations, and articles on environmental issues, such as water usage. Organize the materials into four categories: personal, local, federal, and international. Use your collection to highlight the issues that concern you most. Determine ways in which a resolution could be approached for each issue. Design a flowchart for each issue, showing the problem and your hypothetical solution. Include brief cost/benefit analyses.

Use Figure 25.6 to answer the following.

1. Where are the regions of significant over-draft located?
2. Is the level of water use in these areas a local issue or a national issue? Explain.
3. How might the global ecosystem be affected by this intense water usage?
4. Predict changes that may occur in the light- and dark-shaded regions as agricultural methods allow more efficient water usage.

ACTIVITY 25.2

Answers and teaching strategies on page T127.

PROBLEM

How do you decide which community-owned lands should be developed and which ones should be left as open space?

MATERIALS

- colored pencils
- notebook

INFERENCE

After reading through the activity, make an inference about the value of open space in your community.

PROCEDURE

1. Walk around your neighborhood or community, noticing the open spaces, including gardens, lawns, parks, and playing fields.
2. In your notebook, make a scale map of your neighborhood, and shade in the areas that are open spaces. Write down the approximate percentage of land that is open space.
3. After you have finished shading in the open areas, choose one prime open space in a central location. Now consider constructing a much-needed community medical clinic on this site.
4. Do library research to find out which species, if any, would be affected by building in this open space. To help you sort your data, copy the following questions into your notebook, leaving spaces for the answers:
   - How many km² would the clinic occupy?
   - How many km² do you estimate would be used for parking?
   - What is the total number of km² lost to this building site?
   - How many animal species would be displaced by the building?
   - Would any species be driven completely from its habitat?
   - What is the total potential loss of wildlife?
5. Contact several local government officials, and ask them what the potential positive effects of building a clinic in your community would be. In your notebook, answer the questions in Step 4. List the potential benefits to the community, such as increased revenues, as well as any negative effects you may be told about.

ANALYSIS

1. What would be the economic advantages to the community of building a clinic on this site? Would there be any economic disadvantages?
2. Consider the long-range effects on your neighborhood. How would the community ecosystem be affected by building a clinic?

CONCLUSION

1. Based on your research, what are the positive effects of building a clinic in the open space in your community?
2. Conduct a class discussion about the positive and negative environmental effects for the neighborhood. In the long run, which do you think is more important to the community: open spaces or increased revenues?

SOLID WASTE MANAGEMENT

Solid waste management is the fastest growing environmental field, and will continue to grow in the foreseeable future. How people in the United States dispose of more than 180 million metric tons of solid waste every year is the responsibility of solid waste managers. Solid waste management utilizes proven methods to reduce the amount and potential hazards of solid wastes, and manages conservation programs that reduce the production of solid wastes.

People in solid waste management are generally involved in one of four specialty areas:

- Recycling, which involves recovering materials from the waste stream and separating them into reusable goods.
- Sanitary landfills, where almost three-fourths of all municipal solid waste is deposited.
- Source reduction, which keeps solid wastes out of the waste stream by encouraging companies to use less packaging.
- Clean waste combustion (or waste-to-energy combustion), which produces energy through the burning of clean wastes.

About 40 percent of those in solid waste management are in the public sector, working at the state and local levels. There are a few federal agencies that hire solid waste managers, but the federal government usually turns over the responsibility for solid waste management to the states and local areas where the solid waste is generated.

The private sector accounts for 45 percent of the people employed in the solid waste field. As the year 2000 approaches, the trend is for this sector to continue to be dominated by several large waste disposal companies. The time is gone when family-run companies dominated the business. New laws and technology have made it extremely costly to run a solid waste disposal company, which is something that cannot be done on a small scale because the equipment is so expensive. The nonprofit sector employs about 15 percent of the solid waste managers, and most of those work for small, locally-based recycling agencies.

People enter the solid waste management field from a variety of educational backgrounds. Some feel it is essential to have an advanced degree before entering the job market. Others suggest obtaining a bachelor's degree (and doing plenty of volunteer and internship work), then securing an entry-level position and working in the field to acquire experience. Once you have identified your special interest area, you can obtain an advanced degree.

SOLID WASTE CONSULTANTS ▶

These professionals design, build, and operate new landfill sites that are safe and effective, and renovate older sites. Landfills have become high-technology systems, and consultants are needed who can work with collection, emission, and groundwater-monitoring systems.

RECYCLING COORDINATORS ▲

There may be more new positions for recycling coordinators than almost any environmental career students could choose. It is a career that appeals to environmental generalists, and the formal education a person obtains is not as important as a demonstrated ability to organize and get things done, create a team, and manage diligently.

Recycling coordinators design and manage recycling programs, find markets for collected goods, and educate the public about the need to decrease the amount of solid waste that goes into landfills.

SOLID WASTE BUDGET SPECIALISTS ▼

These people are the financial experts in the solid waste management field. They provide the dollar figures that determine whether a particular program or site is going to be financially effective, and what the present and future costs of such systems will be. Because these programs are so costly and time-consuming, these financial experts play important roles in making financial projections that often determine whether a site will be developed or not.

ENVIRONMENTAL ENGINEERS ▲

Environmental engineers design systems and processes to reduce and recycle solid wastes, and treat potentially hazardous waste water. Environmental engineers may design programs to reduce the amount of paper used in a large corporation, or they may devise methods to recycle and reuse styrofoam packaging materials.

FOR MORE INFORMATION:

Air and Waste Management Association
P.O. Box 2861
Pittsburgh, PA 15230
(412) 232–3444

National Recycling Coalition
1101 30th Street NW, Suite 305
Washington, DC 20007
(202) 625–6406

National Solid Waste Management Association
(Publishes the monthly *Waste Age* and the bimonthly *Recycling Times*; offers internships)
1730 Rhode Island Avenue NW, Suite 1000
Washington, DC 20036
(202) 659–4613

METRIC CONVERSIONS

Metric Units	Metric to English	English to Metric
Length		
meter (m) = 100 cm	1 m = 3.28 feet 1 m = 1.09 yards	1 foot = 0.305 m 1 yard = 0.914 m
kilometer (km) = 1000 m	1 km = 0.62 mile	1 mile = 1.609 km
centimeter (cm) = 0.01 m	1 cm = 0.39 inch	1 foot = 0.305 m 1 foot = 30.5 cm
millimeter (mm) = 1000 m	1 mm = .039 inch	1 inch = 2.54 cm
micron (μm) = 10^{-6} m		
nanometer (nm) = 10^{-9} m		
Area		
square meter (m^2) = 10 000 cm^2	1 m = 1.1960 square yards	1 square yard = 0.8361 m^2 1 square foot = .0929 m^2
square kilometer (km^2) = 100 hectares	1 km = 0.3861 square mile	1 square mile = 2.590 km^2
hectare (ha) = 10 000 square meters	1 ha = 2.471 acres	1 acre = 0.4047 ha
square centimeters (cm^2) = 100 mm	1 cm = 0.155 square inch	1 square inch = 6.4516 cm^2
Mass		
gram (g) = 1000 mg	1 g = 0.0353 ounce	1 ounce = 28.35 g
kilogram (kg) = 1000 g	1 kg = 2.205 pounds	1 pound = 4536 kg
milligram (mg) = 0.001 g		
microgram (μg) = 10^{-6} g		
Volume (Solids)		
1 cubic meter (m^3) = 1 000 000 (cm)	1 m = 1.3080 cubic yards 1 m = 35.315 cubic feet	1 cubic yard = 0.7646 m^3 1 cubic foot = 0.0283 m^3
1 cubic centimeter (cm^3) = 1000 (mm)	1 cm = 0.0610 cubic inch	1 cubic inch = 16.387 cm^3
Volume (Liquids)		
liter (L) = 1000 milliliters	1 L = 1.06 quarts	1 quart = 0.941 L
kiloliter (kL) = 1000 liters	1 kL = 264.17 gallons	1 gallon = 3.7851 L
milliliter (mL) = 0.001 liter	1 mL = 0.034 fluid ounce	1 pint = 0.471 L
microliter (μL) = 0.000001 liter		1 fluid ounce = 29.57 mL

Periodic Table of the Elements

This numbering system is used by the International Union of Pure and Applied Chemistry (IUPAC)

Legend:
- **11** — Atomic number
- **Na** — Element symbol
- Sodium — Element name
- 22.990 — Average atomic mass

1	2	3	4	5	6	7	8	9	10	11	12	13	14	15	16	17	18
1 **H** Hydrogen 1.0079																	2 **He** Helium 4.0026
3 **Li** Lithium 6.941	4 **Be** Beryllium 9.0122											5 **B** Boron 10.81	6 **C** Carbon 12.011	7 **N** Nitrogen 14.007	8 **O** Oxygen 15.999	9 **F** Fluorine 18.998	10 **Ne** Neon 20.179
11 **Na** Sodium 22.990	12 **Mg** Magnesium 24.305											13 **Al** Aluminum 26.982	14 **Si** Silicon 28.086	15 **P** Phosphorus 30.974	16 **S** Sulfur 32.06	17 **Cl** Chlorine 35.453	18 **Ar** Argon 39.948
19 **K** Potassium 39.098	20 **Ca** Calcium 40.08	21 **Sc** Scandium 44.956	22 **Ti** Titanium 47.90	23 **V** Vanadium 50.941	24 **Cr** Chromium 51.996	25 **Mn** Manganese 54.938	26 **Fe** Iron 55.847	27 **Co** Cobalt 58.933	28 **Ni** Nickel 58.71	29 **Cu** Copper 63.546	30 **Zn** Zinc 65.38	31 **Ga** Gallium 69.72	32 **Ge** Germanium 72.59	33 **As** Arsenic 74.922	34 **Se** Selenium 78.96	35 **Br** Bromine 79.904	36 **Kr** Krypton 83.80
37 **Rb** Rubidium 85.468	38 **Sr** Strontium 87.62	39 **Y** Yttrium 88.906	40 **Zr** Zirconium 91.22	41 **Nb** Niobium 92.906	42 **Mo** Molybdenum 95.94	43 **Tc** Technetium (97)	44 **Ru** Ruthenium 101.07	45 **Rh** Rhodium 102.91	46 **Pd** Palladium 106.4	47 **Ag** Silver 107.87	48 **Cd** Cadmium 112.41	49 **In** Indium 114.82	50 **Sn** Tin 118.69	51 **Sb** Antimony 121.75	52 **Te** Tellurium 127.60	53 **I** Iodine 126.90	54 **Xe** Xenon 131.30
55 **Cs** Cesium 132.91	56 **Ba** Barium 137.33	71 **Lu** Lutetium 174.97	72 **Hf** Hafnium 178.49	73 **Ta** Tantalum 180.95	74 **W** Tungsten 183.85	75 **Re** Rhenium 186.21	76 **Os** Osmium 190.2	77 **Ir** Iridium 192.22	78 **Pt** Platinum 195.09	79 **Au** Gold 196.97	80 **Hg** Mercury 200.59	81 **Tl** Thallium 204.37	82 **Pb** Lead 207.2	83 **Bi** Bismuth 208.98	84 **Po** Polonium (209)	85 **At** Astatine (210)	86 **Rn** Radon (222)
87 **Fr** Francium (223)	88 **Ra** Radium 226.03	103 **Lr** Lawrencium (260)	104 **Unq** (261)	105 **Unp** (262)	106 **Unh** (263)	107 **Uns** (264)	108 **Uno** (265)	109 **Une** (266)									

Lanthanide Series

57 **La** Lanthanum 138.91	58 **Ce** Cerium 140.12	59 **Pr** Praseodymium 140.91	60 **Nd** Neodymium 144.24	61 **Pm** Promethium (145)	62 **Sm** Samarium 150.4	63 **Eu** Europium 151.96	64 **Gd** Gadolinium 157.25	65 **Tb** Terbium 158.93	66 **Dy** Dysprosium 162.50	67 **Ho** Holmium 164.93	68 **Er** Erbium 167.26	69 **Tm** Thulium 168.93	70 **Yb** Ytterbium 173.04

Actinide Series

89 **Ac** Actinium (227)	90 **Th** Thorium 232.04	91 **Pa** Protactinium 231.04	92 **U** Uranium 238.03	93 **Np** Neptunium 237.05	94 **Pu** Plutonium (244)	95 **Am** Americium (243)	96 **Cm** Curium (247)	97 **Bk** Berkelium (247)	98 **Cf** Californium (251)	99 **Es** Einsteinium (254)	100 **Fm** Fermium (257)	101 **Md** Mendelevium (258)	102 **No** Nobelium (259)

Word Part	Meaning	Example
a-, an-	not, without	abiotic
aero-	air	aeration
agri-	field, farm	agriculture
aqua-	water	aquatic
bio-	life	biosphere
-cide	kill	pesticide
de-	from	detritus
decid-	fall down	deciduous
demo-	people	demography
eco-	house	ecosystem
gen-	produce, make	generator
geo-	earth	geology
-graph	written	biography
hetero-	mixed, different	heterotroph
homo-, homeo-	same	homogenious
hydro-	water	hydroelectric
hyper-	above, over	hyperactive
hypo-	under, beneath	hypothesis
iso-	equivalent	isotope
-logy	study	biology
mal-	bad, faulty	malnutrition
macro-	large	macronutrient
micro-	small	microscope
-meter	measure	kilometer
mono-	single	monoculture
para-	beside, along	parasite
patho-	suffering	pathogen
phos-, phot-	light	photic
phyto-	plant, plantlike	phytoplankton
poly-	many	polyunsaturated
sol-	sun	solar
syn-	put together	synthesis
sub-	under, beneath	subside
-troph	nourishment	autotroph
therm-	heat	thermosphere
-thesis	position, proposal	hypothesis
zoo-	animal	zooplankton

Environmental Organizations and Periodicals

Conservation International
1015 18th Street, N.W., Suite 1000
Washington, DC 20036
(202) 429-5660
Periodical: *Orion Nature Quarterly*

The Cousteau Society
870 Greenbrier Circle, Suite 402
Chesapeake, VA 23320
(804) 523-9335

Earth Action Network
P.O. Box 6667
Syracuse, NY 13217
Periodical: *E: The Environmental
        Magazine*

Earth Island Institute
300 Broadway, Suite 28
San Francisco, CA 94133
(415) 788-3666

Greenpeace USA, Inc.
1436 U Street, N.W.
Washington, DC 20009
(202) 462-1177
Periodical: *Greenpeace Magazine*

High Country News
P.O. Box 1090
Paonia, CO 81428

League of Conservation Voters
1707 L Street, N.W., Suite 550
Washington, DC 20036
(202) 785-8683

National Audubon Society
700 Broadway
New York, NY 10003
(212) 797-3000
Periodical: *Audubon*

**National Parks and
Conservation Association**
1015 31st Street, N.W.
Washington, DC 20007
(202) 944-8530
Periodical: *National Parks and
        Conservation Magazine*

National Wildlife Federation
1412 16th Street, N.W.
Washington, DC 20036
(202) 797-6800
Periodicals: *National Wildlife
        International Wildlife*

Rainforest Action Network
450 Sansome, Suite 700
San Francisco, CA 94111
(415) 398-4404

Sierra Club
730 Polk Street
San Francisco, CA 94109
(415) 776-2211
Periodical: *Sierra*

**Texas Natural Resources
Conservation Commission**
P.O. Box 13087
Austin, TX 78711
1-800-64-TEXAS
Publications: Various information packets
        available on request

**United Nations
Environment Programme**
United Nations, Rm. DC2-0803
New York, NY 10017
(212) 963-8138

World Wildlife Fund
1250 24th Street, N.W.
Washington, DC 20037
(202)293-4800

WorldWatch Institute
1776 Massachusetts Avenue, N.W.
Washington, DC 200036
(202)452-1999
Periodicals: *WorldWatch
        State of the World*

GLOSSARY

Key Terms are defined in the glossary to clarify their meaning in the text. The numbers following the definitions correspond to sections in the text.

In the text some terms and names have been respelled as an aid to pronunciation. A key to pronouncing the respelled words appears here.

Pronounciation Key

Like other words in this book, the term *aquifer* has been respelled to indicate its pronunciation: AWK-weh-fer. A hyphen is used between syllables. Capital letters mean that a syllable should be spoken with stress.

Pronounce "a" as in hat

ah	father
ar	tar
ay	say
ayr	air
e, eh	hen
ee	bee
eer	deer
er	her
g	go
i, ih	him
j	jet
k	car
ng	ring
o	frog
oh	no
oo	soon
or	for
ow	plow
oy	boy
sh	she
th	think
u, uh	sun
y	kite
z	zebra
zh	measure

abiotic factor   a nonliving part of the environment *2.3*

acid precipitation   rain or snow that is more acidic than normal precipitation *22.3*

active solar heating system   a system using devices to collect, store, and circulate heat produced from solar energy *17.1*

aeration   a water treatment method where cleaned and filtered water is exposed to air and sunlight *20.3*

aerogenerator   a windmill used to generate electricity; also called a wind turbine generator *17.3*

agribusiness   large corporations that have taken over much of U.S. agriculture using large, expensive farm equipment instead of human labor *14.3*

agricultural revolution   occurred around 8000 B.C. when hunters and gatherers began to develop farming techniques, and learned to domesticate animals *13.1*

agricultural society   a society where crops are grown and people have specialized roles *12.2*

air pollution   harmful substances released into the air *22.1*

alien species   a non-native species introduced to an area by humans *23.1*

alpha particle   a large particle made up of two protons and two neutrons, given off by radioactive atoms *16.1*

anthracite coal   a metamorphic rock that has been changed from sedimentary bituminous coal into hard coal by extreme pressure and heat *15.2*

aphotic zone   in a body of water, the layer of water below the photic zone that receives no sunlight *10.1*

aquaculture   the commercial production of fish in a controlled, maintained environment *14.2*

aquatic   describes a habitat where the organisms live in or on water *10.1*

aquifer   an underground layer of porous rock that contains water *1.2, 20.2*

artesian well   a well in which water flows to the surface due to high pressure underground *1.2*

atmosphere   the layer of gases that surrounds Earth *1.1*

atomic number   the number of protons in the atoms of a given element *16.1*

autotroph   a producer that makes its own food;

autotroph   a producer that makes its own food; the first trophic level in an ecosystem *4.1*

bedrock   the combination of the igneous, metamorphic, and sedimentary rock of the lithosphere that exists as mountains, cliffs, or low-lying plains *18.3*

benthic zone   the floor of a body of water *10.1*

beta particle   a high-speed electron given off by radioactive atoms *16.1*

bioconversion   the conversion of organic materials into fuels *15.4*

biodegradable   describes substances that decompose easily and enrich the soil *19.4*

biodiversity   the variety of species in an ecosystem *3.3, 23.1*

biological magnification   the increasing concentration of a pollutant in organisms at higher trophic levels in a food web *4.2*

biomass   the total amount of organic matter present in a trophic level *4.3*

biomass fuel   a fuel, such as wood, formed from the products of living organisms *15.4*

biome   a major type of ecosystem with distinctive temperature, rainfall, and organisms *6.3*

biomedical revolution   an occurrence of the twentieth century that has resulted in population growth because the death rate has decreased as many life-threatening diseases have been controlled by antibiotics, vaccines, and modern hygiene techniques *13.1*

biosphere   the combined parts of the lithosphere, hydrosphere, and atmosphere where life exists *1.4*

biotic factor   a living part of the environment *2.3*

bituminous coal   an abundant, soft coal found deep in Earth's crust *15.2*

brackish   describes water that is more saline than fresh water, but less saline than ocean water *10.1*

breeder reactor   a reactor that generates fuel as it works *16.2*

bubonic plague   a plague that struck much of Europe and Asia in the mid-fourteenth century, resulting in the deaths of about 25 percent of the adult populations of these areas; also known as the Black Death *13.1*

bunchgrass   a short, fine-bladed grass that grows in a clump *8.2*

buttress   a ridge of wood on the trunk of a rainforest tree that provides support for the tree *9.3*

cancer   a disease where cells grow abnormally and out of control *22.2*

canopy   the highest layer of a deciduous forest *9.2*

carbohydrate   a compound of carbon, hydrogen, and oxygen in a 1:2:1 ratio *14.1*

carnivore   an organism that captures and eats herbivores or other carnivores *4.1*

carrying capacity   the number of individuals of a species that can be supported by an ecosystem *5.3*

cash crop   a crop grown for the purpose of export sale *14.2*

chain reaction   the continuous action of neutrons splitting atomic nuclei *16.2*

chaos theory   a type of mathematics that suggests that ecosystems may be sensitive to even very small changes, and that the beginning state of an ecosystem is crucial to its later development *6.3*

chemical and biological treatment plants   treatment plants where some hazardous wastes are treated and made harmless (neutralized), then safely disposed of *19.4*

chlorofluorocarbon (CFC)   a compound of carbon, chlorine, and fluorine once used in refrigerators, air conditioners, aerosol cans, and in the production of styrofoam *22.1*

clay soil   soil that contains grains smaller than 0.002 mm in diameter *18.3*

climax community   a diverse community that does not undergo further succession *6.2*

coagulant   a chemical that is added to water to aid in the settling process *20.3*

coevolution   the process where species interact so closely with one another that they adapt to one another *5.2*

commensalism   a symbiotic relationship that benefits one of the organisms and neither helps nor harms the other organism *6.1*

community   all the populations that live and interact in the same environment *3.3*

compaction   a process where the space decreases between the particles of soil, preventing the flow of air and water, which makes the soil very hard and less able to absorb moisture *18.4*

competitive exclusion   the extinction of a population due to direct competition with another species for a particular resource in a niche *5.1*

compost pile   a combination of plant waste and food waste collected together to form a type of humus *19.4*

conductor   any material through which heat and electricity flow relatively freely *18.1*

conifer   a tree that produces seed cones *6.4, 9.1*

conservation a strategy to reduce the use of resources through decreased demand and increased efficiency *24.1*

consumer an organism that cannot make its own food *4.1*

continental shelf the shallow border that surrounds the continents *11.2*

contour farming a soil conservation method of plowing along the slope instead of across the slope *19.3*

control an experimental situation where the variable being tested is missing *2.2*

control rod rod of neutron-absorbing material used to regulate the chain reaction in a nuclear reactor *16.2*

controlled incineration the burning of wastes at extremely high temperatures *19.4*

convergent evolution the independent development of similar adaptations in two species with similar niches *5.2*

corrosive wastes a type of hazardous wastes that can eat through steel and many other types of materials *19.2*

cost/benefit analysis the analysis of the social costs versus the social benefits of an activity or policy.

crop rotation a farming method where the type of crop grown in a particular area is changed on a regular cycle *14.4*

deciduous describes a tree that sheds its leaves during a particular season each year *6.4, 9.2*

decomposer a bacterium or fungus that consumes the bodies of dead organisms and other organic wastes *4.1*

deep-well injection a disposal method where liquid hazardous wastes are pumped deep into porous rocks below drinking-water aquifers *19.4*

deforestation the destruction of forestlands as a result of human activity *9.3*

demand the amount of a resource that people desire and are willing to purchase *25.1*

demography the science of the changing vital statistics in a human population *13.2*

density-dependent limiting factor a limiting factor that is dependent on population size *5.3*

density-independent limiting factor a limiting factor that affects the same percentage of a population regardless of its size *5.3*

desalination a water treatment method where salts are removed from water *20.3*

desert a biome occurring throughout the world characterized by low humidity, high summer temperatures, and low annual rainfall *6.4, 7.1*

desert-grassland boundary an area between a desert and a grassland where increased rainfall enables some grasses to grow *8.1*

desertification the processs of changing semiarid land into desert as a result of human activity *7.2, 19.3*

detritus tiny pieces of dead organic material that are food for organisms at the base of an aquatic food web *11.1*

distillation a water treatment method where salt water is heated to boiling and salts separate out from the water vapor *20.3*

dormant a condition of an organism when the life processes within the body slow down *3.2*

doubling time of a population determines how long it will take, at the present rate of growth, for a particular population to double its size *13.2*

dredging a mining method that involves the scraping or vacuuming of desirable minerals from ocean floors, beaches, or streambeds *18.2*

drip (or trickle) irrigation an overhead irrigation method that uses tubing to deliver small quantities of water directly to the root system of plants *20.1*

drought season in grassland areas, long periods of little or no rain *8.1*

ductile any material that can be pulled and stretched into wires *18.2*

ecological pyramid a diagram that shows the relative amounts of energy in different trophic levels in an ecosystem *4.3*

ecosystem all the communities that live in an area together with the abiotic factors in the environment *3.3*

El Niño a disturbance of ocean winds and currents when a warm-water current lasts for several months along the western coast of South America *3.1*

emphysema a disease in which the tiny air sacs in the lungs break down *22.2*

environment everything that surrounds a particular organism *2.3*

equilibrium a state of balance between opposing forces *6.3*

erosion the wearing away of land by weather and water; a natural process where soil is lost, transported, and reformed *3.1, 14.4, 19.3*

essential amino acid   one of eight amino acids that humans must obtain from food to remain healthy *14.1*

estuary   a region of water where a freshwater source meets salt water from the ocean *11.2*

ethic   a guideline or rule for determining what is right and what is wrong *12.3*

eutrophication   the process in which lakes and ponds receive runoff rich in life-supporting plant nutrients *21.2*

evaporation   the movement of water into the atmosphere as it changes from a liquid to a gas *4.4*

evergreen   a tree that does not lose its leaves at a given time every year *9.1*

evolution   a gradual change in a population of organisms over time *5.2*

experimental variable   the variable being tested in an experiment *2.2*

exponential growth   population growth in which the rate of growth in each generation is a multiple of the previous generation *5.3*

extinction   the disappearance of a species from all or part of its geographical range *23.1*

famine   a severe food shortage that causes starvation and death to the inhabitants in a specific area *13.1*

filtration   a water treatment method where water is passed through screens to trap particles *20.3*

flood irrigation   a type of irrigation where flat expanses of land are flooded *20.1*

flowing-water ecosystem   a freshwater environment on land such as a river, stream, creek, or brook *10.3*

fluorescent light   a type of lighting that uses less energy than incandescent light and produces little heat *24.1*

food chain   a series of organisms that transfer food between the trophic levels in an ecosystem *4.2*

food web   a network of food chains representing the feeding relationships among the organisms in an ecosystem *4.2*

fossil fuel   fuel derived from the remains of organisms that lived long ago *15.1*

freezing   a water treatment method where salt water is frozen so that it separates into ice and brine slush; the ice is then melted and used as fresh water *20.3*

frontier ethic   the system of ethics in the modern industrial world, based on the view that humans are apart from nature *12.3*

fuel   any substance from which energy can be obtained *15.1*

fundamental niche   the theoretical niche that an organism can occupy *5.1*

furrow irrigation   a type of irrigation where water is released into ditches that have been dug between crop rows *20.1*

Gaia hypothesis   states that Earth is a single, living organism that regulates itself to maintain life *12.1*

gamma ray   a form of elecromagnetic radiation given off by the decay of unstable atomic nuclei *16.1*

gene bank   a secure place where seeds, plants, and genetic material are stored *23.4*

generalized species   a species that occupies a wide niche *5.2*

geographical range   the total area in which a species can live *3.3*

geothermal energy   heat energy that is generated deep within Earth *17.4*

germ theory of disease   developed about 300 years ago, this theory identified bacteria and other microorganisms as the agents responsible for many diseases *13.1*

global warming   an increase in Earth's average surface temperature caused by an increase in greenhouse gases *22.3*

grassland   an ecosystem where there is too much water to form a desert, but not enough water to support a forest *8.1*

greenhouse effect   the trapping of radiated heat by gases in the atmosphere *3.1, 22.3*

greenhouse gas   an atmospheric gas that traps heat *22.3*

Green Revolution   the development of new, disease-resistant strains of rice and wheat, plus the use of expensive modern farming methods, machinery, and technology that has brought about huge crops and lowered the overall price of the world's main food crops *14.2*

groundwater   water contained in porous or jointed bedrock *20.2*

growth rate of a population   arrived at by subtracting the death rate of a population from the birth rate *13.2*

habitat   an environment where a particular species lives *3.3*

habitat destruction   disturbing the part of an ecosystem that an organism needs to survive *23.1*

half-life the amount of time it takes half the atoms in a sample of a radioactive element to decay *16.1*

hazardous wastes solid, liquid, or gaseous wastes that are potentially harmful to humans and the environment, even in low concentrations *19.2*

heavy metal a poisonous metallic element with a high atomic mass *21.2*

herbivore an organism that eats only plants *4.1*

heterotroph a consumer that forms the second or higher levels in a trophic system *4.1*

hibernation dormancy in some animals when the heart rate and breathing slow down, the body temperature drops, and the animal enters a sleeplike state *3.2*

high-level wastes radioactive wastes that emit large amounts of radiation *16.3*

horizon a layer of topsoil or subsoil *18.3*

host the organism a parasite feeds on *6.1*

humus a layer of organic matter formed from decaying plant matter *8.2*

hunter–gatherer society a society where people gather natural food, hunt, and are nomadic *12.2*

hydrocarbon a compound made only of carbon and hydrogen *15.1*

hydroelectric power electricity that is produced from the energy of moving water *17.2*

hydrogenate the process of adding more hydrogen to liquid vegetable oils to give the oils more texture *14.1*

hydrosphere the parts of Earth that are made of water *1.1*

hypersaline describes lakes that are more saline than the ocean *10.1*

hypothesis a possible explanation for a set of observations *2.1*

ice age a long period of cooling when glaciers move from the poles and cover much of Earth's surface *3.1*

ice core a long cylinder of ice that is drilled and removed from deep within a sheet of polar ice *22.3*

igneous rock rock that is formed when liquid rock solidifies and cools *1.2*

ignitable wastes hazardous waste substances that can burst into flames at relatively low temperatures *19.2*

incandescent light this traditional type of lighting gives off much of its energy as heat and is less efficient than fluorescent light *24.1*

industrial society a society where the production of food and other products is performed by machines, requiring large amounts of energy and resources *12.2*

integrated pest management (IPM) a farming method that makes use of natural predators to control harmful pests, reducing the use of pesticides *14.4*

intertidal zone the region of shoreline that alternates between periods of exposure and periods of submersion at least twice each day *11.3*

ionosphere a layer of the thermosphere where gas molecules lose electrons and become ions *1.3*

irrigation the process of bringing water to an area for use in growing crops *20.1*

isotopes atoms of the same element that have different atomic masses *16.1*

keystone predator a predator that causes a large increase in the diversity of its habitat *5.1*

kilocalorie (kcal) The amount of energy needed to raise the temperature of 1 kg of water 1°C *14.1*

landfill a site where wastes are disposed of by burial *19.1*

leaching a process where rainwater moving through soil removes and carries away minerals *7.1*

legume a plant that has colonies of nitrogen-fixing bacteria on its roots *4.4*

lichen a plantlike organism that is a mutualistic relationship involving a fungus and an alga *6.2, 7.3*

lignite a soft, brown coal composed of 40 percent carbon *15.2*

limiting factor a factor that slows growth in a population *5.3*

lipid an organic compound that contains three long chains of fatty acids which is a main component of all cell membranes *14.1*

lithosphere the layer of land that forms Earth's surface *1.1*

loam soil type containing roughly equal amounts of clay, sand, and silt particles *18.3*

macronutrient a nutrient that provides the body with energy *14.1*

magma molten rock deep within Earth that becomes lava when it reaches the surface *17.4*

malleable any material that can be hammered and shaped without breaking *18.1*

malnutrition the lack of a specific type of nutrient in the diet *14.1*

mangrove swamp a coastal wetland that occurs in warm climates, characterized by mangrove trees or shrubs and water with little dissolved oxygen *11.3*

marine describes the ocean *11.1*

mass extinction a relatively short period of time during which many species die *23.1*

medical wastes hazardous wastes such as old medicines, lab containers, and specimens, some of which are considered toxic wastes *19.2*

medium-level and low-level wastes radioactive wastes that are not as dangerous as high-level wastes, although a much larger volume of these wastes is generated *16.3*

meltdown the process in which a nuclear chain reaction goes out of control and melts the reactor core *16.3*

mesosphere the layer of the atmosphere beyond the stratosphere, extending about 85 km above Earth's surface *1.3*

metamorphic rock rock that has been transformed by heat, pressure, or both *1.2*

micronutrient a nutrient that provides the body with small amounts of chemicals needed in biochemical reactions *14.1*

migration long-distance seasonal travel by animal populations *7.3*

mineral a naturally occurring, inorganic solid material that has a definite chemical composition, with atoms arranged in a specific pattern *18.1*

monoculture a farming technique in which only the highest dollar-yield crops are grown *14.3*

mutualism a symbiotic relationship where both species benefit *6.1*

natural gas fossil fuel in the gaseous state *15.3*

neritic zone the region between the continental shelf and the surface of the water *11.2*

niche the role of an organism in an ecosystem *5.1*

nitrate an inorganic compound containing three oxygen atoms and one nitrogen atom *4.4*

nitrite an inorganic compound containing two oxygen atoms and one nitrogen atom *4.4*

nocturnal describes animals that sleep during the day and are active at night *7.1*

noise pollution loud, continuous, or high-pitched sounds that are harmful to living things *22.5*

nonrenewable resource a resource that does not regenerate quickly *12.3*

nuclear fission a reaction in which the nucleus of a large atom is split into smaller nuclei, emitting large amounts of energy *16.2*

nuclear fusion the source of the energy given off by the sun, this process occurs when two atomic nuclei fuse to become one larger nucleus *17.4*

nuclear reactor vessel the structure where the fission of U-235 takes place *16.2*

nucleus the cluster of protons and neutrons in the center of an atom *16.1*

nutrient a substance needed by the body for energy, growth, repair, or maintenance *3.2*

ocean current water flow in the ocean in a characteristic pattern *11.1*

oceanic zone the open ocean, the largest zone in the marine biome that is more than 90 percent of the surface area of the world ocean *11.1*

octane (iso-octane) an important component of gasoline that rates the amount of energy contained in a particular gasoline *15.1*

omnivore an organism that eats both producers and consumers *4.1*

open-pit mining a surface mining method in which large machinery is used to dig huge pits where minerals are removed *18.2*

ore a rock that contains a relatively large amount of economically desirable mineral *18.1*

organism any living thing *1.1*

overdraft the process where a body of water is drained faster than it is filled *20.2*

overhead irrigation a type of irrigation method where a sprinkler system waters crops from above the ground *20.1*

oxide a type of gaseous pollutant that is a compound of oxygen and another element *22.1*

ozone an oxygen gas containing three oxygen atoms per molecule *1.3*

ozone depletion a 2 to 3 percent thinning of the global ozone layer that has occurred over the last ten years *22.3*

parasitism a relationship where one organism feeds on the tissues or body fluids of another organism *6.1*

parent rock bedrock that is the source of an area of soil *18.3*

particulate a type of air pollutant made of tiny solids suspended in the atmosphere *22.1*

passive solar heating the process where the sun's energy is collected, stored, and distributed in an enclosed dwelling. *17.1*

pathogen   a parasite, bacterium, or virus that causes diseases in living things *21.1*

pavement   the desert floor made up of hard-baked sand, bare rock particles, or both *7.1*

peat   a brittle, brown plant material used as a fuel that contains a great deal of water and a low percentage of carbon *15.2*

permafrost   the frozen soil below the active zone in tundra regions *7.3*

petroleum   a liquid fossil fuel; also known as crude oil *15.3*

phosphate   a nutrient containing phosphoric acid that can be a pollutant in large amounts *21.4*

photic zone   in a body of water, the top layer of water that receives enough sunlight for photosynthesis to occur *10.1*

photochemical smog   a yellow-brown haze that is formed when sunlight reacts with pollutants produced by cars *22.1*

photovoltaic cell (PV cell)   a device that uses thin wafers of semiconductor material to produce electricity directly from solar energy *17.1*

phytoplankton   plankton that carry out photosynthesis and are the main producers in aquatic biomes *10.2*

pioneer community   the first community to colonize a new habitat *6.2*

plankton   a general term for microorganisms that float near the surface of water *10.2*

policy   an outline of actions, incentives, penalties, and rules that a company, group, or government follows concerning a particular issue *25.1*

pollutant   a harmful material that enters the environment *22.1*

population   all members of a particular species that live in the same area *3.3*

prairie   a grassland area characterized by rolling hills, plains, and sod-forming grasses *6.4, 8.2*

predator   an organism that actively hunts other organisms *5.1, 6.1*

preserve   an area of land or water set aside for the protection of the ecosystem in that area *24.3*

prey   an organism upon which a predator feeds *6.1*

primary succession   the sequence of communities that forms in an originally lifeless habitat *6.2*

producer   an organism that makes its own food from inorganic molecules and energy *4.1*

protein   a large compound of amino acids used by the body to make blood, muscle, and other tissues *14.1*

radiation   alpha and beta particles and gamma rays that are given off in the decaying of unstable nuclei *16.1*

radioactive   describes atoms that emit particles and energy from their nuclei when they decay *16.1*

radioactive decay   the process that occurs when an atom emits radiation and becomes a different element or isotope *16.1*

radioactive wastes   hazardous wastes that give off radiation that is harmful to people and other organisms *19.2, 21.3*

radon   a colorless, odorless, radioactive gas formed by the decay of radium *22.1*

rain forest   a biome with a dense canopy of evergreen, broadleaf trees that receives at least 200 cm of rain each year *6.4, 9.3*

rainshadow effect   occurs when warm, moist air cools and loses most of its moisture as precipitation over the western side of mountainous regions, and the resulting cool, dry air picks up moisture from soil on the eastern side of the mountains *7.2*

rainy season   in a grassland area, part of the cycle of heavy rains that is followed by long periods of little or no rain *8.1*

range of tolerance   the range of temperatures at which an organism can survive *3.2*

reactive waste   an explosive type of hazardous waste *19.2*

realized niche   the actual niche that an organism occupies *5.1*

recycling   reducing resource use by collecting usable waste materials and using them to produce new items *24.2*

reef   a natural structure built on a continental shelf from the shells of small sea animals *11.2*

renewable resource   a resource that regenerates quickly *12.3*

residual soil   soil that sits on top of the parent rock from which it was formed *18.3*

reverse osmosis   a water treatment method where salt water is forced through a strainer to remove the salts *20.3*

rill   a shallow groove carved in the ground by runoff *20.2*

risk assessment   determining how much risk is acceptable in a given situation *25.1*

runner   the long, horizontal stem of many plants that runs below the ground, making the plant resistant to drought, fire, and grazing animals *8.3*

runoff   water from rainfall and melting ice that runs along the ground *20.2*

S-shaped curve   a growth curve with an initial rapid growth rate followed by a slower growth rate *5.3*

salinity   a measure of the dissolved salts in a sample of water *10.1*

salt marsh   a flat, muddy wetland that surrounds estuaries, bays, and lagoons *11.3*

sandy soil   soil where most of the mineral grains vary from 0.5 mm to 2.0 mm *18.3*

sanitary landfill   a landfill where wastes are spread in layers and compacted by bulldozers *19.2*

saturated fat   a fat that contains the maximum number of hydrogen atoms on the fatty acid chains *14.1*

savanna   a tropical grassland ranging from dry scrubland to wet, open woodland *6.4, 8.3*

scavenger   an animal that feeds on the bodies of dead organisms *4.1*

secondary succession   a type of succession that occurs when a community has been cleared by a disturbance that has not destroyed the soil *6.2*

secure chemical landfill   a secure landfill constructed in an area of nonporous bedrock *19.4*

sedimentary rock   rock that is formed when layers of sediments accumulate, compress, and cement together *1.2*

sedimentation   a treatment method where water that has gone through screens is allowed to settle in tanks, with the remaining particles falling to the bottom *20.3*

sediments   small particles that settle to the bottom of a body of water *10.3*

semiarid region   a dry area that borders a desert that supports communities of grasses and shrubs *7.2*

sewage   water that carries organic wastes from humans and industry *21.1*

sewage treatment plant   a facility that processes raw sewage before it is returned to surface water systems *21.1*

shelter belt (windbreak)   a row of trees planted along the outer edges of a field as an aid to reducing erosion *19.3*

silt   soil type with mineral grains between 0.002 mm and 0.05 mm *18.3*

smelting   the process of heating and refining an ore to separate out the valuable minerals *18.1*

sod-forming grass   a grass that forms a mat of soil and roots *8.2*

soil   a mixture of mineral particles from bedrock and organic particles from living and decaying organisms *18.3*

soil profile   a vertical cross section of soil from the ground surface down to bedrock *18.3*

soil water   water that seeps into the ground and fills the spaces between soil particles *20.2*

solar collector   a device used to gather and absorb the sun's energy in a solar heating system *17.1*

solar energy   energy from the sun that is absorbed by plants and used as fuel by virtually all organisms *17.1*

solid wastes   all garbage, refuse, and sludge products from agriculture, forestry, mining, and municipalities *19.1*

source reduction   the lowering of demand for a resource, reducing the amount used and wasted *24.1*

specialized species   an organism that occupies a small niche *5.2*

species   a group of organisms so similar that they breed and produce fertile offspring *3.3*

spoil pile   a mound of mineral wastes deposited outside a mine *18.2*

standing-water ecosystem   a type of freshwater biome such as a lake, pond, or marsh *10.2*

steppe   a grassland area that gets less than 50 cm of rain per year, characterized by short bunchgrasses *6.4, 8.2*

sterilization   a water treatment method where any residual harmful bacteria and microorganisms are destroyed with extreme heat or chemicals *20.3*

stratosphere   the layer of Earth's atmosphere beyond the troposphere, reaching a height of 50 km above Earth *1.3*

strip-cropping   a soil conservation method where farmland is plowed so that the plowed strips are separated by planted strips, reducing soil loss *19.3*

subirrigation   an irrigation system where water is introduced naturally or artificially beneath the soil surface *20.1*

subsidence   a process in which land sinks, due either to the weight of sediments, or the extraction of subsurface water *11.3, 20.2*

substitution   a conservation method where a more plentiful material is used for a product instead of a less plentiful material *18.2*

subsurface mining   a method used to extract mineral deposits from below the surface of Earth *18.2*

succulent   a plant such as a cactus that has thick, water-filled tissues *7.1*

supply   the availability of a resource to be purchased *25.1*

supply-demand curve   represents the relationship between supply, demand, and the purchase price for a particular resource *25.1*

surface water   the water that is above ground in streams, lakes, rivers, and ponds *20.2*

sustainable agriculture   a type of farming based on crop rotation, reduced soil erosion, pest management, and minimum use of soil additives; also called regenerative farming *14.4*

sustainable development   ethic a development plan that meets the current needs of society without limiting the ability of future generations to meet their needs *12.3*

sustainable lifestyle   a way of life that focuses on reducing energy and material consumption *24.1*

symbiosis   a relationship where two species live closely together *6.1*

tailings   low grade ore and other mineral wastes generated by mining *18.2*

tectonic plate   one of several large, movable plates that make up the lithosphere *3.1*

ten percent law   the concept that only 10 percent of the energy that enters a trophic level is passed on to the next trophic level as biomass *4.3*

terracing   a soil conservation method where crops are planted on a series of terraced platforms built into the slope of a hill *19.3*

territorial animal   an animal that maintains a territory with specific boundaries *3.2*

territory   an area claimed as a living space by an individual animal *3.2*

thermal pollution   a large increase in water temperature due to human activity *21.3*

thermonuclear fusion   the process in which the high temperatures in the sun's core cause hydrogen nuclei to fuse, forming helium nuclei; as each helium nucleus forms, a loss of mass occurs. This lost mass is converted to the heat and light energy of the sun. *17.1*

thermosphere   the outer layer of the atmosphere *1.3*

toxic chemical   an element or molecule that is directly harmful to living things *21.2*

toxic wastes   hazardous wastes made of chemicals that are poisonous to humans *19.2*

transpiration   the evaporation of water from the leaves of plants *4.4*

trophic level   a layer in the structure of feeding relationships in an ecosystem *4.1*

tropical zone   an area located at latitudes near the equator that receives direct rays from the sun during most of the year *9.3*

troposphere   the layer of the atmosphere that touches the surface of Earth *1.3*

tuft   a large clump of tall, coarse grass *8.2*

tundra   a cold, windy, dry area just south of the polar ice caps in Alaska, Canada, Greenland, Iceland, Norway, and Asia *6.4, 7.3*

understory   in a forest, trees that are younger and smaller than those of the canopy *9.2*

unpotable   describes water that is polluted and unfit to drink *20.1*

unsaturated fat   a fat with some hydrogen atoms missing from the fatty acid chains *14.1*

variable   any factor that affects the outcome of an experiment *2.2*

vertical feeding pattern   the pattern where different animals eat vegetation at different heights *8.3*

waste exchange   a process where a waste product from one company or industry is used by another company in the production of its products or materials *19.4*

water purification   a treatment method that removes the harmful chemicals and microorganisms that make water unpotable *20.3*

water table   the top of the saturated layer where groundwater collects and saturates the bedrock *20.2*

wetland   an ecosystem in which the roots of plants are submerged under water at least part of the year *10.2*

wilderness   an area where the ecosystem is relatively undisturbed by the activites of humans *23.3*

zone of aeration   the area where water enters an aquifer *20.2*

zone of discharge   the place where water leaves an aquifer and becomes surface water *20.2*

zone of saturation   the saturated rock layer beneath the water table; also called aquifer *1.2, 20.2*

zooplankton   plankton that do not carry out photosynthesis, including microscopic organisms and protozoans *10.2*

INDEX

Page numbers in **boldface** indicate definitions of terms in the text.
Page numbers in *italics* indicate figures or illustrations in the text.

ACKNOWLEDGMENTS

PHOTO ACKNOWLEDGMENTS

Front cover Pat O'Hara/AllStock
Back cover S. Nielsen/DRK Photo
Title page Pat O'Hara/AllStock

Contents
iiiB Alan Blank/Bruce Coleman Inc.
iiiC Dr. Brian Eyden/SPL/Photo Researchers
iiiT William Grenfell/Visuals Unlimited
ivL Michael Fogden/DRK Photo
ivR Kevin Schafer/Tom Stack & Associates
vi Craig Aurness/Woodfin Camp & Associates
viiL Natalie Fobes/AllStock
viiR Don Spiro/Tony Stone Images

Unit 1
xii-1 Art Resource
1 Michael Holford

Chapter 1
2 NASA
5BC Geoffrey Nilsen Photography*
5BL Geoffrey Nilsen Photography*
5BR Geoffrey Nilsen Photography*
5T Alastair Black/Tony Stone Images
7 Albert Copley/Visuals Unlimited
11 Johnny Johnson/DRK Photo
12C Peter Ryan/Scripps/SPL/Photo Researchers
12L Erwin & Peggy Bauer/Bruce Coleman Inc.
12R Darrell Gulin/AllStock
14 Anthony Howarth/SPL/Photo Researchers

Chapter 2
18 Krafft/Explorer/Photo Researchers
20 Dr. Brian Eyden/SPL/Photo Researchers
21 Ray Pfortner/Peter Arnold, Inc.
23 David Austen/Stock, Boston
26C Lori Adamski Peek/Tony Stone Images
26L Lawrence Migdale/Tony Stone Images
26R Guy Marche/AllStock
27 Giraudon/Art Resource
28C Larry Ulrich/Tony Stone Images
28L William Grenfell/Visuals Unlimited
28R D. Cavagnaro/DRK Photo
30B Kim Heacox/DRK Photo
30T Michael Ventura/Bruce Coleman Inc.

Chapter 3
34 T. A. Wiewandt/DRK Photo
37B Alberto Garcia/SABA
37T Tom Bean/DRK Photo
39 John Nees/Animals, Animals
40B J. C. Stevenson/Animals, Animals
40T Dr. Eckart Pott/Bruce Coleman Inc.
41 Allan Tannenbaum/Sygma
48L John Cancalosi/Peter Arnold, Inc.
48R Bob Daemmrich/Uniphoto Picture Agency
49B Russell A. Mittermeier/Bruce Coleman Inc.
49C Brownie Harris/The Stock Market
49T Tomas del Amo/West Stock

Unit 2
50-51 Wayne Lynch/DRK Photo
51 Wendell Metzen/Bruce Coleman Inc.

Chapter 4
52 Gary S. Withey/Bruce Coleman Inc.
53B Manfred Kage/Peter Arnold, Inc.
53T Doug Wechsler/Earth Scenes
54C Renee Lynn/AllStock
54L Steven Fuller/Peter Arnold, Inc.
54R Steve Kraseman/Peter Arnold, Inc.
55 Peter Davey/Bruce Coleman Inc.
63B Bob Torrez/Tony Stone Images
63T Max Winter/AllStock

Chapter 5
72 C. K. Lorenz/Photo Researchers
73 Alan Blank/Bruce Coleman Inc.
74 Anne Wertheim/Animals, Animals
75 Patti Murray/Animals, Animals
77 Mike Bacon/Tom Stack & Associates
78 Patti Murray/Animals, Animals

Chapter 6
88 Dwight R. Kuhn/DRK Photo
90 Tom & Pat Leeson/DRK Photo
91BL Rich Buzzelli/Tom Stack & Associates
91BR M.P.L. Fogden/Bruce Coleman Inc.
91T Jonathan T. Wright/Bruce Coleman Inc.
92 Jeff Foott/Tom Stack & Associates
94B John Shaw/Tom Stack & Associates
94T Sharon Gerig/Tom Stack & Associates
96 Gary Braasch/AllStock
98 Steve Dunwell/The Image Bank
106B Stephen Kraseman/DRK Photo
106T John Eastcott & Yva Momatiuk/The Image Works
107B Lawrence Migdale/Stock, Boston
107TL Earl Roberge/West Stock
107TR Joe McDonald/Animals, Animals

Unit 3
108-109 David Harvey/Woodfin Camp & Associates
109 Michael Fogden/Bruce Coleman Inc.

Chapter 7
110 David Hughes/Bruce Coleman Inc.
111L Carr Clifton/AllStock
111R Tom Bean/DRK Photo
112L K. G. Preston-Mafham/Earth Scenes
112R James R. Simon/Bruce Coleman Inc.
113 J. Cancalosi/Tom Stack & Associates
115 Wendy Watriss/Woodfin Camp & Associates
117L Tom Walker/Stock, Boston
117R David C. Fritts/Animals, Animals
118L G. C. Kelley/Photo Researchers
118R Jeff Lepore/Photo Researchers
119 Thomas Kitchin/Tom Stack & Associates

Chapter 8
124 Joe McDonald/Tom Stack & Associates
125B Fred Whitehead/Earth Scenes
125T Spencer Swanger/Tom Stack & Associates
126BL David Muench/AllStock
126BR Dave Millert/Tom Stack & Associates
126T Grant Heilman/Grant Heilman Photography
127C Phil Schermeister/AllStock
127L R. Van Nostrand/Photo Researchers
127R Stephen J. Krasemann/DRK Photo
128 Runk-Schoenberger/Grant Heilman Photography
129 Greg J. Ryan & Sally A. Beyer/AllStock
130B Tom Walker/AllStock
130T Runk-Schoenberger/Grant Heilman Photography
131 The Bettmann Archive
132 R. F. Head/Earth Scenes

Chapter 9
138 Phil Degginger/Bruce Coleman Inc.
139C Doug Sokell/Tom Stack & Associates
139L S. Nielsen/DRK Photo
139R Spencer Swanger/Tom Stack & Associates
140BL W. E. Ruth/AllStock
140R Leonard Lee Rue III/Bruce Coleman Inc.
140TL Wayne Lankinen/Bruce Coleman Inc.
141L Pat & Tom Leeson/Photo Researchers
141R James Randklev/AllStock
142 Michael P. Gadomski/Photo Researchers
143 John Shaw/Bruce Coleman Inc.
144C Leonard Lee Rue III/Animals, Animals
144L Brian Parker/Tom Stack & Associates
144R Randy Ury/The Stock Market
145 J. H. Robinson/Earth Scenes
146 Geoff Tompkinson/Aspect Picture Library/ The Stock Market
148B Kevin Schafer/AllStock
148C Kevin Schafer/Tom Stack & Associates

148TC Kevin Schafer/Tom Stack & Associates
148TL Michael Fogden/DRK Photo
148TR Michael Fogden/DRK Photo
149 Sam Bryan/Photo Researchers

Chapter 10
154 David Muench/AllStock
158 Harold Taylor Abipp/Oxford Scientific Films/ Animals, Animals
160B Marty Cordano/DRK Photo
160T Vic Beunza/Bruce Coleman Inc.
161 John Shaw/Bruce Coleman Inc.
163 Will & Deni McIntyre/AllStock

Chapter 11
168 James Randklev/AllStock
170L Norbert Wu/The Stock Market
170R Francois Gohier/Photo Researchers
172 Brian Parker/Tom Stack & Associates
173 Ronald L. Sefton/Bruce Coleman Inc.
174 Nicholas Devore III/Bruce Coleman Inc.
175 Pat & Tom Leeson/Photo Researchers
176 John Shaw/Bruce Coleman Inc.
177 Stephen Krasemann/DRK Photo
182 Nikolay Zurek/AllStock
183B Cameramann/The Image Works
183TL David Barnes/AllStock
183TR C. C. Lockwood/Earth Scenes

Unit 4
184-185 Sean Sprague
185 Julie Habel/Westlight

Chapter 12
186 M. P. Kahl/DRK Photo
187 Jet Propulsion Lab/Newell Color Lab
190 Jason Laure/Woodfin Camp & Associates
195 Ben Gibson/Woodfin Camp & Associates

Chapter 13
200 David Pollack/The Stock Market
203 The Bettmann Archive
207 John Livzey/AllStock
208 Bill Wassman/The Stock Market
209 Alon Reininger/Contact Press/Woodfin Camp & Associates

Chapter 14
214 Hilarie Kavanagh/Tony Stone Images
218L Ken Greer/Visuals Unlimited
218R Betty Press/Woodfin Camp & Associates
220 Grant Heilman/Grant Heilman Photography
221B Greg Vaughn/Tom Stack & Associates
221T Clyde H. Smith/Peter Arnold, Inc.
222 G. Prance/Visuals Unlimited
223 Thomas Hovland/Grant Heilman Photography
224 Jack Fields/Photo Researchers
226 Anthony Mercieca Photo/Photo Researchers
230B Jerry Howard/Positive Images
230T Randa Bishop/Uniphoto Picture Agency
231B Ken Graham/AllStock
231C Paul Conklin/Uniphoto Picture Agency
231T Arthur Grace/Stock, Boston

Unit 5
232-233 Art Wolfe/AllStock
233 Gregg Adams/AllStock

Chapter 15
234 Vince Streano/AllStock
235B Larry Lefever/Grant Heilman Photography
235C The Bettmann Archive
235T Erich Lessing/Art Resource
238B Barry L. Runk/Grant Heilman Photography
238C E. R. Degginger/Bruce Coleman Inc.
238T John Colwell/Grant Heilman Photography
241 Michele Burgess/The Stock Market
242 Rafael Macia/Photo Researchers
243 Epipress/Sygma
245 Gary E. Holscher/AllStock

Chapter 16
250 Bernard Hermann
252 Paul Silverman/Fundamental Photographs
257 Doug Wilson/Black Star
258 Sandia National Laboratories/Waste Isolation Pilot Plant
260 Igor Kostin/Imago/Sygma

Chapter 17
264 Otto Rogge/The Stock Market
267B Brian Parker/Tom Stack & Associates
267T T. J. Florian/Rainbow
269 Courtesy General Motors
271B Manfred Gottschalk/Tom Stack & Associates
271T Brian Parker/Tom Stack & Associates
274BR Ken W. Davis/Tom Stack & Associates
274L John Mead/SPL/Photo Researchers
274T Culver Pictures, Inc.
275 Thomas Braise/The Stock Market
276 David Ball/The Stock Market
282 Mugshots/The Stock Market
283B Jeff Zaruba/The Stock Market
283C Dawson Jones, Inc./Uniphoto Picture Agency
283T Joe Sohm/Chromosohm/Uniphoto Picture Agency

Unit 6
284-285 World Photo Service/SuperStock, Inc.
285 Fred J. Maroon/Photo Researchers

Chapter 18
286 J. Kyle Keener/Philadelphia Inquirer Matrix
287BL Geoffrey Nilsen Photography*
287BR Geoffrey Nilsen Photography*
287T Charles Gupton/Stock, Boston
288 Jon Feingersh/Tom Stack & Associates
290B Rod Allin/Tom Stack & Associates
290T Barry L. Runk/Grant Heilman Photography
291T Grant Heilman/Grant Heilman Photography
292 Steve Kaufman/DRK Photo
293 Dan Budnik/Woodfin Camp & Associates
294 Werner Forman Archive/Art Resource
297 Scott Camazine/Photo Researchers
300 Walt Anderson/Tom Stack & Associates

Chapter 19
304 Oliver Strewe/Tony Stone Images
306 Susan Meiselas/Magnum Photos Inc.
308B Eugene Richards/Magnum Photos, Inc.
308C Dilip Mehta/Contact Press Images
308T L. L. T. Rhodes/Tony Stone Images
309 W. Hodges/Westlight
313L Bruce Hands/Tony Stone Images
313R Bob Davis/Woodfin Camp & Associates
314 Louis Psihoyos/Contact Press Images
315 Gabe Palmer/The Stock Market

Chapter 20
322 Tom Bean/AllStock
323B Mark Downey/The Gamma Liaison Network
323T Allan Tannenbaum/Sygma
325BL Shelly Katz/Black Star
325BR Grant Heilman/Grant Heilman Photography
325BR inset Lowell Georgia/Photo Researchers
325TL Grant Heilman/Grant Heilman Photography
325TR Joe Bator/The Stock Market
326 Craig Aurness/Woodfin Camp & Associates
327 Grant Heilman/Grant Heilman Photography
328 Leif Skoogfors/Woodfin Camp & Associates
330 Bruce Dale
332 David Madison/Bruce Coleman Inc.

Chapter 21
338 P. Schutte/SuperStock, Inc.
339 The Bettmann Archive
341C Sinclair Stammers/SPL/Photo Researchers
341L Moredun Animal Health Ltd./SPL/Photo Researchers
341R Moredun Animal Health Ltd./SPL/Photo Researchers
343 Victoria Hurst/Tom Stack & Associates
345L Sygma
345R Natalie Fobes/AllStock
346 Frank P. Rossotto/The Stock Market
349 Grant Heilman/Grant Heilman Photography
351 Frans Lanting/Photo Researchers

Chapter 22
356   D. Logan/AllStock
358B William Johnson/Stock, Boston
358C Norman Owen Tomalin/Bruce Coleman Inc.
358T Don Spiro/Tony Stone Images
361   Richard Packwood/Oxford Scientific Films/Earth Scenes
363B Runk-Schoenberger/Grant Heilman Photography
363T Carlos V. Causo/Bruce Coleman Inc.
364B NASA
364T D. P. Hershkowitz/Bruce Coleman Inc.
367   Tad Ackman/University of New Hampshire
370   Courtesy General Motors
372   Gabe Palmer/The Stock Market
376   Greg Brown/Uniphoto Picture Agency
377B David Aronson/Stock, Boston
377C Mark Burnett/Photo Researchers
377T Pedrick/The Image Works

Unit 7
378-379 Brian A. Vikander/Westlight
379   Stanley Breeden/DRK Photo

Chapter 23
380   Jim Richardson
384   Claus Meyer/Black Star
385   Novosti/Lehtikuva/Woodfin Camp & Associates
387C John Gerlach/Tom Stack & Associates
387L Michael J. Balick/Peter Arnold, Inc.
387R Greg Vaughn/Tom Stack & Associates
388   J. Lotter/Tom Stack & Associates
389   Scott Berner/The Stockhouse
390   Calvin Larsen/Photo Researchers
391   Keith H. Murakami/Tom Stack & Associates

Chapter 24
396   C. Bradley Simmons/Bruce Coleman Inc.
397   Richard Megna/Fundamental Photographs
399   Richard Megna/Fundamental Photographs
400   Peter Beck/The Stock Market
401   Alex Bartel/SPL/Photo Researchers
402L Mark Sherman/Bruce Coleman Inc.
402R Will McIntyre/Photo Researchers
403L H. R. Bramaz/Peter Arnold, Inc.
403R Norman O. Tomalin/Bruce Coleman Inc.
404   Paula Lerner/Woodfin Camp & Associates
405L Roy Toft/Tom Stack & Associates
405R Roy Toft/Tom Stack & Associates

Chapter 25
410   H. Sutton/AllStock
412L IFA/Bruce Coleman Inc.
412R D. Brewster/Bruce Coleman Inc.
413   Byron Augustin/Tom Stack & Associates
415   M. Theiler/Washington Stock Photo
417   Robert E. Daemmrich/Tony Stone Images
419   Natalie B. Fobes/AllStock
421   Jim Richardson
422   Brian Parker/Tom Stack & Associates
426   Michael Ma Po Shum/Tony Stone Images
427B Tom Tracy/AllStock
427C Bill Denison/Uniphoto Picture Agency
427T Will and Deni McIntyre/AllStock

*Photographed expressly for Addison-Wesley Publishing Company, Inc.

ILLUSTRATION CREDITS

Warren Budd & Associates 3, 9, 13, 77, 147, 169, 240, 266, 273, 277, 328

Dave Danz All unit openers symbols and full-page activity leaf pattern art

Mark Foerster 61, 62, 68, 102, 150, 210, 215, 219, 298, 318, 334, 340, 347, 348, 392

Bill Hollowell 268, margin feature art

Marlene May-Howerton 93, 97

Carlyn Iverson 291, 295, 296, 365, 366, 369

Lois Lovejoy 76, 95, 311, 386

Trevin Lowrey 202, 256, 263, 288

Mapping Specialists Ltd. 10, 35, 43, 100–101, 119, 123, 160, 171, 191, 193, 239, 289, 297, 329, 344, 368, 383, 385, 406, 416, 418, 420

Michael Maydak 56, 57, 58

Precision Graphics 4, 6, 25, 33, 59, 61T, 89, 120, 153, 167, 174, 181, 324, 332, 360, 362, 367

Rolin Graphics 42, 44, 128, 132, 133, 134, 305, 307, 315

Margo Stahl-Pronk 114, 156, 162, 164, 292, 299

Beowulf Thorne 8, 24, 74, 80, 81, 82, 83, 84, 205, 206, 216, 217, 229, 236, 237, 249, 254, 258, 272, 281, 306, 312, 371, 381, 382, 398, 401, 411, 413, 414, margin feature art

Sarah Woodward 65, 66, 67, 188, 189, 251, 252, 253, 255, 268T, 278